Cost and Management Accounting

DUNCAN WILLIAMSON

Professor of Accounting

PRENTICE HALL

London New York Toronto Sydney Tokyo Singapore

Madrid Mexico City Munich

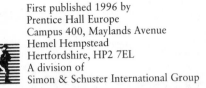

First published 1996 by
Prentice Hall Europe
Campus 400, Maylands Avenue
Hemel Hempstead
Hertfordshire, HP2 7EL
A division of
Simon & Schuster International Group

Typeset in $9\frac{1}{2}$/12 pt Sabon
by PPS, London Road, Amesbury, Wilts.

Printed and bound in Great Britain by
T.J. Press (Padstow) Ltd

Library of Congress Cataloging-in-Publication Data

Williamson, Duncan.
Cost and management accounting / Duncan Williamson.
p. cm.
Includes bibliographical references and index.
ISBN 0-13-205923-1
1. Managerial accounting. 2. Cost accounting. I. Title.
HF5657. 4. W535 1996 95-20704
657'. 42-dc20 CIP

British Library Cataloguing in Publication Data

A catalogue record for this book is available from the British Library

ISBN 0-13-205923-1 (pbk)

1 2 3 4 5 00 99 98 97 96

Contents

Preface

My reason for undertaking the writing of this book stems from the comments I have repeatedly received from my students regarding the texts to which they are referred, and my own dissatisfaction with one or more aspects of existing texts. A common and particular concern is their apparent failure to view the subject matter through the eyes of students. Faced with this underlying dissatisfaction and the trend towards placing a greater emphasis for learning on students, I felt compelled to grasp the nettle. In writing this text, I have therefore attempted to approach it with a student's insight into the problems with which cost and management accounting confronts them.

The objective of this text is to explain and illustrate the principal accounting techniques involved in the production of cost information, and their application to a broad range of managerial decision-making, planning and control activities (including those in divisionalised companies), coupled with a critical evaluation of the underlying concepts and contemporary issues. By embracing both the practical and theoretical strands of management accounting systems, the text provides comprehensive descriptive and analytical coverage.

In this treatment of the subject, the text draws upon and contains many references to empirical research and actual company practices. The relevance, contribution and context of cost and management accounting systems in attaining strategic objectives, and the tensions that often exist between conventional theory and modern practice, are also highlighted through the inclusion of significant material on developments in production systems and advanced manufacturing technologies.

Again with the needs of students in mind, the approach I have taken to the explanation and application of quantitative techniques is generally to integrate them with the particular topic, but to assign more complex aspects to an appendix at the end of the relevant chapter.

Beyond the content and structure of the text, I considered it equally important for the student-centered appoach to extend to the provision of pedagogical features, examples, illustrations and assessment materials, all of which have been carefully conceived and constructed, and which are outlined below. In publishing this text, particular attention has been given to its physical attributes and to the presentation of the material in seeking to make the text an accessible and effective teaching and learning resource; as such, it is hoped that the layout and two-colour design of the text will be appreciated by lecturers and students alike.

This text is written for undergraduate and postgraduate students on introductory to intermediate courses in management accounting, but will be particularly relevant for those who might wish subsequently to undertake an advanced course in the subject, or to enter the accountancy profession. In this respect, it will also be of use to students preparing for the cost and management accounting examinations of professional bodies.

Special features

Each chapter begins with a set of **learning objectives** to highlight what students should be able to accomplish after working through the chapter. This is followed by an **introduction** which provides a preview of the material covered.

Integrated throughout the text are **worked examples** for students to follow through. These develop a technique or concept step by step, and include a fully documented solution and workings. **Cameos** are boxed illustrations that enlarge upon or give case material related to the practical application of a particular topic in a variety of organisations, covering both the manufacturing and service sectors. Many are taken from the activities of actual companies or from my own personal experience.

Chapters end with a **summary**, which highlights and reinforces the main topics covered by the chapter. A list of **key terms** follows in each chapter; these terms are highlighted where they are first encountered and defined in the chapter text, and students are encouraged to check back through the chapter to ensure that they have understood them. This list of key terms also serves as a roadmap for quick revision. Some **recommended reading** is then given containing annotated suggestions of key books or articles that might be read to provide an additional perspective on a topic or to enable it to be studied in a more depth. A full list of chapter **references** follows the assessment materials, and appendices, where present, are at the end of each chapter.

Assessment materials

A further important feature of this text is the comprehensive range of assessment materials provided at the end of each chapter to enable students to consolidate and apply their understanding. These materials have either been developed through extensive class-testing or utilise questions taken from the professional accountancy examinations; all questions and their solutions have been thoroughly checked for their accuracy. There are the following three distinct types.

Review questions

Relatively short and generally descriptive or analytical in their type, these questions are designed to encourage students to revisit, assimilate and critically evaluate the main topics and issues. Outline suggested answers to all these questions are provided in either the Student

Workbook or Teacher's Manual. They are suitable both for assessment and discussion purposes in seminars and tutorials, or as examination material.

Practice questions

These questions are generally of a numerical type and are intended to test the student's capacity to apply the main techniques or concepts. A two-tier grading system (Level I and Level II) has been adopted according to the level of difficulty, providing maximum flexibility in their use. For each chapter, fully worked solutions to two of these questions (identified by the question number in colour) are provided at the end of the text, and further information and annotations are sometimes provided to enhance the material covered in the chapter. The remaining solutions are provided in either the Student Workbook or Teacher's Manual. In addition to providing a means for self-assessment, the practice questions are also suitable for assessment purposes in seminars or examinations.

Projects

Wherever suitable, chapters include these practical assignments, designed to encourage students to look beyond the confines of the text and to promote the benefits of experiential learning. Typically, they require students to relate and critically apply one or more techniques or concepts to a company or organisation with which they are familiar. Guidance on the use of a selection of projects is given in the Teacher's Manual. These projects are particularly suitable where individual or group-assessed coursework is set.

Structure and outline of the text

Figure P.1 illustrates the basic structure and outline of this text. A more detailed description of the role and linkage of the various parts and chapters is given in the introduction to each of the five main parts, however, a summary is given below.

The foundation and framework for the book are laid out in Chapter 1, which provides an overview of cost and management accounting in manufacturing, service and non-profit-making settings. Here we discuss the scope, main functions and purpose of management accounting systems and their organisational context.

In Part I, we address the elements and production of cost information. How the management accountant classifies and codes the costs of an organisation into material, labour and overhead elements is examined in Chapter 2, and we see how this classification system is used to analyse all data in accounts and sub-accounts. An analysis of the behaviour of costs into their fixed and variable components follows in Chapter 3 (which is extended in Chapter 9). Chapters 4 and 5 contain an in depth review of much of the work relevant to cost and management accounting that is being done in the areas of logistics, inventory management and labour costs. Chapters 6 and 7 chart the movement from traditional overhead cost accounting to activity-based cost accounting. We develop the argument that activity-based costing is not new, but that it provides us with a new emphasis and mind-set. Chapter 8 is concerned with the preparation of the job, batch and process cost accounts that enables the management accountant to analyse the costs of his or her organisation. We

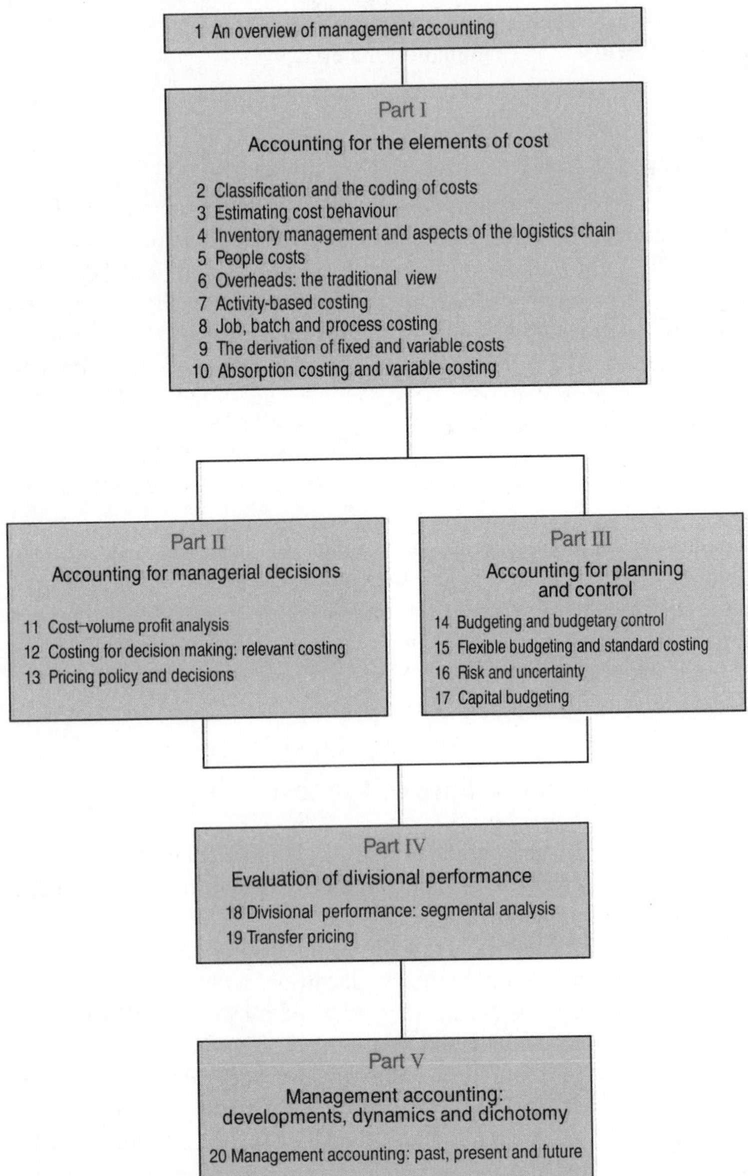

FIGURE P.1 *Structure and outline of the text*

return to the analysis of costs into their fixed and variable components in Chapter 9 when we look at more sophisticated methods of cost behaviour analysis than those we examined in Chapter 3. We also examine how the learning effect arises, and the implications of it for management accountants and their organisations. Together with a knowledge of the classification and coding of costs, an understanding of the behaviour of costs allows the management accountant to employ the concepts of variable costing. Chapter 10 begins our discussion of variable costing by comparing absorption costing and variable costing.

Part II is dedicated to the information that a manager needs in decision making: for example, whether a department that is apparently losing money should be closed; whether it is better to buy in components or make them; how to allocate resources in a situation where the supply of those resources is severely limited, and so on. In Chapters 11 and 12, we develop further our discussion of variable costing. One of the most difficult decisions faced by organisations is that on pricing, and this aspect is dealt with in Chapter 13.

The role of accounting in the planning and control of organisations is the subject of Part III. Why we need to prepare budgets and operate a system of budgetary control is demonstrated in Chapters 14 and 15. Risk and uncertainty are discussed in Chapter 16, and we conclude this part in Chapter 17 with a review of capital budgeting.

The measurement of divisional performance within companies and transfer pricing are two strongly related and problematic sets of issues, and we tackle these in Chapters 18 and 19 respectively in Part IV.

Finally to Part V, where I set out in Chapter 20 what is essentially a personal evaluation of the past, present and future of cost and management accounting, and explore what I believe are some of the remaining tensions between management accounting theory and practice.

Note to students

It might seem a bizarre claim to make of a text, but the material has been written, structured and presented from a student's perspective: that is, I have tried to anticipate all your questions, doubts and fears as we move from topic to topic and chapter to chapter. My advice to you is to read the text carefully. More importantly, don't just read it passively – get involved!

Check back through each chapter to ensure you have understood the key terms and accomplished the learning objectives. Moreover, don't simply accept the solution to a worked example – follow it through conscientiously. By attempting the practice questions and checking your solutions with those provided at the end of the text, you will not only enhance your understanding, but also acquire additional useful information and insights beyond that contained within the chapters themselves. Wherever possible, undertake the projects too. All the students I have taught have benefited from and enjoyed these assignments, since they give the opportunity, individually or as part of a group, to actively develop your knowledge and skills by applying them to actual companies and organisations.

To complement this text, there is a separately published *Student Workbook*, which if you have not already done so, you are recommended to purchase. It is designed to enhance and apply your understanding and skills through allowing you to practise answering the type of questions you will encounter in assessed coursework and examinations. Each chapter in the Workbook corresponds to a chapter in this textbook, each divided into four sections:

1. Outline suggested answers to half of the review questions.
2. Fully worked solutions to the practice questions not given in the text or Teacher's Manual.

3. Additional practice questions.
4. Fully worked solutions to a selection of the additional practice questions.

Note to lecturers

In addition to the accompanying Student Workbook, which is available for students to purchase either separately or as part of the special bundle-pack at a discounted price, this text is supported and complemented by teaching resources comprising the following:

1. *Teacher's Manual*
   Each chapter in the Manual corresponds to a chapter in this textbook, each divided into six sections:
   (a) teaching notes and guidance for each chapter;
   (b) outline suggested answers to half of the review questions;
   (c) fully worked solutions to the practice questions not given in the text or Student Workbook;
   (d) guidance on the use of selected projects;
   (e) additional practice questions; and
   (f) fully worked solutions to a selection of the additional practice questions.
2. *OHP Transparency Masters' Pack*, which contains over 100 of the key tables and illustrations in the text, enlarged for reproduction onto acetates for use in lectures and seminars.

Overall, I hope this book will be judged as a significant new contribution to the teaching and learning of cost and management accounting. It has been developed from my experience of teaching the subject over many years at a variety of levels in both further and higher education, and across three continents. My approach in this text, and the special features and assessment materials it contains, is based upon the fact that not everyone is, or wishes to be, a gifted management accountant. My intention, therefore, is to make management accounting accessible to as many as possible who are prepared to give the time and effort to its study.

Any comments on this book, whether good or bad, will be gratefully accepted.

Duncan Williamson

Acknowledgements

In the Preface, I outlined my reason for undertaking this project. Now thousands of hours later, I am at the stage of believing I have accomplished my objectives and, in the process, have learned a huge amount. In reaching this point, the people mentioned below have helped me beyond their knowing.

First and foremost, my wife Christine and children Daniel, Andrew and Fran, have not only put up with all those hours during which I have been preoccupied, but have also had to read some of the material I have written, or at least have had to listen to me reading out a key passage. They read and listened with an astounding amount of patience, understanding and enthusiasm. Of course, what happened after they left the room I have no way of knowing, but they are deserving of my eternal gratitude. I hope they'll each have the decency to buy a copy too!

It almost goes without saying that my students have had a lot of input into this book. If students knew how much of the role of a guinea pig they are being put through by people like me, they would demand some form of recompense – or more graceful treatment at examination time! I am indebted to the students whom I have taught at: Newcastle College, the University of Sunderland, the University of Malawi, and the Kazakhstan Institute of Management, Economics and Strategic Research. Students are excellent editors and critics, and always like finding errors or omissions. My students have put me right on many occasions and for that I am truly grateful.

The numerous anonymous reviewers of chapter outlines and material throughout the span of this project deserve particular praise. They provided me with constructive criticisms and insights, and have found fault, made suggestions for improvements, and generally given advice that this book has benefited from in large measure. Reviewers have the gift of hindsight and, in this kind of situation, it is an ideal gift – my hearty thanks to them all. In particular, Graham Francis at the University of Hertfordshire has been generous with his time in providing a significant number of refinements to the text. Of course, any errors or omissions that remain are down to me.

Tim Cross and Philip Price also both deserve special mention. Tim read through several chapters of an earlier version of this book for me and made some very valuable comments.

Philip provided me with some of the material on inventory management and logistics, together with several hours of his time, again very valuable.

Perhaps an unusual acknowledgement for a book on cost and management accounting, but I want to give posthumous thanks to Messrs Gilbert and Sullivan. The wit and wisdom of Gilbert and the music of Sullivan enliven the spirits when a problem can't be solved, the spreadsheet simply refuses to work properly, or that vital file has just erased itself! I have listened to *The Mikado*, *HMS Pinafore*, *The Pirates of Penzance*, *Trial by Jury* . . . as I have written this book. For anyone looking for amiable companions during the lonely hours of penmanship, people such as Ko-Ko, Major-General Stanley, and the Duke of Plaza-Toro can be highly recommended.

Andy Goss, and the others of his team whom I have met, have provided me with often needed guidance and assistance. Without their efforts, such a project as this could easily collapse. Sincere thanks to everyone at Prentice Hall who has helped me in any way.

I am grateful to the Chartered Institute of Management Accountants for their permission to use some of their past examination questions and definitions from their official terminology, and to the Chartered Association of Certified Accountants for permission to use some of their past examination questions. In both cases, the solutions I have used are my own.

I should acknowledge the sources of questions and other information I have incorporated into the text but which might not be my own. I like to think that all of the questions and other material have been specially devised for the book, yet I am aware that over the last 15 years or so, I have gathered material from a variety of sources whose authorship now eludes me. It is not my intention to rob anyone of the credit for their work, and I will happily acknowledge all sources for anything that is found not to be mine.

CHAPTER ONE

An overview of management accounting

CHAPTER OBJECTIVES

After reading this chapter you should be able to:

- define management accounting
- distinguish between management accounting, cost accounting and financial accounting
- identify different types of service organisation and the role of management accounting in them
- discuss the role of management accounting in non-profit-making organisations
- identify the traditional and modern purposes of management accounting
- define and discuss responsibility accounting, controllability and controllability filters
- use the meaning of non-financial indicators
- define the source and meaning of value added management

Introduction

This chapter gives an overview of and introduction to cost and management accounting, essentially in two parts. The first part of the chapter deals with cost and management accounting as it is: its definition, how it differs from cost accounting and financial accounting, and the part it can play in service and non-profit-making organisations. The second part of the chapter deals with cost and management accounting and the modern world. Here we look at the way management accounting has been developing over the last two decades or so. This chapter also provides some links with the overview of cost and management accounting and the way that the material is dealt with in the rest of this book.

The Chartered Institute of Management Accountants

The Chartered Institute of Management Accountants of the UK (CIMA) is the premier management accounting body in the UK. CIMA represents the interests of its Fellow and Associate members worldwide, together with the interests of 57,000 registered students, again worldwide. CIMA continually actively supports much empirical and academic work in the development of cost and management accounting as a more appropriate management information support system. To this end, CIMA publishes many books, pamphlets and documents aimed at helping its members, and the wider academic and practitioner community. One of the books that CIMA publishes, with regular updates, is its *Terminology*, CIMA's versions of definitions covering most aspects of management (and other branches of) accounting. Throughout this book, there are references to the CIMA *Terminology*. Whilst the latest available edition of the *Terminology* has been used, there are differences between editions that have sometimes led, to some extent, to an inferior definition being derived in the later edition. Where necessary, an earlier definition has been used in this book.

The substance of management accounting

Definition of management accounting

The term cost accounting is, perhaps, better known than management accounting in many respects in that management accounting is relatively new. Modern definitions, however, include cost accounting as part of management accounting. Because management and cost accounting are so broad in their outlook, the definitions of them need to be comprehensive.

Management accounting is:

> The provision of information required by management for such purposes as:
>
> 1 formulation of policies,
> 2 planning and controlling the activities of the enterprise,
> 3 decision taking on alternative courses of action,
> 4 disclosure to those external to the entity (shareholders and others),
> 5 disclosure to employees,
> 6 safeguarding assets.
>
> The above involves participation in management to ensure that there is effective:
>
> (a) formulation of plans to meet objectives (long-term planning),
> (b) formulation of short-term operation plans (budgeting/profit planning),
> (c) recording of actual transactions (financial accounting and cost accounting),
> (d) corrective action to bring future actual transactions into line (financial control),
> (e) obtaining and controlling finance (treasurership),
> (f) reviewing and reporting on systems and operations (internal audit, management audit).
>
> (CIMA 1989)

This definition is very broad insofar as it says that all accounting is management accounting. In discussing its definition, CIMA goes on to say that treasurership, planning, financial accounting, cost accounting and financial control are all secondary to management accounting; but CIMA further says that internal and external auditing are only partly dependent on management accounting. CIMA's definition includes that management accounting provides information for 'disclosure to those external to the entity (shareholders and others)'. This book is not especially concerned with the disclosure to those external to the organisation. Our interpretation of management accounting is that it is: 'the provision of information required by management'.

Management accounting v. cost accounting

Although CIMA does contrast management and cost accounting, for our purposes assume that management accounting includes cost accounting. Cost accounting is:

> That part of management accounting which establishes budgets and standard costs and actual costs of operations, processes, departments or products and the analysis of variances, profitability or social use of funds.
>
> The use of the term costing is not recommended. (CIMA 1989)

If the two definitions are compared – management accounting with cost accounting – we can see that there are great areas of overlap that enable us to interpret them as if management accounting does include cost accounting.

Throughout this book, we will be using manufacturing industries as our main reference point. However, service industries and non-profit-making organisations are assuming a greater significance in Western economies. Therefore, we will consider examples relating to situations other than manufacturing industry at relevant points.

Management accounting and non-manufacturing organisations

As an indicator of the importance of service organisations in the world economy, a random sample of fifteen developed economies and fifteen developing economies shows the arithmetic mean proportion of the GNP of those countries that was generated by the service sector (see Table 1.1).

The developed economies were drawn from those countries whose GNP per capita exceeded US$10,000 per year in 1991; and the developing economies were drawn from

TABLE 1.1 *Percentage of GNP generated by service sector*

	%
Developed economies	61.5
Developing economies	44.0

Professional services
- people-oriented
- high contact time
  - customisation
  - discretion
- front office process

Examples of professional services include management consultancies and corporate banks

Service shop
- people/equipment-oriented
- medium contact time
  - customisation
  - discretion
- front office/back office process/product

Examples of services shops include hotels and hotel chains, and retail banks

Mass service
- equipment-oriented
- low contact time
  - customisation
  - discretion
- back office product

Examples of a mass service include newsagents and newsagency chains, and public transport companies

FIGURE 1.1 *Definitions and descriptions of the three types of business service (Source: Adapted from Brignall* et al. *(1991 : 242), figure 6)*

those countries whose GNP per capita was less than US$3,000 per year in 1991. Whilst similar information is not available on non-profit-making organisations, Drucker (1989) gives an example of how management accounting thinking is now being used by non-profit-making organisations. His example concerns such organisations as the Girl Scouts and the Salvation Army. He says, speaking of the United States of America, that the non-profit-making sector is by far America's largest employer: 80 million people work as volunteers, each giving an average of nearly five hours per week to one or several non-profit-making organisations. This is equal to ten million full-time jobs. Drucker says:

> Twenty years ago, management was a dirty word for those involved in non-profit-making organisations . . . Now most of them have learned that non-profit-making organisations need management even more than business does, precisely because they lack the discipline of the bottom line. (Drucker 1989)

Drucker goes on to say that this development carries a clear lesson for business: managing the knowledge worker, or white-collar worker, for productivity is the challenge ahead for management:

> The non-profit-making organisations are showing us how to do that. It requires a clear mission, careful placement and continuous learning and teaching, Management By Objectives and self-

> control, high demands but corresponding responsibility and activity for performance and results. (Ibid.)

In Chapter five, we take a detailed look at productivity, including productivity measurement for knowledge workers. In the same way that one manufacturing organisation is different to another one, the same is true of service organisations.

Three types of service business

Brignall *et al.* (1991) quote Fitzgerald *et al.* who classified service businesses into three archetypes: professional services, service shops, mass services. The definitions and descriptions of these three types of service are contained in Figure 1.1. Brignall *et al.* (1991: 242) said:

> The basic conclusion from our small sample (five profit making service organisations) is that cost traceability appears to be high in professional services (small numbers of customers served per day) and low in mass services (a large number of customers serviced per day), with service shops falling in between. These findings have implications for the use of costs in pricing decisions.

By traceability, we mean assigning costs in some way to a cost unit or cost objective, such as the delivery of a pint of milk to your doorstep or a kilometre travelled on a bus. When costs are assigned in such a way we can say with some degree of accuracy what that service actually cost to provide. The point about the traceability of costs in service organisations clearly illustrates that management accounting has a role to play in such organisations. Throughout this book, even when we do not refer to service organisations in particular, bear this point in mind and apply the principles under discussion to service organisations whenever necessary.

Who needs management accounting information and why

Management accounting provides the management of organisations with an information system: it has developed over the centuries in response to management's needs. Stemming from the basic idea that management accounting is a management information system, we need to start our exploration of it in terms of who needs management accounting information and why. The following three examples give simple ideas of who needs information, and what they might need it for.

1. A **managing director** is concerned with all aspects of his or her organisation: taking an overview of everything that is going on. The MD will therefore need to be informed by his or her management accountant on all matters relating to the business.
2. A **distribution manager** may be trying to determine his or her vehicle replacement policy. The distribution manager will know a lot about these vehicles and their characteristics, being the organisation's expert in this area. However, the finer points of terotechnology (that is, trying to assess his or her fleet's life-cycle costs in order to optimise the cost/output relationship) may prove elusive. If so, the job is best left to the management accounting specialist.
3. Suppose the **supervisor** in a factory has been given the job of supervising the completion of job XYZ, and is told to keep costs to a minimum. One of the supervisor's primary concerns may revolve around the grade of labour to use, and its efficiency. The

management accountant can advise the supervisor on costs per hour of each grade of labour as well as on efficiency levels, based on records of previous achievement.

The financial accountant does fulfil a useful role. However, the financial accountant does not provide the kind of managerial information that the supervisor, the distribution manager, and the managing director are looking for when seeking information that will help them in their decision-making role.

Financial accounting does not provide management information

The reason why the financial accountant does not provide managerial information is summarised by Brausch who talks about the American equivalent of Chartered (Financial) Accountants: 'Typically ... they are well versed in financial accounting but have little knowledge of the intricacies inherent to cost management... The evolving attitude is toward an obsession to manage by the numbers ...' (Brausch 1994: 46).

The tables that follow show the usefulness of financial accounting reports when prepared for external publication; they also show why this feature of financial accounting reports is a severe limitation to management information needs.

While the financial accounting report in Table 1.2 is not bad as far as it goes, it does lack vital information for management purposes. The report gives total sales, total cost of sales and total costs: that is, it is an aggregated report. By being an aggregated report, this report hides, for example, the number of products or product lines made by the organisation. Nor does it show whether all products are contributing to profit equally or, maybe, not at all.

One of the functions of management accounting is to disaggregate data for management's use: it breaks down the data so that management can see sales and cost data by product group or product, or sales area, or any other classification required by the organisation's management. Consider, in the light of this function, Table 1.3, the management accounting

TABLE 1.2 *Financial accounting report*

	£	£	%
Sales		165,000	100.0
less: Cost of sales		115,000	69.7
Gross profit		50,000	30.3
less:			
Administration expenses	20,000		
Selling expenses	10,000		
Distribution expenses	5,000	35,000	21.2
Net profit		15,000	9.1

TABLE 1.3 *Management accounting report*

	Total £	Product A £	B £	C £
Sales	165,000	70,000	25,000	70,000
Cost of sales	115,000	46,000	18,000	51,000
Gross profit	50,000	24,000	7,000	19,000
Expenses				
Administration	20,000	7,000	4,000	9,000
Selling	10,000	2,000	3,000	5,000
Distribution	5,000	2,000	1,000	2,000
Total	35,000	11,000	8,000	16,000
Net profit/(loss)	15,000	13,000	(1,000)	3,000

version of the financial report in Table 1.2. Although this statement still lacks much detail, the personal knowledge and experience of the managing director, together with other statements prepared by the management accountant, will fill any gaps. So, data is transformed into information: it has a use now. The managing director now knows that product B is losing £1,000 in the period, and that of £15,000 total net profit, £13,000 comes from product A alone. Questions arising from such information include: Is this acceptable? Should product B be scrapped? If product B should not be scrapped, can its cost structure be changed?

Financial v. management accounting

It might still be easy to conclude that we are saying that financial accounting has no use when management accounting can be provided: this is not true. The CIMA definition links all forms of accountancy, with management accountancy as the common thread. However, financial and management accounting are two separate strands of accountancy. The financial accountant is primarily concerned with the provision of accounting information for those external to the organisation. (Remember point 4 of CIMA's definition of management accounting.) Furthermore the financial accountant's output is required by law for any limited company (such output includes the statutory accounts). Financial accounting embraces the classification and recording of accounting transactions in monetary terms; and it does so whilst working within the framework of both legal and accounting rules and regulations. The financial accountant fulfils the role of stewardship for shareholders and others external to, but having an interest in, the organisation. We can distinguish the work of the financial and management accountants under a number of different headings (see Table 1.4). The main points of discussion arising from Table 1.4 are as follows.

TABLE 1.4 ***Differences between financial and management accounting***

Financial	Management
■ Produce general purpose statements	■ Produce special purpose statements
■ Externally oriented	■ Internally oriented
■ Required by law	■ Prepared as deemed useful
■ Historic orientation	■ Future orientation
■ Highly aggregated	■ Must be very specific
■ Conforms to external standards	■ Has no external standards
■ Emphasises objectivity	■ Emphasises relevance even if it is subjective

General purpose v. specific purpose

The financial accountant's statements (including the trading account, profit and loss account, and balance sheets) are general purpose statements in that they relate to the whole organisation, or to relatively large parts of them, such as divisions and factories. On the other hand, the management accountant's output consists of highly specific statements such as production line A cost schedule.

External or internal orientation

By the nature of the purpose for which the financial accountant's statements are prepared, the financial accountant is concerned mainly with those external to the organisation: shareholders and other stakeholders (such as banks and finance houses). He or she is reporting to people outside the organisation. The management accountant, as we have already said, reports to, and prepares all of his or her statements for, those inside the organisation. Virtually nothing that the management accountant does is for direct external publication.

Legal requirement

The final accounts of limited companies are required by law. Much of the work of the financial accountant is directed at preparing statements that meet the requirements of the Companies Acts and other such legislation. The management accountant has no such obligations. His work is concerned with providing statements that are useful for decision-making purposes, and not because the law says it must be done.

Historic or future orientation

The work of the financial accountant is concerned with history: he or she takes the transactions of the previous accounting period and summarises and analyses them. The management accountant may use historic data for its information content, but the use to which management accountants put that data is concerned with the future: pricing policies; whether to make or buy a spare part; whether to close a department – all issues that are future-oriented.

Aggregation

In the same way that a financial accounting statement is a general purpose statement, it is also highly aggregated. All the sales of a business are added together to appear in the annual report and accounts of that business: this is aggregation. Similarly, the costs of the business are added together for the whole business. The management accountant prepares specific reports that might only relate to a fraction of the business's activities. Hence he or she may prepare dozens of reports for the use of management colleagues.

External standards

The financial accountant has to abide by and conform to external standards such as Statements of Standard Accounting Practice (SSAPs) and Statements of Recommended Practice (SORPs), as well as statute law. The work of the financial accountant is largely governed by external influences and controls. On the other hand, the management accountant is free of virtually all external constraints, concerned only with what his or her management colleagues need, and SSAPs and SORPs do not, by and large, play a significant part in his or her day-to-day activities.

Objectivity

In the ultimate, when presented with any accounting transaction, a room filled with, say, 1,000 financial accountants would provide the same solution to a given problem calling for accounting interpretation. By accounting transaction we mean, for example, paying the rent, paying wages, or receiving sales income, and not adjustments such as depreciation, bad debts, and so on. The financial accountants would all apply the principles of objectivity and only deal with the matters under review in an objective way. Hence all solutions must be the same. If the room were filled with, say, 1,000 management accountants and they were being asked to deliberate on a management accounting problem, there could well be 20, 30 or more different solutions! This is not to say that management accountants do not understand what they might be facing. Rather we are saying that the work of the management accountant is concerned with what is relevant, and what is relevant to one management accountant will not be relevant to me, or you. The management accountant has the luxury of being able to be subjective, providing he or she is dealing with matters that are relevant. The data that the financial accountant classifies and records is the basis of the information that the management accountant further processes and translates into management information. Both types of accountant are dealing with the same basic data; **it is the objectives of what they are doing with those data that is different.**

Given that management accountants are employed to present their management colleagues with management information services, it is crucial that the information provided is useful. One set of problems with management information is that it may be given in such a way that its value is limited. Imagine that we receive information concerning the provision of computing services in our organistion, yet we work for the maintenance and repairs department! Similarly, imagine that I am being held accountable for the lease costs of a machine in the factory when that cost has been negotiated by the board of directors. The point is that if we are to be held responsible for our costs and revenues, we need to have our responsibilities well defined.

Responsibility accounting

Responsibility is a broad concept of crucial importance to an understanding of management accounting; and it is central to any management accounting system. The term responsibility accounting has been developed to encompass these ideas. Responsibility accounting is: 'A system of accounting that segregates revenues and costs into areas of personal responsibility in order to assess the performance attained by persons to whom authority has been assigned' (CIMA 1989).

In order for the management accountant to carry out his duties fully, he or she must be aware of how the organisation is divided into 'areas of personal responsibility'.

Responsibility centres

Responsibility centres, or just centres, are areas of responsibility and can be a person, a room, or an asset. It is useful to think in terms of departments in this context, however. For example, the Accountancy Department will be a cost centre for most organisations; the Marketing Department will be a revenue centre; and the Personnel Department will be a cost centre. Any organisation can be divided into one or more of the following responsibility centres: cost centre; revenue centre; profit centre; and investment centre. Although responsibility accounting can be applied to any organisation, not every organisation will have all types of responsibility centre. For example, an NHS hospital is unlikely to be regarded as an investment centre.

Cost centres

The manager of a cost centre has no revenue responsibilities at all: he or she is only concerned with the costs that centre incurs. This manager, therefore, will take full responsibility for the operation of the centre because his or her efficiency will be measured by the level of expenditure incurred. His or her performance relates to how efficiently he or she manages costs. He or she will have targets set for all costs for which he or she is responsible.

Revenue centres

A revenue centre manager is responsible for the income generated by the centre, but not the profit that might attach to it. A good example of a revenue centre is the marketing or sales department of an organisation. The marketing department has sales targets set for it to achieve, and whether it achieves these targets is the subject of end-of-period review. The performance measure here would be, for example, total sales, perhaps broken down by region and/or product and/or salesperson.

Profit centres

A profit centre is one step down from an investment centre in that the profit centre manager will be responsible only for the rate of profit on sales or income. The manager will not be held responsible for the rate of return on capital employed. Thus he or she is being held responsible for the relationship between net profit and sales or income. The rate of profitability will be set as a target, in advance, and his or her actual performance will be measured against this.

Investment centres

By investment, we mean the total amount invested by way of equity and other shares, reserves and loans in the assets of the organisation. An investment centre is usually the responsibility of the chief executive of an organisation. The responsibility of the chief executive is to ensure an adequate return on this investment. The chief executive's performance will be measured by means of the rate of return on capital employed (ROCE). He or she will be given (or will set) a required rate of return for an accounting period, and it is by the comparison of this target with the actual result that he or she will be judged.

Mixed responsibility centres

The marketing department is an example of a department that might simultaneously have revenue responsibilities and separate cost responsibilities although it is not a profit centre.

There are problems with responsibility centres, despite the benefits of them. For example, in a cost centre environment, we might be tempted always to assume that underspending is a good thing – and it might well be. However, there are times when we might find that underspending has led to problems which would not otherwise have arisen. Underspending on a maintenance contract, for example, would not necessarily be a good thing to do. Underspending on repairs might be equally disastrous.

There are, too, many examples of salespersons generating sales at any cost. A salesperson has a target to achieve, so he or she sets to work achieving it. But if this salesperson is rewarded on the basis of the level of his or sales, that may be causing problems elsewhere in the organisation. A sale generated at any cost could be causing production scheduling problems, logistics problems and so on, and is therefore not to be encouraged.

When looking at managerial performance, we need to take much more of a holistic view than a simplistic view of responsiblity accounting might have us do. In short, managerial performance needs to be viewed as carefully as any other activity. Responsibility accounting calls for wisdom in its establishment.

CAMEO

There are several examples now that illustrate the way that responsibility accounting is being used in a more and more strategic way. The Xerox Corporation is only one example of an organisation that has given a cost centre profit-centre-style responsibilities. The essence of what Xerox has done is to say to its Logistics and Distribution (L&D) cost centre that although it will continue to operate as a cost centre, it must now behave as if it were a profit centre.

L&D now works much more closely with the departments within Xerox that it serves: it analyses customer needs more than ever before so that it now treats a sister department as if it were an external customer. L&D went through a benchmarking process to ensure that it is operating at world-class levels of efficiency and effectiveness.

References: Tucker and Seymour (1985); Allen (1987).

Another problem with responsibility, in addition to it being poorly controlled, as suggested above, is that it can easily be assigned to the wrong centre. There are many examples of managers who are held responsible for a result yet they are not able to control the outcome of that result. To prevent such an outcome as this, we need to be clear as to who precisely should be responsible for which costs. This takes us on to a discussion of controllability.

Controllability

Controlling operations is one of the chief objectives of any manager. A discussion of control in this context follows logically from a discussion of responsibility accounting, and it leads on naturally to a discussion of controllability filters. Ultimately, all costs are controllable, just as, in the long term, all costs are variable. In the ultimate, the organisation can be closed down completely and all costs cease to be incurred. However, we are more interested in discussing the situation with respect to a going concern. On a day-to-day basis, responsibility centre managers can face problems of controllability. Rent of buildings is commonly a centrally negotiated cost, yet the cost of renting a room or area may be allocated to a department or person. However, that manager is not able to control the rent cost allocated to him or her. Nevertheless, managers need to attempt to control their environment. Otherwise, anything that can go out of control will! By control, we mean ensuring that, for example, a cost or profit will remain within limits previously agreed. Thus, to control, we have to be able to observe and measure the cost or profit, and then take any corrective action necessary.

A thermostat is often given as an example of the control cycle. A thermostat can regulate the heat output of a central heating system in a house or office. The desired temperature (the objective) may be set on the thermostat by means of a mechanical or electronic indicator, the central heating system is turned on and the system then runs (inputs and process). According to a predetermined cycle, the thermostat monitors the temperature achieved (output). If the temperature falls within an acceptable range of temperatures, all is well. If, however, the temperature is significantly below the desired temperature, the central heating system will keep running longer to boost the temperature. Similarly, if the temperature is

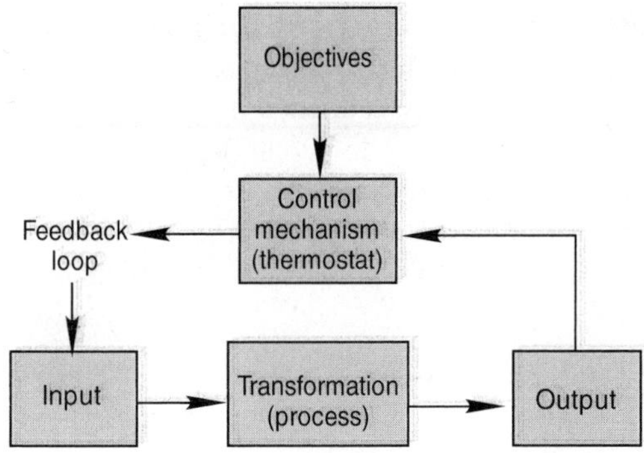

FIGURE 1.2 *Closed loop system*

higher than it should be, the system will shut down until the temperature falls back to an acceptable level. Generalising the idea of the thermostat as an example of the control cycle, we have a closed loop system, as shown in Figure 1.2.

This simplified description shown in Figure 1.2 generally fits the way that a manager controls those aspects of his or her environment for which he or she is being held responsible. There is a significant difference, however, in that a thermostat is an electromechanical device that can be preprogrammed to behave exactly as determined. A manager is a human device subject to many influences. Nevertheless, the thermostat example does outline the control process as applied to the human environment.

As far as managers and their responsibilities are concerned, there are always grey areas: costs and situations where responsibility assignment might not be as clear cut as might otherwise be thought. There are many occasions when we can see that someone has been given the responsibility to undertake a task, but the controllability for at least part of the outcomes lies with someone else.

Controllability filters

Choudhury (1986) describes three controllability filters that help clarify how the management accountant can help management colleagues by distinguishing between costs that are controllable by a specific manager and those that are not. The three filters are: event separation filter; manager separation filter; and period separation filter. Choudhury says that these filters are designed so that they 'exclude "external effects" from the manager's performance'.

Event separation filter

This filter ensures that the manager's performance is not affected by uncertain events outside his or her control: that is, his or her performance should be assessed after allowing for the state of nature that occurred. This allowance can make the manager's performance look better or worse depending on whether the event was favourable or adverse. In the case of an organisation that buys and/or sells from overseas markets, and thus has to engage in buying and selling foreign currencies, we can readily see how an event separation filter should be brought into use. By excluding the effect of currency movements from a foreign subsidiary manager's performance measure, the head office can ensure that he or she does not undertake local currency buying and selling that may be suboptimal from the company's overall perspective.

Manager separation filter

The function of this filter is to insulate the manager's performance evaluation from the effects of the actions of other managers. The manager separation filter is designed not only to isolate one manager's performance from another's, but also to exclude the effects of the superior's decisions from the manager's performance. The decision on establishing and running a head office has little or nothing to do with a manager operating out of, say, a provincial department of that organisation. Nevertheless, it is common to find head office costs being allocated or apportioned to that provincial department. The controllability principle dictates the exclusion of allocated head office costs from the manager's evaluation measures such as return on investment. The problems here include the following:

1. There may be a cost of operating a unit that services more than one manager.
2. There may be a unit that services one manager but investment in the unit was instigated by his or her superior.

Period separation filter

This filter is designed to exclude the effects of past decisions not made by the manager from his or her performance evaluation. This requires that the performance evaluation includes the future effects of a manager's current decision. In some senses this is a minor variant of the manager separation filter. The newly appointed manager of a football team cannot be held responsible for the performance of his new team. We must wait until it is feasible that he could possibly be having some influence over the results of what is, essentially, someone else's team.

Performance reports

This discussion of responsibility accounting and controllability, should help us to appreciate the need for performance reports: that is, formal reports presented regularly to managers that detail how well they have performed in the period under review. Without these reports it will be difficult for anyone to assess the performance of a manager and his or her team. An example of a simplified performance report is shown in Table 1.5.

TABLE 1.5 *Department A performance report*

	Actual £	Budget £	Variance £
Controllable costs			
direct materials	16,500	15,300	1,200 adv.
direct labour	21,000	22,000	1,000 fav.
indirect labour	3,000	3,200	200 fav.
idle time	500	400	100 adv.
fuel	800	1,000	200 fav.
supplies	400	500	100 fav.
stationery	300	280	20 adv.
	42,500	42,680	180 fav.
Uncontrollable costs			
salaries	14,000	14,000	–
depreciation	5,000	5,000	–
insurance	2,000	2,200	200 fav.
	21,000	21,200	200 fav.
Total costs	63,500	63,880	380 fav.

The performance report contained in Table 1.5 not only distinguishes a manager's controllable costs from his or her uncontrollable costs, it also gives him or her information about whether these costs are under control. His or her variances (the differences between actual and budget) are either adv (adverse) or fav (favourable). An adverse variance occurs when a manager's actual expenditure is greater than his or her target or budget allowance. A favourable variance occurs when a manager's actual expenditure is less than his or her allowance. The level of a variance relative to the allowance decides whether an item of expenditure is out of control. In the example above, we can assume that any variance (adverse or favourable) that is more than 5% of budget allowance is out of control. How well has this manager performed this month? Several of this manager's variances are out of control. Direct material is a large cost and the direct materials variance is more than 5% of budget allowance; the indirect labour variance is 6.25% of budget allowance and is also out of control; so is the idle time cost variance, which is 25% of budget allowance.

Management by exception

We have talked about variances as if it is a good idea to investigate every variance that arises. In fact this is rarely a good idea. A good way of illustrating this point is to consider the cyclist cycling down a road when suddenly one of his tyres has a puncture as a result of his having ridden over a piece of broken glass. What does the cyclist do? Does he strip down the bike completely in an attempt to correct his problem, or does he concentrate on the one problem he has and correct for that? It should be obvious that he will only mend the puncture. This is an example of management by exception: that is, dealing only with what varies significantly from the norm. In the case of variance analysis, we would determine by mathematical or statistical means what is normal and what is not, and then deal only with those variances that are significantly different to the norm.

Non-financial indicators

Usually, a performance report is presented as being a document concerned with accounting data; but it is sometimes desirable to include in a performance report non-financial indicators such as ratios. Innes and Mitchell (1990) discuss non-financial measures in relation to performance measurement. Commonly, we think of measuring performance by way of sales figures, net profit and cost expenditures and forget the usefulness of non-financial measures. Innes and Mitchell (1990: 8–9) give an example in their discussion of seven firms in the electronic sector:

> In firm F a major part of the supplementary performance measurement concerned customer satisfaction and was composed entirely of non-financial measures:
>
> - on-time deliveries
> - $\dfrac{\text{number of completed orders shipped}}{\text{total orders shipped}}$
> - current sales order index
> - ageing of past due orders
> - percentage of products rejected in any way by customers
> - product quality index.

We will meet these aspects of management accounting at many points throughout this book.

Traditional purposes of management accounting

If we expand on our discussion now, we can take a look at how management accountants have historically provided a management accounting service. We will then see to some extent how cost and management accounting is developing to deal with the modern world. Traditionally, the purposes of management accounting have been: accounting for product valuation and pricing; policy formulation and planning; decision making; and cost control.

Accounting for product valuation and pricing

Drury (1992) and others talk about the purposes of management accounting as including accounting for stock valuation. What they mean is that the management accountant evaluates the units of production/service at all stages of the production or service provision process. Note, of course, there are no stocks left at the end of a service process: we cannot have a stock of accounting expertise after our annual audit, nor can there be any stocks of servicing work when a machine is serviced. Therefore, we are concerned with the accounting for all elements of cost necessary to arrive at intermediate stage and finished goods valuation, or final service valuation. The methods to be used here apply to all products, all services, and all organisations, including non-profit-making organisations. Accounting for product valuation does, of course, include stock valuation, and we will be discussing stock valuation in Chapter 4.

Economists and accountants have long been involved in the pricing decisions of organisations. A plethora of books and articles are devoted to pricing issues in all sorts of organisations. One area of the work of the management accountant concerns establishing product and service costs for pricing purposes. In Chapter 13, we discuss pricing issues in detail.

Policy formulation and planning

Before management can formulate the policies referred to in CIMA's definition it needs the management accountant to provide it with information relevant to the future. It is this aspect of the purpose of management accounting that gives rise to the view that management accounting is future-oriented, as opposed to the historic orientation of financial accounting. For example, My Company Ltd sets its objectives – what the organisation is to do, and where it wants to go – as the first part of its overall planning and control process. Such objectives will be subjectively determined and, initially, may or may not be attainable. The management accountant's role is to provide financial plans and non-financial plans that explain these objectives. We can assume that My Company Ltd's primary objective is to maximise sales income: the management accountant (working with the managers from the sales, production, personnel, and other departments) will derive financial and non-financial plans consistent with this objective for management's use. The plans derived will show management whether their objectives are attainable or not. When the plans are first drawn up, the bottom line may be found not to be attainable, therefore revisions and modifications will have to be made.

Decision making

One of the primary functions of management is to make decisions; and the management accountant's role is to help management make these decisions. By information for decision making, we mean providing information to help answer the following types of question:

- Should we make our own component parts: that is, can we make this component cheaper than we buy it for, and what are the quality aspects and opportunity costs?
- Is it advisable to close Department X since it is currently making a loss?
- Should we expand output of Product Y?
- Should we invest in new machinery for Product Y?
- Will it prove beneficial to undertake a free gift campaign to boost sales?

We will be examining these types of question at various stages in the book. One of the great strengths of management accounting lies in its ability to act as a vital information source for decision-making purposes.

Cost control

The level of a controllable cost can be influenced by the person that has responsibility for it assigned to him or her. The implications of this are that the management accountant collects and processes cost data which he or she then reports to managerial colleagues. The manager then, performing one of his or her managerial roles, takes any corrective and suitable action in attempting to ensure that the cost remains within the control limits previously agreed. The management accountant has, historically, spent a great deal of time and energy providing information in order for managerial colleagues to control their activities through controlling their costs. However, a lot of evidence has emerged suggesting that the management accountant, and his or her management colleagues, have been wasting their time because of their misplaced emphasis.

A cost can only be controlled if someone is able to influence the level of it. Historically, what has been happening is that a product or service has been designed and produced with between 60% and 80% of its costs already built in, and therefore fixed, *at the design stage*. The implications of built-in costs are that once they're in, they can't be got out simply by tinkering with them. Hence, trying to control a cost that cannot be controlled is a waste of time. The modern management accountant and his or her managerial colleagues now appreciate more than ever the need to control costs before or at the design stage. Closing the stable door after the horse has bolted must be a thing of the past!

Management accounting and the modern world

Newer directions of management accounting

We discussed the traditional purposes of management accounting above when we described such purposes as accounting for product costs and so on. The emphasis of management accounting is now turning more towards the strategic aspects of the organisation. To this end, we will introduce briefly four aspects of the newer ideas of management accounting, which include: activity-based costing; contingency theory; management accounting change; and strategic cost analysis/management.

Activity-based costing

In the first section of this chapter we identified three purposes commonly found in existing management accounting texts. However, with the advent of activity-based costing (ABC), and related developments in that area, new directions in management accounting are being explored. ABC is a new area of study for management accountants, and relatively few organisations have installed an ABC system as yet. Nevertheless, we will see in Chapters 6 and 7 the power of ABC: it is a system which dispels the myth that all costs can be recovered by products or services merely by charging overheads on the basis of an arbitrarily derived chargeout rate. A proper application of ABC ensures that a minimal number of arbitrary decisions are built into cost analysis. Therefore when a cost schedule is prepared by ABC, it will give a highly accurate view of what the cost really is.

Brignall *et al.* (1991: 228) say: 'Focusing on product costs in particular, if they do not reflect the costs of the resources consumed to produce them this could have serious implications for strategic pricing and resource allocation decisions within the firm.' They go on to say:

> The approach (ABC) is to focus on what is generating the cost rather than . . . merely allocating the cost . . . ABC systems allocate costs to functional activity cost pools and then calculate costs to products using individual ABC drivers . . . The central idea, that many individual costs are driven by 'functional activity' rather than volume of output, may enable us to gain a better understanding of indirect cost behaviour. (Ibid.: 232)

Contingency theory

If we were to review cost accounting textbooks from the early to the middle of the twentieth century, we would find examples suggestive of a contingency view of management accounting. Old textbooks give detailed examples of, for example, accounting for the manufacture of motor vehicles, the generation of electricity and so on. The purpose behind such examples was to reflect the fact that each type of organisation has different accounting needs to each other type of organisation. Contingency theorists have taken the view that it is not sufficient simply to speak in terms of the differences between industries and sectors: differences between the various systems and functions of organisations must also be identified.

A lot of useful work has been done by contingency theorists, but this work has a weakness. The fundamental weakness of the academic work on the contingency approach is that it has, on the one hand, accepted that contingency variables must exist, and then, on the other hand, has largely sought to prescribe what those variables will be in any given environment. Something of a paradox! Ezzamel and Hart (1987: 33–6) give a good evaluation of the contingency theory of management accounting. They introduce the contingency theory as follows:

> Through a combination of a priori reasoning and empirical validation, propositions are developed formalising the relationship between the situational contingencies of a firm and the appropriate nature of its information system. Organisational effectiveness, it is argued, will be improved by attaining an appropriate fit between the characteristics of the organisation's situation . . . and the characteristics of its management information systems. (Ibid. 96)

Brignall *et al.* (1991), in discussing product costing in service organisations, reiterate the view of the need for a contingency approach to management accounting. By a contingency approach, we are talking about an organisation designing its management accounting system by taking account of its contingency variables, which include:

- the environment in which the organisation operates;
- the technology the organisation employs;
- organisation size; and
- organisation structure.

Essentially, the contingency approach says that the precise nature of the management accounting system will be contingent upon the nature of the business engaged in. So, a furniture manufacturer will need a different management accounting system from a computer assembler because the contingency variables as between the two organisations are different – the making of furniture is radically different to the assembly of computers. Wilson and Chua (1993: 53) illustrate in outline how such contingency factors impact upon a managerial accounting environment. They impact upon:

- method of budget use;
- method of costing; and
- manipulation of accounting data.

The reasons for such differences might sometimes be obscure, but in general they include the following factors:

1. Large organisations will tend to have sophisticated systems.
2. Organisations with an experienced accountant will tend to have a sophisticated accounting system.
3. Organisations with a trained management accountant, rather than a trained financial accountant, will tend to have a sophisticated management accounting system.
4. Organisations that use computer-based information systems will tend to have sophisticated information reporting systems.

It would be useful, of course, if an organisation could simply turn to a management accounting manual, or a research study, and, taking a variety of factors into account, select the type of management accounting system it needed. It would then know whether to adopt a simple or sophisticated system, a job-costing system, a batch-costing system, or any other kind of management accounting system. Attempts to be more specific, however, usually meet with problems. Karmarkar, Lederer and Zimmerman (1990) tried to find out what determined the kind of cost accounting and production control system an organisation had in place. The starting point of their investigation was to hypothesise that management chooses the type of accounting and control systems depending upon:

> 1) the physical characteristics of the manufacturing process,
> 2) instability of the production process,
> 3) the relative importance of overheads,
> 4) the extent of product competition faced by the firm. (Karmarkar *et al.* 1990: 357)

Unfortunately, they could find few statistical relationships between the variables they set out to study. Hence the type of management accounting system in place in an organisation will be determined by a host of factors, not all of which may be obvious.

Whether they realised it or not, management accountants of yesteryear did not necessarily appreciate the need for a contingency theory of management accounting. Management accountants historically would often use systems and procedures because they had always been found to be effective – like old wives' tales! Now, however, as research and practice become more sophisticated, mere acceptance of accounting routines is not sufficient. However, before moving on to considering some of the newer directions in which management accounting is moving, we should dwell, for a short while, on the directions from which management accounting has come: that is, the traditional purposes of management accounting.

Management accounting change

Innes and Mitchell (1990) investigated the factors that have influenced management accounting change. They investigated seven firms (designated A to G) in the electronics sector. The importance of their paper is, at least in part, that they clearly demonstrate the need for management accounting systems for all organisations, and therefore the changes necessary within an organisation to implement the management accounting system. They list the origins of change as:

- competitive and dynamic market environment
- organisational structure
- production technology
- product cost structure
- management influence
- deteriorating financial performance (Ibid. 9–12)

They say that the consequences of change were that more timely, relevant and comprehensible new information was perceived as improving managerial decisions in areas such as cost reduction, cost control, production location, product quality and performance assessment. They also found that the involvement of accountants in such areas as competitive analysis, design for cost and the calculation of 'landed costs' made managers more cost conscious in their general work.

> In firm D both accountants and managers attributed substantial recent improvements in the net cost of quality merely to the measurement and reporting of the relevant costs for the first time. In two firms, D and E, the abandonment of conventional direct labour hour based production overhead rates and their replacement by alternative methods had significantly affected new product design. In the past, designers faced with high projected labour overhead rates (often over 1,000%) had tried to design labour out of new products. This process had led to a vicious cycle of higher overhead rates and less direct labour, a cycle which had been broken by this costing change. (Ibid. 13, 15)

Lapsley and Pettigrew (1994: 84–92) discuss accounting for change in the context of both private and public sectors. Drawing on two important studies of change, they discuss why the performance of organisations in broadly the same industry, country and product markets differ. Five interrelated factors are postulated for private sector firms:

1. How firms assessed their environment.
2. How they led change.
3. How they linked strategic and operational coherence.
4. How they managed human resources.
5. The management of coherence in the overall change process.

For the public sector organisation, the rate and pace of change was found to vary substantially accross District Health Authorities. The interlinked factors associated with receptivity included:

- Environmental pressure for change.
- The quality and clarity of change goals and strategies.
- Organisational cultures and interorganisational relations supportive of change.
- Availability of key people to lead change.
- The character of manager–clinician relationships.
- Capability in managing the change process.

They discuss the transferability of management accounting practices across private and public sector boundaries. Thus what the private sector can implement successfully may be successfully applied in the public sector. The two lists taken from Lapsley and Pettigrew contain essentially common elements. They do conclude, however, that:

> the public sector may represent a more formidable challenge for manager and management accountant alike. One means by which such changes might be intitiated, managed and accounted for, would be by the application of a broader concept of strategic management accounting which embraces not only consideration of internal–external relationships of costs and service attributes, but also concepts of how changes in service delivery are managed in the new, market oriented, public sector. (Lapsley and Pettigrew 1990: 91–2)

Strategic cost analysis/management

Alongside of all the work done over the last twenty years or so in the area of activity-based costing, throughput costing, target costing and so on, has been a lot of work on strategic cost management. Shank and Govindarajan (1993: 8) entitled their book *Strategic Cost Management: The new tool for competitive advantage*. They say that strategic cost management (SCM) has three underlying themes:

1. value chain analysis;
2. strategic positioning analysis; and
3. cost driver analysis.

They go on to say that accounting exists within a business primarily to facilitate the development and implementation of business strategy and that accounting information plays a role in the cycle that this represents. Perhaps one of the most important messages that they attempt to convey is that accounting is not an end in itself, but only a means to help achieve business success. It follows from this that the management accountant needs to understand his or her environment: that is, to understand the contingency factors that exist within and surround his or her organisation.

Brausch (1994: 45), discussing target costing, says that it (the implementation and operation of such a system) 'presumes interaction between cost accounting and the rest of the firm'. To help with the more strategic aspects of cost and management accounting in his own organisation, Brausch states that their first goal was to separate the functions of managerial and financial accounting. Thus they were separating the need to report within the financial accounting corset of statutes and accounting standards and the management accounting need to provide valuable managerial, strategic information.

In the context of strategic cost management, Shank and Govindarajan (1993: 8) provide three key questions that need to be answered when considering any accounting idea:

1. **Does it serve an identifiable business objective?**
2. **For the objective it is designed to serve, does the accounting idea enhance the chances of attaining the objective?**
3. **Does the objective whose attainment is facilitated by the accounting idea fit strategically with the overall thrust of the business?**

We should bear in mind these three questions as we work our way through this book. Even if we do not specifically pose them, they should be at the forefront of every discussion we have.

CAMEO

The green aspects of cost and management accounting

There are now many areas of both our personal and our business lives that can call upon the skills of the management accountant for assistance. One such area is the environmental (green) aspect of business life. Many people will have heard businesspeople, accountants, and engineers all calling for clemency when laws such as the Clean Air Act are enacted and enforced. The initial knee-jerk reaction of most businesspeople to green legislation is to take us through the economic disasters that are about to befall their business in particular and their industry in general. However, the management accountant's skills can be called upon to help obtain such information as that provided by Frances Cairncross (1995) in her very well written and easy to read book, *Green, Inc.*

One aspect of Cairncross's line of debate concerns green issues and technology. She cites the example of the closed stove (or furnace) and its advantages over the open stove. A closed stove retains a lot of its energy, hence making production or heating operations more cost efficient. Cairncross states that seven times as much electricity can be generated from a tonne of coal now as compared with the turn of the twentieth century. This is good news and might fly in the face of the businessperson's knee-jerk reaction mentioned above. The essence of the green debate is thus twofold: protecting the environment, and cost efficiency. Cairncross and many others are at pains to point out the many benefits that both business and society can derive from the green debate. The examples that Cairncross (1995: 180–3) gives in support of this debate include:

1. Procter & Gamble's detergent 'dosing' ball: the little ball that we put washing detergent into when we use an automatic washing machine. The benefits of this innovation are green and economic: the plastic from which they are made can be recycled; manufacturing costs are reduced; packing and transport costs are reduced; the new products take up a lot less shelf space on supermarket shelves.
2. The example of McDonald's (the fast food organisation) and a management accounting exercise. McDonald's came under pressure to replace their polystyrene packaging with washable and reusable ceramic plates and so on. The outcome of the exercise was that in addition to the arithmetic being wrong, washable plates and similar items were less environmentally friendly.
3. A survey by the MORI (market research) organisation determined the following, from an annual survey of 2,000 adults in Britain:
   (a) in 1990, 23% of the people surveyed claimed to avoid buying products or services of organisations with a poor green record: in 1993, 22% of those surveyed said the same;
   (b) in 1990, 40% of those surveyed bought products made from recycled materials: by 1993, 50% of respondents bought products made from recycled materials.

Another example where we can see the interface between green issues and management accounting issues concerns the transportation of logs of wood. If we harvest wood and ship it to the saw mill in rough logs, we might be able to ship, say, twenty logs on a lorry. If, on the other hand, we partially dress (or prepare) those logs at the forest site, we might be able to transport, say, forty logs. This gives rise to waste at the forest site rather than at the saw mill, but if costed properly the decision to dress at the forest and save on transportation costs, lorry emissions and so on will be beneficial all round.

Introduction to value added management (VAM)

Value added management is concerned with the elimination of those aspects of a process or system that add costs but do not add value. That is, by the end of the relevant part of a process or service which of the following do we observe?

1. Total costs increase and profits decrease
2. Total costs increase and profits increase

If we observe the former situation, we have a value added problem. If we observe the latter situation, we should be pleased. This is so because value added management is concerned to enhance profitability even if costs increase. Such increases in profitability are achieved by increasing sales values over and above any increase in costs that additional aspects to processes or services might incur. Smith (1989: 70) lists the principal concerns of VAM as follows:

- overproduction
- waiting
- transportation (times spent transporting)
- inventory
- motion (non-value-adding movement)
- defects
- unused creativity (ignoring feedback from the shop floor)
- processing (time spent adding value to the product)

VAM is concerned with maximising an organisation's effective use of processing time – the last of the concerns listed above – and minimising the effect of each of the others. It comprises three subsystems:

1. Just in time (JIT)
2. Total quality management (TQM)
3. Total employee involvement

We deal with just-in-time as part of our discussion of accounting for materials in Chapter 4. However, the just-in-time philosophy is essentially based on the idea that carrying stocks of any kind must be considered to be a waste of resources. Apart from stocks held for strategic purposes and for reasons connected with uncertain delivery periods, for example, stocks should not be held, according to the just-in-time philosophy.

Total quality management stems from the desire of organisations to build in reliability to products rather than repair defects out of products. That is, when buying raw materials, we would, using the total quality management philosophy, negotiate with our suppliers to ensure that they are free of all defects. The outcome of defect-free raw materials is that we do not build problems into our processes, hence we have controlled one of the most important variables in the manufacturing process. Similarly, we will control the manufacturing process more carefully under total quality management systems. To do this, we might increase our training inputs, or simply hire better qualified and experienced employees. We are now more certain that the processes and systems will have more reliable outputs. Total quality management is a philosophy, rather than just a set of techniques and directives, in that it requires the management of the organisation to look at what it does from start to finish and consider the quality aspects of what it does at every stage. The examples of raw material inputs and the labour aspects are just two examples of how total quality management looks at the organisation from a quality improvement point of view.

Total employee involvement is an issue that is now discussed at length in some areas. Much work has been done in this field over the last five or six decades, and all studies have arrived at similar conclusions, which we can summarise as follows. If someone is involved in decision making, controlling his or her own sphere of influence and so on, he or she will feel much more responsive towards colleagues and systems. Consequently, employees who participate are happier, more productive, employees. Smith (1989) cites a survey of the motor vehicle industry in 1984 that revealed a cost advantage to Japanese manufacturing relative to the United States of \$2,203 per unit. The survey reveals that almost two-thirds of the manufacturing cost advantage can be ascribed to factors concerned with non-value-adding activities.

A great deal of effort has been put into analysing manufacturing systems, procedures and methods ever since the Industrial Revolution of the eighteenth and nineteenth centuries. One of the biggest problems that has remained with many (if not most) manufacturers world-wide is the problem of the non-value-adding effort expended in bringing finished goods to market. By non-value-adding we mean that something is done to raw materials, semi-finished and finished products that costs money and other resources but which does not enhance the value of the product. For example, moving raw materials from a raw materials storage area to the factory floor costs money, but having moved the materials does not enhance the value of the finished product. Similarly, having semi-finished or finished goods waiting for further processing or sale is expensive but does nothing to convince the customer to pay any more for the goods. VAM seeks to identify and analyse such issues and eradicate them. We can measure value added along the following lines:

$$\text{value added per employee} = \frac{\text{sales value} - \text{materials costs}}{\text{number of employees}}$$

This ratio is used in the same way that any other accounting ratio is used: we monitor the performance of an organisation or department over time or in comparison with other organisations or departments performing the same, or similar, operations. In conclusion, Smith (1989: 73) says that if we apply the principles of value added management, we aim:

To reduce costs by reducing:

Lead times	Changeover time
Inventory	Cycle time
Floor space	Raw material stock
Wastage	Work in progress
Reworking	Interest payments

To increase quality by increasing:
Flexibility
Employee involvement
Productivity

One specific example of the power of VAM can be seen from the example of Toyota Motors in Japan. As a result of the desire to eliminate as much waste as possible from their operations, Toyota reduced the setup time for certain presses to ten minutes. The impact of this is measured when we learn that in the United States, the setup of the same presses can take six hours. As you read through this book, even though specific reference may not be made back to this point, the concepts of value added management, and their impact on JIT, quality management, and employee involvement, should be considered and applied as much as possible. Question everything.

SUMMARY

The main conclusion we should draw from this chapter is that management accounting is an internally based management information system. The management accountant of an organisation works entirely within and for his or her organisation, and only exceptionally will the work of the management accountant ever be known outside that organisation. This chapter shows that the work of management accountants does, in fact, cover every aspect of the work of the organisation that they work in – whether that organisation is a manufacturing organisation, a retail outlet or a hospital. The skills and knowledge that management accountants carry with them are universally applicable. As Drucker (1989) has essentially pointed out, management accountants can work effectively anywhere and contribute positively to the work of any organisation. Lapsley and Pettigrew (1994) also say that the work of the private sector management accountant can be taken and used by his or her public sector counterpart.

This chapter has provided us with an overview of the role the management accountant plays in organising, planning, and controlling his or her organisation. Additionally, the chapter has given us an introduction to the benefits of the outputs of the management accountant, and we have contrasted the output of the management accounting system with the output of the financial accounting system. We have concluded that for a management information system to work effectively, the output of the management accountant has to be detailed and specifically designed for the purpose for which it is needed. The discussion of activity-based costing, just in time and other new techniques, has shown the management accountant working in a dynamic environment. Although the basic techniques of management accounting remain relatively stable, new ones do come along from time to time, and we will be discussing some of these new techniques in this book.

Finally, we have incorporated in our introductory discussion the ideas stemming from general management, and we have considered the impact of global marketing on the ideas behind value added management. This led us to introduce the ideas that surround such techniques as just in time, quality management and employee involvement.

KEY TERMS

You should satisfy yourself that you have noted all of these terms and can define and/or describe their meaning and use, as appropriate.

Cost accounting (p. 2)	Controllability (p. 12)
Management accounting (p. 2)	Control (p. 12)
Service industries (p. 3)	Activity-based costing (ABC) (p. 18)
Terotechnology (p. 5)	Contingency approach (p. 19)
Financial accounting (p. 7)	Value added management (p. 24)
Responsibility accounting (p. 10)	Total quality management (p. 24)
Cost centre (p. 10)	Total employee involvement (p. 25)

RECOMMENDED READING

For a different viewpoint to much of this book see Brignall *et al.* Drucker (1989) is well written and possibly an eye opener, and is recommended at the end of almost every chapter of this book! See also Shank and Govindarajan (1993). Essential reading is Tucker and Seymour (1985). Finally, see Allen (1987), which illustrates that the circumstances described in the Xerox cameo are also occurring in the former Soviet Union.

QUESTIONS

Review questions

1. Define management accounting as concisely as you can.
2. Give examples of who needs management accounting information and why.
3. Highlight the differences between a financial accounting report and a management accounting report.
4. What are the traditional purposes of management accounting?
5. What is responsibility accounting?
6. Describe the three controllability filters discussed in the chapter.
7. What is a performance report, and how should it be used?
8. Define management by exception, and give an example of the application of it.

Answers to review questions 2, 5, 6 and 7 can be found in the Student Workbook.

Graded practice questions

Level I

1. Mrs A. Smith was a marketing executive with a large conglomerate until five years ago, when she was made redundant. Given a reasonable settlement on her redundancy, she invested wisely in her own engineering business. Mr Smith is a mechanical engineer, and the husband and wife are in partnership in this venture. Of late, they have both realised that as the business is growing, they are feeling that they are not entirely in control of their situation. They both feel that they need help from a management accountant.

Required

Detail the advice you would give the Smiths on the aims and outputs of a management accounting system for their business.

2. Information can be described as being provided to management under three different headings: record keeping needs; performance evaluation needs; and decision-making needs. Under which heading do the following properly fall:
   (a) information about expenses contained in an account in the general ledger;
   (b) information relating to leasing a vehicle as opposed to using bank finance to buy it;
   (c) information relating to the cost of making a component rather than buying it in ready made;
   (d) information containing the profitability of a department;
   (e) information concerning how well costs are controlled in the computer department?
3. State whether the activities listed below are financial accounting or management accounting activities:
   (a) a monthly profitability report for a new factory is sent to the bank that helped finance the project;
   (b) the marketing director receives a monthly report concerning the advertising costs for each product line;
   (c) a consolidated income tax return is prepared for a large organisation;
   (d) a company's annual report and accounts is prepared and sent to shareholders;
   (e) each regional sales manager is sent a report showing the actual earnings performance of the operation compared with the expected results;
   (f) a company's auditor requests detailed product cost information during the annual audit;
   (g) monthly payroll costs are summarised, being analysed by department and job responsibilities;
   (h) a detailed analysis of the cost of purchasing or leasing computer equipment is prepared.
4. Management functions are divided as follows: planning; organising; directing; and controlling. How would you classify each of the following:
   (a) the engineering department of a manufacturing organisation predicting the type of vehicle the public will want five years from now;
   (b) comparing actual financial results with those expected for an accounting period;
   (c) allocating resources to four product lines for the next production period;
   (d) a factory manager answering questions raised by five department managers about a new bonus compensation plan recently adopted by the organisation;
   (e) combining separate goals of the segments of a business into overall organisation goals;
   (f) combining budgets of individual segments of a business into an overall organisation's budget;
   (g) evaluating the last quarter's financial performance of a sales territory?
5. Indicate whether each of the following is a long- or short-term decision-making activity:
   (a) a plant manager is evaluating the feasibility of buying a new piece of equipment to take advantage of advances in technology offering substantial cost savings;
   (b) a manufacturing organisation is evaluating the profitability of a proposed plant expansion;
   (c) a marketing manager is trying to decide which products should be listed in the organisation's advertising campaign;
   (d) a factory manager is trying to decide whether to hire a maintenance crew or obtain maintenance services from an outside source;

(e) facing a significant decline in the company's cash balance, the board of directors is evaluating whether a quarterly dividend should be paid and, if so, how much it should be;
(f) the demand for the products produced at an organisation's factory has declined significantly, and the chairman is evaluating whether the plant should be closed or a new product should be added;
(g) an organisation's top management is trying to determine the scope and direction of the research and development activities;
(h) a retailing organisation is considering a price decrease for certain products to meet competition.

6. Which of the following costs are likely to be controllable by the head of a production department in a manufacturing organisation:
(a) price paid for materials;
(b) charge for floor space;
(c) raw materials used;
(d) electricity used for machinery;
(e) machinery depreciation;
(f) direct wages;
(g) insurance of machinery;
(h) share of costs of personnel department.

Level II

7. The following accounts are extracted from the books of Austins Bakery Ltd, a small but highly popular baker in a small town in Northern England.

Bakery appraisal form for the month of October

	Actual	Budget
	£	£
Sales		
Bread	9,500	11,875
Cakes	11,475	14,000
Pies		
meat	3,500	3,375
fruit	1,950	1,450
Sweets	126	60
Total Sales	26,551	30,760
Expenses		
Flour		
wholemeal	1,900	2,200
plain white	2,675	3,300
self-raising white	1,350	1,700
Sugar		
caster	3,500	3,500
icing	950	950

Rates	481	600
Water	300	375
Eggs	500	625
Yeast	75	95
Other shortening	293	265
Jams	100	125
Dried fruit	365	465
Transport	650	815
Salt	5	5
Spices	25	30
Wages	5,600	7,000
Electricity	850	1,060
Overalls replacement	50	60
Telephone	600	550
Cleaning materials	255	320
Wrappings		
baking cases	70	80
plastic bags	150	90
paper bags	95	100
Overalls cleaning	125	100
Meat	400	500
Margarine/butter	865	1,080
Repairs and maintenance	512	640
Depreciation		
plant	300	300
vehicle	150	150
Total expenses	23,191	27,080
Net profit	3,360	3,680

Required

(a) (i) Redraft this report into a much more management friendly format. Include in your solution a variance column.

(ii) Comment on any aspect of the variances you wish.

(b) Make any recommendations you think valid from the information supplied in this question.

Solutions to practice questions 2, 4 and 6 can be found in the Student Workbook. Solutions to practice question numbers in red can be found at the end of this book.

Projects

1. (a) Draw up a list of at least twenty organisations and classify them according to which sector of the economy they operate in: primary; secondary; or tertiary.

   (b) Of those that you classify as being in the tertiary sector (the service sector), further classify

them as: professional services; service shops; mass shops.
Justify your classifications in both (a) and (b).

2. (a) Take any example you wish from part (b) of the first project above and build up an example of the kind of outputs that the management accountant could provide for that organisation. (*Hint*: a simple example would be to take accountancy services from the professional services list and build up a demonstration of the rate to charge per hour for the services provided to its clients.)
   (b) Look for evidence in your community or in newspapers and journals for service sector organisations that demonstrably are using management accounting principles on a regular basis. Discuss the evidence you have found.
3. The privatisation of publicly owned organisations in the United Kingdom is, from a management accounting point of view, based on responsibility accounting and controllability. Discuss the relationship between these two factors in the context of privatisation.

REFERENCES

Allen, B. (1987), 'Make information services pay its way', reprint no. 87102, *Harvard Business Review*.

Brausch, J. M. (1994), 'Beyond ABC: target costing for profit enhancement', *Management Accounting* (NAA) (November), 45–9.

Brignall, T. J., Fitzgerald, L., Johnston, R. and Silvestro, R. (1991), 'Product costing in service organisations', *Management Accounting Resarch*, vol. **2** (4) (December), 227–48.

Cairncross, F. (1995), *Green, Inc.* (Earthscan Publications).

Choudhury, N. (1986), 'Responsibility accounting and controllability', *Accounting and Business Research*, (Summer), 189–98.

CIMA (1989), *Management Accounting Official Terminology* (Chartered Institute of Management Accountants).

Drucker, P. F. (1989), 'What business can learn from nonprofits', *Harvard Business Review* (July–August), 88–93.

Drury, C. (1992), *Management and Cost Accounting*, 3rd edn (Chapman & Hall).

Ezzamel, M. and Hart, H. (1987), *Advanced Management Accounting: An organisational emphasis* (Cassell).

Innes, J. and Mitchell, F. (1990), 'The process of change in management accounting: some field study evidence', *Management Accounting Research,* vol. **1** (1) (March), 3–19.

Lapsley, I. and Pettigrew, A. (1994), 'Meeting the challenge: accounting for change', *Financial accountability and management*, May, 79–92.

Karmarkar, U. S., Lederer, P. J. and Zimmerman, J. L. (1990), 'Choosing manufacturing production control and cost accounting systems', in R. S. Kaplan (ed.), *Measures for Manufacturing Excellence* (Harvard Business School Press).

Shank, J. K. and Govindarajan, V. (1993), *Strategic Cost Management: The new tool for competitive advantage* (Free Press).

Smith, R. B. (1989), 'Competitiveness in the '90s', *Management Accounting* (US) (September), 24–9.

Tucker, F. G. and Seymour, M. Z. (1985), 'A Xerox cost center imitates a profit center', reprint no. 85317, *Harvard Business Review* (May–June).

Wilson, R. M. S. and Chua, W. F. (1993), *Managerial Accounting: Method and meaning*, 2nd edn (Chapman & Hall).

PART ONE

Accounting for the elements of cost

Chapter 1 provided an overview of cost and management accounting as information systems. These systems are part of the overall provision of financial information regarding the internal operation of an organisation, whether that organisation is a manufacturer, a service company or a non-profit-making body.

Part I now deals essentially with the cost accounting aspects of management accounting.

We start by looking in Chapter 2 at the need for, and methods associated with, the classification and coding of cost information. In fact the content of this chapter can be perceived as the foundation for much of the work that is identified as cost and management accounting. Chapter 3 takes a fundamental look at some of the questions relating to the analysis of the behaviour of costs, while Chapters 4, 5 and 6, give a detailed view of the three elements of cost: material, labour and overheads. Looking first at inventory management tand aspects of the logistics chain, we see in Chapter 4 that organisations such as supermarket achains, for example, are using their logistic chains strategically to gain competitive advantage. Similarly, accounting procedure for people costs is more than merely calculating wage costs, as Chapter 5 demonstrates.

Taken together, Chapters 6 and 7 give a detailed review of the theory and practice of accounting for overheads. The more traditional treatment of overheads covered in Chapter 6 provides a platform for Chapter 7 in which we discuss the development of activity-based costing and costing management.

The way in which, for example, a job costing system works – and why we would use a job costing system as opposed to a batch or process costing system – is illustrated in Chapter 8. Further material in Chapter 9 on the derivation of fixed and variable costs makes up the final information needed to allow the use of cost accounting information in a management accounting setting.

An introduction to managerial decision making completes this part in Chapter 10, in which distinction is drawn between absorption costing and variable costing.

CHAPTER TWO

Classification and the coding of costs

CHAPTER OBJECTIVES

After reading this chapter you should be able to:

- appreciate what is meant by cost classification
- understand classification for cost accounting
- understand classification for decision making
- understand the link between the clasification and coding of costs
- appreciate the need for the coding of costs

Introduction

This section is concerned with the classification of costs but starts with the classification and coding system found in a library. The reason for the apparent contradiction is that most, if not all, readers of this book will be able to confirm the workings of the classification and coding system in a library with little difficulty. Libraries could not function without a classification and coding system: without such a system, the only way of storing books and periodicals would be on a 'stack them as they come' basis. Trying to find a book in a library that does not use a classification and coding system would be a nightmare! For an accountant in a large business, the same problem would apply: unless costs and revenues are fully classified and coded, trying to keep track of profits and losses would be impossible.

The historic cost and historic revenue information we are discussing in management accounting is exactly the same cost and revenue information dealt with by the financial accountant. However, financial accounting is concerned only with the nature of the cost or revenue: for example, whether a cost is wages, rent or raw material. Management accounting, on the other hand, is concerned with the purpose of the cost. For example, whether the wages cost is incurred by manufacturing, maintenance or administration; and, if it is for manufacturing, whether it is a direct or indirect cost. If we look at the work of the financial accountant, we see that when an invoice arrives for payment, or when the payroll is being analysed, one of the first things that happens is that an allocation is made to a division, department or product, so that the correct account can be debited in the purchases or general ledger. The only way such an allocation can be made is if the costs associated with that invoice or payroll charge have been classified in the first place. Without classification, all charges could end up in the same account, or there may be no way of deciding how much of a cost belongs to department A as opposed to departments B, C and D.

Classification is: 'The arrangement of items in logical groups having regard to their nature (subjective classification) or purpose (objective classification) (CIMA 1991). CIMA says that subjective classification is used to indicate the nature of the expenditure (for example, materials, or labour) whereas objective classification tells us, for instance, which cost centre or cost unit is to be charged. We will look at two different, but complementary, cost classification schemes. In the first scheme, we will look at the general classification of costs for a manufacturer that allows us to build up the costs of making a product, or providing a service, in such a way that we can say with confidence that a computer costs £x to make or that it costs y per page to provide a word processing service. Furthermore, the classification allows the management accountant to advise his or her management colleagues in the organisation precisely how the cost came to be £x for the computer or £y for the word processing service. The second cost classification scheme concerns the abstract division of costs into such categories as:

- absorbed versus marginal;
- sunk versus committed; and
- opportunity versus incremental.

In general, scheme one will be used for cost accounting, cost determination purposes; whereas scheme two will be used for decision-making purposes.

Cost classification scheme one: classification for cost accounting

The management accountant can accumulate the costs of the products made in his or her organisation on a cost card. A cost card is record of all of the materials, labour, and overhead costs incurred in the processing of a job, product or service.

If we had not classified costs at all, the cost card could only look like the cost card in Table 2.1. Without classification, the cost of every product made can only be an average of all costs divided by the total number of units made. This would not necessarily be a serious problem if only one product were being made, but in the real world, how many computer manufacturers are there who only make one model with no model variations? And how many word processing bureaux only ever process one type of document? As soon as a model is varied, its cost structure relative to the initial model will probably change. Therefore an average cost becomes more unrepresentative of reality, the more variations of a model there are.

TABLE 2.1 *Cost card (1): manufacture of ICBM computer model*

Average cost per unit ICBM model computer abc.

Average cost of

$$1 \text{ computer abc} = \frac{\text{Total costs}}{\text{Number of computer abc's made}}$$

When the accountant has a cost classification system, he or she is able to keep track of the organisation's costs in detail; and his or her performance reports, such as Table 2.2, are much more meaningful. With a full classification system, every product and variation can be reported on separately.

TABLE 2.2 *Cost card (2): manufacture of ICBM computer model*

Cost per unit	£	£
Direct materials:		
1		
2		
3	———	
Direct labour:		
A		
S		
F	———	———
Prime cost		
Overheads:		
Supervision		
Electricity		
Insurances		
Indirect labour		
Indirect materials	———	———
Total manufacturing cost		

These issues are vital for the management accountant. If the management accountant did not classify the organisation's costs, the answers to the questions relating to stock valuation, decision making, and controlling the organisation's activities that were highlighted in Chapter 1 would remain unanswered. If the management accounting system could not provide detailed cost summaries, the informational content of the output of the management accounting department would be very low indeed. A total average cost per unit might give some indication of the efficiency of the manufacturing departments, but it does not allow for detailed insights into the quantities and costs of each direct material used in manufacture. Nor does it highlight the relevant direct labour costs of manufacture, while the details of the overhead costs associated with manufacture would remain a mystery.

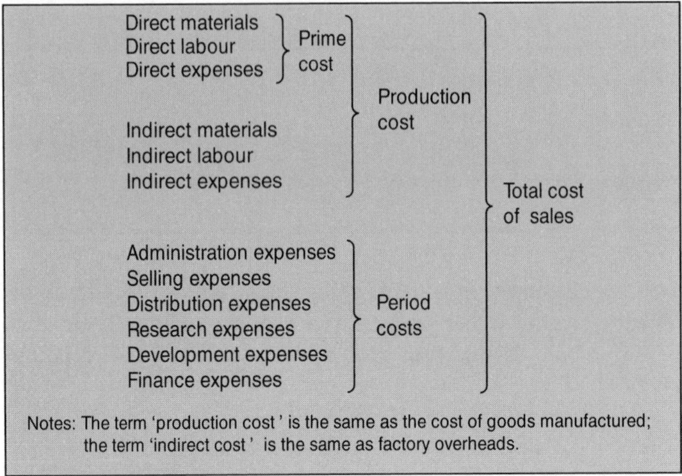

FIGURE 2.1 *General classification system for a manufacturer*

General classification of costs for a manufacturer

The following discussion defines in detail all of the terms used in Figure 2.1, which provides a general classification system for a manufacturer.

The elements of cost

Material costs, labour costs and expense (or overhead) costs are known collectively as the three elements of cost; and although Figure 2.1 gives a simplified view of the classification of costs, by defining each of the terms in the figure, we will see how this scheme will suit any manufacturing organisation.

Direct costs

A direct cost is classified as direct if the element of cost being discussed can be directly associated with the product being manufactured.

1. *Direct materials.* In the case of direct materials, a material is classified as being direct if it is incorporated in the finished product. For example, in the manufacture of wooden furniture, the pieces of wood that are made into chair legs, and the foam padding that goes into the seat of a chair, must both be classified as direct materials.
2. *Direct labour.* As far as direct labour is concerned, the labour costs of the people who prepare the wood that goes into the finished chair and the labour costs of the people who assemble the pieces of the chair are both direct labour costs since those people are directly involved in the making of the finished product.
3. *Direct expense.* A direct expense is usually taken to be a special cost such as the hire of a special machine or tool, the costs of a special design, or the payment of a licence fee

or royalties. It is classified as a direct expense because the cost is directly associated with a particular design or product as opposed to the organisation's normal, everyday, range of products. A furniture manufacturer may make a range of six different designs of dining chairs. All costs of such normal products are classified as normal, under the relevant headings. However, if a customer requests 120 chairs of a special design, all of the costs associated with that special design will be assignable to that design. If, therefore, the manufacturer has to hire a special plane or sawing machine just for that job, these hiring costs will be a direct expense; similarly, the costs incurred by the design department in drawing up the working plans will be a direct expense. The direct materials and direct labour costs will be classified in this situation in the normal way: any direct materials will be debited to the relevant direct materials account, and so on.

Indirect costs

Within the factory environment, any cost that is not a direct cost must be an indirect cost. Therefore, if a material is used in the factory and it is not a direct material, it must be an indirect material. Examples of indirect materials costs include cleaning materials, lubrication oils, grease, and materials that are part of the finished product but that cannot be considered direct materials. This may sound like a contradiction, for a direct material to be classified as an indirect material, but this is not necessarily the case, and for one simple reason. Although the glue used to stick a chair's legs together is most definitely a part of the finished chair, its cost may be insignificant and so it is classified as an indirect cost. Significance, in this context, can be defined in a number of ways. In the case of the glue, it could be that a manufacturer spends £500 on glue in a year in making 200,000 chairs: the average cost of glue per chair is £500 ÷ 200,000 chairs = £0.0025 per chair. If the manufacturer chooses to work to the nearest 0.01 for cost data purposes, the cost of glue is insignificant. Thus the glue is part of the finished product, but the cost is controlled only in total as an indirect cost. There are potentially thousands of different indirect costs; for example in the case of a furniture manufacturer, see Table 2.3.

Product, period and conversion costs

Taken together, the direct and indirect costs make up product costs which CIMA define as: 'The cost of a finished product built up from its cost elements' (CIMA 1991).

All other costs, such as administration costs, selling costs and so on, are known as period costs. CIMA says that period costs are also known as fixed cost and fixed overhead cost, CIMA defines fixed overhead cost as: 'The cost which is incurred for a period, and which, within certain output and turnover limits, tends to be unaffected by fluctuations in the levels of activity (output or turnover)' (CIMA 1991).

Product costs are those costs that are assigned to stocks because they are closely associated with production activities rather than with the passage of time. On the other hand, period costs are charged in the profit and loss account in the period in which they are incurred because they relate to the passage of time, rather than being associated closely with the manufacturing process. Examples of period costs include administration expenses, selling expenses, distribution expenses, research expenses, development expenses, and finance expenses.

TABLE 2.3 *Indirect costs*

Materials	Glue Screws Finishing fabrics Cleaning materials Lubricants
Labour	Supervision Materials handlers Machine setters Maintenance operatives Cleaners Holiday pay Overtime premium
Expenses	Rent Rates Insurance Electricity Water charges Administration costs Depreciation: buildings equipment Maintenance materials Maintenance wages Telephone charges Postal costs Costs of security

1. *Administration expenses.* These are the costs of running the administration side of the business, including the accounting department(s), the legal department, the personnel department, and the computer suite. These include all relevant labour costs and overhead expenses. Corporation tax and value added tax are costs that have to be borne by the business (temporarily, at least, in the case of value added tax), and would be included under the heading of administration expenses.
2. *Selling expenses.* The selling expenses are the costs of running the selling operation of the organisation and include labour and overhead costs, together with any specific selling costs such as trade fair costs and advertising costs.
3. *Distribution expenses.* The distribution expenses cover the costs of moving finished goods from the maker to the buyer. They include not only labour and overheads, but also the costs associated with the storage and moving of goods once the manufacturing departments have finished with them.

Research and development expenses may be shown separately (as in Figure 2.1) or together (see below). Some businesses will have neither expense, others may have one or the other. Research and development costs are those costs that are incurred by many organisations as a result of their efforts to research and introduce newer and better ingredients, components and products.

4. *Research costs*. Research costs belong to the department that carries out the research into new material inputs and so on. For example, a research department may consist of a chemical laboratory, a mechanics laboratory, or a psychology department. The work of such departments may lead to success – in the sense that their output is usable for further development into improved or new products, processes and so on – or failure. The costs of the research department are the subject of financial accounting regulation. SSAP 13 deals with such regulations: 'SSAP 13 divides research costs into (a) applied research, which is the cost of research leading to a specific aim, and (b) basic, or pure, research which is research carried out without a specific aim in mind: these costs are written off in the year in which they are incurred' (Collin and Joliffe 1992).
5. *Development costs*. Again, SSAP 13 deals with development costs, which arise from the department within an organisation that carries out work stemming from, for example, the research department. Additionally, development work may stem from an idea received from an employee or a customer as a result of a suggestion scheme. Collin and Joliffe (1992) state: 'Development costs are the costs of making the commercial products based on the research and, according to SSAP 13, may be deferred and matched against future revenues.'
6. *Finance expenses*. The finance expenses are the costs associated with providing the finance for the organisation. There can sometimes be some confusion as to what constitutes a finance cost. For example, some people will include the cost of bad debts as a finance expense when clearly bad debts are a selling cost. A finance expense relates specifically to the interest costs of debentures, bank loans and mortgages. The dividends on preference and ordinary shares are appropriations of profit, not expenses, and therefore do not feature in this list.

Finally, conversion costs are the costs associated with turning the raw materials into finished products. That is, conversion costs are the direct labour costs, direct expenses and factory overheads. The summary in Figure 2.2 will help us to consolidate all this information.

Cost classification scheme two: classification for decision making

As we will see, with the exception of the final three costs listed below, there are links between pairs of costs, but not necessarily between one of the pairings and another pairing. Hence, the classification that follows introduces costs in pairs and contrasts those pairs:

- Absorbed v. variable costs.
- Sunk and committed costs.
- Opportunity and incremental costs.
- Avoidable v. unavoidable costs.
- Fixed v. variable costs.
- Controllable v. non-controllable costs.
- Standard costs.
- Post-manufacturing costs.
- Life-cycle costs.

Prime cost
- direct materials
- + direct labour
- + direct expenses

Production cost
- prime cost
- + indirect costs

Total cost
- production costs
- + period costs

FIGURE 2.2 *Summary of total costs*

Absorbed v. marginal costs

Absorbed costs

An absorbed cost or overhead is one which is charged to products or services. This commonly means that overhead costs are accumulated department by department or activity pool by activity pool, and then averaged over the number of units produced or prepared. In the simplest of all cases, the following formula is used:

$$\frac{\text{total overhead}}{\text{absorption base}}$$

As an example, assume that the maintenance department has incurred costs of £100,000: these are overhead costs by virtue of the definitions we have discussed under classification scheme one. We need to average these maintenance costs over the 10,000 units we can further assume have been made by this organisation. Hence the average, absorbed, overhead is calculated as follows:

$$\frac{\text{£}100{,}000}{10{,}000 \text{ units}} = \text{£}10 \text{ per unit}$$

Every unit of output will now absorb, or suffer, or be charged £10 by way of its share of maintenance costs. The same analysis applies to all overhead costs, in addition, of course, to maintenance.

Variable costs

Variable costs are those costs that are only incurred if a job or activity is performed. So, if we don't go into town on the bus, we don't need to pay the bus fare: simple! Similarly, if we don't make product X then there must be a whole string of costs that are not incurred. Consequently, the variable costs of making product X are the costs that are incurred simply as a result of having made product X. The concept of variable cost implies that it is a cost that varies with output. Therefore the more of product X that is made, the greater will be the total variable cost. In the case of making furniture, making a batch of 10 chairs will incur, say, wood costs of £200; whereas making 10 batches each of 10 chairs will incur costs of £2,000 (10 batches × £200 wood cost per batch). The distinction between absorption and variable costing will be explored in later chapters when we look at a variety of decision-making situations in which the nature and behaviour of costs is important.

Sunk and committed costs

Sunk costs

A sunk cost is a cost that has already been incurred at the time that a decision is being considered and is therefore not of importance for the new decision under consideration. Sunk costs are often considered alongside variable and relevant costs. Such costs are irrelevant in a decision-making situation because there is nothing that can be done to undo the decision to invest in them. Once a boiler has been installed and paid for, it is sunk; once we have bought and taken delivery of a car it is considered to be a sunk cost investment. A good example of a sunk cost would be covered by the situation where a market research survey has been carried out and all the costs incurred in carrying it out have been paid for. Following on from this survey is a proposal to invest in new machinery to produce a new range of products. The market research survey having already been completed and paid for, it is a sunk cost and not relevant to the decision now in hand.

Committed costs

Committed costs are those costs that need to be incurred in order for the organisation to continue to function but over which management may have little or no discretion. Examples of committed costs include rent of buildings, rates payable to the local authority, and employer's liability insurance.

Opportunity and incremental costs

Opportunity costs

The term opportunity cost, like many such terms used by accountants, is borrowed from economists. An opportunity cost is defined as being the cost of an opportunity forgone. Hence if I decide, on my limited entertaining budget of £300 per annum to travel to Paris, I cannot then follow my favourite football team around the country week after week during the season. The opportunity cost of the holiday in Paris is forgoing following my favourite football team. The concept of opportunity cost thus represents a sacrifice.

Incremental costs

An incremental cost represents the increase of the cost of one alternative over another. Because of this, it is also known as a differential cost, the difference between costs of alternatives. When choosing between two investment opportunities, the incremental cost will be:

Opportunity A	£100,000
Opportunity B	97,500
Incremental cost	£ 2,500

Again, even though the concept of the incremental cost is not a difficult one to grasp, it is widely used in decision making, and we will meet it again later in this book.

Avoidable v. unavoidable (or incurred) costs

Quite simply, if you do not need to incur a cost, it is avoidable. An avoidable cost, therefore, is a cost that would be avoided if a job, process or activity were not undertaken. On the other hand, an unavoidable cost must be incurred whatever the decision that is taken or to be taken. English league football clubs have been put in the position of incurring unavoidable costs by having to turn their stadia into all-seater facilities rather than having all-standing areas, or a mixture of standing and seating areas.

Fixed v. variable costs

We will be talking about fixed and variable costs in much more detail in Chapter 3 when we consider the nature and behaviour of costs. However, we can consider the general implications of the differences between fixed and variable costs here.

A fixed cost is one which tends to remain unchanged despite often wide changes in output or activity. The rent of buildings of an organisation is a good example of a fixed cost. We can determine whether the rent cost is a fixed cost by asking a simple question: If we increase our output by, say, 20%, by how much will the rent cost increase? If the answer is that there will be no change to the level of the rent cost, then we can conclude that we are probably dealing with a fixed cost. A variable cost is one that tends to vary with the level of output. Raw material costs is a good example of a variable cost. For every chair we make in our furniture factory, we will use, say, 5 metres of wood strips at a cost of, say, £3: thus, if we make one chair, we use £3 of wood; 10 chairs need £30 worth of wood and so on. The costs vary in proportion to output as does the amount of raw material. In Chapter 3 we will also discuss semi-variable costs, but these are not described here.

Controllable v. non controllable costs

A controllable cost is one that can be controlled by the relevant responsibility centre manager; and a non-controllable cost is one that the responsibility centre is unable to control, or influence. We discussed these issues in detail in chapter 1: review that chapter if there is any aspect of these costs that presents problems for you.

Standard costs

Standard costs are predetermined costs of a unit of input of material, labour or overheads. Standards are developed by means of detailed assessments of: material input requirements; the amount and values of labour required to complete given tasks; and the value of overheads to be incurred in a job, process or activity. We will be discussing the setting of standards and standard costs in Chapter 16 of this book.

Post-manufacturing costs

For some organisations, post-manufacturing costs can be significant. Here, we are dealing with costs that are incurred once the goods have left the factory. In the case of a white goods manufacturer (for example, washing machines), the post-manufacturing costs might include installation costs (for instance, plumbing in automatic washing machines) and the costs of the one- or two-year guarantee that typically will accompany such goods. We might have a problem here in the sense that these post-manufacturing costs are non-value adding. Depending upon where we draw the line in terms of the end of the production process, customising products can incur post-manufacturing costs that do add value. In the case of customised motor cars, for example, we have the car already manufactured: it has been sold and could be driven as any other normal car. However, the owner of a vehicle might now want different wheels, different interior trim, and a modified engine. The job now will incur further costs but there will be an additional amount of revenue that will not only match those costs, but should provide additional profit, hence value, too.

Some organisations can make a virtue out of their post-manufacturing activities! Take the example of a fine wine or Scotch whisky club and we have the perfect example of value adding post-manufacturing activities.

CAMEO

There are organisations whose task it is to store good quality wines and/or spirits once they have been produced. The problem here is that storage of itself is an activity that incurs costs but not normally any revenue or benefit: it is a non-value adding activity. The solution to this problem is to create a service that will add value to the storage of these products.

Both wines and spirits, of the requisite quality and character, need to be stored post production before they are drinkable; and the storage costs are high, even in the Highlands of Scotland where many Scotch whiskies are made. Add to the simple storage problem the fact that these products need to be kept for several years and these organisations have a serious non-value adding headache.

For many years now vintners have underwritten at least part of their wine storage costs by putting together, all at once or in stages, a cellar of wines for their clients. Typically what happens is that the client will select one or more cases of a certain wine to be held in storage until it is ready for drinking. The key, however, is that the client will pay in full for the wines as they are ordered and pay storage charges too.

In such a way, the vintner has not only eliminated storage costs for the wines he or she is able to sell in this way but, since he or she has created a service (selecting, presenting, storing and delivering the wines), he or she can charge a premium for the entire service offered.

Many Scotch distilleries are now actively selling their immature whiskies along the same lines as vintners with their wines. It should be stressed that although the wines or whisky have been sold, it is not uncommon for the goods to remain in storage on site until they are mature/drinkable.

Post-production costs are relevant to product introduction and retention decisions. Consequently, post-manufacturing costs need to be identified, recorded and controlled as carefully as possible.

Life-cycle costing

Life-cycle costing is:

> The practice of obtaining, over their life-times, the best use of physical assets at the lowest total cost to the entity (terotechnology). This is achieved through a combination of management, financial, engineering and other disciplines. (CIMA 1991)
>
> Life-cycle costing deals explicitly with the relationship between what a customer pays for a product and the total cost the customer incurs over the life cycle of using the product. (Shank and Govindarajan 1993: 15)

Life-cycle costing was hotly discussed during the 1970s by the management accounting profession and has evidently become important for many organisations. One of the reasons for the hot debate in the 1970s resulted from the realisation that: 'experience has shown that up to 90% of the producer's costs for a product are committed during the planning and design stages' (Yoshikawa *et al.* 1993: 166–7). Additionally: 'In the future, a greater percentage of product cost will be allocated to the engineering phase' (Berliner and Brimson 1988: 33).

Therefore, life-cycle costing has to be a vital consideration for any management accountant. The effect of life-cycle costing is that in the case of asset acquisition, for example, not only will the direct costs of buying, installing and operating such assets be taken into account, but so also will be the longer-term costs such as repairs, maintenance, upgrading, and replacement. It is because of such techniques as life-cycle costing that the management accountant requires a broad education and a flair for acquiring skills and knowledge that cut across all disciplines within his or her employing organisation. The best management accountant is the one who spends a significant amount of time during his or her early days with the organisation learning industrial, engineering and other such disciplines relevant to that organisation. Thereafter, the good management accountant will update such knowledge and skills by walking round the facility on a regular basis.

Coding of costs

Classification of costs takes place so that the management accountant can place each item of revenue and expenditure in its relevant slot within the overall accounting structure. We have discussed the cost structure above in detail; but not the revenue structure. However, we are aware now that as far as costs are concerned, whenever we buy or acquire anything that has a value, that value will be identified as a product or as a period cost. If it is found to be a product cost, it will be subclassified, first, as a direct or indirect cost, and then as a material, labour or overhead cost, and so on. Another reason why we classify our costs is to enable the management accountant to code them. A code is: 'A system of symbols designed to be applied to a classified set of items to give a brief accurate reference, facilitating entry, collation and analysis' (CIMA 1991).

An organisation does not have to use a coding system, of course, but one example will illustrate how useful coding systems are.

The UK postcode system

Although this section is concerned with the coding of costs, the following cameo has little to do with them, in the context of this chapter. The example of the UK postcode is included here since most, if not all, readers of this book will be familiar with it or a similar system.

CAMEO

The UK postcode is an alphanumeric code consisting of up to eight characters that is included in the address on every envelope and parcel sent through the Royal Mail. By alphanumeric we mean that the code is a mixture of both letters and numbers. For example, CB3 0PN will give you a small area of Cambridge; SR4 7JS would give you a road in Sunderland. By combining the house's (or building's) street number and the postcode we have covered every single postal address in the United Kingdom. At the time of writing, the UK postcode system deals with 1.7 million postcodes and 24.5 million associated addresses: all from a maximum of 8 characters plus street, house or apartment number.

To demonstrate how effective the postcode is, organisations now use the post office postcode database to assist them in their everyday operations. For example, there is a holiday-letting agency that uses the postcode to accurately address and locate their clients. Using the postcode, they claim, cuts by 80% the number of keystrokes their telesales people have to enter. Equally importantly, a customer booking call that used to take three minutes now only takes two minutes. This organisation deals with hundreds of thousands of queries and actions per year.

The postcode example helps to illustrate the effectiveness of using a coding system. It helps the post office to automate its systems and, as a by-product, it helps other organisations make its own work much more efficient. CIMA's definition of a code confirms that a coding system cannot be used without first having classified the organisation's costs.

Motivations for coding

The motivations for coding an organisation's financial transactions include:

- Efficiency of data capture and analysis.
- Frequency of use and familiarity.
- Consistency and understanding of use within the organisation.
- Saving on computer processing time and storage.

- Similar items can be related by means of a coding system, whereas a verbal description could be very inefficient.

A full discussion of coding and coding systems belongs in cost accounting and systems information books, but attempt the questions at the end of this chapter relating to coding and coding systems if you are interested in exploring these aspects further.

Classification, coding and the computer

There are many computer software packages available now for financial and management accountants using personal computers. These software packages range from the simplest cash-book-type program for home-based businesses to very sophisticated general ledger systems for small to medium-sized businesses. For financial and management accountants using mini and mainframe computers, accounting software packages have been around for decades now. As far as computerised accounting systems are concerned, the software developer will have built into the package a classification and coding routine. It will not be possible to enter any data at all that has not already been assigned to one or more ledger account. Hence, the computer-based accounting system is a perfect example of the application of the classification and coding regime outlined under the heading of scheme one in this chapter. A detailed discussion of classification, coding and the computer is, however, best left to a data processing or information systems book.

SUMMARY

This chapter has introduced and developed the meaning of the classification of costs and has given an introduction to the coding of costs.

We have discussed the classification of costs under two separate headings, or schemes. In the first scheme, classification for cost accounting, we looked at costs and their classification for a manufacturer. In the second scheme, classification for decision making, we looked at a whole variety of cost headings that are relevant for managerial analysis. Having discussed classification systems, we introduced the link between the classification and the coding of costs. Coding, we found, follows on directly from the classification regime, and has a number of features and advantages that benefit organisations significantly. Anyone interested in the finer detail of cost-coding systems is referred to a cost accounting or information systems text for a more detailed treatment of this topic.

KEY TERMS

You should satisfy yourself that you have noted all of these terms and can define and/or describe their meaning and use, as appropriate.

Classification (p. 36)	Period costs (p. 39)
Cost card (p. 36)	Administration expense (p. 40)
Average cost per unit (p. 37)	Selling expense (p. 40)
Indirect labour (p. 38)	Research costs (p. 41)
Elements of cost (p. 38)	Conversion cost (p. 41)
Direct expense (p. 38)	Prime cost (p. 42)
Indirect cost (p. 39)	Coding system (p. 47)
Product costs (p. 39)	

RECOMMENDED READING

Lengthy but worth a read is Berliner and Brimson (1988). A standard reader for an alternative view of many points is Shank and Govindarajan (1993), while Yoshikawa *et al.* (1993) provides a well-written review.

QUESTIONS

Review questions

1. What is classification and why is it so important to business organisations?
2. Give a realistic example of each of the following:
   (a) direct material;
   (b) direct labour;
   (c) direct expense;
   (d) indirect material;
   (e) indirect labour;
   (f) indirect expense.
3. What are prime costs?
4. Define product and period costs.
5. Identify the components of conversion costs.
6. Define coding and state why it is important to a business organisation.
7. What are the links between the classification and the coding of accounting transactions?

Answers to review questions 1, 3 and 7 can be found in the Student Workbook.

Graded practice questions

Level I

1. Classify the following costs incurred by a car manufacturer as *product* or *period* costs. Additionally, state whether the product costs are *direct* or *indirect* costs:
   (a) car window glass;
   (b) salaries of legal staff;
   (c) depreciation of word processor in chairman's office;
   (d) cost of factory fire department;
   (e) car tyres;
   (f) car bumpers;

(g) assembly line production employees' wages;
(h) national sales meeting expenses;
(i) overtime premium paid to assembly line workers;
(j) assembly line maintenance employees' wages;
(k) national TV advertising costs;
(l) depreciation of assembly line.

2. Classify the following costs incurred by a cotton cloth manufacturer according to the scheme set out in Figure 2.1 in this chapter:
(a) telephone costs of the administration block;
(b) purchases of raw cotton;
(c) wages of operatives moving materials from spinning to weaving department;
(d) audit fees;
(e) insurance of delivery lorries;
(f) cost of dyes;
(g) salaries of design artists;
(h) carriage on purchases of raw cotton;
(i) salaries of weaving shed supervisors;
(j) continuous stationery and floppy disks for office computer;
(k) advertising of products in national newspapers;
(l) interest on bank overdraft;
(m) maintenance of spinning machines;
(n) wages of weavers;
(o) electricity to power spinning machines and looms;
(p) electricity for heating and lighting general office;
(q) electricity for heating and lighting sales office;
(r) running costs of finished goods stores;
(s) running costs of raw material stores.

3. Prepare manufacturing cost and income statements from the following data for the year ended 31st December:

(a)	£	
Sales	220,000	
Materials purchased	37,000	
Direct labour	17,500	
	opening	closing
Stocks:		
Finished goods	11,500	8,500
Work in progress	13,750	9,000
Raw materials	10,000	11,300

(b) Factory overheads amount to £25,000
(c) Selling expenses are estimated to amount to 26% of sales
(d) Administration expenses are to be charged at 23% of sales
(e) Research and finance expenses are to be shown together as being 12% of sales.

4. The information below relates to The Craft Shop for the month of November.

	£
Rent	12,000*
Electricity and water	4,600*
Advertising	3,350
Sales	175,000
Salaries: selling and distribution (including fringe benefits of £2,500)	12,000
Wages: production (including fringe benefits** of £4,000)	13,000
Purchases:	
timber	24,500
glue, sandpaper, paint	700
office supplies	210

Stocks:***	November 1	November 30
	£	£
Timber	1,200	800
Glue, paint, etc.	250	300
Office supplies	75	90
Finished goods	12,000	8,000

Notes
* 60% of these costs are assigned to manufacturing and 40% to selling and administration.
** Production employee fringe benefits are classified as factory overhead.
*** There is no opening or closing stock of work in progress.

Required

Prepare a statement of cost of goods manufactured and an income statement, and include the following on your statement in addition to any other headings you feel necessary:

(a) direct costs;
(b) prime cost;
(c) indirect costs;
(d) conversion costs.

Level II

5. The following details relate to the Ray Charles Production Company for the month of November:

	£
Sales office equipment rent and maintenance	2,600
Purchases:	
raw materials	70,000

manufacturing supplies	3,500
office supplies	1,200
Sales	425,700
Advertising costs	11,000
Administrative salaries	12,000
Direct labour	104,000
Production employees' fringe benefits	4,000*
Sales commissions	50,000
Production supervisors' salaries	7,200
Depreciation of plant	14,000
Depreciation of office equipment	20,000
Depreciation of salesmen's cars	7,000
Interest on overdraft	2,000
Interest on mortgage	6,000
Plant maintenance	10,000
Plant water and electricity	35,000
Office water and electricity	8,000
Office maintenance	2,000
Production equipment rent	6,000
Office equipment rent	1,300

Note: * Classified as factory overhead

Stocks

	November 1 £	November 30 £
Raw materials	17,000	15,000
Manufacturing supplies	1,500	3,000
Office supplies	600	1,000
Work in progress	51,000	40,000
Finished goods	35,000	27,100

Required

Prepare a statement of cost of goods manufactured and an income statement, and include the following on your statement in addition to any other headings you feel necessary:

(a) direct costs;
(b) prime cost;
(c) indirect costs;
(d) conversion costs.

6. The information below relates to a department store. You are required to devise a cost code to cope with that information.

Departments:
China and cutlery
Sportswear
Children's wear
Children's shoes
Ladies' wear
Ladies' shoes
Men's wear
Men's shoes
Toys and games
Food hall

All departments have purchases; they all have sales assistants; and window/shelf/stand dressers/designers. Every department incurs the following costs: rent, rates, insurance, heating, lighting, depreciation of fixtures and fittings; and all departments have fixtures and fittings, carpets. The china and cutlery, and food hall departments have special fixtures and fittings in addition to ordinary shelves and cupboards: china and cutlery need security cupboards and cases, and the food hall needs refrigerators.

The store also employs people in administration (accounting, personnel, training, welfare) and other ancillary staff (store keepers, cleaners, maintenance, security, lift operators).

Outline a cost code system to deal with purchase and storage of merchandise, the payment of wages and salaries, and all other expenses, and the purchase of fixed assets.

7. When you took up your present position, your business was very small, having an annual turnover of £350,000 and a total work force of five. Now, due to successful sales and marketing efforts by the business, the business has grown such that its turnover is now £4,500,000 per year and it employs 40 people.

   As the accountant of this business, you feel it is necessary to rationalise your financial operations and install a full classification and coding system for all revenues, costs and balance sheet items, prior to the computerisation of the accounting function (which you anticipate to be about two years away from now).

   You are required to write an introductory memorandum to your managing director supporting your assertion that such a classification and coding system is required and requesting support for a consultant to study your present systems; and for the consultant to devise a new coding system for your business.

Solutions to practice questions 2, 3 and 7 can be found in the Student Workbook. Solutions to practice question numbers in red can be found at the end of this book.

Projects

1. Visit two manufacturing units and make careful observations of what happens in a manufacturing process: look at the manufacturing, storage and distribution aspects of the process; and consider how the subject content of this chapter can be applied to the situations you observe during your visit.

   If you are unable to visit a manufacturing operation, find and watch video recordings and/or television programmes that show the manufacture of a product: preferably illustrating the manufacturing, storage and distribution aspects of the product.

2. As you walk around your town or city, look out for the provision of services such as transport, retailing, banking, insurance ... and consider how the subject content of this chapter can be applied to the situations you observe.
3. Compare your observations to projects 1 and 2 above. In what ways (if any) will the application of classification and coding differ between a manufacturing organisation and a service organisation?
4. Find examples of the use of a coding system.
   (a) Identify the type of coding system in use in your example (e.g. sequential, block); and
   (b) Given the context in which you find the code, identify what you consider to be the information that the designer of the code intended the code should contain.

   If possible, link this project with projects 1 and 2 above.
5. (a) Compare the ISBNs on any three books you can find. Do all the books have a ten digit ISBN?; are all ISBNs presented in the same way as the *CIMA Terminology* book?: 0 901308 67 6, suggesting a four-facet code.
   (b) Given that hundreds of thousands of books are published throughout the world each year, is a ten-digit code likely to be sufficient in the long run? Think about this very carefully and determine the way the structure of an ISBN works.
   (c) Assuming that more books are published than can be coped with by a ten-digit code, how might the ISBN code structure be modified?

REFERENCES

Berliner, C. and Brimson, J. A. (1988), *Cost Management for Today's Advanced Manufacturing: The CAM-I conceptual design* (Harvard Business School Press).

CIMA (1991), *Management Accounting Official Terminology* (Chartered Institute of Management Accountants).

Collin, P. H. and Joliffe, A. (1992), *Dictionary of Accounting* Peter Collin Publishing).

Shank, J. K. and Govindarajan, V. (1993), *Strategic Cost Management: The new tool for competitive advantage* (Free Press).

Yoshikawa, T., Innes, J., Mitchell, F. and Tanaka, M. (1993), *Contemporary Cost Management* (Chapman & Hall).

CHAPTER THREE

Estimating cost behaviour

CHAPTER OBJECTIVES

After reading this chapter you should be able to:

- define the meaning of cost behaviour
- appreciate the scattergraph method of cost behaviour determination
- appreciate the high–low method of cost behaviour determination
- appreciate the importance of the relevant range in cost behaviour determination
- discuss various aspects of linearity of cost data
- understand the problems surrounding data collection

Introduction

It should be stressed at the beginning of this chapter that it is introductory in nature only: it is a preparation for Chapter 9, 'The derivation of fixed and variable costs'. The purpose of this chapter is to introduce the ideas surrounding the way that costs tend to behave. By cost behaviour we mean the way that a cost can be estimated to be fixed, variable or semi-variable. We also mean, by cost behaviour, the way that a cost might behave in a linear or a non-linear way. This chapter is concerned to distinguish between the variability of costs and the linearity of costs.

Mathematical conventions

In this chapter we will be using a little bit of mathematics. So that it does not come as too much of a shock to us all, the following conventions are introduced now. We will be developing arguments surrounding the function of a straight line. This means that we will be looking at the following functions:

(1) $y = \mathrm{a}$

(2) $y = bx$

(3) $y = \mathrm{a} + bx$

Function (1) is taken to represent that the value of the dependent variable, y, is equal to a; and a, then, is a fixed cost. Function (2) is taken to represent that the value of the dependent variable y is equal to b multiplied by x. In the examples in this chapter, this means that b, the variable cost per unit, multiplied by x, the volume of output, represents the total variable cost of something. Function (3) is taken to represent a semi-variable cost. That is, y is equal to the sum of the fixed cost element, a, and the total variable cost, bx. These ideas will be developed when we look at scattergraphs later in the chapter.

Furthermore, in the section concerned with linearity, whether we are dealing with straight lines or curves, we will come across a further convention: the use of subscripts. If we have a function in which we find that there is more than one variable cost, it is usual to represent them as follows:

$$y = \mathrm{a} + b_1x + b_2x + b_3x$$

That is, each variable cost is assigned the letter b and is further assigned a subscript number: ranging here from 1 to 3. In this example, the function contains three different variable costs per unit. This means that we are dealing with a situation whereby we multiply each variable cost per unit (variable cost per unit one is represented by b_1, variable cost per unit two is represented by b_2 and variable cost per unit three is represented by b_3) by the output and then add the result of that to the fixed costs, a, and obtain an estimate of total costs. We will see these conventions used in this chapter.

Meaning of cost behaviour: definition, description and scattergraphs

Examples of cost behaviour include such situations as, whether the cost of rent increases, decreases or remains unchanged if the level of output is increased. Let us suppose that our organisation decides to increase the number of units we make from 1,000 units per year to 1,200 units per year. Are we likely to spend more on people costs as a result of this change? The issues we are facing in this chapter relate to fixed and variable cost behaviour. In the next section we look at cost behaviour in three stages: first, we describe the three types of cost we are aiming to identify; secondly, we will apply our definitions to numeric data; and thirdly, we plot these numeric data on scattergraphs in a final attempt to appreciate the meaning of the different types of cost behaviour.

Fixed, variable and semi-variable costs

In general, as we saw in Chapter 2, if a cost remains unchanged, despite even a relatively large change in the level of output or activity, then we can conclude that the cost is a fixed cost. We would normally conclude that the rental costs of a building or machine would be a fixed cost because a fixed cost does not change, no matter how many units our organisation makes. Even if output were nil, we would still incur the rental cost.

If a cost changes in direct proportion to any change in the level of output or activity, then that cost is said to be a variable cost. If an organisation's labour cost is a direct cost, we would expect, in general terms, to find that the more units we made, the more would be incurred in labour costs. Again, generally speaking, for a one unit increase in output or activity, we would expect a one unit increase in direct labour costs. This is an example of a variable cost.

A semi-variable cost (sometimes known as a semi-fixed cost) is a mixed cost that has both a fixed and a variable element to it. Telephone costs are an example of a semi-variable cost. This is so because a typical telephone account has a fixed rental charge and a variable cost per unit of telephone time used per call. This means that the total telephone cost is a mixture of fixed and variable costs.

Numeric illustration of cost behaviour

The data in Table 3.1, showing three historic costs incurred by an organisation, help us to appreciate cost behaviour in a practical way. Look at Table 3.1 and, without reference to anything else, prove that the titles fixed, variable and semi-variable do describe the way that these costs behave.

It should be clear that it is not always easy, merely by looking at the data in such a table, to see how any of these costs are behaving. One feature of the discussion so far has been that we have talked about the three types of costs in an abstract way. The best way of discussing and appreciating cost behaviour is to plot them onto a scattergraph.

TABLE 3.1 *Illustration of the basic behaviour of costs*

Output (units)	Fixed costs	Variable costs	Semi-variable costs
0	5,000	0	5,000
100	5,000	1,000	6,000
200	5,000	2,000	7,000
300	5,000	3,000	8,000
400	5,000	4,000	9,000
500	5,000	5,000	10,000
600	5,000	6,000	11,000
700	5,000	7,000	12,000
800	5,000	8,000	13,000
900	5,000	9,000	14,000
1,000	5,000	10,000	15,000

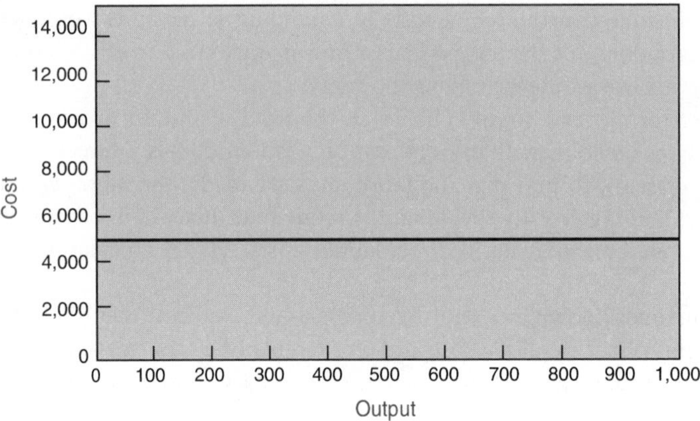

FIGURE 3.1 *Normal presentation of fixed costs*

Scattergraphs

A scattergraph is a graph or chart onto which is plotted raw data. It is called a scattergraph because, in most cases, data will appear to be scattered over the area of the graph. In spite of this, however, the first three scattergraphs we are considering contain data that are far from scattered: Figures 3.1, 3.2 and 3.3 show straight line scattergraphs. Nevertheless, merely because data is not scattered in an irregular fashion, does not mean that we are not dealing with a scattergraph! The benefit of plotting such data on a graph is that a visual image is created which clearly arranges the data in a way that gives maximum impact. The three figures translate Table 3.1 into visual images that are far simpler to interpret than trying to unravel the behaviour from lists of numbers: a picture paints a thousand words! In every graph in this chapter we are faced with the following conventions:

1. The independent variable – the x variable, the horizontal axis – represents output (production or sales, for example).
2. The dependent variable – the y variable, the vertical axis – represents total costs.

Figure 3.1 illustrates the behaviour of the fixed costs found in the fixed cost column of Table 3.1. The graph illustrates, for example, the case of rent, where the rent does not change irrespective of whether the output is 0 units or 1,000 units: it does not matter how many units are made, the rent does not change. Algebraically, a fixed cost graph is represented by

$$y = \text{a}$$

where y is the total cost and 'a' is the fixed cost value.

Figure 3.2 shows graphically the variable cost data from Table 3.1. This figure shows a perfectly variable cost: there is a direct link between the numbers of units made or provided and the material, labour or overhead inputs into the units, direct materials being an excellent example here. Algebraically, a variable cost graph is represented by

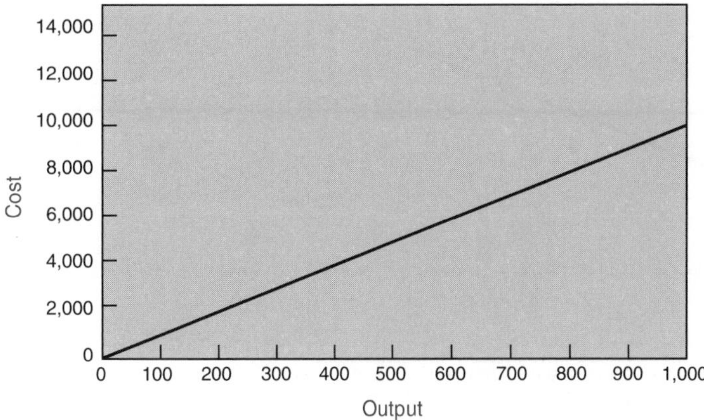

FIGURE 3.2 *A perfectly variable cost*

$$y = bx$$

where:

'y' is the total cost;
'b' is the variable cost per unit; and
'x' is the number of units of output.

In Figure 3.3 we see how a semi-variable cost behaves when the cost is plotted against output. An example of a semi-variable cost, as we discussed above, is a telephone account: this is a semi-variable cost because there is a standing charge payable every period that does not vary with the number and duration of calls made, and there is a variable cost per unit. Algebraically, following the mathematical conventions we introduced earlier in this chapter, a semi-variable cost graph is represented by

$$y = \mathrm{a} + bx$$

where:

'y' is the total cost;
'a' is the fixed cost value;
'b' is the variable cost per unit; and
'x' is the number of units of output.

Analysis of accounts method of cost behaviour estimation

By way of a summary of this introduction, Table 3.2 shows a few examples of costs that we can generally classify as fixed, or variable, or semi-variable costs. Table 3.2 is constructed in line with the analysis of accounts method of cost behaviour determination. The analysis of accounts method assigns behaviour to a cost on the grounds that it seems sensible that

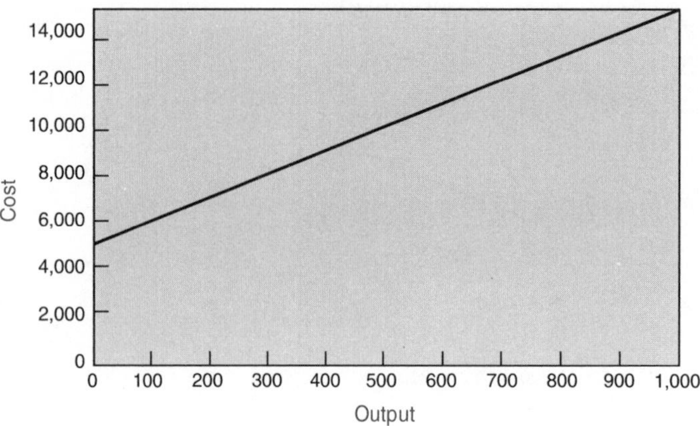

FIGURE 3.3 *Semi-variable cost*

it should behave that way. Rent is commonly given as the best example of the application of such a classification. The way the analysis of accounts method works is based on the 'everyone would classify a cost in this way' approach. That is, if we take the case of the rent cost of a room or building and analyse that cost over a range of levels of output, we would expect to find that even though output levels change significantly, the rent cost will remain static. The same kind of analysis can be applied to all costs and the conclusions would be, as in the case of Table 3.2:

- rent costs are fixed costs;
- management salary costs are fixed costs;
- direct material costs are variable costs;
- telephone costs are semi-variable costs;

and so on.

Hence, whenever we look at a rental cost, we automatically say that it is a fixed cost ... direct material costs are variable ... and telephone costs are semi-variable. Note, in Table 3.2, that items are occasionally shown in two columns at the same time. This is fine providing we realise that, as in this instance, electricity might be variable for my business because I

TABLE 3.2 *Analysis of accounts method*

Fixed costs	Variable costs	Semi-variable costs
Rent	Direct materials	Electricity
Depreciation	Direct labour	Telephone
Insurances	Water	Gas
Management salaries	Power	Pension costs
Rates	Goods received	Travel
Wages of guards	Electricity	
Supervision costs		

have negotiated with the electricity supply company for it to be that way. Your company, on the other hand, might still be in the position of having a standing charge and variable cost per unit elements to your electricity costs; hence, in your case it is a semi-variable cost.

Be aware that the analysis of accounts method is subject to significant qualification. There may be many costs that can easily be classified under the heading of fixed, variable and semi-variable. However, there are also many costs that simply defy classification without first having analysed them very carefully. The intuitive classification system that is described by the analysis of accounts method is only to be used for rough and ready calculations: that is, where there is no alternative (for example, lack of other information available), or where the costs are known to fit within such a classification.

Arithmetical estimation of cost behaviour

Whilst graphical analysis is very useful, and indeed it is recommended that we start almost any analysis of cost behaviour by drawing a scattergraph, there are problems with it. One of the problems with graphical analysis is that it often simply is not accurate enough. Even with very sophisticated spreadsheet and statistics packages that are readily available for most computers, graphs can still turn out to be difficult to interpret. The simplest problem of all is that the lines that are drawn onto a graph are too thick to enable an accurate reading. Alternatively, drawing graphs badly by, for example, breaking axes in an inappropriate way, by working with inappropriate scales, all lead to problems with interpreting graphs. Additionally, arithmetical methods are usually able to give highly accurate results to even the most difficult problems. Consequently, a firm estimate of cost estimation might be done by means of graphical analysis, but then an arithmetical solution ought to be sought. We can best illustrate the arithmetical estimation of cost behaviour by working through an example.

WORKED EXAMPLE 3.1

Using the algebraic method first, we can calculate the cost of making a batch of 5,000 dining chairs, when:

- The cost of wood and other materials amounts to £10.50 per chair.
- Direct labour costs £17.50 per chair.
- Variable factory overheads amount to £7.00 per chair.
- Fixed factory overheads amount to £100,000 for the period.

Solution to Worked example 3.1

Algebraic method

Approach 1

To find total variable costs, one approach is to add together all of the variable costs per unit to give:

$$
\begin{aligned}
'b' &= \text{materials} + \text{labour} + \text{factory overheads}\\
&= £10.50 + £17.50 + £7.00\\
&= £35 \text{ total variable cost per unit.}
\end{aligned}
$$

Therefore, where 'x' = 5,000 (chairs),

$$
\begin{aligned}
'y' &= \text{total variable costs}\\
&= bx = £35 \times 5{,}000\\
&= £175{,}000
\end{aligned}
$$

where 'a' = fixed costs = £100,000,

$$
\begin{aligned}
y &= a + bx\\
&= £100{,}000 + 175{,}000\\
&= £275{,}000.
\end{aligned}
$$

Approach 2

As an alternative to this method, we consider each variable cost per unit on its own, and change the cost function to become:

$$y = a + b_1x + b_2x + b_3x$$

where:

b_1 = the variable material cost per unit;
b_2 = the variable labour cost per unit; and
b_3 = the variable factory overhead cost per unit.

This gives:

$$
\begin{aligned}
y &= a + b_1x + b_2x + b_3x\\
&= £100{,}000 + £10.50 \times 5{,}000 + £17.50 \times 5{,}000 + £7.00 \times 5{,}000\\
&= £100{,}000 + £175{,}000\\
&= £275{,}000
\end{aligned}
$$

As an alternative to the algebraic method of cost behaviour determination, we can use the accounting format for presentation: this is shown in Table 3.3.

The high–low method

One quick and easy way of determining cost behaviour is to use the high–low method. This method is quick and easy because it only needs two elements of data for each of the '*x*' and the 'y' variables. The two elements of data needed are the high reading for the variables and the low reading for the variables.

TABLE 3.3 Cost card for sets of dining chairs

	5,000 chairs £
Direct materials:	
Wood and other materials	52,500
Direct labour:	
Labour costs	87,500
Factory overheads:	
Variable costs	35,000
Fixed costs	100,000
Total costs	275,000

By 'high' in this method we mean the value for the '*y*' variable, given the highest value of the '*x*' variable. By 'low' we mean the '*y*' variable associated with the lowest value for the '*x*' variable. Two examples will help us sort this out fully: refer to Table 3.4 for these examples.

For Product 1, the high and low values we are looking for are:

	'*x*' variable	'*y*' variable
high	500	3,650
low	0	2,000

For Product 2, the high and low values we are looking for are:

	'*x*' variable	'*y*' variable
high	500	4,400
low	0	3,000

This confirms that the high and low values of the '*y*' variable depend on the high and low values of the '*x*' variable. This means that the high value for costs for Product 1 is taken

TABLE 3.4 *High and low values of 'x' and 'y' variables*

Product 1		Product 2	
output (x)	costs (y)	output (x)	costs (y)
0	2,000	0	3,000
100	2,500	100	3,600
200	2,900	200	4,300
300	3,300	300	4,200
400	3,700	400	4,500
500	3,650	500	4,400

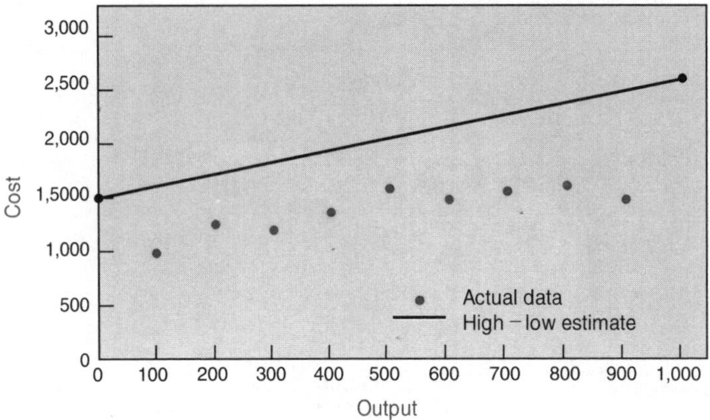

FIGURE 3.4(a) *High–low estimate: unreasonable*

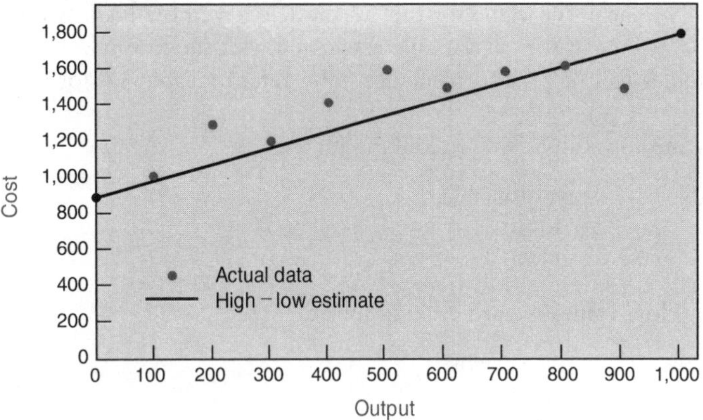

FIGURE 3.4(b) *High–low estimate: reasonable*

as £3,650. Note that £3,650 is taken as the high value even though it is not highest cost value in absolute terms.

Consider Figures 3.4(a) and 3.4(b) (which are *not* based on the data for products 1 and 2). In Figure 3.4(a) we see a situation where the high and low readings suggest that costs are behaving in a way that is clearly not the case. By joining the two extreme values, an estimate of $y = a + bx$ is given that does not have much bearing on reality: it is misleading. Figure 3.4(b), on the other hand, gives a more reasonable estimate of $y = a + bx$. It can do this in this case because there does appear to be *some* relationship between the 'x' and the 'y' variables. We do not have to draw a diagram to estimate the values of 'a' and 'b', we can do that arithmetically.

Arithmetical estimation using the high-low method

Let us take the example of Product 1 and estimate 'a' and '*b*' from there.

For Product 1, the high and low values we determined above are:

	'*x*' variable	'*y*' variable
high	500	3,650
low	0	2,000

We find the estimate of the '*b*' variable first by taking the differences between the two elements of data and calculating the average cost per unit, '*b*':

	'*x*' variable	'*y*' variable
high	500	3,650
low	0	2,000
difference	500	1,650

Therefore, '*b*' = £1,650 ÷ 500 units = £3.30.

The reasoning here is that the total cost changes only because the variable cost element of it has changed: the more units we make, the higher total costs become. The fixed cost component of total costs remains unchanged, despite even large fluctuations in output. Consequently, if we identify the total change in total costs and divide it by the total change in output, we obtain an estimate of the rate of change, '*b*'. To calculate the value for 'a', we substitute for '*b*' in either the high or low data. Using the high data for substitution purposes, the total cost at 500 units of output is:

$$£3{,}650 = \text{a} + £3.30 \times 500 \text{ units}$$

Therefore:

$$\begin{aligned} \text{a} &= £3{,}650 - (£3.30 \times 500) \\ &= £3{,}650 - £1{,}650 \\ &= £2{,}000 \end{aligned}$$

We can now conclude that:

$$y = \text{a} + bx = £2{,}000 + £3.30\text{x}$$

Check that by using the low data, you would obtain the same value for 'a' as we have just done here; and you should repeat this process for Product 2 from the example introduced above.

Using the $y = \text{a} + bx$ estimates

Having found estimates for 'a' and '*b*', we should practise using them.

WORKED EXAMPLE 3.2

Calculate the value of 'y' for product 1 when:

1. $x = 300$ units
2. $x = 600$ units

Solution to worked example 3.2

1. $y = a + bx = £2{,}000 + £3.3$ per unit × 300 units
   $= £2{,}000 + £990$
   $= £2{,}990$
2. $y = a + bx = £2{,}000 + £3.3$ per unit × 600 units
   $= £2{,}000 + £1{,}980$
   $= £3{,}980$

We need to stress that the high–low method is subject to enormous limitations: if the data we are analysing are either non-linear or follow no real pattern, the high–low method may be wholly inappropriate. As we mentioned above, these representations of fixed, variable and semi-variable costs are somewhat simplistic: one factor that they have failed to take into account is that of the relevant range. The relevant range refers to the levels of output or activity over which an organisation has directly relevant experience. Thus, if an organisation says its variable costs are £3.00 per unit, we should immediately be on our guard because the statement needs to be qualified by relating the variable cost to a range of output.

The relevant range

The relevant range is the range of output or activity over which the organisation has actually produced or for which it has collected detailed cost estimates as a result, for example, of a budgeting or *ad hoc* costing exercise. The implications of the behaviour of costs outside an organisation's relevant range can be dramatic. Figure 3.5 helps to illustrate this point.

In Figure 3.5 the relevant range, the range of output over which the organisation has had direct experience, is from 400 to 800 units of output. Outside that range, the fixed costs are quite likely to change. In this example, detailed examination of the organisation's situation could reveal that if output falls below 400 units, then some of the fixed costs may be eliminated or reduced: that is, a building that the organisation currently uses could be surplus to requirements if output falls below 400 units, therefore all its attendant fixed costs can be eliminated. Similarly, at an output level below 400 units, there will be less need for supervisors and managers, and their costs can thus be reduced. On the other hand, when output rises above 800 units, more machinery could be required, more supervisors and managers may be needed. Therefore, fixed costs will rise when the organisation starts to

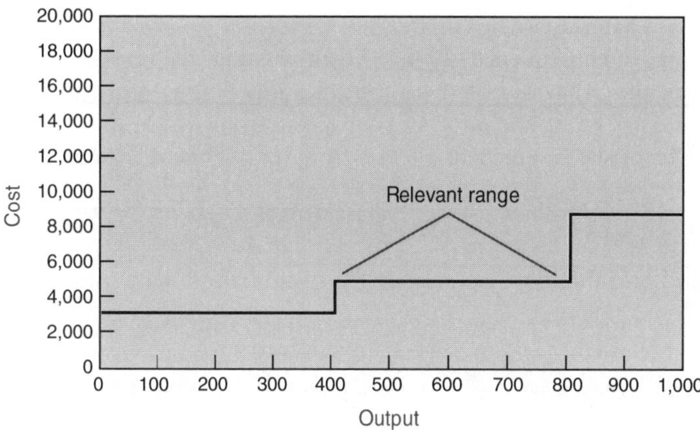

FIGURE 3.5 *Fixed costs and the relevant range*

produce at a level above its current relevant range if extra machinery, building space, supervision and so on are needed. Figure 3.5, incidentally, shows the behaviour of a step cost. A step cost is so called because the cost increases in steps (or jumps) such that over one range of output the cost remains fixed. When the next range of output is considered, the cost can be seen to have increased, and then remains fixed over the whole of the new range. If this happens over, say, three or more ranges of output, as is the case in Figure 3.5, a step function arises. Figure 3.6 shows how variable costs might behave both inside and outside the relevant range. This figure also illustrates the problems of making predictions based only on data contained within the relevant range.

The relevant range shows a cost that is apparently linear; and based on that linear behaviour, a linear cost function for all levels of output is predicted. Look at the true behaviour, however. Below the relevant range, the cost function shows a cost increasing at a decreasing rate per unit. Above the relevant range, the cost function shows a cost increasing

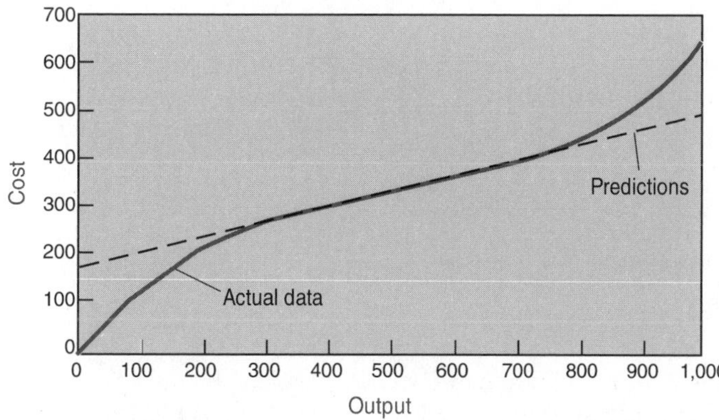

FIGURE 3.6 *Variable costs and the relevant range*

at an increasing rate per unit. Whatever else this figure shows, it does not show a truly linear cost across all levels of output. In consequence of what we know about the relevant range, whenever anyone talks about the behaviour of their costs, we now know to ask whether that person is talking about costs he or she knows about (costs from within the relevant range) or costs about which he or she is speculating (costs from outside the relevant range).

CAMEO

Estimating fixed and variable cost behaviour from published accounts

There are times when we might wish to estimate, for example, the way that our competitors' costs are behaving; or we might want to carry out a cost behaviour exercise on an organisation that we might be interested in buying. Whatever our motivation for carrying out such an exercise, elementary cost behaviour analysis can be drawn from published accounting statements. The data below are derived from the information contained in the annual report and accounts of an international hotel chain.

Year	Operating costs
84	1,423.3
83	1,293.5
82	1,190.5
81	1,107.2
80	966.3
79	681.9
78	650.4
77	614.4
76	583.1
75	565.0
74	564.9

Carrying out a high–low analysis of these data allows us to estimate the variable and fixed costs as follows:

	Year	Costs
	84	1,423.30
	74	564.90
Difference	10	858.40
Variable costs		85.840
Fixed costs		−5,787.26

Hence, we conclude that our estimate of $Y = a + bX$ is:

$$Y = -5{,}787.26 + 85.840X$$

where: X is the year under review.

Rather a strange result for the fixed costs – a negative amount. Consider this result carefully since it does have a meaning, but further analysis is called for resolve this potential problem.

We will return to this example in another cameo in Chapter 9.

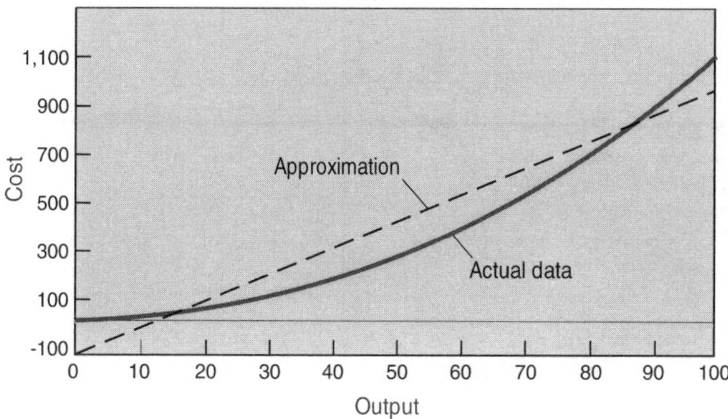

FIGURE 3.7 *Linear approximation: an overall line of best fit*

Linearity

Figures 3.1 to 3.3 assumed that all costs behaved in a perfectly linear way: thus, $y = a + bx$. By behaving in a linear way, we mean all costs can be described by a straight line. A straight line can be perfectly horizontal and represent a fixed cost; or it can slope at an angle and represent a variable cost. Whilst the assumption of linearity makes life simple for us, it is not wholly realistic. In reality, costs are often described by curves. By non-linearity, we might find that a cost is not capable of being described by a straight line: it might behave in the way that $y = a + bx^2$ would. If a cost does behave in a non-linear fashion, life could become difficult for us because the mathematics of such functions can be difficult. Nevertheless it is possible for a cost to be non-linear and for us to be able to make estimates of its behaviour by means of linear approximation.

By linear approximation, we mean either **assuming** that the data behaves linearly and drawing a line of best fit over it, or breaking the costs down into sections and drawing a line of best fit for each section. Figures 3.7 and 3.8 illustrate these points.

Figure 3.7 shows the actual data given by $y = bx^2$ and the linear approximation of it: $y = a + bx = -100 + 10x$. All that has happened is that to make the mathematics simpler, the approximation is added somewhere in the middle of the data so that when a linear approximation is made, it should give a reasonable estimate of the cost. To make a linear approximation, all we have to do is to mark off on our linear approximation curve, the cost relative to the level of output that we wish to provide an estimate of cost for. Table 3.5 compares the actual values with the approximated values derived from Figure 3.7, to show how accurate an approximation we have obtained. The residuals column (actual less estimate) gives some large values. This version of linear approximation is only useful when absolute accuracy is not vital.

In Figure 3.8, we see a more helpful set of approximations. These approximations are an example of a piecewise linear estimation in that the actual costs are broken into pieces or segments and a linear approximation applied to each separate segment. In this figure,

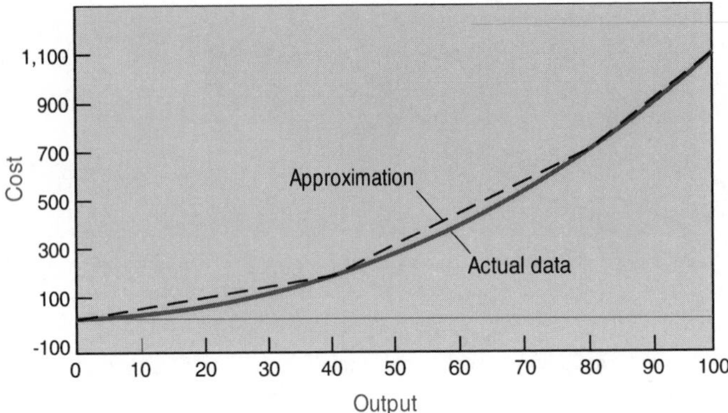

FIGURE 3.8 *Linear approximation: piecewise line of best fit*

TABLE 3.5 ***Comparison of actual and approximated values in Figure 3.7***

Output (units)	Actual Data	Estimate $y = -100 + 10x$	Residuals
0	0	−100	−100
10	10	0	10
20	40	100	60
30	90	200	110
40	160	300	140
50	250	400	150
60	360	500	140
70	490	600	110
80	640	700	60
90	810	800	−10
100	1000	900	−100

therefore, there are three segments with which to approximate costs. Segment one runs from 0 units of output to 39.9 units of output, segment two runs from 40 units of output to 79.9 units of output, and segment three runs from 80 units of output to 100 units of output. Calling these segments, or pieces, 1, 2, and 3, we have:

$$y_1 = a + bx = 0 + 4x$$
$$y_2 = a + bx = -320 + 12x$$
$$y_3 = a + bx = -800 + 18x$$

These estimates are based on the high–low estimates derived from the curves shown in Figure 3.8; the data in Table 3.6 can also be used for the same purpose. A piecewise linear estimation is more accurate than a single-line approximation because, by having several segments across the curve, each individual approximation can lie very close to the original. In piecewise linear approximation, therefore, there need not be too much margin of error when estimates are being derived.

Table 3.6 provides similar comparisons for the new approximations to those given in Table 3.5 for Figure 3.7. The main point to notice here is that the residuals are much smaller than in Table 3.6. Thus, as we said above, piecewise linear approximation gives consistently more accurate results than simple linear approximation.

We should now ask the question whether, in the real world, linear approximation of costs is a useful and realistic approach to take. After all, our arguments so far have only been based on assumed data.

TABLE 3.6 *Comparison of actual and approximated values in Figure 3.8*

Output (units)	Actual Data	Estimate	Residuals	
0	0	0	0	$y_1 = 0 + 4x$
10	10	40	30	
20	40	80	40	
30	90	120	30	
40	160	160	0	
50	250	280	30	$y_2 = -320 + 12x$
60	360	400	40	
70	490	520	30	
80	640	640	0	
90	810	820	10	$y_3 = -800 + 18x$
100	1000	1000	0	

Linear approximations justified

One justification for linear approximations comes from the fact that we are usually dealing with the behaviour of costs within the relevant range; and within the relevant range, costs may not fluctuate except in a restricted or limited way. A further justification for this assertion comes from Johnson (1960: 165) who provides evidence to show that linearity can be reasonably assumed. He cites an example of production function estimates and he concludes: 'The cubic and quadratic terms in [the formulæ derived in the case study] give no improvement over the linear function also derived.' Another study cited by Johnson, of the administrative costs and scale of operations in the US Electric Power Industry, shows: 'The administrative costs were plotted against the value of plant less depreciation (taken as a measure of the scale of operation) and the following relationship resulted . . . ' (ibid. 161).

The relationship that resulted showed an almost linear approximation of the administrative costs (in fact, the study gave a coefficient of correlation (the '*r*' value) of 0.951, where, of course, an '*r*' value of 1.0 denotes a perfectly linear relationship). So, although we might be making estimates of costs, there is evidence that such estimates might not be too unrealistic. In certain circumstances linear approximations can be acceptable. The major thought to be borne in mind when trying to determine the component parts of total cost is that we need to know the cost we are dealing with. To this end, first plot the cost data on a graph and then, secondly, assess whether a linear approximation would be a reasonable approach to take. If a linear approximation seems inappropriate, turn to Chapter 9 for advice!

Management policy and cost behaviour

A further dimension to the nature and behaviour of costs debate is that of management policy. Management policy is often set so that a cost is not a fixed or variable cost in the sense discussed above: that is, a cost may behave the way it does because it has been deliberately set to behave that way as part of management's overall allocation of costs throughout the organisation. As an example of management policy affecting cost behaviour, consider the allocation to academic departments of a university's library operating costs. In this case, the allocation of library costs is determined by the management of the University; and it is based on $y = a + bx$ where $a = £30,000$ and $b = £20$ for every full-time student in each department. This translates into $y = £30,000 + £20x$. Thus, the accountancy department, which has 700 full-time students, will have £30,000 + £20 × 700 = £44,000 allocated to it for the year.

Identifying such influences as management policy on cost behaviour is important, otherwise attempting to analyse cost behaviour could prove to be a problem if, for example, the wrong independent variable (the 'x' variable) is used. If we set out to determine the way the library costs behave relative to each academic department, without knowing that management had predetermined the allocation method, we could waste a great deal of time attempting to derive values for 'a' and 'b'. Furthermore, although we would derive values for 'a' and 'b', they could well be wrong. The most likely reason they might be wrong could be that we might choose numbers of total book issues to staff and students in each department as the independent variable rather than the number of full-time students. In this sort of situation we could base our budgetary allocations on our findings, only to discover later that we are wrong and have to change them in line with management policy. (Note that we are not implying that the number of students is the correct basis for estimating library usage costs. We are using this example for demonstration purposes only.)

Horngren and Sundem (1987: 227) provide a diagram that gives us a further insight into fixed and variable costs:

Fixed costs	Variable costs
Committed Discretionary	Engineered Discretionary

The insight this diagram gives is that it helps us to expand on management policy and cost behaviour. We will deal with the fixed costs first.

Committed fixed costs

Committed fixed costs arise from the strategic direction dictated by the management of an organisation. These costs include rent, rates, insurance and supervisory salaries. They are strategic in the sense that they are dominated by the long-term plans of the organisation. If the organisation expects activity to be low over the next '*n*' years, the management of that organisation will not invest as heavily in land, buildings, machinery and equipment as it would if activity were forecast to be much higher. Such costs are committed costs because short-term management decisions cannot change these costs. The costs cannot be changed because of the nature of the investment in the assets and/or the contractual obligations arising from these committed costs. Be aware, however, that my long-term viewpoint and your long-term viewpoint could be significantly different to each other. If I am a manufacturer of cars, my commitment to certain costs could last for years, whereas your commitment, if you are a market trader, might only last for a week or two. The other aspect of committed fixed costs is that they are incurred even when output is zero: that is, they do not change as activity changes.

Discretionary fixed costs

The best-known examples of discretionary fixed costs include advertising costs, sales promotion costs, research expenses, development expenses, and charitable and political donations. Unfortunately, many organisations regard education and training costs as discretionary costs too. These costs are usually determined as part of the annual budgeting process for the coming budget period only (hence, they are not strategic, unlike committed fixed costs); and in any period, any or all of these costs will reflect the objectives of the management that sets them. For example, a managing director, keen to support handicapped children's charities, could well ensure charitable donations are high and aimed at that target. The objective of this policy is to show his or her organisation to be one that cares for the less fortunate child in the community. It is sometimes said that there is no optimum relationship between a discretionary fixed cost and the benefits received (Horngren and Sundem (1987: 229–30) make this very point). However, there are examples of organisations that, for example, set their advertising budget at, say, 3% of sales for a period. The figure of 3% can be arrived at either intuitively (the management just feels 3% is correct) or statistically. By using statistical methods, a relationship between advertising and sales and/or profits can sometimes be determined, and the optimal (or near optimal) level of expenditure set. Let us now turn to the variable costs.

Engineered variable costs

The term engineered variable costs is used to reflect the nature of the precision of the inputs into, and control over, a process. Making a chair, for example, in engineering terms, requires, say, one piece of wood measuring 3 m × 4 cm × 2 cm: this means that every chair needs this amount of wood. Therefore, to make six chairs, six pieces of wood of 3 m × 4 cm × 2 cm would be required, for 24 chairs, 24 pieces of wood measuring 3 m × 4 cm × 2 cm would be required, and so on. The same arguments apply to the other direct materials and direct labour requirements for the chairs. Where possible, an engineering approach should be encouraged because in such a case all inputs can be reasonably accurately anticipated and any deviations from them analysed by way of variance analysis (to be discussed in chapters 15 and 16). The Japanese approach to engineered costs is enshrined in what they call cost tables. In the discussions about engineered costs and cost tables in this book, we will be discussing them in very simplistic terms. However, we should bear in mind that a cost table for a motor car needs to take full account of the 20,000 or so parts that each vehicle contains. We discuss cost tables in further detail in Chapter 9.

Discretionary variable costs

Discretionary variable costs are those variable costs that are incurred or reduced or eliminated as needs arise. Labour overtime cost is a good example. Based on budgeting estimates, the labour cost might be set at £300,000. If activity increases unexpectedly, overtime could be worked at a cost of an extra £10,000. When activity falls, overtime disappears: it is a discretionary cost. A further example of a discretionary variable cost would be Christmas party costs. When a business is performing well, it could, as a motivational gesture, pay for staff parties at Christmas. If an economic downturn occurs, the management could well decide that this cost should no longer be incurred: thus it is a discretionary cost since it can be withdrawn.

Data collection and its problems

Finally, in this chapter, we should appreciate that up to now, we have simply assumed that data is available to us without having to collect it; or without having to think about the implications of collecting it. As with any other data collection activity, the collection of cost and output data is not without problems. Let's have a look at several issues connected with data collection.

Volume of data

For reasons of space, clarity and cost of preparation, most textbook examples tend to show the determination of cost behaviour based on six or twelve months' data only. In reality, this small volume of data will be insufficient for most purposes: as a minimum, weekly or daily data should be gathered and made available to the analyst. Working with weekly or daily data for one year would give 48–50 or 280–300 data points per year for weekly or daily data respectively (based on actual working days per year). Having access to so many data points avoids the averaging of data that monthly data could easily include. A better position to be in would be to use several years' worth of data rather than just one year's worth. We must be careful here, however, in that production methods can change in the medium to long term: more advanced machinery used, changes in raw material specifications, and computerisation are some examples that could each change the relationship between inputs and output, and consequently cost behaviour.

Recording problems

The actual recording and transmission of data is not without its problems, either. Clerical error can give rise to errors and omissions. If data is not collected at the time output is produced, there is no guarantee that the knowledge can be calculated or even assumed: it may be lost for ever. Similarly, an error in recording could give rise to errors such as the transposition of figures, or the moving of a decimal point: 457 instead of 475, or 45.7 instead of 4.57.

Costs of collection

From the way that organisations are structured, or the way that textbooks are often written, it can easily be assumed that collecting cost data costs nothing. We need to consider how true it is to say that collection costs can be very high. If we take the example of a small cost office in, say, a medium-sized company, we might find a supervisor; two clerks, one secretary/typist, and fittings, furniture, and equipment, together with the central administration costs that go into supporting this office (personnel costs, head office costs and so on). The costs of operating this office are relatively high: the cost of collecting and processing information by the cost office is a significant cost. Thus before we consider whether any new information should be collected and/or processed, we have to consider the impact that such a change in the costs to be collected will have on this already significant cost.

Outliers

Outliers or extreme values also have to be contended with. An outlier is a value that lies well outside the range of most (if not all) of the other data that has been collected. Outliers can arise because of sudden, but short-lived, changes in the levels of activity, or because of a strike or machine breakdown.

Anyone involved with data processing or studying data processing will be aware of such data collection problems. However, we have to guard against compartmentalising functions in an organisation. Merely because we feel a topic or problem belongs under the heading of another function or subject, is not cause for us to dismiss it as 'not my problem, old boy'. If an issue is a problem, it affects everyone. A management accountant's data are as liable to corruption as is anyone else's.

SUMMARY

We have looked in detail in this chapter at the introductory issues surrounding cost behaviour. We looked at the distinction between fixed costs, variable costs, and semi-variable costs. We also considered an introduction to the algebraic nature of the behaviour costs. One of the fundamental points that we stressed concerning the analysis of cost behaviour was that the first thing we should do before getting involved in tedious or difficult calculations is to plot all relevant data on a graph first. Plotting data on a graph gives a visual image of the data, and from this image, it can often be seen immediately whether a linear or non-linear cost is being dealt with.

We also discussed two points of vital importance that are often overlooked in other texts: first, that managerial action and decisions can, and often do, influence the way that a cost behaves; and secondly, we pointed out that the collection of data and its transmission and use is subject to error. The errors to which data may be subjected include: collecting too small a sample, not being aware of changes in technology or specifications, and being faced with outliers.

Perhaps the most important point to make about this chapter is that before we try to apply the material from it in reality, we need to be aware that the methods discussed are simple. This means that we could not usefully use the analysis of accounts method in a sophisticated setting and hope to arrive at a credible solution to our estimation of cost behaviour problems. This chapter is an introduction to the more advanced techniques we will be meeting in Chapter 9.

KEY TERMS

You should satisfy yourself that you have noted all of these terms and can define and/or describe their meaning and use, as appropriate.

Cost behaviour (p. 55)
Fixed cost (p. 56)
Variable cost (p. 57)
Semi-variable cost (p. 57)
Independent variable (p. 58)
Analysis of accounts method (p. 59)
Determination (p. 62)
High–low method (p. 62)
Step cost (p. 67)
Linear approximation (p. 69)
Piecewise linear estimation (p. 69)
Management policy (p. 72)
Committed fixed cost (p. 72)
Discretionary fixed cost (p. 73)
Engineered variable cost (p. 73)
Data collection (p. 74)
Volume of data (p. 74)
Outliers (p. 75)

RECOMMENDED READING

Further information in Chapter 9 of this book! A good treatment by an evergreen, Horngren and Sundem (1987)

QUESTIONS

Review questions

1. Discuss what you mean by the behaviour of costs.
2. Explain why a fixed cost is said to be fixed.
3. Explain why a variable cost is said to be variable.
4. What is the significance of the function $y = a + bx$?
5. What is the relevant range and why is it important to a full understanding of the behaviour of costs?
6. Explain the term 'linear approximation'.
7. Explain the term 'piecewise linear approximation'.
8. What part can management policy play in the analysis of cost behaviour?

Answers to review questions 2, 4, 6 and 8 can be found in the Student Workbook.

Graded practice questions

Level I

1. Calculate the cost of making 20,000 dining chairs given the following costs:

   - cost of wood and other materials amounts to £10.50 per chair;
   - direct labour costs £17.50 per chair;
   - variable factory overheads amount to £7.00 per chair; and
   - fixed factory overheads amount to £100,000 for the period.

   Present your answer:

   (a) in algebraic form; and
   (b) in cost card form.

2. Plot the following data on two separate graphs: graph one for the variable costs and graph two for the fixed costs; and comment on the saying, 'the more we make, the cheaper our production costs are'.

Output (units)	Variable costs per unit £	Fixed costs per unit £
0	2.00	∞
100	2.00	100.000
200	2.00	50.000
300	2.00	33.333
400	2.00	25.000
500	2.00	20.000
600	2.00	16.667
700	2.00	14.286
800	2.00	12.500
900	2.00	11.111
1,000	2.00	10.000

3. A company has analysed its costs and determined the figures given below. Illustrate this situation by means of a graph.

Output ranges	Total fixed costs £	Variable costs per unit £
0–10,000	50,000	7.00
10,001–20,000	65,000	7.00
20,001–30,000	65,000	6.50

4. Express each of the examples below in the form of an algebraic expression:
   (a) The fixed costs are £20,000 and variable costs are £3 per unit.

(b) The fixed costs of making a product are £5,000 and the total costs of making 500 units are £10,000.

(c) The total cost of making 20,000 units is £50,000 and the total costs of making 30,000 are £70,000.

(d) The total cost of producing 5,000 units of a product is £100,000. The variable cost per unit is £15.

(e) The total cost of producing 100 units is £30,000 and the variable cost is equal to £0.50 times the square of the output.

Level II

5. Your Company Ltd makes one type of wooden toy. In November, Your Company made 500 units of this toy and it incurred the following costs:

Variable costs	£
Preparing and carpentry:	
wood	2,000
labour	5,000
Assembly:	
dowling (wood)	800
screws	100
glue	10
sandpaper	20
labour	4,000
Finishing and upholstery:	
foam rubber	650
fabric	1,250
paint	900
labour	3,000
Fixed costs	
Supervision costs	900
Electricity and gas	470
Depreciation of machinery	250
Rent, rates and insurance	650

Prepare a statement showing total cost and cost per toy of:

(a) direct material;
(b) direct labour;
(c) variable factory overheads; and
(d) fixed factory overheads.

6. The Business Assistance Bureau (BAB) offers a word processing service to the business community. A representative month's data for the word processing pool shows:

- Income at £50,000.
- 50 reams of A4-size paper used at £2 per ream (one ream contains 500 sheets of paper). This paper is used both for the final drafts and for photocopying extra copies
- A total of 20 printer ribbons are used in the printing process, and they cost £5.00 each.
- 100 floppy discs costing £0.25 each are used.
- The electricity costs for the period amount to £100 plus £0.50 per ream of paper used.
- Every job has a binder or special cover. Each of these binders costs £4.00
- Photocopying costs for the period are made up of a fixed cost element of £250 and a variable cost of £0.05 per page. On average, photocopying accounts for 90 pages per word processing job performed.
- The wages for the typists amount to £1 per page typed. Each word processing job averages 10 pages of script.
- Depreciation for the period amounts to £1,500 for the computer hardware; £500 for the software and £2,000 for the furniture and fittings.
- Supervision/quality control costs for the period amount to £1,000

Prepare an income statement for the word processing pool for the period under review, showing:

(a) variable costs;
(b) fixed costs; and
(c) word processing profit.

7. The following data are actual second-hand prices of two different motor cars. The prices relate to the second-hand value of a vehicle in 'A1' condition.

Range Rover
Five-door automatic
station wagon

Age (years)	A1 price £
7	5,325
6	7,800
5.5	8,850
5	9,525
4.5	10,750
4	11,400
3.5	13,525
3	14,175
2.5	14,925
2	15,750
1.5	17,125
1	17,925
0	19,475

Rolls-Royce Corniche
Two-door automatic

Age (years)	A1 price £
9	29,400
8	33,150
7	35,775
6	40,750
5.5	47,775
5	56,725
4.5	58,400
4	62,025
3.5	65,025
3	71,675
2.5	75,650
2	85,350
1.5	89,200
1.0	94,600
0.5	97,975
0	110,025

Note: an age of zero years indicates a car that is second-hand but is less than six months old.

From these data, estimate for each vehicle:

(a) an annual value for depreciation; and

(b) the method of depreciation you feel is demonstrated by these results.

Solutions to practice questions 1, 4 and 5 can be found in the Student Workbook. Solutions to practice question numbers in red can be found at the end of this book.

Projects

1. Find three sets of annual reports and accounts: one for an extractive industry organisation; another for a manufacturing business; and the other for a retailing or other service-based organisation. For this project, all sets of reports and accounts need to include several years' worth of accounting data in them.

   (a) (i) From the data in the reports and accounts, estimate the total costs of the organisation for each year for which you have data.

   (ii) Determine the behaviour of the total costs from the data extracted in (i).

   (b) If the annual reports and accounts provide sufficient detail, determine the fixed and variable elements of, for example, manufacturing costs, administration costs, selling costs, research costs, and so on.

REFERENCES

Johnson, J. (1960), *Statistical Cost Analysis* (McGraw-Hill). Book Company New York.

Horngren, C. T. and Sundem, G. (1987), *An Introduction to Management Accounting* (Prentice Hall).

CHAPTER FOUR

Inventory management and aspects of the logistics chain

CHAPTER OBJECTIVES

After reading this chapter you should be able to:

- discuss the need for holding inventory
- understand the materials control cycle and its component parts
- appreciate the calculation of inventory value by several pricing methods
- understand the ways to optimise investments in inventory
- appreciate the reorder point, MRPI and MRPII methods
- understand and evaluate the just-in-time method of production and material control
- understand the JIT/EOQ model of stock investment optimisation.

Introduction

To avoid any confusion, the term 'inventory' is used in this chapter in preference to the term 'stock'. Inventory consists of goods and materials held for later use. We see inventory in the form of spare parts in an engineering workshop; as raw materials in a factory; and food and drink in a supermarket. We will generally find inventory classified under three headings:

1. raw materials;
2. work in progress; and
3. finished goods.

Just look at the balance sheet of almost any organisation and there will be inventories of one form or another. Even the management accountant's office could be holding inventories of pens, pencils and paper: that is, stationery inventories. We can see the importance of materials at both a micro and macro level by consulting the annual reports and accounts of organisations, and also government statistics. Table 4.1, drawn from a sample of organisations from around the world, shows an average (arithmetic mean) percentage of inventory to total assets of 17.92%, which helps to illustrate the importance of inventories to a wide variety of organisations. Whether they are manufacturers or service-based organisations, the table shows that for every £1 invested in fixed assets, 17.92p is invested in inventories. For a very large organisation with total assets of, say, £2 billion, this represents an inventory holding of £358.4 million. A small organisation with total assets of £100,000 has an inventory holding of £17,920 to look after.

The *Annual Census of Production* published recently by HMSO showed that materials cost as a percentage of value of gross output for two groups of manufacturers is as follows:

	%
Textiles	63
Timber	63

TABLE 4.1 *Average (arithmetic mean) percentage of inventory to total assets*

	Stocks as a % of total assets	Industry category
United Kingdom		
Independent radio station	0.68	service
Producer and seller of naturally based cosmetics manufacturer	30.34	
		service
Hotel group	0.36	service
Manufacturer of branded consumer goods manufacturer	23.93	manufacturer
United States of America		
Telecommunications	9.65	service
Manufacturer of microchips	10.31	manufacturer
Toy company manufacturer	10.46	
Republic of South Africa		
Food retailing	45.40	service
Butchery	30.16	manufacturer
		service
Average investment in stocks	17.92	

Putting this information with data for gross output for these industry groups gives us the value of materials consumed or used in the UK economy in the year to which these data relate (see Table 4.2). This level of material consumption represents £120 for every man, woman and child in the United Kingdom at 1980 prices – and this is for two industries only!

TABLE 4.2 ***Gross output of materials and value consumed***

Category	Gross output (£m.)	Materials as a % of gross output	Materials consumed (£m.)
Textiles	5,140.1	63.0	3,238.26
Timber	5,216.0	63.0	3,286.08
	10,356.1		6,524.34

Source: Abstracted from Annual Census of Production, HMSO.

Why hold inventory?

We now know what inventory is, and we also know how important it is at the micro and macro level. However, we need to consider why organisations hold inventory. After all, we know inventory consumes a large amount of resources, and later in this chapter we are going to discuss how to optimise our investment in inventories. There are many reasons why organisations hold stock, including the following:

- As buffer stocks to counter both general and specific risks of a stockout.
- To take advantage of discounts.
- To take advantage of holding gains.
- To take advantage of currency fluctuations.

First, an organisation holds what are called buffer stocks in order to prevent a stockout: that is, the situation when inventories fall to zero yet there is unsatisfied demand for those inventories. There are many reasons why inventories fall to zero, including the general problems of a sudden and unexpected increase in demand for the material or product. Similarly, accidents in the storage area, theft of some or all of the inventory and so on, all contribute to the risk of not holding inventory. Historically, buffer stocks were held to ward off the fear of a stockout; this seems to have been done irrespective of the cost of holding inventories, to some extent. By a specific risk of a stockout we mean that a particular event is likely to happen and we are attempting to guard against that. We might consider the case of import quotas within the European Community. It is well established now that many products generated within the EC are subject to import/export restrictions. If it is felt that our organisation will suffer from these restrictions, we might hold inventories to prevent stockouts arising from such problems.

Secondly, organisations may, from time to time, be offered cash and/or quantity discounts that make it attractive to buy inventories in advance of their being used. In such cases, assuming the calculations have been done correctly, it is worthwhile holding inventory in a warehouse or other storage area instead of waiting for deliveries to be made on another basis.

Thirdly, organisations often hold inventories to take advantage of holding gains. In a period of inflation, or shortage of goods or materials, there are often gains to be made simply by holding inventories in order to use them later or to sell them at a profit. In such cases, the original cost price will be, say, £5 per unit and the replacement price/selling price may be, say, £7 only a little while later. Again assuming the calculations have been done correctly, it may be worthwhile to buy inventory at £5 per unit and hold it until the unit cost is £7 at which time full advantage can be taken of the difference of £2 per unit.

Fourthly, an organisation that deals across national boundaries and between different currencies may see an opportunity to hold stocks on the basis that their own currency is about to move favourably with respect to another currency. If that other currency is used in a market in which our organisation can sell its products, holding inventories to wait for such favourable currency movements will make economic sense.

Lastly, many organisations worldwide now use just-in-time (JIT) inventory control methods, and even they hold stocks. It is often felt that JIT means that there is no inventory at all in an organisation, but this is not true. JIT might mean the virtual elimination of some kinds of inventory, but organisations still require other types of inventories. Indeed, some or all of the reasons given above for the justification of inventory holding can equally well apply to the JIT organisation. Tragically, the Japanese company Toyota, a JIT organisation, discovered a need for holding inventory at the beginning of 1995 when an earthquake rocked part of Japan and cut its supply chain. Within a very short period of time after the earthquake, a Toyota plant that was not damaged by the earthquake at all ran out of component parts for the vehicles it was manufacturing. We will discuss JIT methods later in this chapter.

Inventory control

Since inventories form such an important part of the overall investments of many organisations around the world, it should be clear to us all that this investment has to be controlled. We need to be confident that what we think we have in inventory, we do actually have; and that the investment in inventories is at a reasonable and desirable level.

Inventory control is: 'The systematic regulation of inventory levels' (CIMA 1991). Because inventories represent such large investments and have to be controlled, systematic procedures need to be adopted for inventory control. Figure 4.1 illustrates an overview of the materials control cycle

An overview of the materials control cycle

The main stages in the materials control cycle are as follows:

1. Raising a purchase requisition.
2. Placing an order.
3. Receiving the goods and raising a goods received note.
4. Inspecting the goods.
5. Taking the goods into stores and entering the items on its bin card.

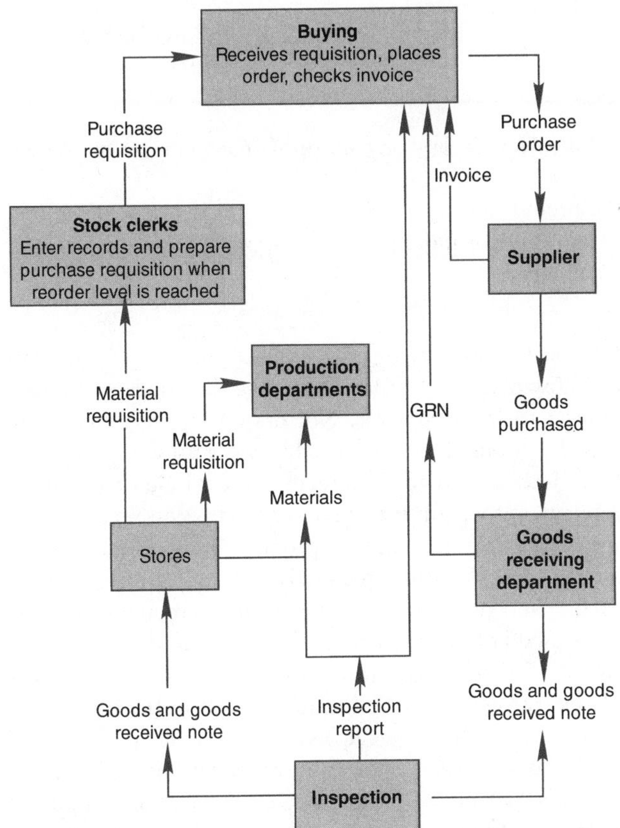

FIGURE 4.1 *The materials control cycle*

6. Issuing the goods to production or warehouse/shop (also of relevance here might be materials transfer notes and materials returned notes).
7. Maintaining a stores ledger card.

For a detailed view of the materials control cycle, consult a textbook on logistics, or a detailed cost accounting textbook. Some of the references given at the end of this chapter will prove useful in this context. However, the following is a brief summary of the cycle.

The materials control cycle really should keep going round and round, just like any other cycle. If we start at the point where an item in inventory has just been used up, we can follow through the cycle stage by stage. We must fully appreciate that there are significant opportunities for fraud at every stage of the materials control cycle, and we must guard against such opportunities by implementing and applying appropriate steps to reduce or prevent such fraud. Given that one of the tasks of stores clerks and controllers is maintaining inventories in their optimum condition and quantity, as soon as an item reaches the level at which it should be replenished they must request that the buyer, or purchasing officer, places an order for more of that item or good.

Once the buyer receives the request, he or she will do one of the following three things with it:

1. If a decision has already been taken not to buy any more of that item, he or she will take no action.
2. Place a purchase order with the preferred supplier.
3. Issue a request for quotations from three or more potential suppliers prior to placing an order, along the lines of step 2 above.

Assuming the buyer has decided to place an order, and has gone through all the relevant ordering procedures, he or she will now place that order. Receiving the goods and raising a goods received note must be subject to strict controls. Not only must we generate the relevant control documents such as the goods received note, but we must ensure that the goods are fully checked, counted and accounted for before they are handed over to the stores, or to the inspection department. Inspection may take place now, on receipt, or at some later stage: for example, just before they are used by production, or are sold in the store, or as they arrive in the storage area. When the materials or goods are issued from sthe storage area, there must be full and accurate documentation accompanying every transaction. Proper documentation is used both by the accounting staff and the stores staff. There are accounting implications for all inventory movements in addition to the storage implications. Materials may simply be transferred from the storage area to the production area, or from the store to the showroom. In this case requests for materials or goods are exactly as implied by the materials control cycle figure. Alternatively, goods may be transferred from one department to another one. Consider the case where department A has taken delivery of materials from the store but has not used them all. It might transfer them to department B, which it knows needs them. In this case, there is no problem with such a transfer providing the relevant transfer notes are completed, fully accounting for the transfer from 'A' to 'B'. Similarly, the excess materials in department A may be sent back to the store, in which circumstance a materials returns note would be generated.

At the same time that all of these receipts, transfers and returns are taking place, the stores control department will be maintaining a stores ledger card for every item in inventory. The stores ledger card contains all relevant details relating to the movement of inventory items as well as their associated cost. It is a fully detailed document and must periodically be reconciled with the bin card that is kept with the materials or goods in the store, but which contains only quantity information: that is, the number, weight, volume, not the values.

Inventory control procedures

One of the most effective ways of ensuring our investment in inventories under control is to check all items in inventory on a regular basis. Once a physical check has been carried out, the results can be compared with the theoretical or book inventories and any discrepancies noted and acted on. There are three chief methods of inventory checking: perpetual inventory; continuous inventory checking; and annual inventory check.

Perpetual inventory

Perpetual inventory is concerned with: 'The recording as they occur of receipts, issues, and the resulting balances of individual items of inventory in either quantity or quantity and value' (CIMA 1991). The term perpetual inventory usually refers to a system of inventory control rather than an inventory-taking system. Nevertheless it can play a part in inventory-taking procedures. With perpetual inventory, every item of inventory usually has its own stores ledger card, and as any transaction affecting an item takes place, the stores ledger card is updated, whether it be an issue or receipt of goods. At any time, therefore, the balance in inventory of the item is known, and can simply be read from the stores ledger card. This balance is the 'book inventory' or theoretical balance and can be used as a check on the physical balance in the stores and on the bin card. The book and the physical balances ought to agree at all stages, of course, but for reasons we will discuss below, discrepancies do sometimes arise.

Continuous and annual inventory checking

We can distinguish between continuous inventory checking and the annual inventory check by discussing CIMA's (1991) definition of the two:

> Continuous stock taking is the process of counting and valuing selected items at different times on a rotating basis.
>
> A process whereby all inventory items are physically counted and then valued (periodic inventory checking).

The annual inventory check is an example of a periodic inventory check. Continuous inventory checking may take place on a daily, weekly, or monthly basis, depending on how many items of inventory an organisation has. With this method, the physical and book inventories are continuously being reconciled. In any accounting period (usually taken to be one year) all stores items should be physically checked at least once. To achieve the counting of all items at least once in an accounting period, the people carrying out the checks should choose their daily, weekly, or monthly checking allocation on a random basis: in this way, every inventory item has an equal chance of being checked at any time; and in the long run, all items will be checked at least once. In addition to the use of random numbers ensuring that all items are checked at least once in the accounting period, it also ensures that at any time any item may be checked, which ensures that the storekeeper is unable to anticipate the items that are due for checking, and thus any discrepancies will remain untampered with. Continuous inventory checking can usefully use the perpetual inventory records. In this way, not only can the physical and theoretical balances be checked against each other, but also any discrepancies can be corrected for, after all necessary investigations are carried out into how they occurred. Any discrepancies that arise must be reported and dealt with immediately; the more serious discrepancies may be a matter for a change of policy or police action. We will deal specifically below with the sorts of discrepancies that might arise.

Annual inventory check

The annual inventory check is a periodic inventory check and is most usually carried out as part of the annual audit. With the annual inventory check, all items in inventory are checked at one time (for a large organisation this may take as long as a week, and some organisations have to close down in order to carry out the annual inventory check). Because the annual inventory check is usually carried out as part of the annual audit, there will usually be an external auditor in attendance at the inventory check (or at least at part of it), which ensures that the results obtained are open to independent scrutiny. The annual inventory check can also usefully use the perpetual inventory records: the physical and theoretical balances are checked against each other, and any discrepancies corrected for, after all necessary investigations are carried out into how they occurred.

We have now seen the financial reason for controlling inventories: they represent a large investment across many organisations. Are there any other reasons for controlling inventories?

Non-financial reasons for controlling inventory

Although the subheading is non-financial reasons, this is only indirectly true. Ultimately these reasons come to represent pounds and pence. We can identify four main non-financial reasons for controlling inventories: obsolescence and waste; deterioration; shrinkage; and clerical and similar errors.

Obsolescence and waste

By obsolescence we mean that items held in inventory, like a computer or other advanced design machine, might be superseded by a more up-to-date version. By waste we mean that something held in inventory has been trodden on, evaporated, or gone bad, and is no longer available for use. In the case of obsolescence there may be a salvage value attached to it: that is, it may be possible to sell the item for something less than its full value. But in the case of waste, the items are valueless.

Deterioration

By deterioration we mean that items held in store have undergone a change so that the value of those items is reduced. For example, in a retail supermarket, goods that have passed their 'sell by' date have deteriorated – they are no longer considered to be in prime condition – and such items can be found at marked-down prices.

Shrinkage

Shrinkage is the term that retailers use for theft. The longer an item is left in storage, the greater risk there is that it will be stolen. Obviously, when an item of inventory has been stolen, it is not available for sale, and the organisation that has lost the item(s) has lost its investment and earning capacity from the item(s).

Clerical and similar errors

The term clerical and similar errors covers a multitude of sins. It ranges from the transposition of a figure to the complete omission of a transaction. Although clerical errors may be minor in nature, on average, their effects are often felt for a long time. Clerical and similar errors include

1. Incorrectly writing up the stores records. For example, an addition or subtraction error, or missing out a receipt into stores.
2. 'Breaking bulk' and incorrectly recording the issue. This means, for example, taking small amounts from a much larger amount. Taking a few kilogrammes of material from a one tonne container many times can lead to, say, 800 kilogrammes having been removed but only 5 kilogrammes remaining in the container! The problem here will be inaccurate measurement of issues, which is a difficult problem to overcome unless more effort and attention is given to the weighing or measuring procedures.
3. It is possible that items returned to stores (via a materials returns note), may be incorrectly recorded on their return. For example, recording 85 litres as 58 litres means that there will be 27 litres more in the store than the theoretical records allow for. Similarly, recording the items as brass screw grade 15 instead of the proper title of brass screw grade 5 will mean a similar problem for storekeeper and accountant alike.
4. One error very difficult to account for is when items are inadvertently over- or under-issued: the equivalent of receiving too much or too little change at a fast-food restaurant, or at the railway station! The problem here, of course, is that the store-keeper will suddenly find he or she has more on the shelf of an item than he or she considers there should be – or too little. The storekeeper will then be at a loss to explain where the extra came from; or where the balance missing has gone to. The only solution to this problem (assuming it is a rare event) is to encourage storekeepers to be more careful with their handling and giving out of materials.

Pricing stores issues

Statement of Standard Accounting Practice number 9 (SSAP 9): Stocks and Work in Progress

One vital area of concern to all accountants is the valuation of inventories: so much so that SSAP 9 was issued to help deal with the problem. In its preamble, SSAP 9 states: 'No area of accounting has produced wider differences than the valuation of inventory and work in progress.' Therefore, SSAP 9 was issued with the following objectives:

1. To narrow the areas of difference and variation in accounting practice on inventory and work in progress; and
2. To ensure adequate disclosure in the accounts.

SSAP 9 calls for:

> the amount at which inventories and work in progress, other than long-term contract work in progress, are stated in periodic published accounts, should be the total of the lower of cost and net realisable value of the separate items of inventory and work in progress, or of groups of similar items.

We should appreciate that stating the cost of an item is easier said than done! Nevertheless, SSAP 9 defines cost as:

> Expenditure incurred in the normal course of business in bringing the product or service to its present location and condition. This expenditure includes both:
>
> *Cost of Purchase*: the purchase price including such items as import duties and handling costs and deducting such items as trade discounts and rebates; and
>
> *Cost of Conversion*: the direct costs, production overheads and any other attributable overheads. Production overheads are defined as those incurred in respect of materials, labour and services for production based on the *normal* level of activity.

Net realisable value (NRV) is defined as

> The estimated selling price less all costs to complete and all costs relating to the sale of the products.

In arriving at values of inventories for balance sheet purposes, then, the management accountant has to determine the cost and the NRV of the inventories, and state the value of those inventories at the lower of the two. The going concern concept is a vital element of the need to value inventories at the lower of cost and net realisable value. If the organisation we were looking at were not a going concern, we would be looking at a different basis of valuation of the inventories.

Surveys carried out by various chartered accountancy firms throughout the United Kingdom reveal that there are in excess of one hundred different ways in which items that have been taken into storage by an organisation can be valued for usage, transfer, or resale purposes. This hardly reflects credit on the objective of SSAP 9 that sought to 'to narrow the areas of difference and variation in accounting practice on inventory and work in progress'.

If we were to look at all these different ways, we could fill an entire book on that topic alone. However, we are concerned with looking at only a small fraction of the methods available.

Thus in many cases, there is no problem concerning the valuation of stores and issues from stores. For example, in the case of large items such as the purchase and sale of motor vehicles, where few items are being traded in at any one time, there will be little difficulty in keeping track of a vehicle and its cost. In the case of an item of inventory which is being traded in large quantities, keeping track of the precise costs per unit may be a problem. It is this latter example that we will be following through in the discussion that follows.

The answer to the question of why we need different methods for the valuation of issues from stores is best illustrated with an example.

WORKED EXAMPLE 4.1

A Business Ltd buys 50 units for resale on a particular date at £3 per unit; a week later it buys a further 25 units of the same goods at £3.10 per unit; and a week after this transaction, it buys a further 30 units, this time at £3.25 per unit. A Business Ltd now attracts a customer who buys 80 units and pays a total of £400.

Required

Calculate the cost of sales of the deal done with the customer.

Solution to Worked example 4.1

This example is designed specifically to illustrate that there are several ways in which the answer can be arrived at. In terms of units, all answers will be the same. In terms of values, there are potentially dozens of different solutions. The solution that follows gives the results of three different inventory valuation methods, after which we work through those methods in detail. The cost of sales is the cost of the goods that have been sold: that is, the 80 units.

FIFO

The FIFO basis is the First In First Out method whereby we price materials 'using, first, the purchase price of the oldest unit in inventory' (CIMA 1991). The workings for the above example for the FIFO method are, in simplified form:

1. Total issues, working from the oldest units to the newest units:

	£
50 units bought at £3.00	150.00
25 units bought at £3.10	77.50
5 units bought at £3.25	16.25
Total cost of sales	243.75

2. Closing inventory: 25 units at 3.25 per unit = £81.25

Check that you follow the method used here.

LIFO

The LIFO basis is the Last In First Out method whereby we price material 'using the purchase price of the latest unit in inventory' (CIMA 1991). The workings for the above example for the LIFO method are, in simplified form:

1. total issues, working from the newest units to the oldest units:

	£
30 units bought at £3.25	97.50
25 units bought at £3.10	77.50
25 units bought at £3.00	75.00
Total cost of sales	250.00

2. Closing inventory: 25 units at £3.00 per unit = £75.00

Check that you follow the method used here.

AvCo

AvCo, the weighted average cost method, is defined by CIMA as 'The total cost of an item of material in inventory divided by the total quantity in inventory' (CIMA 1991). The workings for the above example for the AvCo method are, in simplified form:

1. Total issues, working on the basis that all issues are priced at the arithmetic mean of all relevant prices:

	£
80 units bought at £3.09524	247.62

2. Closing inventory: 25 units at £3.09524 = £77.381

Check that you follow the method used here.

Each of these methods is a valid way of accounting for the issue prices of inventories: even though they each provide us with a different value!

Inventory valuation and inflation

At many times over the last three or four decades, there have been many debates and discussions over which method of inventory valuation should be preferred. First, we ought to be aware that over one hundred different methods for valuing inventories have been recorded as having been used in any one year over a cross section of organisations in the United Kingdom. Secondly, the impact of inflation or deflation on inventory valuation methods and thus on the profitability of organisations, is a constant source of articles in academic and accounting journals.

The worked example we have just worked through will help us to illustrate the nature of the problem organisations face in periods of inflation. In the worked example, we simulated a period of inflation when the buying price of the goods rose from £3 per unit to £3.10 per aunit and then to £3.25 per unit. The results we found were that, using each of the three methods demonstrated, cost of sales were:

FIFO	£243.75
LIFO	250.00
AvCo	247.62

If we assume, for the sake of this demonstration, that the sales value of these goods is £600, the gross profit results for each of the three methods is:

FIFO	£356.25
LIFO	350.00
AvCo	352.38

These results are general results in that:

1. FIFO will always give a higher profit result than either the LIFO method or the AvCo method during a period of inflation.
2. LIFO will always give the lowest gross profit return of the three methods in a period of inflation.
3. In a period of deflation, the converse is true: FIFO gives the lowest and LIFO the highest profits.

Do these results have any significance other than we can predict their outcome, given sufficient data? The answer to this is yes! Organisations are keen to minimise their taxation liabilities and will wish to choose the inventory valuation method that allows them to do that. LIFO in a period of inflation returns the lowest profit figure and therefore will generate the lowest tax demand. However, until recently, the LIFO method was barely acceptable in a UK setting, although in the United States it has been widely acceptable since 1947.

The above debate has confined itself to the income statement in that we have concerned ourselves only with profitability. What about the balance sheet? Inventories appear on the balance sheet, as we are aware. From what we know of the worked example, the closing inventory values for each of the three methods are:

FIFO	£81.250
LIFO	75.000
AvCo	77.381

Hence, in the balance sheet for this organisation, we have current assets with one or other of these values. If we are using the FIFO method of inventory valuation, we have assets that include £81.250 worth of inventory; for LIFO it is £75.000; and for AvCo it is £77.381. Generally, in a period of inflation, FIFO gives the highest current asset value and LIFO the lowest. Is there a problem here? Again, the answer is yes! When we come to evaluate this organisation, the value of assets will be important since such ratios as the current ratio, acid test ratio, return on capital employed and so on will all be affected by the value of current assets. Therefore, the inventory valuation method we use will have an impact on the way analysts, creditors, and financiers will view our organisation.

We appear now to have two problems: income statement and balance sheet. Is there a solution to these problems? If we take a full view of the final accounts of the organisation, we find, taking the FIFO view under inflationary conditions, that profit is higher under this method, the current assets are higher and shareholders' funds are higher. From a book keeping point of view, everything works out well.

However, because of the possible impact of inflation and the choice of inventory valuation method, a combination of both the FIFO and LIFO methods have been considered for use by organisations. See Welton, Friedlob, Gray and Sloan (1987) and Edwards and Barrack (1987) for full discussion on this issue. Welton *et al.* (1987: 53) propose a combined LIFO/FIFO financial statement presentation consisting of:

1. LIFO inventory valuation of cost of goods sold, net income, and retained earnings,
2. FIFO inventory valuation in the balance sheet (via an allowance to adjust the LIFO ending inventory valuation to FIFO), and
3. A valuation account to adjust owners' equity for the resulting gross amount of unrealised gain (loss).

Welton *et al.* work through a reasonably extensive example in discussing how their proposed method works; and they use the method on real data for companies such as Allied Stores, Ames Department Stores, and FW Woolworth.

Edwards and Barrack provide us with a much more comprehensive example of the LIFO/FIFO method. They also provide a much more extensive and wide ranging debate. There are many issues to consider within this debate, of course, and they discuss: inflation and deflation; cash flows; relevance, reliability, representative faithfulness, and comparability; historical cost; disclosures; articulation; income tax; materiality; conservatism; benefits v. costs; and LIFO conformity requirements. This list helps to demonstrate that this debate is very wide ranging in nature.

We need to question, however, the realism on which this LIFO/FIFO debate is based. Whilst both articles referred to above give a good discussion on the issues involved, and they present many credible arguments for considering adopting the method, we should ask: Why bother? Is it really worth the effort? Furthermore, can all organisations really run two inventory valuation systems concurrently? Edwards and Barrack are very dismissive of this problem: they say the increased costs associated with changing to LIFO/FIFO procedures are very nominal. We must also appreciate that both articles are concerned with demonstrating a particular method and so there is an element of vested interest in the line of debate they follow. Nevertheless, other solutions to the problems must be available. In the simplest of all worlds, the AvCo method might suit everyone's purpose: and AvCo does not lead to the need for adjustments hither and yon, or to the tinkering around with national legislation and accounting standards!

This is potentially a never-ending source of debate, and at the end of this discussion we might be tempted cynically to conclude that the LIFO/FIFO alternative is merely a way of tinkering around with numbers and merely gives management accountants the opportunity to show off their skills!

Optimising our investment in inventories

As we have already agreed in this chapter, a manager's objective must be to optimise the organisation's investment in materials. This means that he or she wishes to set at an optimum level the following factors: reorder quantity; reorder level; maximum inventory level; and minimum inventory level.

Reorder quantity

The reorder quantity is also known as the economic order quantity, and we will be using the abbreviation EOQ throughout this discussion to reflect this more usual name. The EOQ model is widely written about in management accounting books, journals and magazines. It determines the optimal number of units to buy at any one time by taking into account such factors as the costs of storing materials and the costs of ordering (or procuring) materials. The application of the EOQ model is relatively straight forward, even though the derivation of the formula we will be using relies on the application of the differential calculus (not to be discussed here). The EOQ model can be used in one of two ways: the trial and error method; and the formula method.

The trial and error method

This method seeks to minimise total relevant annual costs by means of a series of guesses, and by doing so the economic order quantity is found. The following example will clarify the issues involved.

TABLE 4.3 ***Trial and error method for finding the EOQ***

	Options						
	1	2	3	4	5	6	7
Order quantity	60	80	120	160	240	480	4,800
Number of orders	80	60	40	30	20	10	1
Average stocks	30	40	60	80	120	240	2,400
Ordering costs (£)	2,000	1,500	1,000	750	500	250	25
Holding costs (£)	281	375	563	750	1,125	2,250	22,500
Total (£)	2,281	1,875	1,563	1,500	1,625	2,500	22,525

Assume the total requirements for material X for MyCo Ltd is 4,800 units per year. An analysis of recent purchases and storage costs shows that total ordering costs average £25 per order and storage costs are £9.375 per unit. Table 4.3 shows some of the options open to MyCo and the costs stemming from them.

The table helps to illustrate why this method is known as the trial and error method: we do not know, before we start working, what the economic order quantity is, so we have a few guesses. During the first few guesses, we might find the EOQ, and we might not! Table 4.3 does, however, include the EOQ – it is 160 units per order (we will verify this when we work through the formula method). The component parts of table 4.3, apart from the order quantity, are:

1. *Number of orders* This is the total annual demand divided by the number of units per order. If we need 1,000 units, and we order them in batches of 100 units, that will mean that we need to place 10 orders (1,000 units needed ÷ 100 units per order).
2. *Average inventories* On average, assuming that inventories are being used at a uniform rate, the average number of units in inventory over the period will be the number of units ordered divided by 2.
3. *Ordering costs* This figure is the number of orders placed multiplied by the cost of placing each order.
4. *Holding costs* These costs are also known as the storage costs, and represent the cost of holding goods in the store. They are calculated by multiplying the cost per unit to store the goods by the average number of units in inventory.

Since table 4.3 gives us a result of the EOQ being 160 units, the total materials cost (ordering and holding) is £1,500 for the year for material X. Notice, we are excluding the actual purchase cost of the material and aspects such as discounts are not allowed for.

Graphical presentation of the EOQ method

Rather than relying on the trial and error method, that may not reveal the correct solution initially (although for the example dealt with so far it has), we can prepare a graph to help

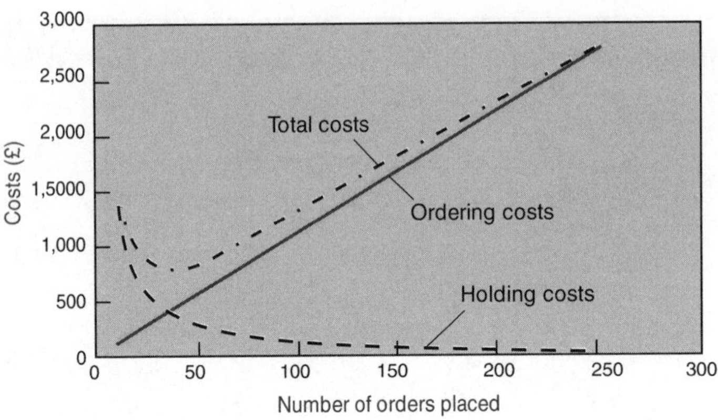

FIGURE 4.2 *Demonstration of the EOQ method*

us with our analysis. Figure 4.2 gives the result that the optimal number of orders to place each year is $33\frac{1}{3}$, and the number of units to buy for each order is 150. Check from the graph that you agree with this. The graph also illustrates a very useful point relating to sensitivity analysis.

Sensitivity analysis

Sensitivity analysis is a routine in which we take a given scenario and make changes to the variables built into that scenario to establish that the changes made will significantly affect the outcome. This means looking at a situation to determine how critical are our assumptions or data to changes, however small or large. In the case of Figure 4.2, we have agreed that 150 units is the optimal number of units to buy each time an order is placed. However, if we study the graph for a few moments we can see that if we bought, say, 140 units or 175 units, we would not be making that much of a mistake. If we did buy the wrong amounts each time, providing the amount was not that far away from the EOQ amount, our organisation would not suffer unduly: we would not be acting optimally, but we would not be acting irresponsibly either. **The EOQ model is generally insensitive to changes around the EOQ: small errors in the numbers to be ordered do not make much difference to the overall result.**

The formula method

This method is both more scientifically based and more direct than the trial and error method. It is scientifically based because it is a mathematically based formula derived using the differential calculus. It is more direct because with only a small series of calculations, the precise solution is found. This means, as we will see shortly, that providing we know the ordering costs per order, the holding costs per unit and the annual demand, we can calculate the EOQ directly.

The EOQ formula

The EOQ is found where:

annual ordering costs = annual carrying costs

and the formula for determining this is:

$$\text{EOQ} = \sqrt{\frac{2 \times \text{annual demand} \times \text{cost of placing an order}}{\text{unit holding cost per unit per year}}}$$

Taking the data from the example, above, we can confirm the EOQ for MyCo Ltd:

$$\text{EOQ} = \sqrt{\frac{2 \times 4{,}800 \times \pounds 25}{\pounds 9.375}}$$

$$= \sqrt{25{,}600}$$

$$= 160 \text{ units}$$

As we found using the trial and error method, the EOQ is 160 units. Sometimes the holding costs are given in a different format to the one presented so far. The data for the above example may be presented, other things being equal, as:

holding cost = purchase cost per unit of the material + storage costs %.

This can be translated by way of an example. Assume the same data as for the previous example, plus the following new information. We are now told that the purchase cost per unit of the material is £18.75 and that it costs the organisation 50% of this cost to store that unit for a year: hence, the storage cost is:

$$\pounds 18.75 \times 50\%$$

$$= \pounds 9.375$$

This can then be used in the way we have already presented. Alternatively, we would change the formula, as follows:

$$\text{EOQ} = \sqrt{\frac{2 \times \text{annual demand} \times \text{cost of placing an order}}{\text{unit cost price for the material} \times \text{cost of materials storage}}}$$

We would then apply this formula in full:

$$\text{EOQ} = \sqrt{\frac{2 \times 4{,}800 \times \pounds 25}{\pounds 18.75 \times 50}}$$

$$= \sqrt{25{,}600}$$

$$= 160 \text{ units}$$

Assumptions of the EOQ model

A variety of assumptions have to be made in order to use the EOQ model. The full list of assumptions is:

- Demand is known and occurs evenly throughout the period.
- There are no quantity discounts.
- Ordering costs vary directly with the number of orders.
- Holding costs vary directly with the average inventory.

We do not need to discuss these assumptions in any great detail since they are built into the EOQ formula: however, anyone who challenges the assumptions must remodel the formula. (In the case of just-in-time purchasing and procurement procedures, this model needs to be remodelled to fit those particular circumstances: see below for a full discussion of the JIT/EOQ model.)

At the same time that we can set the EOQ within fairly well-defined limits, we can do the same for the other aspects of inventories that we mentioned earlier: reorder, maximum and minimum inventory level. We can look at each of these in turn now. We should bear in mind throughout this discussion that a variety of assumptions are built into these formulæ. We will discuss the more important ones, but the lesser ones may simply be left as implicit.

Reorder level

The 1991 edition of CIMA's *Terminology* does not define the inventory reorder level. In the previous edition, the reorder level was defined as: 'A quantity of materials fixed in advance at which inventory levels should be reordered' (CIMA 1991).

One formula for finding the reorder level is

maximum usage × maximum reorder period

This is the most pessimistic version of the formulæ that could be used to determine the reorder level. Being optimistic we would use:

minimum usage × minimum reorder period

The first of these two formulæ is pessimistic in that it assumes an order needs to be placed as far in advance as possible so that the organisation does not run out of inventory of that particular material. By allowing for the maximum usage (the quickest possible rate of usage) and the maximum reorder period (the slowest time that it could possibly take), we are allowing for the worst possible scenario. For example, if my organisation uses Brand X at the maximum rate of 100 units per day, and the longest possible reorder period (allowing for ordering delays, postal delays, bad weather condition and so on) is 30 days, the reorder level will be, at its most pessimistic:

100 units per day × 30 days

= 3,000 units

That is, when the inventory reaches 3,000 units, we must place an order to replenish the inventories of this item. If, on the other hand, we were to be optimistic, we might set our reorder level as:

50 units per day × 20 days

= 1,000 units

There is thus a large difference between the optimistic and the pessimistic. We should therefore now ask the question: Which formula should we use, or should we devise a totally different one? The answer is that our attitude to risk, coupled with our experience of running our organisation, will tell us whether we should be optimistic, pessimistic, or somewhere in between.

Maximum inventory level

The maximum inventory level – not defined by CIMA – is the level of inventory that we should never exceed, and it is set in a similar way to the way in which the reorder level is set, using a simple formula. The formula that follows is based on an optimistic outlook:

Reorder level – (minimum usage × minimum reorder period) + EOQ

This is an optimistic version of the formula since it only allows for the minimum usage and reorder periods. Alternatively, being most pessimistic, we have:

Reorder level – (maximum usage × maximum reorder period) + EOQ

Note that the reorder level is part of the formula for setting the maximum inventory level. This should be set in a consistent manner with the maximum inventory level calculation.

The formula we should use here is:

Reorder level – (minimum usage × minimum reorder period) + EOQ

Using the data from the previous examples, and being told that, for EOQ purposes, the annual usage is 30,000 units, the ordering cost is £11.25 per order and the storage cost is £7.50 per unit, the maximum inventory level will be:

3,000 units – (50 × 20) + 300

= 2,700 units

Note that the figure of 300 is the EOQ derived from the additional data.

This formula assumes that the best possible conditions are used. The reasoning behind this version of the formula being used is that it ensures that, even if there is an unexpectedly quick delivery, and, at the same time, there is also low demand being experienced within the organisation, the inventories should not exceed the maximum inventory levels agreed.

Minimum inventory level

The minimum inventory level is the level of inventories below which we should not allow inventory levels to fall, otherwise known as a buffer inventory. The reason for having a minimum inventory is to prevent the organisation experiencing 'stockouts': that is, the position of having no inventories of the relevant material at all. The danger with a stockout is that production or operations could be severely curtailed, or even halted altogether, at great cost to the organisation. The sort of costs that arise as a result of a stockout include the opportunity costs associated with losing business. If I cannot supply you with the service I normally provide, and you are not prepared to wait until I can provide it again, I have lost the amount of contribution I would have earned from you. The minimum inventory may be used in emergencies, however. If, for some reason, deliveries were not being made, we might have to dip into our buffer inventories to prevent ourselves from suffering from a stockout. As soon as normal deliveries resume, the minimum inventory must be replaced. The formula that sets the minimum inventory level is

Reorder level – (average usage × average reorder period)

This version of the formula assumes average conditions prevail. Under average conditions, this minimum inventory would not be needed. Applying the formula, when the average usage is 80 units and the average reorder period is 25 days:

2,700 – (80 × 25)

700 units

Average inventory level

We often need to know the average level of inventory holdings when, for example, we need to calculate the rate of inventory turnover. There are two formulæ to use here:

(a) $\dfrac{(\text{maximum inventory level} + \text{minimum inventory level})}{2}$

and

(b) minimum inventory level + (reorder quantity ÷ 2)

There is no reason why these two formulæ should give the same value for the average inventory – even for the same item of inventory, for the same organisation, at the same time! An example will clarify this point.

The maximum inventory level for a Splodger is 400 units, the minimum inventory level is 150 units and the reorder quantity has been set at 200 units. Calculating the average inventory level for the Splodger using each of the two formulæ above, we find:

(a) (400 + 150) ÷ 2 = 275 units

(b) 150 units + (200 ÷ 2) = 250 units

Further considerations and inventory control

In the simplest of all situations, what we have talked about in this chapter so far is universally applicable. Whenever inventories are held we need to consider carefully the recording and analysis of them; and inventory records provide the management accountant with a great deal of very important information. Studies have shown that we need not, however, always be too concerned with everything that we carry in inventory. For example, there are those items we have or use that are small and are relatively inexpensive. In terms of cost classification, small, inexpensive items are often classified as factory overhead items, rather than classifying them as a direct material cost. Glue that is used to make furniture may be a case in point in this argument.

Pareto analysis

Taking this argument a stage further, we can consider Pareto analysis. To use this method, we have to classify our inventories according to:

Category	Characteristics
A	Items of considerable value
B	Items of medium value
C	Items of low value

When an average store room is analysed, we usually find the following:

Category	% of total value	% of total quantity
A	70	10
B	20	20
C	10	70

That is, the items of considerable value account for 70% of the total value of the organisation's investment in inventories, yet these items account for only 10% of the total quantity of items held in inventory: so out of 10,000 units of inventory, 1,000 represent category A items, and of a total inventory value of £100,000, category A items account for £70,000. The same interpretation applies to category B and C items. The implications of this analysis are that category A items should be very carefully controlled. Full and detailed records must be kept of all of these items at all times; and very strict levels of inventory should be maintained. Category B items should be subject to the normal materials control routine, but inventory levels (minimum, maximum and so on) need not be strictly adhered to. Category C items may be uncontrolled except in total: that is, they may be issued by the tonne, or the box rather than individually.

The Pareto method is an application of the management by exception principle: we are only concerned with what is exceptional. Category C items of inventory are not exceptional and therefore we should not bother too much over what is happening to them. The danger

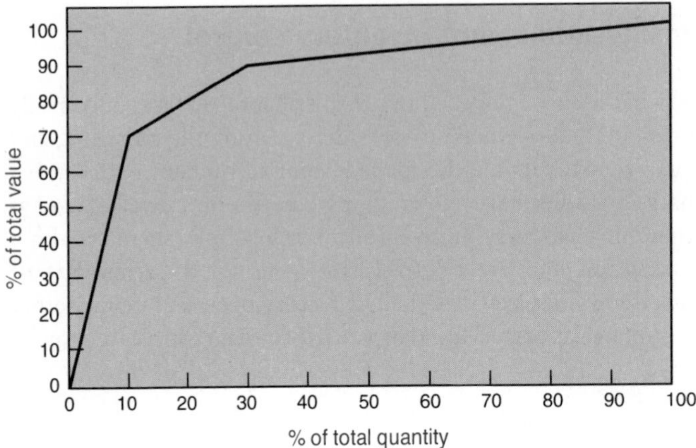

FIGURE 4.3 *Pareto method of stock control*

with applying the Pareto method is that management may become complacent and allow, say, category C items to be subject to misuse or gross misuse, and they could end up as category B items because of the amount of fraud and/or inefficiency surrounding them. The Lorenz curve is a useful device for demonstrating the Pareto method. Translating the discussion above into Table 4.4, and then plotting the Lorenz curve from there gives Figure 4.3.

TABLE 4.4 *Data for the Lorenz curve to illustrate the Pareto method*

Cumulative value (%)	Cumulative items (%)
0	0
70	10
90	30
100	100

This is a very simple representation of the Pareto method but it does help us to visualise the nature of the problem associated with the importance of linking value and quantity.

Reorder point

McLeod (1993: 645) says that:

> After the first computers were successfully applied in the accounting area, they were given the task of controlling inventory. The most simple approach is a reactive one of waiting for an item to reach a particular level and then triggering a purchase order or a production process. The

> item level that serves as the trigger is called the reorder point, and a system that bases the purchasing decision on the reorder point is called a reorder point system.

This is a simple application of materials control in a computer-based environment. Essentially, this early computer application took a manual procedure and computerised it. The important point stemming from this development is that computerisation did not make the procedure any more proactive.

Materials requirements planning (MRPI)

Materials requirements planning (MRPI) is an example of a proactive materials strategy. MRPI was developed in the early 1960s, and it works by looking into the future and identifying the materials that will be needed, their quantities, and the dates that they will be needed. In contrast to reorder point systems, MRPI is a time-based system. Looking back over value added management, we can appreciate the many areas that MRPI sought to impact positively. If we can act proactively on one or more of the non-value adding features of an organisation, we can, for example, influence inventory levels, wastage, raw material inventories, work in progress, among others. Additionally, if we are really anticipating our production and supply requirements properly, we are almost certain to gain flexibility and then, by ensuring employee involvement, we can increase our levels of productivity.

Materials resource planning (MRPII)

Proactive though it was, MRPI still did not go far enough. Hence the development of materials resource planning (MRPII), which can cover the entire organisation's activities.

> An MRPII system integrates all of the processes within manufacturing that deal with materials management. It also interfaces with other CBIS sub systems ... (McLeod 1993: 650)

(Note: a CBIS is a computer-based information system.)

In diagrammatic terms, an MRPII system works as shown in Figure 4.4, which demonstrates, for example, that the production staff will prepare a production schedule of each product to be manufactured during, say, the next three months. Based on this schedule, the MRPII program will determine precisely what quantities of raw material, components and so on are required to enable this schedule to be completed, and at what times. Once MRPII has drafted its own schedule, the purchasing department can then buy materials and components against that schedule. Automatically, in addition to the involvement of production and purchasing functions, the accounting department, receiving department, and all other relevant departments, get involved in the MRPII system. Figure 4.5 illustrates the relationships between MRPI, MRPII and the way that manufacturing co-ordinates its resources. The figure helps to show that whilst we now have MRPII, MRPI is not dead and forgotten, it does still exist by linking the movement of materials with MRPII via the bill of materials.

MRPI is also effective in not only linking into MRPII, but also in setting up an effective inventory control mechanism that is vital for the full and effective use of MRPII and JIT.

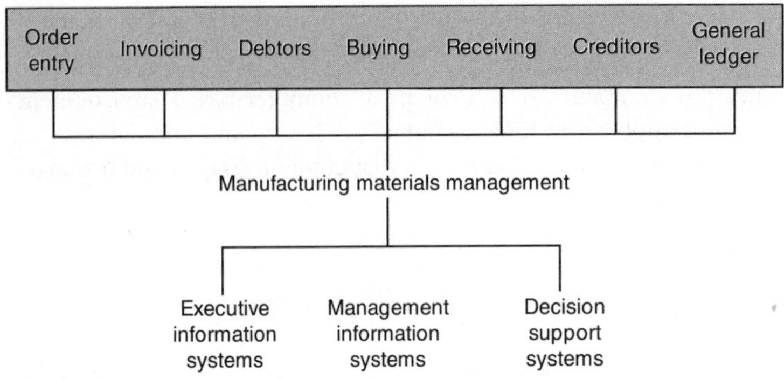

FIGURE 4.4 *The layout of an MRPII system*

If the MRPII system is effective it ensures that inventory levels are reduced. McLeod (1993: 651–2) lists five potential benefits from using the MRPII system:

1 more efficient use of resources
2 better priority planning
3 improved customer service
4 improved employee morale
5 better management information

He goes on to say that the MRP 'family' represented the mainstream activity of North American and European manufacturers in applying the computer as an information system. He also says that the Japanese have taken MRPII one or more stage further by using and popularising the just-in-time approach to production and inventory control.

Just in time (JIT)

Cushing and Romney (1990) view JIT as an extension of MRP. JIT has the aim of eliminating as far as possible all manufacturing and finished goods inventories. It does this by ensuring that nothing is made or processed that is not needed. Thus it is a demand pull manufacturing system. The implications for an organisation of using the JIT system are tremendous and involve total quality management, with a need to redesign plant layout, reschedule receipts of raw materials and the delivery of finished goods, as well as the redesign of the accounting system of the organisation. McIlhattan (1987: 23) defines JIT as:

> the constant and relentless pursuit for the elimination of waste, with waste being defined as anything that does not add value to a product – inspection, queue time, and inventory.

Although this is a starting point to our discussion, it does not give us a deep insight into precisely what JIT is. In an ideal JIT system, the throughput time for a part or product will exactly equal its processing time. The throughput time is defined by Kaplan and Atkinson (1989: 412) as:

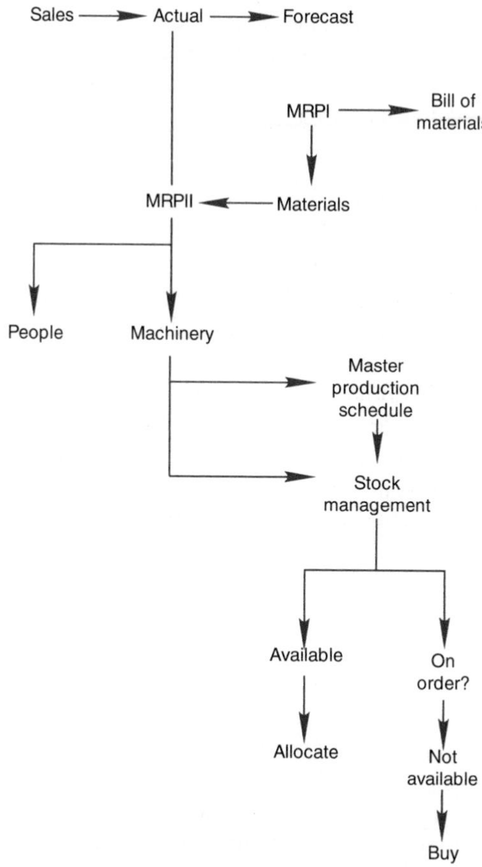

Note: a bill of materials is the list of parts and subassemblies, with their quantities, that go into the manufacture of finished goods. In the case of the manufacture of a 40-cm neck long-sleeved shirt, the bill of materials would show: the length of fabric required; cotton or polyester cotton or nylon; the number, type and quality of buttons; the collar and cuff stiffeners; and the amount, type and colour of thread to sew it all together with. Notice also that actual sales are compared with sales forecast as well as people requirements, machinery requirements, together with the master production schedule.

FIGURE 4.5 *MRPII: its links with sales, MRPI and manufacturing resources*

processing time + inspection time
+ conveyance time + waiting time

The significance of this relationship is spelled out by Kaplan and Atkinson (and many others) when they say that, relating to organisations that have not introduced MRPII and JIT:'In many factories, processing time is less than 10% of throughput time . . . ' (ibid. 412).

McIlhattan (1987: 21) introduces JIT by way of what we can call the '10% factor'. He says:

> In many organisations, the amount of process time is much less than 10% of the total manufacturing lead time and cost . . . associated with manufacturing a salable item. Therefore, over 90% of the manufacturing lead time associated with a product adds cost, but no value to the product. It is this premise that leads to the JIT philosophy that reducing lead time will reduce total cost.

He maintains that by not recognising the importance of the 10% factor, organisations are calculating senseless costs for products, costs that do not bear any relationship to reality. Along with activity-based costing, JIT requires an investigation into and the application of cost drivers. One key result of the application of JIT is the way that customer and supplier have to work together. In order to apply JIT, we need to be absolutely certain that, as the supplier, you can actually get your goods to my work benches or shop at precisely the moment that I need them, otherwise, I will have to keep buffer inventories, and defeat the whole process! Providing this can be done, surveys and discussions show that both manufacturing and service industries are more efficient and productive as a result. To implement JIT properly, however, everyone has to work to very high levels of efficiency. Furthermore to use the method properly usually means that the number of suppliers that an organisation will deal with will be reduced, so there are many cost savings to be had here too.

Zero defects

In addition to the materials handling and storage implications of JIT, the customer's needs extend to having very high-quality requirements for the materials and components he or she is using. If an organisation is living on the edge of its usage cycle by using JIT, it needs to be confident that the materials it is receiving now and putting into operation immediately will not cause any problems. The supplier will need to provide strict guarantees relating to quality control, and the quest for zero defects is important in this context. Again, this development has significant implications for the efficiency with which customers and suppliers are operating. Schniederjans (1993: 26) summarises the management principles of JIT, which, he says, include:

1. Cut lot sizes and increase frequency of orders
2. Cut buffer inventory
3. Cut purchasing costs
4. Improve material handling
5. Seek zero inventory
6. Seek reliable suppliers

As any organisation that has installed a JIT system knows, one of the key aspects to its success is the organisation's links with its suppliers. Due to the need to reduce inventories, but at the same time keeping production flowing smoothly, suppliers have to deliver lower volumes but more frequently. For example, instead of delivering five tonnes of raw materials every week, a supplier may now have to agree to deliver one tonne every day. Additionally, JIT requires that there is very little, if any, leeway for error. Hence, suppliers now have to guarantee higher quality of materials delivered than ever before. Supplier and customer alike must strive to ensure zero defects enter the manufacturing process since any stoppage due to defects can be catastrophic for the manufacturer. The more finely tuned the JIT system, the more susceptible it is to delivery and quality problems. As a result, most JIT manufacturers certify their suppliers. Usually, only a small handful of carefully chosen suppliers are certified, based on their commitment to reliability and quality control. Thus vendor selection does not have to be performed each time the product is ordered since, having been chosen, it is incorporated in the master inventory record for the product.

Such links as are being described here are called co-makeship and have been seen as important beneficial spin-offs from the JIT system. More than ever before, relationships between supplier and customer are closer and more realistic. In addition to a supplier being carefully selected and certified, it is well documented that design engineers, for example, work with the raw material and component suppliers to ensure that everything is as it should be. Supplier and customer work together rather than seeing each other as enemies trying to outdo each other.

The Chrysler Corporation of the Unted States adopted the JIT production philosophy in the early 1980s; and to encourage suppliers to supply just in time to their assembly plants, they offered long-term supply contracts – and a long-term contract will be seen as attractive by most, if not all, suppliers (see Addonzio 1991: 7). Schniederjans (1993) again summarises for us, this time the characteristics of the supplier/manufacturer relationship:

1 long-term contracts
2 improved accuracy of order filling
3 improved quality
4 order flexibility
5 small lots ordered frequently
6 continuous improvement in the partnership

Layout of organisations and JIT

JIT calls for more frequent deliveries of goods in smaller quantities, at predetermined time slots, to the specific locations that require them, as opposed to infrequent larger deliveries to a central receiving and storage area. JIT systems are designed to reduce or ultimately eliminate cost of materials handling and storage. If an organisation is no longer stockpiling raw materials, and is manufacturing in response to demand pull conditions, then there is much less of a need for storage space. Indeed, there is much less need for space throughout the whole manufacturing part of the organisation if JIT systems are adopted. If a central storage place is to be eliminated, and deliveries are required that go directly to the shop floor or to the showroom, it is possible that plant and machinery have to be moved around, or shelves and counters have to moved. Additionally, since more and more frequent deliveries will have to be made by suppliers, alterations may have to be made to delivery bays; and delivery procedures will doubtless have to change. As an overall analysis of factory layout under JIT, all we need to realise, in summary, is that there may be no raw material storage or inspection areas. Raw materials and components are delivered directly to the shop floor; and given the quest for zero defects, there is no need to inspect incoming goods since they will be assumed to be perfect. Similarly, there is no finished goods storage area since everything made has already been demanded, so shipment is virtually immediate upon being finished.

CAMEO

Tesco is a high-profile example of an organisation that is making huge strides in its quest to become the UK's foremost supermarket chain. Tesco is using JIT and other inventory control and distribution methods to help it in its development. To help it use JIT methods, it is using laser technology in its distribution chain. Laser technology is being used to help with assigning cartons of produce to lorries and hence to its stores on a constant replenishment basis. Such constant replenishment allows the stores themselves to hold less inventory of each item, thus allowing them to hold a wider variety of items in inventory.

Tesco now has less than two weeks' supply of produce in its inventories and 40% of its items for sale go straight to stores rather than languishing in a warehouse somewhere. Additionally, because of the introduction of JIT, Tesco has been able to reclaim large amounts of storage space to use as selling space.

The impact the introduction of such sophisticated inventory and distribution control methods is having on Tesco is perhaps best demonstrated by the following:

> Every day Tesco sends 1,000 lorry loads of goods on their way to its stores. Before it installed its new systems, up to nine times as many lorries (many of them half empty) have been reported as having been used to achieve the same inventory replenishment objectives.

Reference: *The Economist* (1995)

JIT and electronic data interchange (EDI)

Although it may not have become apparent yet, JIT does rely more and more on the exchange and gathering of information by using modern telecommunications and computer technology. In fact, it seems fair to say that on-line purchasing and inventory data processing systems are essential to the use of JIT. Unless there is real time access to up-to-date inventory levels and other related information, there is little likelihood that JIT will succeed. One of the significant uses of such on-line, real time, knowledge is that if there is a delay to a delivery, the inventory management department can, for example, monitor the inventory holding situation and take immediate action to correct the problems. Many supplier–customer communications are now carried on largely by paperless trading systems such as EDI networking arrangements: invoices and orders are no longer sent by post, or collected by a salesman. Such details are electronically transferred between computers down standard telephone lines. Finally, organisations such as large supermarket chains have their checkout equipment linked into the JIT system through their data-capturing electronic point-of-sale (EPOS) systems. Allied to the use of laser (bar code) technology, inventory records are continuously updated as customers pass through the checkout with their baskets of purchases.

All of this electronically processed information feeds into the management information system (MIS) and is used for up-to-date decision making. Statistical and other software enhancements can be added to the basic recording software to provide analyses of sales and delivery data, thus ensuring the manager is not only up to date but is also aware of the implications of what is happening in his or her organisation. For EDI to be implemented successfully, it has to be appreciated that it is, for a large organisation, a 24 hours a day, seven days a week and 365 days a year commitment. One of the biggest obstacles to the transfer of documents and transactions between different organisations must be that there is no guarantee that the computer system I use is the same one that you use; and that the two will be able to communicate with each other. This is a problem, but it has been overcome!

Third-party networks exist which allow us to transmit our documents to a computer bureau. The bureau, in turn, retransmits the data to our supplier, the ultimate recipient of the data we were sending. The basis of this system is that our computer can communicate with the bureau's computer, and the bureau's computer can communicate with our supplier's computer. So, even though we and our supplier have incompatible systems, using a third-party network overcomes the difficulty.

JIT and management accounting

One of the key features of JIT as far as the management accountant is concerned is that a simplification of product costing procedures has become possible. This is achieved by attaching costs only to finished output and abandoning any attempt to track and cost work in progress through production systems. Thus only when finished production is notified are costs transferred from the individual cost element (materials, overheads) accounts to cost it. The accounting system, if it works in the way suggested above is then known as a backflush cost accounting system. Backflushing is particularly appropriate in the JIT environment:

> Whenever a product is completed all the materials and components are identified via the bill of materials and removed from the MRP system's records ... the use of backflushing has two important considerations:
>
> - the system treats all materials as being available even though some have become part of the product (they really are in process but the system does not know it). [They are in inventory only one to two days, therefore the risk of a stockout is small.]
> - because materials are removed from system records only when the product is completed, they carry no overhead whilst they are in process. [This is no problem because work in progress should be small anyway.] (Dugdale and Shrimpton 1990: 41)

With JIT the importance of inventory valuation methods such as FIFO and LIFO dwindles. If JIT is applied in its extreme form, there will be only negligible differences between the inventory values derived from each method since what is received is being used immediately. At the period end there may be no inventories of anything; and only minor issue valuation differences will arise.

The benefits of JIT

Addonzio (1991: 9) gives the following as the benefits of JIT production for suppliers and carriers:

- reduced inventory of up to 75%;
- reduced machine tooling changeover of up to 20%;
- improved use of floor space;
- reduced equipment and staffing requirements;
- reduced unplanned and non-structured routes; and
- improved carrier/supplier relations.

It is worth pointing out the true scale of the potential savings as far as investments in inventories are concerned. In Chrysler's case, even though they did really reduce their inventory holdings by $1 billion, they still have several billion dollars worth of inventories left to hold and finance. This is not to say that JIT has actually failed them. What this means is that there are often inventories in addition to raw materials and components, and these may not be as susceptible to such savings as JIT can give to raw materials and components. Furthermore it is rarely possible to eliminate inventories altogether. At one extreme, the quantity and value of inventories will include the materials and components just delivered but not yet used, but which are at a low level. At the other extreme, an organisation might prefer to keep two or three days worth of buffer inventories, just in case the just in time system fails for some reason. In order to achieve fully the levels of saving that have been made by using JIT systems, Pareto analysis is usually applied by management to ensure, using management by exception, that time is not wasted on category C inventory items. Remember, Pareto analysis categorises inventories as A, B or C items: A items are high-value and low-volume goods; B items are medium-value and medium-volume goods; and C items are low-value and high-volume goods. By concentrating on the A items of inventory first, management concentrates on eliminating the high-value items first. Eventually, when the JIT system is running properly, management will then seek to make savings with category B items, and finally category C items. Given the success that many organisations have had, and are having, with JIT, the application of the advantages given above to our own organisations will become appealing.

Bailes and Kliensorge (1992: 29) report in glowing terms the success that JIT has provided for Oregon Cutting Systems (OCS) within five years of JIT being in operation there. Some of the many benefits reported are:

Table 1/Reported improvements at Oregon Cutting Systems

- Die change cut from 6.5 hours to 1 minute and 40 seconds
- Space requirement cut 40%
- Lead times cut from 21 days to three days
- Inventory down 50%
- Reduction of 30% to 40% in the amount of floor space required for manufacturing
- Setup time for a punch press was reduced from 3 hours to 4.5 minutes
- An 80% reduction in defects with no increase in quality costs
- A 50% reduction in scrap, sort, and rework

Again, note that inventories have not disappeared altogether: in the case of the Oregon Cutting Systems organisation, inventories were down 50% – not 100%.

Why doesn't everyone implement JIT then?

Walleigh (1986) challenged every manufacturer to say why they have not yet used JIT. What Walleigh does is to list seven different excuses commonly given by manufacturers as to why they either have not considered JIT or have rejected it. Just two should be enough to illustrate the thrust of Walleigh's argument:

Excuse number three

Our batch-oriented materials planning and control system won't allow us to operate in a JIT mode. We need to install a JIT software package before we can convert our production operation.

Excuse number seven

Our factory is operating okay already. We don't need to put in the effort to convert our operations to JIT.

Walleigh goes to great lengths to explain away why these two excuses are really not tenable: together with the other five excuses he tries to demolish! To accompany reading Walleigh's article, the interested reader might care to look at Wheatley (1992) who suggests it takes only a week to become a master of JIT! In reality, of course, the practice will be different to the theory: once JIT has been properly planned and implemented, users can master its practicalities in a week. Wheatley's book gives a good account of the needs of JIT and factory layout.

Disadvantages of JIT

Normally, if there is an advantage to something, someone somewhere will find a disadvantage! JIT has many good features, but it does have its down side. Carter and Price (1993) provide us with five problems associated with JIT:

(a) problems if orders are delivered late
(b) or not enough parts arrive
(c) or wrong parts arrive
(d) dangers associated with single sourcing
(e) shortages of skilled staff

CAMEOS

Three stories will help to enhance these disadvantages: all of the stories are true!

First, there is the story of the driver who was standing in for the regular driver who was sick. When it came to the time for the stand-in driver to eat, he stopped his lorry at a transport café and ate . . . what he did not know was that his lorry contained vital materials needed JIT by the destination organisation. An irate plant manager had to drive off in search of the lorry, its driver and contents, and once he had found them, explain to the driver how important it was that he didn't just take his meal break when he thought fit!

The second story concerns the football club that wanted to build a new stadium in which to play its games. The site for the stadium was eventually chosen . . . next to a large car manufacturing plant. When the official enquiry came to seek objections to the building of the new stadium, the car manufacturer objected: the traffic generated by the new stadium will, on match days, interfere with JIT deliveries. At the time of writing no solution has been found to this problem but several possible solutions do exist, including:

- build the stadium elsewhere;
- the car manufacturer liaises with the football club and increases its deliveries before and/or after match days;
- the football club compensates the car manufacturer for any losses incurred;
- separate roads/slip roads are built to feed the stadium.

The third story concerns the earthquake that devastated large parts of Kobe, Japan, early in 1995 (referred to above when we discussed why organisations hold inventory). Toyota was operating its factory away from the area that was devastated by the earthquake but its supply lines were affected by it. Hence, within 12 hours of the earthquake having happened, Toyota had run out of some of the components it needed to continue with the production of its vehicles. Production ceased until further components could be supplied.

Given the nature of JIT, however, the problems facing car manufacturer and football club can be overcome by the accurate planning of the manufacturer and real co-operation between the two organisations. The Toyota story could have happened almost anywhere, of course, and such catastrophes are beyond the control of man. However, when earthquakes do happen, they are no respecter of JIT!

Who wants JIT?

If we look at JIT carefully, we can gain a most interesting insight into the oganisational aspects of it. We begin by asking the question: Who wants JIT? Just a few examples to illustrate the implications of this far reaching question.

Does the production manger want JIT? The answer may be no, he or she does not. Take a look at what it means to that manager to implement JIT. The factory layout has to be redesigned; he or she has to accept greater risks that deliveries of materials may be late, which means that production has to stop. He or she may have no buffer inventories whatsoever to cope with late deliveries. Bear in mind that one of the most significant reasons for holding inventory is to offset the risk of a stockout: no inventory, no production; no production, no sale; no sale, no profit.

Does the accountant want a JIT system? To operate a JIT system in full, the accountant now has to implement a new system of ordering and paying for goods: that is, electronic transfers and communications. The audit trail may be less secure than it was. Although safeguards will be built in to the EDI and allied systems, computer-based fraud can be spectacular in terms of the amount of money that can be embezzled.

Does the buyer want JIT? To operate a JIT system, he or she needs to monitor suppliers frequently to ensure that their delivery record is acceptable, and he or she may also have to monitor the supplier's materials quality record more frequently than ever before. The buyer may constantly have to be looking for new suppliers, or, at least, new specifications as designers and shop floor personnel suggest manufacturing improvements . . .

There are many people throughout the organisation who may not want to implement JIT at all. Yet JIT is implemented and often brings great rewards to the organisations implementing it. What, then, is the driving force behind JIT? The answer has to be the final profit figure, and the balance sheet values of inventories. In the final analysis, it is possibly the shareholder who is most keen to see JIT implemented in an organisation. Managers who are looking over their shoulders to see whether they have the support of their shareholders will be keenest to improve their end-of-year results in the ways that JIT can allow. JIT covers the whole organisation. It is not just an inventory control method, even though it does have significant implications for inventory control.

Kanban

Reflecting the Japanese birthplace of JIT, Toyota of Japan brought the word *kanban* into the management accountant's vocabulary. *Kanban* is a card based production control system where the cards act as triggers for the production and movement of items. There are specific rules associated with these *kanban* that must be followed strictly. For example, if *kanban* are not physically attached to the unit, transfer the unit to the next stage in the process or process it, as relevant. If *kanban* are attached to the unit, do nothing to that unit. The main operating rules of *kanban* ensure that there will be no overproduction or accumulation of excess inventories.

The JIT/EOQ model

We saw the EOQ model earlier in this chapter. As we said there, the EOQ model is built on the foundation of a variety of assumptions. Furthermore we said that these assumptions should be changed if the basic situation on which our organisation operates is changed. The JIT system is based on fundamentally different lines to conventional material control systems, therefore, we should now compare the original EOQ model with the JIT/EOQ model. Schniederjans (1993) provides a series of refinements to the traditional EOQ model for JIT purposes. Based on his formulæ and analysis, the following is an explanation of how the new models work. Schniederjans calls his formulæ the JIT/EOQ formulæ: we will do the same here in deference to his work. The following formulæ all relate to the JIT/EOQ:

order quantity (Q_n) $= \sqrt{n} * Q^*$

total annual cost $T_{\text{jit}} = \dfrac{CQ^*}{2n} + \dfrac{OD}{Q^*} = \dfrac{1}{\sqrt{n}}(T^*)$

delivery quantity (q) $= Q_n$

n

savings by switching to JIT/EOQ = S

$$\left[1 - \frac{1}{\sqrt{n}}\right]^{(T^*)}$$

optimal number of deliveries $= n_m$

$$\left[\frac{Q^*}{m}\right]^2$$

where: m is the maximum inventory capacity level

optimal number of deliveries = n_a

$$\left[\frac{Q^*}{2a}\right]^2$$

where: a is the targeted level of average on-hand inventory

optimal number of deliveries = n_p

$$\frac{1}{(1-p)^2}$$

where: p is the desired prespecified percentage total cost savings

WORKED EXAMPLE 4.2 (based on Schniederjans)

Assume that the annual demand for a component that is bought from an outside supplier is 80,000 units and the carrying costs per unit amount to £2 per year; the ordering costs per order are found to be £65. The company to which these data relate currently operates an EOQ systems of inventory control and is assessing whether to implement the JIT philosophy.

Required

Assess the impact of changing to the JIT philosophy as opposed to remaining with the EOQ method.

Solution to Worked example 4.2

demand	80,000	D
carrying cost	2	C
ordering cost	65	O
number of deliveries	2	n

EOQ results

EOQ (Q^*) =	2,280.35
(T^*) =	£4,560.70

JIT Results

Qn =	3,224.90
Tjit =	£3,224.90
q =	1,612.45
s =	£1,335.80

The interpretation of these results is that under the EOQ system, the economic order quantity is 2,280.35 units and total costs are £4,560.70; with JIT, however, the economic order quantity becomes 3,224.90 units with total costs of £3,224.90, the JIT delivery quantity is 1,612.45 units, and the savings made by switching to the JIT method is £1,335.80.

WORKED EXAMPLE 4.2 EXTENSION 1

Suppose now that the company has a storage limit of only 500 units.

Required

Calculate the number of deliveries, the JIT/EOQ, the total annual cost and the delivery quantity.

Solution to Worked example 4.2 extension 1

storage limit $m =$ 500
$nm =$ 20.80 deliveries
$Qn =$ 10,400 units
$Tjit =$ £1,000
$q =$ 500 number of units per delivery

Notice what has happened: we have reduced the lot size, from 1,612.45 to 500, and the total annual costs associated with these components has fallen from £3,224.90 to £1,000. For simplicity's sake, we assume that part deliveries are possible and do not upset the JIT cost relationships.

WORKED EXAMPLE 4.2 EXTENSION 2

The company's managing director, hearing of the benefits that most other organisations achieve when switching from EOQ to JIT, announces that he expects the switch to JIT to save his organisation 45% of total annual inventory costs.

Required

Based on the managing director's announcement, calculate the optimal number of deliveries, the order quantity and the total annual costs; based on a starting point of the original EOQ being 2,280.35 units.

Solution to Worked example 4.2 extension 2

percentage improvement = 0.45p
$np =$ 3.3058 deliveries
$Qn =$ 4,146 units
$Tjit =$ £2,508.38

As we should expect, the new total annual cost is 45% lower than the original total annual cost, when the EOQ was 2,280.35 units.

WORKED EXAMPLE 4.2 EXTENSION 3

Finally, we can assume that the company says it wants no more than, say, 300 units in inventory at any one time.

Required

Calculate, based on the initial EOQ results, the optimal number of deliveries, the order quantity and the total annual cost of this new just in time situation.

Solution to Worked example 4.2 extension 3

target inventory holdings $a =$ 300

$na =$ 14.44 deliveries

$Qn =$ 8,666.66 units

$Tjit =$ £1,200.18

SUMMARY

This chapter showed us the importance of holding inventories as well as the many issues surrounding the control of them. The chapter highlighted the links between inventories and total assets.

We discussed many of the issues concerning accounting for materials in a modern environment, and discussed, in outline, the basic materials control cycle and several of the mathematical models that accompany it. The models we discussed included the EOQ model, reorder level, and the maximum and minimum inventory level models. We considered some of the implications of the Pareto technique as applied to inventory control and then went on to discuss the more modern theories surrounding materials control including *kanban*, MRPI and MRPII together with a thorough review of just-in-time procedures and the associated developments to the EOQ model, the JIT/EOQ model.

Given the importance of the holding of inventory, as clearly demonstrated in the early parts of this chapter, we need to make ourselves aware of the role of the management accountant. Organisations like Tesco, a service organisation, are demonstrably implementing sophisticated inventory control techniques. Perhaps the most important point to be made about organisations like Tesco is that they are looking at their operations from a total logistics chain point of view, not simply inventory control. This chapter has attempted to give us an insight into some of the many aspects of the logistics chain. The management accountant can no longer merely look at inventory, entreat the stores controller to keep everything tidy, and hope for the best. In the world-class organisation, management is concerned to get rid of as many non-value adding activities as possible; and inventories are often the first target in the war against non-value adding activities.

Many of the ideas in this chapter are new ideas: they have been developed within the last decade or so. Yet most organisations have still to consider them, let alone implement them. Any organisation considering an inventory control benchmarking exercise needs to look to organisations such as Tesco for examples of industry best practice. We should be wary, however, of looking to implement all of the new ideas in this chapter. As an example, consider JIT. It is now accepted that the implementation of JIT methodology has led to increased traffic pollution since there are now, in some cases, more lorries driving along the highways and byways more frequently than before. Furthermore, when something goes wrong with the supply chain, JIT often breaks down.

EDI is a significant, positive, achievement for many organisations yet it is fraught with problems. It offers the potential for fraud, while smaller organisations cannot benefit from it because they cannot afford the investment needed to install the EDI infrastructure. Most importantly of all, though, is the attitude of management who refuse to consider implementing these modern methods: they will go to the ends of the earth to justify why they should remain firmly ensconced in the mid-twentieth century, at the latest! The management accountant has an educating role to play here. This chapter should be used as your teaching tool, for inventory control purposes!

KEY TERMS

You should satisfy yourself that you have noted all of these terms and can define and/or describe their meaning and use, as appropriate.

JIT (p. 84)	LIFO (p. 91)
Inventory control (p. 84)	AvCo (p. 91)
Materials control cycle (p. 84)	Economic order quantity (p. 94)
SSAP 9 (p. 89)	Pareto analysis (p. 101)
FIFO (p. 91)	Zero defects (p. 106)

RECOMMENDED READING

Bailes and Kliensorge (1992): The accent here is on JIT and it's readable. Berliner and Brimson is an old one now but has a lot of useful insights. See also Cobb (1991); *The Economist* (1995) is short and indicative of what's happening in the best British supermarkets. Edwards and Barrack (1987) provide an American view of LIFO/FIFO but are worth a read to see what's going through their minds. An integrated view of JIT can be found in McIlhattan (1987), Sadhwani and Sarhan (1987), and Walleigh (1986). More American concerns over LIFO/FIFO in Welton *et al.* (1987).

QUESTIONS

Review questions

1. Why is inventory control such an important topic for management accountants to study?

2. Review the main stages in the material control cycle.
3. Draft a form, or report, to accompany each stage of the material control cycle.
4. Distinguish perpetual inventory from continuous stocktaking and the annual stock take.
5. Define each of FIFO, LIFO, and AvCo. Give a simple example to demonstrate how each method works.
6. What are the arguments in favour of a centralised storage facility?
7. What is the EOQ method? Briefly discuss the assumptions on which it is based.
8. How is Pareto analysis said to apply to inventory control?

Answers to review questions 1, 4, 6 and 8 can be found in the Student Workbook.

Graded practice questions

Level I

1. Applying the 'lower of cost and net realisable value' rule in SSAP 9, determine the value per unit that should be applied to each of the following:

	Purchase price	Selling price	cost to complete and sell
	£	£	£
(a)	1.34	1.44	0.08
(b)	4.40	4.44	0.24
(c)	0.38	0.48	0.06
(d)	1.86	1.94	0.10

2. Calculate the:
   (a) reorder level;
   (b) minimum stock level;
   (c) maximum stock level; and
   (d) average stock level

   in each of the following two cases:

Case 1

The average usage in an organisation is 3,000 units, the minimum usage has been determined to be 2,200 units, the maximum usage is felt to be 4,200 units, the lead time is 10 to 14 weeks, and the reorder quantity is 35,000 units. Normal consumption is equal to the minimum usage plus half the difference between the minimum and maximum usage; and the normal lead time is 12 weeks.

Case 2

The reorder quantity for another organisation is 6,000 units. The budget shows that the maximum usage should be 1,500 units per month, the minimum usage should be 800 units per month. The average usage is 1,200 units per month. The estimated delivery period is a maximum of four months and minimum of two months and averages three months.

3. Two items X and Y are used as follows:

Normal usage	500 per week of each
Minimum usage	250 per week of each
Maximum usage	750 per week of each
Reorder quantity	X: 600 units; and Y: 1,000 units
Reorder period	X: 4 to 6 weeks; and Y: 2 to 4 weeks

Calculate for each of X and Y:

(a) reorder level;
(b) minimum stock level;
(c) maximum stock level; and
(d) average stock level.

4. (a) What is the difference between the economic order quantity and the economic batch quantity?
   (b) Calculate the economic order quantity in each of the following circumstances:

	Demand (pa)	Cost of ordering (£)	Price of materials per unit (£)	Cost of storage as a % of price (pa)
(i)	43,750	2.00	5.00	14.0
(ii)	18,000	6.50	9.75	15.0
(iii)	50,000	5.00	1.00	0.5

5. Fransco Ltd had receipts and issues of a material for the first quarter of 1993:

	Receipts/*Issues* Quantity	Price £
1 January	1,500	4.40
5	*600*	
3 February	250	4.80
10	400	5.00
19	*600*	
3 March	400	5.20
21	*600*	

Required

Draft the stores ledger card using each of the

(a) FIFO method
(b) LIFO method
(c) AvCo method

Level II

6. To which of FIFO and LIFO do each of the following advantages apply?:

   (a) Corresponds exactly to the physical movement of items.
   (b) Overstates stock turnover in a period of inflation.
   (c) Matches current costs with current revenues.
   (d) Depresses profits in a period of inflation.
   (e) Values stocks approximately at replacement cost.
   (f) Matches old costs with new prices.
   (g) Gives lower profits in a period of deflation.

   Fully illustrate your answers.

7. Fill in the gaps in the following table

	Demand (pa)	Cost of ordering (£)	Cost of storage per unit (£)	EOQ
(a)	24,500	5.00	0.50	
(b)	13,000	16.00		750
(c)	5,000		0.38	200
(d)		3.00	4.80	100
(e)	66,000	7.00		555
(f)	10,000	10.00		1,000

Solutions to practice questions 1, 3 and 5 can be found in the Student Workbook. Solutions to practice question numbers in red can be found at the end of this book.

REFERENCES

Addonzio, M. L. (1991), 'Chrysler Corporation: JIT and EDI', Case No. 9–191–146 (Harvard Business School Press).

Armitage, H. M. and Atkinson, A. A.(1990), 'The choice of productivity measures in organizations', in R. S. Kaplan (ed.), *Measures for Manufacturing Excellence* (Harvard Business School Press).

Bailes, J. C. and Kliensorge, I. K. (1992), 'Cutting waste with JIT', *Management Accounting* (US) (May), 28–32.

Berliner, C. and Brimson, J. A. (1988), *Cost Management for Today's Advanced Manufacturing: The CAM-I conceptual design* (Harvard Business School Press).

Carter, R. J. and Price, P. M. (1993), *Integrated Materials Management* (M+E Handbook).

CIMA (1991) *Management Accounting Official Terminology* (Chartered Institute of Management Accountants).

Cobb, I. (1991), 'Understanding and working with JIT', *Management Accounting* (CIMA) (February), 44–6.

Cushing, B. E. and Romney, M. B. (1990), *Accounting Information Systems*, 5th edn, World Student Series (Addison-Wesley).

Dugdale, D. and Shrimpton, S. (1990), 'Product Costing in a JIT Environment', *Management Accounting* (CIMA), 40–2, March.

Economist, The (1995), 'British supermarkets: Tesco's new tricks', (21 April).

Edwards, J. D. and Barrack, J. B. (1987), 'A new method of inventory accounting', *Management Accounting* (NAA) (November), 49–56.

Kaplan, R. S. and Atkinson, A. A. (1989), *Advanced Management Accounting*, 2nd edn (Prentice Hall).

McIlhattan, R. D. (1987), 'How cost management systems can support the JIT philosophy', *Management Accounting* (NAA) (December), 20–6.

McLeod, R. Jr (1993), *Management Information Systems: A study of computer-based information systems*, 5th edn (Macmillan).

Sadhwani, A. T. and Sarhan, M. H. (1987), 'Electronic systems enhance JIT operations', *Management Accounting* (NAA) (December), 25–30.

Schniederjans, M. J. (1993), *Topics in Just-in-Time Management* (Allyn & Bacon).

Walleigh, R. C. (1986), 'What's your excuse for not using JIT?', *Harvard Business Review* (Mar.–Apr.), 38–43.

Welton, R. E., Friedlob, T., Gray F. R. and Sloan, J. D. (1987), 'LIFO/FIFO: a simple solution to inventory disclosure problems', *Management Accounting* (NAA) (October), 52–56.

Wheatley, M. (1992), *Understanding Just in Time in a week* (British Institute of Management).

CHAPTER FIVE

People costs

CHAPTER OBJECTIVES

After reading this chapter you should be able to:

- discuss the importance of people costs
- apreciate the meaning of the new manufacturing environment and its impact on accounting for people
- distinguish between direct and direct and indirect people costs under certain conditions
- understand the elements in the make up of people remuneration
- calculate earnings using various people remuneration methods
- discuss the important factors surrounding people productivity
- be able to calculate labour turnover measures and contrast them with measures of labour stability.

Introduction

To reflect the way that the structure of the UK workforce is changing, this chapter is entitled people costs rather than labour costs. At several points in this chapter we discuss the changing nature of the modern employee. We need to stress that whilst many employees have been and always will be direct labour employees along the lines they were last year, the year before, the year before that . . . many more are changing their work role for ever. For the employees who have changed their role, by becoming a non-production-oriented worker, we need to reconsider the way they are viewed and treated. For example, in the modern manufacturing environment we now have the concept of the machine minder rather than the machine operative. Machine minders may be skilled but their influence over output is much more limited than the machine operator. Machine minders may work with computer-controlled machines, for example, whereas machine operators work with old fashioned, directly controllable machines. This chapter should be read in the context of the modern manufacturing environment.

Importance of people costs

In the last ten years or so there has been much debate in the management accounting literature on the subject of the changing importance of people costs. Develin (1990) have shown that between the years 1960 and 1986, direct labour costs in UK manufacturing fell by 32% as a proportion of total costs: with total costs defined as being:

direct materials + direct labour + direct expenses + overheads

Over the same period, overheads increased by 45% as a proportion of total costs. Develin & Partners illustrate that direct labour accounted for approximately 14% of total costs by 1986; whereas in 1960 they accounted for approximately 21% of total costs. Even if the labour cost is not the single most important cost, it is still a significant cost – 14% of total costs represents a large amount of money – and therefore needs to be controlled carefully. An organisation with annual total costs of £250 million, for example, is spending £35,000,000 each year on its direct labour requirements – a large amount in absolute terms by anyone's standards. Böer (1994) takes a different perspective on the relative importance of people costs when he discusses them in an article devoted to dispelling five modern management accounting myths. Using data from the United States he demonstrates that for a large proportion of a sample of 459 US manufacturing organisations, people costs as a percentage of sales fall in the range 6% to 20%, in 1987. Böer's data spans the period 1849 to 1987: he demonstrates that at its peak, people costs accounted for only 23% of sales; and that was in 1849. Figure 5.1 is derived from Böer's data:

Figure 5.1 also shows the cumulative frequency of the importance of people costs across the whole sample of data. Böer's argument is that people costs have never been a significant cost in US manufacturing organisations; they have always represented only a relatively small part of total costs. Material costs are much more significant, having remained at 55% of total sales for the entire period 1849 to 1987. However, in service industries or organisations, people costs still often represent relatively very large proportions of the total costs of the organisation. In the case of labour intensive organisations such as accounting firms, the health service and education, it is not difficult to imagine that up to 70% of total costs are represented by people costs. A London-based bank, operating largely in Hong Kong, has people costs of 56.5% of total costs and a Danish civil engineering consultancy with a turnover of approximately £80 million per year shows their personnel costs as being 68.8% of their total costs.

A second issue of vital concern to a study of direct labour cost is the realisation that it may be a fixed cost rather than a variable cost. In terms of basic cost analysis, it is commonly assumed that direct labour cost is variable: it is a direct cost and the amount of direct labour inputs varies with output. The analysis of accounts cost estimation method we discussed in Chapter 3 classifies direct labour cost as a variable cost, for example. The reality is that direct labour cost is often found to be fixed cost. It is often simply not the case that the level of inputs of direct labour can be varied, in the short run at least.

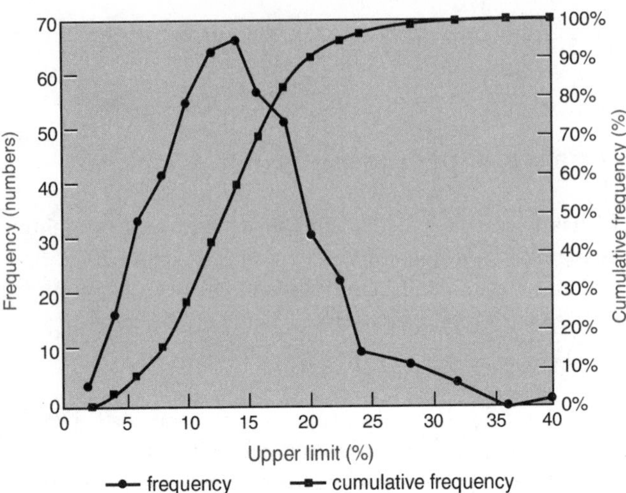

FIGURE 5.1 *Labour percentage of sales (Source: Böer (1994))*

Thirdly, despite the lessening importance of direct labour costs, we ought to remember that the economically active population of the United Kingdom is still well over 20 million people. From a macro economic point of view, therefore, total labour costs are of vital concern.

The new manufacturing environment

The discussion above has arisen because of what is called the 'new manufacturing environment'. The term 'new manufacturing environment' refers to the situation whereby we now have global rather than national or regional markets for our products. Additionally, in order to compete in these global markets, many organisations are being forced to invest heavily in new, often highly sophisticated, equipment and procedures to help them to be more competitive:

> The ... equipment is intended to reduce labour costs ... The shift from labour to equipment changes both the proportion and characteristics of manufacturing costs. Labour decreases, overhead increases, variable costs drop, fixed costs and the break even point rise.
>
> Howell and Soucy (1987: 44)

In addition to direct labour costs being reduced in significance, the new manufacturing environment means organisations are forced to compete at world-class levels in factors such as higher quality, greater reliability and faster delivery times. Berlant, Browning and Foster

(1990: 180) provide an extreme illustration for Hewlett Packard of the effects on people costs of the new manufacturing environment:

> In 1986, we eliminated the direct labour category altogether by combining it with overheads ... direct labour had shrunk to a very small proportion of total product costs. The year we finally eliminated direct labour, it was averaging less than 2% of total manufacturing costs. Yet we were spending a lot of time tracking it. We estimated that 30 minutes direct labour time per person each day was spent on vouchering labour time directly to individual products.

Not all organisations have changed their cost structures as radically as Hewlett Packard. Indeed, there are many organisations that are still competing effectively but have not changed their processes or cost structures. Nevertheless we need to be aware that if we are operating in the new manufacturing environment, direct labour cannot be regarded as important as it used to be. Notice, where labour is the single most important cost, it is also the most sensitive cost to any changes. We can see the relative importance of people costs in Table 5.1 where they are the single most important cost, and we reduce each of the three elements of cost in turn by 10%. The effects on profit would be as shown in the table. Similarly, if the costs were to increase by 10%, profit would fall by similar amounts.

People costs: direct or indirect

There are times when it is not clear whether a cost is a direct cost or an indirect cost. When we discussed the classification of costs in Chapter 2, we saw examples of costs that could easily be classified as either direct or indirect. There are elements of people cost to which this applies: overtime costs, bonus payments and holiday pay are potential problem areas in this regard. The following cameo helps to illustrate a potential overtime analysis problem for many organisations.

TABLE 5.1 ***Relative importance of people costs***

	Present structure	Effects of a 10% reduction in		
		Materials	Labour	Overheads
Materials	300	270	300	300
Labour	500	500	450	500
Overheads	200	200	200	180
Profit	50	80	100	70
Total	1,050	1,050	1,050	1,050
Increase in profit (£)		30	50	20

Fridgereps	**Invoice**	**Number:** **Date:**
High class refrigerator repairs and servicing. All makes and models looked at.		
Customer details: ______________		
Materials: spares and sundries		£15.00
Labour		30.00
Overtime		10.00
Administration etc		17.50
Amount due		£72.50

FIGURE 5.2 *Fridgereps invoice*

CAMEO

Fridgereps is a refrigerator repair and servicing organisation, owned and run by Sam Weller. Mr Blunt, a regular customer, brought his old fridge in one Wednesday afternoon and said, 'The usual, Sam,' and off he went. Five days later Mr Blunt returned to collect his fridge and he was presented with the invoice (see Figure 5.2).

The ensuing conversation went as follows:

Mr B: What's this? Why have I been charged for overtime?

SAM: Because we had to repair your fridge late on Thursday evening, Mr Blunt.

Mr B: That's not my problem, get rid of it.

SAM: We're busy Mr Blunt and that's the only time we had to do your fridge.

Mr B: You could have done it during daytime on Friday, surely?

SAM: No. My work schedule pencilled you in for Thursday evening. Sorry, that's the way it is Mr Blunt.

If you were Sam's management accountant what would you advise Sam to do now? Should Mr Blunt have the overtime recorded on his invoice, as was the case?

The reason for charging the overtime premium to a specific job or product depends on the reason for the overtime work. In the case of Mr Blunt, he should not be charged the overtime because, as Sam said, he pencilled Mr Blunt's fridge in for Thursday evening, but he could easily have put someone else's job there if he had wished. Mr Blunt was right, the fact that his fridge was worked on during overtime hours was no fault of his own. In this case, the normal case, the overtime costs would be classified as an indirect labour cost. On the other hand, if Mr Blunt had said something like, 'I don't care how you do it, Sam, but I must have that fridge back first thing Friday morning', then Sam could legitimately have charged the overtime premium to Mr Blunt's job since Sam was being given the go ahead to work on the fridge at any time of the day or night to fit in with current work schedules. Now we are in the situation where the overtime cost is a direct (directly attributable) people cost.

Notice, we are talking only about the overtime **premium**: the amount over and above the basic rate of pay that is paid to reward someone for working during what would otherwise be their leisure time. This should make sense because all of the time that someone works on a job will be charged at the basic rate: whether the work is done at 5 am, 10 am, or 8 pm. The disputed amount concerns the extra payment made for working outside normal basic hours: that is, the overtime premium.

Bonus payments may also be an area of concern to the management accountant. Bonus payments made, say, on an annual basis may be averaged out over the year. For example, suppose my organisation pays a bonus equal to three weeks' pay at the year end. Spreading the bonus cost over the year so that production can be charged its full value will be done by accruing the liability for the bonus and charging the factory overheads account. When the bonus is paid the liability account is cleared by debiting it. The benefit of accruing such bonus payments and debiting them to factory overheads allows the organisation to incorporate the costs in the overhead absorption rates.

Holiday pay is dealt with in a very similar way to the bonus payment. It is a general cost and is debited to the factory overhead account as it is earned. Therefore, if I am paid £400 weekly and I am entitled to, say, two weeks' paid holiday per year, the cost of that holiday pay will be accrued evenly over the year. This would be recorded as, per week:

	£
Payroll costs	dr 400
Overheads: holiday pay accrual	dr 16

The calculation for the amount of the holiday pay is:

$$\frac{\text{£400 per week} \times \text{2 weeks' holiday entitlement}}{\text{50 weeks worked during the year}}$$

Make-up of people costs

The simple view of people costs is that they consist of gross pay, overtime, bonuses and government taxes or subsidies. However, there are a number of costs which do not appear in the payroll that are also of vital importance to an organisation. Total people costs include the following categories:

1. remuneration;
2. direct fringe benefits;
3. statutory costs;
4. recruitment costs;
5. training costs;
6. relocation costs;
7. learning costs;
8. support/social costs; and
9. personnel administration costs.

Examples of many of the actual costs included in just three of these categories include:

Remuneration

- basic pay
- bonus pay
- overtime pay
- shift premium
- merit awards
- responsibility allowances

Recruitment

- pre-recruitment:
  job specifications
  briefing personnel department
  setting up recruitment process search
- advertising – direct and indirect
- postage and stationery – direct and indirect
- candidate evaluation
- interviewing, including travel and subsistence
- bought in selection costs – such as a recruitment bureau
- selection tests – bought in or costs of administration
- induction
- inducement to move
- induction/orientation programme

Leaving costs

- loss of production – between loss and effective replacement
- statutory redundancy payments (if appropriate)
- *ex gratia* payments
- retirement payments (excluding pensions)

From these three examples, we can see that people costs and their control may not simply be a case of controlling direct labour costs or indirect labour costs. There is, therefore, a lot more to people costs than merely what appears on a pay slip and in the payroll. (See practice question 4 at the end of the chapter for further consideration of the make-up of people costs.)

People remuneration methods

For many workers, their remuneration is based on attendance. They simply arrive at work, stay there for a number of hours per day, carry out their duties, return home and then get paid at the end of the week or month. For other workers, their remuneration is based on the quantity and quality of their work: that is, the more good units they make or provide, the higher their pay.

Time-based remuneration methods

Basically, with a time-based system of remuneration, an employee is paid for time attended: a rate per hour will be determined which will be multiplied by the number of hours attended. Thus gross pay (E) is:

$$E = CHW \times RH$$

where

$CHW =$ clock hours worked
$RH =$ rate per hour

So, by attending work for a week in which I work 35 hours, and being paid at the rate of £4 per hour, my gross pay is:

35 hours × £4 per hour = £140 for the week

Overtime payments

It is commonly found with the basic time-based system that an overtime rate will be applied to any time spent at work over and above the agreed basic working week. Furthermore there are often graded overtime rates that are applied depending on the time of day or the day of the week that the overtime is worked. For example, Precision Discs Ltd operates a time-based remuneration system, and for one grade of employee, the basic and overtime rates are:

	Basic element		Overtime premium
basic rate	£3 per hour		
overtime rate 1	£3 per hour	+	50% of basic rate
overtime rate 2	£3 per hour	+	100% of basic rate
overtime rate 3	£3 per hour	+	200% of basic rate

Thus:

1. Overtime rate 1 operates at any time that attendance at work is required during the week but when attendance is outside the basic working hours.
2. Overtime rate 2 applies for any work carried out on Saturday.
3. Overtime rate 3 applies to any work performed on Sunday.

The basis for setting the overtime premium reflects the importance of opportunities foregone in working at the relevant time. For Precision Discs Ltd, the management obviously feel that Sunday is an important day for employees since it is prepared to pay £9 per hour rather than £3 per hour for any work done on that day. An alternative method of paying for overtime work is to offer time rather than cash. Some organisations do not pay overtime in cash at all; instead they allow the employee to take time off in lieu of payment for the extra time worked. Therefore, depending on whether a premium is applied, if I work an extra day, over and above my basic time, in a month, I will be allowed an extra day's holiday (assuming no premium is applied). Flexitime systems are a good example of where such time off in lieu of payment is often the basis for overtime working. These systems offer the advantage of being easy to understand by everyone, and where the quantity of work is important rather than the quality, these systems are appropriate. Wage bargaining is also simplified because for every grade or group of employees there is only one rate to set. The systems are also very usefully applied when it would be inappropriate to try to install an incentive scheme, such as in a clerical environment where an incentive scheme may be inappropriate. Time-based remuneration schemes are also appropriate where people have little or no control over the outputs of the process they are supervising: for example, in chemical plants and textile mills.

Surveys of selections of industries around the world show a variety of refinements and additions to time-based systems: for example, shift premia, dirt money, and unsocial hours payments. Depending on the precise nature of the addition, the gross pay will be affected. A shift premium, for example, may be a weekly sum, whereas an unsocial hours payment may be paid for at an hourly rate, as and when unsocial hours are worked.

Incentive payment schemes

The general purpose of an incentive payment scheme is to tie earnings to output with the aim of increasing output or guaranteeing a minimum level of quality of output. Even a brief survey of management accounting books, journal articles, and books and articles in other related fields shows that there are many schemes we could discuss under the heading of incentive payment schemes. Many of these schemes have been in existence for a long time (see Williamson (1989) for more discussion on this point). Textbooks normally ask us to assume that organisation A employs scheme X . . . and only scheme X. However, in reality, organisation A might be using two or more such schemes: it would do so because scheme X applies to one part of the organisation, while scheme Y applies better to work in another part of the organisation. Similarly, texts imply that once a scheme is in place it remains in place: Williamson illustrates that incentive payment schemes are used in a more dynamic environment than other authors would have us believe (see Table 5.2).

TABLE 5.2 *Changes in the use of reward schemes over a 5-year period*

	% of establishments		
Type of scheme	Abandoned	Introduced	Current
PBR	29	28	47
Incentive bonus	38	45	41
Measured daywork	12	15	12

Note: PBR = payment by results.
Source: Williamson (1989: 40).

As circumstances demand, schemes are abandoned and introduced as necessary. Lloyd (1976) reports schemes being in place, for example, for ten years, but then having to be replaced. One of the reasons given by Lloyd for the abandonment of schemes is that 'they invite exploitation and manipulation over a period': after a while a scheme loses some of its motivating force and a new system needs to be introduced. Before we discuss individual methods in detail, we should say something about the importance of such schemes. In 1986 30.5% of all males and 16% of all females in employment in the United Kingdom received payment by results (PBR) payments; these payments accounted for 19.45% and 15.8% of gross average earnings (for those in receipt of PBR payments) for male and female workers respectively. In manual occupations, 19.5% and 25.5% of gross average earnings came from PBR payments for male and female workers respectively. Since there is such a large range of schemes to choose from, we must confine ourselves to the study of a selection only.

Piecework

Straight piecework is the name given to the scheme that pays a fixed rate for every good unit of output that is made or provided, and earnings are calculated by using a simple formula:

Earnings = number of units × Rate per unit; or

$E = NU \times RU$

Note that we are talking about payment for good units of output. If someone works at a very rapid pace and produces, say, 1,000 units in a day when everyone else averages only 750 units in a day, we would be foolish if we paid for all 1,000 units unless we were satisfied that the units were usable. If 300 of those 1,000 units were substandard, the employee should only be paid for the 700 good units; otherwise, everyone could increase their rate of output and earn a lot more than they are currently doing, and at the same time, the reject rate will increase dramatically. Graphically, straight piecework earnings behave as Figure 5.3 shows.

Straight piecework earnings behave exactly in the same way that a perfectly variable cost does: earnings increase in direct proportion to output.

Derivation of a piece rate

Piece rates are usually based on the hourly rate for the grade of people concerned, but to provide an incentive to work harder, an inducement is added. The following example shows how the piece rates can be determined.

Basic hourly rate	£1.50
rate of inducement for piecework	20%
Therefore, adjusted hourly rate	£1.50 × 1.2 = £1.80

If we assume that 10 units are expected to be produced per hour, the rate per piece becomes

£1.80 ÷ 10 units per hour = £0.18 per piece.

So, for every good unit produced, the employees will receive £0.18. Piecework should only be considered as a valid incentive scheme when employees can influence their rate of output.

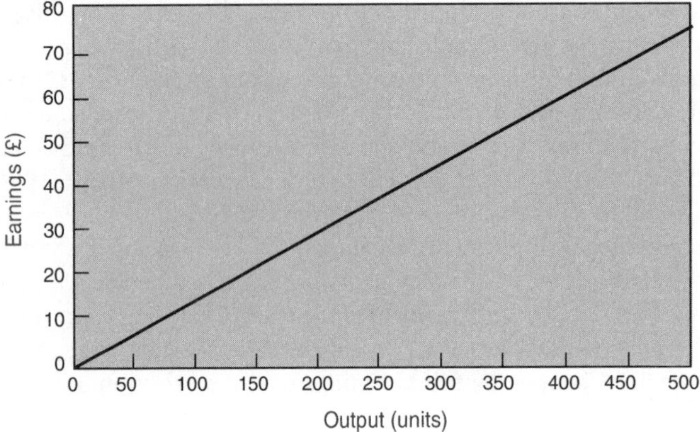

FIGURE 5.3 *Straight piecework*

If the machinery on which the employee works, for example, determines the rate of output, a piecework scheme cannot provide any incentive to that employee since the rate at which output can be achieved is outside his or her personal control.

Piecework with a guaranteed time rate

Commonly, if, due to power failure, for example, or the lack of arrival of materials at the correct time or place, an employee cannot produce, he or she will have a guaranteed or fall-back rate. Sometimes an 'in lieu' bonus is payable when production or output has to stop, thus ensuring a minimum level of earnings when problems are outside the control of individual employees. In such a case their total earnings will behave as Figure 5.4 illustrates.

In algebraic terms, the piecework with guaranteed time rate scheme is represented as follows:

$$E = NU \times RU \geqslant CHW \times RH$$

That is, the piecework earnings ($NU \times RU$) must be greater than or equal to the time based earnings ($CHW \times RH$), otherwise the guaranteed basic wage is paid. The danger with the guaranteed time rate scheme is that employees may be satisfied with the guaranteed time rate, and thus lose the effect of the incentive element of the scheme. However, if the scheme is properly devised, the guaranteed earnings will not be sufficient to encourage the less well-motivated employees to sit back and underachieve.

The average management accounting textbook talks about incentive payments schemes that were devised in the late nineteenth and early twentieth centuries. However, a lot must have happened in the meantime to encourage the development of new schemes, surely? What has happened over the last hundred years or so is that the schemes designed 80, 90 or even a hundred years ago have either been retained or developed; the development has been such, however, that the basic features of the scheme have been retained. Consequently, we will be looking at some of these old favourites as well as some newer schemes.

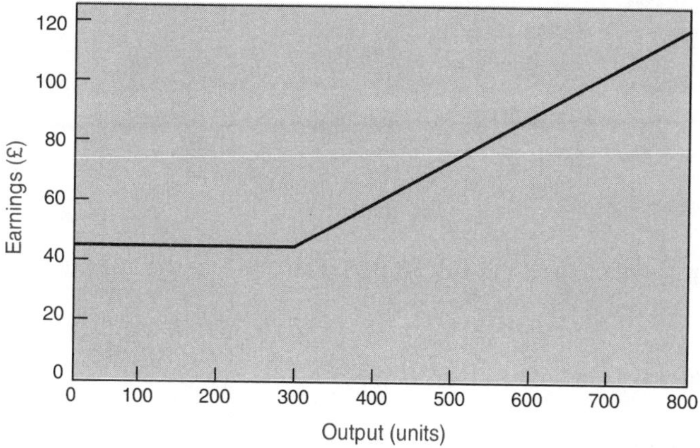

FIGURE 5.4 *Piecework with guaranteed time rate*

75–100 straight proportional scheme

There are three critical features of this type of scheme:

1. standard performance is taken as being 100;
2. the bonus begins to be earned when an employee's performance exceeds 75; and
3. the bonus is $33\frac{1}{3}\%$ of the job rate for a performance of 100, and below and above it is in direct proportion.

Authorised downtime: stoppage time may or may not be built in, and the precise amount of authorised downtime must vary according to circumstances. An example will help us to see how the scheme operates.

WORKED EXAMPLE 5.1

Clock hours worked	8 hours
less: Authorised downtime (waiting etc.)	$1\frac{1}{2}$ hours
Net operating hours	$6\frac{1}{2}$ hours

The standard time allowed in minutes per unit is 6 minutes. Assume that 50 units are produced and the hourly rate of pay is £5.50.

Solution to Worked example 5.1

The total standard time allowed, from the above data, is:

6 minutes per unit × 50 units made = 300 minutes

The total net operating time (in minutes) is:

$6\frac{1}{2}$ hours × 60 minutes per hour = 390 minutes

Therefore, operator performance is

$$\frac{300 \text{ minutes allowed}}{390 \text{ minutes taken}} \times 100$$

= 76.92307%

The calculation of the bonus is: 76.92307% exceeds 75 by 1.92307%, and because 100 exceeds 75 by 25, and the bonus is $33\frac{1}{3}$%, it follows that:

$$\frac{1.92307\%}{25\%} \text{ of } 33\tfrac{1}{3}\% = 2.56409\%$$

Therefore the bonus is 2.56409% of the job rate of £5.50:

= £0.14102

The total rate per operating hour becomes:

£5.50 + £0.14102 = £5.64102

and total earnings are:

$6\frac{1}{2}$ hours × £5.64102	=	£36.6666 +
$1\frac{1}{2}$ hours × £5.50	=	£8.2500
Earnings		£44.9166
		(rounded to £44.92)

Diagrammatically this scheme behaves as shown in Figure 5.5.

Group bonus schemes

By a group bonus scheme we mean a scheme whereby all members of a group, department or section are working on the same or related work and they earn a bonus as a group, department or section. The value of such a scheme is that employees are encouraged to work together, and to a large extent, the success of the scheme, and therefore the group, depends on developing a team spirit. One of the key reasons why group, as opposed to individual, incentive schemes are used in some situations is that it is often impossible to identify the work of any single member of a group: for example, on a car assembly line, everyone is adding value as the cars move along the line but it would be impossible to say with any confidence the full value of each individual. Additionally, an individual cannot increase his or her output without the co-operation of the entire group of people working on the assembly line. The way a group bonus scheme works is that each employee in the group receives an hourly rate for production up to the standard level of output. Units produced in excess of the standard are seen as being time saved by the whole group, and each employee is paid a bonus for this time saved. One big advantage of group bonus plans

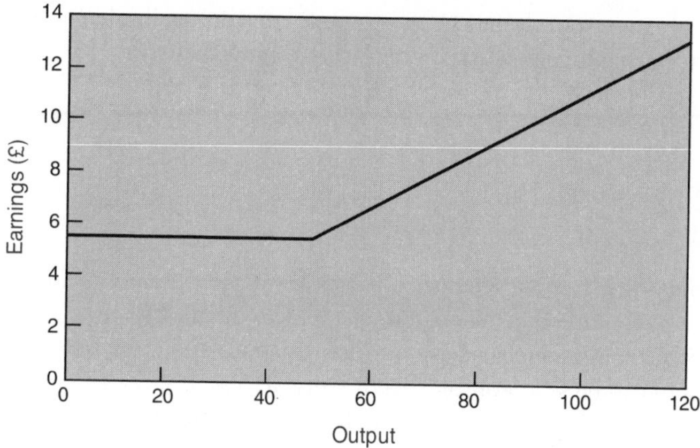

FIGURE 5.5 *75–100 straight proportional scheme*

is that they can save significantly on clerical effort: if the basic calculation for the group is to identify the time taken and time saved, this calculation needs to be done once only since the answer applies to every member of the group.

It should be appreciated that group bonus schemes will vary between organisations: indeed there could be as many variations as there are organisations. The illustration that follows, therefore, is one possible way for the scheme to operate. The standard production rate is fixed at 30 units per day, and it is agreed that for every 20% increase in production, a bonus of £1,000 will be shared equally among the 10 members of the group, and pro rata. In one day, 45 units were produced, which represents an increase over standard output of:

$$\frac{15}{30} \times 100 = 50\%$$

By proportion (pro rata), the amount of bonus earned is calculated by:

$$\frac{\text{excess of actual output over standard}}{\text{bonus increment}} \times \text{bonus earned}$$

$$\frac{50\%}{20\%} \times £1{,}000$$

$$= £2{,}500$$

Therefore, each member will receive:

$$£2{,}500 \div 10 \text{ members} = £250$$

as their share of the total bonus available.

One variation that is worthy of mention is that the amount of bonus each employee receives might be paid according to his or her basic hourly rate of pay: thus, for example, someone earning £5 per hour will receive more than someone earning £4.75 per hour.

Group plans need not be tied only to output. It may be worthwhile considering implementing schemes, for instance, to reduce accidents at work by declaring a bonus when an accident has not happened for a specified period of time; or when the reject rate remains below a predetermined level.

Other incentive schemes

There is therefore a wide variety of incentive schemes and variations on schemes available throughout the world, and we have looked at just a few of them in detail. Other schemes worthy of a mention are profit sharing schemes, share options schemes, and co-partnership schemes. Although these schemes can be very complex to organise and set up, the principles on which they are based are very simple, as the names of all three schemes suggest.

Also there are two incentive payment schemes that have been used in the United Kingdom which do not rely on time or manufacturing output. First, Austin Rover cars used to use 'A customer quality rating (CQR)' system as a basis for calculating bonus payments for employees. This quality rating is based on the number of faults found in vehicles made by the organisation, and a bonus is paid on the basis of a 13-week average of the bonus ratings. Secondly, Pearl Assurance were reported to have operated an efficiency-based scheme for white-collar employees.

Goal congruence

The variety of incentive payment schemes devised and in use tell us a great deal about the objectives of the people who institute such schemes. Without an incentive, none of us would work too hard (on average). In order to overcome the problem of motivation, therefore, methods have to be found to encourage goal congruence: that is, you work hard for me, and I will reward you well. For some people, simply being paid a basic wage is not enough, they need a challenge. Incentive payment schemes can provide that challenge: the harder one works, the greater the financial (and other) rewards that follow. If the incentive scheme is designed properly, the employee's personal objectives of adequate motivation and reward will complement the employer's objectives of cost minimisation, thus achieving goal congruence. In turn, this will match shareholders' objectives of adequate returns on their investment.

Questioning performance-related pay

Recent discussion on performance-related pay (the situation where an employee's earnings are related to his level of output or efficiency) casts a rather large shadow over whether it is such a good idea. Writing in the *Financial Times*, David Goodhart (1993), summarises a debate which suggests that PRP does more to demotivate than to motivate staff, and neither helps to retain high performers nor disturb poor performers. If this is true, Goodhart asks, what explains PRP's continuing popularity? He gives three sets of reasons:

1. PRP helps organisations to change their culture, to improve employer and employee relationships.
2. PRP is one way in which 'flatter' organisations can reward people since there are fewer opportunities for promotion.
3. PRP schemes can save the organisation money.

Furthermore, Goodhart says, PRP schemes can help to reward the effective efficient employee over and above the employee who does just enough to avoid the sack. Lucy Kellaway, writing in the same edition of the *Financial Times*, adds a further dimension to the concerns expressed over PRP when she discusses an article from the *Harvard Business Review* written by Alfie Kohn. Kohn argues that 'incentives are . . . hopeless at motivating senior and junior employees. Surveys have failed to establish any link between top pay and company performance.'

> Kohn cites the example of a mid western manufacturing company, where an incentive system for welders was suddenly dropped. Productivity fell initially, but after a few months was back where it had been before. (Kellaway 1993)

Not everyone agrees with Kohn, of course, and a closer look at his article and Kellaway's discussion of it will help with our understanding of the issues involved.

Labour performance reports

One of the primary objectives of paying wages is to reward people for their efforts on behalf of the organisation. As management accountants, we are concerned that the data coming out of the wages system can usefully be turned into information. The information derived from the wages system data can be used by management to assess the effectiveness of its labour force, whether the organisation is overmanned, or whether a department is understaffed. Every organisation will have its own reporting system, but the following ideas are indicative of the kind of performance reports that management accountants can generate for their management colleagues. Once a full analysis of labour costs is done, the relevant performance reports can be prepared and distributed. A whole variety of reports can be prepared. For example:

- direct labour cost reports;
- indirect labour cost reports;
- departmental labour cost reports;
- job labour cost reports;
- idle time reports;
- daily labour reports;
- weekly labour reports.

The reports that an organisation actually prepares are the ones that are needed by management. Two labour reports are given in Tables 5.3 and 5.4. Note that the titles in the daily idle time report are fixed: that is, once the report has been circulated once or twice, the titles used must remain the same day after day. Therefore, although it is not shown in Table 5.4, there has to be the flexibility to allow for extra headings, or to have a 'Sundry' or 'Others' column.

TABLE 5.3 ***Labour cost report***

Labour cost report								**Week ending:**
Dept	Labour type	Actual			Budgeted			
		This week £	Last week £	Year to date £	This week £	Last week £	Year to date £	
Sawing	Direct							
	Indirect							
	Total							
Dressing	Direct							
	Indirect							
	Total							
Assembly	Direct							
	Indirect							
	Total							

TABLE 5.4 ***Labour idle time***

Daily idle time report											**Date:**
Dept	Total DLH	Productive DLH		Idle time due to:							
				Maint		No mats		Trans		Total	
		Amt	%	Amt	%	Amt	%	Amt	%	Amt	%
A	1,000	800	80	150	15			50	5	200	20
B	1,900	1,710	90					190	10	190	10
C	850	765	90			85	10			85	10
D	300	255	85	15	5	15	5	15	5	45	15

Note: Abbreviations:
DLH is direct labour hours
Amt is the amount or number of hours
maint is maintenance
nomats is no materials (waiting for materials to be delivered)
Trans is waiting for transport

Productivity

One aspect of the performance of people that must be of prime concern to management, but which has not yet emerged from our discussions, concerns productivity. We should appreciate that productivity is a subject that has been, and must continue to be, a topic which is widely discussed throughout all industries. In the 1960s in the United Kingdom, trade unions and management were often locked in heated debates over pay awards that centred around productivity deals. Reading newspapers today will still illustrate the importance of productivity: many references to it can still be found when pay awards are under negotiation, or when organisations are trying to rationalise their operations.

Economic impact of productivity

In the United Kingdom from the 1950s to the 1980s, productivity was a key word. When employees were discussing pay awards, the central argument very commonly centred around how the award was to be financed: through higher prices, lower profits, reduced capital investment, redundancies, closure . . .

Chew (1988: 110) says: 'Productivity is not about high wages. High wages can present a problem, not because workers are paid too much but because they produce too little.'

If a pay award of x% is to be granted, productivity needs to rise by y% so that the organisation remains competitive, maintains profit, and does not have to cut capital investment. In our discussion we have highlighted measures concerning 'single factor productivity measures' (ibid.), such as output per labour hour or output per machine. Chew warns against being overelaborate in designing productivity measures: 'If the people who use an index cannot understand it at a gut level, it probably will not affect their decisions and priorities' (ibid. 114).

Economically, productivity has much to offer. An example will illustrate the point. Mr Albertson is a skilled technician. When he first arrived at the Toburg Brewery, it took him 1 hour 40 minutes to carry out a maintenance procedure on one of the brewery's items of plant. Now, six years later, Mr Albertson has become much more proficient and familiar with Toburg's plant and equipment and the job that used to take 1 hour 40 minutes takes him only 23 minutes, and no other factor inputs are involved now than were used six years ago. In cost terms, assuming a rate of pay of £3 per hour (at constant values) and an overhead absorption rate for his services of 200% of his people cost, the maintenance procedure Mr Albertson is carrying out cost

$$1^{40}/_{60} \times (£3 + (200\% \times £3)) = £15$$

six years ago; and today that procedure costs:

$$23/60 \times (£3 + (200\% \times £3)) = £8.625$$

A saving of £6.375 per procedure: all due to productivity.

The discussion that follows draws distinctions between manufacturing and white collar productivity. The essence of this distinction is to illustrate that anyone who works or performs a task should be subject to productivity analysis. We should always look at ourselves and our colleagues and ask ourselves whether we could be working better: that is, quicker, more effectively, more efficiently, and so on. Productivity is defined as the relationship between the units of output and the units of input:

$$\text{Productivity} = \frac{\text{output}}{\text{input}}$$

Although the definition is very simple on the face of it, problems arise immediately with some of the terms. What is output, for example? In what units are the inputs measured? Furthermore, productivity is normally defined in terms of manufacturing processes and organisations, but white collar productivity is also measurable and important.

Manufacturing productivity

Examples of manufacturing productivity and its impact on people costs are legion in a manufacturing environment. For example, an oil refinery produces 500,000 litres of refined oil in 20 hours; thus, the rate at which oil is refined is

$$\frac{500{,}000 \text{ litres}}{20 \text{ hours}}$$

$= 25{,}000$ litres per hour

Of itself, this figure is just a bit of data. It does not really help management to know that output for one 20-hour period was at the rate of 25,000 litres per hour. We can convert these data into information by, for example, creating an index of oil refined. We can generate such an index by assuming further refining data:

	Day 1	Day 2	Day 3	Day 4
Oil refined / Hours/time	500,000 / 20	519,750 / 21	453,600 / 18	484,000 / 22
Output per hour	25,000	24,750	25,200	22,000

The index is constructed by taking day 1 as the base point, or benchmark, and expressing all of the other output figures as a percentage of that:

Index	100.00	99.00	100.80	88.00

The index gives us a relative measure of the rate of output or productivity for this oil-refining business. The index can be plotted on a graph, and progress monitored, as in Figure 5.6.

Note that the vertical scale on Figure 5.6 has been 'broken' to start at an index of 50. This is merely to emphasise the change in the index numbers over time. Plotting the index number over a more prolonged time scale will give an excellent overview of how productivity is behaving. One problem this analysis has not revealed concerns the inputs. To what do the hours relate? Are they total people hours, direct labour hours, or machine hours? As we have said previously, we have to find the input measure that most realistically reflects the driving of the process and that determines the outputs. In the case of refining oil, the most sensible input measure will relate to a machine- or technology-based measure. Therefore, in such a case, the result will be output per machine hour, or similar.

White-collar productivity

Judging by the contents of management accounting textbooks, management accountants usually ignore white-collar productivity. It is, though, an aspect of business and commerce

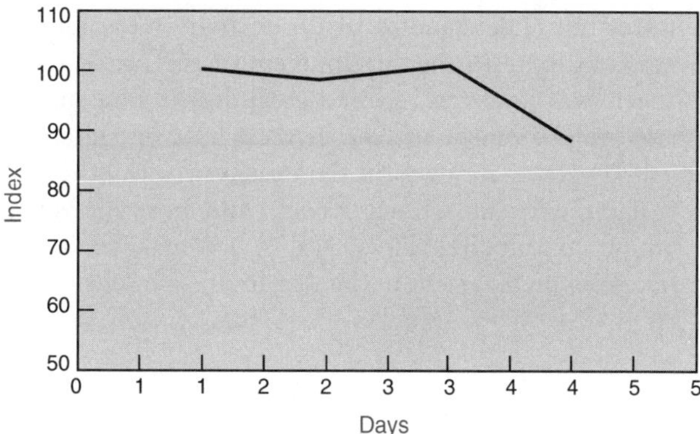

FIGURE 5.6 *Oil refinery productivity index*

that is gaining in importance. Gass, Bentson and McMakin (1987) give us an insight into white-collar productivity in their host organisation (United Service Automobile Association (USAA 1986)) in San Antonio, Texas. They were given the job of devising white-collar productivity measures. One of their biggest problems was that they had no measures to work from, so they had to devise their own! A reading of Gass *et al.* shows how they set about the problem of answering the question concerning measurement of white-collar productivity in their organisation, a service-based organisation. The output of their efforts includes such measures as those described in Table 5.5.

Gass *et al.* do point out that what works for you might not work for me. This is a point that Lloyd (1976) stresses in her report. Because of the range of industries, the types of jobs, and the variations in size, location, production methods and types of employees covered by such schemes, each scheme for each organisation has to be considered on its merits and tailor-made to fit.

TABLE 5.5 ***White-collar productivity methods***

Efficiency measures (quantity/volume related)	Effectiveness (quality/service related)
$\frac{\text{number of entries}}{\text{FTEs}}$	$\frac{\text{number of due dates met}}{\text{total number of due dates}}$
$\frac{\text{number of reports filed}}{\text{FTEs}}$	$\frac{\text{total records samples by the system}}{\text{total data element errors by the system}}$

Note: FTEs are full time equivalent staff numbers.
Source: Adapted from Gass *et al.* (1987).

One most important way that ensures full understanding of productivity measurement understanding is by having employees contribute to the development of the productivity measure that they will be working to achieve. Gass *et al.* spent a great deal of time on the implementation of a productivity-based improvement scheme in their host organisation. They spell out the need to involve employees at all levels in the design of such schemes. Involvement by employees helps to ensure the scheme will work better and more effectively than one that is merely imposed without consultation. Lloyd (1976: 19) makes a list of devices that can be used to ensure employee involvement in the design of such schemes:

- written communication
- general circulars
- briefing groups
- notice boards
- house journals
- verbal communication

Communication of ideas does not just happen: it has to be made to happen. Lloyd's list shows some of the ways we can all co-operate to achieve our aims.

CAMEO

White-collar productivity and the civil service

One of the first measures that Britain's Deputy Prime Minister, Michael Heseltine, announced, in August 1995, was that he was waging war on white-collar productivity in the UK civil service. There is nothing remarkable in this, of course, since we ought to expect our public servants to be as efficient as possible. However, the most interesting point about this measure is the extent of the savings that have been claimed to be possible – and they are all coming from white-collar productivity.

Mr Heseltine announced the results of studies by external consultants, civil servants and 'professionals' (this latter term is not defined!). The conclusions of the studies, commissioned by the Prime Minister a year earlier, are that £90 million per year will be saved if the necessary reforms are put into operation. The police could save £30 million by cutting out 6 million pieces of paper; the number of school forms could be cut by 11 million per year; and doctors would be able to cut back on 15 million forms per year. At the Home Office, much of the £30 million to be saved will result from using fixed penalty notices instead of individual actions against motoring offenders. Similarly, if all the measures identified relating to education are implemented, and merely ten minutes per week of head teacher time could be saved, this in turn would save £5 million in salary costs alone. As far as the point relating to head teacher time is concerned, it is fair to say that those savings would come in the form of opportunity costs.

For further discussion on these points see both *The Times* and the *Guardian* newspapers of 1 August 1995.

Labour turnover

When we were looking at the make-up of people costs, we considered, for example, the many costs associated with employees being recruited and leaving an organisation. Because such costs can be extensive, we need to consider controlling them. The first step in controlling such costs is to find out what is driving them. Labour turnover is one reason why recruitment and leaving costs exist. In some organisations it is the only driver, in other organisations it may be a minor reason. If we assume labour turnover is a significant issue in an organisation, we need to measure it and assess its significance. Although there can be practical difficulties with the formulæ, they give us a starting point:

1. $\dfrac{\text{number of leavers replaced}}{\text{average number of employees}} \times 100$
2. $\dfrac{\text{number leaving whether replaced or not}}{\text{average number of employees}} \times 100$
3. $\dfrac{\text{new engagements and employees leaving}}{\text{average number of employees}} \times 100$

The kind of problems raised by these formulæ include that formulæ number (2) will be distorted when, for example, employees are being dismissed because of a contraction of the business; and using an average of the number of employees can be misleading if the method of calculating the average is incorrect.

WORKED EXAMPLE 5.2

Use each of the three labour turnover formulæ to assess the labour turnover position of AY Ltd over each of the last three months

	Jan.	Feb.	Mar.
Total employees at the start	400	420	415
Total employees at the end	420	415	405
Total leavers	30	28	51

Solution to Worked example 5.2

Before we assess the labour turnover rate, we have to assess how many new recruits we had during the periods under review:

	Jan.	Feb.	Mar.
Total employees at the start	400	420	415
New starters	50	23	41
	450	443	456
Total employees at the end	420	415	405
Total leavers	30	28	51

This schedule works like a trading account, and new starters – the figure we have to calculate – is found by difference. It is the only figure in the table we do not know at the start of the exercise. The average number of employees is the average of the employees at the start and at the end of the period.

Thus, using the three formulæ, labour turnover is as follows:

	Jan.	Feb.	Mar.
1.	30 ÷ 410 = 7.32%	23 ÷ 417$\frac{1}{2}$ = 5.51%	41 ÷ 410 = 10.00%
2.	30 ÷ 410 = 7.32%	28 ÷ 417$\frac{1}{2}$ = 6.71%	51 ÷ 410 = 12.44%
3.	50 ÷ 410 = 12.20%	23 ÷ 417$\frac{1}{2}$ = 5.51%	41 ÷ 410 = 10.00%

Three formulæ and three sets of results. The interpretation of these results is that we know from each formula how many employees had to be replaced during the period.

Labour stability: an alternative measure

The Independent Labour Organisation (ILO) (1984: 76) report contains a formula devised by Angela Bowey concerning an alternative measure to the three labour turnover rate formulæ given above. The formula concerns labour stability and it is represented by:

$$\frac{L_n}{n \times N} \times 100$$

where:

N is the total number of employees
n is the number of months over which stability is being measured
L_n is the total length of service in months of the employees concerned measured over the past n months.

This formula expresses stability as a percentage of the maximum possible stability.

> Labour stability measures the ability of the unit to retain its employees, as distinct from labour turnover which measures the rate of replacement of employees. The significant difference between these two measures is illustrated, for instance, where a high labour turnover rate is due mostly to a small proportion of jobs in the units being filled several times in the time period considered. High labour turnover in this example does not indicate low labour stability. (ILO 1984: 76)

If we work through an example incorporating both labour turnover and labour stability we can fully appreciate the difference between them.

WORKED EXAMPLE 5.3

For the six-month period, NW plc had an establishment of 75 people. Of the 75 people, there was a total of 15 leavers, all of whom were replaced. More specifically, though, 72 of the 75 people were employed throughout the whole six-month period, therefore, the 15 leavers represented significant changes in only one or two jobs or positions. The average length of service of the people who had changed jobs during the six-month period is 2 weeks.

Required

Calculate the labour turnover and labour stability rates for NW plc

Solution to Worked example 5.3

Labour turnover

The formula here is to take the 15 replaced leavers as a percentage of the assumed average of 75 employees:

$$15 \div 75 \times 100 = 20\%$$

Labour stability

L_n is the total length of service of all employees for the period: this is 72 employees multiplied by 6 months each, since none of the 72 employees left during the period, and 0.5 months times the 15 employees who came and went during the period. We can assume that 2 weeks is half of a month; N is 75 employees; and n is six months:

$$\frac{L_n}{n \times N} \times 100$$

$$= \frac{(72 \times 6) + (0.5 \times 15)}{6 \times 75} \times 100$$

$$= \frac{432 + 7.5}{450} \times 100$$

$$= \frac{439.5}{450} \times 100$$

$$= 97.67\%$$

The labour turnover rate suggests that the organisation's labour supply is 80% stable (that is, 20% unstable or changing), whereas the labour stability rate says that the labour supply is 97.67% stable. The usefulness of the stability ratio is that it does pick out, even if management were not aware of it before, that although a relatively large number of employees have left and been replaced, the majority of employees have remained in post.

Labour turnover reports

Regular labour turnover reports are needed, in spite of the possible conflicts between the turnover and stability rates, that give a breakdown of the reasons why individuals have left and some assessment of costs made. Analysis can also be made by department, grade of employee, sex and so on. Attempts should also be made to detect any relationships between labour turnover and such factors as the accident rate, transport facilities (for getting to and from work), and alternative employment opportunities.

SUMMARY

This chapter has given a detailed overview many of the issues surrounding accounting for people. We have looked at many aspects of accounting for people from a consideration of the importance of people to incentive payment schemes. A variety of ways in which employees' earnings can be derived were examined, and we looked at very simple time-based methods as well as the often more complicated incentive payment schemes. The idea of goal congruence in the context of remuneration schemes was introduced. When we looked at labour turnover we also considered a more realistic measure of how much an organisation was really suffering from employees leaving and being replaced, and we discussed labour stability. Productivity was another important factor considered when we examined the economic impact of improvements in the rates of output of employees.

There are several key elements to a discussion of people costs. Perhaps the most important element of people costs is that their relative importance is now changing in many societies. We know that as countries move from developing to developed status, the proportion of service-based organisations increases. We also know that as world markets become more globalised and as organisations need to compete more effectively, the relative importance of people in organisations changes. In the new manufacturing environment, we are moving away from the machine operative to the machine minder. In the former case, the operative could have an impact on the output of his or her machine. In the latter case, we have someone whose impact is much less directed to controlling output.

The management accountant needs to be aware of the type of changes affecting his or her organisation:

- Is the organisation moving towards being a world class organisation?
- Is the organisation employing machine minders now rather than machine operators?
- Is the organisation employing more service personnel than direct labour?

The implications of the answers to these kinds of questions are crucial for the survival of the modern organisation. If the management accountant is not fully aware of the direction in which his or her people costs are moving, he or she cannot possibly advise management colleagues about people costs, people cost systems, or the rewards systems that people need in order to help them work more efficiently. For much of this century, people costing systems seemed to change little. We had the productivity debate of the 1960s and 1970s, but many aspects of people reward systems appeared not to change. Now, however, people costing systems of the 1970s and 1980s are already outdated. If an organisation is still using people reward systems that date from two or three decades ago, they may be losing ground in their attempts to become a world-class organisation.

As befits such a dynamic area as people costing, the final sentence in this chapter must be to say to the modern management accountant: history is dead, look to the future!

KEY TERMS

You should satisfy yourself that you have noted all of these terms and can define and/or describe their meaning and use, as appropriate.

Remuneration (p. 127)
Direct fringe benefits (p. 127)
Statutory costs (p. 127)
Overtime (p. 129)
Incentive payment schemes (p. 130)
Payment by results (p. 131)
Group bonus scheme (p. 134)
Productivity (p. 138)
Manufacturing productivity (p. 140)
White-collar productivity (p. 140)
Labour turnover (p. 143)
Labour stability (p. 144)

RECOMMENDED READING

Böer (194) explodes one or two myths, Stateside anyway. There are not many articles in this area, so Chew (1988) is useful in this respect, as is Gass *et al.* (1987). Kellaway (1993) is written by a journalist, so it's readable. Williamson (1989) offers a summary of several schemes.

QUESTIONS

Review questions

1. Categorise labour costs under nine separate headings.
2. What methods are there for recording employees' attendance at work?
3. Outline the procedure for the payment of wages, starting with the collection of attendance times.
4. What performance reports might be generated that will help with the control of labour costs?
5. Overtime is a cost that is borne by all output, not just the output for which it was specifically incurred. What is meant by this statement?
6. Contrast labour turnover and labour stability. Devise and work through an example of your own to answer this question.
7. (a) Define productivity and contrast it with production;
   (b) Chew (1988) says 'Productivity is not about high wages.' What did Chew mean by this statement?

8. Write short notes on each of the following:
   (a) piecework;
   (b) piecework with guaranteed time rates;
   (c) group bonus schemes.

Answers to review questions 5, 6, 7 and 8 can be found in the Student Workbook.

Graded practice questions

Level I

1. Budgeted and actual details for the bread and confectionery shop owned by Saxover Ltd are given below. From these data prepare a labour cost report for the month.

	Budgeted hours	Actual labour	Units produced
Mixing	2,200	£19,596	1,480
Baking	6,640	56,550	1,430
Packing	1,160	7,632	1,360

In addition to the above total data, the following standards relate to the bakery section:

	Standard hours per unit	Standard labour cost per hour (£)
Mixing	0.8	18.30
Baking	2.5	19.50
Packing	0.3	18.00

2. From the data contained in the table below, prepare an analysis of both labour turnover and labour stability. Include in your study both numerical and graphical analyses.

Week	Employees at the start	Employees at the end	New starters
1	75	77	6
2	77	73	0
3	73	73	4
4	73	74	6
5	74	72	3
6	72	76	4
7	78	76	0
8	76	77	2
9	77	75	6
10	75	74	4

For the purposes of the calculation of the labour stability ratio, L_n is based on the average number of employees for each week; and N is based on an establishment of 77 employees for the whole period. Use the second labour turnover formula we discussed in the chapter for the purposes of calculating the labour turnover rates.

3. Rupert's main job is that of management accountant for a large international corporation, but as a member of a service (charity) organisation, Square Table, he often gets involved in community service activities. One of the jobs that Rupert likes doing is cleaning windows at an Old People's Home, and being the type of person he is, he cannot stop thinking about management accounting, even when cleaning windows! For a ten-week period, Rupert collected the following information to enable him to assess the productivity of his Square Table window cleaning team.

Week	Windows Cleaned	Time taken (hours)	Number of cleaners
1	650	33	4
2	695	32	4
3	632	31	5
4	648	36	4
5	635	29	3
6	675	36	5
7	665	37	5
8	600	31	4
9	598	33	5
10	634	35	5

Prepare a numerical and graphical analysis of these data. What conclusions do you draw from your analysis for the Square Table team?

Level II

4. Under the heading of the 'Make up of labour costs' in the chapter, we listed nine categories within which labour costs may be listed: we have discussed six of those categories. List as many examples of costs that could be found under each of the other three categories, which are:

   (a) training costs
   (b) relocation costs
   (c) personnel administration costs

5. (a) Why is labour turnover expensive? List as many possible labour turnover-driven costs as you can. In your list, attempt to give some idea of the relative importance of each of the costs.
   (b) Identify the steps that might be taken to reduce the more important of the labour turnover driven costs that you have listed in part (a) of this question.

6. The accelerating premium bonus scheme is based on the following formula:

   $y = bx^2$

   where:

   y is the factor that determines earnings;
   b is the 'weight' applied to the level of efficiency; and
   x is the level of efficiency achieved, expressed as a decimal.

   For example, standard performance of 100% or 1.0 is 200 units produced, 250 units are actually made, and $b = 0.75$:

$x = 250 \div 200 = 125\% = 1.25$

Therefore:

$$y = 0.75 \times (1.25^2) \\ = 1.171875$$

Earnings for this job or week will therefore be basic pay times y, which is, in this example, if basic pay is £200:

$$£200 \times 1.171875 \\ = £234.375$$

Required

Fill in the table below and plot the results on a graph. George is a supervisor in Department A who is rewarded by means of an accelerating premium bonus scheme, and whose basic pay is £350 per week. Include George's earnings at all nine levels of efficiency shown in your table. Plot these results on a graph and comment on your findings.

	Percentage efficiency								
	80	90	100	110	120	130	140	150	160
ea x									
x^2									
$y = 0.85x^2$									

Is the accelerating premium bonus scheme a regressive or progressive scheme? What limits are there to the potential earnings of an employee under this scheme?

7. Defrauding an organisation via its wages payment system can be easy. Discuss the measures which should be adopted in order to minimise the incidence of fraud in such a situation.

Solutions to practice questions 2, 4 and 7 can be found in the Student Workbook. Solutions to practice question numbers in red can be found at the end of this book.

Projects

Either:

1. Carry out a survey of people in employment in your area to determine the proportion of your sample that are paid in whole or in part by way of an incentive or payment by results scheme. In your survey you should classify your respondents under such headings as:
   (a) male or female;
   (b) manual or white-collar employee;
   (c) proportion of earnings coming from the scheme;
   (d) primary, secondary or tertiary organisation;
   (e) up to 30 years of age or over 30 years of age;
   (f) education: sub 'A' level or post 'A' level;
   (g) whether the scheme has been changed in the last 5 years

Or:

2. Set up an interview with two or three personnel managers and ask them to identify the make-up of the labour costs in their organisation along the lines of the 9-point list we introduced at the start of this chapter. If possible interview personnel managers from different sectors of the economy. Does the make-up of labour costs differ between, say, a profit-making manufacturer and a non-profit-making service organisation?

3. Take a sample of annual reports and accounts and determine the importance of labour costs to the organisations you have chosen. Given our discussion of the 'new manufacturing environment', do you see any evidence to support the theory of the diminishing importance of labour costs in any of the organisations you have chosen to survey? Discuss your findings.

REFERENCES

Berlant, D., Browning, R. and Foster, G. (1990), 'How Hewlett-Packard gets numbers it can trust', *Harvard Business Review* (Jan.–Feb.), 178–83.

Böer, G. (1994), 'Five modern management accounting myths', *Management Accounting* (IMA) (January), 22, 24–7.

Chew, W. B. (1988), 'No-nonsense guide to measuring productivity', *Harvard Business Review* (Jan.–Feb.), 110–18.

Develin & Partners (1990), *Activity-based Cost Management* (Develin & Partners, Management Consultants, 211 Piccadilly, London WIV 9LE).

Gass, G. L., Bentson, R. and McMakin, G. (1987), 'White collar productivity', *Management Accounting* (NAA) (September), 33–8.

Goodhart, D. (1993), 'On the curious appeal of UK performance related pay', *Financial Times* (3 November).

Howell, R. A. and Soucy, S. R. (1987), 'Cost accounting in the new manufacturing environment', *Management Accounting* (NAA) (August), 42–8.

ILO (1984), *Payment by results* (International Labour Organisation, Geneva).

Kellaway, L. (1993), 'Are incentive plans really all they are cracked up to be?', *Financial Times* (3 November).

Lloyd, P. A. (1976), *BIM Management Survey Report* (British Institute of Management).

USAA (1986), *Productivity direction statement 1986* (USAA Property and Casualty Insurance).

Williamson, D. (1989), 'Incentive payment schemes: a revisitation proves worthwhile', *Management Accounting* (CIMA) (March), 40–1.

CHAPTER SIX

Overheads: the traditional view

CHAPTER OBJECTIVES

After reading this chapter you should be able to:

- define cost units and cost objects
- discuss and define overheads and discuss why they are a problem
- describe and apply the 'traditional overhead absorption' bases
- appreciate examples of modern approaches to overhead control
- appreciate the term 'relevance lost' in the context of modern management accounting

Introduction

An overhead is: 'Expenditure on labour, materials, or services which cannot be economically identified with a specific saleable cost unit ...' (CIMA 1991). This definition contains indications of the problems contained in any analysis of overhead costs: an overhead 'cannot be economically identified with a specific saleable cost unit'. CIMA is saying that we can, for example, calculate or determine the **total** cost of rent for our organisation, but we cannot say, automatically, that rent per unit of product or service is £x. Cardullo and Moellenberndt (1987: 39) summarise this problem:

> Cost allocation is a pervasive problem.... The problem exists because of indirect costs. Direct costs can be identified with a single costing unit, but indirect costs are common to two or more costing units.

They confirm something we have agreed several times already: a direct cost is known as a direct cost because it can be directly associated with a product or service. We can see and/or find evidence of a direct cost in a product or service relatively easily, and we can find the direct costs per unit of output relatively easily too. Trying to find evidence of an indirect cost in a product or service can be more difficult when that cost is a common cost. What is the value of insurance per unit of output, or the value of the depreciation of land and buildings, when each cost is common to several departments and/or products or product lines? Accounting for overheads is becoming more sophisticated now because of the changes we have already noted in this book. We already know that because of the changes taking place in both world markets and the technology base of many industries, overheads are becoming more and more important. This chapter reflects the changes in overhead costs being found in industry and commerce. By the end of this chapter we will have seen both traditional and modern ways of dealing with the problems that overheads provide for management accountants.

The importance of overheads

We know from the work of earlier chapters that many organisations are moving their processes away from being labour-based to being more capital intensive. Even only a brief look at the various accountancy journals and magazines published since the mid- to late 1980s will show numerous articles concerned with the **new manufacturing environment**: that is, the shift of emphasis from labour costs to overhead costs, and so on. Develin (1990) illustrates clearly the way that cost structures are reported to have changed in the United Kingdom in the last three decades or so. Develin reports that between 1960 and 1986, for manufacturing organisations the average incidence of overhead costs has increased in real terms by 45%, whereas the incidence of direct labour costs has decreased in real terms by 32%. Direct material costs have remained virtually unchanged, having decreased only 5% in real terms as a proportion of total costs over the period under review. Furthermore, Develin shows that in manufacturing industry, only 27% of overhead costs are controllable. Consequently, overhead costs are increasing over the manufacturing sector, yet they are largely uncontrollable.

The importance of the controllability of overhead costs stems from the well-reported fact that 60–90% of product costs are determined well before the product reaches the marketplace. Develin (1990: 7) reports that: 'In the case of automobile development, 85% of future unit costs are determined by the end of the testing phase.' They go on to say, however, that it is only in the post-production phases that costs are conventionally focused by accountants. Hence accountants are largely wasting their time in manufacturing industries by attempting to control costs that are already built into their products at the conceptual, design, testing and process planning stages. Further, they report that in the financial services sector, the distribution/retail sector and the transport/communication sector, overheads are, on average, approximately 64% controllable, the implication being that service industry organisations are not subject to the same overhead cost control problems as industrial organisations. A similar pattern of cost behaviour has emerged in the United States. As we saw in Chapter 5, Böer (1994: 22) has traced the behaviour of labour and overhead costs in manufacturing industries in the United States from 1849 to 1987, and states:

> even in 1849 production labor was only 23% of sales. That is, as far back as more than 145 years ago labor was not a major proportion of manufacturing costs . . . labor as a percentage of

> sales has not made a sudden drop because of modern manufacturing; rather, it has declined steadily from 23% in 1849 to about 10% in 1987.

Note that Böer is talking about labour costs as a percentage of sales, not as a percentage of total costs. This is because of problems associated with the recording of data. However, Böer gives, perhaps, a more balanced and less histrionic view of the changes in cost structure than many authorities have recently presented! Similarly, Böer shows that, for a selection of the same US data, overhead costs in manufacturing as a percentage of sales have increased from approximately 17.5% to 35.5% from 1974 to 1987; but the data that Böer presents 'indicates a steady upward trend from 1947 to 1971, a downward movement from 1972 to 1980, and a steady increase since then' (ibid.).

Böer concludes his analysis of overhead costs by saying that there has been no sudden upward shift in these costs, but they have shown steady increase over a lengthy period of time. (See the contribution to this debate by Turney (1992) in the section 'The implications of using unreliable cost information' later in this chapter.) The authors of some textbooks and some journal articles would have us believe that in the new manufacturing environment everything is new, including all aspects of a cost and management accounting system. But it is not true to say that everything is new! We will see when we link what we are about to discuss with activity-based costing, that there is significant common ground between the approaches.

Much of what follows has been labelled traditional cost accounting, or the traditional view of overheads. Whilst it is true that the next few sections of this book could have been found in a cost or management accounting textbook published at any time over the last sixty or even seventy years, it is still relevant material. What makes the work we are about to do traditional is that it does not include any detailed discussion of cost pools, cost drivers and so on. Nevertheless, the traditional view we are about to undertake forms the foundation of the more advanced work we will be working through in Chapter 7.

Cost units and cost objects

When we talk about determining the cost of a product or a service we often talk about cost units. A cost unit is a product or service for which we want to find a total cost. A synonym for the term cost unit is cost object or cost objective. Examples of different cost units are as follows:

Business	Cost unit
Furniture making	Tables, chairs
Telephone manufacture	Telephones
Accountant's advice	Chargeable hour
Word processing service	Cost per page/document
Brewing	Barrel, crate

CIMA (1991) gives a more extensive list of cost units than is presented here.

So that we can determine the cost of cost units, we usually combine all of the costs of a function or department into a cost pool for that function or department. 'A cost pool is a collection of related costs, such as production overhead, that is reassigned to cost units. Overheads are often pooled along functional lines' (ibid.).

The basic idea behind a cost pool is that cost items pooled together should relate to the same functional basis. The repairs and maintenance cost pool would include all costs related to the repair and maintenance of machinery, equipment, plant and so on. There may also be sub-pools within each function or department: for instance, the variable cost pool and the fixed cost pool; or the controllable cost pool and the non-controllable cost pool.

Why not just cut out cost assignment to departments and make sure total costs for cost units are found and recorded? We must appreciate that it simply is not possible to calculate the cost of overheads incurred by any department in any complex organisation without some form of assignment. Furthermore, if we did not attempt to calculate overhead costs as accurately as possible, we would lose the management information content of the intermediate cost pool stage.

Absorption costing

Absorption costing, or full costing, is concerned with finding the full cost of a product or service. This means that we need to determine the sum of the fixed, variable and semi-variable costs of a unit, activity, product or service: that is, the full cost.

By absorption we mean: 'Overheads charged to products or services by means of absorption rates' (CIMA 1991). Where an absorption rate is: 'A rate charged to a cost unit intended to account for the overhead at a predetermined level of activity' (ibid.).

The worked example that follows shows how to calculate an overhead absorption rate (OAR), and discusses some of the problems built into such rates.

WORKED EXAMPLE 6.1

MyCo Ltd makes five entirely unrelated products and the total land and buildings rent cost is £90,000 per year. Total output for a year was:

Product	Units
1	4,000
2	6,000
3	1,300
4	18,000
5	700

Calculate the amount of rent to be absorbed by, or charged to, each product made by MyCo Ltd.

Solution to Worked example 6.1

One approach to this problem is to find an average cost per unit of output. Using the easiest of the available methods, we can find an overhead rate per unit for rent costs by applying:

$$\frac{\text{total rent cost}}{\text{total units of output}}$$

In this case, this is:

$$\frac{£90{,}000}{30{,}000 \text{ units}}$$

$= £3$ per unit

Note that the 30,000 units is the total of all of the units produced of all five products made by MyCo Ltd (4,000 + 6,000 + 1,300 + 18,000 + 700 units = 30,000 units). So for every unit of output rent costs an average £3 per unit of output, and therefore we should absorb £3 for rent costs every time a unit of output is produced. If we therefore made 20 units of output, the overhead costs that we would absorb will be:

20 units x 3 per unit = £60.

This is an easy solution, but it could be greatly misleading. By dividing rent by units of output, we have assumed, at least, that all units of output are the same: that is, they are equal in all respects in terms of material inputs, labour inputs and overhead inputs. However, the information we were given tells us that the products were entirely unrelated – potentially radically different in all respects. The implication here is that the overhead cost – rent in this case – may not be related to units of output; it might be better related to, say, the time spent on a machine. If, in the MyCo Ltd example, the machine hours per unit of output, are:

Product	Hours
1	2.5
2	1.0
3	4.0
4	0.1
5	10.0

we can calculate an overhead absorption rate per machine hour based on:

$$\frac{\text{total rent cost}}{\text{total machine hours}}$$

In this case, this is:

$$\frac{£90{,}000}{30{,}000 \text{ hours}}$$

$= £3$ per machine hour

The meaning of this rate is that for every hour a machine is operated, an average of £3 will be incurred by way of overheads. So, if we ran a machine for 10 hours, we would absorb:

10 hours × £3 per machine hours

= £30 for overheads

This, of course, is in addition to any direct costs that will also be incurred.

Note that the total machine hours are made up as follows:

Product	Hours per unit	Units	Total time (hours)
1	2.5	4,000	10,000
2	1.0	6,000	6,000
3	4.0	1,300	5,200
4	0.1	18,000	1,800
5	10.0	700	7,000
Total			30,000

Now, we have two rates: per unit and per machine hour, and they are both £3. By applying these rates and calculating the overheads absorbed by each method, we will see the one serious problem overheads can cause. In the case of each of the two absorption rate methods we have absorbed £90,000 in total for the production we have achieved, but if we look on a product-by-product basis, we can see radical differences between the overheads absorbed. Table 6.1 gives us an insight into the kind of differences the use of different OARs give rise to.

TABLE 6.1 ***Overheads absorption rates: differences***

Product	Units rate of overhead absorption £	Machine hour rate of overhead absorption £	Differences £
1	12,000	30,000	18,000+
2	18,000	18,000	0
3	3,900	15,600	11,700+
4	54,000	5,400	48,600−
5	2,100	21,000	18,900+
Total	90,000	90,000	0

We should work through the arithmetic for Table 6.1 by looking at the workings for products 1 and 2. (If you are uncertain about how the table works, check the calculations for all five products.)

Product 1

per unit rate basis

4,000 units × £3 per unit = £12,000

per machine hour rate basis

4,000 units × $2\frac{1}{2}$ hours per unit × £3 per machine hour

= £30,000

Product 2

per unit rate basis

6,000 units × £3 per unit = £18,000

per machine hour rate basis

6,000 units × 1 hour per unit × £3 per machine hour

= £18,000

The problem shown in Table 6.1 is that the amount of overheads each product will absorb will **depend entirely upon the overhead absorption rate (OAR) used.** Furthermore, if the wrong rate is used, the wrong amount of overheads will be absorbed. In the case of MyCo Ltd, this is most striking in the case of product 4, which shows an absorption difference of 48,600 between the two methods of absorption. Is there a solution to the problems that often arise from overhead absorption? The solution is to ensure that, as far as possible, we use the rate which most closely reflects the way the overhead behaves or is driven. Generally, an overhead absorption rate is:

$$\frac{\text{overhead cost}}{\text{total units of absorption basis}}$$

The arguments relating to absorption of overheads product by product applies equally well to the absorption of overheads by departments, and we will be discussing the points relating to overhead absorption by departments later in this chapter.

Historically, management accounting textbooks have discussed OARs in a simplistic way. A reading of virtually any textbook, or journal, published prior to the mid-1980s will clearly show that OARs are discussed in a very matter of fact way. The general view was that there were just a few OAR methods worthy of consideration, and it is common to find just six of these methods discussed:

1. Units of output rate.
2. Direct labour hours rate.
3. Machine hours rate.
4. Prime cost percentage.
5. Material cost percentage.
6. Wages cost percentage.

Furthermore the view often presented was that of these six bases, the direct labour hour basis was usually the most appropriate since it probably most closely reflected the basis by which overheads were driven. The formulæ for the calculation of the six rates are:

$$\text{units of output rate} = \frac{\text{overheads}}{\text{total units of output}}$$

$$\text{labour hour rate} = \frac{\text{overheads}}{\text{total labour hours worked}}$$

$$\text{machine hour rate} = \frac{\text{overheads}}{\text{total machine hours worked}}$$

$$\text{prime cost percentage} = \frac{\text{overheads}}{\text{total prime costs}} \times 100$$

$$\text{materials cost percentage} = \frac{\text{overheads}}{\text{total material costs}} \times 100$$

$$\text{labour cost percentage} = \frac{\text{overheads}}{\text{total labour costs}} \times 100$$

The following worked example illustrates the way the six methods operate and forms the basis for what we will then discuss.

WORKED EXAMPLE 6.2

The data that follow were extracted from the books of E. I. Patel, manufacturing pharmacist, for the year ended 31 January 1993:

	£
Materials cost	100,000
Labour	150,000
Prime cost	250,000
Overheads	150,000
Total costs	400,000

Additionally, the following details are relevant to the period in question:

Labour hours worked	75,000
Machine hours worked	50,000
Units produced	50,000

Required

1. Calculate the six OARs mentioned above
2. Assume that, of the entire output of 50,000 units from Patel's business, we wish to calculate the total cost of a batch of 3,000 units of a product. The details we have of this batch of 3,000 units of output is that total materials costs amount to £5,000, labour costs were £6,000 (paid at the rate of £2 per hour), and machine hours amounted to 500 hours.

Solution to Worked example 6.2

For this worked example, only the outline solution is given. Check your own workings carefully, however.

1. Applying the above formulæ, gives us:

Units of output rate	£3.0 per unit
Labour hour rate	£2.0 per labour hour
Machine hour rate	£3.0 per machine hour
Prime cost percentage	60
Materials cost percentage	150
Labour cost percentage	100

2. Table 6.2 shows the results of applying the six different OARs to the batch of 3,000 units. Only two of the methods give the same result for the overheads to be absorbed: the labour hour rate and the labour cost percentage methods give the same value for the overheads to be absorbed, £6,000. The arithmetic mean of the six values for the overheads to be absorbed is £6,100 whilst the standard deviation of the values is approximately £2,302 – rather a large spread of the data.

TABLE 6.2 ***Results of application of six different absorption rates***

	Units of output £	Labour hour £	Machine hour £	Prime cost% £	Material cost% £	Labour cost% £
Materials	5,000	5,000	5,000	5,000	5,000	5,000
Labour	6,000	6,000	6,000	6,000	6,000	6,000
Prime cost	11,000	11,000	11,000	11,000	11,000	11,000
Overhead	9,000	6,000	1,500	6,600	7,500	6,000
Totals	20,000	17,000	12,500	17,600	18,500	17,000
Labour hours worked	3,000	3,000	3,000	3,000	3,000	3,000
Machine hours worked	500	500	500	500	500	500
Output (units)	3,000	3,000	3,000	3,000	3,000	3,000

Since we are trying to determine the most accurate estimation of unit costs for our management colleagues, we need to be sure that the OAR we finally use for our calculations is the correct one. Choosing an OAR that is not sufficiently representative of the situation we are trying to depict can have severe business policy implications for our organisation.

CAMEO

Costing for contracting in the NHS

The 1989 'Working for Patients' White Paper established the internal market for health care. This was to be achieved by purchasers (i.e. District Health Authorities and GP fund holders) buying their services from the providers (i.e. hospitals) which offer the greatest value for money in terms of both cost and quality. Competition is used to induce improved performance. The White Paper insisted that hospitals should price their services on a full cost basis and that there should be no planned cross-subsidisation between contracts. The Department of Health initially provided only limited guidance on how this should be achieved and, not surprisingly, used a variety of bases of cost allocation.

In 1990, the Department of Health issued guidelines on the pricing of contracts in the internal market which stated that: 'Prices must be based on full (net) costs such that, for provider's annual assumed volume of service, income from contracts will cover the quantum cost with no planned cross subsidisation between contracts.' In essence prices should be set so income matches the net cost of providing the service. There are three fundamental principles underlying this approach:

1. Prices should be based on costs.
2. Costs should be arrived at on a full cost basis (which includes capital charges).
3. There should be no planned cross-subsidisation between contracts.

Full cost pricing has been a feature of government policy for public services. It is evident in the pricing requirements of contracts for local authority direct service organisations,for central government agencies, and for other commercial style public organisations such as the BBC and British Rail. Full cost pricing entails the allocation of overheads across all services, the calculation of capital charges – often on a current cost basis – and usually forbids cross-subsidisation between services.

Hospital costing systems tended to be able to cost to department or speciality level, which historically had been sufficient for their needs. However, with the advent of the internal market it was important that hospitals quickly developed an insight into cost behaviour patterns within specialities. Simply dividing the total cost of a speciality by its 'activity level' would in most cases be insufficient. This is because the procedures carried out within a speciality vary from case to case and, logically, so do the costs of treatment. In order to cope with the variety of work that arises from patient to patient, costs are calculated for particular treatments related to diagnosis. Thus the cost of a particular type of treatment is calculated by looking at what it would involve for an average patient based on historical trends (casemix). This total cost includes direct costs such as drugs plus indirect costs such as heating and lighting. The actual cost may well differ as no two patients are alike, but as long as the casemix does not change too much, then over time the costs will be recovered. However, as absorbed overheads are included in these costs, hospitals are dependent on achieving planned volume. For this reason it is very important that hospitals accurately monitor their casemix and have an understanding of the breakdown between fixed, variable and semi-variable costs.

Other aspects of this cameo are given in Chapter 13.

Reference: Bowerman and Francis (1995); this case was prepared by Graham Francis.

Business policy implications

The business policy implications for management of the variations in the values derived for the overheads to be absorbed may centre around the setting of selling prices, and therefore the demand for the products. If a manufacturer decided to set his or her selling prices based on his or her costs, and further decided to set the selling price for a batch on the basis of the smallest total cost (that is, the total cost derived from the machine hour rate basis), the manufacturer may well find that he or she sells goods at a loss if production is not especially dependent on the use of machinery. In other words, if the manufacturer is to reasonably choose the machine hour rate method, a significant proportion of his or her output should centre around the use of machinery. On the other hand, if the manufacturer were to choose the labour hour rate, we would expect that the most significant aspects of the work to be carried out by hand-based methods. In the final outcome, however, the manufacturer has limited choice over the OAR method. He or she has to choose the method that makes most sense given his or her individual circumstances. The optimal rate to choose is the one that reflects what is actually driving overhead costs, not the one that will help make selling prices and profit look healthier in the short term. Using an OAR method simply because it helps reflect lower selling prices is not a viable, sustainable, strategy.

Choosing the best overhead absorption rate (OAR)

The units of output OAR basis is satisfactorily used if the organisation is making or providing only one product, or a range of very similar products. If there is more than one product on offer, and/or the products are significantly different to each other, as our examples so far have shown, using this OAR method will not give accurate and consistent results. If we are to use the direct labour hour OAR method, we have to be certain that there is a good relationship between labour hours worked and the incidence of overhead that we are seeking to absorb. Note here again what we have already discussed concerning the new manufacturing environment in Chapter 5. Any shift away from the dominance or importance of labour hours worked in an organisation, may lead to the need to review the OAR method to be used. In the case of a highly automated organisation – for example a car factory – machine hour rates could well be the most sensible basis on which to base OARs. When employees are working in a machine-dominated environment, the use of labour-based rates will be inappropriate, and will probably lead to errors in costings and estimations.

The three cost percentage rates – prime cost, materials cost and labour cost – can all be discussed together. It is possible that, at one time or another, a statistical relationship was found between the incidence of overheads and prime cost, or materials cost, or labour cost. Logically, the method of attaching overhead rates to costs of production is flawed since the method assumes that because, for example, the materials cost is high, the overhead cost must also, therefore, be high. One excellent argument that helps to dispel the myth of a connection between material value and incidence of overheads is the case of the very expensive block of metal that is bought on a just-in-time basis. The metal is received, worked on straight away, and then shipped immediately to the customer for whom the product was intended. This piece of metal will have incurred relatively few overheads since it moved through the organisation very quickly. A second example is that of the raw material which is inexpensive per kilogramme, but is very bulky. It is bought in large quantities, and is stored in a purpose-built warehouse until it is used. If this second material is stored, on average, for two or three months before being used, it will actually incur relatively high amounts of overhead (storage charges, security, materials handling). Yet using the material cost percentage rate of overhead absorption will show that this material absorbs relatively few overheads.

Similar arguments that apply to materials also apply to labour costs, and therefore to prime costs. Cost percentage rates are not sensible rates on which to base OAR methods, unless relationships between such costs are proven to persist over the long term. There are many other overhead absorption bases to discuss and we will be defining and discussing these when we discuss activity-based costing.

The predetermined aspects of OARs

Notice from CIMA's definition of an overhead absorption rate, given above, the use of the word predetermined: this means that the rates are set in advance of their being used. So, if we are going to use an OAR in February, it will have been set in, say, January or December. It is possible that an OAR will be set for an entire financial year as part of the annual budgeting process. To do this, we modify the OAR formulæ to read:

$$\frac{\text{budgeted total overheads}}{\text{budgeted absorption basis}}$$

The most significant problem to be encountered when attempting to set a predetermined OAR is of deciding on a relevant activity level. There is a variety of levels of activity that could be used in setting predetermined OARs. For example:

- theoretical (or ideal) activity;
- practical activity;
- expected actual activity;
- normal activity.

The theoretical activity level is known as the ideal activity level because it deals only with what can be achieved when working at 100% of capacity, with no allowances made at all for stoppages for any reason.

Practical activity levels allows for **unavoidable** stoppages, and takes account of the fact that machinery, although it can often work continuously for days and sometimes for weeks, will eventually need to be stopped for maintenance or repair purposes. The practical activity level also allows for late deliveries of materials and labour skills shortages.

If practical activity reflects high levels of efficiency, the expected actual activity level takes matters a stage further and allows for other stoppages and delays due to inefficiencies: it takes a slightly more pessimistic – some would say a more realistic – view of man and machine.

The normal activity rate is based on the idea that the overhead rate should not be changed merely because existing facilities are used to a greater or lesser extent in different periods.

The idea here is that a job or product or service should not cost more to produce in December than it does in January solely because predetermined levels of output varied between the two periods.

As we have said above, when a predetermined OAR is used we apply the OAR to a job or product in order to charge or absorb an amount of overhead to that job or product. It should be expected that the actual overheads incurred will be different to the predetermined overheads. This is fine providing the difference is not excessively large, and that, on average, the differences tend to cancel each other out (this view is in alignment with the normal activity level view).

Consequences of using predetermined OARs: under- and overabsorption of overheads

When a difference between actual overheads and the overheads absorbed does occur, what do we do about it? The following example illustrates this difference and answers the question.

Earlier in the chapter we considered E. I. Patel's manufacturing pharmaceutical business. We are now told that his business's actual overheads to which the batch of 3,000 units relate amounted to £6,453. Using the labour hour rate of overhead absorption, we can calculate the amount of overheads over- or underabsorbed. Overheads absorbed:

= labour hour rate × labour hours for the batch

= £2 per labour hour × 3,000 labour hours

= £6,000

Actual overheads:

= £6,453

Since Patel has absorbed £6,453 − 6,000 = £453 less than the actual overheads incurred, we are dealing with an underabsorption of overheads. The question that must arise from this situation now is: What happens to the difference of £453? If the amount of under- or overabsorption is small, the organisation suffering the difference may quite happily leave the balance in the relevant accounts month after month, accumulating all differences as they arise. Using the normal activity level as the basis of the predetermined OARs, it should be expected that the under- and overabsorption amounts will tend to cancel each other out over the longer term. Hence, many organisations will only write off the balance on the over- and underabsorptions annually. This write off takes place by debiting or crediting the profit and loss account with an under- or overabsorption respectively. In exceptional circumstances, a large over- or underabsorption may occur at any time. In a case such as this that balance can be written off immediately by debiting or crediting the profit and loss account as relevant.

What we have essentially been discussing so far has been the setting of predetermined organisationwide OARs (also known as blanket rates and plant-wide rates). These are OARs that are used for any output or activity taking place anywhere within the organisation. However, in reality, given that the work of any one department can be radically different to the work of any other department in the same organisation, an organisationwide OAR is not a practical idea. For control purposes, therefore, we need departmental overhead absorption rates.

Departmental overhead rates

In the simplest of all examples, we can see why we need departmental overhead rates Assume, for example, that our organisation consists of two departments, A and B. Department A has 30 employees and the employees use no machinery or equipment whatsoever for their work. On the other hand there are only 3 employees in department B and this department is highly mechanised, with very little work being done by hand. If we were to use an organisationwide labour hour rate in this situation, we would be heading for potential problems with department B since only insignificant amounts of work are carried out by labour in that department. The same is true as far as machine hour rates are concerned with department A. When overhead data have already been analysed, those costs are said to be allocated. If a cost is a common cost and can be found in total only, it needs apportioning.

Cost allocation

Cost allocation is: 'That part of cost attribution which charges a specific cost to a cost centre or cost unit' (CIMA 1991).

Cost apportionment

Cost apportionment is: 'That part of cost attribution which shares costs among two or more cost centres or cost units in proportion to the estimated benefit received, using a proxy, e.g. square metres' (CIMA 1991).

Note that many authors of articles and textbooks use the word allocation when they mean apportionment. That is, they discuss overhead cost assignment under the heading of allocation. The definitions just given should clarify the true usage of the words. However, the word used many times in this chapter, assignment, is an all encompassing word that serves all purposes.

Because we are now interested in data provided on a departmental basis, we have a lot more work to do in order to calculate predetermined departmental OARs. The scheme of work to undertake is:

1. Determine the level of activity that is to be classed as normal, and which will be used for all OAR determination.
2. Prepare total and departmental budgets of all overhead expenses for all producing and service departments.
3. Prepare budgetary data that will allow for the apportionment of overhead costs.
4. Allocate and apportion the overheads.
5. Reapportion service department overheads to the producing departments.
6. Calculate the departmental predetermined OARs.

This list is really a plan of attack for dealing with any situation involving the allocation and apportionment of overheads and the calculation of predetermined OARs. Note the following points:

- Step 1, the setting of the normal level of activity, is done as part of the budget preparation routine, and along the lines of the discussion we had earlier in this chapter.
- Steps 2 and 3, the preparation of the departmental budgets and data that allow for the apportionment of overheads, are, again, determined as part of the budgeting routine.

Consider the example in Table 6.3 relating to Meredew plc, which takes us through the overhead aspects of the predetermination of OARs, but assumes that the budgetary aspects are taken care of elsewhere. The data we start with will be taken from the ledgers of the business, together with such analysis of costs as will be found with the payroll: departmental wages analysis.

The summary in Table 6.3 already includes departmental information for four cost headings: these are allocated costs. Such costs as supervision and labour costs can be allocated by means of the analysis of the payroll: it should be easy to discover where each individual has worked, how much he or she has been paid and so on. Finding out where people have spent their time is done by means of clock card analysis, job card analysis, or time sheet analysis. The depreciation of buildings is being set by management, and can therefore be allocated, and the water costs can be allocated because each department is, let's say, having its water usage metered. All other departments need the common overhead costs apportioned to them. That is, no amount of analysis or metering can be, or is being, carried out. Consequently, as CIMA's definition says, we have to estimate the amount of overhead cost that each department should suffer in proportion to the estimated benefit received. The estimation of the benefits received by a department can sometimes cause problems; but in theoretical exercises, the basis on which apportionments are carried out are usually suggested by the problem under consideration. The 'additional information', or its equivalent, is usually the place where the data is given that tells us the basis on which to apportion costs.

TABLE 6.3 ***Departmental factory overhead summary: before apportionment of overheads***

	Production departments			Service departments		
	1	2	3	A	B	Total
Supervision costs	9,000	8,000	8,000	10,000	12,000	47,000
Indirect labour	1,000	2,000	1,000	1,000	1,000	6,000
Indirect materials						35,000
Repairs and maintenance						3,000
Depreciation:						
plant						10,000
buildings	1,250	1,000	1,500	0	0	3,750
Rates						3,000
Electricity						3,500
Water	1,500	1,000	1,000	2,000	1,000	6,500

Table 6.4 below contains the additional information that we are going to use to apportion the remaining overhead costs relating to the departmental factory overhead summary above. If we take the material cost from the departmental summary, and apply the additional information, we will see how the two tables go together. The total value of indirect materials we need to apportion is £35,000 (see the departmental summary for this figure). Table 6.4 of additional information contains six items of information for us to consider for apportionment purposes. The question is: Which of these six bases is the most suitable for apportioning the materials cost? In the absence of any other indications to the contrary, the number of materials requisitions would seem to be the most suitable: that is, the basis that most nearly relates to the behaviour of materials costs. We have arrived at this basis on two grounds:

1. on the ground that it is the one of the six most nearly related to the cost we are seeking to apportion, and;
2. on the ground of elimination of all other bases.

Overhead apportionment calculations

We can work through the calculations now, starting with the indirect materials cost and working our way down the departmental summary until all of the overheads costs have been allocated or apportioned, and departmental totals arrived at.

There are two parts to this calculation, as there are for all overhead cost apportionments:

1. Derive the constant that all other calculations depend upon.
2. Apply the constant department by department.

The constant is the total cost – materials in this case – divided by the total number of units of the apportionment basis – the number of material requisitions in this case:

$$\frac{\text{total overhead being apportioned}}{\text{total units of apportionment base}}$$

TABLE 6.4 ***Additional information to assist apportionment of overheads***

	Production departments			Service departments	
	1	2	3	A	B
KwHrs	20,000	12,000	8,000	0	0
Area (ft^2)	5,250	4,200	6,300	0	0
Material requisitions	20,000	5,000	5,000	15,000	25,000
Maintenance hours	1,500	3,000	3,000	0	1,500
Cost of plant (£)	500,000	350,000	125,000	10,000	15,000

$$\frac{\text{total materials cost}}{\text{total material requisitions}}$$

$$= \frac{£35{,}000}{70{,}000 \text{ requisitions}}$$

$$= £0.50 \text{ per requisition}$$

The **constant** is no more or less than **an average cost per unit of apportionment,** of course. In this example, the indirect materials cost, on average, is £0.50 for every requisition made to stores:

Production departments

1	£0.50 × 20,000 = £10,000
2	£0.50 × 5,000 = £2,500
3	£0.50 × 5,000 = £2,500

Service departments

A	£0.50 × 15,000 = £7,500
B	£0.50 × 25,000 = £12,500
Total	£35,000

Check that the total of these apportionments sum to the total we started with, £35,000. If they do not, there is something wrong with our calculations. These results are then entered into the departmental factory overhead summary in Table 6.5, along with all of the other results that you should now determine.

TABLE 6.5 ***Departmental factory overhead summary: after apportionment of overheads***

	Production departments			Service departments		
	1	2	3	A	B	Total
Supervision costs	9,000	8,000	8,000	10,000	12,000	47,000
Indirect labour	1,000	2,000	1,000	1,000	1,000	6,000
Materials	10,000	2,500	2,500	7,500	12,500	35,000
Repairs and maintenance	500	1,000	1,000	0	500	3,000
Depreciation:						
plant	5,000	3,500	1,250	100	150	10,000
buildings	1,250	1,000	1,500	0	0	3,750
Rates	1,000	800	1,200	0	0	3,000
Electricity	1,750	1,050	700	0	0	3,500
Water	1,500	1,000	1,000	2,000	1,000	6,500
	31,000	20,850	18,150	20,600	27,150	117,750

The totals in Table 6.5 are our estimates of the overhead costs of operating each of the departments within our manufacturing unit: the total overheads for production department 1 amount to £31,000, for production department 2 they are £20,850 and so on. These results form the basis of any performance reports issued to the managers of these departments. Before we calculate the departmental overhead absorption rates, there is one further stage to the work we have to carry out. We have to reapportion the costs of all service departments into the production departments' costs because, although a service department fulfils a useful function, it does not work on the products that are being made. Consequently, it is not possible directly to absorb overhead costs units of output from a service department.

Reapportionment of the service departments' overheads to the production departments

If we left our overhead summary as it currently is, we will not be able to achieve the objective of cost and/or profit assessment. We might argue that it is a waste of time apportioning costs to service departments in the first place, if they are only going to be reapportioned straight away. Arguing this way would cut against the grain of the true management accountant and manager, however, since if the apportionment into the service departments does not take place, how would we know how much those departments are costing to operate?

There are three distinct methods of calculating the reapportionment of costs from the service departments into the production departments:

1. the direct method;
2. the step method, and
3. the algebraic method, which consists of two approaches:
   (a) simultaneous equations; and
   (b) matrix algebra.

The algebraic method is discussed in the appendix to this chapter since it may not be vital for you to consider the two approaches. The direct method uses the bases of apportionment technique that we have been discussing so far: that is, we find a suitable basis of apportionment for each service department and reapportion to the production departments on that basis. The step method bases its reapportionments on the basis of the use to which service departments' services are put by other departments. The algebraic method is an enhancement of the step method and uses either simultaneous equations or matrix algebra to solve the problems that reapportionment can sometimes cause.

The direct method

We can use Meredew plc to illustrate the direct method. The direct method takes the total overheads of £20,600 and £27,150 for service departments A and B respectively as its starting point and reapportions these amounts according to the most appropriate reapportionment basis. We have to know, however, what service each of the two departments provide: let us assume that department A is a central material stores department, and department B is a maintenance department.

TABLE 6.6 *Factory overhead summary*

	Production departments			Service departments		
	1	2	3	A	B	Total
Total(£)	31,000	20,850	18,150	20,600	27,150	117,750
Reapportionments:						
A (stores)	13,734	3,433	3,433	(20,600)	–	–
B (maintenance)	5,430	10,860	10,860	–	(27,150)	–
Total	50,164	35,143	32,443	–	–	117,750

On the basis of the information supplied in this case, and our earlier discussion, we should reapportion the stores department's costs on the basis of the number of material requisitions, and the maintenance department's costs on the basis of the maintenance hours. The totals derived above for the departmental overhead expenditures for Meredew plc and the reapportionments are given in Table 6.6.

So now we have all of the overheads apportioned and reapportioned into the three production departments, and the service department overhead accounts have a zero balance. (Check these calculations carefully, and make sure you agree with them.)

Calculation of the departmental overhead absorption rates

The final step to take in this seemingly very lengthy procedure is to find the departmental overhead rates we have been looking for. Now that we have all of the overheads allocated, apportioned and reapportioned into the production departments, we can carry out that calculation. The last items of information we need for Meredew plc is to be told that departments 1 and 3 use hand-based production methods, whilst department 2 uses machine-based technology. The relevant production hours are:

	Departments 1	2	3
Labour hours	25,082	–	6,488.6
Machine hours	–	3,514.3	–

The departmental overhead absorption rates are now found by dividing the respective departmental overhead expenditures by the OAR base:

$$\frac{\text{£}50{,}164}{25{,}082} \quad \frac{\text{£}35{,}143}{3{,}514.3} \quad \frac{\text{£}32{,}443}{6{,}488.6}$$

= £2 per lh   £10 per mh   £5 per lh

where

lh = labour hour;
mh = machine hour.

Whenever any work is done in department 1, now, overheads are absorbed at the rate of £2 per labour hour, similarly, whenever any work is carried out in departments 2 and 3, the OARs are £10 per machine hour and £5 per labour hour respectively. The implications for this are best illustrated by use of an example.

WORKED EXAMPLE 6.3

Meredew carried out Job ABC recently. Job ABC was worked on in all three production departments and took 4 hours (all labour hours) to pass through department 1; 2 hours 15 minutes to pass through department 2 (of which 1 hour 45 minutes was machine time); and 7 hours to pass through department 3 (90% of which was labour-based time). If the direct materials cost for Job ABC amounted to £275 and the direct labour costs amounted to £350, calculate the total production cost of Job ABC.

Solution to Worked example 6.3

The best approach to this problem is to fill in the summary job card as follows:

Job Card **Job** ABC
Date started **Date completed**
Details ....

Materials	£275.00
Labour	350.00
Overheads	57.00
Production cost	£682.00

Workings

The overheads are derived as follows:

	£
Department 1	
£2 per labour hour × 4 labour hours	= 8.00
Department 2	
£10 per machine hour × 1.75 machine hours	= 17.50
Department 3	
£5 per labour hour × 6.3 labour hours	= 31.50
Total overheads to be absorbed	57.00

The Step Method (the repeated distribution method)

The step method does not rely on reapportionment based on units of output, or machinery value, or the number of people in a department. The method works by someone – probably the management accountant – having analysed the organisation's records and found that on average, say, 25% of service department 1's work is done in or for production department A, and 30% of service department 2's work is done in or for production department B, and so on. The illustrations that follow will demonstrate this point; but first we need to consider the problem of reciprocal service costs.

Reciprocal service costs

One important feature of many organisations that we alluded to when we discussed the direct method of reapportionment was that one service department may carry out work for another service department. This causes a problem of a circular nature in that we may reapportion reciprocal service costs in an infinite loop. For example, when we reapportion service departments 1 and 2, we might find that the two service departments do work for each other. In such circumstances we invoke the repeated distribution method: that is, we accept that although in the extreme this method accepts the infinite loop, the method usually only carries on for four to six iterations at the most: not infinitely! If we reuse the example A Co plc, we will see exactly how the repeated distribution method works. The data for A Co plc are repeated in full here – A Co plc operates five departments, and the overhead distribution summary has been completed to the point where the service department costs are about to be reapportioned:

	Total (£)	Manufacturing (£)	Assembly (£)	Finishing (£)	Power (£)	Administration (£)
Total	71,000	24,000	21,000	18,000	3,000	5,000

We are now given the reapportionment proportions in tabular form:

	Manufacturing (%)	Assembly (%)	Finishing (%)	Power (%)	Administration (%)
Power	30	10	30	–	30
Admin	40	25	25	10	–

The interpretation of these proportions is that of the power department's costs of £3,000, 30% is reapportioned to the manufacturing department, 10% to the assembly department, 30% to the finishing department and 30% to the administration department. Similarly with the administration department's costs. The overhead distribution summary following the use of the repeated distribution method is shown in Table 6.7. (Again, check the workings on which this distribution summary is based.)

TABLE 6.7 *Overhead distribution summary following the use of the repeated distribution method*

	Total	Manufacturing	Assembly	Finishing	Power	Administration
Total	71,000	24,000	21,000	18,000	3,000	5,000
Reapportionments:						
Admin	–	2,000	1,250	1,250	500	−5,000
Power	–	1,050	350	1,050	−3,500	1,050
Admin	–	420	262.5	262.5	105	−1,050
Power	–	31.5	10.5	31.5	−105	31.5
Admin	–	12.6	7.88	7.88	3.15	−31.5
Power	–	0.95	0.32	0.94	−3.15	0.94
Admin	–	0.38	0.24	0.24	0.09	−0.94
Power	–	0.04	0.01	0.04	−0.09	–

As we said above, the repeated distribution method actually runs to between four and six iterations in the normal course of events. In this demonstration there are eight iterations: we could have stopped at six and not lost a great deal of accuracy. As we can see, once we got to six iterations, or reapportionments, we were already down to dealing with values of less than £1. At this stage we can easily stop the process and close off the reapportionments by treating the last iteration as if we were not reapportioning anything into a service department. Although overhead reapportionment does not feature in the discussion, the section that follows contains four references to examples of the way in which world-class organisations are attempting to control their service centre overhead costs. This takes us back a stage, in a sense, to when we discussed the need to appreciate fully that service centre departments must control their overhead costs, and in order to do so, they must know what their costs are! Preparing overhead distribution summaries and reapportionment schedules are relevant to the organisation seeking to control its overhead costs.

In every case, we will see that the control of service centre costs is being carried out by treating cost centres as if they were profit centres. Therefore, we are seeing the application of controllability accounting and responsibility accounting. The following section then leads into a broader discussion of what is wrong with the traditional view of accounting for overheads and the remedy for that problem.

Modern approaches to the control of overhead costs

CAMEO

As far as cost control is concerned, the Weyerhaeuser Company (of the USA, a Fortune 500 company) adopted a novel approach for controlling corporate overhead costs. In 1985, Weyerhaeuser developed the 'charge back' system which gives managers decision rights over activities that consume resources: the Financial Services Department of Weyerhaeuser was set up as if it were a business, selling its services to other departments in the organisation.

One of the key aspects of the Weyerhaeuser system is that:

> Managers of units, if dissatisfied, are free to challenge . . . Likewise, the manager of FSD is free to sell services outside the company. To date, no user unit in Weyerhaeuser Company, has elected to take over any of the services that FSD provides. (Johnson and Loewe 1987: 23)

Additionally, an important benefit of identifying and charging users for overhead activities is the clear identification of users with the demand for services: 'A related benefit of this charge back system is that line and staff groups understand better the nature of the services being provided and their associated costs' (ibid. 24).

The Weyerhaeuser charge-back system helps Weyerhaeuser to appreciate the importance of overhead costs. This is an excellent example of exemplifying the benefits of responsibility accounting, and the application of controllability filters.

Hoshower and Crum (1987) provide a similar example to Johnson and Loewe. They discuss the provision of a cafeteria service in a hospital in the United States. The interesting feature of this case concerns the sudden free-of-charge provision of meals for all employees in this cafeteria:

> The administration believed that the hospital's cost of providing this employee benefit would be low because the kitchen facilities were a fixed cost. Labour costs would also be low because of the mass production of food for the hospital's patients.
>
> However, the hospital's food service costs shot up. An investigation revealed that the employees were wasting large amounts of food. Some were taking several entrees, tasting them, and throwing away the rest. (Hoshower and Crum 1987: 44)

The free-of-charge meals policy was then changed: employees were charged a token amount per meal. The results were that the waste of food declined dramatically and the decrease in the food service department's costs was greater than the revenue generated by the nominal charge. The nominal charge is reported to have amounted to one-third of the price of a dinner.

Whilst much of the rest of Hoshower and Crum's article then goes on to discuss controlling service centre costs from other perspectives, it does illustrate one significant point. In order to control the level of service, the levels of quality of service, and so on, that service must be controllable by the manager of the service centre. Furthermore, a knowledge of costs plays an important role in the control of the service.

In the case of the hospital cafeteria, the hospital's administration became aware of problems with the provision of a free-of-charge service through its accounting system. The hospital's responsibility accounting system revealed problems with a policy that was otherwise laudable in its intent.

References: Johnson and Loewe (1987); Hoshower and Crum (1987).

Before cases such as the Weyerhaeuser and Hospital Cafeteria cases, service centres have been viewed as being cost centres and as such there may have been a tendency not to attempt to control their spending in the way that modern management accounting suggests they should be controlled. There have been other cases reported along the lines of the two we have just discussed (see Allen (1987) and Tucker and Seymour (1985) for two further examples of cost centres being made to work as profit centres), and all these examples show the application of a mixture of traditional management accounting techniques and modern responsibility accounting thinking. However, if we were able to look at the accounting records of the four organisations mentioned in this section of this chapter, we would find much of the technical work familiar to us. What is of concern to us now is that the modern management accountant needs to take the kind of examples just discussed and seek to apply the attitudes underlying them to his or her own situation.

Next, we are about to see examples of where the management accountant has essentially fallen down on the job: and has been doing so for many years. Optimistically, however, we are also about to see how the modern management accountant has overcome these problems.

Implications of using unreliable cost information

If the management accounting system in use in an organisation is not doing what it should do, we might conclude that the information coming out of it is unreliable. The implications for the management of organisations whose cost information is unreliable can be, at the one extreme, that their organisation will fail. Many organisations will, however, muddle along. Turney (1992: 6–19) spells out the implications for an organisation using unreliable cost information. It will be:

- focusing on the wrong markets;
- servicing the wrong customers;
- encouraging costly product designs;
- encouraging costly process designs;
- increasing costs despite cost-cutting programs;
- taking incorrect sourcing decisions.

The reasons why organisations with unreliable cost information will be focusing on the wrong markets and so on are often complicated, but they include organisations basing their selling prices on their costs. If the cost on which a selling price is based is wrong, then the selling price must be wrong. If the selling price is wrong, products will be being sold that may actually be losing money for the organisation. If losses are being made by products, the organisation may be focusing its attention on entirely the wrong market. It may be selling a whole line of products and services that are causing it more problems than it solves. The problem with the inappropriate plant-wide overhead absorption rate is that it does not allow the organisation to cost and price accurately non-standard products. Since the rate is inappropriate, a product may be incurring overheads at a rate that is several times faster than the cost system is reporting. Hence products and services that appear profitable are, on deeper analysis, loss-making.

Turney's heading of 'costly product designs' is interesting. He declares that:

> Ford Motor and others have estimated that as much as 60–80% of costs over a product's life cycle are already locked in by the time product design is completed. This rises to 90–95% by the time design of the production process is completed. (ibid. 9)

The philosophy behind this finding is similar to the philosophy behind total quality management and GIGO (garbage in, garbage out): what goes into the product or service or process determines what happens to that product, service or process. Unless the cost system is adequate, it may not allow management the flexibility they actually have when designing products. This will mean that a product is either overdesigned or too costly compared with what should really be the case. Overall, a cost system that distorts the cost situation can do nothing but harm. It is possible that a cost system may allow us to come within 10–20% of the true costs, but in many cases this just is not close enough.

The case against the traditional system: relevance lost

The subtitle for this section of this chapter comes from Johnson and Kaplan's (1991) book *Relevance Lost: The rise and fall of management accounting*. This book chronicles some of the more serious deficiencies of management accounting. The authors chart the emergence of cost and management accounting from the nineteenth century to the present day. One of their main conclusions is that much of what is deemed modern management accounting practice has been known about since at least 1925.

This section of our text addresses some of the issues that Johnson and Kaplan raise, adds a few more, and then discusses the ways in which the problems revealed are being resolved.

Johnson and Kaplan cite the work of Alexander Hamilton Church, who wrote about some of the problems related to accounting for overheads as long ago as 1910. Church is reported to have said, when discussing the allocation and apportionment of overheads:

> it is a very usual practice to average this large class of expense, and to express its incidence by a simple percentage either upon wages or upon time ... As a guide to actual profitableness of particular classes of work it is valueless and even dangerous. (Johnson and Kaplan 1991: 54)

Church reveals a problem with management accountants that has clearly largely persisted to the present day. There is much evidence that management accounting practices that were already in place by the middle to the end of the nineteenth century are still being used, or at least written about. Williamson (1989) gives examples of labour payment and incentive schemes that were in use by the early part of the twentieth century and which are still being written about in articles and textbooks. There is a disturbing element to this discussion, of course, that is further amplified by the illustration given by Johnson and Kaplan when they discuss the 'engineer "cost accountant"'. It seems clear now, given their evidence, and that of a host of other writers, that the engineer (the production manager, the factory manager, or whatever we might call him or her) has long been dissatisfied with some of the work of the management accountant. We have the phrase 'management by eye' that encapsulates the problems the management accountant faces. Engineers, production managers and marketing managers are well recorded now as having decided that at least some of the information the management accountant is preparing for them is of little use. The non-financial manager has rebelled and is now preparing information for and by him- or herself. These non-financial managers are preparing reports based on data they can relate to and on the basis of which they are managing their parts of their organisation.

Many of the non-financial indicators that are now discussed in accounting texts and journals were created in the factory or in the marketing department. A production engineer can more easily relate to machine time and efficiencies than he or she can to (what are essentially fictitious) standard costs per unit of output, for example. To this end, the production engineer is managing his or her resources using information generated from within his or her own terms of reference.

How do we know our cost accounting system is not meeting its targets?

Cooper (1989: 80, 79) confirms the need to replace a cost system when:

> engineering develops one of its own.
>
> Where the official system used direct labor to allocate costs, the private system used a number of different bases. Also, the engineers tracked costs they considered to be product related but that the official system treated as period expenses. The department ignored the official system and used its private system to steer design work.

There is evidence, of course, that the management accountant is catching up on this debate, but until he or she was faced with the reality of selling goods that the market did not want, he or she seemed unaware that there was a problem. A good example of an organisation that recognised and solved the kind of problem Cooper addressed was Hewlett-Packard (HP). Berlant, Browning and Foster (1990: 179) detail how HP's accounting staff were first made aware that their information outputs were causing problems for manufacturing management, information systems management, procurement management, and so on:

> The goal for accounting, then, was to design a system that would accurately reflect manufacturing costs, use data that manufacturing could collect easily, and meet the legal and practical needs of the accounting function ... We can trace our new cost accounting system to a conversation we had with the production manager.

The sad fact in all the cases we are examining now is that it was not the accountant that found the discrepancies in the accounting data and information he or she was reporting: it was professionals from other disciplines.

What are accountants doing about all of this?

What is the management accountant doing to resolve the apparent crisis in management accounting? How is the management accountant addressing the issues raised above? It seems that his or her work is irrelevant and unwanted. Bright *et al.* (1992) provide insight into what was happening in terms of cost accounting techniques in the UK manufacturing sector in the early 1990s. Their study covered 677 organisations in such industries as primary metals, chemicals and pharmaceuticals, and electronics, with turnovers ranging from less than £15 million per year to more than 1,000 million per year. They found four disturbing features in the replies to their questionnaire:

1. Many of the managers that responded to the questionnaire discussed issues for which they had no definition. That is, even if they did not fully understand the term backflush costing, they were still able to discuss its advantages and disadvantages!
2. Managers reported having introduced one or more of the new accounting techniques into their organisations. However, analysis of the data showed inconsistencies between what was reported as happening and what was clearly happening. At follow-up seminars with the respondents, Bright *et al.* found that managers had, effectively, lied about the installation of new accounting techniques as a result of peer group pressure: 'Accountants ... had wanted to be seen responding positively to new accounting initiatives, many of

which were familiar to other managers because of the wide debate on "relevance"'. (Bright *et al.* 1992: 204).

3. Bright *et al.* clearly found a lack of integration between the factory and the accountant's office. As an example, they cite the case of measuring output and stocks: '43% did not maintain a single inventory record keeping system for both financial and manufacturing purposes' (ibid. 206). So, the factory kept one set of inventory control information and the accountant kept another set!
4. The barriers to the introduction of the 'new' costing techniques and practices foreseen by the managers responding to the questionnaire included:
   (a) cost of change 50%
   (b) lack of relevant skills 46%
   (c) management inertia 35% (ibid. 208).

All rather disturbing evidence for such an important sector of the UK Economy.

Certainly these four pointers from Bright *et al.*'s study give rather a pessimistic view of the contribution of the management accountant to the health and welfare of modern industry, commerce and government. However, much of what they discussed has many positive aspects to it. The good news is that the modern management accountant now has a large battery of skills that his or her late-nineteenth-century equivalent could not have possessed. If we look only at the management accounting syllabuses of both major and minor accounting institutes, the syllabuses of university accounting and business studies degrees and diplomas, and at the syllabuses of courses such as MBAs, we will see that the modern management accountant is now a very sophisticated professional. One of the most important areas of development over the last twenty years or so has been that of activity-based costing (ABC) and activity-based cost management (ABCM). The definition of ABC given by CAM-I of Arlington, Texas is a good one:

> [ABC is] the collection of financial and operational performance information tracing the significant activities of the firm to product costs. (quoted in Raffish 1991)

Whilst much of the work on which ABC and ABCM are based is probably centuries old, the overall methodologies themselves have only recently been recognised. Indeed we will see, when we look at the way ABC and ABCM work, that much of what this chapter has discussed so far resembles the groundwork of ABC systems in many respects. Berlant *et al.* show quite clearly that it is the accountant that has to change. In HP, it was the accounting system that was producing faulty output. The production manager had on his personal computer a 'private accounting system' that reflected the work that his department did: not the work that accounting was hoping he was doing! In concluding their article, Berlant *et al.* (1990: 182–3) say that whilst engineers, designers and accountants still argue about each other's work, they are now arguing over different things. It is no longer the case that everyone has to accept the accountant's answers merely because he or she knows the accounting answers!

> We speak the same language... We have succeeded in creating an accounting system that focuses primarily on the cost of a process... One product designer said it best: 'Finally we have numbers we can have some faith in.' (ibid.)

SUMMARY

This chapter has been concerned with overheads. We have seen the development of the treatment of overheads from their having been recorded in the ledgers of an organisation through to their presentation to cost centre managers for their consideration and action.

We know from what we have discussed in this chapter that overheads are becoming more important as organisations move away from labour-based methods to more capital-intensive methods. We also know that because costs are often common – that is, they are costs incurred on behalf of two or more sections of the business at the same time – there are problems of allocation and apportionment to be tackled. Also of importance to an organisation is the determination of overhead absorption rates, for the recovery of overheads by products and services.

One of the primary purposes of this chapter was to develop what we called the traditional view of accounting for overheads. Modern management accounting theory and practice has now embraced the idea of activity-based costing (ABC) – even if ABC has yet to be implemented on a widespread scale. The final part of this chapter developed the need for the management accountant to consider his or her position. From all over the world evidence is being stacked heavily against the management accountant who is relying on techniques and knowledge that simply cannot to be relied upon any more.

We have been concerned in this chapter to look at the knowledge and techniques that have been used by management accountants for a long time. We did so initially without questioning the overall set of techniques we were discussing. However, we came to appreciate that the modern management accountant needs to look at his or her organisation with a much more critical eye now. It is no longer appropriate for the management accountant to encourage management colleagues to manage their organisation using such devices as plant-wide labour hour absorption rates. We can find plenty of evidence that management accountants have used one plant-wide, labour-based, rate to absorb overheads in their organisation. When economic problems set in, labour is commonly laid off and the labour hour rate increases. The labour hour rate in some cases has increased to as much as 1,000%: surely the management accountant should question the validity of such a rate? The worst aspect of the problems enshrined in the debate over inadequate accounting information is the credibility of the management accountant and his work. If the production manager of Hewlett-Packard has to resort to using his or her own, private, control system since he cannot rely on the outputs of the management accounting system, we ought to feel ashamed of ourselves.

Historically, the work of this chapter would have stood alone: that is, the management accountant would have learned the material in it and then tried to apply it. However, the material in this chapter is presented by way of an introduction to the following chapter, Chapter 7, which contains a comprehensive development of much of the work on a system that overcomes many of the problems inherent in the traditional view of absorption-based cost accounting: activity-based costing.

For maximum benefit, you must understand the work of this chapter before moving on to Chapter 7.

KEY TERMS

You should satisfy yourself that you have noted all of these terms and can define and/or describe their meaning and use, as appropriate.

Overheads (p. 152)	Plant wide rate (p. 164)
Cost units (p. 154)	Departmental overhead rate (p. 165)
Cost pool (p. 155)	Reapportionment (p. 169)
Absorption costing (p. 155)	Simultaneous equations (p. 169)
Absorption rate (p. 155)	Step method (p. 172)
Predetermined (p. 163)	Reciprocal service costs (p. 172)
Practical activity (p. 163)	Repeated distribution method (p. 172)
Normal activity (p. 163)	Overhead distribution summary (p. 172)

RECOMMENDED READING

Berlant *et al.* (1990) provides interesting news for management accountants. More myths are exploded by Böer (1994). Who **really** does what, and again one or two interesting insights, are described in Bright *et al.* (1992). Elphick (1985) reassures us that we are not wasting our time. Johnson and Kaplan (1991) is a classic that must be read. Piper and Walley (1990) provide something of an alternative view that got them a mauling from Robin Cooper. See also Piper and Walley (1991). Shank and Govindarajan (1993) is still essential reading.

QUESTIONS

Review questions

1. Why is it felt that overheads are gaining in importance for businesses throughout the world? And why are overheads considered to be a problem for accountants and managers?
2. What is overhead absorption?
3. Does the fact that we can calculate six different overhead rates for any one department or project mean that there are six possible selling prices that we can set?
4. Why should we use predetermined overhead absorption rates rather than actual rates? And why should we use departmental rates rather than blanket, or organisationwide, rates?
5. Why do we reapportion the overheads from a service department?
6. What are reciprocal service costs? How might we deal with the problem of reciprocal service costs?
7. Briefly describe each of the following in the context of overhead reapportionment:
   (a) the specified order of closing method;
   (b) the repeated distribution method;
   (c) the simultaneous equation method;
   (d) the matrix algebra method;

8. The matrix algebra method of overhead reapportionment is appropriate only for those organisations that have (a) a qualified accountant working for them and (b) a computer with the relevant software. Discuss this assertion.

Answers to review questions 1, 2, 5 and 8 can be found in the Student Workbook.

Graded practice questions

Level I

1. (a) How is it possible to *allocate* an overhead cost, as opposed to apportioning it? In answering this question, give at least four different examples to illustrate your points.
   (b) Assume that Mr A operates one organisation and Mr B operates another one. Both organisations employ the same accountant on a part-time basis, and she is consistent in the way she applies her accounting skills and knowledge. The overhead absorption rate derived for Mr A's organisation is radically different to the value of the overhead absorption rate for Mr B's organisation. Given that both organisations operate within the same sector of the economy, can we conclude that one organisation is more efficient than the other one?
2. Under what circumstances can a single organisation-wide overhead absorption rate be considered appropriate?
3. Suggest bases of apportionment for each of the following service departments:
   (a) building maintenance
   (b) power
   (c) inspection and packing
   (d) machine shop
   (e) cafeteria
   (f) personnel
   (g) purchasing
   (h) stores
4. What would be an appropriate basis for apportioning each of the following factory overhead expenses to departments?
   (a) depreciation on buildings
   (b) depreciation on machinery
   (c) rates
   (d) insurance on the machinery
   (e) heating
   (f) lighting
   (g) indirect materials
   (h) indirect wages
   (i) repairs to machinery
5. Midland Ltd operates a factory with three departments A, B, and C. The monthly factory overheads for the departments are:

	£
A	24,000
B	20,000
C	12,600

The production data are

	Departments A	B	C
Materials used (£)	20,000	10,000	10,000
Direct wages cost (£)	16,000	15,000	8,400
Direct labour hours ('000)	16	10	7

During the month under consideration, a job, Job 1-2-3, passed through the organisation: relevant details as below:

	Departments A	B	C
Materials used (£)	12.00	14.00	12.00
Direct wages cost (£)	13.00	13.50	12.50
Direct labour hours	11	9	10

Required

Find the cost of Job 1-2-3, assuming that the overheads are absorbed by output on the basis of:

(a) direct wages cost; and
(b) direct labour hours.

6. Omar Selim (Egypt) plc uses the direct labour hours method of overhead absorption for jobs being worked on in departments A and B. The company expects each production department to use 30,000 direct labour hours during the year. The predetermined overhead rates for the year are:

	Departments A	B
	£	£
Variable cost per hour	0.75	0.65
Fixed cost per hour	2.50	2.85

During the year both departments A and B used 28,000 direct labour hours in their departments. Factory overhead costs incurred during the year were as follows:

	£
Maintenance	20,000
Factory services	60,000
department A	42,000
department B	62,000

In determining absorption rates at the beginning of the year, cost allocations were made as follows: maintenance to factory services, 20%; to department A, 50%; to department B, 30%. Factory services was apportioned on the basis of direct labour hours.

Required

Determine the under- or overrecovery of overhead for each production department (A and B).

Level II

7. Having carried out the allocation and apportionment process of its operations, the management accountant of Flowers Ltd is left with the reapportionments to carry out. The data below represent the current state of the overhead distribution summary and the additional detail that is needed to answer the question that follows:

Flowers Ltd: Overhead distribution summary

Month of ______________

	Production			Service	
	M	T	F	A	B
	£	£	£	£	£
Total b/d	25,000	20,000	30,000	10,000	20,000

Reapportionment percentages

	Production			Service	
	M	T	F	A	B
A (%)	30	20	25	0	25
B (%)	20	25	30	25	0

direct labour hours	17,300	7,300	41,200
tonne miles	346,000	29,200	4,120

Required

(a) Reapportion the service department overheads into the production departments on the basis of *each* of:
   (i) the repeated distribution method;
   (ii) the simultaneous equations method;
   (iii) the matrix algebra method.

(b) Calculate overhead absorption rates for each production department based on each of:
   (i) direct labour hours;
   (ii) number of tonne miles.

Solutions to practice questions 2, 4 and 6 can be found in the Student Workbook. Solutions to practice question numbers in red can be found at the end of this book.

Projects

1. If you work in a manufacturing organisation, attempt to discover the methods used for allocating and apportioning overheads. Are methods such as the repeated distribution and simultaneous equations method used?
2. If you work in a service-based organisation, attempt to discover the methods used for allocating and apportioning overheads. Are methods such as the repeated distribution and simultaneous equations method used?
3. From whatever sources you can find, try to determine the *levels* of overhead suffered by organisations: classify your findings in terms of primary, secondary and tertiary organisations, as well as profit-making and non-profit-making organisations. (Sources such as annual reports and accounts, Extel cards, newspapers such as the *Financial Times*, magazines such as the *Investors Chronicle*, should all be helpful here, as well as trade magazines.)

   Do your findings support the view expressed in Chapter 6 that overheads are becoming more important for organisations?
4. Create a SPREADSHEET MACRO to solve any problems such as the ones found in the appendix to this chapter. You should build in sufficient flexibility to allow for any number of service departments (within the limits of the software, that is).

Appendix: The algebraic method of service department reapportionment

The algebraic method of service department overhead reapportionment involves using simultaneous equations and matrix algebra. We will start with the simultaneous equation method and then move on to the matrix method. We might have doubts that we are taking a sledge-hammer to crack a nut in considering the algebraic approaches to service department reapportionment. We might feel this in the sense that all of the knowledge and effort required to set up and solve simultaneous equations and matrices is apparently not in proportion to the complexity of the situations we are dealing with. So far this has been true of the materials presented in this book. In reality, however, the situation often becomes overwhelmingly larger. Consider what Elphick (1985: 22) has to say:

'For comparatively small allocation problems, involving up to 50 service centres the simultaneous equations can be readily solved using the matrix inversion function of APL on a microcomputer', and he used allocation matrices to solve allocation problems: 'for an allocation problem with 1,714 internal centres, 704 external centres and 5,247 internal flows' (ibid. 24). (Note that the internal flows are those relating to the service centres and the external flows are those involving the production departments.)

These two quotations show that Elphick considers a 50 service centre problem to be small! While his organisation (ICI plc) deals with reapportionments involving in excess of 1,700 service departments, the techniques we are discussing here are basically the ones Elphick is describing. We are not wasting our time!

Simultaneous equations

Simultaneous equations generally look like:

$$2x + 3y = 24 \qquad (6.1)$$
$$5x + 7y = 58 \qquad (6.2)$$

In both equations (6.1) and (6.2), the 'x' and the 'y' variables have the same values: in this case 'x' = 6 and 'y' = 4 in both equations. Usually, of course, we do not know that $x = 6$ and $y = 4$ until we solve the equations! We can set up simultaneous equations for the situation summarised below: Andrew's Rat Paper Business Ltd

	Production			Service	
	A	B	C	X	Y
	£	£	£	£	£
Total	25,000	20,000	36,750	10,000	7,500

Reapportionment percentages

	Production			Service	
	A	B	C	X	Y
X (%)	30	20	40	–	10
Y (%)	25	15	35	25	–

If we let x be the total overheads of service department X; and we let y be the total overhead of service department Y, we can say:

$$x = 10{,}000 + 0.25y \qquad (6.1)$$
$$y = 7{,}500 + 0.10x \qquad (6.2)$$

That is, the total overheads allocated, apportioned and reapportioned into department X amount to the £10,000 allocated and apportioned as per the overhead distribution summary plus the 25% of department Y's costs that are reapportioned into it. Similarly, the total overheads allocated, apportioned and reapportioned into department Y amount to the £7,500 allocated and apportioned as per the overhead distribution summary plus the 10% of department X's costs that are reapportioned into it. Furthermore we can express the overheads situation in the production departments in a similar way:

$$\mathrm{A} = 25{,}000 + 0.3x + 0.25y \qquad (6.3)$$

$$\mathrm{B} = 20{,}000 + 0.2x + 0.15y \qquad (6.4)$$

$$\mathrm{C} = 36{,}750 + 0.4x + 0.35y \qquad (6.5)$$

Where:

A is the total overhead of production department A after all reapportionments have taken place;
B is the total overhead of production department B after all reapportionments have taken place; and

C is the total overhead of production department C after all reapportionments have taken place.

Concentrating on equations (6.1) and (6.2) for now, we rearrange the equations we have derived and solve for 'x' and 'y' respectively:

$$x - 0.25y = 10{,}000 \tag{6.1}$$

$$-0.10x + y = 7{,}500 \tag{6.2}$$

We can solve these equations in one of two ways (and we will consider equations (6.3), (6.4), and (6.5) later):

by substitution; and
by elimination.

Both methods will give exactly the same results, if done properly, although only the substitution method will be demonstrated here.

By **substitution** we mean that we can substitute as follows:

$$x - 0.25(7{,}500 + 0.10x) = 10{,}000 \tag{6.6}$$

That is, from the information we have, we know that $y = 7{,}500 + 0.1x$; therefore, all we do is substitute $7{,}500 + 0.1x$ whenever we see 'y'. We can now solve for 'x' relatively straightforwardly:

solving for 'x' in equation (6.6):

$$x - 0.25 \times (7{,}500 + 0.10x) = 10{,}000$$

removing the terms from the brackets, gives:

$$x - 1{,}875 - 0.025x = 10{,}000$$

rearranging (and notice any sign changes):

$$x - 0.025x = 10{,}000 + 1{,}875$$

combining the 'x' and numerical values:

$$0.975x = 11{,}875$$

therefore, 'x' equals:

$$x = \frac{11{,}875}{0.975}$$

$$= 12{,}179.48718$$

We now use this value for 'x' in order to find a value for 'y'. We do this by putting 12,179.48718 whenever we find 'x', in either of equations (6.1) or (6.2). We will use equation (6.2) for this demonstration, although using equation (6.1) would give exactly the same solution:

equation (6.2) is:

$$-0.10x + y = 7{,}500 \tag{6.2}$$

substitute for the value of 'x' that we have just determined:

$$-0.10(12{,}179.48718) + y = 7{,}500$$

remove the brackets:

$$-1{,}217.948718 + y = 7{,}500$$

rearranging (notice the change of sign in front of 1,217.948718):

$$y = 7{,}500 + 1{,}217.948718$$

therefore:

$$y = 8{,}717.948718$$

In summary, we have:

$$x = 12{,}179.48718$$

$$y = 8{,}717.948718$$

What do these results mean, however? What does, for example, $x = 12{,}179.48718$ tell us?

The meaning of the '*x*' and '*y*' variables

If we were to have carried out the repeated distribution method of overhead reapportionment for Andrew's Rat Paper and added together, first of all, all of the **positive** values in the Department X column, we would find:

$$10{,}000 + 2{,}125 + 53.13 + 1.33 + 0.00 = 12{,}179.46;$$

and when we add together all of the **positive** values in the Department Y column, we find:

$$7{,}500 + 212.50 + 5.31 + 0.13 = 8{,}719.94$$

Within a very small margin of error, these two results correspond to the values for 'x' and 'y' respectively. The differences, therefore, between the repeated distribution and the simultaneous equation methods are:

	Repeated distribution	Simultaneous equation	Differences
$x =$	12,179.46	12,179.48718	0.027180
$y =$	8,717.94	8,717.948718	0.008718

Not significant differences at all.

The simultaneous equation method is the more accurate of the two methods, as we have already said.

Finding the values for the production departments

We can use these values now to find the values for A, B, and C, by substitution in equations (6.3), (6.4), and (6.5):

$$A = 25{,}000\ (0.3 \times 12{,}179.48718) + (0.25 \times 8{,}717.948718)$$
$$B = 20{,}000\ (0.2 \times 12{,}179.48718) + (0.15 \times 8{,}717.948718)$$
$$C = 36{,}750\ (0.4 \times 12{,}179.48718) + (0.35 \times 8{,}717.948718)$$

The results are:

$$A = 30{,}833.33333$$
$$B = 23{,}743.58974$$
$$C = 44{,}673.07692$$

Interpretation of results

We can determine the meaning of the results we have just found for A, B, and C by looking back at Andrew's Rat Paper overhead distribution summary that we prepared under the direct method. The final line of that statement is shown below:

	Production			Service	
	A	B	C	X	Y
	£	£	£	£	£
Total	30,833.32	23,743.58	44,673.09	–	–

We can see that what the simultaneous equations method does is to give us the final fully apportioned and reapportioned overheads for all production departments without the need to carry out the repeated distribution, two-step, or any other similar method.

Matrices

Matrix algebra is learned in schools now, and most readers of this book will doubtless be familiar with it. This section is an extension of the simultaneous equations method, since matrix algebra is ideally suited to solving such problems. We will work through examples with which we are already familiar, so that it is only the matrix algebra that is new. We are going to start by solving the reapportionment problem contained in A Co plc:

$$x - 0.10y = 3{,}000 \qquad (6.1)$$

$$-0.30x + y = 5{,}000 \qquad (6.2)$$

Translated into matrix format gives:

$$\begin{bmatrix} 1 & -0.1 \\ -0.3 & 1 \end{bmatrix} \begin{bmatrix} x \\ y \end{bmatrix} = \begin{bmatrix} 3{,}000 \\ 5{,}000 \end{bmatrix}$$

We will be using the most direct method to solve this problem by matrix algebra. What we do to is to set up a partitioned matrix and solve for 'x' and 'y'; where row one relates to 'x' and row two relates to 'y'.

$$\left[\begin{array}{cc|c} 1 & -0.1 & 3{,}000 \\ -0.3 & 1 & 5{,}000 \end{array}\right]$$

Ultimately we are looking to replace the left-hand side of this partitioned matrix by a unit matrix. We do this by a series of multiplications, divisions, additions and subtractions, as necessary. A 2×2 unit matrix looks as follows:

$$\begin{bmatrix} 1 & 0 \\ 0 & 1 \end{bmatrix}$$

The rest of this example will proceed on the basis that this methodology is understood. There will always be several steps or iterations to such problems; and, remember, there are many ways to solve them. The calculations you might carry out could be different to the ones you see here. There is often nothing wrong with this providing both sets of solutions are efficient and correct!

For A Co plc:

Step 1: add 0.3 times row 1 to row 2 (leaving row one unchanged)

0.3 times row 1 plus row two is:

$$\begin{array}{rrr|r} & 0.3 & -0.3 & 900\ + \\ & -0.3 & 1 & 5{,}000 \\ = & 0 & 0.97 & 5{,}900 \end{array}$$

$$\left[\begin{array}{cc|c} 1 & -0.1 & 3{,}000 \\ 0 & 0.97 & 5{,}900 \end{array}\right]$$

Step 2: divide the new row 2 by 0.97.

the new row two divided by 0.97 is:

$$0 \quad 1 \quad | \; 6{,}082.474227$$

$$\left[\begin{array}{cc|c} 1 & -0.1 & 3{,}000 \\ 0 & 1 & 6{,}082.474227 \end{array}\right]$$

(Recognise anything here?)

Step 3: add 0.1 times row 2 to row 1.

0.1 multiplied by the revised row two plus row one is:

$$\begin{array}{rr|l} 0 & 0.1 & 608.2474227 + \\ 1 & -0.1 & 3{,}000 \\ =1 & 0 & 3{,}608.2474227 \end{array}$$

$$\left[\begin{array}{cc|l} 1 & 0 & 3{,}608.247227 \\ 0 & 1 & 6{,}082{,}474227 \end{array}\right]$$

After only three iterations we have achieved our objective of having turned the left-hand side of the partitioned matrix into a unit matrix, and at the same time we can see that we have solved for the values of 'x' and 'y'. We have:

$x = 3{,}608.247227$
$y = 6{,}082.474227$

We can use these results now, as we did with the simultaneous equations method to find the values for the final overheads for the production departments: we are not showing this step here, however.

Matrix algebra and three or more variables

As we saw in the quotation from Elphick, matrix algebra can easily cope with more than two variables (especially when a computer is used). We should take a look at a three-variable situation, at least to see what the problem looks like!

WORKED EXAMPLE 6.4

Sloth plc has three service departments that have overheads to reapportion. All of the relevant details are given below:

	Production departments				Service departments		
	1	2	3	4	A	B	C
Total overheads (£)	10,000	20,000	15,000	10,000	10,000	5,000	15,000

Reapportionment percentages:

	Production departments				Service departments		
	1	2	3	4	A	B	C
SDA (%)	20	10	30	20	–	10	10
SDB (%)	5	35	20	10	20	–	10
SDC (%)	10	10	30	5	20	25	–

Where SDA, SDB, and SDC represent the reapportionment percentages for service department A, B, and C respectively.

Required

By the use of matrix algebra, reapportion the service department overheads into the production departments, and derive a total value for overheads for all of the production departments.

Solution to Worked example 6.4

Rather than work through the whole of the solution to this problem, the solution that follows merely illustrates the setting up of the simultaneous equations and matrices. The solution then shows the initial and then final matrices only, but not the intermediate matrices. The starting point to solving such problems is to set up the simultaneous equations and then set up and solve the matrices. We will see this step by step.

Derive the simultaneous equations

1. Let A be the total overheads of service department A including all of the reapportionments of the service departments B and C.
2. Let B be the total overheads of service department B including all of the reapportionments of the service departments A and C.
3. Let C be the total overheads of service department C including all of the reapportionments of the service departments A and B.

The equations, then, are:

$$A = 10{,}000 \qquad + 0.20B + 0.20C \tag{6.6}$$
$$B = 5{,}000 + 0.10A \qquad + 0.25C \tag{6.7}$$
$$C = 15{,}000 + 0.10A + 0.10C \tag{6.8}$$

Rearranging these equations to get all of the A, B, and C variables on the left-hand side, and all of the numerical values on the right-hand side of the equations, makes them more manageable:

$$A - 0.20B - 0.20C = 10{,}000 \tag{6.6}$$
$$-0.10A + \quad B - 0.26C = 5{,}000 \tag{6.7}$$
$$-0.10A - 0.10B \qquad C = 15{,}000 \tag{6.8}$$

Set up the initial partitioned matrix

$$\left[\begin{array}{ccc|c} 1 & -0.20 & -0.20 & 10{,}000 \\ -0.10 & 1 & -0.25 & 5{,}000 \\ -0.10 & -0.10 & 1 & 15{,}000 \end{array}\right]$$

When we have solved this problem, the result in the top row of the right-hand side of the partitioned matrix gives us the value of 'x', the value in the second row of the matrix will be the value of 'y' and the result in the bottom row will be the value of 'z'. We have reached the final matrix when the left-hand side of the partitioned matrix reaches unity, as seen below:

$$\left[\begin{array}{ccc|c} 1 & 0 & 0 & 15{,}732.7586 \\ 0 & 1 & 0 & 10{,}991.3793 \\ 0 & 0 & 1 & 17{,}672.4138 \end{array}\right]$$

The values for *A*, *B*, and *C*, reading down the right hand column of the matrix are, respectively:

$A = £15{,}732.7586$
$B = £10{,}991.3793$
$C = £17{,}672.4138$

As before, we can now use these results to find the values of the final overheads for the production departments, as we did with the simultaneous equations method, but that aspect of this exercise is not shown here.

Matrix algebra and the power of the computer

Those of us who have access to such spreadsheeting software as Lotus 1-2-3, will be able to use the power of that software to solve much larger reapportionment problems than the 'three by three' problem we have just worked through. The later versions of Lotus 1-2-3 spreadsheet software can easily deal with the size of matrices we are discussing here. Using its matrix inversion and multiplication commands, such software can solve a reapportionment problem involving in excess of ninety different service departments. The procedures for solving such problems are very straightforward, and can be mastered within minutes by anyone, even those who may be only slightly familiar with Lotus 1-2-3 commands and procedures. Dedicated Operations Research software can cope with much larger problems, of course. The following two problems that are designed to be solved by Lotus 1-2-3 rather than by hand. Attempt these problems only if you want to.

Solving reapportionment of overheads problems by computer

The precise and detailed instructions needed to operate these commands are not given here, but they can be found easily in the manual that came with your version of the software, or in reference books specially written for the software. Many other spreadsheeting software packages will also be able to solve matrices such as the ones we are dealing with here. Again, if you are using other software, check your manuals or reference texts for guidance.

PROBLEM 6.1

Four-service department problem.

The information supplied for you to program your spreadsheet for this reapportionment problem involving four-service departments is given below.

Distribution summary

	Service departments			
	A	B	C	D
Total	20,000	20,000	15,000	25,000

For this exercise, only the service departments' reapportionment and overheads data are supplied. The relevant portion of the reapportionment percentage table is:

	A	B	C	D
SDA (%)	0	5	20	15
SDB (%)	25	0	10	15
SDC (%)	15	10	0	25
SDD (%)	5	25	10	0

where SDA tells us the proportions in which service department A's overheads is reapportioned to the other service departments, SDB tells us the proportions in which service department B's overheads is reapportioned, and so on.

Solution to Problem 6.1

All of this translates into the following simultaneous equations:

$$
\begin{aligned}
A &= 20{,}000 + \ 0.25B + 0.15C + 0.05D \ldots (1)\\
B &= 20{,}000 + 0.05A + \ 0.10C + 0.25D \ldots (2)\\
C &= 15{,}000 + 0.20A + 0.10B + \ 0.10D \ldots (3)\\
D &= 25{,}000 + 0.15A + 0.15B + 0.25C \qquad \ldots (4)
\end{aligned}
$$

where A is the total overhead of service department A, after all reapportionments; B is the total overhead of service department B, after all reapportionments; and so on.

Rearranging these equations gives:

$$
\begin{aligned}
A - 0.25B - 0.15C - 0.05D &= 20{,}000 \ldots (1)\\
-0.05A + B - 0.10C - 0.25D &= 20{,}000 \ldots (2)\\
-0.20A - 0.10B + C - 0.10D &= 15{,}000 \ldots (3)\\
-0.15A - 0.15B - 0.25C + D &= 25{,}000 \ldots (4)
\end{aligned}
$$

Translating these equations into matrix form, we have:

$$\left[\begin{array}{rrrr|r} 1 & -0.25 & -0.15 & -0.05 & 20{,}000 \\ -0.05 & 1 & -0.10 & -0.25 & 20{,}000 \\ -0.20 & -0.10 & 1 & -0.10 & 15{,}000 \\ -0.15 & -0.15 & -0.25 & 1 & 25{,}000 \end{array}\right]$$

Finally, by using Lotus 1-2-3, and without showing the intermediate workings, as we have been doing above, the results are:

A = £35,547.02
B = £35,566.22
C = £29,982.28
D = £43,162.56

In a full version of such a question we would now apply these results to the production departments, and reapportion the service department overheads in full. Since this demonstration is purely concerned with demonstrating the application of matrix algebra, there is no need to do this.

PROBLEM 6.2

Six service department problem.

This problem concerns an organisation where there are six service departments, and our task is to use matrix algebra to solve the organisation's reapportionment problem. As with Problem 6.1 in this appendix, no production department data is given since the problem is devised to allow for the solution by using computer software.

Distribution summary

	Service departments					
	A	B	C	D	E	F
Total	10,000	16,000	17,000	55,000	57,000	17,000

The relevant portion of the reapportionment percentage table:

	A	B	C	D	E	F
SDA (%)	0	5	15	10	5	10
SDB (%)	5	0	10	10	5	15
SDC (%)	10	15	0	15	5	5
SDD (%)	5	10	5	0	25	5
SDE (%)	10	10	15	5	0	5
SDF (%)	5	5	5	10	15	0

where SDA tells us the proportions in which service department A's overheads is reapportioned to the other service departments, SDB tells us the proportions in which service department B's overheads is reapportioned, and so on.

Solution to Problem 6.2

All of this translates into the following simultaneous equations:

$$A = 10{,}000 + 0.05B + 0.15C + 0.10D + 0.05E + 0.10F \quad (1)$$
$$B = 16{,}000 + 0.05A + 0.10C + 0.10D + 0.05E + 0.15F \quad (2)$$
$$C = 17{,}000 + 0.10A + 0.15B + 0.15D + 0.05E + 0.05F \quad (3)$$
$$D = 55{,}000 + 0.05A + 0.10B + 0.05C + 0.25E + 0.05F \quad (4)$$
$$E = 57{,}000 + 0.10A + 0.10B + 0.15C + 0.05D + 0.05F \quad (5)$$
$$F = 17{,}000 + 0.05A + 0.05B + 0.05C + 0.10D + 0.15E \quad (6)$$

Where A is the total overhead of service department A, after all reapportionments; B is the total overhead of service department B, after all reapportionments; and so on.

Rearranging these equations gives:

$$A - .05B - .15C - .05D - .05E - .10F = 10{,}000 \quad (1)$$
$$-.05A + B - .10C - .10D - .05E - .15F = 16{,}000 \quad (2)$$
$$-.10A - .15B + C - .15D - .05E - .05F = 17{,}000 \quad (3)$$
$$-.05A - .10B - .05C + D - .25E - .05F = 55{,}000 \quad (4)$$
$$-.10A - .10B - .15C - .05D + E - .05F = 57{,}000 \quad (5)$$
$$-.05A - .05B - .05C - .10D - .15E + F = 17{,}000 \quad (6)$$

Translating these equations into matrix form, we have:

$$\left[\begin{array}{rrrrrr|r} 1 & -0.05 & -0.15 & -0.05 & -0.05 & -0.10 & 10{,}000 \\ -0.05 & 1 & -0.10 & -0.10 & -0.05 & -0.15 & 16{,}000 \\ -0.10 & -0.15 & 1 & -0.15 & -0.05 & -0.05 & 17{,}000 \\ -0.05 & -0.10 & -0.05 & 1 & -0.25 & -0.05 & 55{,}000 \\ -0.10 & -0.10 & -0.15 & -0.05 & 1 & -0.05 & 57{,}000 \\ -0.05 & -0.05 & -0.05 & -0.10 & -0.15 & 1 & 17{,}000 \end{array}\right]$$

Finally, by using Lotus 1-2-3, and again without showing the intermediate workings, as we have been doing above, the results are:

A = £31,140.35
B = £40,774.72
C = £44,889.44
D = £84,343.70
E = £77,285.48
F = £42,867.42

REFERENCES

Allen, B. (1987), 'Make information services pay its way' reprint no. 87102, *Harvard Business Review.*

Berlant, D., Browning, R. and Foster, G. (1990), 'How Hewlett-Packard gets numbers it can trust' *Harvard Business Review* (Jan.–Feb.), 178–80 and 182–3.

Böer, G. (1994), 'Five modern management accounting myths', *Management Accounting* (NAA) January pp 22 + 24–27.

Bowerman, M. and Francis, G. (1995), 'Costing for contracting in the NHS – a case study', *Journal of Applied Accounting Research*, 2(2).

Bright, J., Davies, R. E., Downes, C. A. and Sweeting, R. C. (1992), 'The deployment of costing techniques and practices: a UK study', *Management Accounting Research* vol. 3 (September), 201–11.

Cardullo, J. P. and Moellenberndt, R. A. (1987), 'The cost allocation problem in a telecommunications company', *Management Accounting* (NAA) (September), 39–44.

CIMA (1991), *Management Accounting Official Terminology* (Chartered Institute of Management Accountants).

Cooper, R. (1989), 'You need a new cost system when . . . ' *Harvard Business Review* (Jan.–Feb.), 77–82.

Cooper, R. and Kaplan, R. S. (1987), 'How cost accounting systematically distorts product costs', in W. J. Bruns and R. S. Kaplan, *Accounting and Management: Field study perspectives* (Harvard Business School).

Develin (1990) *Activity-based cost management* (Develin & Partners, Management Consultants, 21 Piccadilly, London W1V 9LE).

Elphick, C. (1985), 'Cost allocation: a new approach', *Management Accounting* (CIMA) (December), 22–6.

Hoshower, L. B. and Crum, R. P. (1987), 'Controlling service center costs', *Management Accounting* (NAA) (November), 44–8.

Johnson, H. T. and Kaplan, R. S. (1991), *Relevance Lost: The rise and fall of management accounting*, 2nd edn (Harvard Business School Press).

Johnson, H. T. and Loewe, D. A. (1987), 'How Weyerhauser manages corporate overhead costs', *Management Accounting* (NAA) (August), 20–6.

Piper, J. A. and Walley, P. (1990), 'Testing ABC logic', *Management Accounting* (CIMA) (September), 37–42.

Piper, J. A. and Walley, P. (1991) 'ABC relevance not found', *Management Accounting* (CIMA) (March), 42, 44, 54.

Raffish, N. (1991), 'How much does that product really cost', *Management Accounting* (NAA) (March), 36–9.

Shank, J. K. and Govindarajan, V. (1993), *Strategic Cost Management: The new tool for competitive advantage* (The Free Press).

Tucker, F. G. and Seymour, M. Z. (1985), 'A Xerox center imitates a profit center', reprint no. 85317 *Harvard Business Review* (May–June).

Turney, P. B. B. (1992), *Common Cents: The ABC performance breakthrough* (Cost Technology).

Williamson, D. (1989), 'Incentive payment schemes: a revisitation proves worthwhile', *Management Accounting* (CIMA) (March), 40–1.

CHAPTER SEVEN

Activity-based costing

CHAPTER OBJECTIVES

After reading this chapter you should be able to:

- discuss the definition, meaning and implementation of activity-based costing
- appreciate the various steps involved in the implementation of ABC systems together with some of its problems
- appreciate the changes that ABC makes to cost accounting procedures
- understand how the ABC method works in detail
- understand the implications of ABC for organisations
- discuss whether ABC always provides benefits for organisations
- discuss some of the interim verdicts on ABC accounting
- appreciate the nature and meaning of strategic management accounting

Introduction

In Chapter 6 we looked at accounting for overhead costs. We saw many of the aspects of what we called traditional overhead analysis and then went on to look at more modern aspects of overhead cost analysis. In this chapter we will look in detail at activity-based costing (ABC) and activity-based costing management (ABCM). We know ABC is not new. We saw in Chapter 6 that ABC has been discussed under different names for at least two decades now. We also appreciated that the concepts on which ABC is based are probably centuries old. Nevertheless, ABC has led to a change of mind set for many management accountants. Chapter 6 led us through several cases where the management accountant went through the equivalent of the conversion on the road to Damascus. There are a few review points that are worthwhile looking at before moving forward with the ABC debate.

ABC does not solve all of the management accountant's overhead assignment problems: 'Costs may still require some element of arbitrary apportionment, for example, where they represent resources shared by more than one product and where jointness exists in the use of cost drivers' (Mitchell 1994: 266). Mitchell goes on to discuss, however, why such assignments are not necessarily a bad thing:

> allocation can provide a means of rationing shared resources. Overhead rates represent a set of taxes on the use of these resources . . . cost allocation can reduce prerequisite [sic: surely perquisite?] consumption by managers. ABC can contribute directly here by strengthening the monitoring capacity of the costing system through the visibility which it brings to the 'hidden factory' of overhead services. ABC also provides a direct control link between providers of activities and the users of their output. The existence of cost driver rates provides the mechanism for the cross charging of costs which will initiate the type of monitoring behaviour described above. (ibid. 269)

This view, as given by Mitchell, probably clarifies many of the accusations that ABC is not wholly new. The assignment of overheads still takes place, first, because it is necessary for ABC to work, and secondly, because it does provide some useful functions, such as we see from Mitchell's work.

Background to ABC: the generation of reliable cost information

There are three key areas of ABC:

1. Product cost differentiation.
2. Activities and their cost drivers.
3. Identification of non-value added cost improvement opportunities

In the early days of the history of cost accounting, from the middle of the nineteenth century to the mid-1970s, management accountants who needed to would happily allocate and apportion overhead costs on bases that were considered fair at the time. A study of cost accounting techniques from this period will reveal that the kind of apportionment bases we discussed in Chapter 6 were widely applied. Several studies have shown that organisations were quite happy to recover their overheads by using a single plant-wide overhead absorption rate. A survey reported in 1988 that in the United States almost one-third of companies canvassed used a single plant-wide overhead absorption rate. A similar study of UK management accounting practice revealed that small business organisations tended to use a single plant-wide overhead absorption rate, as did some larger organisations with high overhead costs (see Drury (1989) for further details).

The product and service costs derived from traditional allocation and apportionment methods were used, even though they may have been inappropriate, for a number of reasons:

- Overheads were relatively unimportant, as a proportion of total costs.
- When organisations were labour intensive, rather than capital intensive, the direct labour hour rate basis of apportionment of overheads was a sufficiently appropriate method to use.
- Before the advent of computerisation and office automation, ABC could only have meant an even more massive bureaucracy than before.
- All organisations were behaving the same way, so it was unnecessary to develop such innovations as ABC.
- Competition, if it existed, was relatively regional, not global, so detailed cost knowledge was not vitally important.
- Organisations were much less diversified than they are now, so there was little impetus to increase management's cost awareness.

Whilst these reasons will not be applicable to all organisations, they do indicate the nature of the need for ABC. In an increasingly automated, globally competitive, environment an organisation's management must have reliable cost information: 'Unreliable cost information is an open invitation to disaster' (Turney 1992: 5).

Reliable cost information is now considered by many to help with an organisation's competitive advantage. In the same way that the application of information and computer technology has given many organisations a competitive advantage, the reliability of cost information also gives an organisation a leading edge over other organisations whose cost information is not so reliable. The organisation that depends only on unreliable cost information must be in a weaker position than the organisation that has reliable cost information. If cost information is unreliable, it is also difficult to control. There is evidence to suggest that, in the case of the automobile manufacturing industry, only 15% of direct costs are controllable by management; even variable costs are not controllable in the short term. However, controllable overhead costs amount to 27% of total product costs.

In the service sector of an economy, of course, the gains to be made can be significantly greater. This will be true when overhead costs account for as much as 60%, or more, of total costs. In the case of overheads, therefore, there is much more scope to influence total costs through monitoring and controlling overhead costs than there is in trying to control the direct costs. ABC is, rightly, concerned largely with monitoring and controlling overhead costs.

The benefits of ABC: diversity and complexity

A simple example will show how ABC generates more accurate product and service costs. ABC recognises that it is activities that cause costs to change, and that the cost of these activities should be based on such activities. For example, this means that if a fork-lift truck is being used to move raw materials from one area of a warehouse to another, the costs of using that fork-lift truck must be identified with such movement, and not simply calculated on an arbitrary basis. Identifying costs with their activity bases means more than ever that the management accountant has to understand the nature of the production and service process, whether his or her organisation is a manufacturing or service organisation.

WORKED EXAMPLE 7.1

Product Zed passes through a variety of stages when being converted from raw materials to finished product. Throughout the production process, 4 direct labour hours are needed to carry out the conversion process in making 50 units; and quality control will spend 30 minutes on attempting to ensure that the product meets the strict requirements of the organisation's customers. The quality control overheads are absorbed at the rate of either £50 per quality control hour or £65 per direct labour hour.

Required

Using the direct labour hour basis (conventional costing) and the ABC method, determine the overhead costs of the product.

Solution to Worked example 7.1

We need, first, to determine the activity from which the quality control overheads are derived. Under the conventional costing system, the implication here is that the direct labour hour basis would have been used to recover (absorb) the quality control overheads. Using ABC, we would say that the reason for the existence of the quality control overheads is the act of quality control: that is, the need to check to ensure that what the customer gets is what he or she wants. In this case, the activity base of quality control is the time spent on controlling quality. The solution to this problem is therefore as follows:

	Traditional costing	ABC
	Direct labour hour basis	Quality control hour basis
Overheads absorbed	4 dlh × £65 per dlh = £260	$\frac{1}{2}$ qch × £50 per qch = £25
Overheads absorbed per unit	£260 ÷ 50 units = £5.2	£25 ÷ 50 units = £0.5

where:

dlh = direct labour hours; and
qch = quality control hours.

A simplified example, but it does illustrate the possible distortion that the conventional costing system can lead to. If an inappropriate overhead absorption basis is used to calculate product or service costs, the costs reported will be unreliable. Using ABC, we have an overhead cost of £0.50 per unit of output rather than the £5.20 per unit under the traditional cost accounting system. We should be able to agree that ABC is giving us the more realistic view of the costs. The realistic view comes from using the correct cost driver; that is, we have identified the reason behind the existence of the activity being undertaken (quality control). The activity is **driving** the cost. Without the cost driver, there would be no cost to worry about. A cost driver is

'An activity which generates cost' (CIMA 1991).

The examples just worked through give us an insight into what Cooper and Kaplan (1987) and others call complexity related costs. The conclusion drawn from a complex situation is that costs vary with the range of items produced, not with the volume of items produced. Cooper and Kaplan give the following example to illustrate this point:

Plant A	Plant B
Makes 1 million of A	Makes 100,000 of A + 900,000 of 199 similar products
Simple environment, few set-ups, stock movements, etc.	Complex: 200 products, frequent set-ups, stock movements, etc.

The reasoning here is quite straightforward, in that when 100,000 of the product are made, together with the other 199 products, the infrastructure required to manage this diverse range, must be more complex than in the situation where only one product is made. The diversity of 200 products will involve many machine setups and startups, stock movements, supervision and inspection problems, and so on. The problem is, however, that a traditional cost accounting view does not appreciate the significance of diversity. For example, as Cooper and Kaplan point out, if a product with a production run of 800 units is made, it will be allocated 0.08% of the production overheads (assuming a units of output overhead absorption rate), whereas a run of 100,000 units of a product would be allocated the same *proportion* of production overheads, 10% in this example. Relatively, both the 800 units and the 100,000 units are being charged with the same overheads, but they are not driving the overheads equally. The benefits of ABC, then, are that it addresses the issues of where costs come from, and by doing so, it also addresses the issue of diversity and complexity of cthe production/service structure.

Shank and Govindarajan (1993: 16) introduced an interesting example into the discussion on production complexities. When discussing complexity in the automobile industry the question was asked: 'how long would it take in [a] minimum efficient scale assembly plant to produce one of every possible end unit combinations for the automobile company?' The answers were:

Honda	45 minutes
Toyota	1 day
Chrysler	220,000 years
General Motors	7,800,000,000,000,000 years 36 trillion years for any one model. There were 200 different models under production at the time.

Shank and Govindarajan (ibid.) record that: 'Whatever advantages GM enjoyed in economies of scale, technology, experience and vertical scope, they more than lost in the diseconomies of product line complexity.' The minimum efficient scale assembly plant they refer to produces one car per minute for 16 hours a day, 250 days a year.

As a side issue, to some extent, an interesting debate took place over the period September 1990 to March 1991 between two British-based academics, Piper and Walley, and Cooper, one of the leaders in ABC development. Although the debate became a little personalised at one stage, it did raise the issue of whether ABC does indeed succeed as a result of costs resulting from activities. Piper and Walley (1990) maintain that it is decisions and not activities that cause costs. They opened the debate in September 1990 and Cooper (1990) replied in the following November. Piper and Walley (1991) had the final word in March of the following year. A reading of the three articles will help with the understanding of the usefulness of ABC and ABCM.

Why organisations use ABC systems

Bailey (1991) carried out a survey into the implementation of ABC by ten UK companies. This survey gives a reasonable insight into how ABC can or cannot help with the issues we have been discussing. Although Bailey did report problems with ABC implementation, he concluded that respondents felt the benefits outweighed the problems (see Table 7.1).

TABLE 7.1 *Benefits of ABC system (1)*

Benefits	% of sample	Probably leading to:
Greater accuracy in product costing	100	Improved pricing, make-or-buy decisions.
Greater involvement of production managers	90	Improved cost awareness, feeling of ownership, interaction.
Improved management information	70	Greater awareness of departmental managers, better product design, strategy improved, management control, and quality management.
Improved profitability	40	
Reduction in costs	60	Greater profitability, improved investment, performance enhanced, business opportunities.

Bailey also reported on the perceived benefits of ABC (see Table 7.2).

TABLE 7.2 *Benefits of ABC system (2)*

	Motivation to consider ABC (%)	Resulting benefits reported (%)
More accurate product costing	80	100
Better management information	50	70

Having set the scene for ABC, we can now turn our attention to a more detailed view of how ABC works overall.

ABC: design and implementation

Cooper (1990) outlined five steps that need to be identified for an ABC system:

1. Aggregate actions into activities.
2. Report the cost of activities.
3. Identify activity centres.
4. Select first-stage cost drivers.
5. Select second-stage cost drivers.

An action is any process that we might carry out – switching on machinery, securing a wheel to a car, programming a computer, are all actions. Actions become activities when we take a series of actions and make them into a complete whole, such as a complete job or a complete stage of a job. Similarly, the aggregation of activities leads to their being centres. An activity centre is a segment of an organisation or production process for which management wants to report the cost of activities performed separately.

Cost drivers are, as we agreed above, the activities that determine, or help us to determine, why a cost arose. Most of the ABC literature shows that cost drivers are found in two stages of the ABC process:

1. First-stage cost drivers trace the costs of inputs into cost pools in each activity centre. Each cost pool represents an activity performed in that centre
2. Second-stage cost drivers trace the costs of cost pools into product costs.

Keys (1994: 34), however, advocates a three-stage ABC process:

> **stage 1**: assign the cost to the year in which the cost produces benefit.
> **stage 2**: assign the current year's cost to activities (ABC system) or departments (traditional system).
> **stage 3**: assign each activity cost or each department cost to products or customers.

He makes the indisputable argument that if this stage 1 procedure is not followed properly: 'inaccuracy of assigning in one stage tends to be cumulative in later stages' (ibid.).

The kinds of costs that Keys sees as often being attributed to the wrong year include management salaries, depreciation, planning and designing new products, start-up costs of new methods, and training costs. Given the concepts and conventions of financial accounting, we should realise that there is nothing new in what Keys is saying; the matching or accruals concept takes care of this assignment problem. However, Keys is probably the first writer to overtly link matching expenditure to benefit received in the context of ABC. Whether we accept that ABC is a two-stage or three-stage process, there are further fundamental questions that need resolution – problems facing designers of ABC systems.

Some of the problems facing the designers of an ABC system in an organisation are:

- How many activity centres should there be?
- How many cost pools should there be?
- Which cost drivers should we use?

As we should expect with a system as product- and organisation-specific as ABC, there are no ready solutions to these questions. General guidance, however, says that the solutions to these questions depend on such matters as:

- product diversity
- the relative costs of the activities aggregated
- batch size diversity
- the ease of obtaining cost driver data
- the behaviour induced by the cost driver.

Each of these matters will vary according to the organisation being dealt with. The solution for my organisation may well be entirely different to the solution for your organisation.

There is no simple, general, guidance that can be given to answer the question of how many activity centres and cost pools an organisation should install within its ABC system. However, as far as possible, common sense should prevail! Taking the definition of an activity centre literally might lead us to draw the conclusion that our organisation has 200 activity centres. Imagine the bureaucracy surrounding 200 activity centres, with each centre subdivided into one or more cost pools. Most organisations installing an ABC system have to arrive at a compromise – the trade-off between accuracy and precision. Accuracy means providing information that is acceptably legitimate – it may be 90% of the truth. Precision pmeans that the information is 100% legitimate.

Setting up a realistic ABC system and accepting the accuracy/precision trade-off, activity centres will often consist of several activity areas being added together or aggregated. Rather than 200 activity centres, therefore, there will only be, say, 30. Similarly with cost pools. There is no theoretical answer or formula that will allow us to derive how many cost pools an organisation should have. The management accountant must have an eye for a sensible level of aggregation in his or her acceptance of the trade-off between accuracy and precision, in the same way that he or she has for activity centres. There is a problem with the aggregation of activities into activity centres, of course, namely, that the number of activities is potentially infinitely large across an organisation. To overcome this problem, many actions will need to be aggregated. Such aggregations may be so arbitrary that they tend to lead to the arbitrary allocation of overheads. If this becomes the case ABC may lose many of its benefits. These problems are common to both traditional and activity-based costing.

Cost drivers tell the management accountant why an activity has been carried out, and the level of effort required to carry out that activity. Examples of cost drivers include:

- the number of production runs;
- the number of goods received transactions;
- the number of quality control inspections;
- the number of patients admitted to a hospital;
- the number of punctures repaired.

Although we know what a cost driver is, we still have the difficulty of agreeing precisely how to choose one. In some cases, a cost driver will suggest itself very easily. In the case of a puncture repairing service, the number of punctured tyres repaired will almost certainly be one of the cost drivers (if not the only one). In other cases, it may not be so obvious at all. In such circumstances, the management accountant will have to liaise with colleagues and collect perhaps several series of data for analysis in order to determine what the driver should be. This means that, in some cases, there will be instances where direct labour hours,

TABLE 7.3 *ABC analysis for raw materials handling*

Functional area	Raw material purchase	Raw materials warehouse	Raw materials dispensing
Activity	Purchase raw materials	Receiving and issuing	Dispensing
Cost pool	Raw materials buying and handling		
Cost driver	Number of issues		
Cost item	Product		
General ledger Administration Materials Manufacturing cost code			

Source: Bhimani and Pigott (1992: 124).

materials-related information, the number of setups, and so on, may all be possible cost drivers. The key to managing costs by using ABC techniques means that data collection is the most important function of the management accounting system. Table 7.3 shows the cost pool and driver aspects of raw materials handling.

In the case where there may be several alternative cost drivers, the management accountant will have to carry out correlation, regression, graphical analysis, or other statistical analysis, on the data and its interaction with the activity being analysed. There is always the possibility in these instances that when a cost driver needs to be analysed in this way, the analysis may need to be carried out on a regular basis. The reason for such regular checking will be because as, for example, the product mix changes, the relationship between cost driver and activity **may** also change. Bhimani and Pigott (1992: 127) confirm the real role that management accountants seem to have played in the development of ABC systems in organisations:

> The implementation of ABC had relied on accountants gaining an appreciation of manufacturing processes, operational issues and production activities and had created the perception among factory and Head Office managers that the accounting data emanating from the . . . plant was now more firmly grounded in organisational processes than being independently prepared in the abstract by the conventional accounting system.

Does ABC mean major changes to cost accounting?

Turney (1992) and others state categorically that the implementation of ABC systems automatically leads to drastic changes to the whole of the cost accounting scheme of things. In other words, once ABC is implemented, all other elements of the cost accounting routine must then change. That possibly being true, we need to ask the questions: why is this chapter Chapter 7, and not Chapter 1; and why is this book dealing with many traditional cost accounting views and not the new ones? The answer is that although ABC has been implemented by many organisations, it is by no means universally applied, and the traditional view of cost accounting in any case still has, and will continue to have, a significant impact on a management accountant's view on life. The other aspect to traditional cost accounting methods is that they will continue to be of direct relevance to non-financial managers too.

How ABC works

We are now able to discuss the way that ABC works in reality. The best way to see how ABC works is to consider an example that compares the traditional cost accounting approach with the ABC approach. When the necessary calculations are completed, we will be able to make a much better judgement of the appropriateness of ABC in any given situation.

WORKED EXAMPLE 7.2

This example is very similar to the example in Drury's (1989) article. Although it is lengthy both to read and to work through, it does illustrate many of the points that need to be appreciated for the work of this chapter and subject. There are some significant differences between Drury's explanations and the ones given here. The information in Table 7.4 provides details of the costs, volume and transaction cost drivers for a period in respect of XYZ Ltd.

TABLE 7.4 *Details of the costs, volume and transaction cost drivers for a period for XYZ Ltd*

Product	A	B	C	Total
Sales and production (units)	90,000	30,000	15,000	135,000
Raw materials usage (units)	10.0	7.0	14.0	1,320,000
Direct materials cost (£)	30.0	40.0	15.0	4,125,000
Direct labour hours	2.5	3.0	1.5	337,500
Machine hours	5.0	3.0	7.5	652,500
Direct labour cost (£)	20.0	30.0	10.0	2,850,000
Number of production runs	5.0	10.0	50.0	65
Number of deliveries	18.0	7.0	50.0	75
Number of receipts	50.0	70.0	700.0	820
Number of production orders	45.0	25.0	60.0	130
Overhead costs				£
Setup				75,000
Machines				1,000,000
Receiving				900,000
Packing				650,000
Engineering				750,000
				3,375,000

Solution to Worked example 7.2

Along the lines of Drury's article, we will be working through these data three times. First, to see how traditional cost accounting methods might deal with them; secondly, to look at the multiple volume-based overhead method; and, thirdly, to look at the ABC method itself. Shank and Govindarjan (1993: 168) call traditional cost accounting conventional volume-based systems, and modern volume-based systems. Of the three approaches we will be looking at, only ABC, as might be expected by now, will be using all of the data in any great detail. This is consistent with the general nature of the traditional method, and the only slightly more advanced multiple volume method.

Traditional direct labour hours basis

The direct labour hour rate is £10, calculated by dividing the total overheads by the total number of direct labour hours (dlh):

$$\frac{\pounds 3{,}375{,}000}{337{,}500 \text{ dlh}} = \pounds 10 \text{ per direct labour hour}$$

Since we are using the direct labour hour rate method for the absorption of all overheads, the product costs per unit must be:

	A	B	C
	£	£	£
Direct materials	30.0	40.0	15.0
Direct labour	20.0	30.0	10.0
Overheads	25.0	30.0	15.0
Total product cost	75.0	100.0	40.0

The overheads recovered are, of course:

dlh rate × number of dlh per product

For product A, for example, the calculation is:

£10/dlh × 2.5 dlh = £25

Multiple volume-based allocation method

The multiple volume-based allocation method is an advance on the traditional allocation method in that it does make some allowance for activities to influence the absorption of overheads. In this example, and following Drury's lead, we have two absorption rates to apply here: the receiving department overhead rate, and the 'other' overhead rate.

The reasoning here is that the organisation we are simulating is using a two-rate basis of apportioning overheads. First, a material handling overhead rate is used to assign overhead to a separate cost centre and then charge it to production on the basis of the number of receipts. Secondly, all of the other overheads are assigned using a general machine hour rate on the basis that the number of machine hours far exceeds the number of labour hours. Notice here that the rate we are using to assign the materials handling overheads is based on the number of receipts of materials into a department. We are using this rate because the activity of receiving dominates the reason for the existence of the overhead. Drury uses an overhead rate expressed as a percentage of direct materials cost. This is not a rate to be recommended, particularly since tying the assignment of an overhead to the cost of a material is not realistic. As we know, merely because a material is expensive does not mean that its attendant overheads will vary in proportion to it.

The receiving overhead rate is:

$$\frac{\text{total receiving overheads}}{\text{total number of receipts}}$$

$$\frac{£900{,}000}{820}$$

= £1,097.56 per receipt

Using this rate as a constant allows us to evaluate the product overhead apportionments:

overheads per receipt × receipts per product group

For product A:

= £1,097.56 per receipt × 50 receipts

= £54,878

	Product A	B	C
	£	£	£
Overheads apportionment	54,878.0	76,829.3	768,292.7

We then divide these product apportionments by the number of units made for each product, to derive the cost per unit for receiving goods. The calculations here give the following results:

	Product A	B	C
	£	£	£
Cost per unit	0.60976	2.5610	51.2195

Notice, when compared with Drury's method of using the overhead rate as a percentage of direct materials cost, the version presented here gives a radically different result. Had we applied Drury's method, the product receiving cost per unit would have been as follows:

Overhead absorption rate:

$$\frac{£900{,}000}{£4{,}125{,}000} \times 100 = 21.82\%$$

Applying this rate to each product's material costs gives:

	Product A	B	C
	£	£	£
Cost per unit	6.55	8.73	3.27

The method we have used is the more realistic approach since it applies the full spirit of ABC by identifying and using fully the ABC approach. The other overhead rate, the machine hour rate is £3.79. This is calculated by dividing the total other overheads by the number of machine hours applied, or worked. In this case:

$$\frac{\pounds 3{,}375{,}000 - 900{,}000}{652{,}500 \text{ machine hours}} = \pounds 3.79103$$

When multiplied by the number of machine hours per product, this then gives us the cost per unit for other overheads. For example, in the case of product A, the calculation is:

$$\pounds 3.79103 \times 5 \text{ machine hours per unit} = \pounds 18.9655$$

Once all the calculations have been completed, the product cost analysis per unit of each product is:

	A	B	C
	£	£	£
Direct materials	30.0000	40.0000	15.0000
Direct labour	20.0000	30.0000	10.0000
Materials overheads	0.6098	2.5610	51.2195
Other overheads	18.9655	11.3793	28.4483
Total product cost	69.5753	83.9403	104.6678

ABC method

As we said above, to apply the ABC method we need to identify cost drivers for two stages: cost drivers tracing the costs of inputs into cost pools; and cost drivers tracing the cost pools into product costs. The workings that follow illustrate clearly how such cost drivers work through the ABC system in these two stages, an initial overhead rate or amount being further subdivided according to the needs of the situation.

Workings

The machine hour rate is the only rate that is what we might call a traditional rate. All of the other rates we are about to use involve a two-stage process. We will see the elements of these two stages as we get to them.

Machine hour overhead rate:

$$= \frac{\pounds 1{,}000{,}000}{652{,}500 \text{ machine hours}} = \pounds 1.5326$$

This rate is used as normal.

For the set-up costs, we first devise a rate to tell us the cost per set-up: that is, total set-up overheads divided by the number of setups. In this case, this is:

$$\frac{\text{£75,000}}{\text{65 production runs}} = \text{£1,153.85}$$

We will return to this rate shortly.

All of the other rates are calculated similarly. Hence they will be presented now without further comment.

Receiving rate:

$$\frac{\text{£900,000}}{\text{820 receipts}} = \text{£1,097.56}$$

Packing rate:

$$\frac{\text{£650,000}}{\text{75 deliveries}} = \text{£8,666.67}$$

Engineering rate:

$$\frac{\text{£750,000}}{\text{130 production orders}} = \text{£5,769.23}$$

All of this information can now be put together into a cost per unit statement (see Table 7.5), which is the final stage in the whole ABC procedure as far as product cost determination is concerned. We will then work through the calculations.

TABLE 7.5 ***Cost per unit statement for XYZ Ltd***

	A £	B £	C £
Direct materials	30.0000	40.0000	15.0000
Direct labour	20.0000	30.0000	10.0000
Machine overheads	7.6628	4.5977	11.4943
Set-up costs	0.0641	0.3846	3.8462
Receiving costs	0.6098	2.5610	51.2195
Packing costs	1.7333	2.0222	28.8889
Engineering costs	2.8846	4.8077	23.0769
Total costs	£62.9546	84.3732	143.5257

Workings

Machine overheads are found by multiplying the machine hour rate by the number of machine hours per product per unit:

	A	B	C
Machine hour rate (£)	1.5326	1.5326	1.5326
Machine hours	5	3	7.5
Machine overheads (£)	7.6628	4.5977	11.4943

The set-up costs rate we have already is the rate per machine setup. The cost per unit is calculated by multiplying the rate per setup by the number of setups per product and then dividing the results by the total number of units per product:

Set-up cost	A	B	C
per setup (£)	1,153.85	1,153.85	1,153.85
Number of setups	5	10	50
Total set-up costs (£)	5,769.25	11,538.50	57,692.50

These values are then divided by the number of units per product to give us the cost per unit:

Number of units	90,000	30,000	15,000
Cost per unit (£)	0.0641	0.3846	3.8462

The receiving, packing and engineering costs are all calculated in the same way as the set-up costs. There is no need to repeat these calculations, but check that they are understood. Summarising each of these methods now (see Table 7.6), we can see the impact of the different methods on product costs. Assuming that the ABC method is really more effective than the traditional approach, product A shows a cost difference of £42.1085 per unit.

TABLE 7.6 ***Summary of total costs and overheads per unit for XYZ Ltd using each of the three methods***

Summary 1: Total costs per unit (£)

Method	Product		
	A	B	C
Direct labour hours	75.0000	100.0000	40.0000
Multiple volume-based	69.5753	83.9403	104.6678
ABC	62.9546	84.3732	143.5257

TABLE 7.6 Continued

Summary 2: Overheads per unit (£)

Method	Product		
	A	B	C
Direct labour hours	25.0000	30.0000	15.0000
Multiple volume-based	19.5753	13.9403	79.6678
ABC	12.9546	14.3732	118.5257

Summary 3: Overheads as a percentage of total costs (%)

Method	Product		
	A	B	C
Direct labour hours	33.33	30.00	37.50
Multiple volume-based	28.14	16.61	76.11
ABC	20.58	17.04	82.58

The implications of the ABC method

Most writers on ABC, when discussing the advantages of the system, record the following as the principal advantages:

- Product cost accuracy is enhanced.
- Cost data is more comprehensive.
- Greater information is provided for managerial decision making.

These advantages should be appreciated when we consider that ABC attempts to address all of the shortfalls that we addressed in Chapter 6. Management accountants are often accused of not knowing what is happening in their organisations in terms of materials flow, storage, production systems and so forth. This has to be one of the most important advantages of the implementation of systems such as ABC, namely, that the management accountant is working with his or her colleagues to provide them with what they need. Looking at the example we have just worked through in the previous section, there are serious implications for the organisation involved under each of the three advantages listed above. This is so because, for example, product A now seems to have a true unit cost of £62.89 per unit as opposed to the traditionally calculated £105 per unit; similarly, product C's cost has gone from £45 to £139.74 per unit. Similarly, King *et al.*'s (1994: 149–50) study into ABC implementation in the NHS in the United Kingdom showed that information generated through ABC can help hospital management in a number of ways:

- Measuring and improving departmental efficiency.
- Promoting activity provider, activity receiver links.
- Managing costs and strategic planning decision making

Assuming that selling prices are based on costs, what does the organisation in our example do now? Does it reduce the prices of product A and increase the price of product C? A simplistic view says that they should, of course, but the evidence coming out of research into ABC practice is that even though costs are being re-evaluated, prices sometimes do not change – not in the short to medium term at least. The reason why prices are not being changed can be complicated, and include such factors as marketing policies, competitors maintaining their prices at the 'old' levels, and so on. There is, perhaps, a more serious aspect to the resistance to changing selling prices that is discussed by Bhimani and Pigott (1992: 130):

> sales managers did not understand or appreciate the reasons for product cost changes since they had not taken part in developing the ABC system. Their resentment nevertheless tended to diminish once the logic of ABC was explained and the rationale for cost changes indicated.

In order to convince one's colleagues of the worth of one's work, one needs to educate and involve him or her: that is, participation. Along the lines of much of modern management practice and thought, even the management accountant is not always and only concerned with things financial. Mitchell (1994: 272) states:

> In addition to new cost data, ABC generates sets of non-financial measures through the cost driver data which is needed for its implementation in output costing. They typically represent activity output measures and so can provide an indication of throughput which facilitates performance measurement and assessment particularly at an operational level...

An ABC warning

Boons *et al.* (1992: 98) give a warning as far as the design and implementation of an ABC system are concerned when they say:

> A theory of costs should always be built upon a corporate model of the physical and technical production relationships as the main design framework... Any cost accounting model therefore should be designed in such a fashion that it can supply any cost information necessary for attaining an optimal situation.

The management accountant needs to look to his engineering and technical colleagues to help him or her understand his or her environment. We have made this kind of comment at various stages throughout this text.

Furthermore Boons *et al.* paint rather a cynical view of the management accountant:

> ABC starts with aggregating tasks into actions then activities and finally into activity centres. It does so without questioning the present methods of producing/servicing i.e., its design starts from the assumption that the status quo is perfect and contains no inefficiencies or structural flaws. Such problems are consequently built into the ABC system. (ibid. 114)

This is rather a cynical view in that it presupposes that the management accountant simply translates his or her existing imperfect system into a more advanced imperfect system. This is the equivalent of the computer programmer programming a payroll system that does not work: that is, he or she programmes everything correctly, but the manual system on which the program is based is flawed. In such situations, we are possibly no worse off but we certainly are no better off: the danger is, however, that we feel we are better off as a result of implementing a supposedly better system. There are, however, many organisations that have implemented ABC systems now that are reporting most worthwhile benefits.

This is not to say that Boons *et al.* are wrong, but theirs is rather a cynical, sweeping viewpoint.

Does ABC always provide benefits?

A lot of work has been and is being done on ABC: both by academics and by accounting practitioners. Generally speaking, especially in the relatively early days of the debate over the benefits or otherwise of ABC, there was a transatlantic divide: American business organisations seemed to like ABC and implemented it widely; the United Kingdom was sceptical of ABC's benefits and had reservations about implementing it. Kingcott (1991) took, perhaps, the most pessimistic view and accused ABC of being inaccurate, arbitrarily allocating indirect overheads and offering nothing new. He also said that ABC is a mechanical system which can only be the foundation for an inflexible, preprogrammed computer-reporting system. Bromwich and Bhimani (1989) reported that although many organisations had implemented ABC systems, there was at that time insufficient evidence that it had affected profit levels. This should be a wrong conclusion, of course, but it might be explained by the organisational and marketing factors we discussed earlier whereby reported costs are changed but prices are not.

More positively, Aitken (1991) suggests reasons why he believes that the UK view of ABC is less positive than the US view of ABC. He says that in the United Kingdom it is often the finance department/function that is 'responsible for' costs: 'cost ownership belongs to finance'. In the United States, on the other hand, most ABC pioneers originate from within the operations functions. Therefore, those who can change costs are involved from the start. In helping us to consider the proprietary nature of an ABC system, the following is interesting. Innes and Mitchell (1991) carried out an extensive survey of 720 CIMA members: receiving 187 useful replies, their summary findings were:

- more than 50% had not seriously considered implementing ABC;
- aproximately 30% were currently vetting ABC;
- approximately 6% had started implementing ABC; and
- approximately 9% had already rejected ABC.

Of the 11 respondents who had implemented ABC, in 4 cases only the management accountant had been involved in the development work, whereas in 7 of the cases, a multidisciplinary team had done the development work. There is **some** evidence, therefore, that the UK management accountant might be guilty of not involving his or her entire management team in the development of the ABC system.

CAMEO

The Bureau of Engraving and Printing (an agency of the United States Treasury which prints US currency notes, postage stamps and other high-security instruments) is reported by Geiger and Leonard (1991) as having implemented an ABC system. Their results are extremely interesting in view of the discussion we have had concerning the impact that ABC systems can have on organisations. Their initial results showed that only 0.25% ($500,000), approximately, of total costs had been influenced by the change from a traditional cost accounting view to the ABC system view of cost management.

The initial reaction within the Bureau of Engraving and Printing was that the allocation bases they had chosen to use in the ABC system might not represent the true cost drivers. Whilst the outcomes of that debate are not yet published, it is possible that the reason for the apparent failure of ABC in this example is that, although some of the bases of apportionment and cost drivers were changed as from one system to the other, the overall effect of the changes was nil. This is not to say that the Bureau should now abandon the ABC system. After all, we have already agreed that with a change of product mix, the Bureau might find that the traditional and ABC systems then give widely different results.

Reference: Geiger and Leonard (1991a and 1991b).

Bailey (1991) found:

> on average, a company spent £48,500 on implementing ABC systems; and it takes 5.3 people to implement it; one company reduced costing staff from 8 to 5 as a result of implementing an ABC system; the implementation time ranged from 20 to 52 weeks.

Develin (1990) gives an overview of the set up and implementation time for an ABC system. Their experience has shown that it can take anywhere between 14 and 19 weeks from the start of an ABC implementation process to beginning implementation. They then say that it will be 75% implemented within the first year of use and 100% implemented within two years of use. There seems little doubt that the setting up and implementation of an ABC system is both time consuming and costly. There is some evidence that, even having installed and operated an ABC system, management accountants and their organisations may not exactly have entered fully into the spirit of the ABC revolution. Taking data from Bhimani and Pigott we find:

10 areas   35 activities   6 drivers

Basis of the OARs for each of the 6 drivers:

labour hours	13 out of 35
machine hours	9 out of 35
total	22 out of 35 = 63%

(Bhimani and Pigott 1992: 126, table 3)

Here we see the situation whereby ABC has been implemented but of the 6 cost drivers chosen to be used within 10 areas comprising 35 activities, 63% of them are either labour hour or machine hour rates. The question that must be asked is: Has anyone questioned the validity of this situation? After all, ABC concerns itself with overhead cost analysis and control and it seems widely agreed that labour hour rates are no longer important indicators of overhead cost behaviour. Are management accountants really falling back on their old, not so trusted, methods?

A further problem may be that there might be some misunderstandings about where ABC can relevantly be applied. King *et al.* (1994) studied ABC implementation in four NHS hospitals in the United Kingdom; and perhaps the largest problem faced by the hospitals related to the cost structure of service activities, with approximately 70% of costs being direct labour costs. It is clear that ABC has been developed to help organisations analyse and control their overhead costs; it is an overhead accounting methodology. Applying ABC, therefore, in a 70% labour cost environment might not be a wise thing to attempt. Is it the case that both King *et al.* and Bhimani and Pigott are dealing with situations where organisations are attempting to analyse overhead costs that are relatively insignificant *vis à vis* their total costs? If so, they ought to be extremely cautious in interpreting the information that is output from their ABC system. It should be added, however, that King *et al.* do instance the case in their study where overheads account for more than 50% of total costs.

Doyle (1994) takes a somewhat cynical view when he says that all novel management techniques tend to work well in prosperous times but are abandoned when business conditions get tough. Doyle is clearly suggesting that ABC is a potential flash in the pan. Positively, however, he goes on to say that consistent investment in management time to improve accounting methods has been shown to be beneficial. Doyle provides us with a list of problems that ABC can give rise to or suffer from. He discusses the time and effort needed to interview people and collect data, both when installing the system and when operating it. Doyle also points out that the ABC system is onerous where activity chains are long and complex, and where they cross numerous functional boundaries. There is also a danger that ABC will generate excessive detail and costings that may cause potential problems – information overload at the very least. Finally, Doyle says that not only will ABC have a great impact on the organisational culture of the organisation that implements it, but also we should be aware that ABC is not a general purpose tool. This final remark is at variance with the work of Shank and Govindarajan (1993) in that they maintain that ABC can be used within the ambit of strategic cost management and value chain analysis.

ABC: verdicts

ABC is a developing idea – but it is not new. We have admitted that ABC is merely an extension of existing cost accounting techniques and methods. However, there is, with ABC, a mind-set that traditional cost accounting does not have. With ABC we have to be prepared to accept arguments and inputs from colleagues outside the accounting function. As we know already, in order to monitor and control costs effectively, we need to become familiar with production processes, with the way that our organisation's services are provided. More than before, however, ABC is telling us that in order to monitor and control costs fully and effectively, we have to go a stage further: we need to know every aspect of every process, rather than, perhaps, just having a good overview of the whole organisation. ABC can be applied in most organisations no matter what their size. The argument that applies to some management accounting techniques, such as capital budgeting – the argument which says my organisation is just too small, or just too simple, to warrant applying that technique (it would be overkill) – does not apply to ABC. Applied with care and used properly, ABC has a lot to offer all organisations.

The most important issue concerning the implementation and upkeep of the ABC system is the length of time it will take to set up and implement the system, and, following on from that, the cost of setting up and implementing the system. It takes a relatively long time and it is relatively expensive. Hence many small organisations will probably not implement an ABC system. Nevertheless, many organisations have implemented an ABC system, concluding that the trade-off, between, on the one hand, the time and cost and, on the other, the benefits received, is beneficial. As Bailey (1991) found, in addition to the costs of setting up and implementing the ABC system, there can be significant savings, for example in terms of staff costs.

ABC in France

A recent article in the American *Management Accounting* journal demonstrates the operation of ABC in two French organisations. The authors of the article (Bescos and Mendoza 1995) claim that ABC has been a long time coming to France and suggest several reasons why this should be. However, they point out that both the organisations under discussion started looking at ABC systems in 1988 or 1989. By any standards, this is not late. However, Bescos and Mendoza do give valuable insights into French culture that might ring true elsewhere – or might certainly be factors to take into consideration elsewhere. Bescos and Mendoza discuss the implications of university-educated people versus people trained on the job. The problem here is that graduates see themselves as being more noble than their technical counterparts and this leads to relationship difficulties. Furthermore ABC was introduced into the two organisations at a time of economic hardship when there were layoffs within the organisations and morale was low. Hence implementing a system such as ABC, which should lead to greater efficiencies, was looked upon with suspicion in that it might lead to even more redundancies.

Otherwise, the French experience seems to match that of the United Kingdom and the United States, except that implementation costs seem extremely high by comparison: $500,000 in the case of one of the organisations.

Strategic management accounting

CIMA (1989) defines strategic management accounting as: 'The preparation and presentation of information for decision making, laying particular stress on external factors.'

Shank and Govindarajan (1993) provide a detailed view of the role of the management accountant in providing strategic cost management information. They go to great lengths to dispel many of the myths surrounding the supposed modern view of management accounting. Whilst not everyone agrees with their views, they are certainly of interest to us here. One of the key issues discussed by Shank and Govindarajan concerns value chains and the part they can play in the life of the management accountant:

> The value chain for any firm is the linked set of value creating activities all the way from basic raw material sources for component suppliers through to the ultimate end use product delivered into the final consumers' hands. (ibid. 13)

Shank and Govindarajan go on to tell us that the value chain breaks down an industry into its distinct strategic activities; they give as an example the paper products industry. This example shows the value chain starting with the farming of trees, while the final part of the chain is the customer who is using the output from the industry. The end user is someone who buys cardboard or paper either directly or indirectly: for instance when buying a packet of corn flakes or a box of matches or a writing pad. Weyerhaeuser, the paper products organisation in the United States that we discussed in Chapter 6, plays a role in all parts of its value chain except that it is not involved in the logging part of the chain. Similarly, the organisation Tetra Pak is concerned only with converting finished paper and card into consumer products, which it then distributes to end-use customers. The concept of the value chain will be clearer if we realise that Weyerhaeuser is a fully vertically integrated organisation within the paper products industry: that is, Weyerhaeuser is involved in all seven stages of the paper products value chain, according to Shank and Govindarajan.

The usefulness of value chain analysis becomes apparent when we take an analytical view of an industry such as paper products. When we carry out a ratio analysis exercise on an industry or an organisation, one of our starting points is the recognition that each industry and organisation has its own unique features. Shank and Govindarajan (1993: 53) say that organisations within one chain can compete effectively with other organisations within that chain:

> only by understanding the total value chain and cost drivers that regulate each activity . . . Each value activity [and therefore value chain] has a unique set of cost drivers that explain variations in costs in that activity.

We often still hear, unfortunately, that the working capital ratio is ideally found to have a value of 2 : 1. It is perfectly clear, however, that in the retail distribution trade, a negative working capital ratio is not unheard of. In fact, it is commonly found that a working capital ratio of much less than 1 : 1 exists in the retail trade. Similarly with other organisations in other industries and sectors, we need to look at each case individually and then we should agree with Shank and Govindrajan. Accepting their view of value chain analysis leads us to conclude that ABC at least should be playing a vital role in the strategic management of organisations. Only by looking carefully at an organisation and identifying its cost drivers and so on can an organisation fully understand its cost structure, and from that point how it can compete effectively with other organisations in their value chain. In addition to simply acknowledging that the value chain exists and then using that knowledge, Shank and Govindarajan demonstrate how value chain analysis provides a superior view of an organisation's activities over a period. Taking traditional DuPont analysis shows, for an airline organisation, that profit margins increased year by year, ticket sales increased over the same period, operating expenses per dollar of sales fell, and asset turnover was improved. Taking a value analysis viewpoint of this airline organisation, Shank and Govindarajan

(1993: 65–72) demonstrate that although the DuPont analysis shows an improving situation, in reality matters are not necessarily so straightforward.

Doyle (1994) highlights a point that must be of vital concern to today's management accountant. Doyle says that much managerial effort over the last ten to fifteen years has been wasted in that organisations have made efforts to reduce costs, downsize, control labour costs, and so on. Doyle then concludes that senior management must now focus its attention where it belongs: that is, on retaining the customer and remaining competitive. The point that Doyle makes raises a vital question for our discussion: What are the implications of a strategic cost management viewpoint for today's management accountant?

Wilson and Chua (1993: 185), using the work of Simmonds from the early 1980s, emphasises the important elements of strategic management accounting:

- real costs and prices;
- volume;
- market share;
- cash flow; and
- the proportion demanded of an enterprise's total resources

Putting together Simmonds' analysis with CIMA's definition of strategic management accounting, we can clearly see the work that today's management accountant must now become involved in. Take an example of an organisation seeking to increase its sales levels relative to others in the industry and we see that the management accountant's job is to assess not only his or her own organisation's real costs and prices, but also those of its competitors. Shank and Govindarajan (1993), in their example of the analysis of an airline organisation, provide clear guidance on the strategic nature of modern management accounting as applied to the kind of cases we are discussing here.

Pogue (1990: 65) gives an indication of the kind of work he feels a strategically oriented management accountant would do in the requirements of a case study he devised for CIMA's *Management Accounting* journal. He asks that the management accountant prepares

- a budgeted monthly profit and loss account
- a budgeted monthly cash flow statement
- a comparison of the profit/loss with the cash flow balance ...
- a learning curve graph showing the average labour batch times

Thus we see that the strategically oriented management accountant is working in accordance with CIMA's basic definition of management accounting, which we have discussed in previous chapters. His or her work extends beyond the historical analysis of internal events.

This brief introduction to strategic management accounting helps us to appreciate the work that we will be looking at in the chapters concerned with decision making, including cost volume profit analysis and relevant costs. We need to realise, however, that despite the fact that writers such as Simmonds have been working in this area for over a decade now, much of the work on strategic management accounting is recent. Of the references shown at the end of this chapter, 85% of them are dated later than 1990.

The prime message connected with strategic management accounting is that we have to take a longer-term view of our environment than we might previously have done.

SUMMARY

This chapter has given a detailed review of activity-based costing (ABC). We have learned that although there is essentially nothing technically different about ABC from what we have studied in previous chapters, ABC does encompass a new philosophy of cost monitoring and cost control.

We saw that ABC does allocate and apportion overhead costs, as does traditional cost accounting; it reports costs on a departmental, cost centre, or other appropriate basis; and it helps management make informed decisions relating to pricing, special decisions, stock valuation and so on. The key message we learned from analysing ABC is that by using it in an organisation, the management of that organisation can usually place a lot more faith in the outputs of the ABC system than was perhaps the case before. The chapter concluded by looking at ABC from two points of view:

1. whether ABC is the panacea to overhead cost control that its proponents say it is; and
2. how ABC and strategic management accounting are recognised as becoming more and more important tools in the armoury of the modern management accountant.

The key conclusion from our review of activity-based costing should be that it represents a long stride forward along the road to a more ideal management accounting system, but that it is still flawed. There are several headings under which we can question the work of the activity-based costing system. The work of Bright *et al* (1992) revealed that there might be a management accountant education problem: that is, there are issues on which the management accountant has a view, but which he or she cannot really discuss on a critical level. If this is the problem, continuing education programmes are required. If education is not the problem there is a possibility that it is a case of old habits dying hard. The management accountant could be happily wrapped up in the methods that have traditionally been used and can find no reason to change. If an organisation is profitable, why change a winning team? The fact that the organisation could be more profitable and more efficient has yet to be fully considered.

Activity-based costing systems are relatively expensive to introduce. The French experience shows horrific set-up costs, but this level of cost has yet to be reported from elsewhere, although it is always an expensive project to undertake. Similarly, activity-based costing does generate the need for a more bureaucratic regime than the traditional system; this seems to be axiomatic. We should also admit that activity-based costing does not solve all management's informational problems. We have reviewed evidence which says that arbitrary assignments of overheads are still made. At the moment, there is no system that sensibly and universally solves all overhead assignment problems. Such problems can be solved, but often only at even greater expense. On the other hand, we need to appreciate that the margin of arbitrary assignment may only be small, and the true impact of such arbitrariness could mean that only, say, 4–5% of accuracy is lost.

Finally, there is some opposition to the foundations of activity-based costing insofar as some writers argue that it does not go back far enough into the core of the management system. We have the argument that it is not activities which drives the incidence of costs, but decisions. In other words, it is the decision to do 'X' that overrides all other aspects of 'X', not the way in which 'X' works or the activities within it.

KEY TERMS

You should satisfy yourself that you have noted all of these terms and can define and/or describe their meaning and use, as appropriate.

Activity-based costing (ABC) (p. 197)	Activity centre (p. 203)
Traditional cost accounting (p. 200)	First-stage cost driver (p. 203)
Cost driver (p. 200)	Cost pools (p. 203)
Complexity related cost (p. 200)	Second-stage cost driver (p. 203)
Activity (p. 203)	Multiple volume-based allocation method (p. 207)

RECOMMENDED READING

ABC works in the United States and Aitken (1991) shows how. How the United Kingdom was faring in Bailey (1991), and France in Bescos and Mendoza (1995). Suggestions and warnings are provided by Bhimani and Pigott (1992), but not exactly whoopee news for ABC from Bromwich and Bhimani (1989). Cooper and Kaplan (1987) is one of their several classics and must be read. Geiger and Leonard (1991a and b) show how putting in ABC might not appear to change things. Some good news and some errors made are revealed in this good paper by King *et al.* (1994). Keep reading Shank and Govindarajan (1993).

QUESTIONS

Review questions

1. Why is 'traditional' costing so reluctant to be displaced by ABC?
2. What are the implications of using unreliable cost information?
3. What are the implications of product diversity and complexity on a cost accounting system?
4. Why does an organisation seem to want to implement an ABC system?
5. What are cost pools and cost drivers?
6. How can an organisation establish cost drivers for itself?
7. Does an ABC system always provide the benefits that are claimed for it? What is the experience of the Bureau of Engraving and Printing in this respect?

Answers to review questions 2, 4, 5 and 7 can be found in the Student Workbook.

Graded practice questions

Level II

1. Having attended a CIMA course on ABC you decide to experiment by applying the principles of ABC to the four products currently made and sold by your company. Details of the four products and relevant information are given below for each product:

Product	A	B	C	D
Output in units	120	100	80	120
Costs per unit:				
direct material (£)	40	50	30	60
direct labour (£)	28	21	14	21
Machine hours (per unit)	4	3	2	3

The four products are similar and are usually produced in production runs of 20 units and sold in batches of 10 units.

The production overhead is currently absorbed by using a machine hour rate, and the total of the production overhead for the period has been analysed as follows:

Machine department costs (rent, business rates, depreciation and supervision)	£10,430
Set-up costs	5,250
Stores receiving	3,600
Inspection/quality control	2,100
Materials handling and dispatch	4,620

You have ascertained that the 'cost drivers' to be used are as listed below for the overhead costs shown:

Cost	Cost driver
■ Set-up costs	Number of production runs
■ Stores receiving	Requisitions raised
■ Inspection/quality control	Number of production runs
■ Materials handling and dispatch	Orders executed

The number of requisitions raised on the stores was 20 for each product and the number of orders executed was 42, each order being for a batch of 10 of a product.

Required

(a) Calculate the total costs for each product if all overhead costs are absorbed on a machine hour basis; (4 marks)

(b) Calculate the total costs for each product, using activity-based costing. (7 marks)

(c) Calculate and list the unit product costs from your figures in (a) and (b) above, to show the differences and to comment briefly on any conclusions which may be drawn which could have pricing and profit implications. (4 marks)

(Total: 15 marks)

(CIMA Cost Accounting, November 1991)

The solution to this practice question can be found at the end of this book.

Note

In view of the relative lack of concrete examples on which to draw as a basis for reasonable questions, the following sources do provide further problems that you might care to try to analyse:

Morse W. J., Davis, J. R. and Hartgraves, A. L. (1991), *Management Accounting*, 3rd edn (Addison-Wesley), chapter 13. See, particularly, pp. 605–12. Additionally, they have a number of ABC questions at the end of chapter 13 that provide useful experience.

See also the Harvard Business School Case number 9–190–025: McMullen and Worby (A) (Abridged). This case is written by Robin Cooper and Kenneth Merchant, and although it was originally written a long time ago, it has recently been abridged and provides excellent practice for the keen student and practitioner.

Projects

1. Find as many articles and books as possible of the ones listed at the end of the chapter and make yourself familiar with the arguments surrounding ABC. Look, particularly, for any trends that might have emerged in where ABC is being applied. Is there a pattern to the types of organisation that is applying, or considering applying, ABC?

   You should also determine why an organisation that has looked at ABC should have rejected its implementation.

   Finally, do you detect, for example, an Atlantic divide over ABC? Does there really appear to be a difference between the British and American approaches to ABC? Analyse any differences you find.

REFERENCES

Aitken, N.(1991), 'How ABC is cutting costs in US companies', *Management Accounting* (CIMA) (November) 42, 59.

Bailey, J. (1991), 'Implementation of ABC systems by UK companies', *Management Accounting* (CIMA) (February), 30–2.

Bescos, P.-L. and Mendoza, C. (1995), 'ABC in France', *Management Accounting* (NAA) (April), 33–41.

Bhimani, A. and Pigott, D. (1992), 'Implementing ABC: a case study of organizational and behavioural consequences' *Management Accounting Research* vol. 3, pp. 119–32.

Boons, A. A. M., Roberts, H. J. E. and Roozen, F. A. (1992), 'Contrasting activity-based costing with the German/Dutch cost pool method', *Management Accounting Research* vol. 3, pp. 97–117.

Bright, J., Davies, R. E., Downes, C. A. and Sweeting, R. C. (1992), 'The deployment of costing techniques and practices: a UK study', *Management Accounting Research* vol. 3 (September), 201–11.

Bromwich, M. and Bhimani, A. (1989), *Management Accounting: Evolution not revolution* (CIMA).

CIMA (1991), *Management Accounting Official Terminology* (Chartered Institute of Management Accountants).

Cooper, R. (1990), '5 steps to ABC system design', *Accountancy* (November) 78–81.

Cooper, R. and Kaplan, R. S. (1987), 'How cost accounting systematically distorts product costs', in W. J. Bruns and R. S. Kaplan (1987), *Accounting and Management: Field study perspectives* (Harvard Business School).

Develin (1990) *Activity-based Cost Management* (Develin & Partners, Management Consultants, 211 Piccadilly, London W1V 9LE).

Doyle, D. (1994), *Cost Control: A strategic guide*, Financial Skills Series (Kogan Page).

Drury, C. (1989), 'Activity-based costing', *Management Accounting* (CIMA) (September), 60–3, 66.

Geiger, D. and Leonard, H. (1991a), 'The Bureau of Engraving and Printing: determining the true cost of money (A)', Case No. 9–191–094 (Harvard Business School).

Geiger, D. and Leonard, H. (1991b), 'The Bureau of Engraving and Printing: determining the true cost of money (B)' Case No. 9–191–095 (Harvard Business School).

Innes, J. and Mitchell, F. (1991), 'ABC: a survey of CIMA members', *Management Accounting* (CIMA) (October), 28–30.

Keys, D. E. (1994), 'Tracing costs in the three stages of activity-based management', *Journal of Cost Management*, 30–7, Winter.

King, M., Lapsley, I., Mitchell, F. and Moyes, J. (1994), 'Costing needs and practices in a changing environment: the potential for ABC in the NHS', *Financial Accountability & Management*, **10** (2) (May), 142–60.

Kingcott, T. (1991), 'Opportunity-based accounting: better than ABC?', *Management Accounting* (CIMA) (October), 36–7, 48.

Mitchell, F. (1994), 'A commentary on the applications of activity-based costing', *Management Accounting Research* vol. 5, 261–77.

Piper, J. A. and Walley, P. (1990), 'Testing ABC logic', *Management Accounting* (September), 37–42.

Piper, J. A. and Walley, P. (1991), 'ABC relevance not found', *Management Accounting* (March), 42, 44, 54.

Pogue, G. (1990), 'Case study in strategic management accounting', *Management Accounting* (CIMA) (May), 64–5, 66.

Shank, J. K. and Govindarajan, V. (1993), *Strategic Cost Management: The new tool for competitive advantage* (The Free Press).

Turney, P. B. B. (1992), *Common Cents: The ABC performance breakthrough* (Cost Technology).

Wilson, R. M. S. and Chua, W. F. (1993), *Managerial Accounting: Method and meaning*, 2nd edn (Chapman & Hall).

CHAPTER EIGHT

Job, batch and process costing

CHAPTER OBJECTIVES

After reading this chapter you should be able to:

- describe basic product costing systems
- define what is meant by a job and job costing
- understand examples of job costing situations
- carry out job costing bookkeeping entries
- define what is meant by a batch and batch costing
- define what is meant by a process contract and process contract costing
- understand the accounting requirements of process costing

Introduction

The basic aim of this chapter is to introduce to the reader some of the practical applications of the work of the cost accountant. To an extent, the value of the work of this chapter is questionable for some organisations in that they are now working with more sophisticated models. However, one of the aims of this book is to encourage the reader to look at his or her accounting environment and question the role of management accounting in it. Here we encourage the reader to take both simple and complex business and commercial situations and apply cost and management accounting principles to them, and we start by looking at examples of where job costing is applicable in simple situations. We then move on to examples of the application of process costing in more complex situations. Remember, we have discussed at length in Chapters 6 and 7 the criticism that management accountants have received around the world for their lack of knowledge of, or attention to, jobbing, batch and processing systems and procedures in the organisations in which they work. This chapter helps the reader to overcome such deficiencies by encouraging him or her to consider the nature and meaning of the work of his or her organisation.

In between job costing and process costing is batch costing. Batch costing can apply in both simple and complex situations, and in the material that follows we discuss aspects of these elements. One aspect that is worthy of prime consideration relates to losses and gains in processing situations. The reason for examining losses and gains in processing situations is that it provides an opportunity to investigate what should happen when a gain or a loss is known to occur in a process. We discuss in full how such gains and losses are dealt with as they arise, and the implications of gains and losses that are not anticipated. This chapter does not, however, cover the bookkeeping aspects of job, batch or process costing, except very briefly in the introductory parts of the discussion on process costing.

Basic product costing systems

CIMA (1991) gives a diagram that outlines the elements of a product costing system, in which a product costing system is broken down into four elements:

1. overall control system;
2. basic product costing system;
3. treatment of fixed production overhead; and
4. method of cost control. (CIMA 1991: 29, Figure 3.1)

In this chapter we are concerned with the second of these four elements, the basic product costing system, and we have in the first part of Figure 8.1 the part of CIMA's figure 3.1 that relates to this element. Specific order costing is defined as: 'The basic cost accounting method applicable where work consists of separate contracts, jobs or batches' (CIMA 1991).

Job costing

We can start our discussion of the basic product costing systems with a discussion of job costing. A **job** is defined as: 'A customer order or task of relatively short duration' (ibid.); and **job costing** as: 'A form of specific order costing; the attribution of cost to jobs' (ibid.).

With job costing, we are dealing with one-off situations, with organisations that carry out functions and services on a one-at-a-time basis. Good examples of job costing situations include jobbing builders, who will provide a householder, or a shop owner, or a factory owner with a service that they provide for no one else. The jobbing builder will build an extension, or renovate some property to a design that will probably not be copied anywhere else at any time: in other words, it is a one-off job. Even though many jobbing enterprises are small scale, we are not suggesting that all jobbing enterprises are undertaken on a small scale. An engineering shop may be working on a job for a customer that takes several months and many man and machine hours to complete. A batch of a good or service provided by an organisation for a customer may consist of a batch of several hundred items, each selling for hundreds if not thousands of pounds.

For specific orders
• Job costing
• Contract costing
• Batch costing
For continuous operations
• Process costing

FIGURE 8.1 *Basic product costing system (Source: Adapted from CIMA (1991), figure 3.1)*

Examples of job costing situations

Examples of job costing situations that are relatively easy to describe follow. Studying such situations will give us a much greater insight into the work and environment of a jobbing organisation.

CAMEO

Making a sheet steel trailer for carrying a motor cycle

Imagine you are a motor cycle enthusiast and you need to transport your new, large motor cycle to rallies. You need a trailer that can be attached to the back of your car or van. You approach Friendly Freddie, jobbing sheet metal worker for help. The process you and Freddie go through is detailed below:

1. Negotiate the order, agree a specification for the trailer.
2. Draw up and agree the plans.
3. Materials required and acquired:
   - sheet steel for the overall box;
   - steel strips for reinforcing strips and chassis;
   - steel rods for axle;
   - welding rods;
   - wood for floor boards;
   - plastic edging strips;
   - wheels;
   - paint: priming, undercoat, and finish;
   - sundry screws, rivets, etc.

(Assume for simplicity that the electrical work and the attachment device (for attaching the trailer to the other vehicle) are added by another contractor.)

4. Carry out the job:
   - transfer plan onto sheet steel;
   - cut out sheet steel;
   - shape and weld sheet steel into a box shape measure, cut and fix reinforcing strips and chassis;
   - measure cut and fix axle;

- fix wheels;
- fit and secure floor boards;
- smooth over all welds, rivets and so on;
- apply paint;
- add edging strips.

This describes the way that Friendly Freddie negotiates for, plans for, and carries out the making of a motor cycle trailer. It is a one-off job. There is a strong possibility that Freddie will never make such a trailer again; or if he does, it will not be the same as the one we have described here. Another trailer may be similar, but not the same.

Table 8.1 shows the translation of the trailer-making process into an accounting format by identifying each operation with the cost accumulation aspects of that operation. For the sake of a little simplicity, we have not mentioned the overheads that are inevitably being incurred during this process. We know, of course, that overheads are being incurred at all stages of the process, and can be assumed to be found on every line in the above table.

TABLE 8.1 *Translation of the manufacturing process into an accounting format*

Operation	Cost accumulation
Draw up plans	Paper, pens, labour
Order materials	Labour, clerical
Buy materials	Transport, labour
Transfer plans	Materials, labour
Cut, shape and weld sheet steel	Materials, labour, equipment
Cut, shape and weld steel strips and rods	Materials, labour, equipment
Fix wheels	Materials, labour, equipment
Fix and secure floorboards	Materials, labour, equipment
Smoothing, etc.	Labour, equipment
Paint	Materials, labour
Apply edging strips	Materials, labour

Whilst we have not been especially specific in this cost accumulation diagram, we do get an idea of the way that every operation has a cost implication; and that the accountant is concerned to make sure that every operation be identified and accounted for. Since job costing is concerned with a one-off situation, the accounting aspects of it tend to be uncomplicated.

CAMEO

Providing a monthly accounting computerised service

The Business Service Bureau (BSB) provides a variety of services for the business community. The service that we are interested in is the one whereby BSB prepares final accounts, payroll, and management accounting information for organisations.

This is a standard service, therefore little negotiation will take place. All negotiations will have taken place at the time the service agreement was first entered in to, so this aspect of a contract is not a problem. The procedure is as follows:

- take delivery of documents after month end: invoices, vouchers, bank paying in slips, wages and salary details (hours, bonuses, etc.).
- Classify, sort and document as per instructions.
- Enter all data onto computer input sheets.
- Input data via input sheet into computer.
- Enter month-end adjustments, for example depreciation, accruals and so on.
- Generate hard copy of final accounts, payroll, coin analysis, and custom-designed management accounting reports.

Again, we can translate this process into an accounting format by identifying each operation with the cost accumulation aspects of that operation (see Table 8.2). The point relating to overheads made for Table 8.1 applies to Table 8.2. We have not forgotten about overheads, and they can be assumed to attach to every line.

Operation	Cost accumulation
Classify and sort	Labour
Input data onto input sheets	Materials, labour
Input data into computer	Labour, equipment
Process data	Equipment
Output hard copy	Materials, equipment
Parcel and deliver hard copy	Materials, labour, equipment

To illustrate that we already know enough to provide Friendly Freddie and BSB with a basic job costing service ourselves, we can work through the following example of a jobbing builder, Blantyre Ltd, and prepare the job cost cards for three different jobs that the builder is and has been working on. With Blantyre Ltd, we are not required to work through the cost accumulation process, as we have just done with Freddie and BSB, but we are given sufficient details to complete the relevant documentation.

WORKED EXAMPLE 8.1

Blantyre Ltd is a jobbing builder, specialising in building, extending and renovating houses built for the executive market. As at 1 February 1993, job cost cards were itemised as follows:

Job	Materials	Labour	Overheads	Total
	£	£	£	£
a12b	18,000	15,000	7,000	40,000
a13b	15,000	15,000	5,000	35,000
a14b	8,000	10,000	2,000	20,000
Total				95,000

→

In February, the following took place:

1. Materials requisitioned by site supervisors and foremen:

		£
job	a12b	2,500
	a13b	6,200
	a14b	3,000
Total		11,700

2. Actual labour costs incurred during the month:

	Bricklayers	Carpenters	Plumbers	Total
	£	£	£	£
job a12b	500	500	2,000	3,000
a13b	3,000	2,000	2,500	7,500
a14b	5,000	1,000	650	6,650
Total				17,150

3. Other overhead costs were, for February.

	Bricklayers	Carpenters	Plumbers	Total
	£	£	£	£
Supervision	1,000	1,000	750	2,750
Payroll costs (overtime etc.)	400	600	500	1,500
Depreciation	300	1,200	500	2,000
Miscellaneous	100	150	250	500
Total				£6,750

4. Overheads are absorbed on the basis of direct labour costs and the rates applied during February were:

Bricklayers	120%
Carpenters	150%
Plumbers	175%

5. Jobs a12b and a13b were completed in the month

Required

Set up and complete individual cost cards for job a12b, starting with the balances brought down as at 1 February.

Solution to Worked example 8.1

The only workings that are needed are for the overhead absorption calculations:

we were given the direct labour cost rates for each of the bricklayers, carpenters and plumbers, and we have determined the direct labour costs in the cost card itself. The workings are:

Bricklayers	120% × £500 = £600
Carpenters	150% × 500 = 750
Plumbers	175% × 2,000 = 3,500

Cost Card: Job a12b

Description:———————————

Date started: xx/xx/xx

Date completed: 28/02/93 Location: ___________

	Materials £	Labour £	Overheads £	Total £
Balances b/d	18,000	15,000	7,000	40,000
Incurred in February				
Requisitioned	2,500			2,500
Bricklayers		500	600	1,100
Carpenters		500	750	1,250
Plumbers		2,000	3,500	5,500
Total	20,500	18,000	11,850	50,350

We have been able to work through the previous worked example without difficulty because we have merely been applying what we have already learned from previous chapters. We can therefore conclude at this stage that job costing does not present any insurmountable barriers. Providing we know the overall structure of the job we are costing, we can put together a job cost card, as we have just done.

Batch costing

Batch costing, as the following definitions clearly show, is only a small variation of job costing. A **batch** is: 'A group of similar articles which maintains its identity throughout one or more stages of production and is treated as a cost unit' (CIMA 1991); and **batch costing** is 'A form of specific order costing; the attribution of costs to batches' (ibid).

What we are dealing with when we are considering a batch is a group of items that are closely related, and are being made for a single customer, or are being made all at the same time. The key point for our purposes is that the group of items maintains its identity as a batch: serial numbers, product numbers, production numbers, all identify the goods as a batch. We can easily imagine a batch costing situation if we imagine that Friendly Freddie wins a contract to make, say, a batch of ten motor cycle trailers, all of the same design and specification. Freddie could easily set up and operate a situation whereby the ten trailers are all made and accounted for as a batch of ten units. Additionally, we can imagine a situation in any organisation that carries out jobs, such as Friendly Freddie and BSB, whereby several of the same units are made several times over. Such repetition of units will, we can assume for the purposes of this discussion, constitute a batch. The accumulation and recording of costs under batch costing is very similar to the techniques used with job costing and we need not discuss it separately here. Attempt the relevant questions at the end of this chapter for practice with batch costing questions.

WORKED EXAMPLE 8.2

Linda Shaw uses a batch costing system for her drilling and boring business. She uses a cost plus system of price setting and sets a mark up of 25% on sales values. Administration costs are absorbed at the rate of 10% of selling price, whereas factory overheads are absorbed at the rate of £12 per direct labour hour for Department C and £9 per direct labour hour for Department L.

Batch C-A.RL consists of 1,000 shafts to be drilled and bored, and the following costs have been incurred on it:

Dept C	500 direct labour hours at £10 per hour
Dept L	750 direct labour hours at £8 per hour

Direct materials costing £6,475 have also been used on batch C-A.RL.

Required

In drawing up a batch cost card show

1. the total cost and total cost per unit; and
2. the selling price and selling price per unit

Solution to Worked example 8.2

Linda Shaw's batch cost card problem should help to confirm that, having mastered job costing situations, there is not a great deal of effort required to complete a batch cost card. The calculations for this batch cost card come under two headings: direct labour hour calculations; and algebraic calculations.

Direct labour hour calculations

There are two sets of calculations here:

1. The direct labour costs are derived from the number of direct labour hours (dlh) worked and the rate of pay per hour. They are:

   Department C = 500 dlh × £10 = £5,000
   Department L = 750 dlh × £8 = £6,000

2. The factory overheads are absorbed on the basis of a direct labour hour rate:

   Department C = 500 dlh × £12 = £6,000
   Department L = 750 dlh × £9 = £6,750

Algebraic calculations

The 'algebraic calculations' concern the derivation of the administration costs and the mark-up (profit) figures. These calculations are algebraic because, for the administration costs, we are told that these costs amount to 10% of the selling price, but we do not know the selling price until we have worked out the administration costs (and the mark-up) – a seemingly insoluble problem! We can set out the solution to this problem as follows:

	£	%
Total factory costs	30,225	65
Administration costs	?	10
Total costs	?	75
Mark-up (profit)	?	25
Selling price	46,500	100

This layout tells us that since administration costs are 10% of the selling price, and the mark-up is 25% of the selling price, the selling price can be set at 100% and therefore the total factory costs must be

65% = (100% – (25% + 10%)).

Knowing these relationships allows us to find the unknowns:

Administration costs:

= total factory costs ÷ 65 × 10
= £30,225 ÷ 65 × 10
= £4,650

Mark-up
= total factory costs ÷ 65 × 25
= £30,225 ÷ 65 × 25
= £11,625

Once we have found that the administration costs are £4,650, we could then add that to the total factory costs to derive the total costs of £30,225 + £4,650 = £34,875. Once we have found the total costs, we can find the mark-up by means of the following calculation:

Mark-up:

= total costs ÷ 75 × 25
= £34,875 ÷ 75 × 25
= £11,625

Batch Cost Card
C-A.RL: 1,000 shafts, drilled and bored
Date started: xx/xx/xx
Date completed: xx/xx/xx

	Total	Per unit
Materials		6,475
Labour:		
Department C	5,000	
Department L	6,000	11,000
Factory overheads:		
Department C	6,000	
Department I	6,750	12,750
Total factory costs		30,225
Administration costs		4,650
Total costs		34,875
Mark-up (profit)		11,625
Selling price		46,500

Process costing

The nature of processing industries

Definitions are a good indication of where to go and what to look for. Earlier in this chapter we looked at part of Figure 3.1 from CIMA (1991). If we now look at the second part of our Figure 8.1, we can expand that diagram and see where process costing lies.

Process costing is part of the basic product costing systems scheme, according to CIMA, who define process costing, under the heading of continuous operation/process costing, as:

'The costing method applicable where goods or services result from a sequence of continuous or repetitive operations or processes. Costs are averaged over the units produced during the period' (CIMA 1991). This definition can suggest that the subject content of job costing etc., could be classified as process costing since many jobs could be the subject of repetitive processes or operations. By process costing, we mean the situation such as the processing of chemicals, the manufacture of textiles, cardboard, and cars, and the canning of fruit and vegetables. We are concerned with process costing to look at operations and systems whereby a product or service moves from one stage of a process to another until a product is completed. An example will help clarify the issue.

CAMEO

Manufacture of cardboard

Cardboard is an apparently simple, everyday product; and yet it is complicated to make – complicated in the sense that the number of processes that the product has to go through are diverse.

The basic processes required to make cardboard are:

Process 1 Wood chips, pulp or recycled materials are mixed with water and turned into a slurry

Process 2 The slurry is transferred by pipes to forming machines where the cardboard is built up layer by layer. A lot of the moisture is pressed out of the cardboard during this process.

Process 3 In some cases, specialised coatings are put onto the cardboard (this process is optional). Look at a cardboard match box: it will probably have grey cardboard with a white or yellow layer as the top (coating) layer.

Process 4 The cardboard is heat dried, to drive out most of the remaining moisture.

Process 5 The finished cardboard is coiled onto beams ready for sale or cutting; each beam will contain several tonnes of cardboard. These rolls will all tend to be the same standard width as each other, the width of the roll being determined by the width of the machine.

Process 6 As the cardboard is being made, it automatically comes out with a rough, or deckle, edge. Customers rarely want a deckle edge. The rolls are sent through trimming machines to trim the long edge of the cardboard. The off-cut cardboard produced as a result of this trimming exercise can be put back through the process from the slurry-making stage.

Unless process 7 is required, these rolls may now be ready for despatch. However, if a customer requires cardboard sheets or smaller width rolls, a further stage in the process is required:

Process 7 The large roll of cardboard on a beam is uncoiled and fed through a cutting machine. In this machine, sheets of cardboard can be prepared to the customer's specifications. The sheets are then wrapped, as necessary, ready for despatch.

Process 1: slurry making
- materials
- labour
- overheads

Process 2: forming
- labour
- overheads

Process 3: coating
- materials
- labour
- overheads

Process 4: drying
- labour
- overheads

Process 5: take off
- labour
- overheads

Process 6: trimming
- labour
- overheads

Process 7: cutting
- labour
- overheads

FIGURE 8.2 *Cost accumulation in the cardboard manufacturing process*

Cost accumulation

For the simplest types of cardboard, and as far as cost accumulation is concerned, the majority of raw materials are put into process at the slurry-making process. If a cardboard has to be coated, as per Process 3, further materials will be added there. Labour and overhead costs are being incurred all of the time, however.

With process costing, we need to accumulate costs process by process, or stage by stage. In the case of the manufacture of cardboard, we can simplify cost accumulation as in Figure 8.2. (We can assume that the cardboard we are costing is a coated cardboard).

For every process of cardboard manufacturing, detailed records have to be kept relating to materials, labour and overheads; they cannot just be accumulated at the time the product is completed. This means that all employees have to be aware of their role in the cost accumulation process. All information must be collected carefully and passed on as soon as it is possible to do so. Although the machinery and technology required for cardboard manufacture is very expensive, the overall process is relatively simple to comprehend. Contrast that now with the manufacture of motor vehicles. An average motor car is made up of in excess of 20,000 different parts, ranging from wheels and tyres, to windscreens and electronic components. Motor car assembly is a long, involved, technical procedure that must be very carefully divided into processes. Consequently, the costing system has to be equally sophisticated.

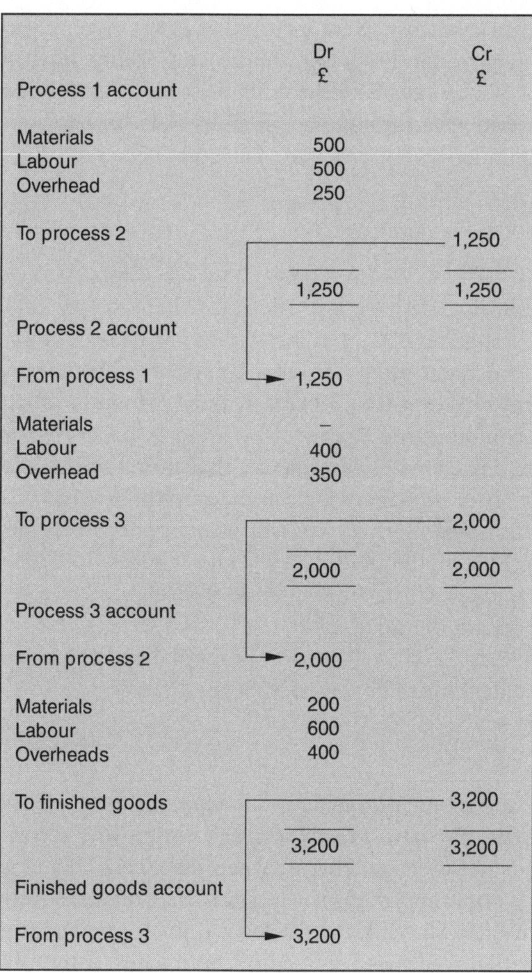

	Dr £	Cr £
Process 1 account		
Materials	500	
Labour	500	
Overhead	250	
To process 2		1,250
	1,250	1,250
Process 2 account		
From process 1	1,250	
Materials	–	
Labour	400	
Overhead	350	
To process 3		2,000
	2,000	2,000
Process 3 account		
From process 2	2,000	
Materials	200	
Labour	600	
Overheads	400	
To finished goods		3,200
	3,200	3,200
Finished goods account		
From process 3	3,200	

FIGURE 8.3 *Simplified ledger accounts*

Process cost accounts

Using assumed data and a vertical layout, we can see the overall make-up of process cost accounts for a three process operation or product. The accounts that are shown in Figure 8.3 are really full and proper ledger accounts, although their presentation has been greatly simplified here for demonstration purposes.

It should be relatively simple to assess what is happening through the three processes, as far as materials, labour and overheads are concerned. Additionally, we can see that when the end of Process 1 has been reached, the products are transferred to Process 2, then onto Process 3, and at the end of Process 3 they are considered complete and are transferred to finished goods stocks.

Similarly, we can see that labour and overhead costs were incurred at every stage in the making of the goods, but materials were incurred in Process 1 and Process 3 only, further materials not being required in Process 2. We can evaluate the costs per unit at each stage in the production process when we are told that the number of units that have passed through the three processes in the period under review is 1,000. The costs per unit are:

Process 1: £1,250 ÷ 1,000 units = £1.250 per unit
Process 2: £2,000 ÷ 1,000 units = £2.000 per unit
Process 3: £3,200 ÷ 1,000 units = £3.200 per unit

What we have considered so far is simplistic. We have just calculated the costs per unit on the basis that 1,000 units came out of Processes 1, 2, and 3 – without any losses at all. In most circumstances, what goes into a process is often not what comes out. This means that if, say, 1,000 units worth of resources were put into Process 1, only 950 units worth of output may have emerged. The same could be true of Processes 2 and 3, or any other process for that matter. It is also possible, in certain circumstances, that more units come out at the end of a process than could have been anticipated, given the amount of resources that went into the process; this can be true when moisture content is an important factor. If the water content of one batch of concrete should be, say, 10% and it turns out to be 12%, then the final weight of the batch of concrete will be different from the weight expected – unless the masses and densities of all inputs are the same, of course!

The consideration of production losses leads us on to discussion of normal and abnormal losses and gains in production. Again, the definitions of these terms will help us.

Normal loss

A normal loss is one which is unavoidable and is uncontrollable and is a natural consequence of the production or service providing process. We have already seen an example of a normal loss: when the cardboard is trimmed of its deckle edge: that is, when the rough edging is trimmed to make it a neat edge. The key point about normal losses is that they are fully expected and probably quantifiable in advance. So, with the cardboard, if we know that a strip two centimetres wide is the amount that is always trimmed off both sides of the roll of finished cardboard, we can anticipate the amount and value of the trimmings. The following example helps us to understand the implications of normal losses:

WORKED EXAMPLE 8.3

1,000 units of materials worth £10,000 were put into a process in March. Additionally, labour costs of £20,000, and overheads costing £15,000 were incurred. Outputs from the process amounted to 900 units. The normal yield is 90% of the inputs of materials, and the loss of materials in process is treated as waste.

Required

Calculate the average cost per unit for units reaching the end of this process.

Solution to Worked example 8.3

The normal loss is shown as an output in the process account. It amounts to a weight of 100 units, based on the inputs of 1,000 units and the normal yield of 90% of materials input.

The cost per unit, on which all valuations are based, is calculated by using the following formula:

Cost per unit:

$$= \frac{\text{normal costs}}{\text{normal output}}$$

$$= \frac{£10{,}000 + 20{,}000 + 15{,}000}{900 \text{ units}}$$

$$= £50 \text{ per unit}$$

All good units of output are valued at this rate now.

What is happening here is that the normal loss is being 'discounted' by being deleted from the good output. This means that the total costs of output are applied only to the normal good units: 90% of the raw material inputs. Normal loss has no value; it is expected to be lost and may play no further part in the costing process. The materials, labour and overhead costs expended on the normal loss are, therefore, being written off (or discounted as we said above).

Normal losses with a scrap value

So far we have assumed that normal losses are considered to be waste: that is, they have no scrap value. We must consider the case now where the losses do have a scrap value. When losses have a scrap value, the formula for determining the average normal cost per unit needs to be modified as follows:

Cost per unit:

$$= \frac{\text{normal costs} - \text{scrap value of normal loss}}{\text{normal output}}$$

The effect of the change is that the scrap value of the losses is used to offset the normal production values of the inputs into production.

WORKED EXAMPLE 8.4

1,000 units of a material worth £1,000 were put into a process in March. Additionally, labour costs of £2,000, and overheads costing £1,700 were incurred. Outputs from the process amounted to 900 units. The normal yield is 90% of the inputs of materials. The loss of materials in process is sold for £2 per unit.

Required

Calculate the average cost per unit for units reaching the end of this process.

Solution to Worked example 8.4

The normal loss amounts to 100 units. We know this because we are told that the normal yield is 900 units (90% of the inputs of materials), and the materials weigh 1,000 units. The scrap value of the normal loss is 100 units at £2 per unit: a total of £200 to take credit for.

Applying the formula we have just discussed allows us to calculate the cost per unit of good output:

Cost per unit

$$= \frac{(\text{£}1{,}000 + 2{,}000 + 1{,}700) - \text{£}200}{900 \text{ units}}$$

$$= \frac{\text{£}4{,}500}{900 \text{ units}}$$

$$= \text{£}5 \text{ per unit}$$

Thus the value of the output transferred to the next process must be the yield of 900 units multiplied by the £5 per unit we have just calculated, that is, £4,500.

It should be noted that in many cases, a process can lead to the gaining of units. As with losses, gains can be either normal or abnormal. As we will see, gains are dealt with in the same manner as are losses, and we will consider examples of them as our discussion progresses. (Throughout the following examples, in which we are introducing abnormal losses and gains, only one process will be demonstrated: this is purely for demonstration purposes.)

Abnormal losses

Unfortunately, it will rarely be the case that only normal losses will be incurred. For a variety of reasons, organisations will incur losses in excess of those expected. Thus they will be suffering abnormal losses. This section considers how we should be dealing with abnormal losses in process accounts. By definition an abnormal loss arises by chance or by poor management of resources, and is both controllable and unexpected.

Cardboard again gives us an example of an abnormal loss. On many occasions throughout a normal working week, the cardboard may break as it is passing through the machine. The reason for the break can range from operator error to poor raw materials. Once the cardboard has broken, it usually takes a while to feed it back into the machine. The lost output is an example of an abnormal loss, since it is unexpected and largely controllable. There may be elements of predictability about breakages, and in such cases, there may be both normal and abnormal aspects to such breakages.

The first point to note about abnormal losses is that they must be valued at their full accounting value. Unlike normal losses which have their value absorbed into the unit cost of the good units, the abnormal losses are shown at their true cost to the organisation. The main reason for this is so that the manager of the process can appreciate the full impact of his or her inefficiencies: that is, the greater the value of such losses, the greater his or her incentive to put matters right.

WORKED EXAMPLE 8.5

The inputs put into a process in February were: 2,000 units of materials, valued at £4,000; and labour and overheads costing £8,000 and £6,000 respectively. Outputs from the process amounted to 1,700 units. The normal loss is 10% of the inputs of materials. The loss of materials in process is not sold.

Required

Calculate the average cost per unit for units reaching the end of this process.

Solution to Worked example 8.5

The normal output or normal yield is 90% of 2,000 units, which is 1,800 units, while the abnormal loss amounts to the normal yield less the actual yield:

1,800 units − 1,700 units = 100 units

As far as costs per unit are concerned, since the losses have no scrap value, we are merely dividing normal costs by normal outputs:

Cost per unit

$$= \frac{\text{£}4{,}000 + 8{,}000 + 6{,}000}{1{,}800 \text{ units}}$$

$$= \frac{\text{£}18{,}000}{1{,}800 \text{ units}}$$

= £10 per unit

The normal output or yield of 1,800 units used in the cost per unit calculation is equal to the total of the abnormal loss and the transfer to the following process. This is consistent with the idea of valuing the abnormal loss at its full economic value. There is no other way of performing this calculation.

Abnormal gains

On a good day, not only will there be no abnormal loss, but there might actually be a situation where the yield is higher than that normally expected. In such a situation, we are dealing with an abnormal gain. As we will see, the accounting for an abnormal gain may cause us a few problems to start with because we always have to account for the normal loss in full. Working through the following example will clarify this point, however. As with the abnormal loss, we will keep the work as simple as possible by assuming that there is no scrap value for the losses.

WORKED EXAMPLE 8.6

The inputs put into a process in March were as follows:

	Units	£
Materials	1,000	2,000
Labour		4,000
Overheads		3,000

Outputs from the process amounted to 920 units. The normal loss is 10% of the inputs of materials. The loss of materials in process is not sold.

Required

Calculate the average cost per unit for units reaching the end of this process.

Solution to Worked example 8.6

The normal loss is 10% of the inputs of 1,000 units which is 100 units. The actual yield is greater than the normal or expected yield of total inputs less normal loss:

920 units − 900 units = 20 units

This excess output represents an abnormal gain.

The cost per unit is, as has been the case so far, based on normal costs and inputs. This gives us the same view of the value of abnormal gains as we had on abnormal losses.

Abnormal gains are valued at their full economic value, at least for management control purposes:

Cost per unit

$$= \frac{£2{,}000 + 4{,}000 + 3{,}000}{900 \text{ units}}$$

$$= \frac{£9{,}000}{900 \text{ units}}$$

$$= £10 \text{ per unit}$$

Abnormal gains and scrap values

We should consider the case now where we not only have an abnormal gain, but we can also sell the losses. The following worked example illustrates the points.

WORKED EXAMPLE 8.7

The inputs put into a process in March were as follows: materials 1,000 units at £1,000; labour at £2,000; and overheads at £1,700. Outputs from the process amounted to 930 units. The normal loss is 10% of the inputs of materials. The loss of materials in process is sold for £2 per unit.

Required

Calculate the average cost per unit for units reaching the end of this process.

Solution to Worked example 8.7

The normal loss is 10% of the inputs of 1,000 units, so it is 100 units. Actual output of 930 units is 30 units greater than the normal output of 900 units, therefore the abnormal gain must be 30 units. The scrap value of the normal loss is 100 units at £2 per unit which is £200.

The cost per unit of normal output is:

$$= \frac{(£1{,}000 + 2{,}000 + 1{,}700) - £200}{900 \text{ units}}$$

$$= \frac{£4{,}500}{900 \text{ units}}$$

$$= £5 \text{ per unit}$$

The normal loss takes full credit for all of the units that were expected to be lost, even though only 70 units of the 100 units expected to be lost actually were lost. To offset this apparent discrepancy, we have the abnormal gain of 30 units valued at its full economic value. Contained within the value of the abnormal gain is the value of the normal loss that was not lost.

Work in progress

Evaluating work in progress in process costing situations is often not just a matter of someone just going along a cardboard-making machine, or looking along a car assembly line and counting up how many items of 'X' there are in progress and how many units of 'Y' there are in progress, and then declaring he has the work-in-progress value for the period end. There are usually complications.

Take the making of cars as an example. Let us assume that at the end of an accounting period, the assembly line for vehicles will be stopped and there will be cars at a whole variety of stages of output. Some will have just started being made, others will have a chassis, four wheels and the body; and others will have chassis, wheels, body, seats, and engine: and so it goes on. At any one time, all units in progress will be at different stages of completion. As far as the accountant is concerned, the stage of completion that a car has reached is vital knowledge because at each stage each vehicle will contain different levels of materials, labour, and overhead inputs. The car with only the chassis, the wheels and the body clearly contains fewer parts and materials than the car that consists of the chassis, wheels, body, seats and engine. The first of these two cars in progress will have been worked on to a lesser extent than the second car, and will therefore contain a lesser charge for materials, labour and overheads.

Given this sort of situation in a process industry, we need a method that will allow us to deal with items in progress that are not at the same stage of completion as each other. The device that has been developed to deal with this situation is known as equivalent units. We should be aware, however, that many processing organisations never have any work in progress, and for them the concept of equivalent units is irrelevant. Cardboard manufacturers who simply make one standard size of board and do nothing with it once it comes off the machine will have no work in progress. Cardboard cannot really be partly finished. Dairies that simply bottle milk will have no work in progress since the milk being processed needs to be fresh and will not be stored in process. Consequently, the next section is concerned with organisations such as motor vehicle manufacturers that can and do have work that is partly finished at the end of an accounting period.

Equivalent units

Equivalent units are defined as: 'Notional whole units representing uncompleted work. Used to apportion costs between work in process and completed output' (CIMA 1991). When

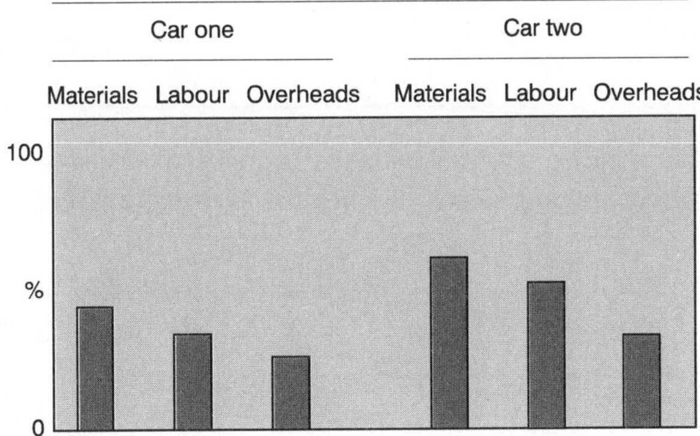

FIGURE 8.4 *Format for equivalent whole units*

we represent our work in progress as equivalent whole units, we are dealing with notional whole units of output. As CIMA says, we are doing this for cost accounting purposes, so that we can estimate as accurately as possible the cost of completed output and stocks of work in progress. Figure 8.4 helps us appreciate the full implications of equivalent units. In this figure, we are dealing with the two in-progress cars that we have just been discussing. Reading down the figure, we have an estimate of the amount of each of materials, labour and overheads that each uncompleted car contains.

For the two cars, reading from Figure 8.4, we have car one having 30% of all of the materials it will have put into it, whereas car two has 50% of its material inputs already complete. Car one has 20% of its labour inputs and car two 40% of its labour inputs already complete. The overhead expenditure amounts to 10% complete for car one and 20% for car two. Whilst Figure 8.4 is suggesting that every car will be assessed for its degree of completion as an individual item of work in progress, it is probably true to say that when there are large numbers of items involved, or complex technical situations to cope with, work-in-progress degrees of completion will be designated by areas of the factory, department, or division. This means that the car factory might split the assembly line into ten areas, and within area one, for example, all cars will be assumed to have, say, 10% of materials, 5% of labour and 3% of overheads already spent on them; in area two the proportions could be 15%, 10% and 10% for materials labour and overheads respectively.

If every item of work in progress were dealt with individually, the costs of stock valuation could be prohibitive, since all work in progress would have to be fully assessed individually. Such assessments would take a long time and be very expensive for most medium- to large-size organisations. In terms of equivalent units, car one is worth 30% of a complete car in terms of materials, 20% complete in terms of labour and 10% complete in terms of overheads. We can talk, therefore, in terms of 30% of a car for materials usage and work-in-progress valuation, and so on. We can now work through a more detailed example that will allow us to take the arguments we have just seen and build on them for cost accounting purposes. The following example is concerned with closing work in progress.

WORKED EXAMPLE 8.8

In March, an organisation had spent £9,000 on inputting 1,000 units into a process, together with £5,040 worth of labour and £5,394 worth of overheads. At the end of the period, 900 completed units were recorded as having been finished, and 100 units remained in work in progress closing stock. The work in progress had reached the following stages of completion:

	%
Materials	100
Labour	60
Overheads	30

Required

Calculate the average cost per unit for units reaching the end of this process together with the total costs of all units reaching the end of the process.

Solution to Worked example 8.8

As far as the completed units are concerned, we already know how to deal with them. We need to concentrate on the work in progress. Since materials inputs in the work in progress amount to 100%, we are saying that all of the material that will be put into these products has already gone into them. With labour and overheads, there is a further 40% and 70% to be spent on them, respectively.

We can now prepare a statement of evaluation in which we identify all equivalent units. This enables us to calculate a cost per equivalent unit, and, finally, we can work out a full cost per unit for transfers out, work in progress, and normal and abnormal losses and gains.

Calculation of equivalent units

Materials:	
completed units	900
work in progress 100 units x 100%	100
equivalent units	1,000
Labour:	
completed units	900
work in progress 100 units × 60%	60
equivalent units	960
Overheads:	
completed units	900
work in progress 100 units x 30%	30
equivalent units	930

Costs per equivalent unit

Materials
£9,000 ÷ 1,000 equivalent units (eu)
= £9.00 per eu
Labour
£5,040 ÷ 960 eu
= £5.25 per eu
Overheads
£5,394 ÷ 930 eu
= £5.80 per eu

Value of the work in progress

		£
Materials	100 eu × £ 9.00 per eu =	900
Labour	60 eu × £ 5.25 per eu =	315
Overheads	30 eu × £ 5.80 per eu =	174
Totals	£ 20.05	1,389

Value of transfer of completed goods to subsequent process

The 900 units of goods that have been recorded as having been completed and transferred out of the process are valued at the total cost per eu of £20.05:

900 completed units x £20.05 = £18,045

Opening stocks of work in progress

The previous worked example concerned the situations where there was closing work in progress. The following worked example adds the further consideration of opening work in progress. We need to be aware from now on that since we are dealing with stocks, we need to consider stock valuation methods. In the context of stocks of work in progress in process costing situations, the two methods we will discuss are the first in, first out (FIFO) method and the weighted average method. The FIFO method of valuing the stocks of work in progress assumes that the opening stock of goods brought down from the previous period are to be worked on first and are therefore always assumed to have been completed in the current period (unless, of course, we are dealing with a very lengthy process when units take a long time to move from the start to the end of all necessary processes). The weighted average method assumes that units of output cannot be separated out, and therefore the only way to value stocks is to average the values.

FIFO method of valuation

WORKED EXAMPLE 8.9

In April, the opening work in progress of 100 units had a value of £700, and was completed as follows:

	%
Materials	85
Labour	65
Overheads	50

During April materials, labour and overheads were added as follows: materials 1,000 units, with a value of £7,385; labour with a value of £6,510; and overheads with a value of £5,665. At the end of the period there were 200 units of production still incomplete, and the production manager estimated that the degree of completion of the closing stock of work in progress was:

	%
Materials	70
Labour	50
Overheads	30

The number of units of completed, good units of output was 900.

Required

Calculate the average cost per unit for units reaching the end of this process together with the total costs of all units reaching the end of the process.

Solution to Worked example 8.9

Since the FIFO method assumes that it is possible to split out individual units, and that the opening units of work in progress are to be completed during the period, we need to calculate the equivalent units in three separate stages: opening work in progress; the units started and completed in the period; and the closing work in progress.

Opening work in progress

As we are trying to assess the costs that relate to units completed during the period under review, we only need take account of the work done during the period. The calculation that follows reflects this. For example, the opening stock of work in progress is 85% complete as far as its material inputs are concerned, therefore, only 100% – 85% = 15% further is required to be added for this period. Similarly with labour and overheads. Consequently the equivalent units for the work in progress b/d are:

Materials	100 units × 15% = 15 eu
Labour	100 units × 35% = 35 eu
Overheads	100 units × 50% = 50 eu

Units started and completed in the period

The question tells us that 900 units were completed during the period. We obviously must accept this to be true, but we need to adjust that figure to find how many units were actually both started and completed in the period.

Since 900 units were completed in the period, and since 100 units of opening work in progress are assumed to have been completed in the period, then 800 units must have been both started and completed in the period. These units are 100% complete in all respects.

Closing work in progress

This calculation is familiar, and is similar to the calculation we have completed for the opening work in progress:

Materials	200 units × 70% = 140 eu
Labour	200 units × 50% = 100 eu
Overheads	200 units × 30% = 60 eu

Summary of equivalent units

In order to evaluate the work in progress (WIP) and the production units, we should summarise what we have:

	Equivalent units Materials	Labour	Overheads	Total
Opening WIP	15	35	50	100
Started and completed	800	800	800	800
Closing WIP	140	100	60	200
	955	935	910	1,100

Note that the total column is not the sum of the individual columns. The total column represents the number of units that each aspect of output or stock represents, and are the values found in the process account. The individual column detail represents the equivalent units for stock and valuation purposes. We can extend this table now to allow for the evaluation of the various aspects of output:

Evaluation statement

	Materials	Labour	Overheads	Total
Total costs (£)(1)	7,385	6,510	5,665	19,560
Equivalent units (from previous table) (2)	955	935	910	1,100
Cost per eu (£) (1)/(2) = (3)	7.733	6.963	6.225	20.921

In the case of the cost per eu, the total of £20.92 is now the total of the individual columns, and it these values that we use to evaluate the costs of processing the units worked on during the period. Note that the balance brought down on the work-in-progress account is kept separate, as the FIFO method dictates it must.

Evaluation

	Materials	Labour	Overheads	Total
	£	£	£	£
Opening WIP, to finish	115.995	243.705	311.250	670.95
Started and completed	6,186.400	5,570.400	4,980.000	16,736.80
Closing WIP	1,082.620	696.300	373.500	2,152.42
	7,385.015	6,510.405	5,664.750	19,560.17

This evaluation statement is made up of multiplying each of the equivalent units by the cost per equivalent unit. For example, for materials, the opening WIP to finish is made up of the equivalent units for this category of 15 eu, multiplied by the cost per eu of £7.733, which gives £115.995. All of the other costs in the evaluation statement are derived in this way.

Note that the totals arrived at in the evaluation statement must agree with the total costs given in the first part of the overall evaluation statement. This must be true since all we are doing with the procedure we are carrying out here is allocating and apportioning those selfsame total costs. However, in this demonstration, the rounding errors that have arisen from the calculations have been left in; it is a simple task simply to remove them at any stage.

Units transferred out

The value of the units transferred out of this process is made up of the opening work in progress value brought down, plus the value of the materials, labour and overhead costs added during the period, plus the value of the materials, labour and overheads spent on the units that were started and completed during the period.

	£
Work in progress:	
brought down	700.00
added this period	670.95
Units started and completed this period	16,736.80
	18,107.75

The weighted average method of valuation

The weighted average method of valuation of production costs is based on the fact that, given the nature of the process we are dealing with, we may not split out the various degrees of completion and we cannot be certain that what was in progress at the start of the period actually was completed during the period. We can rework the previous example to illustrate how the weighted average method works. The information given for that exercise needs to be changed a little, to help make it a more realistic weighted average, rather than a FIFO based exercise.

WORKED EXAMPLE 8.10

In April, the opening work in progress of 100 units had a value of £700, and that value was broken down as follows:

	£
Materials	400
Labour	200
Overheads	100

During April materials, labour and overheads were added as follows: materials 1,000 units, with a value of £7,385; labour with a value of £6,510; and overheads with a value of £5,665. At the end of the period there were 200 units of production still incomplete, and the production manager estimated that the degree of completion of the closing stock of work in progress was:

	%
Materials	70
Labour	50
Overheads	30

The number of units of completed, good units of output was 900.

Required

Calculate the average cost per unit for units reaching the end of this process together with the total costs of all units reaching the end of the process.

Solution to Worked example 8.10

Because we will be averaging many of the figures given, there are fewer workings for this method than there were with the FIFO method. We can go straight to the evaluation statement.

Evaluation statement

	Materials	Labour	Overheads	Total
	£	£	£	£
Work in progress b/d	400	200	100	700
Costs for the period	7,385	6,510	5,665	19,560
	7,785	6,710	5,765	20,260

We are not given the equivalent units for the opening stock of the work in progress, but we are given the information for the closing stock of work in progress. The table we should draft, therefore, for the number of units processed is:

	Materials £	Labour £	Overheads £	Total £
Completed units	900	900	900	900
Work in progress c/d	140	100	60	200
Equivalent units	1,040	1,000	960	1,100

Check that you can see where the work in progress costs per eu have come from.

Costs per eu (£)	7.486	6.710	6.005	20.201

Evaluation

	Materials £	Labour £	Overheads £	Total £
Completed units	6,737.40	6,039.00	5,404.50	18,180.90
Work in progress c/d	1,048.04	671.00	360.30	2,079.34
	7,785.44	6,710.00	5,764.80	20,260.24

We need now to look at losses in process and how to deal with them as far as their impact on work in progress is concerned, and also their FIFO and weighted average implications.

Losses in process

In many industries, losses can happen at any point in a process: they can occur at almost the very beginning of a process, and they can happen at the inspection stage at the end of a process. Our task is to carry out the cost accounting procedures that will enable us to identify the true costs per unit, no matter when the units are deemed lost. The following worked example helps to illustrate the points involved.

WORKED EXAMPLE 8.11

In February 5,000 units of Product A were put into process, and the inputs during the period were:

	£
Materials	15,000
Labour	10,000
Overheads	7,500

At the end of the period, 500 units of product were still in process, and their various degrees of completion were:

	%
Materials	75
Labour	50
Overheads	25

An allowance is made for normal losses in process of 10% of the units put into the process. All losses can be sold, and they have a scrap value of £5 per unit. The units scrapped in this period were scrapped at the following degrees of completion:

	%
Materials	80
Labour	70
Overheads	50

A total of 3,800 units were transferred out of the process.

Required

Using the weighted average method of valuation, carry out the relevant calculations for this process for February. Work to three decimal places whenever necessary.

Solution to Worked example 8.11

The first, and most important point to appreciate about this example, is that it specifies that we have to use the weighted average method of evaluation.

Note that rounding errors are left in the solution that follows. Again, these are not serious errors and should not cause any problems. They are left in so that there is no misunderstanding about how the individual parts of the solutions are derived. The most efficient way to work through this exercise is, as in the previous few examples, to work down the statement of evaluation, in which we can identify the relevant costs for the period, the equivalent units, and, from there, the costs per equivalent unit.

Note also that when we worked through the exercises dealing with normal losses and abnormal losses and gains, we deducted the value of any scrap values from the process account without difficulty. Now, however, we have the complication of the split according to the various degrees of completion of the elements of cost. The rule that is adopted to cope with the question of how to deal with scrap values is to deduct the scrap values from the material costs, as is demonstrated below.

Evaluation statement

	Materials	Labour	Overheads	Total
	£	£	£	£
Costs incurred in February	15,000	10,000	7,500	32,500
Scrap value of normal loss	(2,500)	–	–	2,500
	12,500	10,000	7,500	30,000

Prove the following equivalent unit values and make sure you agree with them

	Materials	Labour	Overheads	Total
Completed units	3,800	3,800	3,800	3,800
Normal loss	–	–	–	500
Abnormal loss	160	140	100	200
Work in progress c/d	375	250	125	500
	4,335	4,190	4,025	5,000

Remember that the normal loss units are not valued, as part of the overall cost per equivalent unit. The cost per equivalent unit is based on normal outputs, and the normal loss is excluded from the calculation so that the costs of those units are fairly spread across the normal good units of output. The abnormal units are, of course, included as part of the calculations since they need to be fully evaluated, for management and cost control reasons, as discussed earlier in the chapter.

	£	£	£	£
Costs per eu	2.884	2.387	1.864	7.135

Evaluation

	Materials	Labour	Overheads	Total
	£	£	£	£
Completed units	10,959.20	9,070.60	7,083.20	27,113.00
Normal loss	–	–	–	–

Abnormal loss	461.44	334.18	186.40	982.02
Work in progress c/d	1,081.50	596.75	233.00	1,911.25
	12,502.14	10,001.53	7,502.60	30,006.27

Multiprocess situations

We are now at the stage, having looked in detail at losses and gains in process, and the impact of varying degrees of completion on work in progress, where we can open our discussion by looking at multiprocess organisations. All of the examples that follow concern multiprocess organisations and situations. With multiprocess situations we see units being transferred from process one to process two to process three . . . and with the transfer of goods comes transfers of costs. We should find that the transfers of costs do not present us with any technical problems that we have not already covered in this chapter. Working through an exercise with a multiprocess dimension built in will illustrate all of the points we need to be aware of.

WORKED EXAMPLE 8.12

Nathan Walsh operates a small chemical processing factory on the west cost of Wales. In March, Walsh recorded the details relating to his factory.

At the beginning of March he brought forward from February work in progress valued at £3,000 representing 500 units. The degree of completion of those units of work in progress were estimated to be materials 80%, labour 70%, and overheads 20%.

During March, Walsh transferred in 3,600 units from Process 1 at a value of £15,000, and added materials worth £10,000, labour worth £7,500 and overheads worth £3,500.

At the end of March, Walsh had 400 units started but not yet complete: he estimated that the degree of completion of these units was that 100% of the material inputs, 70% of labour inputs, and 50% of overhead inputs had all been made.

Walsh makes an allowance of 10% of the input from the materials transferred in from the previous process as a normal loss. Of the units lost in production, 250 of the normal loss units are sold, and all of the abnormal loss units are sold. Saleable scrapped units have a scrap value of £4 per unit. All losses are determined at the end of the process, and are therefore fully complete as per materials, labour and overheads.

Transfer of 3,190 units, as complete, was made to Process 3.

Required

Prepare all of the necessary calculations and statements for Walsh's business.

Solution to Worked example 8.12

In reality, company policy would say whether the FIFO or weighted average method of valuation should be used. In exercises such as this one, we have to decide which method to use: depending on the information supplied. In this case, we have been given a detailed breakdown of the opening and closing work in progress in terms of the degrees of completion, so we should use the FIFO method of valuation. Had we been given only the total value, and cost element breakdown of the work in progress, then we would have concluded that Walsh was using the weighted average method of valuation.

We should start our workings by calculating the normal loss, and whether there is an abnormal loss or gain.

Normal and abnormal losses

The normal loss amounts to 10% of the inputs transferred in from the previous process, Process 1. Since the inputs from Process 1 are 3,600 units, the normal loss must be:

10% × 3,600 units = 360 units.

The abnormal loss is 150 units because, given the inputs and outputs from the process, 3,340 units should have been transferred to Process 3, yet only 3,190 units were transferred. The difference of 150 units represents the shortfall, the abnormal loss. The workings for the abnormal loss are:

		Units
From Process 1		3,600
WIP b/d		500
		4,100
less:		
WIP c/d	400	
Normal loss	360	760
Transferable to Process 3		3,340
Transferred to Process 3		3,190
Abnormal loss		150

Completing the evaluation statement now will give the rest of the information needed to complete the process and other accounts that we are required to complete.

Since only 250 units of the normal loss of 360 units are sold, the scrap value of the normal loss is:

250 units × £4 per unit = £1,000

Equivalent units

The equivalent units are the work in progress b/d: that is, the amount of work to complete this period:

Materials 500 units × 20% = 100 eu
Labour 500 units × 30% = 150 eu
Overheads 500 units × 80% = 400 eu

Make sure this calculation is well understood: the reason we are taking account only of the work to complete the opening work in progress is because all of the work to date has already been accounted for. We have already taken account of the 80% of the material input into these units, so we only need to add the costs of the 20% material input that is about to be made. Similarly with labour and overhead costs.

Started and completed

To calculate the units both started and completed, we start with the units put into the process (the 3,600 units transferred in this case) and then subtract those units not yet completed in the period (normal and abnormal losses and the work in progress carried down). If necessary, we would then add any units gained: that is, normal and abnormal gains. The units started and completed are always 100% complete in all respects.

		Units
Transferred from process 1		3,600
less:		
Normal loss	360	
Abnormal loss	150	
Work in progress c/d	400	910
Started and completed		2,690

Abnormal loss

Materials 150 units × 100% = 150 eu
Labour 150 units × 100% = 150 eu
Overheads 150 units × 100% = 150 eu

Work in progress c/d:

Materials 400 units × 100% = 400 eu
Labour 400 units × 70% = 280 eu
Overheads 400 units × 50% = 200 eu

Evaluation statement

Total costs

	Process 1	Materials	Labour	Overheads	Total
	£	£	£	£	£
Costs	15,000	10,000	7,500	3,500	36,000
Normal loss:					
scrap value		(1,000)			(1,000)
	15,000	9,000	7,500	3,500	35,000

In the statement that follows, notice that there is no provision for the opening work in progress to take a value as far as the transfer of materials from Process 1 is concerned. The reason for this is that, in the absence of any information to the contrary, the opening work in progress has already gone through Process 1 and been fully evaluated for that purpose. It must not take further costs from that process.

Equivalent units

	Process 1	Materials	Labour	Overheads	Total
	£	£	£	£	£
Work in progress b/d	–	100	150	400	500
Started and completed	2,690	2,690	2,690	2,690	2,690
Normal loss	–	–	–	–	360
Abnormal loss	150	150	150	150	150
Work in progress c/d	400	400	280	200	400
	3,240	3,340	3,270	3,440	4,100
	£	£	£	£	£
Cost per eu (£)	4.6296	2.6946	2.2934	1.0174	10.6350

Evaluation

Note the point above, under equivalent units, about the opening work in progress being exempt from further Process 1 valuations.

	Process 1	Materials	Labour	Overheads	Total
	£	£	£	£	£
Work in progress b/d	–	269.46	344.01	406.96	1,020.43
Started and completed	12,453.62	7,248.47	6,619.25	2,736.81	28,608.16
Normal loss	–	–	–	–	–
Abnormal loss	694.44	404.19	344.01	152.01	1,595.25
Work in progress c/d	1,851.84	1,077.84	642.15	203.48	3,775.31
	14,999.90	8,999.96	7,949.42	3.499.26	34,999.15

This solution shows the calculations worked to two places of decimals for the evaluation statement. Although this gives us an apparently messy evaluation statement, it gives more realistic values.

Value of the transfer to process 3

In the process account that we are now about to prepare, we need to allow for one more calculation: the value of the units transferred to process 3 is made up of three separate amounts: the amount relating to each of the work in progress brought down; the additional expenditure on the work in progress brought down; and the units started and completed during the period. The relevant amounts are:

	£
Work in progress b/d:	
opening costs	3,000.00
Work in progress b/d:	
additional costs	1,020.43
Started and completed:	
costs incurred	28,608.16
	£32,628.59

To within £0.85, this process account balances. Again, a very small rounding error accounts for the difference.

In many process costing situations, there will arise cases where there will be one process (or a series of processes) and several products. The best example of multiproduct outputs is a petroleum refinery: there are potentially hundreds, if not thousands, of different products that can be made from one raw material input. The purpose of this final part of the chapter, therefore, is to account for all of the potential different products that can arise. Essentially, we are dealing with two separate situations: the situation where by-products arise, and the situation where joint products arise. We will look at each in turn.

By-products

A by-product is: 'Output of some value produced incidentally in manufacturing something else (main product)' (CIMA 1991). In terms of the definition, 'some value' means small value. A by-product is something that is considered an output of a process, but just by the way, it has a resale value. Other outputs from processes are waste and have no scrap or resale value; and yet other outputs are joint products, with relatively large resale values. If we return to our cardboard processing example from earlier in the chapter, we can find examples of by-products. When a large roll of cardboard is cut into strips or sheets, for example, apart from the deckle edge, there may be 'oddments' produced. Oddments are pieces of cardboard that are perfectly good, but they are of an odd size. If a market can be found for the oddments, they have a value and can be classed as by-products; they will not be sold for their full economic value. Depending upon the industry, process, or material, a by-product might arise at any time. In some cases, a by-product may arise only at the end of the final process; in other cases, by-products might arise at the end of every process.

Unfortunately, in theory at least, the methods of accounting for by-products are often considered to be unsatisfactory – they are not particularly scientifically based! Nevertheless, the discussion that follows provides us with reasonable solutions to the problem of finding realistic values to by-product situations.

WORKED EXAMPLE 8.13

5,000 units of Wye were processed to completion at a cost of £50,000. The Wye sells for £25 per unit. In addition to the 5,000 units of Wye, 50 units of Aye were produced which were sold at £5 per unit (a total of £250).

Aye is considered to be a by-product of the process, and in order to sell it, a further £150 has to be spent on it (this expenditure covers such items as special packaging, further processing and so on).

Required

Calculate the gross profit for the period.

Solution to Worked example 8.13

We can present our solution in one of three main ways:

1. We could calculate the net realisable value of the by-product and deduct that from the total costs of production of the main or joint products. We can then determine the gross profit.
2. We could evaluate the total costs, and total revenues and put them together to determine the gross profit.
3. We could treat the by-product as a joint product, and proceed appropriately.

We will be demonstrating the joint product approach shortly: concentrate on the other two methods for now.

Gross profit via the net realisable value

	£	£	£
Sales value of Wye			
(5,000 units × £25/unit)			125,000
less: Net production costs			
Completion costs of Wye		50,000	
less:			
Sales of Aye	250		
Processing Aye costs	(150)	100	49,900
Gross profit			£75,100

Gross profit via the total costs

	£	£
Sales value of: Wye		125,000
Aye		250
		125,250
less: Production costs		
Completion costs of Wye	50,000	
Further processing costs of Aye	150	50,150
Gross profit		75,100

Note that the gross profit is the same whichever of the two approaches is taken.

Joint products

Joint products are: 'Two or more products separated in processing, each having a sufficiently high saleable value to merit recognition as a main product' (CIMA 1991) and a joint cost is: 'The cost of a process which results in more than one main product' (ibid.).

When we dealt with a by-product we dealt with one main product and a minor, almost insignificant, product. With joint products we are dealing with situations where there are two or more equally important products. In the simplest of cases, the joint products arise and are made together, and are finished together. Our mission, then, is to find a cost per product. In this simple case, we use one of the methods we are about to discuss, and apply what we have found to stock valuations, profit calculations and so on. On the other hand, there are cases where joint products are split off at a certain point, and then one or more of them is sent for further processing. From the time of the split-off, the products are recognised as being separately identifiable. In this case, we need to determine not only the joint costs, but also the post-split-off costs as well. Again, we will be looking at that below. We can represent these situations diagrammatically, as in Figure 8.5.

There are a number of ways in which the joint products of an organisation may be valued, and we will be looking at two of those ways:

1. the physical units basis of valuing products; and
2. the sales value basis of valuing products.

The physical units basis

With the physical units basis, the joint costs are apportioned over the joint products in direct proportion to the physical weight or volume of the products. This method has the advantage of simplicity. The method assumes that it is possible to determine the weight or volume of the output, and then by simple arithmetic – such as we saw when we were apportioning overheads between departments – share the costs over the relevant products. Three products,

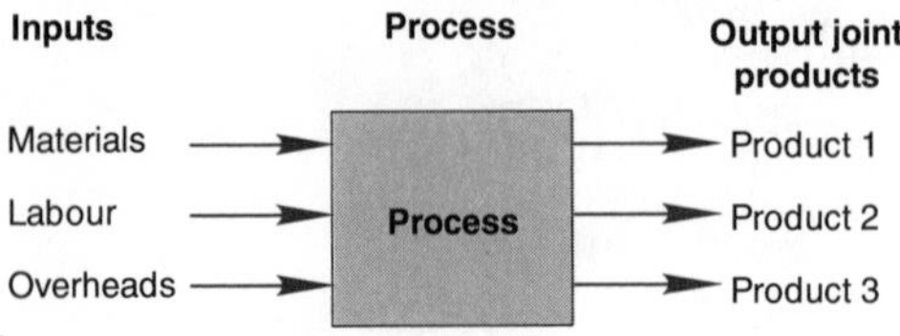

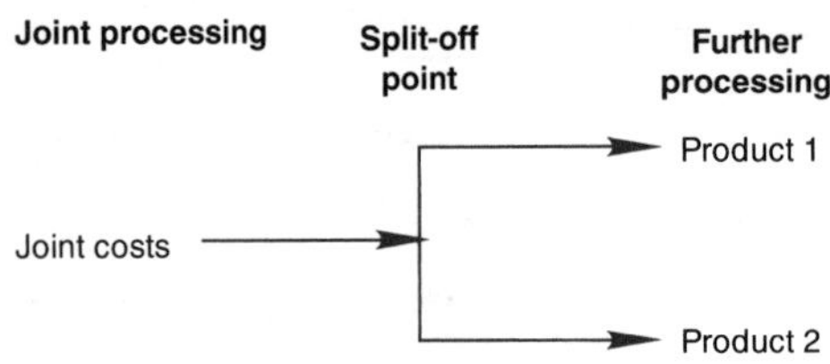

FIGURE 8.5 *Joint product situations*

1, 2, and 3, are produced in a process. Up until the time they are extracted from the process, these products are joint products, and the total costs incurred during processing amounts to £100,000. Output details are as below:

Product 1	30,000 kilogrammes
Product 2	50,000 kilogrammes
Product 3	20,000 kilogrammes

The apportionment of the costs is based on the average cost per unit of output (kilogrammes in this case). The result of this calculation is a constant to be used for all products:

$$\frac{\text{total joint processing costs}}{\text{total output in kilogrammes}}$$

In this case, we have:

$$\frac{\pounds 100{,}000}{100{,}000 \text{ units}} = \pounds 1 \text{ per unit}$$

Applying this constant to the individual outputs gives:

		£
Product 1	30,000 units × £1 per unit =	30,000
Product 2	50,000 units × £1 per unit =	50,000
Product 3	20,000 units × £1 per unit =	20,000
Total		£100,000

Assuming the sales values given in the profit statement below, we can calculate the profit per product.

Profit statement

	Product 1	Product 2	Product 3	Total
	£	£	£	£
Sales value	80,000	95,000	75,000	250,000
less: Apportioned costs	30,000	50,000	20,000	100,000
Profit	50,000	45,000	55,000	150,000

The sales value basis

The physical units basis of joint product cost apportionment has given us a relatively easy method for evaluating the profit, average costs and so on for each joint product. The sales value basis, which is based, literally, on the value of the sales derived from each of the joint products, gives us an alternative view of the apportionment of costs, and a different level of profit, product by product. Using the data from the physical units method, we can recalculate the cost apportionment and profit per product. The apportionment of the costs is based on the average cost per unit of sales. The result of this calculation is a constant to be used for all products:

$$\frac{\text{total joint processing costs}}{\text{total sales values}}$$

In this case, we have:

$$\frac{\pounds 100{,}000}{250{,}000 \text{ units}} = \pounds 0.4 \text{ per unit}$$

Applying this constant to the individual outputs gives:

Product 1	80,000 units × £0.4 per unit =	£32,000
Product 2	95,000 units × £0.4 per unit =	£38,000
Product 3	75,000 units × £0.4 per unit =	£30,000
		£100,000

Profit statement

	Product 1	Product 2	Product 3	Total
	£	£	£	£
Sales value	80,000	95,000	75,000	250,000
less: Apportioned costs	32,000	38,000	30,000	100,000
Profit	48,000	57,000	45,000	150,000

Comparing the two methods of joint cost apportionment shows the extent of the differences between the levels of profit reported by them:

	Product 1	Product 2	Product 3	Total
Sales value (£)	80,000	95,000	75,000	250,000
Profits reported:				
Physical units (£)	50,000	45,000	55,000	150,000
As a % of sales	62.50	47.37	73.33	60.00
Sales value (£)	48,000	57,000	45,000	150,000
As a % of sales	60.00	60.00	60.00	60.00

The sales value method returns profit levels of 60% of sales: every product shows profits of 60% of sales. The physical units basis shows profit margins ranging from 47% to 73%. Arithmetically, the sales value basis always gives such consistent results: the profit margin will always be the same from product to product. Checking the arithmetic will show us that this must be so. In the sales value method, costs are apportioned in direct proportion to the sales value, therefore, every product has the same relative portion of costs assigned to it. This also must always be true.

Other issues

Usry *et al.* (1988) discuss an interesting problem that some organisations will face when applying the physical units basis. They talk of the manufacture of coke. In the manufacture of coke, products that are produced such as coke, coal tar, benzol, sulphate of ammonia and gas are all measured in different units. For example, coke will be measured in tonnes, coal tar in litres, and gas in cubic metres. The management accountant working in situations such as these needs to take full account of these problems, and determine solutions to them. With the correct conversion factors this will not be a problem, but the management accountant needs to be aware of the situation. Usry *et al.* also discuss a method not discussed here: the weighted average method where weight factors are assigned to products. The weights are assigned in an attempt to allow for variations in size of units, difficulty of manufacture, amount of materials used and so on. Any system such as this is bound to lead to anomalies, and would be better disregarded in favour of the application of an activity-based costing approach.

Joint products that need further processing: notional sales value method

It often happens that, having produced joint products, some or all of those products need further processing to make them saleable. The method of cost apportionment usually demonstrated in these circumstances is the notional sales value method. The notional sales value referred to is an entirely fictitious figure made up of the final sales value and the subsequent processing costs. For example, if Product 1 had a final sales value of £5,000 and subsequent processing costs from the split-off point of £3,000, the notional sales value used to apportion the joint costs would be £5,000 – 3,000 = £2,000. The idea behind the notional sales value method is that the organisation is committed to using the sales value method of joint cost apportionment, but at the split-off point there is no sales value. Consequently, a sales value has to be arrived at in one way or another, and the notional sales value is an acceptable way of doing that. The problem presented by the joint products with further processing situations can best be demonstrated by means of a worked example.

WORKED EXAMPLE 8.14

A process has joint costs of £5,350 and produces products A and B, both of which are processed further before they can be sold. In March, 2 tonnes of A were produced, and 4.5 tonnes of B. The costs incurred in further processing the two products amounted to £3,000 for A and £2,500 for B. The selling price of A is £6,000 per tonne and for B it is £4,500 per tonne.

Required

Apportion the joint costs and hence determine the profit per product. Show your results in a profit statement.

Solution to Worked example 8.14

Total sales values:

product A = £6,000 per tonne × 2 tonnes = £12,000
product B = £4,500 per tonne × 4.5 tonnes = £20,250

Notional sales values:

	Final sales values (£)		Subsequent processing costs (£)		Notional sales values (£)
Product A	12,000	−	3,000	=	9,000
Product B	20,250	−	2,500	=	17,750
					26,750

The formula for apportioning the joint costs is now:

$$\frac{\text{total joint costs}}{\text{total notional sales value}}$$

$$= \frac{£5,350}{£26,750} = £0.2$$

Applying this rate to the notional sales values gives the apportioned joint costs of:

Product A = £ 9,000 × £0.2 = £1,800
Product B = £17,750 × £0.2 = £3,550

£5,350

Profit statement

	Product A	Product B	Total
	£	£	£
Final sales value	12,000	20,250	32,250
less:			
Apportioned costs	1,800	3,550	5,350
Subsequent costs	3,000	2,500	5,500
	7,200	14,200	21,400

SUMMARY

This concludes our look at basic product costing systems for specific orders. This chapter has covered three systems for dealing with situations where a one-off job, batch and process has been worked on.

We have considered a series of situations relevant to job or batch processes. We have analysed those situations from both a product flow point of view, and from a costing point of view. Overall we have found that a job costing system is probably the simplest of all costing systems to employ. We then dealt with the more complicated processes where we were faced with a continuous flow of production, such as can be found in a chemical factory, a car factory, or a baked bean cannery.

The process costing model was developed by identifying a process costing situation and working through the various stages or processes involved. We became aware that an organisation may make a product or provide a service that develops at various different stages: the examples of cardboard making and motor vehicle manufacture were discussed in detail. The question of how to deal with losses and gains that arise during the various processes was also considered. Losses and gains arise for a variety of reasons, including loss of weight or volume, or gains in weight or volume.

Finally, we dealt with the situation whereby a process gave rise to by-products, outputs from a process which are of little economic value. We also discussed the problems of joint products, whereby two or more products emerged from a process, all having a relatively large economic value.

KEY TERMS

You should satisfy yourself that you have noted all of these terms and can define and/or describe their meaning and use, as appropriate.

Job costing (p. 225)	Notional whole units (p. 244)
Process costing (p. 225)	Degree of completion (p. 245)
Batch costing (p. 226)	First in, first out (FIFO) (p. 247)
Normal yield (p. 239)	Started and completed (p. 249)
Waste (p. 239)	By-products (p. 259)
Abnormal gain and loss (p. 240)	Joint products (p. 259)
Work in progress (p. 244)	Physical units basis (p. 261)
Equivalent units (p. 244)	Sales value basis (p. 263)

RECOMMENDED READING

Apart from textbooks, not a lot is written about this subject that needs to be recommended!

QUESTIONS

Review questions

1. Give examples of situations in which job, batch, and process costing respectively are most appropriately used.
2. Describe and give an example of a job cost card. Is there any managerial information contained in a job cost card?
3. What are normal losses and normal gains? And what are abnormal losses and gains?
4. Define what is meant by an equivalent unit. Give examples of equivalent units, other than the ones found in this chapter.
5. Why do we need the FIFO and the average cost valuation methods in process costing?
6. Distinguish between by-products and joint products.
7. What is a split-off point and what might its significance be?
8. In what three ways might joint product costs be apportioned to products?

Answers to review questions 1, 3, 4 and 6 can be found in the Student Workbook.

Practice questions

Level I

1. Prepare a table of data to show the derivation of the economic batch size to be produced under the following circumstances:

   Each setup costs a total of £5.40 to carry out; and the variable cost per unit is £0.40. This business has an annual demand for 81,000 units of its product but has capacity to make 202,500. The carrying costs amount to £0.072 per unit per year, and the interest rate suffered by the organisation is 18% per year.

2. In the context of process costing:
   (a) define the term 'joint costs';
   (b) ilustrate the meaning of the term 'equivalent units'.

Level II

3. Ellen Shapiro makes consumer goods on a jobbing basis. On 1 January 1993, Shapiro's business had an opening stock of work in progress of £50,000, made up as follows:

Job	Direct materials	Direct labour	Factory overheads
10	12,000	5,000	3,000
11	9,000	9,000	2,000
12	3,000	4,000	3,000

During the month of January, the following transactions took place:

(a) Materials requisitioned from stores for production:

Job 11	15,000
Job 12	8,000
Job 13	19,000
Indirect materials	4,000

(b) The payment of wages during January was as follows:

Job 10	5,000
Job 11	2,000
Job 12	10,000
Job 13	8,000
Indirect labour	6,000

The number of direct labour hours used for each job were:

Job 10	550
Job 11	270
Job 12	1,200
Job 13	800

(c) The factory overhead absorption rate used by Shapiro's business is £7.50 per direct labour hour
(d) At the end of January, Jobs 10 and 11 had been fully completed and despatched to their respective customers
(e) Factory overheads amounting to £15,000 were incurred in addition to the overheads declared above.

Required

(a) Prepare a combined summary job cost card for all four jobs.
(b) Record January's activities in the journal.
(c) Prepare the factory overhead account for January and discuss the balance carried down on that account.

4. My Company Ltd operates two processing departments, A and B. The details for March for both departments are:

	Process A		Process B	
	%	Units	%	Units
Work in progress b/d		200		80
Degree of completion:				
Process A				
materials	100			
labour	25			
overheads	25			
Process B				
labour		60		
overheads		60		
Put into processes during the period		4,000		3,750
		4,200		3,830
	%	Units	%	Units
To process B		3,750		3,400
work in progress c/d		450		430
degree of completion:				
Process A				
materials	100			
labour	60			
overheads	60			
Process B				
labour			80	
overheads			80	
	4,200		3,830	

Required

Prepare the equivalent units part of the evaluation statement for My Company Limited for April using FIFO.

5. For each of the two independent sets of information below:
   (a) find the equivalent unit of production using the weighted average method;
   (b) find the equivalent unit of production using the FIFO method;
   (c) find the unit cost using the weighted average method;

(d) find the unit cost using the FIFO method;
(e) for both valuation methods find the work in progress carried down; and
(f) for both valuation methods find the cost of units transferred to finished goods stocks.

	Set 1	Set 2
	Units	Units
Work in progress b/d	10,000	20,000
To subsequent process	160,000	220,000
Work in progress c/d	12,000	24,000
Degrees of completion:		
	%	%
Work in progress b/d	50	70
Work in progress c/d	75	80
	£	£
Work in progress b/d	26,420	13,240
Incurred in the period	932,400	477,120

6. Lawrence Ltd operates a manufacturing plant to produce a single product. The product passes through two distinct processes: known as process 1 and process 2. The following data relate to the operation of process 1 for February and March.

	February units	March units
Work in progress b/d	0	600
Put into process	12,400	13,100
Transferred to process 2	11,800	13,300
Work in progress c/d	600	400
Degree of completion of work in progress c/d:		
	%	%
Materials	90	50
Labour and overheads	60	30
Processing costs:		
	£	£
Materials	258,640	271,760
Labour and overheads	526,860	569,770

The following data relate to the operation of process 2 for February and March. Note that process 2 simply processes the transfer in from process 1; no further materials are added during this process.

	February units	March units
Work in progress b/d	0	1,000
Put into process	11,800	13,300
Transferred to process 2	10,800	13,800
Work in progress c/d	1,000	500

Degree of completion of work in progress c/d

	%	%
From process 1	100	100
Labour and overheads	80	70

Processing costs

	£	£
Labour and overheads	212,750	237,620

Required

For both the FIFO and the Weighted Average valuation methods, calculate the costs of production, transfer costs, and stock values for each process: working to four decimal places when appropriate. As far as process 2 is concerned, assume that the costs transferred in are the FIFO costs of process 1.

7. A cleansing agent is manufactured from the input of three ingredients. At 1 December there was no work in progress. During December the three ingredients A, B and C, were put into the process in the following quantities.

A 2,000 kilos at 80p kilo
B 3,000 kilos at 50p kilo
C 6,000 kilos at 40p kilo

Additionally, labour working 941 hours and being paid £4 per hour was incurred, and overheads were recovered on the basis of 50% of labour cost. There was no loss in process. Output was 8,600 kilos.

The remaining items in work in progress were assessed by the company's works manager as follows:

- complete so far as materials were concerned
- one-quarter of the items were 60% complete for labour and overheads
- three-quarters were 25% complete for labour and overheads.

Required:

(a) A cleansing agent process statement, showing clearly the cost of the output and work in progress carried forward. (16 marks)

(b) Define the following terms, give examples, and explain how they would be accounted for in process costing:

(i) by-products; (6 marks)
(ii) abnormal gain; (3 marks)
(iii) equivalent units. (3 marks)

(Total 28 marks)
AAT Cost Accounting and Budgeting
December 1984

Solutions to practice questions 2 and 3 can be found in the Student Workbook. Solutions to practice question numbers in red can be found at the end of this book.

REFERENCES

CIMA (1991), *Management Accounting Official Terminology* (Chartered Institute of Management Accountants).

Usry, M. F., Hammer, L. H., Matz, A. (1988) *Cost Accounting: planning and control*, 9th edn (South Western Publishing).

CHAPTER NINE

The derivation of fixed and variable costs

CHAPTER OBJECTIVES

After reading this chapter you should be able to:

- describe three methods of cost behaviour analysis:
  - the inspection of accounts method
  - the engineering method
  - the ordinary least-squares method
- undertake ordinary least squares analyses of accounting data
- understand and discuss the limitations of cost behaviour analysis
- appreciate the learning curve phenomenon
- carry out mathematical analyses of learning curve data
- discuss the continuing relevance of learning curve analysis
- appreciate the practical implications of using learning curve theory
- understand various applications of learning curve analysis

Introduction

In Chapter 3 we looked at the scattergraph, high–low and linear approximation methods of cost behaviour analysis. The aim of those methods is to take a cost and, all other things being equal, separate out the fixed costs from the variable costs so that a function such as

$$Y' = \mathrm{a} + bX$$

could be derived. We know from Chapter 3 that a function such as $Y' = \mathrm{a} + bX$ enables us to predict the level of fixed ('a') and variable costs ('bX') at any level of output, not just the levels that we have direct experience of. In this chapter we will not only be using the ideas contained in Chapter 3, but we will also be adding to them by considering the following alternative methods of cost behaviour analysis:

- the inspection of accounts method
- the engineering method; and
- the ordinary least-squares method (OLS)

and we will be revising the high–low and scattergraph methods as necessary.

Inspection of accounts method

This method is also known as the account classification method and is based on the function

total cost = fixed cost + variable cost

which, for our purposes, is equivalent to the function

$Y' = a + bX$

With the inspection of accounts method a decision is taken at some stage which classifies a cost as either a fixed cost or a variable cost. Accountants and managers often use this method without necessarily being aware of doing so. The inspection of accounts method is based to a large extent on intuition, and to a further extent on what has always been believed to be the case. A few examples will illustrate how the method works. If we ask ourselves to say, generally, whether direct labour costs are fixed or variable, most of us would reply that they are variable costs (the more of a product or service we complete, the more direct labour must have been employed). Similarly, is direct material a fixed or variable cost? Again, the answer received would be that it is a variable cost (for the same reason as applied to direct labour). Rent would be classified by everyone as a fixed cost, as would insurances, administration salaries, and so on. This is the inspection of accounts method. The inspection of accounts method is based on the 'everyone would classify this cost as fixed cost and that cost as variable cost' analysis. Therefore, we say, just by looking at the nature of an expense, we know what its behaviour is.

WORKED EXAMPLE 9.1

We can calculate the fixed and variable costs for an organisation based on the data in the table below by using this method:

Cost	Total (£)
Direct materials	75,000
Direct labour	53,000
Indirect materials	37,000
Indirect labour	22,000
Rent and rates	12,000
Insurance	10,500
Administration overhead	6,500
	216,000

The output of finished goods to which these data relate is 12,800 units.

Required

1. Using the inspection of accounts method, estimate the variable and fixed cost elements of the total costs given below.
2. Using the output information also given, estimate the total cost function for this organisation.
3. Estimate, based on the function derived in section 1 above, the total costs when output reaches 5,000, 7,000 and 10,000 units.

Solution to Worked example 9.1

Based on the ideas we have already discussed, that direct costs are variable, rent and rates are fixed, and so on, fixed and variable costs for this organisation are:

Cost	Total	Fixed	Variable
	£	£	£
Direct materials	75,000		75,000
Direct labour	53,000		53,000
Indirect materials	37,000	37,000	
Indirect labour	22,000	22,000	
Rent and rates	12,000	12,000	
Insurance	10,500	10,500	
Administration Overhead	6,500	6,500	
	216,000	88,000	128,000

Using the algebraic notation from Chapter 3:

Fixed costs $= a =$ £88,000

Variable costs per unit $= b = \dfrac{£128,000}{12,800 \text{ units}}$

$= £10$ per unit

Therefore, our function to estimate total costs is:

$Y' = a + bX = £88,000 + £10X$

We would estimate, based on this function, that total costs would be, for 5,000, 7,000 and 10,000 units:

	Total costs (Y′) £	Fixed costs (a) £	Variable costs (bX) £
5,000 units	138,000	88,000	50,000
7,000 units	158,000	88,000	70,000
10,000 units	188,000	88,000	100,000

Check the calculations to your own satisfaction.

Problems with the inspection of accounts method

There are serious problems with the inspection of accounts method that make it useful only for providing us with crude estimates of what the true situation might be. The inspection of accounts method is entirely subjective: it is based on the way we feel a cost ought to behave. Take direct labour as an example. Intuitively, it seems obvious that the more we make of a product, the more direct labour must be employed; therefore, direct labour costs must be greater the more we make. However, direct labour costs can be a fixed cost to a large extent, in that the number of people needed to operate machinery, or to provide a given level of service must be set at a particular level for safety reasons, for operational reasons, and so on. Even when we do find that the cost **used to** behave in the way that the inspection of accounts method is saying, that information may be out of date: the factory or workshop may have been reorganised, new technology may have been installed, new agreements with trade unions may have been reached, or new efficiency and productivity methods may have been implemented. Hence the precise behaviour of the cost has changed. By using the inspection of accounts method, we use only the latest information available, and base our analysis on a classification made, perhaps, years ago.

Berliner and Brimson (1988: 25), referring to the increase in technological advances in use in many industries and organisations, state:

> As a result of changes in the manufacturing environment, several cost management issues have become more prominent. . . . As manufacturing facilities have become increasingly automated, cost behaviour patterns have changed.

Note, however, that not all manufacturers have found these changes. There are still many manufacturers who have yet to be touched by such technological changes as those discussed by Berliner and Brimson. For the less technologically advanced organisations, older techniques and situations will still apply. Finally, the inspection of accounts method does not make any allowance for semi-variable costs. We have seen from the discussion we have had that we define costs as being either fixed or variable, and we made no attempt to define them in terms of semi-variability. This is clearly a severe limitation of the method since a very wide variety of costs are semi-variable in nature: telephone and electricity costs are examples of semi-variable costs.

The engineering or technical estimate method

The second method, the engineering method, has a great deal to commend it since it is based on scientific or technical estimates of what is (and should be) happening. The name 'engineering' may be offputting to those of us that work in a non-engineering environment. However, the alternative title of technical estimate is perfectly acceptable. In essence, the way that the engineering method works is that all products and services are defined in terms of a series of technical estimates, or chemical formulæ, or recipes. The accountant then applies the costs to them. We can see the usefulness of the engineering method by considering an example.

WORKED EXAMPLE 9.2

The basic technical requirements for the manufacture of a dining table might be:

7 metres of wood @ 4 cm × 4 cm
4 metres of wood @ 8 cm × 4 cm
1 piece of plywood @ 1.5 m × 1 m × 1 cm

Required

Assuming a simple linear relationship between the quantity of the inputs and the number of tables made, estimate the quantity of each of the three inputs needed to make 10 dining tables.

Solution to Worked example 9.2

All we have to do here to provide ourselves with the quantity of the ingredients needed to be bought or requisitioned from stores is to multiply each of the ingredients by 10 (the number of tables required to be made). Hence, our estimate of the material inputs to make 10 dining tables is:

70 metres of wood @ 4 cm × 4 cm
40 metres of wood @ 8 cm × 4 cm
10 pieces of plywood @ 1.5 m × 1 m × 1 cm

This is all there is to the basic idea behind an engineering or technical estimate. Providing the formula or recipe is correct, the engineering method gives us a very good view of the estimate of costs. Although we have not seen this aspect yet, the engineering method can easily deal with fixed costs. The estimate would also include details of the electricity required to run the various machines needed to make the tables. All the information relating to the making of the tables comes under the heading of engineering or technical information, and can be determined in advance. In Japan, there is an approach to the engineering or technical estimate method that is worthy of our consideration: that is, cost tables.

Cost tables: the Japanese equivalent of the engineering method

Cost tables are, strictly speaking, the application of the engineering method we are currently discussing; and we will doubtless come across them more and more in our reading. Yoshikawa *et al.* (1993) discuss cost tables. A cost table is: 'a measurement to decide cost and to be able to evaluate the cost of not only existing products but also future products at the very beginning of the design process' (Yoshikawa *et al.* 1993: 88, quoting Sato 1965). In Japan, cost tables: 'were traditionally classed according to the area in which they would be used. Thus tables existed for design, manufacturing, purchasing and distribution' (ibid.).

This demonstrates that a cost table takes the engineering method of cost estimation outside the factory. It can be applied to virtually the whole organisation. We also need to appreciate the potential size of a cost table. If we agree that a cost table covers an entire product from start to finish, we are dealing with, in the motor vehicle manufacturing industry, a product with thousands of parts and several aspects to the manufacturing process. Thus in a motor vehicle manufacturing plant, we will have a cost table broken down into several functional areas containing, overall, all the parts and operations that go into making the vehicles. Yoshikawa *et al.* give several examples of the considerations that need to be included in a cost table. As one example, they discuss the properties of a cogwheel being manufactured (either alone or as part of a larger product) under the heading of cost table by factor analysis. The two aspects to the manufacture of the cogwheel are design and production. Under the design aspects are factors such as:

- model;
- number of teeth;
- width of teeth;
- weight of material; and
- diameter of shaft.

Under the production aspects are such factors as

- whether it needs forging;
- whether it needs filing;
- whether it needs the corners rounding off.

Similarly, they discuss the technical formulæ that engineers need to use in estimating the theoretical properties of a product. These properties are taken from the design of the product and the nature of the materials used by the product. Multiple regression formulæ would be used where relevant; and Yoshikawa *et al.* give examples of the kind of formulæ that would be used in a cost table in chapter 7 of their book. Cost tables also contain actual data, of course, whenever possible. Finally, cost tables can be relatively easily linked to the computer-aided design software that many organisations use now; and the data contained in cost tables is commonly held in databases that all relevant employees, designers, engineers and accoutants, have access to. In terms of size, Yoshikawa *et al.* (1993: 104) give us a good insight into this aspect when they say: 'The compilation of cost tables requires a great deal of work with two or three cost accountants working full time to maintain cost tables in a factory with, say, around 6,000 employees.'

The engineering method and standard costing

The engineering method is closely related to standard costing. With standard costing we have standard inputs, based on standard recipes, formulations and so on. There is no difference between what we have been doing here, and the way that standard costing works. The engineering method is a very useful starting point in the assessment of costs because of its use of standards, formulæ, and recipes. It shows us the way the process or product or service should behave. Kaplan and Atkinson (1989: 93) state:

> Engineering studies require direct physical observation of the production process. Such studies are most useful for understanding repetitive processes that have a well defined relationship between inputs and outputs. The studies are generally expensive and are typically performed to improve the efficiency of the process, not just to set cost standards

Whilst this observation is generally true, it does miss the point to some extent. On the face of it, Kaplan and Atkinson are correct: such engineering studies could be costly, especially for a highly complex set of operations. However, when an operation is initially being set up, and perhaps when standards are being set or reviewed, a great deal of useful engineering information will be gathered and be available for accounting use. In simple environments, such as small-scale sherry fermentation, the amount of engineering data required by the accountant is not enormous and it is not onerous for the wine chemist or engineer to provide such data. Even in large organisations, engineering data are not **necessarily** difficult to gather, providing the process under review is clearly defined, logically set out and is easily accessible. Where Kaplan and Atkinson are perfectly correct concerns the indirect costs. As we know from Chapter 6, indirect costs (overheads) are problematic. Even with the engineering method, many problems will be encountered when attempting to assess cost functions for indirect costs.

The ordinary least-squares method

The method of ordinary least squares (OLS), or regression analysis, gives a statistical fit to the data which bisects the data exactly. Remember that in Chapter 3 we used the line of best fit, employing scattergraphs. When fitting lines of best fit by inspection, there is an infinite number of possible solutions to the function $Y' = a + bX$, because there is an infinite number of places on any graph on which to place a line of best fit. OLS takes away the uncertainty with the line of best fit since there is only one line which exactly bisects the data we are analysing. In the OLS, the line of best fit is called the regression line: that is, where we are regressing one variable on another variable:

> in regression analysis, the regression line is a line that summarises the relationship between an independent variable, X, and a dependent variable, Y, while also minimising the errors made when the equation of that line is used to estimate Y from X. (Kohler 1985)

The reason the method is called the OLS method is that it minimises the sum of the squared vertical distances between observations and the line. That is, when we draw on a line of best fit, we can evaluate the distance between an actual data point and the line of best fit. When we find the square of all of these distances and add them together, the smallest possible value for this sum is found by OLS. (At the end of this chapter there is a worksheet that takes us through all of the steps of regression and correlation analysis. The worksheet will help with our learning and understanding of the OLS process.)

OLS and the normal equations

To arrive at the sum of squared vertical distances, OLS uses what statisticians call the *normal equations*, these are:

$$\Sigma Y = na + b\Sigma X$$

$$\Sigma XY = \mathrm{a}\Sigma X + b\Sigma X^2$$

By solving these equations, we obtain the values for 'a' and 'b' that we use in our total cost function $Y' = \mathrm{a} + bX$.

OLS, therefore, is the statistical method that allows us to find the optimum values for 'a' and 'b', given any set of data. Whether the data under review lie close to the OLS line of best fit we will discuss later, but for now we can assume there is no problem of goodness of fit. The following worked example will illustrate how the normal equations are used.

WORKED EXAMPLE 9.3

In the table below, X relates to the independent variable of a situation, and Y relates to the dependent variable of the same situation. For example, X could be the number of machine hours operated by a machine and Y could be the expenditure on maintenance of the same machine. X is the independent variable assuming the time that the machine is operated does not depend upon the amount of money spent on maintenance. On the other hand, maintenance expenditure, we are saying, depends on the length of time that the machine is operated.

X	Y
425	1,000
320	900
125	520
290	1,100
380	900
260	750
190	600
520	1,150
360	900
190	500
3,060	8,320

Required

Expand the data in the table and solve the normal equations. By doing so derive the total cost function.

Solution to Worked example 9.3

Solving the normal equations manually (without the aid of a computer, that is) can be a time consuming and not particularly inspiring thing to do. However, it should not prove especially difficult. All we have to do is to identify from the normal equations what variables we need to use or to calculate, and take it from there. We need to expand the table given in the example, to find values for ΣX, ΣY, ΣXY, and ΣX^2. The table below shows the expansions needed:

X	Y	XY	X^2
425	1,000	425,000	180,625
320	900	288,000	102,400
125	520	65,000	15,625
290	1,100	319,000	84,100
380	900	342,000	144,400
260	750	195,000	67,600
190	600	114,000	36,100
520	1,150	598,000	270,400
360	900	324,000	129,600
190	500	95,000	36,100
ΣX 3,060	ΣY 8,320	ΣXY 2,765,000	ΣX^2 1,066,950

We can now substitute the relevant values in the normal equations, including the value 'n', which is the number of observations, 10.

$$\Sigma y = na + b\Sigma x \qquad (9.1)$$

$$\Sigma xy = a\Sigma x + b\Sigma x^2 \qquad (9.2)$$

$$8{,}320 = 10\text{a} + 3{,}060b \qquad (9.1)$$

$$2{,}765{,}000 = 3{,}060\text{a} + 1{,}066{,}950b \qquad (9.2)$$

We are dealing with simultaneous equations here. We can solve for 'b' in this case by the substitution method we used in Chapter 6 when dealing with reciprocal service department overheads.

$$8{,}320 = 10\text{a} + 3{,}060\,\frac{(-3{,}060\text{a} + 2{,}765{,}000)}{1{,}066{,}950}$$

$$8{,}320 = 10\text{a} - 8.78\text{a} + 7{,}929.98$$

$$-10\text{a} + 8.78\text{a} = -8{,}320 + 7{,}929.98$$

$$-1.22\text{a} = -390.02$$

Therefore:

$$\text{a} = 318.65$$

Substitute for 'a' now in equation (9.2):

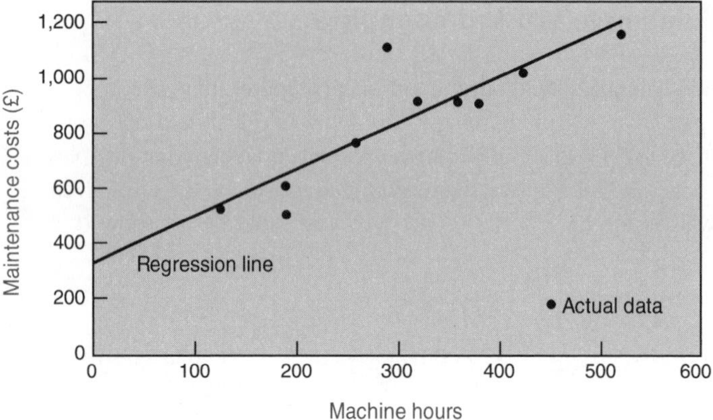

FIGURE 9.1 *Least squares: regression line*

$$2,765,000 = 3,060 \times 318.65 + 1,066,950b$$
$$2,765,000 = 975,066.68 + 1,066,950b$$
$$2,765,000 - 975,066.68 = 1,066,950b$$
$$1,789,933.32 = 1,066,950b$$

Therefore:

$$b = \frac{1,789,933.32}{1,066,950}$$
$$= 1.68$$

It follows from these calculations that (rounding off to two decimal places)

$$Y' = a + bX$$
$$= Y' = 318.65 + 1.68X$$

Plotting the actual data and the regression line derived from the normal equations on a graph gives Figure 9.1.

The slope of the line of best fit is 1.68 (the value of 'b') and the intercept term is 318.65 (the value of 'a'). The line of best fit is plotted by using the total cost function to estimate the values of maintenance costs at the various values of X.

CAMEO

Estimating fixed and variable cost behaviour from published accounts

In Chapter 3, we looked at the operating cost data for an international hotel chain. The data are repeated below. The purpose of this cameo is to analyse these data in more detail.

Year	Operating costs
84	1,423.3
83	1,293.5
82	1,190.5
81	1,107.2
80	966.3
79	681.9
78	650.4
77	614.4
76	583.1
75	565.0
74	564.9

In Chapter 3, we simply carried out a high–low analysis of the above data and obtained the result:

$$Y = -5{,}787.26 + 85.840X$$

where X is the value of the year under review.

Additional information in this organisation's annual report and accounts shows as follows:

Year	Number of hotels	Number of table games	Number of restaurants
84	1,696	612	312
83	1,707	453	309
82	1,744	483	311
81	1,751	463	343
80	1,755	445	375
79	1,741	45	364
78	1,718	0	0
77	1,700	0	0
76	1,713	0	0
75	1,714	0	0
74	1,688	0	0

From these additional pieces of information we can see immediately that we need to revise our cost behaviour estimates, since the organisation changed the basis of its operations significantly from 1979 onwards.

Taking a piecewise view of the data, a high–low analysis of these data would now show radically revised estimates of fixed and variable cost behaviour analysis for the periods 1974–9 and 1980–4. However, taking a more scientific view for the purposes of this cameo, the ordinary least squares results of the analysis of these data gives fixed and variable cost estimates as per the following:

$$Y = -6{,}542.2 + 93.91X$$

where X is the year and Y are the operating costs. Note that we still have the unusual estimate of fixed costs – unusual in that it is negative.

You should take the opportunity now to analyse these data further. Carry out a piecewise analysis in an attempt to determine realistic and usable estimates of fixed and variable costs from this organisation for the period under review. To carryout the piecewise estimates, use the data split into the periods suggested above: 1974–9 and 1980–4.

Issues in cost behaviour estimation

Before we accept wholeheartedly cost behaviour analysis from a statistical, or other, point of view, there are a number of factors that we need to clarify.

Cause and effect

We may be forgiven for putting all of our trust in a statistical method that gives us a result suggesting a relationship between '*X*' and '*Y*'. There is no guarantee, however, just because the relationship between '*X*' and '*Y*' may be statistically highly significant, that '*X*' causes '*Y*' to happen, or change. Spurious correlation occurs where two variables may be highly correlated, but there is no real relation between them at all: examples such as the growth in the money supply in the UK and the growth in the incidence of tuberculosis in Glasgow being highly correlated are proven to be spurious! Taking full account of such issues as cause and effect will help in selecting the correct '*X*' variable to match to the proper '*Y*' variable.

Changing technology

An organisation attempting to estimate its cost function(s) must allow for changes in technology: already made, or about to be made. Increasing the level of capital investment at the expense of labour intensity must have a significant impact on the behaviour of costs: moving from a highly variable to a highly fixed position, perhaps. If such changes in technology are contemplated, a new cost behaviour analysis must be carried out.

Extent of the data

Although we have worked through a number of examples in this chapter based on 10 bits of data, in reality this is nowhere near a sufficient amount of data on which to base serious cost behaviour estimations. From a statistical point of view alone, 30 observations will be our minimum required number of observations if proper tests for normality of data can be carried out with the utmost confidence. In most organisations, data can be collected regularly, and, especially with the advent of personal computers, can now be analysed very easily using spreadsheet and statistical packages. There is no need for us to stint ourselves on data collection!

Management policy and cost behaviour analysis

There are cases where management have set cost levels on one basis or another but the accountant or cost analyst is unaware of the fact! If management has decided that a university library is to have an allocation of, say, £10,000 plus £5 for every student, then it should come as no surprise when the cost analyst finds that the total cost function for the library is

$$Y' \quad a + bX = 10{,}000 + 5x$$

Similarly, there is no need for the analyst to have carried out his or her exercise if management has already decided on its allocation policy!

Linearity

We have dealt with all of the data in the exercises in this chapter as if they were linear data. We never allowed for the data to be non-linear. We do need to be aware, of course, that non-linear data do exist. Later in this chapter we discuss some of the issues facing us when confronted by non-linear data: in this case learning curve analysis. We can ease the problem of non-linearity in a case such as learning curve analysis by transforming our data by logarithms. Logarithmic transformation is not especially difficult, and we could, if we wished, return to cost behaviour determination exercises where a cost can be seen to be behaving in a non-linear way. We will not be doing this, however, but feel free to do this yourself!

The relevant range

Perhaps the most dangerous problem with cost behaviour estimation comes when accountants and others are tempted to make predictions for events outside the relevant range. Estimates based on data are only to be made within the relevant range, and estimates based on data outside the relevant range must be treated with great caution. See Chapter 3 for a detailed discussion of the significance of the relevant range.

The learning curve

A knowledge of learning curves is important for the management accountant because their effects can be pervasive. Although a lot of the work that has been done on learning curves concentrates on the labour content of them, work has been done to demonstrate that learning curves can apply even when the labour element of a job or process is relatively small. A good example of the way managers and accountants often react when facing a learning situation is demonstrated clearly in the Harvard Business School case concerning the Morrin

Aircraft Company, which can be found in Anthony and Reece (1989: 571–5). In this case there is the situation where one manager of an organisation clearly understands learning curve theory and its application whereas the manager of another company clearly understands nothing about learning curves. Given the situation in the Morrin case, it is apparent that misunderstandings as far as learning curves are concerned can lead to serious tensions between managers of the same organisation, or between managers of different organisations who may be negotiating a contract. This discussion concerns the theory and practice of learning curves, but concludes by questioning the way that they have been applied historically.

Whilst this chapter is concerned with the learning curve, we should be aware that there is also the experience curve. The experience curve is, essentially, the learning curve applied to the whole organisation, rather than just being applied to one job, task, or manufacturing costs. Consideration of the experience curve is of importance to industry and commerce, but further discussion of it is not part of the discussion that follows.

The learning curve: definition and theory

The learning curve: 'shows the relationship between labour time per unit and cumulative units produced' (CIMA 1991). The essence of learning curve theory, as it applies to labour hours, is that when we carry out an action more than once, we tend to carry out the action more quickly the more we repeat the action.

Background to learning curves

Hirschmann (1964: 125) says:

> No matter what products you manufacture or what type of operations you manage, there is a good possibility that you can ... Profit from the learning curve. The learning curve ... is an underlying natural characteristic of organised activity ...

Although the first article written on the subject of learning curves in an industrial setting did not appear until 1936, Hirschmann reports that Henry Ford was effectively using the benefits of the learning curve as early as 1909. Perhaps more interestingly, from a historical point of view, churches and cathedrals built in many parts of Europe at least from the Middle Ages onwards demonstrate that learning curves may have been known about even by then. If we look at any medieval church we can see stone and wood carvings repeated around the walls and roof of the church. Thus, the craftsman was carving the same design over and over again – assuming one man did several or all of the carvings.

The experience curve

Consider any action you perform during any average day: tying your shoe lace, making a cup of tea, or answering the questions from this book. When you first performed such an action you will have taken a certain length of time; when you performed that action again (assuming the conditions under which the action was repeated are the same as they were previously), you will almost certainly have performed it more quickly. The third time you performed the action, you will have been quicker still; and so it goes on.

The point relating to the labour content of a job or operation is important: that is, as Hirschmann (1964: 126) illustrates, the higher the labour content of a job, the greater is the scope for the learning curve to take effect. However, even when the content of a job or process is not entirely labour based, the learning curve effect can still be found (see Pattison and Teplitz 1989). The greater our experience of a situation, the more efficient we are at dealing with it. This is the essence of learning curve theory.

Table 9.1 and Figure 9.2 illustrate what happens as we improve as a result of repeating an action. In Table 9.1, we can imagine that we perform a task for the first time, and it takes us 50 hours to complete. The second time we perform the same task, under the same conditions, we might take only 40 hours or 30 hours, and so on. Table 9.1 is illustrating what is known as an 80% learning curve. This means that as a job (or batch in terms of Table 9.1) is repeated, we learn at the rate of 80%. Working down the table will help us to understand what this means. When we undertake batch 1 of a job or process, we take a total of 50 hours to complete it. When we learn at the rate of 80% (we will discuss this aspect later), we will complete batch 2 in 40 hours (80% of 50 hours). Learning at the rate of 80% allows us to complete batch 4 in only 32 hours (80% of 40 hours), and so on. The total time taken for the relevant number of batches is calculated by multiplying the number of batches by the cumulative average time (CAT). So, if 16 batches have been carried out or made, the total time taken to do that is:

16 batches × 20.48 hours per batch = 327.68 hours

Note that because of the mathematics involved, this tabular presentation has to use the cumulative average times at the doubling point: that is, we are concerned with what happens after 1 batch, 2 batches, 4 batches, 8 batches . . . and not every batch. We will be using the mathematical approach below to eliminate this problem.

Figure 9.2 confirms what Table 9.1 has shown us.

TABLE 9.1 ***An 80% learning rate***

Batches	Cumulative average time (hrs)	Total time (hrs)
1	50.00	50.00
2	40.00	80.00
4	32.00	128.00
8	25.60	204.80
16	20.48	327.68
32	16.38	524.29
64	13.11	838.86
128	10.49	1,342.18

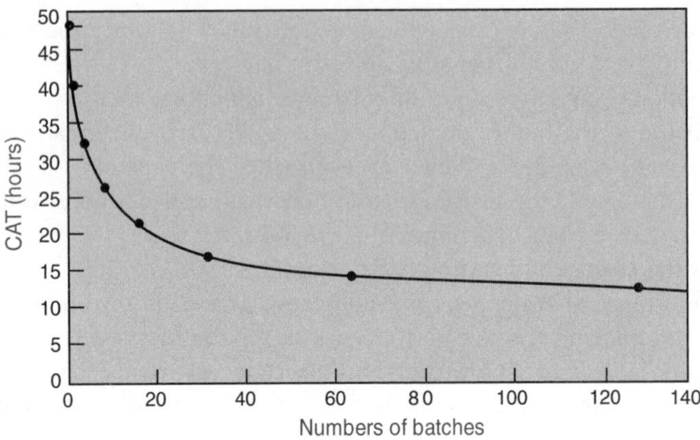

FIGURE 9.2 *Cumulative average time (80% curve)*

Cessation of learning: the steady state

Eventually, the effects of learning must, and do, wear off. Apart from a 100% learning curve, which is a perfectly horizontal line, all curves that demonstrate some learning behave this way. All learning curves slope downwards from left to right and eventually level off: that is, the steady state. There is nothing especially unusual about the way the learning curve behaves, but there are three points to be made about the cessation of learning:

1. **It is inevitable.** If learning is taking place at a constant, or near constant rate, then eventually the learning curve will level off. Eventually we will achieve a level of skill and dexterity on which we cannot improve.
2. **We should know it exists.** Knowing about learning rates and their effect on costs, times and so on is vital. Organisations have fallen foul because they failed to allow for the learning effect when they were tendering for contracts. Similarly, if we are keen to win a special order and we do not take allowance of the learning effect, we might assume that we have less labour time available to us than we have. With learning we know that the eventual cumulative average time for a job might be five hours per batch, whereas without learning it might be twenty-five hours per batch. Not allowing for the learning effect could reduce our ability to compete effectively and thus cost us business, contribution and profit.
3. **Where are we on the learning curve?** We may already be partly experienced at a job when we decide to assess our learning rate. In this case, we have to be very careful about our calculations. In looking at any situation where the person performing a job already has some experience of it, we should ask the question: What are the implications of already being part of the way down the learning curve?

The benefits of learning

Imagine a situation where learning did not take place (a 100% learning rate). Taking the case of the job first encountered in Table 9.1, when no learning is taking place, we complete

TABLE 9.2 Comparison of the effects of learning and non-learning on labour hours

	Learning at 80%		Non-learning (100%)	
Batches	Cumulative average time (hrs)	Total time (hrs)	Cumulative average time (hrs)	Total time (hrs)
1	50.00	50.00	50.00	50
2	40.00	80.00	50.00	100
4	32.00	128.00	50.00	200
8	25.60	204.80	50.00	400
16	20.48	327.68	50.00	800
32	16.38	524.29	50.00	1,600
64	13.11	838.86	50.00	3,200
128	10.49	1,342.18	50.00	6,400

batch 1 in 50 hours, and we complete batch 2 in 50 hours: a total of 100 hours taken. We take 50 hours for **every** batch we complete if we are unable to learn as we go. Comparing the two situations now in Table 9.2, in terms of labour hours and costs, we can see the benefits of learning. The table illustrates the labour hours position clearly:

To complete 128 batches	Total time taken (hrs)
With learning	1,342.18
Without learning	6,400.00

Table 9.3 shows the effect that non-learning and learning has on the costs of the job or batch being completed. For this example, we are assuming that: we are paid a labour hour rate of £1.20 per hour; fixed costs of £8,500 apply to the job we are completing; 128 batches are being completed. The workings here concern only the multiplication of the

TABLE 9.3 Comparison of the effects of learning and non-learning on job costs

Costs	No learning effect	80% learning effect	60% learning effect
Total hours	6,400.00	1,342.18	
Labour rate (£)	1.20	1.20	
Direct labour costs (£)	7,680.00	1,610.61	
Fixed costs (£)	8,500.00	8,500.00	
Total costs (£)	16,180.00	10,110.61	9,707.96

labour rate per hour (£1.20 per hour) by the total hours derived previously. For the non-learning situation, the calculation is:

£1.20 per hour × 6,400 hours = £7,680

For the 80% learning situation, the calculation is:

£1.20 per hour × 1,342.18 hours = £1,610.61

The difference between the non-learning and learning situations is that total costs amount to £16,180 for the 128 batches when learning does not take place, as opposed to £10,110.61 when an 80% learning rate is present – a very significant difference between the two situations. Complete the 60% learning effect column to your own satisfaction. Rather than relying on the tabular approach, we can take a mathematical approach now to solving our learning-effect problems. The mathematical approach allows us a great deal more flexibility since by using it we can calculate the cumulative average time (CAT) taken for **any number** of batches or jobs completed.

The learning curve formula

The basic learning curve formula is:

$$Y = aX^{b}$$

where:

Y = cumulative average time (or cost)
a = time (or cost) for the **first** unit or batch
X = cumulative production or batches completed
b = the learning exponent

furthermore:

$$b = \frac{\ln \text{ learning rate}}{\ln 2}$$

where ln means the natural logarithm of, and the learning rate is expressed as a decimal

Note:

1. The precise derivation of this formula and 'b' is not important.
2. Some books show b as a negative:

$$Y = aX^{-b}$$

This is fine providing that the sign is used carefully.

Applying the formula to our first example – where our initial batch time for the first batch was 50 hours, we have just completed the batch 128, and the learning rate is 80% – will help us to understand how the formula is used:

$$Y = 50 \times 128^{-0.32193}$$
$$= 10.48567$$

This is very near to the result of 10.49 we saw when we first worked through that example.

Note: $b = \ln\ 0.80 \div \ln\ 2 = -0.32193$

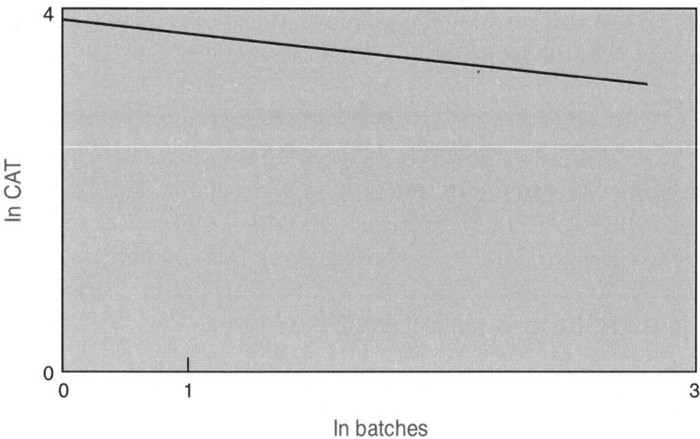

FIGURE 9.3 *Log log learning curve*

Logarithms and the learning curve formula

When dealing with the sort of situation we have just been using to find the cumulative average time, we have been dealing with curves and values raised to a power. Figure 9.3 illustrates what happens when we transform the cumulative average time (CAT) formula by the use of logarithms: we are now dealing with much straighter lines. The benefits of transforming our formulæ with logarithms is that it allows us to deal with straighter lines, and this makes our analysis and interpretation of data much more straightforward. Figure 9.3 is based on a learning rate of 80%, a time for the first batch of 50 hours and the CAT and number of batches as shown in Table 9.4. Figure 9.3 helps to illustrate the point that if we need to analyse the data we have to work on for learning curve purposes, we have now derived a straight line, and estimates from straight lines are much easier to deal with than true curves. Working through Table 9.4 shows us how Figure 9.3 was derived.

TABLE 9.4 *Logarithmic data for an 80% learning curve*

Batch number	ln of batch number time (hrs)	Cumulative average time (hrs)	ln of cumulative average time (hrs)
1	0.00	50.00	3.91
2	0.69	40.00	3.69
3	1.10	35.11	3.56
4	1.39	32.00	3.47
5	1.61	29.78	3.39
6	1.79	28.08	3.34
7	1.95	26.72	3.29
8	2.08	25.60	3.24
9	2.20	24.65	3.20
10	2.30	23.83	3.17

Table 9.4 shows that Figure 9.3 is based on a log log graph: that is, both 'x' and 'y' axes are transformed by logarithms. To find the logarithm of the batch number, we look up the batch number in a table of natural logarithms, or use the ln function on a calculator. For example, the natural logarithm of 1 (ln(1)) is 0 (zero), the natural logarithm of 2 is 0.69315 and so on. Similarly, to find the logarithm of the CAT, we look up the cumulative average time in a table of natural logarithms, or use the ln function on a calculator. For example, the natural logarithm of 50 (ln(50)) is 3.91202, the natural logarithm of 40 is 3.68888 and so on. Note that whilst we are using natural logarithms throughout this chapter, we could just as well be using logarithms to any other base, and the solutions would be the same.

When using natural logarithms, the basic formula $Y = aX^b$ becomes:

$$\ln Y = \ln a + (b \times \ln X)$$

where the definitions of Y, a, X, and b are all as before; and ln Y, for example, means the natural logarithm of Y.

WORKED EXAMPLE 9.4

A contract is signed for 45 batches. We want to anticipate the total number of hours it will take to complete those 45 batches given a time to completion of 50 hours for batch 1 and a learning rate of 80%.

Solution to Worked example 9.4

Using our new formula:

$$\ln Y = \ln a + (b \times \ln X)$$

ln a becomes ln 50 (logarithm of the hours for the first batch);

b is -0.3219 (this reflects an 80% learning rate);

ln X becomes ln 45 (logarithm of the number of batches to be completed).

Therefore:

$$\ln Y = \ln 100 + (-0.3219) \times \ln 45$$

$$= 4.6052 + (-0.3219)\ (3.80666)$$

$$= 3.3798$$

As this result stands, it is not the final piece of information we need, because 3.3798 is still in logarithmic format. We have to translate this into 'real numbers'. To do this involves the use of 'e', the basis of natural logarithms. This stems from that fact that 'e' is that 'irrational' (and constant) number almost equal to 2.7183 that is the basis of natural logarithms. It does not matter if you know nothing else about 'e' except that you should find it on your calculator! Consequently, the CAT, in hours per batch, is

$e^{\ln Y} = e^{3.3798}$

$= 2.7183^{3.3798}$

= 29.366 hours per batch

Finally, the total time to be taken to complete the 45 batches is:

45 batches × 29.366 hours per batch

= 1,321.47 hours

Sensitivity analysis

Learning curves are very sensitive to change, hence the need for sensitivity analysis. Even small changes can have a large impact on costs, times, and the other factors that are touched by learning curves. Table 9.5 illustrates the sensitive nature of learning curves, and clearly shows that making only a small error in the estimation of the learning rate – say, 82.5% instead of 80% – will lead to a significant distortion of labour costs. At low levels of output or achievement, the errors do not seem that large, but at higher levels of output, the differences are relatively and absolutely large. At 500 units, for example, the total labour costs are £66,831 when the learning rate is 82.5%, but it is only £50,717 when the learning rate is 80%. Mistakes with learning curve assessment can be costly: they are important.

TABLE 9.5 *Sensitivity of learning curve information*

Time to complete unit 1	50			
Labour cost per hour	£15			
Quantity produced	Learning curve			
	90.0%	85.0%	82.5%	80.0%
'b'	−0.1520	−0.2345	−0.2775	−0.3219
	£	£	£	£
10	5,285	4,371	3,958	3,574
50	20,691	14,986	12,662	10,644
100	37,244	25,476	20,893	17,030
200	67,039	43,309	34,473	27,247
500	145,807	87,341	66,831	50,717

Source: Adapted from Hirsch and Louderback (1986: 901).

Manipulating the learning curve formula

We can manipulate the learning curve formula now to enable us to find out any one aspect of the situation, given all other aspects of the situation.

For example, we can manipulate the learning curve formula to tell us: the number of batches, given the CAT; the incremental time between two different numbers of batches; and the learning rate given all other data.

The number of batches given the CAT

We may have a budgetary or physical constraint built into the time our organisation has available to work on contracts or batches that are undertaken in addition to our normal workload. Therefore, we might ask, for example, given the situation of an 80% learning curve and a time for batch 1 of 50 hours, how many batches must we complete in order to achieve CATs of: 20 hours; 10 hours; and 5 hours. (Assume part batches may be made in complying with these requests.)

To solve this problem, we have to rearrange our formula $\ln Y = \ln a + (b \times \ln X)$, which tells us the value of the CAT, so that it tells us the value of X, the number of batches to be made – given values for Y, a, and *b*. The basic formula needs revising, and its derivation is:

$$\ln Y = \ln a + (b \times \ln X)$$

$$\frac{\ln Y}{b} = \ln a + \ln X$$

$$\frac{\ln Y - \ln a}{b} = \ln X$$

Thus,:

$$\ln X = \frac{\ln Y - \ln a}{b}$$

Working through the problem where we are trying to find the number of batches (X) to guarantee us a CAT of 20 hours:

$$\ln X = \frac{\ln 20 - \ln 50}{-0.3219}$$

$$= \frac{2.9957 - 3.9120}{-0.3219}$$

$$= 2.8463$$

$$X = e^{2.8463}$$

Therefore:

$$X = 17.2232 \text{ batches}$$

The incremental time between two different numbers of batches

On certain occasions, it might be desirable to know how many hours it should take to produce between, say, 45 and 61 batches. That is, what is the incremental time to be taken by completing batches 45 to 61 inclusive? This would be the case when we have already finished 44 batches, and we receive an order for a further 17 batches. A modification of the initial formula allows us to work this through:

$$\ln XY = \ln a + (b + 1)\ln X$$

Here, $\ln XY$ gives us the **total time for** X batches.

WORKED EXAMPLE 9.5

Given a time of 100 hours for the first batch, and an 80% learning rate, we need to know the number of hours that should be taken to complete batches 45 to 61.

Solution to Worked example 9.5

We need to do two calculations here. Initially, we calculate the total number of hours to complete 44 batches:

$$\begin{aligned}\ln XY &= \ln 100 + (-0.3219 + 1)\ln 44 \\ &= 4.6052 + (0.6781)\,(3.7842) \\ &= 7.1713\end{aligned}$$

Therefore:

$$e^{XY} = 1{,}301.48 \text{ hours}$$

The second calculation reveals the total number of hours needed to complete 61 batches:

$$\begin{aligned}\ln XY &= \ln 100 + (-0.3219 + 1)\ln 61 \\ &= 4.6052 + (0.6781)\,(4.1109) \\ &= 7.3928\end{aligned}$$

Therefore:

$$e^{XY} = 1{,}624.22 \text{ hours}$$

Finally, the total hours required to produce batches 45 to 61 is the difference between the time to complete 44 and 61 batches:

$$\begin{aligned}&1{,}624.22 - 1301.48 \text{ hours} \\ &= 322.74 \text{ hours}\end{aligned}$$

The learning rate given all other data

The final manipulation we need to discuss concerns finding the learning rate, given the performance of the person or the people that have achieved a certain level of output and efficiency. For much of our discussion so far, we have talked about an 80% learning curve. We also said that it seems that an 80% learning curve is 'typically observed'. Whilst this may be true in general terms, there are times when one would need to know the precise rate at which a particular individual or group of individuals is or are learning – simply because the true rate of learning will vary from individual to individual and from situation to situation. If individuals or groups are learning at different rates, even small differences may be significant. Any significant difference between learning rates from person to person and group to group can have a significant impact on average and total costs, as we saw under the heading of sensitivity analysis. To demonstrate the calculation of the rate of learning, we can use some data that was collected in response to a group of students carrying out a set task.

WORKED EXAMPLE 9.6

The data in Table 9.6 below represent the trial numbers and trial times of a student carrying out a simple activity ten times. The raw data are already transformed by natural logarithms.

TABLE 9.6 *Results of student X in carrying out an activity ten times*

Trial number	ln of trial number	Time taken (secs)	Cumulative average time (hrs)	ln of cumulative average time
1	0.00000	67	67.00	4.2047
2	0.69315	57	62.00	4.1271
3	1.09861	40	54.67	4.0013
4	1.38629	38	50.50	3.9220
5	1.60944	42	48.80	3.8877
6	1.79176	33	46.17	3.8323
7	1.94591	35	44.57	3.7971
8	2.07944	49	45.12	3.8094
9	2.19723	31	43.56	3.7740
10	2.30259	27	41.90	3.7353

Solution to Worked example 9.6

There are three basic methods for calculating the learning rate: the high–low method; the scattergraph method; and the ordinary least-squares (OLS) method. We will be employing all three methods, using the data presented in Table 9.6. The section that follows is relatively brief since we have seen the technical content of it in previous chapters. We should now be confident about working through each of these three methods, so we will not discuss them in great detail here, as we use them in this example.

High–low method

Using this method, we estimate the value of 'b' by taking notice only of the highest and the lowest values we have recorded for the number of units and the average time per unit. The trial number is the independent (X) variable, and the CAT is the dependent (Y) variable:

$$b = \frac{\text{high lnCAT} - \text{low lnCAT}}{\text{high lntrial number} - \text{low lntrial number}} \qquad b = \frac{3.7353 - 4.2047}{2.30259 - 0.00000}$$

$$b = -0.20386$$

Notice which of the lnCAT values is considered the high value: this is determined by the independent variable. Therefore, the high lnCAT is 3.7353 and **not** 4.2047. This is because trial number 10 is the high trial number and since the trial number is the independent variable, this dominates the CAT. Now, because 'b' equals the logarithm of the learning rate divided by the logarithm of 2, we have:

$$-0.20386 = \text{lnlearning rate/ln2}$$

$$-0.20386 = \text{lnlearning rate/0.6932}$$

$$\text{lnlearning rate} = 0.6932 \times -0.20386$$
$$\text{lnlearning rate} = -0.14132$$

If the logarithm of the learning rate is -0.14132, the learning rate we are looking for is:

$$\text{learning rate} = 0.8682 = 86.82\%$$

So, we can conclude from this high–low estimate that this student, performing this simple activity, learns at a rate of 86.82%.

The high–low method and graphical analysis

The high–low method can also be carried out using graphical analysis. We plot on a graph only the high and low values respectively for both the number of trials and their corresponding CATs and draw a line though the resulting points we have plotted. Extending this line if necessary to the vertical axis gives the estimated value for 'a'. See Figure 9.4 to see the data from Table 9.6 plotted on a log log graph.

The value of 'b' from such a graph is found by estimating the slope of the curve drawn. To estimate the value for 'b' take the values at the two points on the high–low curve we have just drawn on Figure 9.4, and proceed as follows.

Applying the formula from the previous section:

$$b = \frac{\text{high ln CAT} - \text{low ln CAT}}{\text{high ln trial number} - \text{low ln trial number}}$$

gives:

$$b = \frac{3.7353 - 4.2047}{2.3026 - 0.0000} = -0.20385651$$

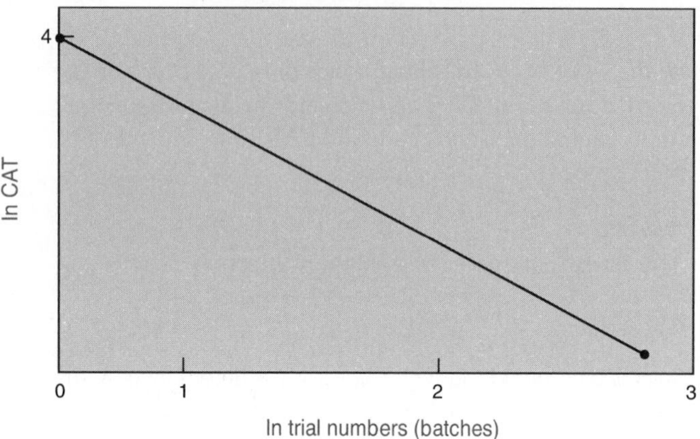

FIGURE 9.4 *High–low estimation of the learning rate*

(Note that the result is negative because we are dealing with a negative slope: a curve that slopes downwards from left to right.)

Since

$$b = \frac{\ln \text{ learning rate}}{\ln 2}$$

$$-0.20385651 = \frac{\ln \text{ learning rate}}{0.69315}$$

therefore:

$$\ln \text{ learning rate} = -0.20385651 \times 0.69315$$
$$= -0.1413031399$$

and therefore:

$$e^{-0.141303} = 0.8682 = 86.82\%$$

This student's learning rate is therefore 86.82% for this activity.

Scattergraph method

You should refer to Figure 9.5 for the whole of this section.

The scattergraph method relies on us using our judgement, based on all of the data, of where the line of best fit of the data should lie. By visual inspection, we would draw the line of best fit on Figure 9.5 and proceed as per the graphical analysis for the high–low method for estimating the value of 'a'. To estimate the value for '*b*', the slope of the curve, take any point you wish on the line of best fit you have drawn in and proceed as follows.

For demonstration purposes, we can imagine a line of best fit which gives

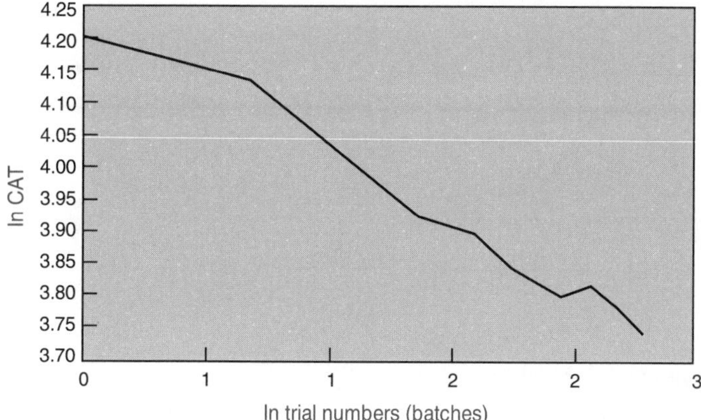

FIGURE 9.5 *Log log graph of student performing a simple activity*

lntrial number	lnCAT
0.00	4.20
2.00	3.85

Estimating the slope gives:

$$b = \frac{3.85 - 4.2}{2.00 - 0.00} = -0.175$$

and since

$$b = \frac{\ln \text{ learning rate}}{\ln 2}$$

$$-0.175 = \frac{\ln \text{ learning rate}}{0.69315}$$

Therefore:

$$\begin{aligned} \ln \text{ learning rate} &= -0.175 \times 0.69315 \\ &= -0.12130125 \end{aligned}$$

and therefore:

$$e^{-0.12130125} = 0.8858 = 88.58\%$$

Note that since these calculations are based on the above line of best fit, you may not arrive at exactly the same answer.

Ordinary least-squares analysis

Using the ordinary least squares (OLS) method on the data relating to student *X* in the previous worked example, we obtain the following:

X = lntrial numbers and Y = lnCAT

Constant (ln a)	4.22889
r^2	0.98
X Coefficient (*b*)	−0.21173

Translating these outputs into a more familiar form gives:

$$\ln Y = \ln a + (b \times \ln X)$$

$$= 4.22889 + (-0.21173 \times \ln X)$$

Hence, the learning rate can now be calculated:

$$-0.21173 = \text{lnlearning rate}/0.6931$$

Therefore:

$$\text{lnlearning rate} = -0.14676$$

giving:

$$\text{learning rate} = 0.8635 = 86.35\%$$

Comparison of the OLS results using logarithmic and original data

Earlier in the chapter we said that we transform the data relating to learning curve analysis so that we can deal with data that tend to form straight lines on a graph. As a partial proof of that assertion, the r^2 value obtained by regressing the original (raw) values for the trial numbers on the original CATs, is

$$r^2 = 0.86$$

This compares with the r^2 value of 0.98 when logarithms are used. Whilst an r^2 value of 0.86 is not bad, a value of 0.98 does represent a near straight line. Transforming by logarithms should help us to achieve enhanced results.

Summary of the benefits of the three methods

The various results obtained by the three methods are:

Method used	Learning rate (%)
High–low method	86.82
Scattergraph method	88.58
OLS	86.35

Since we are dealing with data transformed by logarithms, the results we obtain are close to each other, whatever method we use to assess the learning rate. Given the high values for r^2 we have for the transformed data, this should not be surprising. Furthermore, any result stemming from the scattergraph method should not be too far removed from the result we have here. Of the three methods, the regression analysis method would tend to be the most acceptable one because it gives the most reliable results of the three over any set of data. Providing that the data are reasonable, that the people being studied have not entered their non-learning phase, and that they are still learning reasonably consistently, good estimates of the rate will be given. The final conclusion, then, is that for initial estimations, we could with reasonable confidence use the high–low method and the scattergraph method to estimate the learning rates of employees, or groups of employees, although, we must bear in mind what we said about the sensitivity of learning curve analysis when finalising quotations, cost estimates, and so on.

Practical implications of learning curve analysis

Are learning curves still relevant?

The title of this section is adapted from an article published in 1989:

> With the increase in the number of flexible manufacturing systems (FMS), some experts have questioned the applicability of the learning curve as a management tool in the new manufacturing environment. They assume that more sophisticated technology requires highly skilled workers who are typically salaried employees. (Pattison and Teplitz 1989: 37)

Pattison and Teplitz go on to say that the problem here must be that wage costs in such situations are fixed, and any reduction in labour hours will have little impact on labour costs. They demonstrate that in the FMS environment, total cost reductions can come from a variety of sources, which leads them to suggest that we should talk in terms of a 'cost-improvement curve' or an 'organizational-experience curve'. The sources of the total cost reductions cited by Pattison and Teplitz are shown in Table 9.7.

TABLE 9.7 *Sources of total cost reductions*

Source of cost reduction	Percentage reduction
Material	4.0
Miscellaneous	5.0
Production control	5.0
Industrial engineering	6.5
Workers and direct supervision:	
Learning	24.5
Tooling	25.0
Engineering	30.0

Source: Pattison and Teplitz (1989: 39), Figure 2.

Hence, even in the new manufacturing environment, there is evidence that learning does take place, and that contributions towards cost reductions can come from several sources. By ignoring labour learning, Pattison and Teplitz maintain that: 'labour time and the resultant cost will be overestimated by denying the existence of the "organizational-experience curve"' (ibid. 40).

Learning curves do have a relevance, then, even in the most sophisticated of environments. Furthermore we should redress the balance somewhat and realise that many organisations are not in, and may never move fully into, the new manufacturing environment. Consequently, 'traditional' organisations can still gain significantly by addressing relevant learning issues within its labour force. Abernathy and Wayne (1974. 109–10) make us aware that whilst the application of the learning curve is useful, we need to be aware that it has its limitations:

> While pursuit of the learning curve can reap great benefits, the manufacturer will find it has a 'bottom' unless he maintains flexibility. . . The learning curve relationship is important in planning because it means that increasing a company's product volume and market share will also bring cost advantages over the competition. . . However, other results that are not planned, foreseen, or desired may grow out of such a market penetration/cost reduction progression. Reduced flexibility, a loss of innovative capability, and higher overhead may accompany efforts to cut costs.

Abernathy and Wayne are concerned that by concentrating on the learning curve and its application within an organisation, management can easily lose sight of the more organisationwide view that consideration of the experience effect or curve can give. Their article gives many insights into the problems of a rigid application of the learning curve, and a reading of it will be beneficial.

The practical use of learning curves

Shank and Govindarajan (1993: 145–6) record that there may be a pattern to the way that learning curves are derived. They say:

> Problems addressable within one . . . department . . . tended to have short and steep learning curves. Problems that required coordination across organizational subunit boundaries but that were still addressable within one organization (multiple department within a division) tended to have longer learning curves. Finally, problems that required cooperation and coordination across independent organizations (a customer/supplier linkage) tended to have the longest and flattest learning curves.
>
> An organisation that is looking to maximise its benefit from using learning curve theory, therefore, needs to assess the kind of organisational situation for which it is trying to quantify its learning experiences.

Is a learning rate of 80% a typical rate?

Although the early studies in the aircraft industry reported a learning rate of 80% – and most, if not all, sources quote a typical learning rate of 80% for most, if not all, situations – this rate of learning is open to question. Whilst writing this book, I have carried out many experiments designed to assess people's rate of learning. The experiments have been designed to test situations where the guinea pig was absolutely unfamiliar with the exercise; and separate situations where the guinea pig already had some experience. To date, a learning rate of 80% has rarely been found – and these experiments have been carried out on three continents! Before dismissing the 80% learning rate that is widely quoted, bear in mind that the experiments referred to here are all designed to test human learning, and not technological or organisational learning.

Applications of learning curve analysis

Learning curve analysis can be used to help management with a wide range of decisions. The following list is indicative of the kind of problems it can help to solve:

- quotations and bids for contracts;
- stock valuation;
- production planning;
- production scheduling;
- standard setting;
- budgeting.

To practise using learning curve theory within these contexts, see the practice questions for this chapter.

A warning from strategic management accounting

Shank and Govindarajan (1993) say that log log graphs are a well-known mathematical trick and that simply transforming data by logarithms is not sufficient to win an argument! However, whether we accept that view or not, they do make the valid point that by relying on learning curve analysis, we might be in danger of relying on single variable cost analysis. Shank and Govindarajan point out that there may be more than one critical cost driver to account for. Hence, even if the learning effect is important for our organisation, do not dismiss other factors that might explain cost behaviour. Learning curves are one tool only in the armoury of the modern management accountant and they should be used wisely.

SUMMARY

In this chapter, we have enhanced the discussion of cost behaviour analysis and cost function estimation that we started in Chapter 3. We have introduced two new non-mathematical techniques: the inspection of accounts, and engineering methods. We have also discussed the ordinary least-squares method; and considered learning curve analysis in detail.

We saw with the ordinary least-squares method that we can make very accurate predictions of cost functions from any data, whether we are attempting to assess the fixed and variable cost split, or analysing a learning situation. We discussed such issues as cause and effect, changes to technology, and management policy influences on cost behaviour analysis. Along with much else that is currently under review in management accounting, the way that cost behaviour is estimated is also subject to review. In this chapter, we mentioned cost tables and linked them with Japanese thinking. Cost tables are reported as being widely used in Japan, yet many management accountants in Europe will never have heard of them. This should not be depressing, since European management accountants will have looked at such cost estimation under the heading of the engineering method of cost behaviour estimation. The engineering method of cost behaviour estimation, and cost tables, therefore, are used simply because they contain all the information needed to account for the cost of a product or service. In many organisations there will be no need for any other method than the engineering method. Consequently, in these instances the use of OLS will be irrelevant. OLS will have its place, however, in organisations that use cost tables if arbitrary estimates of certain costs are to be minimised.

There are many stories concerning organisations and governments that did not, initially, take the learning effect into account when negotiating contracts. The outcome of such omissions has been that organisations have set their selling prices at far too high a level to win a contract. Alternatively, the organisation has been paid the full amount for the work done, only to be forced to pay back some of the money because it was considered to have been pricing unfairly! The sole reason for having to repay the money was because of ignorance over the application of the learning effect.

The second part of this chapter has shown what is meant by the learning curve. We also discussed learning rates and the many applications of learning curve theory in a variety of settings. The worked examples presented the following kinds of applications:

- budgeting;
- standard setting;
- production planning; and
- production scheduling.

Finally, the chapter looked at some of the practical implications of learning curve analysis including the idea that an 80% learning rate may not be typical and that care needs to be exercised in using learning curves in reality. Not everyone agrees with the importance of learning about learning curves! Indeed, as we saw, Shank and Govindarajan (1993) positively mistrust them. However, we have seen evidence that applying a knowledge of learning curves will stand us in good stead when negotiating contracts, when attempting to analyse the cost structure of a competitor or a potential supplier, and so on. Although the mathematics of learning curves can be offputting to some of us, programming a spreadsheet to do such work will help enormously. After this has been done once, reusing that spreadsheet should be simplicity itself!

Worksheet: regression and correlation

Put your data in the table that follows and then put all of your workings down the right hand side of the page.

Regression

1. Complete the table below, data line by data line:

X	Y	XY	X^2	Y'	$(Y - Y')^2$	$(Y - \bar{Y})^2$

2. Solve the 'normal equations':

(a) $\Sigma y = n\text{a} + b\Sigma x$

(b) $\Sigma xy = a\Sigma x + b\Sigma x^2$

3. Analyse the regression line:

(a) standard error of the estimate:

$$S_e = \sqrt{\frac{\Sigma(Y - Y')^2}{n - 2}}$$

(b) confidence intervals:

$$Y' \pm (t_\alpha)(S_e)$$

at n − 2 degrees of freedom

Correlation

1. (a) coefficient of determination: r^2

$$r^2 = 1 - \frac{\Sigma(y - y')^2}{\Sigma(y - \bar{y})^2}$$

(b) coefficient of correlation: r

$$r = \sqrt{r^2}$$

2. Standard error of the 'b' coefficient:

$$S_b = \frac{S_e}{\sqrt{\Sigma x^2 - \bar{n}x^2}}$$

3. The confidence interval is calculated by:

$$B = b \pm t_\alpha \frac{S_e}{\sqrt{\Sigma x^2 - \bar{n}x^2}}$$

KEY TERMS

You should satisfy yourself that you have noted all of these terms and can define and/or describe their meaning and use, as appropriate.

Ordinary least-squares method (OLS) (p. 274)	Steady state (p. 288)
High–low (p. 274)	Cessation of learning (p. 288)
Scattergraph (p. 274)	Learning rate (p. 288)
Learning curve (p. 286)	Cumulative average time (CAT) (p. 290)
Experience curve (p. 286)	Natural logarithms (p. 292)
80% learning curve (p. 287)	Sensitivity analysis (p. 293)
Doubling point (p. 287)	Incremental time (p. 293)

RECOMMENDED READING

Abernathy and Wayne (1974) state that learning curve theory is not all positive, while Allan and Hammond (1975) say that it makes our thinking strategic. Berliner and Brimson (1988) is one of the books that is continually recommended, and another winner on learning curves is Hirschmann (1964). A good account and with loads of end-of-chapter questions that are suited to computer analysis is contained in Kaplan and Atkinson (1989). I personally like Kohler (1985); it's full of excellence. Pattison and Teplitz (1989) gives answers to things that many authors didn't even think to question. And, of course, Shank and Govindarajan (1993) again.

QUESTIONS

Review questions

1. Discuss the deficiencies of the inspection of accounts method.
2. What are the deficiencies of the engineering method?
3. In what ways is the OLS method useful in cost behaviour analysis?
4. Define the learning curve; and discuss the doubling point in the context of learning curve theory?
5. Under what conditions might a learning rate of greater than 100% be achieved?
6. What does the term 'cessation of learning' mean?
7. Discuss the following formulæ:

$$Y = aX^b$$

$$\ln XY = \ln a + (b + 1)\ln X$$

$$\ln X = \frac{\ln Y - \ln a}{b}$$

8. What aspects of management accounting does learning curve theory assist with?

Answers to review questions 1, 3, 4 and 8 can be found in the Student Workbook.

Practice questions

Level I

1. Use the inspection of accounts method to determine the behaviour of the costs found in the table of information given below.

Cost	Amount £
Raw materials	43,000
Supervisory salaries	35,000
Overtime premium	5,500
Power for machinery	50,000
Direct wages	97,500
Sundry materials	1,000
Management salaries	70,000

The output relating to these costs was 40,000 units.

2. The following data relate to the manufacture of high-quality motor cars and motor cycles:

Cars and bikes made ('000)	Total costs (£m.)
385	9,400
410	11,420

450	13,738
465	16,155
482	17,778
480	17,177
490	19,085
510	24,092
540	26,129
550	26,780

(a) Using whichever method of regression equation estimation you deem is most suitable, estimate the fixed and variable cost elements of total cost for this business.

(b) Prepare a scattergraph of the above data and plot the regression line derived from your regression equation.

(c) Prepare confidence bands based on the standard errors of the estimate and the coefficient for these data. (Use the worksheet found at the end of the chapter to help with this part of the question.)

3. The transport department of the Norwest Council operates a large fleet of assorted vehicles. These vehicles are used as the need arises by the various departments of the Council. Each month a statement is prepared for the transport department comparing actual results with budget.

One of the items in the transport department's monthly statement is the cost of vehicle maintenance. This maintenance is carried out by the employees of the department.

To facilitate his control the transport manager has asked that future statements should show vehicle maintenance costs analysed into fixed and variable costs.

Data for the six months from January to June 1982 inclusive are as follows:

1982	Vehicle maintenance cost (£)	Vehicle running hours
January	13,600	2,100
February	15,800	2,800
March	14,500	2,200
April	16,200	3,000
May	14,900	2,600
June	15,000	2,500

Required

(a) (i) Analyse the vehicle maintenance costs into fixed and variable costs by means of a graph, based on the data given.

(ii) Prove your results by utilising the least-squares method.

(b) Discuss briefly how you would propose to calculate rates for charging out the total costs incurred to the user departments.

(20 marks)
CIMA Cost Accounting 2
November 1982

4. Imagine a member of staff of the work study department is observing you with a view to assessing your learning rate for the job you do. You know that the learning rate she records will be used to set your piecework rates, but you do not trust her to come up with an answer that will be helpful to you.

Required

Explain how you might cheat on your learning curve in this situation, and therefore enhance your earnings, at least in the short term.

Level II

5. You are currently working through a mountain of data relating to a new service your organisation is about to provide, and your Director of Services has presented you with the following.

Memorandum

To: The Management Accountant
From: Services Director
Date: xx/xx/xx
Subject: Cost breakdown for service X

As per our discussion of yesterday, I have attached the information you were asking for on service X. As far as I can tell, the estimates I am giving you are the best estimates my chaps can provide. The precise nature of the work, though, is certain. All of the processes and procedures I am giving you will work exactly the way I am telling you here.

Best of luck!

Working paper: cost etc. data on Service X.

The service we provide under the heading of Service X entails the following procedures (times in brackets represent standard times spent on the activity):

(a) An order is received by telephone (3 minutes).
(b) That order is passed to a progress clerk (5 minutes).
(c) The progress clerk checks the availability of personnel from the register of available service personnel, and draws up Service X work schedule (5 minutes).
(d) The schedule is passed over to a service executive manager who ensures the schedule is circulated to the available service personnel (20 minutes), and that affirmative responses are received that the job can be completed by them (10 minutes).
(e) The job is carried out and a work ticket confirming the completion of the work and the payment for the job has been received and is being banked, according to company procedures (120 minutes).

Recovery rates for personnel involved in providing Service X:

	Per hour (£)
Telephonist	12.50
Progress clerk	15.00
Service executive manager	12.50
Service personnel	13.75

Consumables for each 'unit' of Service X consist of 3 kg of Sudso powder at £1.50 per kg, and 100 ml of Deterjo at £10 per litre. Additionally, machinery and equipment, depreciated at the rate of £6 per hour, is used in providing Service X for 100 of the 120 minutes allocated to each 'unit' of Service X provided.

Required

Calculate the cost per unit of Service X

6. The managers of MTGG Ltd expect that the number of units its new product will sell will be 50,000 units in the next two years if the selling price is set at £50, and 25,000 units if the price is set at £55.

   The management accountant has estimated that for the first 1,000 the unit costs per unit will be:

	£
Materials	25
Direct labour and variable overhead	20

   Direct labour and variable overhead are expected to drop, reflecting an 85% learning curve, which is what the rate the firm has tended to experience on its new products.

Required

Which of the selling prices would you charge? Justify your answer.

7. A Company Ltd has received an order for 35 newly designed machines. The customer says she needs all of the machines delivered as soon as possible. The Production Manager of A Company Ltd is not at all certain that he has the capacity to be able to make all 35 machines. Having checked his budgets, targets, and revised schedules, the Production Manager has the following information to hand:

Estimated hours for first machine	450
Estimated learning rate (%)	75
Total labour hours available until year end	11,000
Labour hours committed on existing orders	7,500

   The Production Manager is keen to ensure that he does not interrupt any of his existing schedules and orders.

Required

(a) Will the firm will be able to finish the order by the year end?

(b) What is the learning rate at which Y exactly equals the number of available labour hours for the rest of the financial year? Discuss your findings.

8. Barrett O'Flaherty plans to make a product called the Timmy. The Timmy is made by means of a labour intensive process. O'Flaherty believes that because of this there will be significant learning effect implications for it.

   Each unit of the Timmy needs 50 units of raw materials at a cost of £30 per unit; the standard direct labour hour rate is £12.50 per direct labour hour; the variable production overhead assigned to production is assigned at the rate of £20 per direct labour hour; and total fixed costs amount to £54,480. O'Flaherty intends to add a mark-up of 30% on variable manufacturing costs in setting the initial selling price for all of his organisation's products.

So far, two batches (16 units) of the Timmy have been made, and the relevant details are:

(a) Batch one: 8 units requiring a total of 3,200 direct labour hours
(b) Batch two: 8 units requiring a total of 2,240 direct labour hours

Required

(a) from the information supplied, what is the learning rate applicable to the direct labour hours needed to produce the Timmy?
(b) Determine the standard direct labour hours which O'Flaherty should establish for each unit of the Timmy, given that O'Flaherty feels that the standard should be based on his experience of the learning curve which says that the average hours per unit for batches three and four should be the basis of the standard labour hours needed.
(c) Having completed the 4 batches, O'Flaherty then received an order for a further 4 batches. What price should O'Flaherty charge for the additional 4 batches?
(d) What are the limitations of learning curve theory?

Solutions to practice questions 1, 4 and 5 can be found in the Student Workbook. Solutions to practice question numbers in red can be found at the end of this book.

Projects

1. From any source, preferably a source that can usefully be applied to management accounting, collect a series of data that can be analysed into the equivalent of fixed and variable classifications using some or all of the techniques we have discussed in this chapter.
2. Determining an individual's learning rate need not be difficult. To determine your own rate of learning, or the rate of learning of a friend, devise a simple exercise, or use a small jigsaw or similar toy that a 2- or 3-year-old child would use. Try to use a toy with which the 'guinea pig' will not be too familiar!

   Once the exercise has been set, the guinea pig should perform the same exercise repetitively for, say, 10 to 15 trials. The exact time it takes the guinea pig to perform each trial being carefully noted. Ensure the trials are carried out with the aim of being as efficient and effective as possible – racing to become as fast as possible is not necessarily a useful thing to try to do. Once all of the data has been collected, carry out as many learning curve related calculations as you feel necessary. As a minimum, determine the learning rate of the guinea pig.
3. To assess the implications of estimating learning rates erroneously, test your guinea pig from project 1 again, and with the same exercise. Carry out the same number of trials, recording the trial times carefully.

   (a) What conclusions can be drawn from assessing learning rates when the guinea pig is already part of the way down his or her learning curve for that activity?
   (b) Were the results derived from project 1 any help in predicting the results of this project?

REFERENCES

Abernathy, W. J. and Wayne, K. (1974), 'Limits of the learning curve', *Harvard Business Review* 52 (5) (Sept.–Oct.)109–19.

Allan, G. B. and Hammond, J. S. III (1975), 'Note on the use of experience curves in competitive decision making', Note 175–174 (Harvard Business School).

Anthony, R. N. and Reece, J. S. (1989), *Accounting: Text and cases*, 8th edn (Irwin).

Berliner, C. and Brimson, J. A. (eds) (1988), *Cost Management for Today's Advanced Manufacturing: The CAM-I conceptual design* (Harvard Business School Press).

CIMA (1991) *Management Accounting Official Terminology* (Chartered Institute of Managemet Accountants).

Hirsch, M. L. Jr and Louderback, J. G. III (1986), *Cost Accounting: Accumulation, analysis, and use*, 2nd edn (Kent Publishing).

Hirschmann, W. B. (1964), 'Profit from the learning curve', *Harvard Business Review* 42 (1) (Jan.–Feb.), 125–39.

Kaplan, R. S. and Atkinson, A. A. (1989), *Advanced Management Accounting*, 2nd edn (Prentice Hall).

Kohler, H. (1985), *Statistics for Business and Economics* (Scott, Foresman).

Pattison, D. D. and Teplitz, C. J. (1989), 'Are learning curves still relevant?', *Management Accounting* (NAA) (February), 37–40.

Shank, J. K. and Govindarajan, V. (1993), *Strategic Cost Management: The new tool for competitive advantage* (The Free Press).

Yoshikawa, T., Innes, J., Mitchell, F. and Tanaka, M. (1993), *Contemporary Cost Management* (Chapman & Hall).

CHAPTER TEN

Absorption costing and variable costing

CHAPTER OBJECTIVES

After reading this chapter you should be able to:

- define variable and absorption costing
- appreciate the difference between absorption and variable costing
- prepare absorption costing statements
- prepare variable costing statements
- account for under- and over recovery of overheads
- appreciate the types of decisions that variable costing can help with
- appreciate the limitations of the variable costing approach to managerial decision making

Introduction

This chapter is the first of four chapters in the section concerning itself with accounting for managerial decision making. Although we have discussed many aspects of accounting for the elements of cost, together with activity-based costing and accounting for jobs, batches and processes, there are still further avenues to explore as far as managerial decision making is concerned. This chapter introduces several of the basic ideas underlying management accounting and managerial decision making. Primarily, this chapter is devoted to variable costing; but there is a significant part of the discussion devoted to absorption costing.

Variable costing versus absorption costing

Variable costing is often seen as being a kind of opposite of absorption costing. Absorption costing is otherwise known as full costing and concerns itself with trying to ensure that every single cost arising within an organisation, process or job is allowed for. We saw much evidence of this approach in Chapters 6, 7 and 8. Variable costing, on the other hand, takes a more realistic view than absorption costing in many instances, by taking account only of what is relevant to a decision. Variable costing takes the view that fixed costs are sunk costs and are therefore not relevant for decision-making purposes. Once a fixed cost is deemed to be non-relevant it is treated as being written off in the period in which it is incurred. Before we contrast the absorption and variable costing approaches we should define our terms. Variable costing is called marginal costing by CIMA and defined as: 'The accounting system in which variable costs are charged to cost units and fixed costs of the period are written-off in full against the aggregate contribution. It has special value in decision-making' (CIMA 1991). Similarly, CIMA uses the term marginal cost rather than a variable cost and defines it as: 'The cost of one unit of a product or service which would be avoided if the unit were not produced or provided' (ibid.). Much of the literature on management accounting has deferred to economics literature by using the terms marginal cost and marginal costing rather than variable cost and costing. Whilst the terms are synonymous, it is more convenient for us to use the latter two terms.

The implications of the definition of variable costing – which says that it is only the variable costs that are charged to cost units, with the fixed costs being written off in the relevant period – can be clearly seen when we examine the differences between the absorption approach and the variable costing approache to the preparation of cost and profit statements. In Chapters 6, 7 and 8 in particular, we discussed accounting for overheads, activity-based costing, and job, batch and process costing respectively, and in those chapters we took the absorption costing view. We found that absorption costing is: 'The procedure which charges fixed as well as variable overhead to cost units' (CIMA 1991).

What this means is that, taking a very simplified view, the absorption cost of a cost unit is the sum of all costs: fixed and variable, product and period. This is irrespective of whether that cost is a cash cost or an accrued cost. To find the average cost of a cost unit, we divide the total (absorption or full) cost by the total number of cost units involved. There are a variety of problems inherent in the absorption costing method that we should identify and discuss. A discussion of the problems of absorption costing will help us to appreciate the advantages of the variable costing approach for managerial decision-making purposes.

Problems with the absorption costing approach

1. Whenever we are dealing with a fixed or semi-variable cost, we come across the problem of changes in volume of output. The argument, of course, is that the more we make of a product, the lower the average fixed cost per unit. The converse is also true: the less we make, the higher the average fixed cost per unit. Thus changes in volumes of output can have an effect on our costings, based purely on the behaviour of a cost.

2. One or more of the costs that are often taken into account in arriving at an absorption cost for a cost unit may not be relevant for the purposes for which the costing was being prepared. A cost such as fixed asset depreciation is often included as part of the absorption cost of a product, yet the capital cost of fixed assets is a sunk cost: that is, it is no longer a cash cost, and is not relevant to the cost units being prepared today. The absorption

costing approach, by including such accrued, sunk, costs is tending to assess long-term costs and apply them to short-term situations.

3. The concept of relevance is also important when we consider the levels of output we might use to calculate costs per cost unit. Such calculations will often be carried out based on, for example, the volumes of output found in the annual budget. The point at issue here is that for day-to-day costing purposes, the annual budget, and the basis on which it was drafted, may have no relevance. This is because on any given day an opportunity might present itself that is either unforeseen by the budget, or would not be accounted for in the budget. For example, a coach party arriving at a country inn and offering to pay £150 providing all members of the party can be given a Ploughman's Lunch, as opposed to paying the menu stated price of £250 for the same meal for the same number of people.

Variable costing overcomes all the difficulties of absorption costing as far as managerial decision making is concerned.

Illustration of the two approaches

The following example of the unit costs of a product shows the basic difference between these two approaches:

	£
Absorption cost per unit:	
direct materials	7
direct labour	8
variable factory overheads	4
fixed factory overheads	9
Total absorption cost	28
Variable cost per unit:	
direct materials	7
direct labour	8
variable factory overheads	4
Total variable cost	19

What we are saying here is that, given the nature of a fixed cost (that it does not change in the short term, irrespective of even large changes in output) the only relevant costs for managerial decision-making purposes are variable costs. We do not need to know that the fixed factory overheads are £9 per unit, as far as a short-term decision relating to the product above is concerned. An example of the sort of decision we are talking about would include, say, that selling 100 units of the product that the above costing data relates to. Let's say the sale of these 100 units can be regarded as a once-only opportunity; that we have the units in stock; and that selling and replacing them will not lead to the business incurring any further fixed costs. Even without knowing the selling price for these 100 units, we should be clear in our minds that the fixed costs are not relevant to this decision. Since we are told that they will not change as a result of the decision, whether we decide to sell the 100 units or not, they are irrelevant. This is the basis of variable costing.

Contribution: the key to understanding variable costing

Of all the words, phrases and definitions we could discuss under the heading of management accounting and managerial decision making, the single most important word is contribution. Not only is much of the work of this part of this book dependent upon this key word, but we could find it in use in a whole variety of situations including, Part Four of this book. Contribution is simply defined as being the contribution that sales make towards fixed costs and profit, and algebraically it is defined as:

sales − variable costs = contribution = fixed costs + profit

Contribution is what is left from sales revenue after we have paid out our variable costs; and out of that contribution we must then pay for fixed costs. Once we have paid for fixed costs out of our contribution, we have a profit or loss. In decision-making terms, we will see that if a short-term opportunity gives rise to a positive contribution we would, generally, consider accepting that opportunity. This is so because we take the view that any short-term opportunity will have no influence on the level of fixed costs; hence fixed costs are irrelevant and the value of the contribution is the only signal we need in terms of acceptance or rejection of such an opportunity.

The preparation of financial statements

A more comprehensive example of the preparation of accounting statements shows us the full implications of the differences between the absorption costing and variable costing methods.

WORKED EXAMPLE 10.1

My Company Ltd makes and sells two different products The Hay and The Bea. We have taken the necessary information from the accounts of the business, as follows:

		The Hay	The Bea
Per unit		£	£
Sales price		30	40
Direct labour costs		5	9
Variable production overheads		4	8
Direct material costs		7	5
Total units		Units	Units
Output:	December	700	800
	January	350	500
Sales:	December	600	700
	January	400	400

Fixed overheads:	£
December	9,200
January	5,400

There were no stocks of either product at the start of December. For every unit of The Hay produced, one hour's worth of labour is applied, and for every unit of The Bea produced, two hours' worth of labour is applied.

Required

Prepare statements for The Hay for December and January showing the profit, and closing stock valuations using the absorption and variable costing techniques.

Solution to Worked example 10.1

Follow through the fully worked solution now for The Hay.
Workings: The Hay

1. We need to sort out the balances in stock at the ends of the periods before we try to prepare the income statements.

Schedule of stocks (units)	December units	January units
Opening stocks	nil	100
plus: Production	700	350
	700	450
less: Sales	600	400
closing stocks	100	50

2. A second issue is the apportionment of fixed overheads. There are three possible bases for apportionment, based on the information supplied. The first basis is to apportion on the basis of the number of labour hours worked for each product; the second basis is to apportion the costs on the basis of the number of cost units of each product made; the third basis for apportioning the fixed costs is to do so in proportion to the number of units sold. The workings for each of these are:

Labour hours basis

December

$$\frac{\text{fixed overheads}}{\text{total labour hours}} = \frac{\text{average fixed cost}}{\text{per labour hour}}$$

$$= \frac{£9,200}{(700 \times 1 \text{ hour}) + (800 \times 2 \text{ hours})}$$

$$= \frac{£9,200}{2,300 \text{ hours}} = £4 \text{ per labour hour}$$

Note, that in the calculation of the total labour hours, we need to take the hours for both products into account, because the fixed overheads relate to both products and the overheads need to be apportioned to both products. The calculation of the total labour hours is the number of cost units of The Hay made multiplied by the number of labour hours per unit, plus the number of cost units of The Bea made multiplied by the number of labour hours per unit.

January

$$= \frac{£5,400}{(350 \times 1 \text{ hour}) + (500 \times 2 \text{ hours})}$$

$$= \frac{£5,400}{1,350 \text{ hours}} = £4 \text{ per labour hour}$$

Units of output basis

The mechanics of this method are very similar to the mechanics of the labour hour approach. There is a significant difference, of course, and that is that the denominator is now the total units of output. The workings are:

December

$$\frac{\text{fixed overheads}}{\text{total units produced}} = \frac{\text{average fixed cost}}{\text{per units produed}}$$

$$= \frac{£9,200}{700 \text{ units} + 800 \text{ units}}$$

$$= \frac{£9,200}{1,500 \text{ units}} = £6.13 \text{ per unit}$$

January

$$= \frac{£5,400}{350 \text{ units} + 500 \text{ units}}$$

$$= \frac{£5,400}{850 \text{ units}} = £10.82 \text{ per unit}$$

Sales units basis

This method is identical to the units of output basis except that the number of units sold is the denominator rather than the number of units made.

December

$$\frac{\text{fixed overheads}}{\text{total units sold}} = \frac{\text{average fixed cost}}{\text{per units sold}}$$

$$= \frac{£9{,}200}{600 \text{ units} + 700 \text{ units}}$$

$$= \frac{£9{,}200}{1{,}300 \text{ units}} = £7.08 \text{ per unit}$$

January

$$= \frac{£5{,}400}{400 \text{ units} + 400 \text{ units}}$$

$$= \frac{£5{,}400}{800 \text{ units}} = £6.75 \text{ per unit}$$

These rates are then multiplied by the relevant base as necessary. Before we do this, we need to make a decision on which of the three rates we should use. Because there is no guarantee that there are any similarities in the nature of the different products made and sold, it is wise to choose the labour hour rate for fixed cost apportionment. We will incorporate these rates in the statements that we can now prepare.

Absorption costing statements

The traditional absorption method shows fixed costs added to all other costs in order to arrive at an average cost for total costs, stock valuations and profit purposes.

Absorption costing profit statement The Hay

December

	£	£
Sales		18,000
Manufacturing cost of sales:		
Materials	4,900	
Labour	3,500	
Variable overheads	2,800	
Fixed overheads	2,800	
	14,000	
less: Closing stock	2,000	
Cost of sales		12,000
Profit		6,000

Workings to accompany December's profit statement

Total sales:

= £30 per unit × 600 units sold

= £18,000

Total direct materials:

= £7 per unit × 700 units made

= £4,900

Total direct labour:

= £5 per unit × 700 units made

= £3,500

Total variable overheads:

= £4 per unit × 700 units made

= £2,800

Fixed overheads:

= £4 per labour hour × (700 units made × 1 labour hour per unit)

= £4 × 700

= £2,800

Closing stocks are valued as follows:

cost per unit × number of cost units in stock

$$= \frac{\text{Total manufacturing costs}}{\text{Total units made}} \times 100 \text{ units}$$

$$= \frac{£14{,}000}{700 \text{ units}} \times 100 \text{ units}$$

= £20 per unit × 100 units

= £2,000

Note that the question had direct materials as the last of the direct costs: for presentation purposes, it has been moved to the top of the list. This makes these profit statements consistent with the layouts that we have previously encountered.

Absorption costing profit statement The Hay

January

	£	£
Sales		12,000
Manufacturing cost of sales:		
Materials	2,450	
Labour	1,750	
Variable overheads	1,400	
Fixed overheads	1,400	
	7,000	
plus: Opening stock	2,000	
less: Closing stock	1,000	
Cost of sales		8,000
Profit		4,000

Workings to accompany January's profit statement

All calculations, except for stocks, are virtually identical to the calculations just seen in the December statement. They are not repeated here. The opening stock is December's closing stock brought down. Note that this stock is valued at £20 per unit. The closing stock is also valued at £20 per unit, since none of the costs making up total costs have changed. The calculation is:

$$\frac{\text{£}7{,}000}{350 \text{ units made}} \times 50 \text{ units}$$

$$= \text{£}20 \times 50 \text{ units}$$

$$= \text{£}1{,}000$$

For future reference, you should note that whether we were using the FIFO, the LIFO, or any other stock valuation method, all units would have been valued at £20 per unit in this example.

Variable costing statements

Variable costing profit statement The Hay

December

	£	£
Sales		18,000
Variable manufacturing cost of sales:		
Materials	4,900	
Labour	3,500	
Variable overheads	2,800	
	11,200	

less: Closing stock	1,600	
Variable cost of sales		9,600
Contribution		8,400
less: Fixed costs		2,800
Profit		5,600

With this statement we see immediately the meaning of the term contribution and what we mean by the fixed costs being written off in the period in which they are incurred. Closing stocks are valued on the basis of variable cost only. The fixed cost is written off in full against the total contribution.

Workings for December's profit statement

Although the calculations for the variable costing method are very similar to those for the absorption costing method, they are repeated here.

Total sales:

= £30 per unit × 600 units sold

= £18,000

Total direct materials:

= £7 per unit × 700 units made

= £4,900

Total direct labour:

= £5 per unit × 700 units made

= £3,500

Total variable overheads:

= £4 per unit × 700 units made

= £2,800

Closing stocks are valued as follows:

cost per unit × number of units in stock

$$= \frac{\text{Total variable manufacturing costs}}{\text{Total units made}} \times 100 \text{ units}$$

$$= \frac{£14{,}000}{700 \text{ units}} \times 100 \text{ units}$$

= £20 per unit × 100 units

= £2,000

Fixed overheads:

= £4 per labour hour × (700 units made × 1 labour hour per unit)

= £4 × 700

= £2,800

Variable costing profit statement The Hay

January

	£	£
Sales		12,000
Variable manufacturing cost of sales:		
Materials	2,450	
Labour	1,750	
Variable overheads	1,400	
	5,600	
plus: Opening stock	1,600	
less: Closing stock	800	
Variable cost of sales		6,400
Contribution		5,600
less: Fixed costs		1,400
Profit		4,200

Workings for January's profit statement

As with January's absorption costing profit statement, only the stock valuation calculations are repeated here. The opening stock is December's closing stock brought down. Notice, this stock is valued at the variable cost of £16 per unit. The closing stock is also valued at £16 per unit, since none of the costs making up total variable costs have changed. The calculation is:

$$\frac{£5{,}600}{350 \text{ units made}} \times 50 \text{ units}$$

= £16 × 50 units

= £800

Again, for future reference, you should note that whether we were using the FIFO, the LIFO, or any other stock valuation method, all units would have been valued at £16 per unit in this example.

Summary of statements The Hay

Summarising the results of these presentations gives:

	Absorption costing	Variable costing
December's profit	£6,000	£5,600
January's profit	£4,000	£4,200
Total	10,000	9,800

Absorption costing profit versus variable costing profit

Looking at this summary, we might well ask the question: Does absorption costing make us richer?' Briefly, the answer is no! In the long term, the differences between the two methods disappear. The difference in the level of profit reported on a period-by-period basis is real: it does exist. The difference is due to the different valuations placed on stocks by the different methods.

Let us take a look at the workings for the two methods to see the explanation for what is happening. The absorption costing value for stock is £20 per unit; and variable costing values stocks at £16 per unit. In December, the total closing stock value for the absorption costing method is £2,000 and the profit is £6,000; and for the variable costing method, closing stock is valued at £1,600 and the profit is £5,600. The difference in profit figures arrived at by the two methods in December is

£6,000 – £5,600 = £400;

and the difference between the values of closing stock arrived at by the two methods in December is

£2,000 – £1,600 = £400

The reason for the periodic differences in the profits reported by the different methods is due to the differences in the values placed on stocks. The reason for the differences in stock values is explained entirely by the inclusion or exclusion of fixed costs from that valuation. However, if, for example, in the case of The Hay, the opening stock and the closing stock (at the beginning of December and the end of January, respectively) had both been nil, there would have been no difference in the overall profits reported by the two methods. There could still have been differences, however, on a period-by-period basis. In the long term, it does not matter which method is used, since the profits will be the same under each method.

Under- and overrecovery of overheads

In Chapter 6, we looked at the under- and overrecovery of overheads in an absorption costing situation. We looked at the over- and underabsorption of overheads when we looked at the implications of using predetermined overhead absorption rates. The examples we have been working through in this chapter contain the same implications for under- and overrecovery of overheads as we found in Chapter 6. In absorption costing, we absorb overheads by means of the fixed overhead absorption rate (FOAR): this means that if, for example, the FOAR is £2 per direct labour hour, and the number of direct labour hours actually worked is 1,000, we will absorb £2 × 1,000 = £2,000 for the period; and we will absorb this amount irrespective of the fixed overheads actually incurred. Thus, if the actual overheads for the period were £2,500, in this example, we would have underabsorbed, or underrecovered them by £500. Had the actual overheads been £1,750 for the period under review, we would have overabsorbed or overrecovered the overheads by the difference of £250.

In summary, the amount by which we have under- or overrecovered our overheads for a period is calculated by taking the difference, if any, between the overheads absorbed by production or output and determining whether the amount absorbed is greater than or less than the amount actually incurred. If the amount absorbed is greater than the amount incurred, overheads have been overrecovered; and if the amount absorbed is less than the amount incurred, overheads have been underrecovered. The accounting treatment of the under- and overrecovery of overheads is dealt with in Worked example 10.2.

Finally, we could ask the question: Why do we allow ourselves to be put in the position of absorbing the wrong amount into products in the first place? After all, if we absorb the overheads actually incurred, there would surely be no under- or overrecovery? The sentiments being expressed here are valid to a point. We could make sure we absorbed only the actual overheads and get rid of the need for under- and overrecovery adjustments. However, the only way to do this is to wait until the relevant period has finished so that total actual overheads can be calculated. After all, we cannot know what our actual overheads are until they have been incurred. The problem we have, of course, is that estimates, quotations and invoices need to be prepared much more frequently than at the end of a period. To do this requires the use of a predetermined overhead recovery rate, and the use of such a rate will almost inevitably lead to the under- and overrecovery of overheads.

Variable costing and the recovery of overheads

Because of the way in which variable costing works, there is no over- and underrecovery of overheads. Since fixed costs are written off in the period in which they are incurred, there is no absorption of overheads. In the following example, therefore, there is no allowance for the over- and underrecovery of overheads. The example that follows shows all of the new features relating to the over- and underrecovery of overheads.

WORKED EXAMPLE 10.2

Bateman Ltd began its operations as a bow tie manufacturer on 1 January 1991. The accounting records for the first two years of operations revealed the following:

	1991	1992
	£	£
Sales revenues	108,000	96,000
Variable manufacturing costs	57,000	66,000
Fixed manufacturing costs	20,000	20,000
Selling and administration costs	32,000	32,000
Units produced	9,500	11,000
Units sold	9,000	8,000

The normal output level is 10,000 units per month; there were no units of work in progress at the end of 1991 or 1992; and selling and administration costs are entirely fixed.

Required

Prepare profit statements for each of 1991 and 1992 for each of the absorption costing and variable costing methods.

Solution to Worked example 10.2

Bateman Ltd profit statements for the years 1992 and 1992

Schedule of stocks (units)

	1991	1992
Opening stocks	–	500
plus: Production	9,500	11,000
	9,500	11,500
less: Sales	9,000	8,000
Closing stocks	500	3,500

Fixed overhead absorption rate

$$\frac{\text{total fixed overheads}}{\text{normal output}}$$

$$= \frac{£20,000}{10,000 \text{ units}}$$

$$= £2 \text{ per unit}$$

Variable cost per unit

The variable cost per unit is constant at £6 per unit. This can be verified by dividing the total variable cost for either year and dividing it by the production for either year, and the result will be £6 per unit in each case.

Absorption costing

	1991		1992	
	£	£	£	£
Sales		108,000		96,000
Manufacturing costs:				
variable	57,000		66,000	
fixed (absorbed)	19,000		22,000	
	76,000		88,000	
plus: Opening stock	–		4,000	
less: Closing stock	4,000		28,000	
	72,000		64,000	
(Over)/underrecovery of fixed costs	1,000		(2,000)	
		71,000		62,000
Gross profit		37,000		34,000
Selling and administration costs		32,000		32,000
Net profit/(loss)		5,000		2,000

Variable costing

	1991		1992	
	£	£	£	£
Sales		108,000		96,000
Variable costs of manufacturing:				
Variable costs	57,000		60,000	
plus: Opening stock	–		3,000	
less: Closing stock	3,000		21,000	
		54,000		42,000
Contribution		54,000		54,000
Fixed manufacturing costs		20,000		20,000
Gross profit		34,000		34,000
Selling and administration costs		32,000		32,000
Net profit		2,000		2,000

The uses of the variable costing presentation

Now that we have mastered the techniques of absorption and variable costing as far as cost and profit statements are concerned, we need now to consider the consequences of what we are doing. Why bother with variable costing statements? Management accounting serves the needs of management, of those in the organisation responsible for attaining the objectives of the organisation. Hence we should look at variable costing to see how it helps management to meet these objectives. Statutes as well as Statement of Standard Accounting Practice (SSAP) 9 do not permit variable costing statements to be used for publication purposes in the United Kingdom. They do so on the grounds that **all** costs have to be matched with the revenue that they give rise to, and variable costing does not allow for this. The variable costing approach of writing off, in full, fixed costs in the period in which they are incurred is not an acceptable procedure. More important from a managerial point of view is the argument that the variable costing approach of the separation of fixed and variable costs helps with the understanding of financial statements. Specifically, such a separation and presentation of information shows clearly how costs are assigned to stocks, and it simplifies the statements in more general terms.

Types of decisions that variable costing helps with

We could say that all managerial decisions can usefully be influenced by variable costing, and there would be a large element of truth in that. However, we should spell out precisely what sort of decisions we are talking about. Variable costing helps with: *ad hoc* decisions; make or buy decisions; close a department decisions; limiting factor analysis; sell or process further decisions; and many more.

It is for these purposes that we might prepare variable costing statements. When we talk about profit planning and pricing, we mean profit planning and pricing in the short term. Such decisions to be taken in the short term include selling units of output at less than full cost: for example, hotel rooms are often sold at less than full cost at weekends. We might pay, say, £50 per night for a room at the Sea View Hotel as long as we stay on both Friday and Saturday nights and at least pay for breakfast there on Saturday and Sunday mornings. The usual price for such a room might be £80 or £100 per night. Pricing decisions such as this one are based on variable costing principles (whether those carrying out such pricing policies are aware of it or not!) Decisions such as these should be based on variable costing principles and a variable costing profit statement needs to be prepared to help management appreciate the variable costing approach. We will develop these latter ideas in full in Chapter 11.

Limitations of variable costing

Authors like Shank and Govindarajan (1993) are now preaching the gospel that does not really accord with variable costing! They have put into rather bilious terms what has been felt, and written about, for a relatively long time now. There are many limitations to variable costing. The following discussion covers some of them. The distinction between fixed, variable and semi-variable costs is by no means certain. We cannot guarantee, even after the most exhaustive analysis, that the split we have arrived at in fixed and variable costs is as true as we might be representing. In many situations, estimating the true behaviour of costs might prove elusive. Labour costs might of themselves cause us many problems.

> The 'ratchet effect' may also operate in respect of direct wages insofar as, in the very short run, decreases in output may not necessarily be accompanied by reductions in variable costs, whereas for increases in output the wages costs would tend to increase. (Ezzamel and Hart 1987: 169)

The debate on activity-based costing has shown that costs may not only be related to output. Relating costs to activities other than final output now has a lot of credibility. Hence the variable cost approach of thinking in terms of variability with output may not go far enough. The nature of the time horizon normally applied to variable costing is one that Shank and Govindarajan rightly object to. If we are concerning ourselves with the short term, as we are with variable costing, then what of the long term? Will the long term automatically take care of itself? The answer is no. More importantly, what is management's attitude to the time horizon and variable costing? There has been a lot of discussion over the last three decades or so about short termism and management action. There are many examples where management are accused of taking a short-term view of their business at the expense of the long term. Whilst such discussions are aimed generally at short termism and the immediate optimisation of managerial bonus payments, there are other more strategic implications to consider. If managers are concerned to apply variable costing, they may be losing sight of the longer-term objectives of the organisation.

The linearity of costs is another problem area that we have discussed several times now. We know from the work of people such as Johnson (1960) that linearity is both a problem and not a problem. We know that some costs are demonstrably non-linear, yet Johnson shows that even so, a linear approximation is sufficient to get round this problem. Nevertheless, linearity is a problem that cannot simply be dismissed and it will haunt the management accountant who ignores it without careful analysis.

SUMMARY

The purpose of this chapter has been twofold. First, it has introduced the idea of variable costing; and secondly, it has contrasted variable costing with the more familiar absorption costing.

Having introduced variable costing, and the vital concept of contribution, we saw that absorption costing is a costing method that essentially takes all costs, fixed and variable, and assigns them to products. Variable costing, on the other hand, breaks down all costs into their fixed and variable components, assigns only the variable costs to products or services, and writes off the fixed costs in their entirety in the period in which they are incurred. In the short term these two methods report different profit figures, given the same accounting inputs. In the long term, however, there is no difference between the two methods as far as profits are concerned.

We have introduced the justification for the use of variable costing statements for internal reporting purposes in the light of various Statutes and SSAP 9 that say that variable costing is not acceptable for external reporting purposes in the United Kingdom. We will develop these ideas in greater detail in the following chapter.

Finally, we took a critical view of variable costing in relation to managerial decision making.

KEY TERMS

You should satisfy yourself that you have noted all of these terms and can define and/or describe their meaning and use, as appropriate.

Variable costing (p. 313)	Under- and overrecovery of overheads (p. 325)
Absorption costing (p. 313)	Fixed overhead (p. 325)
Full costing (p. 313)	SSAP 9 (p. 328)
Contribution (p. 316)	Variable costing statements (p. 328)

RECOMMENDED READING

Definite, realistic insights from Darlington *et al.* (1992). Johnson (1960) is now fairly old, but it has a lot of useful commendably researched material in it. And Shank and Govindarajan (1993), of course.

QUESTIONS

Review questions

1. The basic problem with the variable costing approach is that it tends to assess long-term costs and apply them to short-term decisions. Explain this comment.
2. Distinguish between variable costs and variable costing.
3. What does the term 'contribution' mean in a variable costing context?
4. Distinguish between gross contribution and net contribution.
5. What justifications are there for excluding fixed manufacturing costs from stock values under variable costing?

Answers to review questions 3 and 5 can be found in the Student Workbook.

Graded practice questions

Level I

1. What arguments are there for and against using variable costing? Assuming that the quantity of closing stocks is higher than the quantity of opening stocks, the profit derived from the variable costing method would be different from the profit derived using the absorption costing method. By way of an illustration of your own devising, demonstrate whether the profit would be higher or lower under variable costing than it would be under absorption costing.

2. Consider each of the following three situations separately:

   (a) What would be the profit under variable costing given the following facts? An organisation reported a profit of £250,000 using absorption costing with a fixed overhead absorption rate of £25 per unit. Stock at the end of the period was 2,000 units lower than at the beginning of the period.

   (b) Evaluate the difference between sales and output assuming that the profit reported by an organisation was £250,000 under variable costing and £200,000 under absorption costing. The fixed overhead absorption rate was £12.50 per unit.

(c) Calculate in units the difference between the opening and closing stocks if an organisation having a profit of £150,000 under variable costing and £250,000 under absorption costing had a fixed overhead absorption rate of £5 per unit.

3. (a) From the unit information for one product prepare profit statements for June and July using both absorption and variable costing.

	£	£
Selling price		30.00
Production costs:		
variable	13.75	
fixed	8.75	
Selling and administration costs:		
variable	1.25	
fixed	3.75	

The unit costs are based on the normal budget volume of 8,000 units per month. During June, the organisation produced 7,500 units and sold 7,000 units. During July, the organisation made 8,500 units and sold 9,000 units. At the start of June the opening stock consisted of 400 units, valued at the costs shown above.

(b) Where relevant, calculate the gross profit, net profit and contribution to sales ratios from the above data.

(See question 7 for an extension to this question.)

Level II

4. From the point of view of the Inland Revenue, what would happen if variable costing were made acceptable for income tax purposes? Illustrate your answer.

5. (a) The following data relate to one product. For both November and December, prepare: (i) the absorption costing and (ii) the variable costing profit statements.
(b) calculate the gross profit, net profit and contribution: sales ratios where possible.

Data

- Sales: November 5,000 units; December, 8,000 units.
- Production: November 7,000 units; December 5,000 units.
- Selling price is £90 per unit for both months.
- Variable cost of production is £55 per unit for both months.
- Fixed costs of production are £130,000 per period and the normal level of output is 8,000 units per month.
- Selling and administration costs amount to £60,000 per month; and they are entirely fixed in behaviour.
- Opening stocks of goods at the start of November was 1,000 units, valued in line with SSAP 9.

6. You recently asked the accountant of the factory of which you are the managing director to cost out the donation of small packets of sweets to be used as gifts and prizes at a charity

fund-raising event. The accountant agreed and said the sweets cost 90 pence per packet. Feeling this to be a typical accountant's answer, you investigated further! The Accounting Department provided the following information:

> The retail selling price per packet is £1.60, and the trade price to retailers is £1.20 per packet. The costs to make and sell the sweets comprise, per packet: basic ingredients £0.40; direct labour £0.25; factory overheads £0.15; and selling and administration overheads £0.10. Therefore the total cost is £0.90 per packet, and this gives the factory a profit of £0.30 per packet.

Both manufacturing, and selling and administrative overheads can be regarded as fixed.

Required

Prepare a note to send to the Accountant of the factory detailing what you consider to be a fair cost. Illustrate your answer.

7. (This question is an extension of question 3.) From the unit information for one product, prepare profit statements for June and July using both absorption and variable costing. Use whichever method of stock valuation your prefer, from a choice of FIFO and LIFO.

Details for June:	£	£
Selling price		30.00
Production costs:		
variable	13.75	
fixed	8.75	
Selling and administration costs:		
variable	1.25	
fixed	3.75	
Details for July:		
Selling price		30.00
Production costs:		
variable	15.00	
fixed	10.00	
Selling and administration costs:		
variable	1.50	
fixed	4.00	

The unit costs are based on the normal budget volume of 8,000 units per month. During June, the organisation produced 7,500 units and sold 7,000 units. During July, the organisation made 8,500 units and sold 9,000 units. Opening stocks as at the start of June, as per question 4, were 400 units.

Solutions to practice questions 1, 6 and 7 can be found in the Student Workbook. Solutions to practice question numbers in red can be found at the end of this book.

Projects

1. Look for evidence of the application of variable costing principles in the business community involving:

(a) discounted air and coach fares offered by transport organisations; and
(b) special deals being offered by hotels and hotel chains

Comment on the ways in which variable costing might be influencing the discounting etc. of the prices normally charged by the organisations you study.

2. In the United Kingdom in 1991/92, for example, apparently huge cash incentives were offered by motor vehicle dealers to customers, in an attempt to increase the turnover of their showrooms. Consider the role of variable costing in the pricing of motor vehicles in a recession.

REFERENCES

CIMA (1991), *Management Accounting Official Terminology* (Chartered Institute of Management Accounting).

Darlington, J., Innes, J., Mitchell, F. and Woodward, J. (1992), 'Throughput accounting: the Garrett Automotive experience', *Management Accounting* (CIMA) (April), 32, 33, 35 and 38.

Ezzamel, M. and Hart, H. (1987), *Advanced Management Accounting: An organisational emphasis* (Cassell Educational).

Hirsch, M. L. and Louderback, J. G. III (1986), *Cost Accounting: Accumulation, analysis, and use*, 2nd edn (Kent Publishing Company), Boston.

Johnson, J. (1960), *Statistical cost analysis* McGraw-Hill Book Company New York.

Shank, J. K. and Govindarajan, V. (1993), *Strategic Cost Management: The new tool for competitive advantage* (The Free Press).

PART TWO

Accounting for managerial decisions

The general theme of Part II is managerial decisions and the ways in which management accountants can assist their managerial colleagues in their decision making. There is a natural progression from Part I, which was concerned with the bases of management accounting. In Part II we can now begin to use that base.

Chapter 11 is concerned with cost–volume profit analysis: that is, the relationship that exists between costs, volumes of output, and profits. Here we have to appreciate the nature and behaviour of costs, and their division into fixed, variable and semi-variable components. We also take a mathematical and a graphical view of cost–volume profit analysis. Thus by the end of the chapter, we should be able to analyse the accounting information of an organisation in order to determine its breakeven position, margin of safety, and so on.

From a decision-making point of view, Chapter 12 is particularly significant. It follows on from the previous chapter by taking a variable costing view of accounting information and applying it to business decisions. In this way, management accountants can help to resolve such questions as, for example: whether to close an apparently loss-making department; when to make or buy in a particular component; the allocation of scarce resources, and so on.

The issue of pricing policies and decisions is taken up in Chapter 13. This is one of the most important topics that managers have to deal with, and, because there are so many possible ways in which pricing problems might be resolved, it is a contentious area.

CHAPTER ELEVEN

Cost–volume profit analysis

CHAPTER OBJECTIVES

After reading this chapter you should be able to:

- define what is meant by cost–volume profit analysis and breakeven analysis
- define contribution and construct contribution charts, profit volume charts and multi-product profit volume charts
- carry out sensitivity analysis on CVP data
- critically examine the assumptions of cost–volume profit analysis
- use mathematical methods to conduct cost–volume profit analyses
- undertake decision tree and normal probability examinations of cost–volume profit analysis under uncertainty

Introduction

Cost volume profit (CVP) analysis follows on directly from the previous chapter, variable costing. This means that the principles derived and applied in the previous chapter are applicable here. We will also see that the limitations of variable costing apply to CVP analysis too. In fact, in this chapter, we examine the problems with the assumptions of CVP analysis in detail. In terms of the volume aspect of CVP analysis, we mean the relationship between output or activity and costs or profits. That is, we assume that if volume changes, so will costs and profit. It is useful for us also to appreciate the links between this chapter and other, previous, chapters. The work we have already done on estimating the behaviour of costs can be highly relevant to the work of this chapter. In order for CVP analysis to have any value, we need to be able to distinguish between our fixed, variable and semi-variable costs. Hence, the management accountant of an organisation trying to apply CVP analysis needs first to estimate cost behaviour. There are potential links with other chapters too: the discussions on material and people costs; activity-based costing; job costing and so on.

Whilst direct reference is not necessarily made in this chapter to other chapters, we can envisage a situation where CVP links in with a discussion of each subject area.

Breakeven analysis is the first aspect of CVP analysis that we will be looking at. With breakeven analysis we are concerned to look at an organisation to try to assess the point at which neither a profit nor a loss is made. The advantage for an organisation of knowing its breakeven point is that it knows the extent of any leeway it has when it comes to reacting to competitive pressures, economic upheavals and so on.

Breakeven analysis

A knowledge of breakeven analysis is useful from a managerial decision-making point of view for a variety of reasons. The primary reason for studying it is so that we can identify for any organisation the level at which it is operating at any time in relation to its breakeven point. In times of depression or recession, or intense competition within an industry, profit margins may be being squeezed to such an extent that management may need to keep a daily watch on pricing policies. Breakeven analysis takes an organisation and combines knowledge of its sales and costs in ways that illustrate whether it is operating near to or far away from its breakeven point. So, if an organisation is operating at levels of output near to its breakeven point, even small changes in activity may mean the difference between profit and loss, or even between survival and non-survival. Similarly, an organisation operating at levels of activity significantly away from its breakeven point has a large margin of safety, and will benefit from knowing that this is the case. It will then know that it has relatively large margins for manoeuvre even if there is competition from within its industry. Without a knowledge of its breakeven point, an organisation will be putting itself at a disadvantage: with such knowledge the organisation can act on any of its variables in response to changes in levels of competition, performance of the economy and so on.

Graphical analysis of the breakeven point

The best way to illustrate breakeven analysis is graphically. The remainder of this section therefore centres around a variety of breakeven and profit charts. Many of the charts we will be using are based on the simple scenario outlined in the following basic data: *An organisation has revenues of £10 per unit and a maximum activity level of 800 units; fixed costs are £3,000; and total costs amount to £6,200 at 800 units* (see Figure 11.1). (Note that the abbreviations used throughout this book TR, TC, FC, VC represent total revenue, total cost, fixed cost, and variable cost respectively.)

In Figure 11.1, the vertical axis has the title, 'Revenues, costs, and profits'. On this axis, all three of these variables can be measured. We can assess, at any level of output, the sales values, the total costs, and the amount of profit or loss being achieved at these levels of output. The amount of profit or loss is determined by finding the difference between the total revenue and total cost curves at any level of activity. All we have done in Figure 11.1 is to plot the data supplied and then, assuming linearity, joined these data points to their relevant place on the vertical axis. The sales line must pass through the origin. In the case

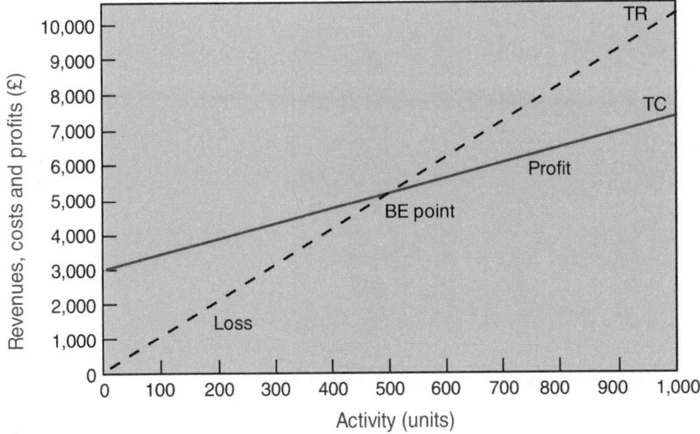

FIGURE 11.1 *Basic breakeven chart*

of total costs, we have joined that with the vertical axis at the level of fixed costs, because, at zero activity, total costs equal fixed costs. Figure 11.1 is a basic chart that achieves our objectives. When we plot the total revenue of an organisation against the total costs of that organisation, we have a graph that shows where these two curves cross each other: this is the breakeven point of that organisation. On this graph, we can see that the breakeven point of this organisation is 500 units of activity, or £5,000 revenue.

We can expand on this basic diagram and include the fixed cost curve (see Figure 11.2). Although the breakeven point does not change as a result of having added this extra information, we do now see more clearly the influence that fixed costs have on the breakeven

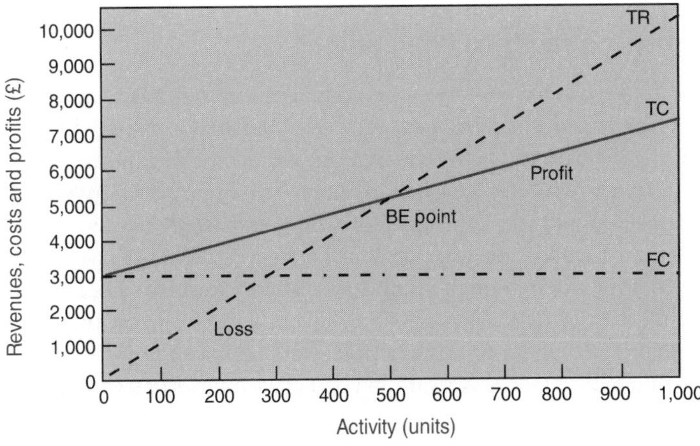

FIGURE 11.2 *Enhanced breakeven chart*

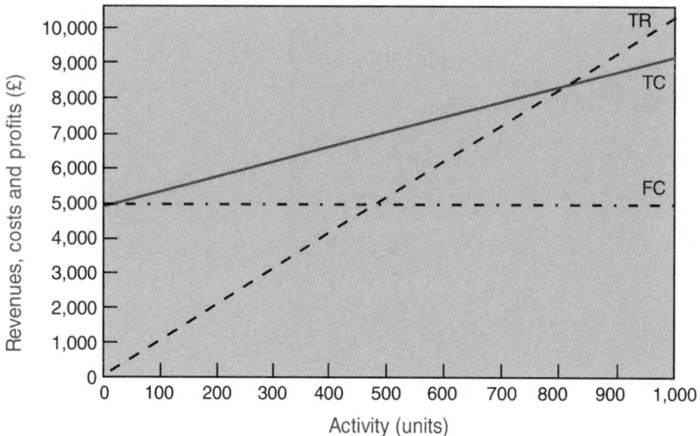

FIGURE 11.3 *High fixed costs breakeven chart*

point and profits; and we can deduce the level of variable costs by subtracting the value of fixed costs from the value of total costs at any level of activity we choose. For example, at the breakeven point, variable costs amount to total costs less fixed costs: that is, £5,000 – £3,000 = £2,000. Similarly, we can deduce the variable costs per unit from the same information. We have just found total variable costs of £2,000, when activity is 500 units. Therefore the variable cost per unit is:

$$\frac{£2{,}000}{500 \text{ units}}$$

$$= £4 \text{ per unit}$$

The influence of fixed costs on the breakeven point

Figures 11.3 and 11.4 illustrate the difference between an organisation that has a high level of fixed costs and a low level of fixed costs respectively. The high fixed cost business is vulnerable to small fluctuations in activity, whereas the low fixed cost organisation can withstand large changes in activity before it gets into trouble. For Figure 11.3, we have changed the basic data: the revenues are the same as before, but now we are assuming that fixed costs are £5,000 rather than £3,000. The effect that a change in fixed costs has should be obvious. The fact that fixed costs are now high relative to all other variables, means that the breakeven point has shifted to the right. The new breakeven point is at just over 833 units – a significant increase from 500 units. In this example, the breakeven point is almost off the graph: this organisation will have to operate beyond maximum sales (previously given as 800 units) to show any profit at all. Even a small downward change in the level of activity for this organisation would have serious consequences, since it would almost immediately move into a loss-making position.

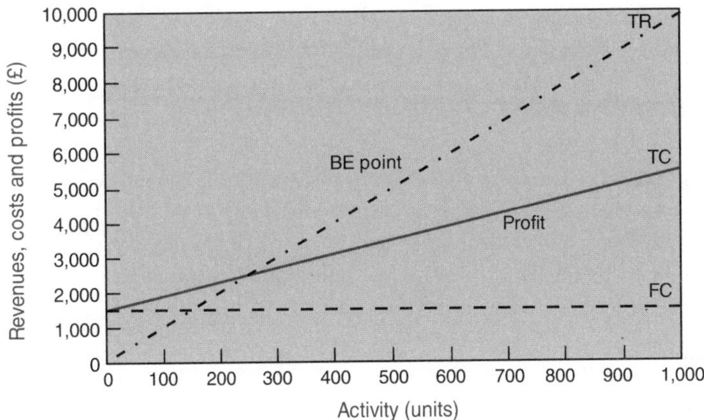

FIGURE 11.4 *Low fixed costs breakeven chart*

Now consider Figure 11.4, where fixed costs are £1,500 (and all other data remain the same). Fixed costs are so low in this figure, relative to all other variables, that the breakeven point shifts leftwards dramatically. An organisation with a relatively low level of fixed costs has much more freedom of action (a greater margin of safety) than the organisation depicted in Figure 11.3. Such freedom of action stems from the organisation being in the position of having maximum sales of 800 units, yet the breakeven point is only 250 units. This represents a large margin of safety for the organisation. We discuss margin of safety in more detail below.

Contribution

We defined the term contribution in Chapter 10 in terms of sales, variable costs and fixed costs. We said that an understanding of the term 'contribution' is crucial to an understanding of much of the work that goes into the use of breakeven and CVP analyses. We must discuss this idea again in some detail before we can continue with our discussion of breakeven analysis.

Contribution (which is also known as contribution margin and sometimes marginal income) is the sales value less variable cost of sales. Expressed in algebraic terms:

$$\text{contribution} = \text{sales} - \text{variable cost of sales}$$

$$= S - VC$$

This is total contribution. We will find it useful to make a distinction between gross contribution and net contribution.

1. **Gross contribution** is the contribution identifiable with manufacturing or operations. In this example, it is sales less variable manufacturing costs.
2. **Net contribution** is the gross contribution less the other (non-manufacturing) variable costs; or sales less total variable costs.

It is sometimes helpful to calculate the two different values for contribution since it gives further insights into managerial performance. For example, when output and sales are 50,000 units, the selling price per unit is £5; variable production costs per unit amount to £2.75; and variable administration costs are £0.50 per unit. The gross and net contributions are as shown in Table 11.1.

The contribution ratios express the rate at which contribution is generated by an organisation, or product, or service, rather than expressing contribution in absolute terms. Older definitions call this ratio the profit/volume ratio or P/V ratio: this is not a very helpful alternative title, but we ought to be aware of it since we will almost certainly come across it in our reading. In the example above, the gross C/S ratio is, using the total sales and contribution information:

$$\frac{£112{,}500}{£250{,}000} = 0.45 \text{ or } 45\%$$

or, using the unit sales and contribution information:

TABLE 11.1 ***Gross and net contributions***

	£
In total:	
Sales	250,000
less: Variable production costs	137,500
Gross Contribution	112,500
less: Variable Administration costs	25,000
Net Contribution	87,500
	£
Per unit:	
Sales	5.00
less: Variable costs	2.75
Gross Contribution	2.25
less: Variable Administration costs	0.50
Net Contribution	1.75

As a ratio:

The basic C/S ratio is:

$$\frac{\text{Contribution}}{\text{Sales}}$$

And we can modify the C/S ratio to incorporate the variations of gross and net contribution:

$$\text{Gross C/S ratio} = \frac{\text{Gross contribution}}{\text{Sales}}$$

$$\text{Net C/S ratio} = \frac{\text{Net contribution}}{\text{Sales}}$$

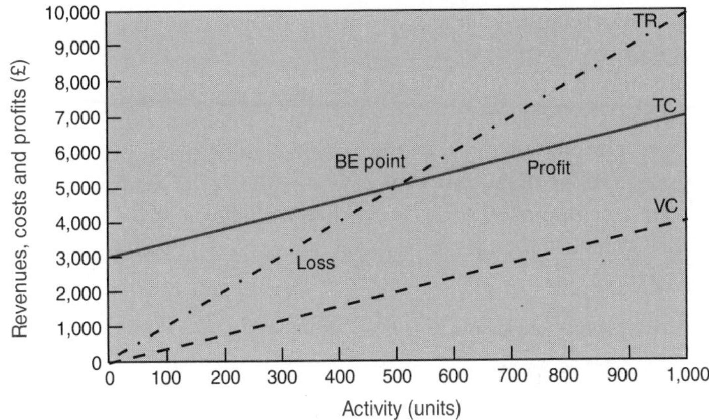

FIGURE 11.5 *Contribution breakeven chart*

$$\frac{£2.25}{£5.00} = 0.45 \text{ or } 45\%$$

Note, that the ratio can be expressed as a decimal or as a percentage. Either presentation is acceptable, and the answers using either presentation will be identical. The net C/S ratio is:

$$\frac{£87,500}{£250,000} = 0.35 \text{ or } 35\%$$

Contribution chart

Unlike previous diagrams we have considered, Figure 11.5 includes the variable cost curve. It is based on the basic data presented above, with the addition that the variable cost is confirmed at £4 per unit. Fixed costs return to their original value of £3,000.

From this graph we can see not only the total revenue curve and the total cost curve, but we now have a view on fixed costs, variable costs and contribution. It is because it includes the ability to deduce the value of contribution that it is often known as a contribution chart. So at any level of output, we can assess contribution by calculating the difference between the total revenue and the variable cost. At a sales level of 300 units, total revenues less variable costs amount to £1,800; at sales of 800 units, the contribution is £4,800. The level of fixed costs can be deduced from Figure 11.5 by subtracting the value of variable costs from the value of total costs at any point.

The margin of safety

When we first started discussing breakeven analysis in this chapter, we used the term margin of safety. We said: an organisation operating at levels of activity significantly away from its breakeven point has a large margin of safety, and will benefit from knowing that this is the case. It will then know that it has relatively large margins for manoeuvre even if there is competition from within its industry.

The idea of the margin of safety is a very useful one because, as we have just reminded ourselves, we know that the margin of safety contains information about how 'safe' an organisation is from changes in any one or more of the variables influencing profit levels. To calculate the margin of safety of an organisation, we need to know its maximum sales (or normal sales, or actual sales, or budgeted sales, depending on what it is we are trying to assess) and the level of sales at its breakeven point. From our basic data we find that the value of the margin of safety is:

maximum sales – sales at the breakeven point

$$= (£10 \text{ per unit} \times 800 \text{ units}) - £5{,}000$$

$$= £8{,}000 - £5{,}000$$

$$= £3{,}000$$

It is very common to express the margin of safety either in unit terms:

maximum sales units – sales units at the breakeven point

$$= 800 \text{ units} - 500 \text{ units}$$

$$= 300 \text{ units}$$

or as a fraction or percentage. The percentage calculation here, based on values, is:

$$\frac{\text{maximum sales} - \text{breakeven sales}}{\text{maximum sales}} \times 100$$

$$= \frac{£8{,}000 - £5{,}000}{£8{,}000} \times 100$$

$$= \frac{£3{,}000}{£8{,}000} \times 100$$

$$= 37.50\%$$

Verify that the same result is obtained when using the unit values to calculate the margin of safety percentage, as is obtained here using total values.

It is sometimes said that when an organisation is currently operating at a loss (that is, to the left of its breakeven point), its margin of safety turns into its margin of danger. This change of name is the result of authors trying to be inventive. It is not in the least a useful change of name!

The unit breakeven chart

Usry, Hammer and Matz (1988) provide us with a different form of breakeven chart: the unit breakeven chart or, as they actually call it, a unit profit graph. They base their example on normal capacity being 100%, and all other levels of capacity stemming from there. The

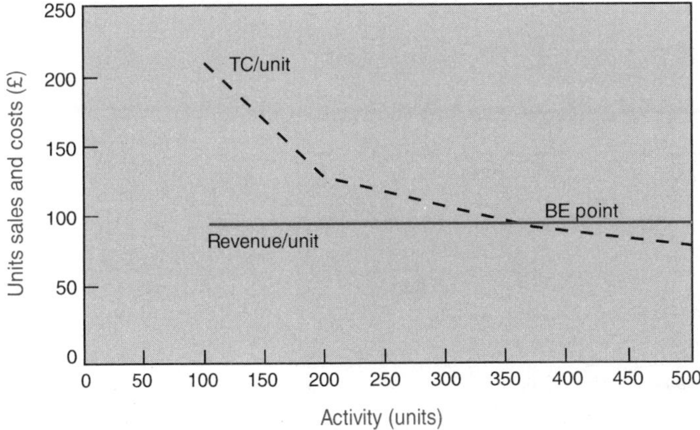

FIGURE 11.6 *Unit breakeven chart*

point of preparing a unit breakeven chart is that it shows the effects on costs and profit of varying volume or activity. More specifically, say Usry *et al.* (1988: 620), these graphs show 'vividly the influence of fixed costs on the product unit cost'. This is true. We can see the way that the total cost per unit curve falls dramatically over the earlier levels of output, which is perfectly consistent with the behaviour of fixed costs per unit. The data on which Figure 11.6 is based, which demonstrates the unit breakeven chart, is as follows: normal capacity is 500 units; the product is sold at £100 per unit; variable cost per unit is £60; and total fixed cost amounts to £15,000. Table 11.2 gives these data in tabular form per unit.

The profit/volume (P/V) chart

The breakeven chart is a very useful form of presentation of organisational data. From these charts we can not only see the breakeven point of the organisation, but we can also evaluate the contribution, variable cost per unit, and so on. An alternative form of presentation is the profit/volume (p/v) chart. The p/v chart gives much of the same information as the breakeven chart, but in a different way. Using the basic data from the early part of the

TABLE 11.2 *Data for unit breakeven chart*

	Units					
	100	200	300	375	400	500
Variable cost/unit	60	60	60	60	60.0	60
Fixed cost/unit	150	75	50	40	37.5	30
Total cost/unit	210	135	110	100	97.5	90
Selling price/unit	100	100	100	100	100.0	100
Profit/(loss)/unit	−110	−35	−10	0	2.5	10

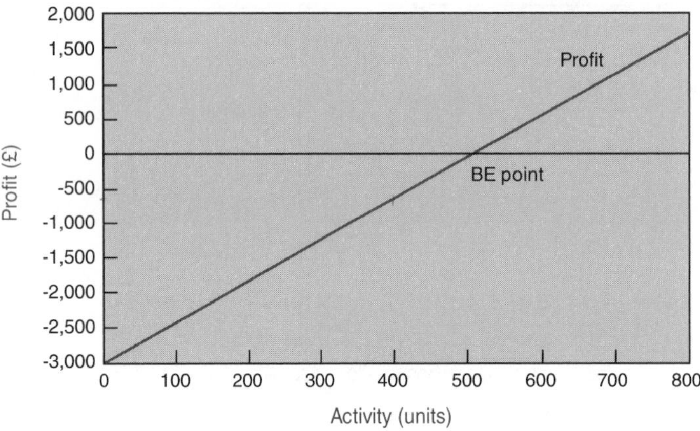

FIGURE 11.7 *Profit/volume chart*

chapter, Figure 11.7 is a p/v chart. An inspection of this p/v chart confirms the results we obtained when we used a breakeven chart: namely, when activity is zero units, profit is a negative amount, which equals the fixed costs; the breakeven point is 500 units and represents £5,000 worth of revenue; and at 800 units maximum sales, total profit is £1,800.

The main advantage of the p/v chart is that it is less involved than the breakeven chart. It does have the drawback, however, that it is not as informative as the breakeven chart: the breakeven chart contains cost information as well as profit information.

The multiproduct p/v chart

Most organisations that manufacture, trade or provide a service, do so with a portfolio of more than one product. Consequently, we should consider how to deal with the situation where there is more than one product, or product group, to contend with. Table 11.3 reflects the standard mix of an organisation whose total revenue is £220,000, total variable costs amount to £126,000, and total fixed costs amount to £44,000.

TABLE 11.3 ***Standard mix of an organisation***

Product	Revenue (£)	Variable costs (£)	Contribution (£)	C/S ratio (%)	Rank
1	50,000	35,000	15,000	30	3
2	30,000	9,000	21,000	70	1
3	75,000	30,000	45,000	60	2
4	65,000	52,000	13,000	20	4
Total	220,000	126,000	94,000		
less: Fixed costs			44,000		
Profit			50,000		

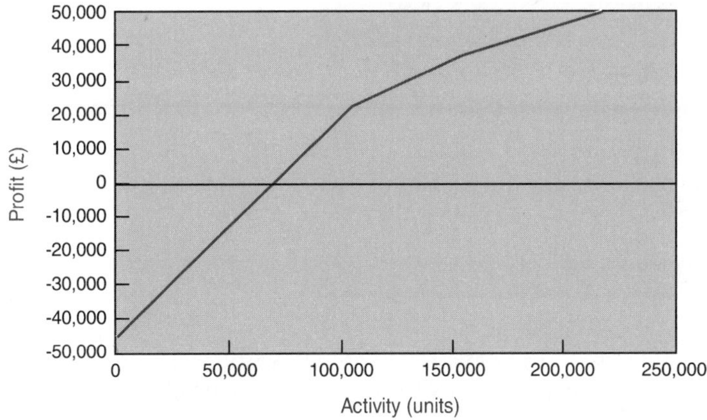

FIGURE 11.8 *Multiproduct p/v chart*

Now that we have these data, we can prepare an enhanced p/v chart that will incorporate the data (see Figure 11.8). We have added a new curve to the p/v chart: this is a piecewise curve showing, product by product, the contribution derived. This curve is plotted as follows:

1. From the contributions in Table 11.3, rank the products in order: the highest C/S ratio is ranked first, the second highest is ranked second, and so on.
2. Take the first-ranked product and plot for it two points on the graph:
   (a) point one starts where the original curve starts: at zero activity and profit of −£44,000 (that is, fixed costs);
   (b) the next point is at the coordinates where activity = £30,000 (sales for product 2 (the highest-ranked product)), and profit = −£23,000 (that is, profit at zero activity, and profit now that product 2 has been made and sold = −£44,000 + £21,000 (the contribution for product 2)).
3. Take the second-ranked product and plot for it two points on the graph:
   (a) the first coordinate for this curve starts at the second point of the previous curve: at £30,000 sales and −£23,000 profit;
   (b) the second coordinate is found at £105,000 (total of revenues for products 2 and 3 (ranked one and two respectively)) and profit = £22,000 (the total of the contributions so far: (£44,000) + 21,000 + 45,000).

And so it goes on until all products have been plotted. In summary, the coordinates for all products for this example are given in Table 11.4.

The multiproduct p/v chart presents management with a pictorial representation of all of its organisation's activities. As far as each product is concerned, the steeper the profit line of each product, the greater its contribution. In the example above, product 2 has the steeper slope, followed by product 3, then product 1, and finally product 4. The slope of the product lines for each product is perfectly consistent with the C/S ratios for that product. For example, the slope of the profit line for product 2 is 0.7; for product 3 it is 0.6 . . . these are exactly

TABLE 11.4 *Coordinates for a multiproduct p/v chart*

Products rank order	Cumulative sales (£)	Cumulative profit (£)
Initial	0	−44,000
Product 2	30,000	−23,000
Product 3	105,000	22,000
Product 1	155,000	37,000
Product 4	220,000	50,000

the same as the products' C/S ratios. A product with a negative C/S ratio will have a negative slope. We can change Table 11.3 so that product 4 has sales of £65,000 but a variable cost of £78,000. This gives a negative contribution and a negative slope to its profit line, as Table 11.5 and Figure 11.9 clearly show.

The negative slope for product 4 can be seen on Figure 11.9 without difficulty. The straight line we see in Figure 11.9 is drawn by joining the first and last data points on the piecewise, or kinked, curve. This straight line represents the profit line for the organisation as a whole, and would be the profit line we would draw for this organisation if we did not have any detailed product data. This tells us that the breakeven point is approximately 140,000 units, and may be a misleading result, as we will see below.

Sensitivity analysis

CVP analysis allows the management accountant and his or her management colleagues to analyse costs and revenues and their interrelationships in as much detail as necessary. Such analysis is usually called sensitivity analysis, because it assesses the sensitivity of one variable to changes in one or more other variables. What we normally do here is to take a basic case

TABLE 11.5 *Coordinates for a multiproduct p/v chart, including a negative C/S ratio*

Product	Revenue (£)	Variable costs (£)	Contribution	C/S ratio (%)	Rank
1	50,000	35,000	15,000	30	3
2	30,000	9,000	21,000	70	1
3	75,000	30,000	45,000	60	2
4	65,000	78,000	−13,000	−20	4
Total	220,000	152,000	68,000		
less: Fixed costs			44,000		
Profit			24,000		

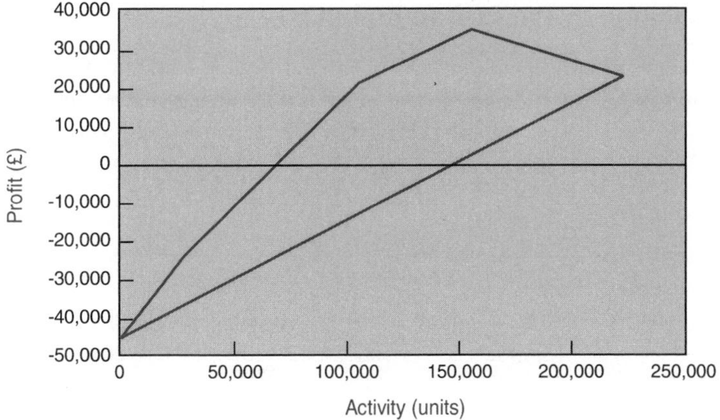

FIGURE 11.9 *Multiproduct p/v chart, including a negative C/S ratio*

– say, the 100% level of output – and then test what would happen if, for the sake of argument, the level of output were to change to 80%. We manipulate our cost structure to reflect the change from 100% to 80% by making the relevant changes to the fixed and variable cost and revenue elements. In this case we would see the sensitivity of the various cost elements to a change in the level of output of 20%. The relevant range is an important consideration at this stage. The following example illustrates the meaning of sensitivity analysis.

WORKED EXAMPLE 11.1

For An Organisation, 100% of normal sales is £100,000 at £5 per unit, the total fixed costs are £55,000 and variable costs per unit are £1.75. This gives a net profit of:

Sales	£100,000
Variable costs	35,000
Contribution	65,000
Fixed costs	55,000
Net profit	£10,000

Note that the total number of units at 100% normal sales level is 20,000 (this is £100,000 total sales divided by the £5 per unit selling price).

Required

Calculate the net profit at 120%, 110%, 90%, and 80% normal sales.

Solution to Worked example 11.1

The following table shows the sensitivity of the relevant variables to changes in output, as demanded by the question. What we are seeing here is the way that sales values and variable costs change in response to predetermined changes in the volume of sales. Selling prices per unit and variable costs per unit remain unaffected by the volume changes:

	Percentage of normal sales				
	100%	120%	110%	90%	80%
	£	£	£	£	£
Sales	100,000	120,000	110,000	90,000	80,000
Variable costs	35,000	42,000	38,500	31,500	28,000
Contribution	65,000	78,000	71,500	58,500	52,000
Fixed costs	55,000	55,000	55,000	55,000	55,000
Net profit	10,000	23,000	16,500	3,500	(3,000)

When we are dealing with a change in sales volume from 100% to 120%, we merely multiply sales values and variable costs at the 100% level by 120% (or 1.2). For example, at 100% of normal output, sales are £100,000; therefore, at 120% of normal output, sales will be £100,000 × 1.2 = £120,000. Fixed relationships remain fixed, of course. If the management of An Organisation were intending to take volume-based decisions, this kind of table would prove of enormous benefit to them in their search for making the optimal decision.

The p/v chart and fixed-cost changes

Earlier in this chapter, when we discussed the contribution to sales (C/S) ratio, we dismissed the expression p/v as being old fashioned. In the context of breakeven and similar charts, the expression p/v is useful and it is widely used by management accountants. The p/v charts that follow are so called because they demonstrate the relationship between the **level of profit** and the **volume of activity** or output that gives rise to that profit. The p/v chart can also be used with dramatic effect to show the effect of changes in policy. Taking the example we have just worked through, we can assume, all other things remaining as they are, that the fixed costs change because of an increase in fixed asset investment: they increase from £55,000 to £75,000. The effect on the profit line is shown in Figure 11.10. As we can see in Figure 11.10, the profit line shifts downwards to the right, from profit 1 to profit 2.

CAMEO

The reality of fixed costs

A lot has been written about the nature and theory of fixed costs. We know from the work of this chapter that fixed costs are those costs that remain fixed despite wide fluctuations in output. We also know how to plot fixed costs on a graph. However, where we often fall down is when we come to assess the practical implications of fixed costs for an organisation. What we are about to discuss applies to all organisations, whether they are commercial organisations, manufacturers, banks, or even a football club. To help illustrate the potential problems that fixed cost levels can cause, we will look at two entirely unrelated organisations: a steel fabricating partnership, and a premier league football club.

Steel fabricating partnership

In this context, fabricating means, for example, taking sheet steel and making such products as ovens to be found in Indian and Chinese takeaways, refrigeration shelves to be found in pubs and clubs, motor bike trailers, guards for industrial machinery, and so on.

In this case, fixed costs became highly relevant only when what was a successful partnership broke down. In the first instance this partnership was formed when two friends combined finance on the one hand and technical expertise and business contacts on the other. The partnership was formed to fabricate sheet steel as outlined above and quickly established itself as the provider of high-quality, reliable products and services. Within two years it was trading at a turnover level in excess of £200,000.

A clash of personalities, differences in management style, and financial jealousies led to the dissolution of the partnership during the third year of its operation. The settlement that dissolved the partnership was reasonably amicable and it left Partner A with his original capital plus a share of the estimated value added that he felt he should derive from the business; financially he was happy. Partner B was not a wealthy person, and in order to buy out Partner A he had to take on large levels of debt. Partner B also had to take on debt to finance a company car, and, not too long into his new business life, he had leased a small fleet of top-of-the-range vans.

Cutting a long story short, all we need to be aware of is that Partner B now has a highly geared, or highly leveraged, business. The effect of such high gearing is that Partner B is constantly chasing work, and working 15 to 18-hour days to ensure that his business stays afloat. We hear such stories every day, of course – of the owner or manager whose life is spent at the office or at the factory – and we accept it as necessary. In this case, it is the effect of fixed costs that is making such a work style necessary.

Assume that Partner B has effectively borrowed £150,000 to finance his business, and the repayment costs of that debt (capital and interest) each year is £30,000. We now see that this business has a fixed finance cost of £30,000, much of which, in this case, is avoidable. The implications of this level of fixed finance cost are that Partner B probably needs to find work worth £100,000 each year *merely to finance his debt*. This covers the £30,000 finance costs, overheads, wages, and profit margin associated with the extra work. In this example, Partner B can be seen running around the country finding work. The work that comes in may be a £25,000 order or a £150 order – all such work is taken. Partner B rarely has time to explain properly to his staff what they need to do, consequently a lot of mistakes are made: products are assembled wrongly, incorrect materials are used in contravention of the customer's specifications, and so on. In this case, high gearing is being compounded with managerial inappropriateness. Some very expensive mistakes are being made.

A Premier League football club

It is fair to say that everyone who knows anything about British league football knows that it is operated in the realms of Peter Pan and Pride and Prejudice: on the level of a fairy tale and the romantic hero and heroine who can both contrive to live happily ever after!

In the middle of 1995, a firm of chartered accountants published a report on the state of the English Football League. This survey was carried out by Touche Ross and involved the accounts of all league clubs for the years 1993/1994. The effect of fixed costs on a football club are adequately demonstrated by considering a club that was relegated from the Premier League to Division One. The problem for the relegated club is not just the loss of prestige – the opportunity to see the great names of the game at their home stadium. Premier League players demand Premier League wages. Generally these will take the form of fixed costs, although a player can be transferred at very short notice and his entire wage bill avoided by not replacing him – this does not seem to happen very often, however.

In today's relegated Premier League club, however, life is even more difficult than it used to be. Along with the burden of larger salaries than Division One can usually support, the club has to contend with losing virtually all of the substantial – and guaranteed, as long as they're in the Premier League – revenue from television fees; turnover, like attendances, will probably fall; and the value of the club's players will probably fall too (this is usually only important when they are transferred, and liquidated). Take a look at the accounts of a Premier League club that becomes a Division One club and see the financial impact of the sudden change of status on that club. You will see that much of the financial problem revolves around the impact of fixed costs.

Reference: For an example of the kind of discussion emanating from Touche Ross's survey of football club accounts, see the *Sunday Times* Sports Section, 6 August 1995, p. 13.

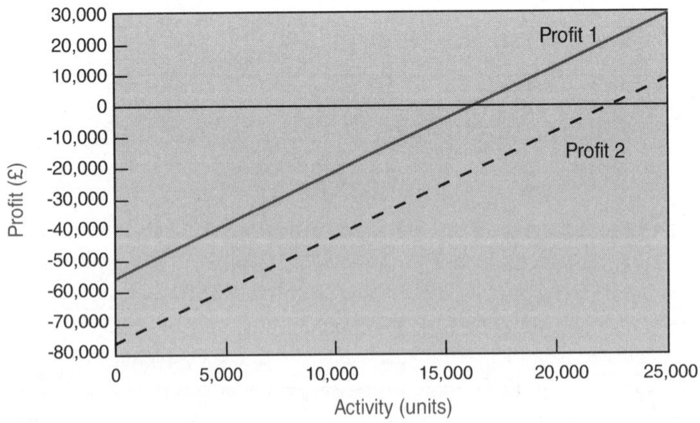

FIGURE 11.10 *P/v chart and fixed cost changes*

Assumptions of CVP analysis

Up to this point we have accepted that when we draw a breakeven chart or a p/v chart, it contains nothing but straight lines. The reason we have been able to do this is because of the assumptions built into the management accountant's CVP model. These assumptions can be accused of making the CVP model unrealistic, but they do help us with our analysis. Without the assumptions, we would be forced to use, to a greater or lesser extent, such techniques as the differential calculus, polynomial equations and so forth. For most purposes, these assumptions are very useful; and they simplify our work significantly (see Table 11.6).

Whilst these assumptions do provide us with a useful framework on which to base our discussion, they are often exceedingly simplistic. The following discussion highlights the major difficulties with these assumptions. The following section may be skipped, however, if you are not concerned with exploring the assumptions on which CVP analysis is based.

Cost–volume profit analysis: its assumptions and their pitfalls

The importance of identifying and criticising the underlying assumptions of cost volume profit analysis (CVP analysis) rests on the practical application of CVP analysis: anyone who has ever tried (or anyone who may wish to try) to apply CVP analysis in reality, whilst also trying to apply the substance of this chapter, will have found severe difficulties. This discussion will help us solve those problems. In any discussion of CVP analysis, any lecturer, manual or accountant will frequently be heard to say something along the lines of 'Let's assume for a moment that fixed costs remain fixed, even if output changes by a relatively large amount . . .' or 'Of course, the selling price in this example is constant over the whole range of output . . .'. There is little doubt that CVP analysis is useful in its proper context; and there are many decisions made which positively shout out that CVP analysis has been employed: examples such as reduced price midday meals in restaurants compared to evening meals in the same restaurant, or reduced weekend rates in hotels. All such examples are based on CVP reasoning; and there is little doubt that in the short term, at least, these special deals attract clients who would otherwise not be attracted in, and thus help to increase a business's contribution. Nevertheless, there are problems with CVP analysis when it comes to applying it. How many student accountants or young accountants have gone to work

TABLE 11.6 *Assumptions built into the CVP model*

The assumptions are:

1. All costs can be classified into their fixed and variable elements.
2. Fixed costs remain fixed over a wide range of activity.
3. Variable costs vary directly with activity.
4. Selling prices are constant per unit.
5. Only levels of activity affect costs and revenues.
6. Usually only one product is effectively dealt with.
7. Uncertainty does not exist.

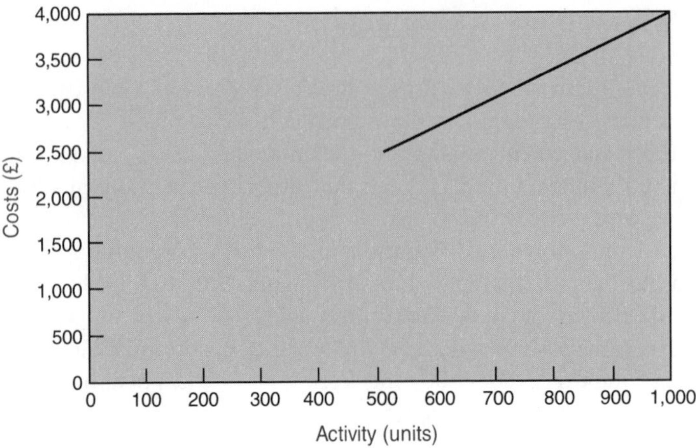

FIGURE 11.11 *Regression line derived from total costs*

following a riveting read of a chapter on CVP analysis determined to calculate his or her firm's breakeven point, only to find that reality is much more complex than the theory might have them believe?! Such problems are centred around the underlying assumptions on which CVP analysis is based. Nevertheless it is frequently found that students are quite happy to apply CVP analysis principles in theoretical settings but may be unaware of these assumptions and how restrictive they really are. Let us look at the assumptions one by one and analyse their limitations as we go.

1 All costs can be analysed into their fixed and variable elements

When we talk about fixed and variable costs, we usually assume that it is possible to take a look at individual or total costs and split them into their fixed and variable elements. However, if we look at any organisation of a reasonably large size, we will quickly appreciate that not only might there be several hundred different costs comprising total cost but also that there are many forces acting on those costs (cost drivers, in activity-based costing parlance, for example). Consequently, it cannot be a simple matter of a few minutes' analysis and the fixed and variable split has been fully explained. Splitting out fixed and variable costs can be a long, time-consuming process; and techniques such as the inspection of accounts method really are not suitable if the analysis is to be realistic. At the very least, some kind of statistical or mathematical analysis will have to be undertaken. For example, I undertook this kind of an exercise with a student recently and it took many man hours for us to research the organisation, set up and work a spreadsheet, analyse the results, and then present our preliminary findings. To refine such a model to a satisfactorily usable state would take many more hours. This is not to suggest that the splitting of fixed and variable costs cannot be done.

Consider Figure 11.11 (which we can assume for the sake of the discussion is the regression line derived from an analysis of a business's total costs), suggest the level of fixed costs, and hence calculate a variable cost per unit. Figure 11.11 is suggesting a regression equation of:

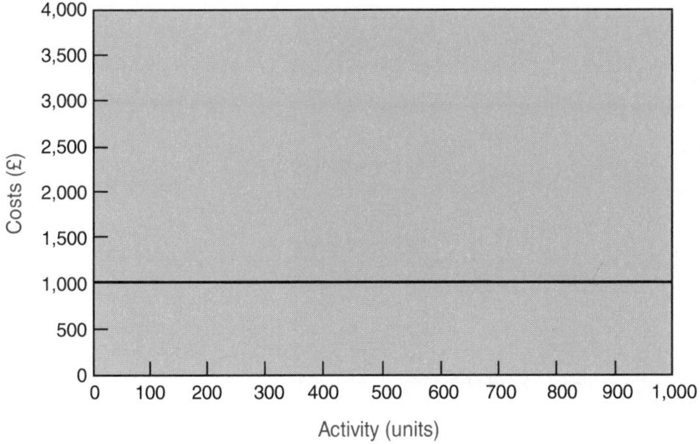

FIGURE 11.12 *Common view of fixed costs*

$$y = a + bx = 1{,}000 + 3x$$

which, in the present context, will be interpreted as: the fixed cost for the business is £1,000, and the variable cost per unit is £3. It should be remembered that Figure 11.11 refers to the whole business and, as we have already agreed, a reasonably large business is complex. Consequently, although a statistical analysis can be carried out, its results will not always be as simple to interpret as the assumptions on which CVP analysis, and the example surrounding Figure 11.11 would have us believe. Imagine the problems which must be faced by the analyst trying to cope with the kind of cost portrayed in Figure 11.15: no longer a straight line at all; and such cost profiles are likely to be the normal – as opposed to straight lines, that is.

Assessing the fixed and variable cost split can be fraught with difficulties and may at best be a highly subjective exercise.

2 Fixed costs remain fixed even over a wide range of activity.

This is another simplifying assumption which helps to keep the arithmetic of CVP analysis simple but which does not help those of us who wish to apply the techniques. The common view of fixed costs is given in Figure 11.12. However, the serious error contained in such charts as Figure 11.12 is that it ignores (or merely assumes away) the importance of the relevant range. The relevant range is the range of levels of activity over which the business has direct experience. That is, it has probably produced at or over that range of outputs; or it has studied such levels of output carefully. Hence, no business will know what its fixed costs will be outside its relevant range; and there is no guarantee that fixed costs will remain fixed if the business produces at a level of output not previously experienced – whether through expansion or contraction. Figure 11.13 illustrates a more realistic scenario, in which a fixed cost can change as a result of a change in output level to a level outside the relevant

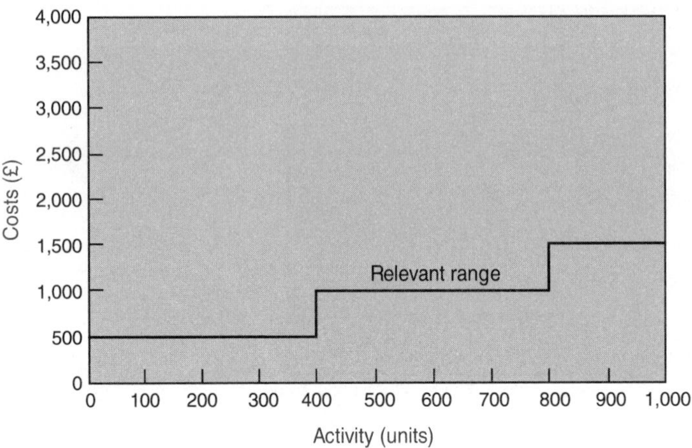

FIGURE 11.13 *Realistic view of fixed costs*

range. The relevant range in Figure 11.13 is represented as 401 units to 800 units. The reasons why fixed costs will change in such a way for, say, a reduction in output include: managers and supervisors being laid off as no longer required at reduced levels of output; machinery sold; and buildings sold or not rented any more. A similar analysis applies to an increase in output and fixed costs.

3 Variable costs always vary directly with activity.

We have here a nice neat assumption which might be true in some circumstances. It is possible for a cost to be truly variable and behave in a perfectly linear way. However, it is still useful to explore here the more likely exceptions to that behaviour. Figure 11.14 demonstrates how a perfectly variable cost behaves.

In reality, of course, a whole host of forces can act upon a cost which is deemed to be variable. For example, once a business grows beyond a certain size it can then enjoy the benefits of greater volume. Such benefits include being awarded trade discounts, being offered cash discounts now that it can obtain credit, and quantity discounts because it can now buy in greater bulk. These changes to the basic assumption of linearity mean that when Figure 11.14 shows a perfectly straight line, reality could be more like Figure 11.15 where we can easily be dealing with a situation in which variable costs are essentially variable but not perfectly variable. In the case of Figure 11.15, we see a true curve; and any analysis of an estimation of a precise relationship between variable cost and output will yield a solution, but not a linear one. Again, since any reasonably large business will have many such costs, isolating the variability of all such costs can be a considerable task.

There are many variations on the possible shapes which a variable cost curve might assume. For example, it might be the case that at higher levels of output a variable cost curve starts to slope upwards again, having initially behaved like the curve in Figure 11.15. Such a situation would hold when diseconomies of scale or increasing import tariffs were being imposed, for example.

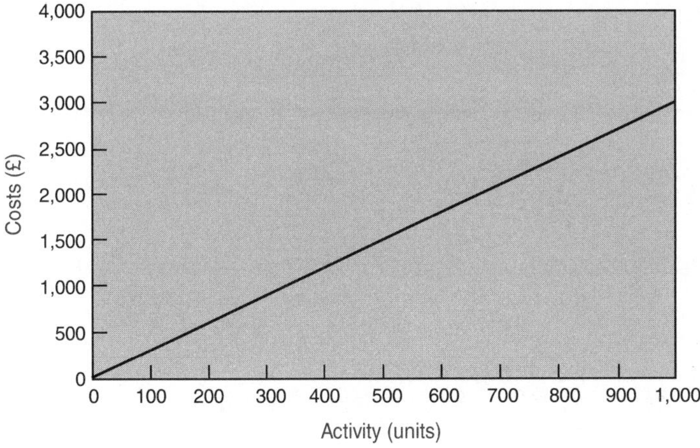

FIGURE 11.14 *Variable cost behaviour*

4 Selling prices are constant per unit.

A very similar series of arguments holds for selling prices as held for variable costs. There is no reason why any business needs to sell to all of its customers at the same price for all products. We could also easily demonstrate that different prices are offered for different levels of purchasing: for example, discounts for bulk buying. The hypothesis of supply and demand also dictates that the higher the price, the fewer will be sold; and the lower the price the more will be sold. Figure 11.16 combines the basic assumed sales curve and a more realistic sales curve based on the arguments just put forward. Again, when we consider the realistic side of total sales a true curve emerges; and again, this means that any analysis

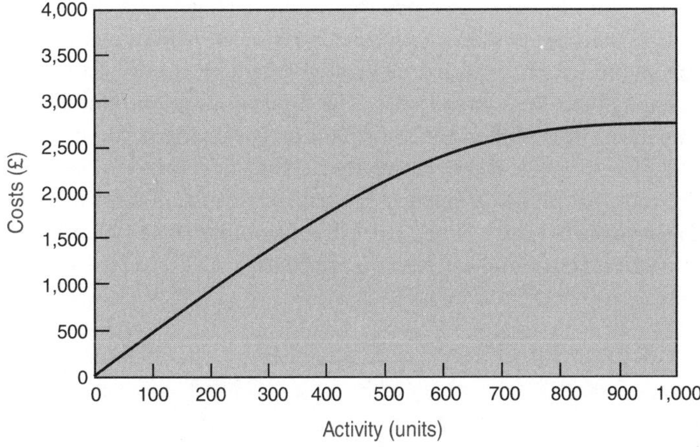

FIGURE 11.15 *Realistic view of variable costs*

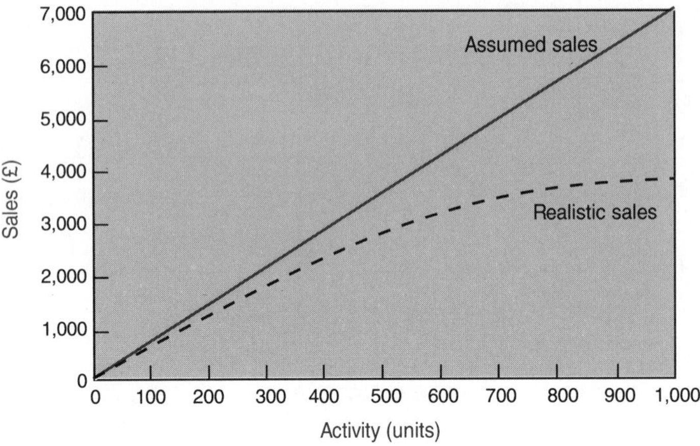

FIGURE 11.16 *Assumed sales and realistic sales*

of sales immediately becomes more difficult than the basic assumptions of CVP analysis would have us believe.

As with the variable cost curve, there are potentially many shapes which the sales curve could take on. Figure 11.16 gives only one variation from the usually assumed straight line.

5 Only levels of activity affect costs and revenues

This, to some extent, is the worst of all of the assumptions from the point of view of a realistic application of CVP analysis. It is the worst because it denies the existence of such things as labour efficiency and changes to labour efficiency. The learning effect is ignored, or assumed away, by this assumption, of course. Along with all of the discussion so far, there are many reasons why a total cost or a cost per unit might change, and changes in the level of output is only one of these reasons. Consider your own environment. Why might any one of the costs with which you are associated change? In the case of a manufacturer, costs might change because someone has improved the way an operation is performed. The operator has moved his or her bench around or has changed the order in which he or she performs the operations. If the operator then spends less time on the work or produces better quality output, his or her efficiency has improved and the cost per unit will also have improved. The reason for this change in cost is in no part solely due to the restrictive assumption of output being the only determinant of cost.

6 Usually only one product can be effectively dealt with

One-product business

The reason for this assumption rests on the mathematics involved if more than one product is assumed to be made. Although it is not the purpose of this discussion to go too deeply

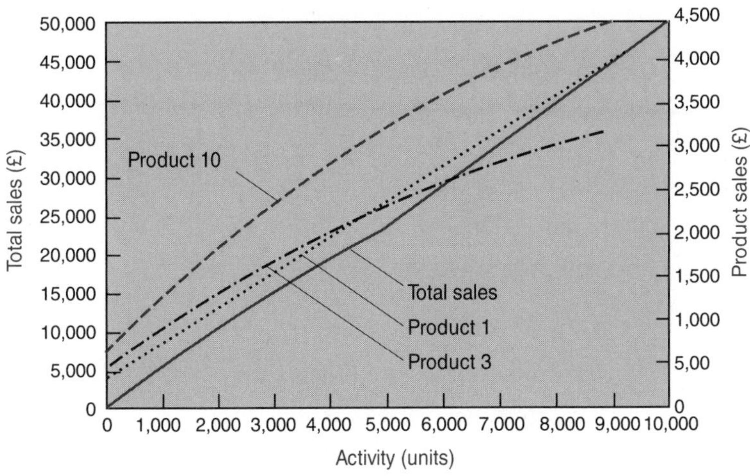

FIGURE 11.17 *Multiproduct business*

into such issues, we should be aware that trying to model a multiproduct business in terms of CVP analysis can become very frustrating indeed. Consider Figure 11.17, which represents a ten-product business – all products have different characteristics, as we can see from the three products included in the graph.

Within this multiproduct business representation, there are six prices, all of which are subject to different levels of variability. The purpose of Figure 11.17 is to demonstrate that simply analysing the total sales curve, and ignoring its constituent parts, is likely to lead to serious errors of judgement or decision making. The total sales curve is almost a straight line, but any one of the individual sales curves for any product can be significantly different to a straight line; as is the case, especially, with products 3 and 10. Any simplistic attempt at unravelling this business is destined to fail. Even the mathematical model for this relatively simple ten-product business could run to several complete lines across an A4 page. Such a model is not too unmanageable for most of us, but it is unwieldy and cannot be readily simplified just for the sake of argument. The same arguments would apply equally well to the variable and fixed costs (although they have been excluded from Figure 11.17).

Sales mix issues

The sales mix argument is a straightforward one and it deals with the contribution to sales ratio (the C/S ratio). If a business makes two products, for example, one with a C/S ratio of 80% and the other with a C/S ratio of 70%, the average C/S ratio will not be 75% (which would be the simple average of the two C/S ratios). The average C/S ratio has to be based on the weighted average of the two, and the value of this weighted average will vary as the sales mix varies. For example, consider the weighted averages in each of the following cases for the business just introduced:

Sales mix (i)	Product 1	Product 2
Sales (units)	100,000	200,000
Sales (£)	500,000	300,000
C/S ratio(as given above)	80%	70%

The weighted average C/S ratio is:

$$\frac{\text{total contribution}}{\text{total sales}} = \frac{(£500{,}000 \times 80\%) + (£300{,}000 \times 70\%)}{£500{,}000 + 300{,}000}$$

$$= 76.25\%$$

Sales mix (ii)	Product 1	Product 2
Sales (units)	300,000	350,000
Sales (£)	1,500,000	525,000
C/S ratio	80%	70%

The weighted average C/S ratio is:

$$\frac{\text{total contribution}}{\text{total sales}} = \frac{(£1{,}500{,}000 \times 80\%) + (£525{,}000 \times 70\%)}{£1{,}500{,}000 + 525{,}000}$$

$$= 77.41\%$$

By changing the sales mix, in a situation where the values of the C/S ratio change from product to product, the weighted average value of all C/S ratios also changes. Unless this point is appreciated, the results of any CVP analysis could easily be invalidated.

7 Uncertainty does not exist

The final assumption underlying CVP analysis is that there is no such thing as uncertainty. Everything is known and knowable to 100% certainty levels: prices are sure; variability of cost is certain; and there is nothing so certain as the level of fixed cost! It should be clear, however, that the only certainty about certainty is that it is certain not to exist! Indeed, as has been said and widely quoted many times, the only things certain in this world are death and taxes – CVP analysis was not included on that list! In this discussion of the assumptions of CVP analysis, we have highlighted a wide range of views. We have not done so in order to dismiss everything learned in this chapter, or from other sources, but so that when CVP analysis is being considered, it can now be considered from a much firmer basis. By pointing out the weaknesses of the assumptions on which CVP analysis is based, the requirements for a more rigorous study can be developed.

More specific CVP relationships

We have now worked our way through a series of examples and explanations of the way in which CVP analysis works, but we have worked on a fairly simplistic level. The following explanation shows a set of more specific CVP relationships.

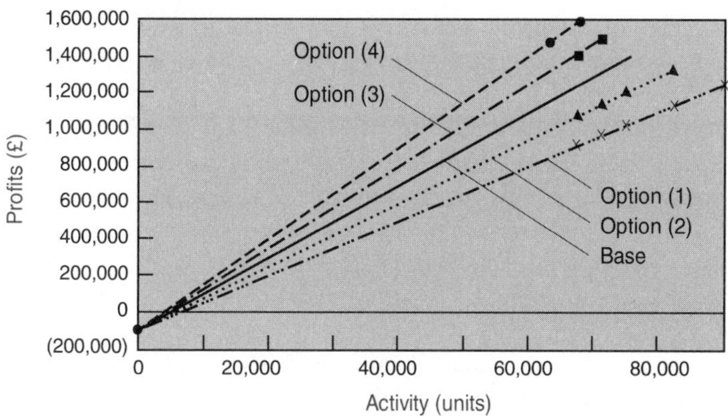

FIGURE 11.18 *Multiline p/v chart*

MyCo Ltd is aware of the economist's hypothesis of supply and demand: the MD said at a recent board meeting: 'If we increase our prices, our sales volume is bound to fall. On the other hand, if we reduce our prices, sales volume should increase. Look at our alternatives. Ted [the management accountant], I want you to carry out an analysis for us of the effects of the following options:

1. a 10% decrease in prices, to give a 20% increase in volume;
2. a 5% decrease in prices, to give a 10% increase in volume;
3. a 5% increase in prices, to give a 5% decrease in volume; and
4. a 10% increase in prices, to give a 10% decrease in volume.

Assume, that variable costs per unit and total fixed costs remain constant.'

The data Ted has to work on are that: the current selling price per unit is £50; sales volume before any of these alterations are made is 75,000 units; variable cost per unit is £30; and total fixed costs are £100,000. As part of his workings, Ted presents a multiline p/v chart, as in Figure 11.18. Each line represents one of the four alternative options Ted had to work on, plus his base case. Although it looks a little confusing to start with, this chart indicates the changes that the alternatives make to the profitability of the organisation: the steeper the slope of the profit line, the more profitable that option is. In this example, option 4 (a 10% increase in prices, to give a 10% decrease in volume) is the best of the alternatives. Although we haven't seen the table of supporting calculations that Ted prepared for his presentation, these will, of course, support his multiline p/v chart

Mathematical analysis

Although graphical analysis is very useful, it is a clumsy device if all we need to know is the revenue at the breakeven point; or the effects on profit of a simple change in prices and volumes. Management accountants have developed a number of useful arithmetical formulæ that reduce the workload of cost volume profit analysis and, at the same time, increase its accuracy. One of the problems with graphical analysis is the way we draw our graphs. Some of us are not very good at drawing them; and with a poorly drawn graph, we often get poor results. Even well-constructed graphs are not always as accurate as we would like, if only because of the thickness of the lines we draw. This is still true despite the advanced graphics-driven computer software that is now readily available. The fact that we can use a spreadsheet or statistics package to generate our charts does not mean that they are necessarily any easier to use, or any more reliable than the charts we used to draw by hand. The formulæ we are going to look at will enable us to find the number of units an organisation needs to provide in order to generate a net profit of £30,000, or a net profit of £3.5 million. Similarly, the formulæ can tell us what the value of sales will be at the organisation's breakeven point. We will look at these formulæ in detail now, and we will also find them useful in the next chapter when we discuss CVP analysis and decision making.

Formula to find the number of units to be sold or provided

The starting point of the derivation of the formulæ is the basic profit formula:

profit = total revenue − total costs

= total revenue − (fixed costs + variable costs)

and

total revenue = revenue per unit × number of units

variable cost = variable cost per unit × number of units

WORKED EXAMPLE 11.2

1. If revenue per unit is £10, total units are 1,000, fixed costs amount to £2,000 and the variable cost per unit is £6, calculate the organisation's profit, using the above formula.
2. Suppose now we were told that all of the above data were given, except the number of units, and that the profit is to be £5,000 rather than £2,000. How many units must be sold to generate the profit of £5,000?

Solution to Worked example 11.2

1. The calculations are based, straightforwardly, on the formulæ we have just been discussing:

Profit

= £10 × 1,000 units − (£2,000 + (£6 × 1,000 units))

= £10,000 − (£2,000 + £6,000)

= £2,000

2. Again, the calculations needed for this part of the solution are reasonably simple:

Let x = number of units sold.

Profit

$$\left.\begin{aligned} &= £5{,}000 = £10x - (£2{,}000 + (£6x)) \\ &= £5{,}000 = £10x - £2{,}000 - £6x \\ &= £5{,}000 = £4x - £2{,}000 \\ &= £5{,}000 + £2{,}000 = £4x \end{aligned}\right\}$$

Notice the way the sign in front of the £2,000 and the £6x change when they are taken from their bracket

Therefore, dividing both sides by 4:

$$x = \frac{£5{,}000 + 2{,}000}{£4}$$

x = 1,750 units

We can prove that this result is correct:

	£
Sales (1,750 units × £10 per unit)	17,500
Variable costs (1,750 units × £6 per unit)	10,500
Contribution	7,000
Fixed costs	2,000
Net profit	5,000

WORKED EXAMPLE 11.3

Find the number of units to be sold or provided to find the profit shown in each case below:

	Specified profit per unit (£)	Total fixed costs (£)	Variable costs per unit (£)	Profit required
1.	10.00	100,000	7.50	50,000
2.	0.05	75,000	0.0325	60,000
3.	175.50	570,000	160.00	0
4.	26.00	1,300,000	22.00	0

Solution to Worked example 11.3

We could work through each of these problems in full by setting out the workings as we have done above. However, there is little point in doing this since we would always return to the same point in every solution:

$$x = \frac{\text{total fixed costs} + \text{specified profit}}{\text{contribution per unit}}$$

Applying this formula gives:

1. $$\frac{£100{,}000 + 50{,}000}{£2.5} = \frac{£150{,}000}{£2.5}$$

   = 60,000 units

   Where the contribution per unit is

   £10 − £7.50 = £2.50

2. $$\frac{£75{,}000 + 60{,}000}{£0.0175} = \frac{£135{,}000}{£0.0175}$$

   = 7,714,285.714 units

   Where the contribution per unit is:

   £0.05 − £0.0325 = £0.0175

3. $$\frac{£570{,}000 + 0}{£15} = \frac{£570{,}000}{£15}$$

   = 38,000 units

Where the contribution per unit is:

   £175.5 − £160 = £15.50

4. $$\frac{£1{,}300{,}000 + 0}{£4} = \frac{£1{,}300{,}000}{£4}$$

   = 325,000 units

   Where the contribution per unit is

   £26 − £22 = £4

To finish off this section, it is worth pointing out that although we have considered two formulæ here, there is really only one:

$$x = \frac{\text{total fixed costs} + \text{specified profit}}{\text{contribution per unit}}$$

This formula is normally simply written as:

$$x = \frac{\text{total fixed costs}}{\text{contribution per unit}}$$

However, appreciating the first version of this formula will help us to understand situations that involve calculating the required value of sales to achieve a specified (target) profit. This formula will give us the value of x, the number of units sold or needed to be produced at any level of profit, whether it be £0 or £2 billion. As far as the breakeven situation is concerned, all we need to realise is that at the breakeven point, profit is £0.

Formula to find the sales value of the units sold or provided

In the previous section we found the value 'x', which represented the number of units to be sold or provided. It does not take much of a leap to revise the formula we devised in that section when we realise that to find the value of the units to be sold or provided means that we are looking for: 'x' multiplied by the revenue per unit, which can be represented by 'TR/unit x'. This gives us our new formula:

$$\text{sales value} = \frac{\text{TFC} + \text{profit}}{\text{TR/unit} - \text{VC/unit}} \cdot \text{TR/unit}$$

Note that this is exactly the same formula as before except that we have multiplied both sides of it by 'TR/unit' (the sales value). We can simplify this formula and make it user friendly for us! The formula becomes:

$$\text{sales value} = \text{TFC} + \text{profit} \cdot \frac{\text{TR/unit}}{\text{TR/unit} - \text{VC/unit}}$$

$$= \text{TFC} + \text{profit} \cdot \frac{1}{\text{C/S ratio}}$$

$$= \frac{\text{TFC} + \text{profit}}{\text{C/S ratio}}$$

Generally speaking, to calculate the sales value of sales output to achieve a given profit, divide total fixed cost plus profit by the C/S ratio. For example, calculate the sales value of sales to achieve a profit of £30,000, given total fixed costs of £40,000 and variable costs of £40,000 when sales are worth £100,000. Apply the new formula:

$$\text{sales value} = \frac{\text{TFC} + \text{profit}}{\text{C/S ratio}}$$

the C/S ratio = 0.6

To keep our work as simple as possible, leave the C/S ratio in the form of a decimal. Thus, sales value equals:

$$\text{TR/unit } x = \frac{£40{,}000 + 30{,}000}{0.60}$$

$$= \frac{£70{,}000}{0.60}$$

$$= £116{,}666.67$$

As with the previous formula, to find sales units, this formula will provide the solution for any level of profit: even the breakeven point. There is no need for more than one formula here. As we agreed in the previous section, we only have to remember that at the breakeven point, profit is equal to £0, and the rest of the workings follow automatically. Apply the new formula now in Worked example 11.4.

WORKED EXAMPLE 11.4

Calculate the sales value of sales to achieve the profit given in the following table:

	TR	TFC	TVC	Profit
	£	£	£	£
1.	200,000	150,000	20,000	25,000
2.	75,000	45,000	20,000	0

Work to two decimal places for your final answer.

Solution to Worked example 11.4

1. C/S ratio = (£200,000 − £20,000) ÷ £200,000 = 0.9

Therefore:

sales value = (£150,000 + £25,000) ÷ 0.9

= £194,444.44

2. C/S ratio = (£75,000 − £20,000) ÷ £75,000

= 0.7333

Therefore:

sales value = (£45,000 + 0) ÷ 0.7333

= £61,363.64

The two examples we have just worked through used total sales and cost information: The formula works equally well with unit sales and cost information, as relevant.

WORKED EXAMPLE 11.5

Calculate the sales value of sales to achieve the profit given in the following table:

	TR/unit	TFC	VC/unit	Profit
	£	£	£	£
1.	13	700,000	11	100,000
2.	90	40,000	75	0

Work to two decimal places for your final answer.

Solution to Worked example 11.5

1. C/S ratio = (£13 − 11) ÷ £13

   = 0.15385

   Therefore:

   sales value = (£700,000 + 100,000) ÷ 0.15385

   = £5,199,870

2. C/S ratio = (£90 − £75) ÷ £90

   = 0.16667

   Therefore:

   sales value = (£40,000 + 0) ÷ 0.16667

   = £240,000

Summary of the benefits of the formula method

Having looked at both the graphical method and the formula method of analysing CVP situations, we should say that when all we are doing is to try to find the breakeven point, or output to give a certain profit, the formula method is preferred to the graphical method. There are three main reasons why this is the case:

1. It is much less time consuming than the graphical method.
2. It is generally more accurate than the graphical method.
3. It can be used to predict sales values and volumes at the breakeven level, and sales values and volumes at any other level, much more directly than the graphical method.

Summary of the benefits of the graphical method

Having praised the formula method, the graphical method has its benefits too.

1. It provides a pictorial representation of the situation.
2. A graph can summarise a very large amount of data.
3. It saves the reader from having to wade through, potentially, thousands of numbers and calculations.
4. It complements the formula method.

CVP analysis and breakeven analysis using more realistic data

All examples illustrated so far have presented data in a simplified manner. The selling price per unit has been given, or is very simple to deduce; and variable costs are given in total, and with units either given or easy to find, so that the variable cost per unit can be derived simply. In reality, however, data will be presented more awkwardly, but the same responses will be required of us.

Have a look at the sort of example reality has to offer and see how we should deal with it.

WORKED EXAMPLE 11.6

My Company has extracted the following data from its accounting records for January, February, and March for this year:

	Sales	Total Costs
	£	£
January	140,000	112,000
February	154,000	119,980
March	170,000	129,100

Sales are all made at £1 per unit.

Required

Calculate:

1. the variable cost per unit;
2. the total fixed costs;
3. the C/S ratio;
4. the breakeven point;
5. the profit for April if sales are £160,000 in that month.

Solution to Worked example 11.6

Although the presentation of data in this example is different to the presentations we have seen so far, there is absolutely nothing new in it. We do, however, have to recall techniques from earlier chapters to help us sort out the information.

1. We can use the high–low method here to help us sort out the fixed from the variable costs. (In a more extended example, we might be wiser to use the scattergraph or ordinary least squares method here.) The workings are familiar, from Chapter 3. The 'high' (where the independent variable is sales units) is data for March and the low is data for January.

   All sales are made at the rate of £1 per unit, so the calculation of sales units is very straightforward:

Variable costs per unit

	Sales (units)	Total costs (£)
High	170,000	129,100
Low	140,000	112,000
Difference	30,000	17,100

Therefore, the variable cost per unit:

$$= \frac{£17,100}{30,000 \text{ units}}$$

$$= £0.57 \text{ per unit}$$

2. Using the solution to part (1) of this exercise, we can find the fixed cost, by substituting the variable cost per unit in March's data:

   total cost = fixed cost + variable cost

   = £129,100 = fixed cost + (£0.57 per unit × 170,000 units)

   = £129,100 = fixed cost + £96,900

   Therefore:

   £129,100 – £96,600 = fixed cost

   fixed cost = £32,200

3. Having sorted out parts (1) and (2), which are the most difficult parts of the question, this part, and the other parts, then become as straightforward as any other CVP analysis question:

   C/S ratio = £1 – 0.57 ÷ £1 = 0.43 or 43%

4. The breakeven point value:

   = £32,200 ÷ 0.43

= £74,883.72

and the breakeven point volume:

= £32,200 ÷ 0.43

= 74,883.72 units

There is no mistake here: the answers are remarkably similar. The reason is that the C/S ratio (as a decimal) and the contribution per unit are both 43% or 0.43. Consequently, the solutions will consist of exactly the same numbers.

To verify there is no mistake, we should prove our workings to ensure that 74,883.72 units does return a profit of £0: that is, it is the breakeven volume.

Sales	£74,883.72
Variable costs:	
(£0.57 per unit × 74,883.72 units)	42,683.72
Contribution	32,200.00
Fixed costs	32,200.00
Net profit	0.00

5. If sales are £160,000 for April, then the profit for April will be:

Sales:	
(must be 160,000 units, at £1 per unit)	£160,000
Variable costs:	
(160,000 units × £0.57 per unit)	91,200
Contribution	68,800
Fixed costs	32,200
Net profit	£36,600

Uncertainty and CVP analysis

Since CVP models are assumed to be used for short-term planning, we would be wise to extend such models to include a more realistic view of how costs and revenues might behave. In traditional models, sales and costs are assumed to be known with 100% certainty. In models attempting to cater for uncertainty, some attempt is made to assign possible outcomes to a series of revenues, costs and outcomes. We will look at two techniques in an attempt to deal with decision making under uncertainty: decision trees; and normal probability distribution.

Decision trees

A probability decision tree is a diagram showing the possible values of the variables and the possibilities of each possible outcome. Once the full evaluation of outcomes is complete, expected values are easily developed.

WORKED EXAMPLE 11.7

Price plc wishes to evaluate whether to undertake production of a new product that has a life of one year. It is felt that fixed costs of £450,000 are certain but that other variables are uncertain. After lengthy investigation, management determined the following outcomes and subjective probabilities.

Sales units	Probabilities	Contribution margin Value (£)	Probabilities
300,000	0.3	5	0.4
200,000	0.5	4	0.6
120,000	0.2		

Solution to Worked example 11.7

Table 11.7 shows the solution in the form of a decision tree.

TABLE 11.7 *Decision tree for Price plc*

Sales volume (units) and probability	Contribution margin probability	Total contribution margin	Fixed costs	Profit	Combined probability	Expected value
300,000	5	1,500,000	450,000	1,050,000		
0.3	0.4				0.12	126,000
	4	1,200,000	450,000	750,000		
	0.6				0.18	135,000
200,000	5	1,000,000	450,000	550,000		
0.5	0.4				0.3	165,000
	4	800,000	450,000	350,000		
	0.6				0.3	105,000
120,000	5	600,000	450,000	150,000		
0.2	0.4				0.08	12,000
	4	480,000	450,000	30,000		
	0.6				0.12	3,600
Expected payoff						546,600

Reading the table across from left to right, we can see that we incorporate all the data we were given, such that, when the sales volume is set at 300,000 units, there is a 30% probability of this happening. Furthermore there is a probability that with this level of sales, there is a 40% probability that the contribution margin will be £5. We can then calculate the total contribution margin (£5 per unit × 300,000 units) and from there determine the overall profit for this scenario of £1,050,000. Having found the profit level, we apply the combined probability of the two events of 300,000 units being sold at a contribution margin of £5, that is, 30% × 40% = 12%, or 0.12. We then multiply this combined probability by the profit of £1,050,000 to give us the expected value of profit of £126,000. This process is repeated for all of the six possible outcomes, so we get six different profit results and six different expected values. The final calculation is to evaluate the expected payoff, which we do by adding together the six expected values. The interpretation of this decision-tree outcome is that if this project is undertaken, then, assuming the subjective probabilities and outcomes are fulfilled, one of the six payoffs will occur. The expected payoff of £491,600 means that if this project were undertaken many times over, the outturn would be that profit would average £491,600. From such a decision tree, we can construct a probability distribution and from there we can assess the various outcomes and their associated probabilities. Table 11.8 demonstrates the probability distribution for Worked example 11.7.

TABLE 11.8 ***Probability distribution***

Outcome £	Probability	Cumulative probability
30,000	0.12	0.12
150,000	0.08	0.20
350,000	0.30	0.50
550,000	0.20	0.70
750,000	0.18	0.88
1,050,000	0.12	1.00

We can use this probability distribution now to demonstrate the probabilities of achieving a given level of profit. For example, there is a 50% probability of making a profit of at least £350,000, based on these data.

One of the problems with the problem we have just analysed in Worked example 11.7 is that the solution is not sufficiently general. Worked example 11.7 is fine as far as it goes, but we cannot say, for example, what the probability of at least breaking even will be given that analysis We cannot estimate the chances of at least breaking even since the data are incomplete. There is, however, a method available that will allow us to estimate the probability of achieving any level of return, given sufficient input data.

Jaedicke and Robichek's method: normal probability distribution

Jaedicke and Robichek (1964) presented a method for dealing with the CVP situation where knowledge is not certain – thus flying in the face of one of the chief assumptions underlying CVP analysis. Their paper has been the foundation of many further journal articles and sections in textbooks, and their work provides a very useful insight into how to deal with uncertainty in CVP analysis. Although we are trying to eliminate the need for one of the basic assumptions on which CVP analysis is based, we need to start this discussion with another assumption. For Jaedicke and Robichek's approach to work, we must assume that the data we are working on are normally distributed. This means that the values of a variable (x) tend to cluster around the mean but spread out symmetrically in both directions. Any particular normal distribution can be completely determined if the mean and the standard deviation are known. All normal distributions can be made comparable to each other by transforming them into standard normal form which has a zero mean and a standard deviation of unity by the use of the following formula:

$$z = \frac{x - \mu}{\sigma}$$

where:

z is the normal deviate
x is the actual value of the variable x
μ is the mean value
σ is the standard deviation

Remember, from statistics, because of the standard deviation of one for the standard normal distribution, the following important characteristics can be stated:

- the range $\pm$ one standard deviation contains 68.26% of the values of z;
- the range $\pm$ two standard deviations contains 95.44% of the values of z;
- the range $\pm$ three standard deviations contains 99.74% of the values of z.

These relationships are extremely useful because they can be used very simply to estimate relationships. Worked example 11.8 will illustrate precisely how the method works.

WORKED EXAMPLE 11.8

The selling price of a product for the next month is known to be £800 per unit. Sales volume, however, is uncertain. The estimated average sales for the period are 1,600 units; and it is assumed that the probability distribution for the sales volume is normal with a standard deviation of 900 units. Period fixed costs of £375,000 and unit variable costs of £510 are both assumed to be certain.

Required

Calculate:

1. the breakeven point;
2. the probability of at least breaking even;
3. the probability of achieving a profit of £10,000 or more;
4. the probability of incurring a loss of £15,000 or more.

Solution to Worked example 11.8

1. We need to calculate the breakeven point for part 2 of the example anyway, and it is:

$$\frac{\pounds 375{,}000}{\pounds 800 - 510} = 1{,}293 \text{ units}$$

2. To calculate the probability of at least breaking even we use the formula from Jaedicke and Robichek:

$$z = \frac{x - \mu}{\Sigma} = \frac{1{,}293 - 1{,}600}{900} = -0.3411$$

The value of the normal deviate is −0.3411, which we transform into a more usable format by consulting a table of areas under the normal curve. Depending upon the table that we consult, we should eventually derive the value of the probability of at least breaking even of 63.31%. That is, there is an almost two in three chance of making at least some profit (greater than zero). Conversely, the chances of making a loss of one magnitude or another is one in three.

3. The probability of achieving a profit of £10,000 or more is calculated by adapting the basic formula to read that x is equal to the number of units needed to ensure a profit of £10,000: we do this along the lines of the formula found in the section in which we considered the mathematical analysis of CVP:

$$\frac{\pounds 375{,}000 + 10{,}000}{\pounds 800 - 510} = 1{,}328 \text{ units (approximately)}$$

$$z = \frac{x - \mu}{\Sigma} = \frac{1{,}328 - 1{,}600}{900} = -0.3022$$

From the table, this gives a probability of 61.79% of achieving a profit of at least £10,000.

4. The probability of achieving a loss of £15,000 or more is calculated by adapting the basic formula to read that x is equal to the number of units needed to ensure a loss of £15,000. We do this along the lines of the formula found in the section in which we considered the mathematical analysis of CVP:

$$\frac{\pounds 375{,}000 - 15{,}000}{\pounds 800 - 510} = 1{,}241 \text{ units (approximately)}$$

$$z = \frac{x - \mu}{\Sigma} = \frac{1{,}241 - 1{,}600}{900} = -0.3988$$

From the table, this gives a probability of 65.54% of achieving a loss of at least £15,000. Note in this case, we have taken the phrase 'achieving a loss of £15,000 or more' to mean achieving a loss of £15,000 or £14,000 or a profit of £x . . .

The most significant deficiency of this approach is, of course, that we have to assume that the data are normally distributed. Whilst this might be true, only a detailed statistical analysis will prove whether this is true or not. However, Kaplan (1983) says that:

> The use of the normal distribution is a simplifying but not necessary assumption for CVP analysis under uncertainty. ... For example, in order for the normal distribution to be a reasonable characterisation of the sales distribution, the mean must be at least three to five times the standard deviation so that there is virtually no probability of negative sales.

This section has provided an introduction to uncertainty and CVP analysis. For a more detailed treatment of this area, see Kaplan (1983: chapter 6).

SUMMARY

In this chapter we have taken a comprehensive look at breakeven analysis and an introduction to cost volume profit analysis. We have seen numerous examples of the different types of breakeven charts and profit/volume charts that can be drawn and presented as part of a breakeven analysis of an organisation's accounting results, or as part of a special exercise to determine the likely outcomes of certain courses of action. We have also seen that this kind of analysis can be applied to simplified and realistic examples, although we have been made aware that it is based on a number of simplifying assumptions. These assumptions do limit the validity of some of the work we have done in this chapter. Nevertheless we analysed these assumptions in detail to provide a more balanced view of the work we are trying to do.

We then worked through the mathematical approach to CVP analysis, and we determined that although the graphical analysis has much to commend it, the mathematical approach is superior in terms of its accuracy and the greater simplicity that attends it. We concluded the chapter by considering two approaches to dealing with the assumption of certainty of knowledge. We assumed that knowledge is not certain, and we applied both decision tree analysis and the statistical approach surrounding the standard normal distribution to solving problems arising from this assumption. From this examination of these techniques we found that even though the Jaedicke and Robichek method of dealing with uncertainty has much to commend it, it is flawed in that it assumes data are normally distributed.

KEY TERMS

You should satisfy yourself that you have noted all of these terms and can define and/or describe their meaning and use, as appropriate.

Cost–volume profit (CVP) analysis (p. 337)
Breakeven analysis (p. 338)
Breakeven point (p. 338)
High level of fixed costs (p. 340)
Low level of fixed costs (p. 340)
Contribution chart (p. 343)
Margin of safety (p. 343)
Margin of danger (p. 344)
Unit breakeven chart (p. 344)
Profit/volume (p/v) chart (p. 345)
Multiproduct p/v chart (p. 347)
Sensitivity analysis (p. 348)
Assumptions of CVP analysis (p. 353)
Hypothesis of supply and demand (p. 361)
Multiline p/v chart (p. 361)

RECOMMENDED READING

Jaedicke and Robichek (1964) is one of the classics.

QUESTIONS

Review questions

1. Define CVP analysis and breakeven analysis.
2. State the assumptions of CVP analysis.
3. Plot a breakeven chart, given a selling price per unit of £10, a variable cost per unit of £5, and total fixed costs of £20,000.
4. Compare the graph you have drawn for question 4 with a new graph that you now draw. The new graph takes into account the heavy investment in capital equipment carried out by this organisation. The new total fixed costs are £100,000. All other data remains valid.
5. What is the margin of safety?
6. What is a p/v chart? How does it differ from a breakeven chart?
7. What is sensitivity analysis?

Answers to review questions 1, 5, 6 and 7 can be found in the Student Workbook.

Graded practice questions

Level I

1. A company has the following revenues and costs, for the single product that it manufactures: a selling price per unit of £12.00; a variable cost per unit £8.40; annual fixed costs of £720,000; and a normal annual output 540,000 units.
   (a) Calculate the following:
      (i) contribution per unit;
      (ii) c/s ratio;
      (iii) breakeven point in units and value; and
      (iv) margin of safety expressed in units, value and percentage form.

   (b) For each of the following cases, which are to be treated as being separate cases, determine the new C/S ratio and break even point in units:
      (i) decrease in variable costs of £1.20 per unit together with a 20% increase in selling price; and
      (ii) a £143,600 reduction in fixed costs and a 20% increase in variable costs.

2. From the annual data provided, prepare a breakeven chart. Determine the breakeven point and margin of safety from your graph, and prove your results arithmetically.

	£
Sales	900,000
Variable costs	525,000
Fixed costs	225,000

3. (a) B Day Ltd makes one kind of sanitary fitment, and has provided you with the following data:

	£	£	£
Sales			300,000
Direct materials		60,000	
Direct labour		40,000	
		100,000	
Other variable costs	50,000		
Fixed costs	120,000		
		170,000	
			270,000
Net profit			30,000

Prepare a p/v chart from these data, and determine the breakeven point and margin of safety.

(b) Making whatever assumptions you feel necessary, discuss the effects of the following changes to the basic data:

(i) an increase in fixed costs;
(ii) a decrease in variable costs;
(iii) an increase in selling price;
(iv) an increase in sales volume.

Level II

4. The Swish Hotel Co operates a three-star hotel in the centre of a medium- sized town. The hotel is family owned and operated, and it closes down for a total of 25 days every year during which time the family returns home to Hong Kong. All rooms are of the same size and standard as each other. The budget for the coming year is:

Number of rooms	80
Maximum bed days	27,200
Selling rate of a room per day	£60

Costs

	Variable £	Fixed £	Total £
Direct materials and services	150,000	–	150,000
Direct wages and salaries	900,000	–	900,000

Guest services			
Overheads	75,000	125,000	200,000
Hotel administration	125,000	175,000	300,000
	1,250,000	300,000	1,550,000

Calculate

(a) the c/s ratio;
(b) the breakeven point in occupancy and value terms;
(c) the margin of safety;
(d) the effect on the breakeven point if the currently negotiated pay rise for all members of staff of an overall 10% of direct salaries were granted;
(e) (i) the effect on the margin of safety if the proposed extension to the hotel of a further 10 rooms went ahead. (If the extension is undertaken, variable costs rise in line with the change and fixed costs would increase by 20% across the board. Treat this option as independent of part (d) of this question.);
(ii) the room rate if, when the extension is completed, the profit requirement of the family is £150,000 per year.

Once you have found your results, what would be your advice to the family?

5. Santos, a Portuguese hairdresser, operates a one-man hairdressing parlour in a suburb of a large town in the north of England. Currently, he operates from rented premises, for which he pays £250 per calendar month. His electricity bill amounts to an average of £75 per calendar month (this is 10% variable); he employs an odd-job man who sweeps up for him, runs errands, and generally looks after the salon and the patrons: the odd-job man is paid £50 per week, in cash. All other costs amount to £150 per calendar month (these are 25% variable). A haircut at Santos's costs the patron £3: it is a one-style haircut service!

Santos's landlord is currently renovating the row of buildings in which the hairdressing parlour is situated. He has proposed to Santos that he move to the shop next door when it is finished. If he does so, he will have a more modern, compact salon, more suited to his turnover. The rent will remain the same; but because of the general improvements carried out as part of the refurbishment, it will be cheaper to run: the electricity bill can be expected to fall to £60 per calendar month (the variable element will remain at the same absolute level as it is in the old premises); the 'other' costs can be expected to fall to £105 per calendar month (they will still be 25% variable). Any other costs will remain as they are in the present premises.

Calculate:

(a) Santos's current breakeven point, in terms of haircuts and value.
(b) Santos's breakeven point if he moves into the shop next door.
(c) Assume Santos felt benevolent, and any savings from the move would be passed back to his patrons. How much would he charge for a haircut in the new premises to maintain his current profit level if his current level of 450 haircuts per calendar month, on average over a whole year, is maintained.

6. Three products are made and sold by Our Company:

Product	Selling prices (£)	C/S ratio (%)
1	350	10
2	300	20
3	250	40

Total fixed costs are £280,000 per year.

Over the latest few years, half of the total sales volume was made up of sales of product 1, and four times as many units of product 2 were sold as product 3. The chief marketing executive has estimated, from regional and other sales data analysis, that the overall profit picture can be improved by selling the products in a different mix to the current mix. She suggests the following sales mix:

	%
Product 1	30%
Product 2	50
Product 3	20

Required

(a) Prepare a p/v chart for the existing sales mix. Start the horizontal axis at zero units and increase in steps of 1,000 units to 8,000 units.
(b) Superimpose the profit line for the proposed product mix suggested by the chief marketing executive on your original p/v chart.
(c) State your conclusions.

7. (a) The accountant of Laburnum Ltd is preparing documents for a forthcoming meeting of the budget committee. Currently, variable cost is 40% of selling price and total fixed costs are £40,000 per year.

The company uses a historical cost accounting system. There is concern that the level of costs may rise during the ensuing year, and the chairman of the budget committee has expressed interest in a probabilistic approach to an investigation of the effect that this will have on historic cost profits. The accountant is attempting to prepare the documents in a way which will be most helpful to the committee members. He has obtained the following estimates from his colleagues:

Average inflation Rate over ensuing year (%)	Probability
Pessimistic 10%	0.4
Most likely 5%	0.5
Optimistic 1%	0.1
	1.0

Demand at current selling prices (£)	Probability
Pessimistic 50,000	0.3
Most likely 75,000	0.6
Optimistic 100,000	0.1
	1.0

The demand figures are given in terms of sales value at the current level of selling prices, but it is considered that the company could adjust its selling prices in line with the inflation rate without affecting customer demand in real terms.

Some of the company's fixed costs are contractually fixed and some are apportionments of past costs; of the total fixed costs, an estimated 85% will remain constant irrespective of the inflation rate.

Required

(a) Analyse the foregoing information in a way which you consider will assist management with its budgeting problem. Although you should assume that the directors of Laburnum Ltd are solely interested in the effect of inflation on historic cost profits, you should comment on the validity of the accountant's intended approach. As part of your analysis you are required to calculate:

(i) the probability of at least breaking even; and
(ii) the probability of achieving a profit of at least £20,000.

(b) It can be argued that the use of point estimate probabilities (as above) is too unrealistic because it constrains the demand and cost variables to relatively few values. Briefly describe an alternative simulation approach which might meet this objection.

ACCA 2.4 Management Accounting
June 1986

Solutions to practice questions 2, 4 and 5 can be found in the Student Workbook. Solutions to practice question numbers in red can be found at the end of this book.

Projects

1. (a) Extract sales/income and total cost information from any annual report and accounts you have for any organisation. If you have more than, say, five years' worth of data for that organisation, estimate the regression function for costs, so that you have an estimate of total fixed costs, and variable costs per unit. If you have only three or four years' worth of data, use the high–low or scattergraph method to estimate the fixed cost/variable cost split. Use the information you have to estimate the organisation's:

(i) c/s ratio;
(ii) breakeven point; and
(iii) margin of safety (taking the current year's sales as the maximum sales).

Repeat these calculations for each year for which you have data.

(b) If you can get access to organisation data from inside the organisation (legitimately, that is) carry out project 1(a) from that vantage point: analyse the overall figures, then analyse any break down of those data that are available (by sales region, product group, and so on). Compare the results of the overall organisation analysis with the results obtained from the regional, group analysis. Justify any differences you find.

2. Repeat project 1 for an organisation that has different objectives to the organisation you dealt with in project 1. For example,if you analysed a profit making organisation in project 1, analyse a non-profit making organisation for this project. Alternatively, if your organisation in project 1 was a manufacturer, you may wish to choose a commercial or service organisation this time.

   Compare the results you have for project 1 with the results you have for this project. Would you expect to find any significant differences between the results of the two different 'types' of organisation that you have chosen to analyse? Do any significant differences emerge?
3. Find the Annual reports and accounts of what you feel will be a relatively high-fixed-cost business, and obtain the report of an organisation that you feel will be a relatively low-fixed-cost business.

   Carry out a breakeven/CVP analysis of the data you obtain.

   Were you correct? Do the results of your analysis support your prognoses about the relative high- or low-fixed-cost levels? If your hypothesis of high versus low-fixed-cost structure was wrong, find out and justify why you were wrong.

4. Look for evidence from the chairman's statement in the annual report and accounts, and/or in the press or magazines, of what the organisation itself considers to be its breakeven point.

   Carry out an analysis of the data in the annual report and accounts to which the chairman's statements refers. Do you agree with the chairman's statement?

   If you find significant differences between your estimates and the chairman's assertion, account for such a difference. How does it arise do you think?

REFERENCES

Jaedicke, R. K. and Robichek, A. A. (1964), 'Cost volume profit analysis under conditions of uncertainty' *The Accounting Review*, **39** (October), 917–26.

Kaplan, R. S. (1983), *Advanced management accounting*, 1st edn (Prentice Hall).

Usry, M. F., Hammer, L. H. and Matz, A. (1988), *Cost Accounting: planning and control*, 9th edn (South Western Publishing).

CHAPTER TWELVE

Costing for decision making: relevant costing

CHAPTER OBJECTIVES

After reading this chapter you should be able to:

- define relevant, differential and incremental costs
- apply relevant costing
- appreciate the meaning of ad hoc decisions
- apply relevant costing to each one of the following situations: make or buy decisions; close a department decisions; limiting factor analysis, including linear programming; and sell or process further decisions

Introduction

Again, as we work through this chapter, we should see the influence of variable costing. Much of the work of the management accountant in the area of relevant costs is based on his or her variable cost assumptions and definitions. The work we are about to go through has its critics, and we shall be discussing some of these criticisms. Along with variable costing and CVP analysis, there is much contained in this chapter that can be subject to critical review. The problem of short-termism is the potential problem area that first comes to mind.

The term 'opportunity cost' has already been defined in this book. We know it is a term borrowed from economists, and we said an opportunity cost is defined as being the cost of an opportunity forgone. At several points in this chapter, we will come across the opportunity cost concept. However, for what ought to be simple examples, opportunity costs are not labelled as such. The point here is that opportunity costs should be identifiable without any conscious effort. If we fail to take opportunity costs into account, we need to review our understanding of the situation anyway. Nevertheless, at this stage it would be worthwhile attempting practice question 7 at the end of this chapter to test fully your understanding of this term.

Relevant, differential and incremental costs

CIMA (1991) defines each of these terms. Relevant costs are said to be: 'Costs appropriate to aiding the making of specific management decisions.' Differential cost is not defined but **differential costing** is: 'A technique used in the preparation of ad hoc information in which only cost and income differences between alternative courses of action are taken into consideration.' Similarly, incremental cost is not defined but **incremental costing** is: 'A technique used in the preparation of ad hoc information where consideration is given to a range of graduated or stepped changes in the level or nature of activity, and the additional costs and revenues likely to result from each degree of change are presented.'

Relevant costs must be the cash costs of implementing a decision: if a cost is a non-cash cost (such as depreciation), it cannot be relevant and it cannot be differential or incremental. CIMA is trying to convince us that there is a difference to be drawn between the terms 'differential' and 'incremental', when clearly there is not. French (1985: 146), in defining incremental says: 'differential has the same meaning.' Hirsch and Louderback (1986: 133) and Drury (1992: 237) both agree with French: there is no difference between differential and incremental. Furthermore Hirsch and Louderback and Drury agree that relevant costs are the same as differential and incremental costs. The rest of this chapter is concerned with relevant costing.

Applications of relevant costing

In 1982, the British government sent a naval 'task force' to counter the invasion of the Falkland Islands by Argentinian armed forces. Derek Brown (1982) wrote an article for the *Guardian* newspaper in May 1982 concerning the relevant costs of the operation. Extracts from that article will help us to see precisely what is meant by relevant in the context of costing for decision making. The main points arising from this article are:

- The capital cost of the Royal Navy ships in the task force represent a sunk cost (no pun intended!).
- The salaries etc. of the crews of the RN ships and the Marines and soldiers are not incremental costs since they would have to be paid anyway.
- Some chartered ships were used: this does represent an incremental cost.
- The civilian ships were paid a special rate relevant for their volunteer crews.
- Insurance cover for the civilian ships and crews is also likely to end up as a charge to the Government [relevant].
- To replace ships, aircraft and other equipment that were all lost represent real costs: again incremental and therefore relevant.

CAMEO

An update on accounting for the Falklands war

How much does a one-day rail strike cost? This was the question posed in the article by Philip Bassett in *The Times* of 18 July 1995. This is, of course, a relevant costing question exactly along the lines of questioning the true cost of the Falklands war. British Rail (BR) openly stated that a one-day strike costs them £10 million – a train driver loses £70 each in lost wages. Bassett, however, wanted to know how much the strike was costing the UK economy in total. The answer was supplied by the accountancy firm Chantrey Vellacott, the only firm brave enough to venture an estimate, according to Bassett. Vellacott's estimate is:

BR revenue lost	£10 million
Lost output of other workers	£46 million
Total cost to the economy	£56 million

The £46 million is based on an estimate of 1.25 million people being unable to get to work on a strike day, which, in turn, is based on the assumption that 35% of people who normally use the train to get to work cannot get in because of the strike. Finally, and this is the trickiest part, Vellacott then have to estimate the net output value that is lost through the absence of the 1.25 million people. A simple calculation reveals that a total of £46 million is achieved by estimating the net output per day lost from each unproductive employee at £36.8 – although neither Vellacott nor Bassett reveals how that value was arrived at. As Bassett says, most people would find something to argue about in Vellacott's estimates. However, it is clear that strikes exert a cost.

When attempting to assess the relevant cost of doing something, then, we have to be careful to exclude all sunk costs. Those costs incurred before the present project was undertaken or before the situation arose. The replacement of assets lost or used up by the project under review could well be relevant, however. As the article above shows, because the asset was wasted as a direct result of the present project, and needs to be replaced, the cost of replacement will be included as part of the relevant cost of the present project. Do note the point about changes of strategy and technology, however, that were brought out by the article. And we have to be careful to ensure that all other supposed costs are cash costs. Throughout the extracts from the article above, references show clearly that the author of the article was positive in his thinking: all relevant costs are cash costs. It is the kind of analysis we have just seen related to a war situation that we will apply to business and commercial situations. A whole host of managerial decisions can usefully be analysed by means of relevant costing. In the rest of this chapter we will look in detail at some of the types of managerial decisions that relevant costing can help with. The point to remember is that it is only revenues and costs that change as a result of the decision under review that are relevant: any other factor is ignored.

Ad hoc decisions

Restaurants, hotels, and travel companies are good examples of places to find the application of relevant costing to *ad hoc* decisions: that is, decisions for a specific purpose: We will work through a restaurant example to show us why that should be.

WORKED EXAMPLE 12.1

Chompers restaurant can cater for 500 meals per day, although on average it caters for 400 meals. The fixed costs for the restaurant are £1,000 per day and the average selling price for a meal is £5, with the variable costs amounting to £3 per meal.

One day a group of 30 people on a mystery tour arrived at the restaurant and offered to pay a total of £120 if every member of the party could have a full meal each.

Required

Assuming you are the duty manager of Chompers at the time, would you accept this deal?

Solution to Worked example 12.1

You would accept the deal because as a result of it, Chompers would be £30 better off. The workings are as follows:

	£
Increase in revenues	120
less: Increase in costs	90
Increase in contribution	30

Notes

1. The increase in costs is the £3 variable costs per meal for 30 meals, amounting to £90.
2. The restaurant has the capacity to cope: total capacity is 500 meals per day, but at the time the party arrives, only 400 meals are being served.
3. Since the capacity of the restaurant is sufficient, it seems fair to assume that fixed costs will remain unaffected by this decision.

As a result of these deliberations, we can conclude that it is only the increase in revenues and variable costs that are relevant, and our decision is to accept the deal.

Developing the Chompers Restaurant example a little now, imagine that a large mail order business nearby is cutting costs and wishes to close down its own in house restaurant. The managing director of the mail order business contacts you, the manager of Chompers, and puts the following proposal to you: in return for a guaranteed 200 customers per day, every working day, my business will pay you £750 per day to provide a full meal for every one of the 200 people. What is your response to this proposition?

As we should expect, we need to sort out what is relevant and what is not relevant. Although the solution to this problem is not difficult, the layout is slightly different to the first part of the problem.

Workings

We can clarify any possible misunderstandings by working through the detail of the question.

In order for this proposal to be accepted, 100 existing clients would have to be turned away every day. The restaurant has the capacity to cope with 500 meals per day and is currently serving an average of 400 per day. Thus, in order to cope with the extra 200 meals for the mail order business, 100 people need to be displaced. Therefore, although the mail order business is contributing £750 per day, Chompers loses £5 × 100 in normal (old) revenue. Similarly, although Chompers incurs an extra £3 × 200 variable costs in providing the extra meals, £3 × 100 variable costs are saved by not catering for the displaced clients. Incremental costs are, therefore, £300.

Solution

	£
Additional revenues	750
less: Old revenues lost	500
Increase in revenues	250
Additional costs	600
less: Old costs saved	300
Increase in costs	300

Summarising this information, to provide us with a final solution:

	£
Increase in revenues	250
less: Increase in costs	300
(Decrease) in contribution	(50)

The outcome of this proposition would be that Chompers would be £50 per day worse off as a result of accepting it. Your decision must therefore be to reject the proposal. Overall, Chompers would not accept the proposal in the short term. In the long term, if Chompers can be satisfied that the mail order business will be able to guarantee the additional 200 meals per day, it might wish to undertake extensions to its premises in order to cope with both existing and new clients. Following on from such a decision, economies of scale may be secured such that £750 per day is a fair price to pay (economies of scale relating to the variable costs are the consideration here, of course). One of the problems potentially faced by organisations such as Chompers comes when one customer finds out that another customer is receiving a different deal to theirs – especially when the other customer is receiving a better price. In the case of Chompers, the regular customer might easily find himself sitting next to someone from the mail order business who knows about the deal that was done to get her there. If these customers start talking about the special price that the mail order business pays as opposed to the price the regular customer is paying, there might be problems for Chompers.

Make-or-buy decisions

Irrespective of the degree of complexity of problems in reality, concentrate now on the situation where an organisation might find that it is paying more to make some or all of the products or components it uses than it can buy them for. Relevant costing helps management in these situations to sort out what should and should not be done about rectifying such a situation. Working through an example will help us to find out what issues are involved in a make-or-buy decision

WORKED EXAMPLE 12.2

Shingle Ltd currently makes one key component that it uses when it is servicing machinery for its clients. Each component costs £20 to make and the current usage is 10,000 components per year. The fixed costs directly associated with the component total £40,000 per year. These fixed costs would be eliminated if the production of the component ceases. After lengthy negotiations, Pebble plc has offered to supply the components to Shingle at a price of £22 per unit.

Required

1. Determine the differential costs of making and buying the component.
2. Should Shingle accept the offer from Pebble? Justify your answer.
3. What qualitative factors should Shingle take into account in arriving at its decision?
4. In what way, if at all, would your answer to parts 1 and 2 be different if the fixed costs could not be eliminated when the component is supplied by Pebble plc? Explain your answer.

Solution to Worked example 12.2

Deal with the economic arguments first (that is, parts 1 and 2).

1. Making the component:

	£
Variable costs	200,000
Fixed costs	40,000
Total costs	240,000

Buying the component from Pebble plc:

	£
Total buying costs	220,000

Savings gained from buying from Pebble plc:

	£
Total costs of manufacture	240,000
Total buying costs	220,000
Savings	20,000

The workings here are straightforward: Variable costs of making are 10,000 units × £20 per unit = £200,000; and the fixed costs are, simply, £40,000 per year; giving a total cost of manufacture of £240,000.

2. On economic grounds alone, it makes sense to buy in from Pebble plc and cease the manufacture of the components. As a result of taking this decision, Shingle will save £20,000 each year on its servicing operations.
3. We have just said that we have taken the decision to accept the special order on economic grounds. However, it is rarely enough just to consider the economics of such a situation. Let us consider the qualitative grounds on which a special offer such as Shingle and Pebble is decided. There is a great deal we do not know about either Shingle Ltd or Pebble plc, of course, but we are still able to discuss, in general, many of the issues confronting the companies in terms of the special deal we are considering on their behalf. Essentially, we will be looking at the qualitative side of the deal from Shingle's point of view. The significant points include:

   (a) Is Pebble a reliable supplier? Will it be able to maintain supplies at the required level of 10,000 units per year, or is it just trying to get rid of a batch it has filling its warehouse? Maybe Pebble is suffering from temporary excess capacity, and once it has solved its problem, it could leave Shingle in the mire.
   (b) Can Pebble guarantee the level of quality that Shingle is used to? Shingle must make sure that the components it gets from Pebble are at least as good as they can manufacture themselves.
   (c) The savings of buying over making are not that great; they are only of the order of 10% of the buying in price. How long will it be before these savings are wiped out? There may be no guarantee that the savings would be maintained.
   (d) Will there be redundancy costs to be incurred by Shingle, in addition to the costs mentioned? If so, it might make the buying option much less attractive than it currently appears.
   (e) There are also stock holding and working capital implications to take into account. Will Shingle have to buy, say, one month's stocks in advance? If it does, and if it worked on a just-in-time basis before, this is bound to tie up vital capital in stocks that were not previously tied up. This possible problem must be evaluated.
   (f) What will be the effects on morale within Shingle Ltd if a whole section is closed down? Although it is not possible to quantify something as intangible as industrial relations and employee morale, there is no doubt that actions which affect such matters can lead to losses in productivity and therefore profitability. A thorough assessment ought to be made.
   (g) Is Pebble plc the kind of business that investors are happy with? Perks, Rawlinson and Ingram (1992) discussed the issues relating to ethical investment in the United

Kingdom. They found that a whole variety of organisations throughout the country consider aspects such as the environment, waste recycling, drugs, nuclear power, and political contributions as being crucial elements in the invest/do not invest equation. Those organisations that had a perceptibly bad record on such issues were either not considered for investment or may have suffered positive disinvestment. Can Pebble plc be classified as such a non-caring organisation? If relevant, Shingle ought to make itself aware of the facts.

4. If the fixed costs cannot be eliminated, the decision to buy rather than to continue making will be reversed. The calculations are:

   Making the component:

	£
Variable costs	200,000
Fixed costs	40,000
Total cost to manufacture	240,000

   Buying the component from Pebble plc:

	£
Total buying costs	220,000
Fixed costs	40,000
Total costs	260,000

   Extra costs incurred by buying from Pebble plc:

Total costs to manufacture	240,000
Total buying costs	260,000
Extra costs incurred	(20,000)

   The detailed workings for this part of the question are exactly as they are for part 1, except for the inclusion of the fixed costs in the buying-in section of the calculations. The thinking here is that if the fixed costs cannot be eliminated, they must still be incurred; and if they must still be incurred, they are relevant. This is an example of a fixed cost being relevant. In any similar situation, a fixed cost would be relevant. Hence it is not only variable costs that are the relevant cash costs. If the fixed costs cannot be eliminated, therefore, the proposal to buy from Pebble must be rejected.

Closure decisions

The make-or-buy decision is an important decision from many points of view. However, on average, it is a relatively minor problem compared to the next type of issue we are going to deal with. Making or buying a component may be concerned with costs amounting to, say, only 2% or 3% of total costs. A closure decision may relate to a much larger proportion of the costs of the organisation's entire operations. Whatever the precise fraction of the organisation's operations we are dealing with, the point is the closure decision is likely to be of major strategic importance to the organisation taking the decision. Organisations suffering as a result of recession, or downturn in the economy, or those going through a period of reorganisation, are often faced with the decision of whether a department that is currently making a loss should be closed down. The arguments here appear simple: if department 'B' is making a loss, by closing it down, we will no longer incur that loss and hence total profits will increase by the amount of the loss no longer incurred. All other things being equal, this would be true. However, in a divisional organisation it must be exceptionally rare for such a situation to exist. Even when we get rid of an entire division, we will be left with some residual costs (usually the fixed costs that are incurred irrespective of whether that division is open or closed). Such a situation clouds the issues: relevant costing helps us sort out the issues.

One group of issues the modern management accountant faces is that of the social aspect of an organisation's environment. Since the Industrial Revolution at least, businessmen have been taking decisions aimed at maximising the economic return on their organisation's investment. Such decisions would often be taken without any reference to the social aspect of those decisions: unemployment, loss of earnings, loss of self-esteem. Modern society now expects a more responsible attitude of its businessmen: trade unions have played a significant role here, of course, but wider share ownership, globalisation of the marketplace and ethically acceptable investment portfolios are all having an impact on the life of modern business. As far as closure decisions are concerned, then, there are implications for a society which are wider than the organisation seeking to rationalise its operations.

In the 1960s and 1970s, great efforts were made by successive governments to ensure that, when an industry was dying or being significantly rationalised, whole towns, districts or regions were not decimated as a result of the business decisions that were being taken. Arising from such regional policies, employees came to expect protection or sympathetic treatment whenever similar circumstances arose. Stemming from this, we now have influential groups of shareholders and investment organisations that simply will not allow the organisation in which they invest to act without at least considering the social consequences of their actions. Government, too, has played its part. Towns like Corby and Consett have been transformed by government action. First, the government allowed big employers to close down their production facilities in these towns and then they gave substantial assistance to attract new industries into those towns. Whether or not this was the right course of action, there is no doubt that the new industries in those towns are thriving.

The social costs of redundancy payments, unemployment and social security benefits are a drain on the rest of society. The human costs of such actions in the short term at least are also significant for those employees affected. Consider the following example.

WORKED EXAMPLE 12.3

Balty Ltd has three products, and uses joint facilities to produce and sell all three products. Each product is independent of the other two. The relevant data are:

	Product A	B	C	Total
Sales per month (units)	900	1,200	700	–
Selling price (£s per unit)	150	115	175	–
Variable costs (£s per unit)	110	90	150	–
Fixed costs (£s per month)	–	–	–	79,100

As part of a profitability assessment project, fixed costs have been allocated to each of the products at the rate of 20% of the product's sales. The management accountant prepared a profit statement for the three products, as follows:

	Product A	B	C	Total
	£	£	£	£
Sales	135,000	138,000	122,500	395,500
less: Variable costs	99,000	108,000	105,000	312,000
Contribution	36,000	30,000	17,500	83,500
less: Allocated fixed costs	27,000	27,600	24,500	79,100
Net profit/(loss)	9,000	2,400	(7,000)	4,400

Required

On reviewing this statement, the managing director asked the management accountant's opinion on getting rid of product C. The accountant replied immediately that it is rarely the case that eliminating an entire loss-making product group will save as much as it is apparently losing because of the fixed cost implications of the decision. The accountant, therefore, asked for an hour, so that he could redraft the profit statement to try to illustrate what he meant.

Solution to Worked example 12.3

The principal assumption contained in this statement is that, even though product C has been entirely eliminated, the fixed costs allocated to that product remain. That is, since the products were being made and sold using common facilities, there is no saving on the cost of these facilities even now that one of the products has gone. Therefore, the overall profit of £4,400 has turned into an overall loss of £13,100.

	Product A	B	C	Total
	£	£	£	£
Sales	135,000	138,000	–	273,000

less: Variable costs	99,000	108,000	–	207,000
Contribution	36,000	30,000	–	66,000
less: Allocated fixed costs	27,000	27,600	24,500	79,100
Net profit/(loss)	9,000	2,400	(24,500)	(13,100)

Note that whether the assumption concerning the fixed costs is valid in all circumstances is open to question. However, for the purposes of this demonstration, we have assumed that fixed costs remain at their previous level purely to show that if fixed costs cannot be eliminated, then the hoped for savings will not necessarily materialise. If, on the other hand, some of the fixed costs could be saved as a result of eliminating product C, the overall profit would become:

	Level of reduction of fixed costs relating to product C		
	75%	50%	25%
	£	£	£
New total fixed costs	6,125	12,250	18,375
Revised total profit	5,275	(850)	(6,975)

Check these figures for yourself and make sure that you agree with them.

Limiting factor analysis

CIMA (1991) defines the limiting factor or key factor as:

> A factor which at any time or over a period may limit the activity of an entity, often one where there is shortage or difficulty of supply. . . . The limiting factor may change from time to time for the same entity or product. Thus, when raw materials are in short supply, performance or profit may be expressed as per kilo of material, or, in a restricted skilled labour market, as per skilled labour hour. Alternatively, the limiting factor may be one critical process in a chain.

In addition to the terms 'limiting factor' and 'key factor', we could also come across the terms 'budget factor' and 'principal budgeting factor'. Whatever the name given to it, the meaning is the same. So far, whatever we have been discussing, we have assumed that all input and output factors are in unlimited, or at least adequate, supply. However, as the CIMA definition helps to illustrate, there is usually at least one factor for any organisation that is in short supply at any one time. Many textbooks and articles start discussions on limiting factors by assuming that sales or demand is the limiting factor, but the CIMA definition gives materials and a class of labour as being a limiting factor. The limiting factor can be any input or output factor: materials, labour, machine hours, demand, managerial talent, . . . When a factor is limited in supply, it is important that that factor should be identified when it is crucial to the taking and implementation of a managerial decision. From our point of view, limiting factor analysis is usually linked with profit maximisation problems, although it should be said that an understanding of the points surrounding limiting factor analysis is vital to an understanding of budgeting and budgetary control, since, when budgets are being prepared, it is vital that the budget containing the limiting factor is the one that is prepared before all other budgets. Often the most crucial point in limiting factor analysis is in identifying the limiting factor itself – in reality, the existence of the limiting factor will not necessarily be written on the management accountant's office door; it will have to be researched and understood. It should be further appreciated that in some cases there may be no limiting factor.

Profit maximisation and limiting factor analysis

When attempting to assess a profit maximisation position for an organisation, we can adopt a standard routine: that is, *divide the contribution per unit of output or service by the unit of the limiting factor to give the contribution per unit of the limiting factor.* An example will show us why we need to know the contribution per unit of the limiting factor, and what we do with it to find the profit maximising level of output.

WORKED EXAMPLE 12.4

The management accountant of Cobb Ltd, a shoe repair business, has analysed the business's products for his managing director, as below:

	Product		
	A	B	C
Contribution per unit	2.00	2.52	3.75
Therefore, profitability ranking	3	2	1

The management accountant goes on to report, though, that since Cobb Ltd has just scrapped three of its machines, machine hours are now less than the total needed to repair all of the shoes it can repair. In view of this further analysis by the accountant – taking machine hour availability into account – dividing the contribution per unit by the number of units of the limiting factor needed to make the product or provide the service gives the following contribution per machine hour:

	Product		
	A	B	C
Machine hours to repair one pair of shoes	0.50	0.60	1.00
Therefore, the contribution per machine hour	$\frac{£2.00}{0.50}$	$\frac{£2.52}{0.60}$	$\frac{£3.75}{1.00}$
	= £4.00	= £4.20	= £3.75
New contribution per limiting factor rankings	2	1	3

→

When we just take the number of units into account, we conclude that product C is the most profitable product, followed by product B, then product A. Once we find a limiting factor, and adjust the contribution for the factor, we find that, with respect to the limiting factor, product B is now the most profitable product, followed by product A, then product C. The importance of this is that if we did not do this additional analysis, any decisions we might take relating to profit maximisation would be wrong. The interpretation of the contributions per machine hour is that, for product B, for example, a rate of £4.20 per machine hour means that for every machine hour applied to product B, contribution amounting to £4.20 is earned. As far as product A is concerned, every machine hour applied to that product generates £4.00.

What we have done here is to appreciate that machine hours are the limiting factor, and, by expressing contribution per machine hour rather than per unit, we are accepting that it is the rate of profitability per unit of the limiting factor that is the most vital piece of managerial information when trying to determine the profit maximising output for the business as a whole. We can see the full benefits of limiting factor analysis by extending the example.

WORKING EXAMPLE 12.4 EXTENSION 1

Cobb Ltd has total machine hours available of 2,100. Our question is how many units of A, B and C should Cobb Ltd produce in order to maximise its profits, if the expected demand for the products for the coming period is:

	Product		
	A	B	C
Expected demand	300	600	700

Solution to Working example 12.4 Extension 1

The first stage in the calculation is to find out how many machine hours (MH) Cobb Ltd needs in order to meet its expected demand. To do this, we divide the total number of pairs of shoes to be repaired by the number of machine hours required to repair each pair. The formula for this calculation is to divide the expected demand by the time taken per unit: this gives us, in this case, the machine hours needed, product by product.

	Product		
	A	B	C
machine hours required to meet the above demand	$\frac{300}{0.5}$	$\frac{600}{0.6}$	$\frac{700}{1.0}$
Machine hours	600	1,000	700

Adding these machine hours together tells us that 2,300 machine hours would be needed if demand were to be met in full. However, we know that only 2,100 hours are currently available. To sort out this problem, we need to apply the contribution per unit of the limiting factor to the hours needed to arrive at our recommended levels of output to maximise profits. To do this, we work systematically through the demand and the potential production until all available machine hours are exhausted:

Product B

Product B is the most profitable product. We therefore devote as many machine hours as possible to that product in order to maximise the profits of the whole organisation:

Hours required to meet demand	1,000
Pairs of product B to repair	600

Product A

We have used 1,000 of the 2,100 machine hours. We then apply the remaining 1,100 machine hours to the next most profitable product, product A:

Hours required to meet demand	600
Pairs of product A to repair	300

Product C

We have now used 1,600 machine hours of the total 2,100 machine hours available to Cobb Ltd. Finally, in this example, we apply the remaining number of machine hours to the demand for the least profitable product, product C;

Hours required to meet demand	700
Machine hours available	500

Therefore, Cobb Ltd are unable to repair as many pairs of product C as they have demand for. They have to reduce their expectations as follows:

Pairs of product C to repair	500

Summary

In summary, the profit maximising product schedule for Cobb Ltd is:

	Product		
	A	B	C
Machine hours used	600	1,000	500
Pairs repaired	300	600	500
Total contribution	£600	£2,520	£1,875

Therefore the profit-maximising contribution for Cobb Ltd is £4,995.

Check the calculations to satisfy yourself that this is the profit-maximising contribution, and that had we merely taken the contributions per unit as our decision factor, the total contribution would have been £4,537.

Linear programming and multiple constraints

Linear programming is a method of management science that offers one way of making resource allocation decisions in an optimal way. Linear programming has been successfully used at many organisational levels in all types of industries including manufacturing, transport, energy, education, the police force, government and many more. In the appendix to this chapter is a discussion of the way that linear programming works. In the context of this chapter, we are interested in linear programming insofar as it can help us to resolve problems where more than one resource is constrained, or limited in supply.

Once you have read the appendix, consider the following example of the kind of problem that exists: the solution to this problem can be found at the end of the appendix to this chapter.

KimCo makes four types of component for the car industry. Each component requires assembly labour, quality control labour, microprocessors and sundry electronics supplies. Table 12.1 details the requirements, availability and profitability of each component and its inputs.

In this kind of situation, we are required to determine the quantities of the four products that should be manufactured during a period in order to maximise profits. Adding a further constraint tells us that KimCo is contractually obliged to supply forty type 1 components.

The optimal solution is to produce:

76.92 type 1 components
20.51 type 2 components
10.26 type 3 components
0 type 4 components

and the profit for the period will be £506.41. Note that this solution assumes that we are able to make and sell fractions of components. (See p. 420 for the linear programming formulation and solution to this problem.)

TABLE 12.1 ***Requirements, availability and profitability of components***

Resources	Electronic component				Resource available
	Type 1	Type 2	Type 3	Type 4	
Assembly labour	6	5	3.5	4	600 hours
QC labour	1	1.5	1.2	1.2	120 hours
Microprocessor	4	3	3	3	400 units
Sundries	2	2	2	3	300 units
Profit	4.25	6.25	5	4.5	

Sell or process further

For the final demonstration in this chapter, look at the sell or process further situation where a manufacturer has to choose between selling one of his or her products at the end of one production stage or processing it further with resources tied up in a further production stage.

WORKED EXAMPLE 12.5

Carol Co. operates in East Africa. Its main product is rice, and it has paddy fields and a rice processing plant there. At the end of April, Carol has 10,000 kg of rice husks in stock. Rice husks can be burned and the ash residue used to make a cement substitute. The incinerator used for this purpose has, at the moment, the capacity to burn the husks. Alternatively, the husks can be sold to a government agency for £15 per tonne; husk ash sells for £1.70 for a 50 kg bag. The relevant cost for incineration is £0.017 per kg of finished ash, and there is a 20% loss of weight due to the incineration process.

Required

Should Carol Co. burn the husks and prepare the ash, or sell the husks to the government agency?

Solution to Worked example 12.5

The solution to this problem rests on the application of relevant costing. The solution revolves around setting off the revenue from the agency against the revenues and costs of the further processing of the husks into ash. A table such as the one that follows should be prepared for comparison purposes. (Note that 10,000 kg is the same as 10 tonnes.)

The yield from the incinerator is only 8,000 kg, because 10,000 kg is put into the incinerator, but there is a 20% loss of weight during the process. Therefore, with an 80% yield, 10,000 kg input becomes 8,000 kg output.

The revenue from further processing is £1.70 per 50 kg bag. The number of bags that would be sold is:

$$\frac{8{,}000 \text{ kg}}{50 \text{ kg/bag}}$$

$$= 160 \text{ bags}$$

The differential revenues from selling to the government agency and from processing further are as follows:

	Sell to agency £	Process further £
10 tonnes at £15 per tonne revenue	150	–

160 bags × £1.70/bag	–	272
less: Incineration costs		
£0.017/kg × 8,000 kg	–	136
Differential revenue	150	136

The conclusion is that since the government agency generates differential revenue of £150 as opposed to the smaller £136 of the additional processing of the husks, the decision must be to sell to the government agency. Carol will be £150 − £136 = £14 better off as a result.

SUMMARY

In this chapter we have seen some examples of the kinds of situation in which relevant costing is actually applied in industry and commerce. We are aware that relevant costing decisions can be taken involving any situation where two or more alternative courses of action are being considered by the management of an organisation.

We have seen, for example, how to deal with one-off special decisions such as a group of people arriving at a restaurant and offering to pay a lump sum of money in return for a meal for every member of the group. Even though the amount they paid was less than full cost, it was still worth the restaurant's while to accept the deal. We have also seen how to deal with the more strategic aspects of business such as make-or-buy and closure decisions,limiting factor analysis, and sell or process further decisions. Relevant costing is one of the richest areas of management accounting from a decision-making point of view. By taking a decision-relevant view of accounting information, management sees in stark reality the real nature of that decision. The Falklands War, for instance, is more than simply a bloody conflict fought out in a remote area of the world – there were important financial considerations for the participants and society at large. Relevant costing helps us to view the true costs of such actions in a proper perspective.

As modern society becomes more sensitive to economic issues following decades of economic turbulence, together with the rise of pressure groups like Greenpeace and socially aware investors, the onus on businesses to become more profitable at any price has gone. Many of the decisions highlighted in this chapter have a social or environmental connotation to them. We emphasised these kinds of issues when discussing closure decisions. During the major industrial confrontations of the 1970s and 1980s, management accountants were often called in to help one side or the other in a dispute to establish the correctness of the economic claims made by the other side. Examples of such work includes the true costs of extracting a tonne of coal from a coal mine, or the real cost of generating a unit of electricity. Relevant costing plays a vital role here by underlining what should and should not be allowed to be taken into account in deciding what is a true cost – whether under contentious conditions or not!

KEY TERMS

You should satisfy yourself that you have noted all of these terms and can define and/or describe their meaning and use, as appropriate.

Opportunity cost (p. 382)	Closure decision (p. 389)
Relevant cost (p. 383)	Limiting factor (p. 392)
Differential cost (p. 383)	Budget factor (p. 392)
Incremental cost (p. 383)	Principal budgeting factor (p. 392)
Sunk cost (p. 384)	Contribution per unit of the limiting factor (p. 393)
Ad hoc decisions (p. 384)	Sell or process further (p. 397)
Make or buy decision (p. 387)	One-off special decisions (p. 398)
Qualitative factors (p. 387)	

RECOMMENDED READING

Worth a read is Brown (1982).

QUESTIONS

Review questions

1. What is a relevant cost?
2. Distinguish between relevant, differential, and incremental costs.
3. What is meant by the term '*ad hoc* decision'?
4. Describe the components of a make-or-buy decision.
5. What are the factors involved in a 'close a department decision'?
6. What is a limiting factor? By what other names is the limiting factor known?
7. Find evidence in this chapter of an opportunity cost-based situation.

Answers to review questions 1, 3, 5 and 6 can be found in the Student Workbook.

Graded practice questions

Level I

1. Strouzer Ltd can make 4,000 units of its product each year, and the budget for the next year is as follows:

Sales (at £80 per unit)	£240,000
Factory costs:	
variable	£45 per unit
fixed	£22,000
Selling and administration costs:	
variable	£2.90 per unit
fixed	£6,000

Strouzer has been approached by a potential customer who is offering to pay £50 per unit for a guaranteed order of 500 units. As far as variable selling and administration costs are concerned, they will be zero for this order since the potential customer has approached Strouzer directly.

Required:

(a) State whether and why this offer should be accepted.
(b) Assume a production problem means that capacity falls to 3,000 units for the year, with demand staying the same, at 4,000 units per year. What is your advice now?

2. Spry Alive Ltd is currently assessing the introduction of a new product to add to its existing range. Based on an annual output level of 15,000 units, the predicted unit cost of the new product would be:

	£
Direct materials	12.00
Direct labour	2.25
Factory overheads	10.50

Fixed overheads included in the above are £75,000.

One of the component parts of the new product is a specialist part, and every unit of output must have one of these parts in it. Although Spry Alive does not make this component itself at the moment, the cost schedule above assumes that they will do so.

A potential supplier, Mike Fraser (Scotland) Ltd, has offered to supply the component ready assembled at a cost of £6.00 per unit, with a minimum annual order of 7,500 units per year. If Spry Alive accepts this offer, it will be able to reduce the variable labour and variable overhead costs of the new product by 50% and materials cost by £1.00 per unit. If Spry Alive makes the component itself, it will cost £3.00 to make.

Required:

(a) Determine whether Spry Alive should make or buy the component.
(b) What additional factors should Spry Alive consider in deciding whether they should make or buy the component?

3. Peck Holdings prints bingo cards. It operates four large machines each of the same output capacity, and each machine was run at near to its full capacity during 1992. Each machine is depreciated separately using the reducing balance method. Information for each machine is as follows:

	Machine 1	2	3	4
Age (years)	6	5	3	2
Cost (£)	150,000	160,000	175,000	180,000
Operating costs, 1992				
	£	£	£	£
Materials	25,000	26,000	24,500	23,000
Labour	30,000	28,000	32,000	31,500
Maintenance	1,600	1,600	900	850
Depreciation	10,090	15,000	24,000	31,110

Peck's budget for next year shows that output is expected to be less than it was in 1992, so it is being proposed that one machine should be dropped from service. The proposal is to get rid of machine number 4, on the grounds that it has the highest operating costs.

Required:

Do you agree that machine four should be dropped from service? Explain your answer.

Level II

4. Clearex Ltd returned the following statement for the year ended 31 December 1992:

	£	£
Sales		1,440,000
less: Variable costs:		
cost of goods sold	480,000	
selling and administration	132,000	612,000
Contribution		828,000
less: Fixed costs:		
factory overheads	520,000	
selling and administration	210,000	730,000
Net profit		98,000

During the coming year it is expected that variable manufacturing costs will increase by £6 per unit, and fixed manufacturing costs will increase by £48,000.

Required

(a) If sales remain at 12,000 units, what price should Clearex charge to produce the same profit as last year?

(b) Management believes that sales can be increased to 16,000 units if the selling price is lowered to £107. Is this action desirable? Explain your answer.

(c) After taking into consideration the expected increases in costs, what sales volume is needed to earn a profit of £98,000 with a unit selling price of £107?

5. WP Ltd provides a word processing service to the business community and is attempting to move into a higher-quality market than it operates in at the moment. The basic product it presently offers consists of offering a word processing service whereby the output is one copy of the document printed on to plain white 80 gsm bond paper. The document is returned in a simple sky-blue folder bearing the name WP Ltd embossed in claret on the front of the folder.

The premium product it is considering trying to promote would be an enhancement of the basic product just described. The basic product would be passed to a more skilled word processor who would add graphics and other desktop publishing (DTP) enhancements to the document. Two copies of the final document would be provided for the client. The first copy would be printed on to 100 gsm vellum paper, and it would be bound in a claret folder with the name WP Ltd embossed in sky blue at the bottom left-hand corner of the front of the folder; and the client's own logo would be embossed in sky blue in the middle of the cover of the folder. A further copy of the premium-processed document would be presented to the specifications of the basic product.

The revenues for the basic product are £5.00 per page processed or part thereof, irrespective of the number of pages processed; the costs would be £0.40 per page for the paper, £0.50 for the cover, £2.25 per page for the salary costs, and £0.50 per document for the other consumables. Depreciation of the hardware and software is charged at the rate of £1.00 per document.

For the premium product, the revenues are £9.50 per page processed or part thereof, irrespective of the number of pages; the costs are £0.75 per page for the vellum paper plus £0.40 per page for the plain 80 gsm paper, the premium cover costs £1.20 each, and the basic cover cost is as for the basic service, salary costs are £2 per page plus the salary costs for the basic part of the service provided, and other consumables cost a total of £0.75 per document. Depreciation of the hardware and the software amount to £0.30 per document plus the depreciation for the basic part of the service.

Required

(a) Assuming an average document would be 10 pages long for the basic service and 15 pages long for the premium service, and the annual demand for the two services would be 2,686 documents and 1,000 documents for the basic and the premium services respectively, would you advise WP Ltd to move into the premium market?

(b) What factors **apart from** the economic factors should be taken into account before finally deciding on the course of action to be taken?

6. Saddleworth Staithes is the trade name of a rather flamboyant salesman and custom car enthusiast who transforms production model cars into custom cars that sell for between £15,000 and £30,000. The pricing policy of his business is to set prices based on the estimated costs of the direct materials, direct labour, and the business's overheads (manufacturing, selling and administrative). A mark-up of 20% typically is added to the total estimated costs in order to set the selling price per car. As an example, a recent price was established for a car as follows:

	£
Direct materials	5,000
Direct labour	8,000
Overheads	2,000
Total	15,000
Mark up (20%)	3,000
Selling price	18,000

By negotiation with Staithes, customers can often force down the mark-up to as little as 5% over the estimated costs involved. The annual average mark-up typically is 15% because of this policy. The company's accountant has suggested that pricing based on variable costs would be better than the current approach. She has determined that the firm's total overhead is expected to be £180,000, of which £108,000 is fixed. The remainder is variable in proportion to direct labour costs of £720,000. Staithes says that he is in love with the cars that he builds, and is not bothered about too big a profit, but that if the accountant feels the pricing policy needs to be reviewed, she should make her suggestions.

Required

(a) Assume that during a month when the business has spare capacity, a customer rejects both the £18,000 price shown for the car above and a £15,750 offer (the selling price with a 5% mark-up). The customer says he will pay £14,600 for the car. Should the business accept the offer? Explain your answer.

(b) What is the minimum selling price the firm can charge for the car in part (a) without reducing or increasing net income?

(c) What advantages does the policy of basing prices on variable costs have over the policy used historically?

(d) What are the disadvantages of a pricing policy based on variable costs?

7. (a) A small contractor has been asked to quote for a contract which is larger than he would normally consider. The contractor would like to obtain the job as he does have surplus capacity. The estimating and design department has spent 200 hours in preparing drawings and the following cost estimate:

	£
Direct materials:	
3,000 units of X at £10 (original cost)	30,000
(see note 1)	
100 units of Y (charged out using FIFO) (see note 2)	
50 units at £100	5,000
50 units at £125	6,250
(see note 2)	
Direct material to be bought in: (see note 3)	12,000
Direct labour:	
skilled staff (2,720 hours at £5 per hour)	13,600
(see note 4)	
Trainees (1,250 hours at £2 per hour)	2,500
(see note 5)	
One month's depreciation on curing press (see note 6)	1,000
Subcontract work (see note 7)	20,000
Supervisory staff (see note 8)	6,150
Estimating and design department: (see note 9)	
200 hours at £10 per hour	2,000
Overtime premium for 50 hours	500
Administration overhead at 5% of above costs (see note 10)	4,950
	103,950

Notes

The following notes may be relevant:

(1) A sufficient stock of raw material X is held in the stores. It is the residue of a quantity bought some 10 years ago. If this stock is not used on the prospective contract it is unlikely that it will be used in the foreseeable future. The net resale value is thought to be £20,000.

(2) Material Y is regularly used by the contractor on a variety of jobs. The current replacement cost of the material is £130 per unit.
(3) This is the estimated cost of the required material.
(4) Staff are paid on a time basis for a 40-hour week. The labour hour rate includes a charge of 100% of the wage rate to cover labour-related overhead costs. It is estimated that, at the current level of operations, 80% of the overheads are variable. It is considered that one extra worker will be required temporarily for 3 months if the contract is obtained. His salary of £100 per week (and the associated amount of labour related overhead expense) is included in the estimate of £13,600.
(5) No additional trainees would be taken on. The trainees' wage rate is £1 per hour but their time is charged out at £2 to allow for labour-related overhead on the same basis as in note 4 above.
(6) The curing press is normally fully occupied. If it is not being used by the contractor's own workforce it is being hired out at £500 per week. Annual (straight-line) depreciation is £12,000.
(7) This is the estimated cost for the work.
(8) It is not considered that it would be necessary to employ any additional supervisory staff. The estimated cost of £6,150 includes an allowance of £1,000 for overtime which it may be necessary to pay to the supervisors.
(9) The expense of this department is predominantly fixed but the overtime payments were specifically incurred to get the drawings and plans out in time.
(10) The administrative expense is a fixed cost. This is the established method of allocating the cost to specific contracts.

It is considered that any quotation higher than £100,000 will be unsuccessful. You are required to prepare a revised cost estimate using an opportunity cost approach. State whether you consider that the revised calculations can provide support for a quotation below £100,000.

(b) Comment on the use of opportunity cost:

(i) for decision making; and
(ii) for cost control purposes.

ACCA 2.4 Management Accounting
June 1986

Solutions to practice questions 2, 4 and 7 can be found in the Student Workbook. Solutions to practice question numbers in red can be found at the end of this book.

Projects

1. Look for evidence of the use of relevant costing by, for example, restaurants, hotels, and travel companies. Determine what evidence drew you to your conclusion that they are using relevant costing.
2. (a) Analyse the products/services offered by, say, a supermarket. What evidence can you find of a 'sell or process further' decision having been taken? [Hint: examples here include baked beans and curried baked beans; perfume packed in a basic pack, and perfume packaged in a presentation pack; and towels: one towel may be just plain whilst the other may have a lace edge, or have a motif embroidered on it. All items would be sold under the same manufacturer's/brand name].

(b) Analyse the products/services offered by your own organisation. Which products/services are processed further rather than sold at an earlier stage? Attempt to discover the basis on which the decision to process further was taken. Was the decision taken on entirely accounting/economic grounds? If other grounds were considered, what were they?

3. Monitor newspapers and magazines to find examples of businesses that ceased making components/raw materials but still made/sold the same final products or provided the same final service. Try to determine from the article(s) the basis on which the make-or-buy decision was taken.

Appendix: Introduction to linear programming

To help us cope with a variety of problems we might face, it is useful to consider the technique of linear programming. Linear programming is one of the most frequently and successfully applied mathematical approaches to managerial decisions. Linear programming models are used to help us allocate scarce resources to products in such a manner that the profits are maximised or costs are minimised. In this appendix, we will describe how the linear programming technique works by demonstrating its application in terms of some basic problems. We should stress basic problems because computer software that is now widely available has taken the drudgery out of the larger more complex problems that students and academics used to like to solve!

The linear programming (LP) problem

We have already said that LP involves allocating scarce resources among competing products or activities:

- Resources available have a cost and are limited in supply; hence management must determine how best to use these resources.
- Allocations of these resources must be made in relation to an overall objective: for example, maximise profits or minimise costs.

The following worked example will help us appreciate the nature of a maximisation problem and its solution.

WORKED EXAMPLE 12.6

An organisation plc has two machines, 1 and 2; 120 hours of time can be scheduled for machine 1 and 80 hours for machine 2. Production during the scheduling period is limited to two products, A and B. Each unit of A required 2 hours of machine time; and each unit of B required 3 hours on machine 1 and 1.5 hours on machine 2. The contribution margin is £4 per unit of A and £5 per unit of B. There are no difficulties in selling and marketing either product.

Required

Maximise profit in this situation.

Solution to Worked example 12.6

Half of the battle in understanding LP problems rests in the setting up of the LP model. Consider the model for the example very carefully, therefore. In other words, this question means that we need to establish our objective function, maximise our contribution (profit), subject to the following constraints: that machine 1 can only accommodate no more than 120 hours worth of work; machine 2 can only accommodate up to 80 hours worth of work; and neither *a* nor *b* can be negative: they must be greater than or equal to zero (this is the non-negativity constraint). The word 'constraint' means that the expression has a limiting effect: that is, it imposes limitations for the relevant input or variable.

Let:

a be the number of units of product A to be produced;
b be the number of units of product B to be produced;
p be the contribution.

The LP problem can then be set up as follows:

Maximise $p = 4a + 5b$ (contribution)

Subject to: $2a + 3b \leqslant 120$ (machine 1 constraint)
$2a + 1.5b \leqslant 80$ (machine 2 constraint)
$a, b \geqslant 0$ (non-negativity constraint)

In such a relatively simple case as this, we can transform the LP model into simultaneous equations and solve for a and *b*. This will give us the solution we are looking for. Alternatively, we can work through a graphical solution to this problem as well as what is known as the simplex method, involving matrix algebra. The simultaneous equations method first.

Simultaneous equations method

In the solution that follows, we ignore the non-negativity constraints as well as the objective function – we will use these for the graphical solution. So, we start by turning the machinery constraints into equalities:

$$2a + 3b = 120 \quad (12.A1)$$

$$2a + 1.5b = 80 \quad (12.A2)$$

and now we can solve them in the usual way.

In this example, the simplest way to solve for *a* and *b* seems to be subtract equation 12.A1 from equation 12.A2:

$$2a + 3b = 120 \quad (12.A1)$$

$$2a + 1.5b = 80 \quad (12.A2)$$

$$1.5b = 40$$

Therefore:

$$b = 26.\dot{6}\dot{6}$$

By substitution in equation 12.A1:

$$2a + 3 \times 26.\dot{6}\dot{6} = 120$$

$$2a + 80 = 120$$

$$2a = 120 - 80$$

$$a = 20$$

Proof

Substituting for both a and *b* in equation 12.A2 gives:

$$2 \times 20 + 1.5 \times 26.\dot{6}\dot{6} = 80$$

The interpretation of this result is that we need to produce:

20 units of product A; and

$26.\dot{6}\dot{6}$ units of product B

in order to maximise our profits. This means that our maximised profit is:

$$p = 4 \times 20 + 5 \times 26.\dot{6}\dot{6} = £213.\dot{3}\dot{3}$$

All such LP problems can be solved in this way, and the interpretation of the result is as given for this example.

Graphical method

As is usually the case, since we have an algebraic, simultaneous equations solution, we can also find a graphical solution to this problem. All we have to do is to derive the line for the graph that represents the two constraints, for machines 1 and 2, and conforms to the non-negativity constraints, as well as observing any constraints provided by the objective function.

Figure A12.1 shows the graph we need to construct. To plot this graph we use all four constraints now:

$$\begin{aligned} 2a + 3b &= 120 \\ 2a + 1.5b &= 80 \\ a &= 0 \\ b &= 0 \end{aligned}$$

We are dealing with linear constraints, so each equation can be plotted from two points. The intercept points are

- $(a = 0, b = 40)$ and $(a = 60, b = 0)$ for the first equation; and
- $(a = 0, b = 53.\dot{3}\dot{3})$ and $(a = 40, b = 0)$ for the second equation.

Meaning that if we set a to zero in the first equation, then *b* must equal:

$$\frac{120}{3} = 40$$

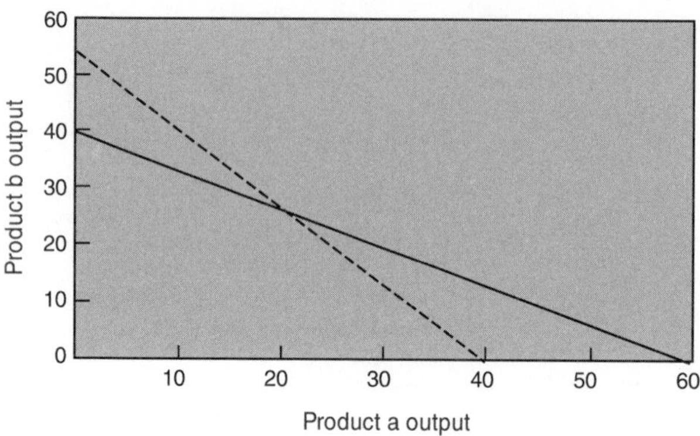

FIGURE A12.1 *Graphical solution to the linear programming problem*

Hence:

$a = 0, b = 40$

and by the same reasoning, when $b = 0, a = 60$.

Similarly for the second equation. We now plot the two points for each function on our graph and obtain Figure A12.1.

We can now read off the solution to this problem by learning two further conventions:

1. In an example such as this, the feasible area is to the left of each of the two lines on the graph. In fact, the total feasible region is that bounded by the the points:

a	b
0,	0
40,	0
20,	$26.\dot{6}\dot{6}$
0,	40

This means that the final solution we are looking for is somewhere within this region.

2. The optimal solution in LP graphs is usually found at one of the extreme points of the graph. In this case, this means at one of the four points:

a	b
0	0
40	0
20	$26.\dot{6}\dot{6}$
0	40

We already know from the algebraic solution that the optimal solution is at the coordinates:

a	b
20	26.66

In terms of the extreme points we saw above, we can show that the optimal profit value is £213.33 from the following table:

a	b	p (£)
0	0	0
40	0	160.00
20	$26.\dot{6}\dot{6}$	213.33
0	40	200.00

All maximisation problems can be approached in the ways we have just seen: both algebraically and graphically. Be aware, however, that the algebraic and graphical solutions become unwieldy with more than two variables. This is why the matrix solutions are preferred to the algebraic and graphical solutions: when there are many variables involved.

Worked example 12.7 takes us through a minimisation problem: we are going to minimise our costs rather than maximise our profits.

WORKED EXAMPLE 12.7

Our Organisation makes an alloy by combining steel and scrap metal. The cost of the steel is £50 per tonne and the cost of scrap is £20 per tonne. For every two tonnes of scrap, at least one tonne of steel is required; and one hour processing time is required for each tonne of steel and four hours processing time for each tonne of scrap. There is a linear relationship between the combination of steel and scrap when making the alloy. During the process, 10% of steel is lost and 20% of the scrap is lost. A minimum of 40 tonnes of alloy must be made but production may exceed demand; and to maintain efficient plant operation, a minimum of 80 hours' processing time must be used. There is no shortage of supply of either steel or scrap.

Required

Find the minimum cost of operating this processing operation.

Solution to Worked example 12.7

Start by setting up the LP formulation.

Let:

a = the number of tonnes of steel;
b = the number of tonnes of scrap;
c = the cost of the alloy.

This gives:

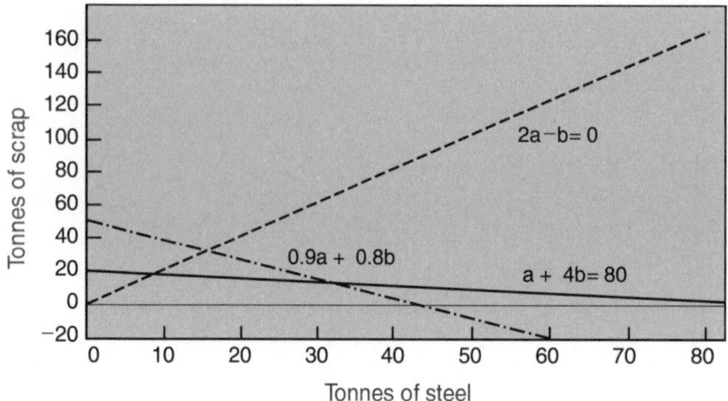

FIGURE A12.2 *Linear programming solution to Worked example 12.7*

Minimise	$c = 50a + 20b$	(cost)
Subject to:	$2a - b \geqslant 0$	(2 tonnes of steel for every 1 of scrap)
	$a + 4b \geqslant 80$	(processing time)
	$0.9a + 0.8b \geqslant 40$	(allows for process losses and minimum volume to be made)
	$a, b \geqslant 0$	(non-negativity)

Notice first of all that in this case the formulation gives rise to expressions that are 'greater than or equal to' ($\geqslant$) rather than 'less than or equal to' ($\leqslant$), as was the case with the maximisation problems.

Solving this problem graphically gives the solution we can see in Figure A12.2. The feasible area of this graph extends outwards from left to right; and the extreme points are:

a	b	c (£)
16	32	1,440
34.32	11.42	1,944.40
80	0	4,000

The optimum combination of steel and scrap, then, is 16 tonnes of steel and 32 tonnes of scrap; giving rise to total costs of £1,440 = (16 × 50) + (32 × 20).

Problems with LP models

There are three potential difficulties that we need to guard against when attempting to solve LP problems:

1. *Non-feasible solutions*, which arise when there is no set of extreme points that simultaneously satisfies all the inequalities or constraints.

2. *Multiple optimal solutions*, which arise when the objective function is parallel to one of the constraints. In such a case we have an infinite number of optimal solutions.
3. *Unbounded solutions*, which arise when the profit function is plotted on a graph and we find that we can continue increasing profit by changing the variables: that is, without limit. In this case, the problem is said to be unbounded.

The simplex method of solving LP problems

The simplex method is based on matrix algebra and can provide much more compact solutions than can the graphical method. The simplex method is ideal for computer programming to assist with the solution of LP problems. Here we will demonstrate the simplex method by working through a problem for which we already have the solution. We will see that the simplex method provides us with information that the algebraic and graphical soltuons do not: that is, opportunity costs and marginal rates of substitution.

The method that follows is a tried and tested method and it is less tedious to work through than other methods we might encounter. However, if you are already used to solving such problems and are happy with the method you use, do not feel obliged to follow the method that is shown here. Further appreciate that this is not a management science or operations research book; therefore you will not find the ultimate logic and reasoning behind what we are about to do. Finally, there are now software packages which are virtually given away that can solve the types of problems we are about to consider. Following the simplex method will allow us to appreciate what the results mean rather than becoming an expert LP solver!

We will rework Worked example 12.6 for the demonstration of the simplex method.

WORKED EXAMPLE 12.8

Take the LP problem found in Worked example 12.6, set up the simplex method tableau, and solve the problem such that you obtain the maximum profit for this situation. The LP problem is repeated below:

Maximise $p = 4a + 5b$ (contribution)

Subject to: $2a + 3b \leqslant 120$ (machine 1 constraint)
$2a + 1.5b \leqslant 80$ (machine 2 constraint)
$a, b \geqslant 0$ (non-negativity constraint)

Solution to Worked example 12.8

The simplex method works by setting up partitioned matrices for us to manipulate. Such matrices are known as a tableau. The demonstration that follows sets up the initial tableau, works through the two iterations necessary to find the optimal profit and then interprets the result. The initial tableau, below, reflects the LP problem. We set down the inequalties from the data supplied and then introduce the slack variables. A slack variable represents the amount that is needed to turn an inequality into an equality. In the case of $2a + 3b \leqslant 120$, there is a value that must be added to $2a + 3b$ that makes the expression equal to 120 rather than less than or equal to. The amount we need to add is called a slack variable. In the initial tableau for this problem, the two slack variables we need are called s_1 and s_2. This means that, for example, rather than having:

$2a + 3b \leqslant 120$ (inequality)

we now have:

$2a + 3b + s_1 = 120$ (equality)

In any initial tableau, slack variables are always given the value of 1. This applies to a less than or equal to inequality as we have here. If we were dealing with a greater than or equal to inequality, we would use **surplus variables** equal to -1. Consider the logic behind this carefully. In the case we are discussing now, then, the addition of slack variables turns our LP model into the following:

Maximise $p = 4a + 5b$

Subject to: $2a + 3b + s_1 = 120$
$2a + 1.5b + s_2 = 80$
$a, b \geqslant 0$

Initial tableau

a	b	s_1	s_2	Quantity
2.0000	3.0000	1.0000	0.0000	120.0000
2.0000	1.5000	0.0000	1.0000	80.0000
−4.0000	−5.0000	0.0000	0.0000	0.0000

Note that the non-negativity constraints have been omitted from this solution since they are not important: they do not affect the decision or the interpretation of it. This means they are redundant, although this is not always the case.

We proceed by finding what are called the pivot column and row, in that order. The pivot column is the column that contains the smallest value in the objective funtion: that is, the final row in the tableau. In this example, the smallest value is -5, hence the pivot column is column b. The pivot row centres on column b and is the row that gives the lowest positive value when the coefficients in column b are divided into the coefficients in the quantity column. This applies to rows 1 and 2 only, not the objective function. In this case, the results of these calculations are 40 for row 1 and 53.33 for row 2. Row 1 returns the lowest positive value, hence our pivot row is row 1.

The aim of what we are looking for is to make the square matrix:

$$\begin{matrix} a1 & b1 \\ a2 & b2 \end{matrix}$$

into a unit matrix; and we do this be means of a series of arithmetical calculations:

1. Divide all terms in row 1 (the pivot row) by 3 (the value of the entry in the pivot cell *b*1).
2. Subtract 1.5 times each term in row 1 from its equivalent term in row 2.
3. Add five times each term in row 1 to its equivalent term in row 3.

When we have finished these calculations, we have iteration 1; check the calculations carefully.

Iteration 1

a	b	s_1	s_2	Quantity
0.6667	1.0000	0.3333	0.0000	40.0000
1.0000	0.0000	−0.5000	1.0000	20.0000
−0.6667	0.0000	1.6667	0.0000	200.0000

We repeat these iterations until we have the unit matrix we are looking for. In the case of iteration 1, we already have the value 1 at position *a*2: this is what we want, of course and the value at *b*2 is also the value we are looking for, 0. Hence we do not need to do anything further to this row. We must use row 2, however, to complete the unit matrix calculations, otherwise we will not find the optimal solution. The calculations needed now relate to iteration 1 only: we have finished with the initial tableau now.

1. Subtract two-thirds of all items in row 2 from their equivalent term in row 1.
2. Add two-thirds of all items in row 2 to their equivalent term in row 3.

This gives us the second iteration and the final tableau, the solution. We know it is the solution because there are no negative values in the objective function. If there were negative values, of course, we would have to carry out another iteration. Generally speaking, the greater the number of variables in an LP problem, the greater the number of iterations required.

Iteration 2 and final tableau

a	b	s_1	s_2	Quantity
0.0000	1.0000	0.6667	−0.6667	26.6667
1.0000	0.0000	−0.5000	1.0000	20.0000
0.0000	0.0000	1.3333	0.6667	213.3333

Interpreting the final tableau

To interpret the final tableau, we start by looking down the *a* and *b* columns and find where there is a value of 1. The value in the quantity column that coincides with that value of 1 is the optimum output value associated with that input variable. In this case, we have an optimal value for *a* of 20 and for *b* it is 26.6667. Furthermore the total profit, taken from the quantity column of the objective function is £213.3333. Look back at the solution to Worked example 12.6 and we find that the results of the two methods (graphical and simplex) are the same!

We now know what our optimum output is. We also now know that there is no spare capacity for either machine in this example. In a case as simple as this, we see that since the unit matrix accounts for rows one and two in the final tableau, there simply cannot be any spare capacity. With larger problems, there may be spare capacity to concern us. The simplex method can allow us to go a stage further with our analysis and investigate our opportunity costs and marginal rates of substitution. The opportunity costs are taken from the objective function in the final tableau. In this case the opportunity costs are 1.3333 for machine 1; and 0.6667 for machine 2. This means that the loss (or gain) of 1 hour of time on machine 1 will lead to a reduction (or increase) in profit of £1.3333; and if we were to lose (or gain) 1 hour of processing time on machine 2, we would lose (or gain) profit of £0.6667.

A more complex illustration in Worked example 12.9 will now help us appreciate further insights into the simplex LP solution.

WORKED EXAMPLE 12.9

The resource allocation problem in one organisation has been modelled as follows:

Let:
- a = the number of units of product a made;
- b = the number of units of product b made;
- z = the total profit for the period.

Maximise	$z = 20a + 40b$	(profit)
Subject to:	$3a + 5b \leqslant 1{,}800$ hours	(labour constraint)
	$a + 5b \leqslant 1{,}000$ hours	(machine constraint)
	$25b \leqslant 3{,}750$ kg	(material constraint)
	$a, b \geqslant 0$	(non-negativity)

Required

Find the combination of the manufacture of a and b that will maximise the total profit for a period.

Solution to Worked example 12.9

We can solve this problem in at least two ways: graphically and by using the simplex method. We will be using the simplex method here.

The initial tableau is:

Initial tableau

a	b	s_1	s_2	s_3	Quantity
3	5	1	0	0	1,800
1	5	0	1	0	1,000
0	25	0	0	1	3,750
(20)	(40)	0	0	0	0

1st iteration

a	b	s_1	s_2	s_3	Quantity
3	0	1	0	0	1,050
1	0	0	1	0	250
0	1	0	0	0	150
(20)	0	0	0	2	6,000

2nd iteration

a	b	s_1	s_2	s_3	Quantity
0	1	(3)	0	300	
1	0	0	1	0	250
0	1	0	0	0	150
0	0	0	20	(2)	11,000

3rd iteration and final tableau

a	b	s_1	s_2	s_3	Quantity
0	0	3	(8)	1	750
1	0	1	(1)	0	400
0	1	0	0	0	120
0	0	6	2	0	12,800

For practice, work through all of the relevant tableaux and iterations for this problem and agree with the final tableau.

The interpretation of this final tableau is

1. We should produce:
   (a) 400 of product *a*; and
   (b) 120 of product *b*;
   Thus giving a profit of £12,800 for the period.
2. There are no unused labour hours and no unused machine hours. We know this because the relevant slack variables do not form part of the final solution. Looking down the s_1 and s_2 columns reveals that even though there is a value of 1 in the s_1 column, it is of no use since in the same row as that 1 is the value of 1 for product *a*. There is no value 1 in the s_2 column. As far as s_3 is concerned, there is a value 1 in that column, and it is the only value 1 in that row. Thus, s_3 has a value of 750: this means that we have 750 kg of materials left unused, with the optimal levels of output.

3. The value of 6 in the objective function of the s_1 column is the shadow price for labour; and the value of 2 in the objective function of the s_2 column is the shadow price for machine hours. s_3 has a zero shadow price as we can see from the 0 value in the objective function of the final tableau.

Shadow prices represent the increase in total profit that can be expected from using one additional unit of that resource. One more labour hour available, would enable us to earn an extra £6; and one more machine hour would enable us to add £2 further to profit. Adding one more unit of materials does nothing for us, of course, since we have spare resources of it. The converse is true here. If we have to reduce these inputs, we lose the equivalent of the values of the shadow prices: that is, they reduce the profit for the period. We could see the effect of such sensitivity analysis by changing the LP model to accommodate such marginal changes.

Applications of linear programming

A large range of business problems can be solved using linear programming. The following list indicates how wide the range is:

- sales force deployment
- dietary inputs for cattle, sheep, pigs
- fertiliser composition
- waste management
- investment planning
- production scheduling
- purchasing
- portfolio selection
- media selection
- capital budgeting
- product mix selection
- cargo loading
- warehouse shipping patterns

Minimisation problems

Although the algorithm on which minimisation problems are founded is the same as for maximisation problems, the mechanics of it are different. We have already seen the graphical solution of such problems and know that such problems are soluble! The following demonstration is entirely worked through using computer software; the full workings are not shown. There are many very good books on management science, operations research and so on that can help with the demonstration of minimisation problems; consulting them will help if you need to solve such problems by hand. There is a simple method for working through a minimisation problem, however: that is, to transform it into a maximisation problem and then solve as normal!

WORKED EXAMPLE 12.10

Consider the following minimisation problem:

Minimise $c = 2a + 1.5b$

Subject to: $400a + 200b \geqslant 2{,}000$
$300a + 600b \geqslant 2{,}400$
$a, b, \geqslant 0$

Required

Use the simplex method, obtain the optimal solution and interpret the results.

Solution to Worked example 12.10

The outline solution here starts with the subtraction of *surplus* variables, as mentioned above, to give us the LP model immediately before we turn it into the simplex format:

minimise $c = 2a + 1.5b$

Subject to: $400a + 200b - s_1 = 2{,}000$
$300a + 600b - s_2 = 2{,}400$
$a, b, \geqslant 0$

The optimum solution shows that costs are minimised at £11 when we combine 4 units of *a* with 2 units of *b*. The shadow prices are £0.004 for constraint 1 and £0.001 for constraint 2. Following through what we said in the introduction to minimisation problems, we should now look at how to transform a minimisation problem into a maximisation problem and then solve that. To achieve our transformation objective, we rotate the problem: the following is the rotation of the minimisation problem, giving us the maximisation problem:

Maximise $-2{,}000y - 2{,}400z$

Subject to: $400y + 300z \geqslant 2$ for profit *a*
$200y + 600z \geqslant 1.5$ for profit *b*
$y, z \geqslant 0$

The solution to this maximisation problem is:

$y = 0.004$
$z = 0.001$

Shadow prices:

$1 = 4$
$2 = 2$

Maximum:

$= -11$

Compare the two solutions, maximise and minimise, and satisfy yourself that the links between them are clear. The essence of this approach is that a maximisation problem is known as a primal problem and a minimisation problem is known as a dual problem. Furthermore, the dual of the dual is the primal! Clark, Hindelang and Pritchard (1989) have an excellent discussion of such matters, and more: well worth a read.

APPENDIX PRACTICE QUESTIONS

A1. Use the graphical solution technique to determine the solution to the following LP problem. This question is set in standardised form and the background data and relationships are ignored.

Maximise $p = 4a + 3b$

Subject to:
$$21a + 16b \leqslant 336$$
$$13a + 25b \leqslant 325$$
$$15a + 18b \leqslant 270$$
$$a, b \geqslant 0$$

A2. Use the graphical solution technique to determine the solution to the following linear programming problem.

Minimise $c = 3a + 2b$

Subject to:
$$2a + b \geqslant 5$$
$$a + 3b \geqslant 6$$
$$a + b \geqslant 4$$
$$a, b \geqslant 0$$

A3. A manufacturer can make three different products during an accounting period. Each of these products requires preparing, sawing, assembly and testing. The maximum number of hours available of each of the processes for the month is shown below. Formulate and solve the linear programming problem by using the simplex method.

	Product A	B	C	Available resource hours
Preparation	1.0	1.5	2.0	200
Sawing	0.6	1.0	0.8	120
Assembly	1.5	2.0	1.4	240
Testing	0.3	0.2	0.2	40
Profit (£)	12.00	18.00	16.00	

Ensure that you build in the non-negativity constraints where appropriate and, if you are using computer software to help you with this problem, include the non-negativity constraints in your initial tableau.

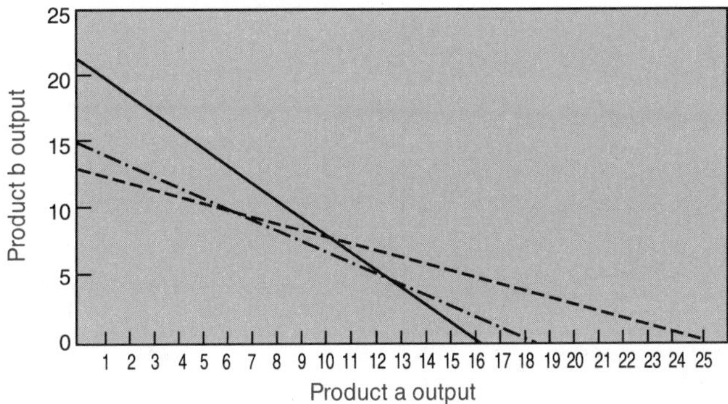

FIGURE A12.3 *Solution to appendix practice question A1*

Solution to appendix practice questions

A1. The graph we are looking for is shown in Figure A12.3. In this example, we have five extreme points; and their associated profit values are:

a	b	p (£)
0	0	0
0	13	39.00
6.38	9.68	54.56
12.45	4.57	63.51
16	0	64.00

We can conclude that the optimal combination to satisfy the objective function is:

$16a + 0b = £64$

On the graph, we see that this is the bottom right-hand feasible corner of the five possible optimal solutions we have considered.

A2. The graph we are looking for is shown below in Figure A12.4. As with Worked example 12.7, the feasible region of this graph is to the right of the extreme points. In this example, we have four extreme points; they and their associated cost values are:

a	b	c (£)
0	5	18
1	3	9
3	1	11
6	0	18

In this case, the optimal solution minimises costs at £9 with outputs of $a + 3b$.

A3. The outline solution to this problem is:

1. Product A	15.385 units made
B	92.308 units made
C	23.077 units made

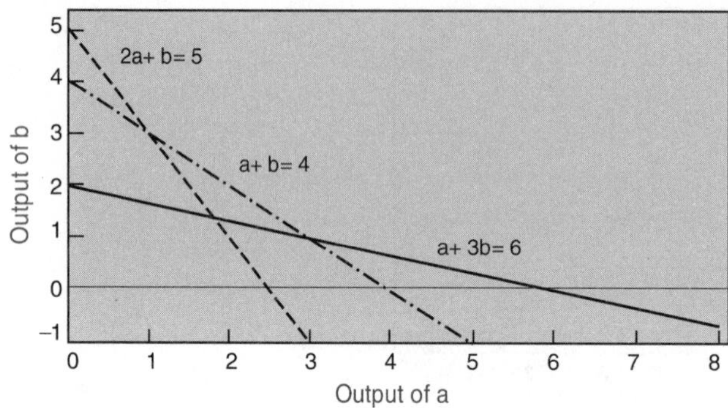

FIGURE A12.4 *Solution to appendix practice question A2*

2. Slack variable 4 is 12.31 hours. This means that variable 4 (the testing hours) is underused by 12.31 hours.
3. The shadow prices are: for constraint 1 2.769
   2 7.692
   3 3.077
   4 0.000

A check on the use of resources shows:

Preparation	200.00 hours used
Sawing	120.00 hours used
Assembly	240.00 hours used
Testing	27.69 hours used:

this reflects the result of 12.31 for slack variable 4.

Solution to KimCo question from the chapter

The LP formulation for this problem is:

Maximise $p = 4.25a + 6.25b + 5c + 4.5d$

Subject to:

$$6a + 5b + 3.5c + 4d \leqslant 600$$
$$a + 1.5b + 1.2c + 1.2d \leqslant 120$$
$$4a + 3b + 3c + 3d \leqslant 400$$
$$2a + 2b + 2c + 3d \leqslant 300$$
$$a \geqslant 40$$
$$b, c, d \geqslant 0$$

There are too many variables to graph this problem, hence the simplex method should be used. The final, optimal tableau is given in Table 12.2.

TABLE 12.2 *Final optimal tableau*

a	b	c	d	s_1	s_2	s_3	s_4	s_5	Quantity
0.00	0.00	0.00	0.12	0.23	−1.15	0.19	0.00	1.00	36.92
0.00	1.00	0.00	0.23	0.46	1.03	−0.95	0.00	0.00	20.51
0.00	0.00	1.00	0.62	−0.77	0.51	1.03	0.00	0.00	10.26
0.00	0.00	0.00	1.08	0.15	−0.77	−0.54	1.00	0.00	84.62
1.00	0.00	0.00	0.12	0.23	−1.15	0.19	0.00	0.00	76.92
0.00	0.00	0.00	0.51	0.02	4.07	0.02	0.00	0.00	506.41

Again, the non-negativity constraints have been left out of this solution since they do not affect anything: everything turns out positive anyway! The beauty of leaving these constraints out is that it makes life easier, especially if we are doing all of the calculations by hand.

This is a relatively complex problem, of course, and the main parts of the solution are:

produce 76.92 units of type 1
produce 20.51 units of type 2
produce 10.26 units of type 3
produce 0.00 units of type 4

The shadow prices are

£0.02 for type 1
£4.07 for type 2
£0.02 for type 3
£0.51for type 4

The unused, and available, resources arising from the optimal solution are:

- 84.62 units of sundries: a further 84.62 units of sundries are available to be used.
- 36.92 units of type 1: the number of units of type 1 product that have been sold in excess of the minimum requirement of 40 units

Table 12.3 shows the use of resources following the optimal allocation of them using the simplex method. This illustrates the way all of the resources are fully used, underused, or not used at all.

TABLE 12.3 *Use of resources*

Profit	£506.41
Assembly hours	600.00 hours used
QC hours	120.00 hours used
Microprocessors	400.00 units used
Sundries	215.38 units used
Type 1	76.92 total unit sales

REFERENCES

Brown, D. (1982), 'The price in cash terms that nobody is counting', *Guardian* (12 May).

CIMA (1991) *Management Accounting Official Terminology* (Chartered Institute of Management Accountants).

Clark, J. J., Hindelang, T. J. and Pritchard, R. E. (1989), *Capital Budgeting: Planning and control of capital expenditures*, 3rd edn (Prentice Hall).

Drury, C. (1992), *Management and Cost Accounting*, 3rd edn (Chapman & Hall).

French, D. (1985), *Dictionary of Accounting Terms* (Financial Training).

Hirsch, M. L. and Louderback, J. G. (1986), *Cost Accounting: Accumulation, analysis, and use,* 2 edn (Kent Publishing).

Perks, R. W., Rawlinson, D. H. and Ingram, L. (1992), 'An exploration of ethical investment in the UK', *British Accounting Review*, **24** (1) (March), 43–65.

CHAPTER THIRTEEN

Pricing policy and decisions

CHAPTER OBJECTIVES

After reading this chapter you should be able to:

- define and describe a variety of methods by which prices are set: absorption cost pricing; variable cost pricing; breakeven point pricing; and rate of return pricing
- appreciate and apply target costing in a pricing setting
- apppreciate target costing's interface with strategic management
- discuss the link between learning curve analysis and product pricing
- discuss a variety of pricing strategies: the product life cycle; price skimming; penetration pricing; and management accounting and pricing strategies

Introduction

As every businessman or -woman knows, the pricing decision is often the most difficult decision they have to make. Trying to assess the price at which a product or service can be sold can be exceptionally difficult. Some organisations are in the fortunate position of being able to charge whatever price they want since they operate as a monopoly. Other organisations have to set a price that the many other manufacturers in the same sector will almost instantly seek to match or undercut. The same is true of the providers of a service.

Primary pricing objectives are generally long run in nature, while pricing decisions themselves are short run. It is an exceptional situation to have a pricing decision remain intact for a lengthy period of time. We can see this is true when we consider the price of a bar of chocolate or a toffee bar: as consumers get used to paying a certain price for the chocolate or toffee bar, manufacturers often need to vary other elements of the marketing effort in order to maintain their customer base. The outcome of maintaining a fixed price for a bar of chocolate has often been that the bar of chocolate itself is reduced in size. By this method, a Jupiter Bar, say, can be kept at 25 pence per bar for lengthy periods of time.

However, the pricing decision is still short run since the price of the product is probably the single most important factor here, and it is the need not to change the price of the bar that diverts our attention from the pricing variable.

In this chapter, we will be concentrating on the setting of prices for profit-making organisations. However, at the end of this chapter we will take a brief review of pricing in the non-profit-making sector of the economy.

Prices and pricing

An economist's definition of a price is that: 'the price of a product is simply the terms on which it can be acquired' (Stigler, quoted in Pitt and Abratt 1987: 13). A marketer's definition of a price is that it is (:) 'the amount of money (and possibly some goods) that is needed to acquire some combination of a product and its accompanying service' (Stanton, quoted in Pitt and Abratt (1987: 13).

A price then, or a selling price, is a transfer of value from one party to a transaction to the other party in the same transaction. Note, in Stanton's definition, that price might include goods (or possibly other services) as well as cash or cash equivalents. Pitt and Abratt then define pricing as being: 'very simply the act of determining price'.

How to spot where pricing is a potential problem

Those of us who have a motor car or motor cycle can easily spot the motoring organisations we deal with who have pricing problems. We can judge the depth of that pricing problem next time we take our car in for its regular 5,000 or 10,000 mile service: just take a look at the invoice given in justification of the overall price of the servicing job. The invoice might read as follows:

	£
Labour 4 hours at £35.00 per hour	140.00
Spares and consumables	15.00
Total before VAT	155.00

How many ordinary garage mechanics are there earning in excess of £63,000 per annum?: that's what the £35 per hour represents! This problem is well explained by McFadden (1990: 38, 40) when he discusses the case of the $7 aspirin to be found in a hospital in the United States. McFadden's article starts:

> In a recent Ann Landers column, a former patient of a Californian hospital complained about being charged $7 for a single aspirin tablet he received during his stay ... according to the Employee Benefits Research Institute, recent studies have indicated that up to 97% of hospital bills are incorrect and only 2% of the incorrect items were in the patient's favor.

He goes on to illustrate his article with a table which includes the news that in the United States an aspirin costs $0.006 per tablet. Where does the rest of the $7 come from? Summarising data from the table in McFadden's article, we have Table 13.1.

TABLE 13.1 ***The $7 aspirin***

	$
Raw materials	0.012
Direct labour	1.214
Indirect labour	0.400
Supplies	0.020
Shared and shifted costs	0.986
Hospital overheads (32.98%)	0.868
Profit	3.500
Total cost per dose	7.000

Source: McFadden (1990).

Our local garage and this Californian hospital have the same pricing problem. Actually, it's a cost accounting problem: one of cost assignment in which no one is really getting fully to grips with sensibly costing products and services. Just to conclude with the legacy of the $7 aspirin, the $7 is made up of:

- the prescribing doctor's time;
- the pharmacist's time;
- the nurse's time;
- the medical records department's efforts; and
- a surcharge for unreimbursed Medicare patient charges

The essence of the problem here is that no one really knows what the true costs are for the service or product under review; but everyone knows it should cost something! So, a bogus cost structure is invented.

Who sets prices in organisations

Many classes of people in organisations will lay claim to being the ones who should be concerned with the setting of prices. Economists discuss pricing issues at length; marketers discuss pricing at length; and over the last two or three decades, accountants have come to discuss pricing at length too!

The economist

The economist discusses pricing in terms of the competitive forces operating in the market in which we might be operating:

1. *Perfect competition* Many sellers and perfect information.
2. *Oligopoly* Few sellers, imperfect information.
3. *Monopoly* One seller, in extreme circumstances.
4. *Monopsony* One buyer.

The marketing manager

The marketing manager discusses pricing in terms of the elements of the marketing mix of his or her organisation, where the marketing mix is the interaction of what are known as the four Ps, namely:

1. Product
2. Price
3. Promotion
4. Place

The marketing manager also discusses pricing in terms of price skimming and penetration pricing and the product life cycle. The marketing manager discusses pricing as one element in the marketing mix.

The management accountant

The management accountant discusses pricing in terms of the accounting bases on which prices may be founded:

1. Absorption cost pricing
2. Variable cost pricing
3. Breakeven pricing
4. Rate of return pricing
5. Target cost pricing
6. Product life cycle pricing

Both the marketing manager and the accountant may discuss pricing in terms of product life cycle pricing. We will be concentrating our discussion in this chapter on the management accountant's approach to pricing.

How organisations set their prices

We might expect, in the simplest of all worlds, that organisations set their selling prices with reference to their cost base. That is, we make product X for £10 per unit, therefore our selling price is at least £10 per unit plus a profit element. Whilst there are many ways in which this profit addition might be arrived at, this approach is only one of many available. Mills (1988) carried out a survey of manufacturing and service organisations in the United Kingdom in an effort to determine how organisations set their prices. Mills found the following methods in use.

	Manufacturing (%)	Services (%)
Used cost-related pricing methods	71	68
Used cost-plus pricing methods	71	65

However, Mills does say that factors other than cost are often taken into account when setting selling prices, most importantly when considering the general level of competitors' prices. Finally, as far as Mills is concerned, he does report that both the manufacturing and the service sectors favour fixed as opposed to variable pricing. Mills's survey confirms the results of previous, similar, surveys, but highlights in more definite terms than before the tendency to modify prices with reference to competitors' prices.

In this section of this chapter, we will look in turn at each of the six pricing methods we listed when discussing the approaches the accountant might take to price determination.

Absorption cost pricing

Absorption-based pricing is also known as full cost pricing. We are familiar with absorption costing from earlier chapters of this book. Consequently, we know what an absorption or full cost is. To establish an absorption cost price, we first determine the absorption cost and then set the price based on that cost.

Cost-plus pricing

The simplest method of cost-based pricing is called cost-plus pricing. The method is called cost plus pricing simply because we take the value of what we believe to be the cost of our product or service and add a profit element. Hence our price is cost plus a profit element. In essence, this method is simple to use since we do not necessarily expect anyone to calculate the profit element in any scientific manner. That is, we simply determine how much profit we think we ought to make and set a cost-plus element based on that target. The illustration in Table 13.2 shows clearly the two general approaches we might take to cost plus pricing.

TABLE 13.2 *Absorption costs for pricing purposes*

	£
Prime cost	10.00
Production overheads:	
variable	5.00
fixed	5.00
Production cost	20.00
Selling and distribution overheads:	
variable	1.50
fixed	1.00
Administration overheads: fixed	1.50
Total costs	24.00

Assuming that the total cost of £24.00 per unit is an acceptable approximation of our real total costs, we now have the basis for setting our cost-plus price. The profit margin might be expressed as a percentage of total cost; or as a percentage of the selling price. If, say, the profit per unit is to be 25% of the total cost, then the profit element is £6.00 per unit and the selling price will be £30.00 per unit. Similarly, if the profit element is to be, say, 40% of the selling price, the profit element will be £16.00 per unit and the selling price, therefore, £40.00 per unit.

Problems with absorption-based pricing methods

The main problem with full cost-based pricing methods centres around overhead absorption. We know from our work on overheads and activity-based costing that predetermined overhead absorption rates need to be based on normal activity levels. Using normal activity levels does not allow us to take account of incremental costs in the way that the variable costing approach does. Following on from the first problem with absorption based pricing methods, we have the problem that the absorption-based price is based on average costs. These average costs are often seen as being benchmarks for pricing decisions. Thus business which may be won at a price less than full cost, but which still covers variable costs and makes a contribution to fixed costs and profit, may be rejected.

In view of the first two problems just highlighted, an organisation following an absorption cost-based regime is vulnerable to the organisation that is using variable costing methods. This situation might lead to the problem whereby the organisation is selling all of its products at full cost, yet is still losing money since the fixed costs are being absorbed at a lower level of output than might otherwise be the case. Furthermore the absorption-based method is not sensitive to capacity bottlenecks within production departments. Applying uniform overhead recovery rates does not distinguish between the scarce resource demands of alternative products. Finally, the absorption-based pricing method, applied literally, will ignore the demand for an organisation's products.

Why does absorption-based pricing persist?

Given Mills's survey, and the problems we have just examined, we must ask the question: Why does absorption-based pricing persist? It seems not to be a good idea, in general. However, we can identify four reasons why absorption-based pricing seems to persist:

1. It is easy to use and understand.
2. There may be too much uncertainty about price output decisions.
3. The method provides stability to pricing decisions, especially if overhead is absorbed on a standard rather than projected level of output.
4. There are difficulties in splitting the fixed and variable cost elements from total costs.

CAMEO

Costing for contracting in the NHS

We first looked at this cameo in Chapter 6, when we examined it from the absorption costing point of view. The second vital aspect of this cameo is its pricing aspect. This cameo deals with the pricing aspects of costing for contracting in the NHS.

We know from Chapter 6 that the 1989 'Working for Patients' White Paper established the internal market for health care. In Chapter 6, we said that this was to be achieved by purchasers (i.e. District Health Authorities and GP fund holders) buying their services from the providers (i.e. hospitals) which offer the greatest value for money in terms of both cost and quality. Competition is used to induce improved performance. The White Paper insisted that hospitals should price their services on a full cost basis and that there should be no planned cross-subsidisation between contracts. In 1990, the Department of Health issued guidelines on the pricing of contracts in the internal market which stated that: 'Prices must be based on full (net) costs such that, for provider's annual assumed volume of service, income from contracts will cover the quantum cost with no planned cross subsidisation between contracts.' So, we said, there are three fundamental principles underlying this approach:

1. Prices should be based on costs.
2. Costs should be arrived at on a full cost basis (which includes capital charges).
3. There should be no planned cross-subsidisation between contracts.

Despite the fact that full cost pricing has been a feature of government policy, it is often difficult to achieve the objectives of that policy. However, a justification for the use of full cost pricing is to facilitate comparison with the private sector. Nevertheless, cost-based pricing is not extensively used in private sector industries. Pricing is often market-led rather than cost led, with such methods as target costing, predatory pricing and price skimming. Furthermore economists believe that the optimal price (Pareto efficient price) should be based in marginal rather than full cost.

The problem faced by management accountants in the NHS is how to cost patient care. By its very nature this task is far more complicated than trying to calculate the cost of producing a unit of manufactured output. Failure to calculate costs correctly should lead to entering contracts at an inopportune price, which could have severe financial consequences for the hospital. In order to cope with this, costs are calculated for particular treatments related to diagnosis. Thus the cost of a particular type of treatment is calculated by looking at what it would involve for an average patient based on historical trends (casemix). This total cost includes direct costs such as drugs plus indirect costs such as heating and lighting.

The ideas given above, together with the ideas discussed in the cameo in Chapter 6 show that cost accounting and pricing practice can be highly related activities. This cameo also helps to demonstrate some of the difficulties of putting together cost accounting and pricing practice. In a complex environment such as the provision of health care, where each case treated can be radically different from every other case, cost-based pricing can illustrate severe limitations of cost accounting. Bowerman and Francis (1995) also admit in their discussion that activity-based costing is not necessarily a sufficient method for solving such cost accounting problems either.

Reference: Bowerman and Francis (1995); this cameo was prepared by Graham Francis.

Variable cost pricing

Variable cost pricing is based on the kind of analysis we have carried out in Chapters 10 to 12 in this book. We first split our costs into their fixed and variable elements and then apply incremental analysis to them. From such an analysis we can determine a variable cost-based price. Variable cost-based pricing seeks to allow an organisation to fix its prices in order to maximise its contribution to fixed costs and profit.

WORKED EXAMPLE 13.1

An organisation employs 20 people who each work 40 hours per week and whose average rate of pay is £3 per direct labour hour. On 1 February the company has to choose between two contracts: with DW plc or HK Ltd; each project starts on 1 March and will last for 13 weeks. Either contract would fully use the organisation's capacity and therefore the contracts cannot both be undertaken at the same time. Standard direct costs for each contract and the best prices that can be obtained are:

	DW plc	HK Ltd
Per dozen:	£	£
direct materials	22.50	7.50
direct labour	7.50	15.00
prime cost	30.00	22.50
selling price	53.75	67.50

The organisation's standard overheads per week are £1,500, of which £1,000 is variable and £500 is fixed. Overheads are absorbed by a standard rate per direct labour hour.

Required

The managing director asks the accountant to:

1. Calculate the total cost per dozen for each contract.
2. Calculate the percentage profit to sale for each contract.
3. State which contract ought to be undertaken.

Solution to Worked example 13.1

1. The number of direct labour hours per contract are calculated from the information that the direct labour hour (DLH) rate of pay is £3 per hour; and the fact that we are given the direct labour cost per dozen units in the information. Thus:

	DW plc	HK Ltd
Number of DLH	£7.50/£3	£15/£3
	= 2.5 hours	= 5 hours

We need this information to enable us to calculate the value of the overheads absorbed.

The total overhead absorption rate is

£1,500/(20 employees × 40 DLH) per week

= £1.875 per DLH

Therefore, the total costs per dozen are:

	DW plc	HK Ltd
	£	£
Prime cost	30.0000	22.500
Overheads at £1.875 per DLH	4.6875	9.375
Total costs	34.6875	31.875

2. The percentage profit to sales is as follows:

	£	£
Selling price	53.7500	67.5000
Total cost	34.6875	31.8750
Profit per dozen	19.0625	35.6250
Profit as a percentage of selling price (%)	35.465	52.78

3. On the face of it, one would recommend the HK Ltd contract since it has a higher profit percentage to sales ratio. However, a more detailed analysis shows the reverse to be the case. Over the duration of the 13-week contract, the number of units that can be made are:

$$\frac{\text{total hours available}}{\text{hours to make one dozen units}}$$

For DW plc this works out as:

$$= \frac{20 \text{ employees} \times 40 \text{ hours per week} \times 13 \text{ weeks}}{2.5 \text{ hours}}$$

= 4,160 dozen

For HK Ltd:

$$= \frac{20 \text{ employees} \times 40 \text{ hours per week} \times 13 \text{ weeks}}{5 \text{ hours}}$$

= 2,080 dozen

The profit statements for each contract are:

	DW plc	HK Ltd
	£	£
Prime costs	124,800	46,800
Overheads	19,500	19,500
Total costs	144,300	66,300
Sales	223,600	140,400
Profit	79,300	74,100

This result is neither wrong nor a paradox. We can explain this result by applying what we already know of limiting factor analysis. Once we recognise that the number of direct labour hours is fixed, this suggests a limiting factor element to this problem. Further analysis shows the contribution per unit of the limiting factor, direct labour hours:

	DW plc	HK Ltd
	£	£
Selling price per dozen	53.75	67.50
Direct materials per dozen	22.50	7.50
Contribution per dozen	31.25	60.00
DLH	2.50 hours	5.00 hours
Contribution per DLH	31.25 ÷ 2.5 = 12.50	60.00 ÷ 5 = 12.00

Note that since the organisation is operating at full capacity, only the direct material costs are variable, all other costs are fixed. Hence we can ignore the other, apparently variable, costs.

CAMEO

Variable cost pricing

Imagine it is July in the United Kingdom and we take a walk down the high street. We come to Lynn Pollu, Travel Agents and see the following sign:

Torremolinos, 7 nights
3 star hotel, full board, sea views, near all amenities
Was £329, now £159, flights included

How it is possible that we can buy a holiday now for £170 less than the previously advertised and binding, price? Remember, many holiday makers will already have paid the £329 full price. The answer is variable cost pricing. The tour operator has sold as many full-price holidays as it thinks it is going to sell and is now discounting as low as possible in order to fill as many seats on the aeroplane and as many beds in the hotel as possible. The price of £159 will be made up of the total variable costs (or an estimate thereof) and a small amount to contribute towards profits – assuming fixed costs have already been at least covered by the full price holidays already bought.

All of this begs the question of why anyone buys a full price if it is certain – and it is almost certain – that eventually the price of the holiday will be discounted. Find out why some people are prepared to pay full price for such holidays.

Breakeven point pricing

Dudik (1989) shows a simple example of the application of breakeven pricing. Breakeven pricing is based on the idea that a selling price needs to be at least equal to the sum of fixed and variable costs. Table 13.3 shows the results of the calculation of breakeven prices for a product over a range of outputs.

A simple idea but it does contain at least two problems. First, the fixed costs per unit depend on the assumptions of units to be made. Thus, in Table 13.3 we see a range of units of output and each level of output gives rise to a different total cost per unit, and therefore a different breakeven selling price. Secondly, in order to be able to calculate the breakeven selling price, based on a knowledge of fixed and variable costs, the split of total costs into their fixed and variable elements has to be able to be carried out. However, in the circumstances given in Dudik's article, this pricing method has something to recommend it.

Rate of return pricing

As a guide for making pricing decisions, management may wish to know what selling price would be required to produce a given rate of return on capital employed. Therefore, with

TABLE 13.3 ***Breakeven prices over a range of outputs***

Number of units	Total fixed costs (£)	Costs per unit (£)		Breakeven prices
		Fixed	Variable	
12,000	226,560	18.880	9.920	28.800
14,000	226,500	16.183	9.920	26.103
16,000	226,560	14.160	9.920	24.080
18,000	226,560	12.587	9.920	22.507
20,000	226,560	11.328	9.920	21.248

this method, pricing starts with the establishment of a planned return on capital employed (ROCE). Secondly, the planned return is then translated into percentage mark-up on costs: this requires an estimate or predetermination of the normal rate of production. Thirdly, the total costs of a year's normal production are estimated, which is then taken as the total annual cost in the relevant computation. Fourthly, the rate of normal capital employed to the year's total annual costs is calculated: that is, the rate of capital turnover. Finally, the rate of capital turnover is multiplied by the planned return on capital employed to give the mark-up percentage to be applied for pricing purposes. This gives:

$$\text{percentage markup} = \frac{\text{capital employed}}{\text{total annual cost}} \times \text{planned ROCE}$$

WORKED EXAMPLE 13.2

An organisation producing jigsaws wishes to obtain an ROCE of 19%. The organisation bases selling prices on normal production levels; and it wishes to know the selling price that will produce this required rate of return. The following estimates have been made:

Variable costs	£0.40 per unit
Fixed costs	£500,000 per year
Normal production	250,000 units
Normal capital employed:	
total	£812,500
variable	£0.25 per unit
fixed	£750,000

Required

Calculate the selling price needed to achieve the planned ROCE to match the organisation's objectives.

Solution to Worked example 13.2

The percentage mark-up on cost required is:

$$= \frac{\text{capital employed}}{\text{total annual cost}} \times \text{planned ROCE}$$

$$= \frac{(250{,}000 \times £0.25) + £750{,}000}{(250{,}000 \times £0.40) + £500{,}000} \times 19\%$$

$$= \frac{£812{,}500}{£600{,}000} \times 19\%$$

$$= 1.354166 \times 19\%$$

$$= 25.73\%$$

The selling price per unit that will produce the required ROCE is:

	£
Variable cost per unit	0.40
Fixed cost per unit	2.00
Total costs	2.40
Mark-up on costs (25.73%)	0.62
Selling price	3.02

The planned mark-up provides a basis for controlling short-term price-making and price-taking decisions; and also for appraising the extent to which these actions direct profits away from the planned ROCE. Rate of return pricing is clearly a variant of absorption pricing. The difference between absorption pricing and rate of return pricing being that rate of return pricing seems to have a more scientifically determined mark-up percentage derivation.

Problems with rate of return pricing

The first problem with the rate of return pricing method is that it is essentially the absorption cost pricing method with a slightly more scientific basis to it. Other than that, it is not a great deal more sophisticated. Imagine the situation of an organisation with many departments and many divisions; and that organisation is decades old, with a constantly fluctuating capital base. How can we be certain of the capital base by department and division? We need to know the capital base of each section of our organisation since we will probably wish or need to establish different planned ROCEs for each area of our business. Again we have the problem of having to deal with normal costs and normal volumes of activity. Only when the actual outturn is the same as the normal levels will there be any congruence between plans and actuals. In certain cases, of course, such variations between normal and actual could be significantly large.

Target costing and pricing

Kato (1993: 36) defines target costing as:

> an activity which is aimed at reducing life cycle costs of new products, while ensuring quality, reliability, and other consumer requirements, by examining all possible ideas for cost reduction at the production planning, research and development, and the prototyping phases of production. But it is not just cost reduction, it is part of a comprehensive strategic management system.

Note that both Kato (1993) and Kato, Böer and Chow (1995) discuss target costing in terms of new product development. Whilst it is clearly the case that target costing is applied to new products, there are examples where target costing, or the equivalent of target costing, can be found applied to existing products.

How target costing applies to existing products

The chocolate bar example given at the beginning of this chapter is one way of meeting the target cost: that is, reduce the size of the finished product. Similarly, a cafetiere bought in 1988 cost approximately £35 in a department store: the equivalent cafetiere is still selling for £35 seven years later. How can the price of the cafetiere have been maintained? When we compare the materials from which the old and the new cafetieres were made we can see precisely how target costing might have been applied. Management have decided that the price of £35 for a cafetiere was a ceiling price in 1988 and is still a ceiling price in 1995. To meet their cost and profit targets, they have changed the material specifications. Target costing and pricing is essentially driven by the needs of the market. Furthermore target costing is based on reality, in that costs do not have to be estimated in advance of manufacture: that is, target costs become actual costs and therefore target prices become the actual price. From this standpoint, target cost-based pricing overcomes many of the disadvantages of the other pricing methods.

The history of target costing in Japan

Target costing has reportedly been in use in Japan for over 30 years (Kato 1993: 36), and a survey shows that 80% of major companies in Japan in assembly type industries have already adopted target costing (ibid.). Furthermore, Kato also reports another survey as showing that 60.6% of companies including those in process type industries use target costing. Kato *et al.* (1995) show some of the results of a survey reported in 1992 of Japanese industry in relation to its take-up of target costing. Table 13.4 shows an extract from this survey.

Sizer (1989: 460) discusses target costing, but he calls it price-minus costing (p460). Sparkes, Buckley and Mirza (1987) say that the term 'price minus' comes from Smyth who coined the phrase in a 1967 article. However, target cost-based pricing is an interesting variation of the methods we have discussed so far since it is the application of lateral thinking to an otherwise potentially hideously difficult problem! Target cost-based pricing works by

TABLE 13.4 *Adoption of target costing by Japanese industries*

Industry	Percentage of respondents using target costing
Food	14
Paper and pulp	0
Steel	23
Electrical	83
Transportation equipment	100
Precision equipment	75

Source: Kato *et al.* (1995: 40), exhibit 1.

management assessing their pricing needs (by way of marketing efforts, for example), and then production departments are told that in order to meet the selling price for this product of £x, the cost price *must* be £x – n. Production therefore make the product for £x – n.

Sparkes *et al.* discuss the differences between Japanese pricing strategies and the strategy of European companies operating in Japan. They discovered that if a selling price was found to be too high for the market to bear, the European company would adjust selling prices by cutting their profit margins. The Japanese companies, on the other hand, because of their target costing approach to pricing, had built into their pricing structure what the market would bear, thus preserving their profit. Sparkes *et al.* claim as theirs the approach that the Japanese take to product pricing and the use of subcontractors and through them the protection of contributions to fixed costs and profit. What they mean is that they may have been the first to describe the approach in Western literature. Sparkes *et al.* make an interesting comment when they say that if selling prices have to fall to 75% of their normal level, a European company's profit disappears, whereas a Japanese company's profit is protected. – interesting, but an oversimplified view suggesting extreme rigidity in European pricing practices.

Target costing and input price changes

How can target costing and target cost-based pricing work if raw materials are currently costing, say, £x? How on earth can production meet such an apparently impossible target? The short answer is for design engineers, production engineers and marketing staff to get together to redesign, remanufacture and resell the product so that they can meet the target cost of £x – n. This seems a reasonable thing to do since we know from previous chapters that up to 80% of a product's cost is designed into products before they even get to the manufacturing stage. Hence if a redesign of a product can take place, then some of that 80% can be got rid of: the cafetiere example above illustrates this approach, is used and works.

Target costing is a philosophy not a cost accounting technique

'Target costing itself is made up of a group of existing techniques, procedures and activities, but reinforced by the target costing philosophy' (Kato 1993: 42). And according to Brausch (1994), target costing is not a costing issue.

Kato (1993: 40) explains why target costing is more than the application of accounting principles to a pricing problem:

> In Japanese target costing, total target profit is based on the medium term profit plans which reflect management and business strategies covering a period of three to five years. It is important to realise that the target profit is not just a target or expectation, it is a commitment agreed upon by every person who has any part in achieving it ... Japanese automobile companies perceive target costs as a commitment. They never expect target costs to change during the development process. Agreed target costs are final.

Participative management and target costing

One of the key issues surrounding budgeting and budgetary control as it is perceived in Europe and America, concerns participation and budget setting. In the context of target costing, Kato *et al.* (1995 : 41) say that every Japanese manager who plays a part in developing the medium-term budgets which target costing become a part of participates in the development of the budget. Furthermore, each manager attends meetings in which the budgets are discussed and he supports his own position on the subjects being discussed at these meetings.

The Japanese solution to input cost problems

The implications of the statement from Kato concerning the achievement or otherwise of the target cost are potentially dangerous, of course. However, in Japan they have at least a partial answer to these problems. If a product takes a long time to develop, and target costing is in use, significant changes to costs that have actually taken place cannot, it seems, be renegotiated into any supply contracts. Consequently, in Japan, they have yet again shrunk the tractor! If a tractor is too large for the field, either increase the size of the field or reduce the size of the tractor. In Japan, they chose the latter course. In the case of target costing, product development times have been slashed. Kato (1993 : 43) reports product development periods as follows:

- 4 years in Japanese automobile companies;
- 5 to 6 years in US automobile companies;
- up to 8 years in European specialty car manufacturers.

Setting a target cost

Kato *et al.* (1995: 41–2) present in diagram form the procedure for setting target costs. Here, however, we will look at the overall method of setting target costs. First, a predecessor product is identified. A predecessor product is one that can be taken as the basis for the current product – perhaps an older version of the current model. Secondly, the management will then review the current production cost of the predecessor product, which will then be adjusted to include any cost reduction ideas for the product that have not yet been implemented. Finally, an 'as-if' cost is calculated. An as-if cost represents the cost of making the product if the company had implemented all available cost reduction activities.

Target costing and strategic management

There are many aspects to target costing that identify the idea as being of strategic management importance to the management accountant and his or her organisation. We have already seen that the target cost becomes integrated into the medium-term financial strategy of the organisation in which target costing is being used. In the two case studies discussed in Kato *et al.* (1995), we see further evidence of the strategic importance of target costing. We learn that target costing has become part of profit management processes. Additionally, we are told that target costing focuses on reducing the life-cycle costs of new products, while also improving their quality and reliability. In the case concerning Daihatsu Motors, we learn that very senior management are involved in the target costing process at the stage when a target cost is finally being decided. Senior management are part of, and give their support to, target costing. In the Matsushita Electric Works case, we learn that target costing was instrumental in helping Matsushita learn a number of lessons relating to the timing of target cost studies: lessons about the design of new products, and about modifications to existing products and procedures. All of the efforts Matsushita put into target costing reaped ample rewards.

Problems stemming from the use of target costing

Kato (1993) reports that there are serious problems being faced in Japan by companies using target costing. Designers and engineers face strict time pressures: we saw above that product development times in Japan can be significantly less than they are in Europe and the United States. Kato further says that even though creative ideas often emerge from the situation in which strict time targets are being aimed at, people in these organisations become tired and exhausted through working long hours and being under severe time pressures. Kato *et al* (1995: 50) confirm the findings of Kato and add two more problems with target costing:

1. **Market confusion** Target costing is a philosophy which means that an organisation interfaces strongly with its market. Kato *et al.* relate the story of two cars being made by Nissan: one car for the Japanese market and another for the European market. The design of both models was tinkered with so much that in the end the two were difficult to tell apart and sales of both dropped significantly.
2. **Organisational conflict** One design engineer became very angry when he heard that an automobile dealer paid to take pictures of customers with their new cars for a custom calendar: 'We work incredibly hard with many hours of overtime to reduce the cost of a vehicle by $3, and the marketing people casually spend this amount to make a calendar.'

Product life-cycle pricing

Although definitions vary, the product life cycle (PLC) generally covers the following phases of a product's life: research; introduction; growth; maturity; and decline. Product life-cycle costing and pricing therefore follow each product across this cycle and monitor prices and profits on a product-by-product basis. Typically, a product earns nothing during the research phase of the cycle and only starts to generate income and profits once the introduction phase has been started. From a product pricing point of view the PLC offers the following insights into potential pricing strategies for a product:

1. **Research/introductory phases** High costs and high prices that will eventually fall
2. **Growth phase** Higher volume of sales and possibly slow competition reaction. This gives a lower price, leading to higher profit and higher market share
3. **Maturity/decline phases** The future is less important. That is, as the product is disappearing, set a selling price that will maximise short-run profits.

We can see the operation of the product life cycle in the microprocessor manufacturing industry. Cats-Baril *et al.* (1988) provide data on the selling prices of microprocessor chips from 1974 onwards. In April 1974 the Intel 8080 chip was selling for $360. By September

1975 the price of a roughly equivalent chip was down to $20. This example is of a rapidly developing product, and the example rests essentially in the research and introductory phases, not even in the maturity or decline phase! A knowledge of a product's life-cycle, and the general way in which product life-cycle costing and pricing works, will assist the manager in setting his or her pricing policy. As a specific example of the application of life-cycle pricing, we need only remind ourselves of the cases discussed in Kato *et al.* (1995).

Pricing policies and learning and experience curves

The work done in Chapter 9 on learning curves is extremely useful for us in connection with product pricing and the setting of pricing policies. If we take almost any of the examples found in Chapter 9, we can see the pricing implications of them. Learning and experience curves fit into the pricing environment especially when selling price follows the cost of manufacture or service provision. Take the example where learning is not allowed or accounted for and a job takes 50 hours to complete the first time it is produced. By the end of the 128th batch, with no learning, we would expect 6,400 hours to have been spent on manufacture. If we now allow for a learning rate of 80%, the labour hours expected to be spent on manufacture would be approximately 1,300.

Pricing strategies

By strategy we mean the art of setting plans and targets in order to operate our organisation more effectively and efficiently. A pricing strategy, therefore, is one by which we set plans and targets for selling prices and total sales in order to achieve the overall aims and objectives of our organisation: 'pricing decisions must be seen as part of an interlinked set of policy decisions including general corporate strategy and component supply decisions' (Sparkes *et al.* 1987).

The product life cycle

As we know, the product life cycle describes the life of a product from its inception through to its death. Pricing strategies need to be developed around a product life cycle, rather than merely setting a selling price in furtherance of a short-term perspective. By taking a life-cycle view, we are taking a long-term, strategic view of our product(s).

Price skimming

A price skimming policy operates by charging high prices for a new product; and once the market is saturated at that price, the price can be lowered in order to attract that part of the market that has not yet been exploited. Price skimming aims at situations where demand is inelastic, where prices are unimportant to the buyer; and where, for example, patent and trademark rights are preventing other suppliers from entering the market. This is important, of course, because with high selling prices and high profits being earned in the early stages of the life of the product, other producers would be enticed into the market, if possible. Similarly, in a price-skimming situation there cannot be close substitutes for the product otherwise there would be elastic demand, and this is inconsistent with the first point in which we agreed that demand for the product would have to be inelastic. The benefit of price skimming for the supplier is that it gives high profits in the short term – but there are no guarantees of profits in the long term.

Penetration pricing

Penetration pricing is, in a sense, the opposite of price skimming. Initially, a low price is charged for new products with the hope that rapid acceptance of the product will be gained. The low price discourages competitors from entering the market and enables the first organisation to establish a large share of the market. Penetration pricing is used where there are close substitutes for the product or where it is easy to enter the market.

Management accounting and pricing strategies

Campbell (1989) points out that the management accountant, the production manager and the marketing manager must all work together in setting pricing strategies. The marketing manager and the production manager need to work together to ensure that the sales force is not simply grabbing as many orders as possible. The problem with order grabbing is that orders will be taken that make neither economic nor production sense. Management accounting needs to be involved in pricing strategies to provide relevant and reliable product cost information. This product cost information can be used to help calculate the profitability or otherwise of make-and-sell decisions. We have discussed pricing, pricing policies and pricing strategies so far in this chapter in the sense that an organisation is selling goods or services to another organisation or consumer.

Target costing

We have seen in the work of Sparkes *et al.* (1987) that target costing and the way it interfaces with pricing has strategic implications. There seems little doubt on this score, given that the nature of target costing is nothing if not a strategic management tool. Target costing, as we have seen, starts with a review of the marketplace, and includes the involvement of senior management in its processes. Target costing is also considered part of an organisation's medium-term profit strategy. Target costing has strategic analysis written through it like letters through a stick of Blackpool rock!

Pricing in non-profit-making organisations

Whilst the subject of pricing in non-profit-making organisations is essentially a whole subject area of its own, Pitt and Abratt (1987: 14) do give us a simplified introduction to the area. They open their discussion of pricing in non-profit-making organisations (NPMOs) with a discussion of opportunity costs, which 'provide a useful construct from which to view the non monetary prices' inherent in NPMOs. They give examples relating to the beneficiaries of the goods and services provided by NMPOs: 'time cost and trouble of travelling a long distance to avail oneself of the organisation's services'; and 'there is the waiting cost – the time spent to take the diagnosis' in the case of a disease detection test by a hospital or similar NPMO. Customers or clients, then, of NPMOs may apparently pay nothing for the service they receive: they may believe they are receiving a free good. However, there are direct costs incurred by them in receiving the service, as Pitt and Abratt describe.

One reason for any organisation charging a price may be the need to recover (even at least in part) costs from those who benefit from the use of the product or service. Secondly the charging of a selling price acts as a motivational device for the client: that is, free goods are sometimes seen as worthless, whereas goods that have an economic penalty attached to them have a concrete value. Thirdly, even in NPMOs, managers of responsibility centres can be assessed against their targets in terms of their inputs and outputs when a selling price is charged.

Pitt and Abratt say that there are occasions when a selling price is inappropriately charged by an NPMO. They cite examples of where the cost of administration of the money received would be outweighed by the administrative effort of accounting for that money: for example, nominal entrance charges to libraries, museums and so on. They conclude by saying that pricing is very different in NPMOs: 'Pricing decisions [in NPMOs] may be rather straightforward, [or] they may be exceedingly complex' (ibid. 15), depending on the situation. All too often the manager in the NPMO may bury his or her head in the sand, hoping the pricing problem may go away! It will not, although pricing in NPMOs is subject to different rules and considerations to profit-making organisations.

SUMMARY

In this chapter we have had a comprehensive overview of both pricing theory and practice. We have found that there are many ways in which prices may be set, whether that price is to be set for the sale of products or services to external customers or not. We have also noted that there are problems with all of the methods which theory might suggest and practice employs.

First, we looked at product pricing and considered the traditional methods of pricing before moving on to the more modern, albeit stress inducing, method of target costing-based pricing. During this discussion we saw that target costing is based on a philosophy rather than a theory or set of practices.

The overall conclusion from a chapter such as this one, devoted to the setting of selling prices is to say that theory and practice may be wildly at variance with each other in this area. A worldwide view of pricing shows a number of influences at work that may override pricing theory: the extent of competition and its intensity has an impact; price regulation by government and trade associations has an impact; the nature of the marketing impetus has an impact. In developing economies, pricing is subject to strange forces. There are multinational organisations moving into new and emerging economies and doing things they would not consider doing at home in order to gain a foothold in the new market. Also in developing economies there is the scarcity factor (supply and demand issues) that dominate pricing issues – as well as the foreigner who knows the price of everything but the value of nothing!

Pricing is a vital concern not only of the accountant, but also of the marketing manager. A review of a selection of marketing books, of which there are many, will help with our further understanding of pricing problems and their resolution.

KEY TERMS

You should satisfy yourself that you have noted all of these terms and can define and/or describe their meaning and use, as appropriate.

Price skimming (p. 426)	Rate of return pricing (p. 426)
Penetration pricing (p. 426)	Target cost pricing (p. 426)
The product life cycle (p. 426)	Product life cycle pricing (p. 426)
Absorption cost pricing (p. 426)	Strategic management (p. 438)
Variable cost pricing (p. 426)	Learning curves and product pricing (p. 440)
Breakeven point pricing (p. 426)	Management accounting in pricing strategies (p. 441)

RECOMMENDED READING

Corey (1980) and (1982) are a good starting point for a general introduction to the issues of pricing in a wider context. Karr (1988) is one of a continuing series of management issues that deals in this case with pricing, and gives the views of people who are in a position to know by way of the solution; Kato (1993) and Kato *et al.* (1995) are up-to-the-minute and inside views on how target costing has helped Japan become a world beater in many areas. McFadden (1990) shows that the Joe's Peanuts case is not necessarily that far-fetched in reality!

QUESTIONS

Review questions

1. Take any organisation with which you are familiar and determine who sets the selling prices in that organisation.
2. Briefly describe how each of the following pricing methods works
   (a) absorption cost pricing;
   (b) variable cost pricing;
   (c) breakeven point pricing; and
   (d) rate of return pricing.
3. What is target costing and how does it work?
4. What links are there between target costing and strategic management?

5. How can an organisation use learning curve analysis in pricing decisions?
6. What role might the product life cycle play in pricing decisions?
7. Describe each of the following pricing strategies
   (a) price skimming; and
   (b) penetration pricing.
8. Can non-profit-making organisations usefully use pricing theory?

Answers to review questions 3, 4, 7 and 8 can be found in the Student Workbook.

Graded practice questions

Level I

1. Steppes Manufacturing Company has experienced intense competition in recent months. However, management still feels that they must maintain the policy of refusing all sales orders unless they receive a 10% return on total unit cost. Orders are rejected daily because of this policy. As a result, finished goods stocks have stockpiled in the warehouse and management is contemplating closing one of its factories.

   Make any suggestions you feel might be of value to the company.

2. GP Ltd is undecided about its pricing policy and is investigating several different cost-based methods. For one of its product lines, the company has determined that direct costs are £45 per unit; indirect costs of all products are 75% of direct costs. The company desires a profit equal to 20% of selling price.
   (a) Determine the mark-up percentage and the selling price, using full cost pricing and variable cost pricing.
   (b) Evaluate the variable cost pricing policy.

3. The management of a local business wishes to earn a 20% return on the £7.7 million assets employed in manufacturing a new product. Annual costs total £3.5 million and the management expects to sell 210,000 units.

   Determine the necessary total sales volume and units sales price to achieve these objectives.

4. After studying the following income statement for its product, the management of C Ltd feels that a reduction in sales price may be justified.

	£	£
Year ended 31 December 19X8		
Sales (200, 000 units)		1,800,000
Variable costs	1,000,000	
Fixed costs	500,000	1,500,000
Profit		300,000

   (a) How much extra volume must be sold in 19X9 to yield an income equal to that earned in 19X8 if decreases of 5%, 10% and 15% in selling prices, respectively, become necessary?
   (b) Why do successive price decreases of equal amounts require progressively larger increases in volume to equalize profits?
   (c) With the limited information given, discuss the factors you would advise management to study before reducing the sales price.

Level II

5. (a) The We Druggem Company is the manufacturer and distributor of a new drug designed as an antidepressant. The company prices the drug at full cost plus 100%. The current variable costs of production are as follows:

Ingredient 'X':	8 milligrams @ £10 per milligram
Labour:	5 minutes @ £80 per hour
Ampoules:	1 @ £1.50 per ampoule

The company's fixed costs (which include the cost of distribution) are currently £320,000 per annum and are absorbed on the basis of budgeted production for the year.

The company is currently setting the price of the drug for the coming year and wishes to take into account expected price increases attached to the various elements of cost. These are as follows:

Element of cost	Expected price increase (%)
Ingredient 'X'	10
Labour rate	50
Ampoules	$33\frac{1}{3}$
Fixed costs	12.5

The company's budgeted production and sales for the coming year are 9,000 ampoules. Calculate:

(i) the selling price of the drug for the coming year on the company's usual basis;
(ii) the company's profit at the budgeted level of activity;
(iii) the breakeven point in units and sales value;
(iv) the contribution/sales ratio;
(v) the maximum amount that the company should be prepared to spend on advertising to increase sales to 10,000 ampoules.

(b) Having received the projected profit figure for the coming year, the chairman of the company has asked the Monopolies and Mergers Commission to help in producing a more sophisticated approach to pricing. They have investigated the market and believe that, with some influence being exercised with clients, the following demand pattern will emerge:

Selling price (£)	Demand (units)
200	17,000
220	16,000
240	15,000
260	11,000
280	9,000
300	7,000

It has been suggested to you that the chairman would appreciate the following information:

(i) the optimal selling price and production level (with supporting calculations) assuming that the demand pattern shown above is accurate;

(ii) the additional profit (if any) compared to the selling price calculated in (a)(i) above;
(iii) the cost per milligram of ingredient 'X' at which the company would be indifferent between charging the price calculated in (a) (i) and (b) (i).

6. Wagner Ltd is about to begin operations using a simple production process to produce two products, A and B. It is the policy of Wagner to operate the new factory at its maximum output in the first year of operations. Cost and production details estimated for the first year are:

Product	Production resources per unit		Variable cost per unit	
	Labour hours	Machine hours	Direct labour	Direct materials
			£	£
A	1	4	5	6
B	8	2	28	16

	Fixed production overheads directly attributable to products (£000s)	Maximum production (000s)
A	120	40
B	280	10

There are also general fixed production overheads concerned in the manufacture of both products but which cannot be directly attributed to either. These general fixed production overheads are estimated at £720,000 for the first year of operations. It is thought that the cost structures of the first year will also be operative in the second.

Both products are new and Wagner is one of the first firms to produce them. Hence in the first year of operations the sales price can be set by Wagner. In the second and subsequent years it is felt that the market for A and B will have become more settled and Wagner will largely conform to the competitive market prices that will become established. The sales manager has researched the first year's market potential and has estimated sales volumes for various ranges of selling price. The details are:

Product A Range of per unit sales prices (£)			Sales volume (000s)	Product B Range of per unit sales prices (£)			Sales volume (000s)
up to		24.00	36	Up to		96.00	11
24.01	to	30.00	32	96.01	to	108.00	10
30.01	to	36.00	18	108.01	to	120.00	9
36.01	to	42.00*	8	120.01	to	132.00	8
				132.01	to	144.00	7
				144.01	to	156.00*	5

Note: * maximum price.

The managing director of Wagner wishes to ascertain the total production cost of A and B as, he says: 'Until we know the per unit cost of production we cannot properly determine the first year's sales price. Price must always ensure that total cost is covered and there is an element of profit. Therefore I feel that the price should be total cost plus 20%. The determination of cost is fairly simple as most costs are clearly attributable to either A or B. The general factory overhead will probably be allocated to the products in accordance with some measure of usage of factory resources such as labour or machine hours. The choice between labour and machine hours is the only problem in determining the cost of each product; but the problem is minor, and so therefore is the problem of pricing.'

(a) Produce statements showing the effect the cost allocation and pricing methods mentioned by the managing director will have on:
   (i) unit costs;
   (ii) closing stock values; and
   (iii) disclosed profit for the first year of operations.

(b) Briefly comment on the results in (a) above and advise the managing director on the validity of using the per unit cost figures produced for pricing decisions.

(c) Provide appropriate statements to the management of Wagner Ltd which will be of direct relevance in assisting the determination of the optimum prices of A and B for the first year of operations. The statements should be designed to provide assistance in each of the following cases:

   (i) Year 2 demand will be below productive capacity.
   (ii) Year 2 demand will be substantially in excess of productive capacity.

In both cases the competitive market sales prices per unit for Year 2 are expected to be

	£
A	30 per unit
B	130 per unit

Clearly specify, and explain, your advice to Wagner for each of the cases described.

Solutions to practice questions 2, 3 and 5 can be found in the Student Workbook. Solutions to practice question numbers in red can be found at the end of this book.

Projects

This is very broad-ranging project that is best broken down into several subprojects. In Chapter 13 we considered a wide variety of pricing situations and strategies: price skimming, product life-cycle pricing, target cost-based prices . . . and so on. Look at any product and attempt to discover the pricing policy or policies used in bringing that product to market. Chapter 13 gave the example of the cafetiere that seems to be priced using a target costing method. How about the pricing of the entrance charge into a football league game? Look at the different English or Scottish leagues and attempt to justify the apparent similarity in prices from division to division despite the wide disparity in the quality of the product from division to division.

REFERENCES

Bowerman, M. and Francis, G. (1995), 'Costing for contracting in the NHS – a case study', *Journal of Applied Accounting Research*, 2 (2).

Brausch, J. M. (1994), 'Beyond ABC: target costing for profit enhancement', *Management Accounting* (NAA) (November), 45.

Campbell, R. J. (1989), 'Pricing strategy in the automotive glass industry', *Management Accounting* (NAA) (July), 26–34.

Cats-Baril, W., Gatti, J. F. and Grinnell, D. J. (1988), 'Transfer pricing in a dynamic market', *Management Accounting* (NAA) (February), 30–3.

Corey, E. R. (1980), 'Note on pricing', Note 580–091 (Harvard Business School).

Corey, E. R. (1982), 'Note on pricing strategies for industrial products', Note 9–582–124. (Harvard Business School), 124

Dudik, T. S. (1989), 'Pricing strategies for manufacturers', *Management Accounting* (NAA) (November), 30–1, 34–7.

Karr, M. (1988), 'The case of the pricing predicament' reprint no. 88205, *Harvard Business Review* (Mar. – Apr.).

Kato, Y. (1993), 'Target costing support systems: lessons from leading Japanese companies', *Management Accounting Research* vol. 4 (March), pp. 33–47.

Kato, Y., Böer, G. and Chow, C. W. (1995), 'Target costing: an integrative, management process', *Journal of Cost Management* (Spring), 39–51.

McFadden, D. W. (1990), 'The legacy of the $7 aspirin', *Management Accounting* (NAA) (April), 38–41.

Mills, R. W. (1988), 'Pricing decisions in UK manufacturing and service companies', *Management Accounting* (CIMA) (November) 38–9.

Pitt, L. F. and Abratt, R. (1987), 'Pricing in non-profit organisation: a framework and conceptual overview', *The Quarterly Review of Marketing* (Spring/Summer), 13–15.

Sizer, J. (1989), *An Insight into Management Accounting* (Penguin Books).

Sparkes, J. R., Buckley, P. J. and Mirza, H. (1987), 'A note on Japanese pricing policy', *Applied Economics*, vol. 19, p.p 729–32.

PART THREE

Accounting for planning and control

With planning and control as its principal subject-matter, there are some potentially significant links between the work of Part III and that of Part II.

Central to Chapters 14 and 15 are the setting of objectives, the drawing up of budgets, and the use of those objectives and budgets. In Chapter 14 we follow the essential steps in establishing budgets for use during the budget period. We look at organisations at the beginning of the budgeting process and then work through that process, including a discussion of some of the behavioural, or non-qualitative, aspects of budgeting. Whilst primarily concerned with the use of the budgets prepared during the budget process, budgetary control is also concerned with what happens after the results of his or her operation are reported to a manager. This latter aspect brings in introductory variance analysis.

In sequence, flexible budgeting and standard costing are the chief topics of Chapter 15, advancing the discussion on budgeting two stages further. Flexible budgeting attempts to place budgetary estimates on a more realistic footing than much of the work in the previous chapter, while standard costing takes a detailed look at each element of cost, each department and each operation. The conclusion reached is that flexible budgeting and standard costing have much to offer managers in the planning and control of their operations.

After dealing with risk uncertainty in Chapter 16, in which we look for the first time in detail at situations where information is not perfectly available, in the next chapter we take a comprehensive view of capital budgeting, that is, the situation where an organisation is seeking to invest in capital assets. All stages of capital budgeting are examined in Chapter 17 – a most important point since many management accounting texts merely look at the capital investment appraisal aspects of the capital budgeting process. The appendix to Chapter 17 gives a solid background to compounding and discounting for those readers who need one.

CHAPTER FOURTEEN

Budgeting and budgetary control

CHAPTER OBJECTIVES

After reading this chapter you should be able to:

- describe the benefits of budgeting and discuss its applicability
- appreciate budgeting as an information and communications system
- describe and discuss the budgeting process
- prepare functional budgets including cash budgets
- prepare a master budget
- discuss the link between budgetary control and variance analysis
- discuss organisational goals and their place in the budgeting model
- discuss a variety of alternative budgeting systems
- appreciate the need for flexible budgeting

Introduction

Budgeting and budgetary control is a set of knowledge and skills from which we can derive significant benefit, no matter whether we are the largest organisation in the world or the poorest individual. The act of budgeting, as this chapter shows, imbues us with a sense of discipline that we cannot gain from anywhere else. The budgeting system is a feed forward system in that by using it we attempt to **anticipate** what we will do, what is going to happen during the budget period. As we will see, however, budgeting has little to offer without its brother, budgetary control. Unless we use and question the budgets we prepared during the budgeting process, we will never establish whether we prepared good, bad or indifferent budgets. Budgetary control is the feedback link that allows us to monitor what actually happened during the budget period, alerts us to what happened that was not in accordance with our plans, and then gives us indications as to what we should then do to correct for what went wrong.

This chapter contains a lot of material that is of a technical nature. The chapter also contains material of a behavioural and organisational nature. Thus, in one chapter we have a wealth of information aimed at broadening our view of both budgeting and budgetary control. By the end of this chapter we will be in a position to establish, run and monitor a budgeting and budgetary control system in any of a variety of organisations.

Definitions

It is common for the definition of a budget to say that a budget is a financial plan. However, as we will see in this chapter, and in many other management accounting texts, there is more to a budget than that. A budget can be a financial plan, it can also be a quantitative plan. That is, a budget can help us anticipate needs of raw materials, people inputs, overhead costs and capital expenditures in terms of quantities other than cash. Thus a budget is a formal plan of action expressed in monetary and other quantitative terms.

> A budget can be drawn up for an entire organization, any segment of the organization such as a department or sales territory or division, or for a significant activity such as the production and sale of a specific product. (Morse and Roth 1988: 387)

Budgetary control is:

> The establishment of budgets relating the responsibilities of executives to the requirements of a policy, and the continuous comparison of actual with budgeted results, either to secure by individual action the objectives of that policy or to provide a basis for its revision. (CIMA 1991)

In outline, a budget is a statement setting out the monetary or numerical aspects of an organisation's plans for the coming week or month or year. Budgetary control is the analysis of what happened when those plans came to be put into practice, and what the organisation did or did not do to correct for any variations from these plans.

The benefits of budgeting

Many of us prepare budgets on a personal level. How much is our income for the month?; How much are we going to spend? Most importantly, is there anything left over? It seems true, however, that many businessmen do not prepare budgets for their businesses. Thus, even though managers prepare budgets for their relatively simple lives, when it comes to the much more complex situation of their business, they prefer to let cash inflows and outflows look after themselves. The purpose of this part of the chapter is to demonstrate that budgets are useful, informative and communicative. We will see that a budget is a necessity not a luxury. We will also see some of the problems underlying organisations: for example, the nature of the organisation and the interactions of the people working in them. By considering these problems, we will be considering ways in which your budgeting system, or the organisation itself, can be changed, if necessary, to overcome them.

By applying the principles of budgeting and budgetary control to our organisation's activities, we gain tremendous benefits. When we prepare our budgets, we are planning. We are forced to consider the future, our methods, our technology, our people and so on. By planning, we at least take an overview of what it is we are budgeting for. Having planned, we are half way towards controlling what we are planning for. Providing we use our plans as targets to be achieved and so forth, we will communicate our findings to the relevant managers and carry out investigations when things do not go according to plan. We then control our operations through our management colleagues taking the necessary corrective action. When we apply the principles of budgeting and budgetary control to our organisation, we help with co-ordination of the various parts of the organisation. When parts of our organisation are interdependent, co-ordination is vital. This is especially true when we are dealing with limiting factors: if a limiting factor impacts on several departments, co-ordination is crucial. Budgeting helps to ensure co-ordination of effort to optimise the application of the limiting factor. Finally, budgeting and budgetary control are prime users of the principles of responsibility accounting. When we set up budget centres – cost centres, profit centres and so on – we do so with the aim of assigning specific targets and deadlines to responsibility centre managers. Budget centre managers have their own budgets: they know what they need to achieve, how to achieve it, what their deadlines are, and so forth.

Applicability of budgeting and budgetary control

Budgeting can be applied to virtually every situation. It does not matter whether we work in the public or private sector of the economy. We may work for a profit-making business or a non-profit-making business. Your company may be engaged in trading, manufacturing, or providing a service. In all of these situations, budgeting and budgetary control is of use to you. As we will see, there are many issues underlying the use of a budgeting system that need careful consideration. For example, we will see that budgeting systems cannot just be imposed on an organisation, nor do they run themselves. Managers at all levels often resent budgets and budget targets for a variety of reasons.

In order for businesses to remain competitive and to progress, or even, in some cases, to survive, more information is needed about the economic environment in which they operate. More information is also needed on day-to-day operations – internally generated information. Accurate, complete information, effectively communicated, is the lifeblood of any organisation; it is the basis on which management must make decisions.

> One of the greatest contributions that a good *management information system* can make is to provide management with time to direct more of its energies to the unsolved human and social problems prevalent in any organisation. (Straat, 329)

Unfortunately, however, from the non-accounting manager's point of view, accounting is a very specialised language, the meaning of much of which is not obvious to the uninitiated. As a result, a communications gap often yawns between a management accountant and an operations manager. Many communications problems arise because managerial accounting reports are primarily quantitative in nature with little or no narrative explanation. Sorting out such communications problems, therefore, should be seen as a priority because of the barrier created by them. The following quotation, whose source is lost in the mists of time, seems to sum up the situation of badly thought out, uncommunicative, budget statements: 'How can I hear what you are saying when what you are is ringing in my ears?'

TABLE 14.1 *Use of appropriate language*

Typical terminology	Appropriate terminology
Allowance for depreciation	Accumulated write-off of original cost of assets
Retained earnings	Profits reinvested in the business
Marketable equity securities	Short-term investment in shares
Trade accounts payable	Amounts payable to creditors
Unearned revenues	Advance payments by customers

All is not lost, of course, because by considering the problems, we can illustrate some of their solutions. Examples of how to improve communications can be demonstrated readily.

Use of appropriate language

Table 14.1 shows the 'Typical terminology', that is, the way the accountant normally speaks or writes. The more 'Appropriate terminology' is one view of how the management accountant might say the same thing but in a more communicative way. By speaking or writing in the more appropriate manner, the management accountant can communicate with his or her audience rather than merely talk at his or her listener.

Use of positive language

The following sentence is an example of passive and negative language: 'Increasing raw materials stocks has not been considered by the manufacturing manager.' It could be replaced with, 'The manufacturing manager should consider increasing raw materials stocks.' to make it much more active and positive. Active and positive language is much easier to read and digest.

Use graphics and design

One of the greatest problems with budgets and budget reports is that they can be absolutely crammed with numbers. The communication of ideas and results can be made much more inspiring with only a minimal use of graphics. Look at the Stamping department report extracted in Table 14.2 and then, for variance analysis purposes only, compare that report with Figure 14.1.

Although we are dealing here with a very simple example, Figure 14.1 does give us more of a ready view of the variances being shown by the Stamping department. At a glance we should appreciate the performance of the Stamping department manager and his team. The table is a clumsy way of portraying accounting information (or any other numerical information for that matter). Nevertheless, tables are a better way of conveying information that paragraphs of narrative. A number of organisations are reported to be using charts

TABLE 14.2 *Stamping department: budget report*

Stamping: department Manager: John Smith

Month of September and year to date, 1995

Direct materials	Current month			Year to date		
	Actual	Budget	Variance	Actual	Budget	Variance
Sheet metal	15,500	15,000	−500	42,000	43,000	1,000
Bands	3,600	2,900	−700	12,400	13,000	600
Pads	1,200	1,500	300	4,200	4,000	−200
Totals	33,150	33,300	150	97,700	101,800	1,400

rather than numerical tables now. Certainly the work of management accountants needs to change if their audience is to remain interested in what they are producing.

Behavioural assumptions

Table 14.3 illustrates some of the behavioural assumptions that have been made, and are now being made, about the reasons for people going to work. We need to consider the behavioural assumptions that we are working on if we are to relate carefully to our client base. What we think of our reasons for working, and the reasons for working that other people have, are bound to influence the way that we report to them, or expect reports from them.

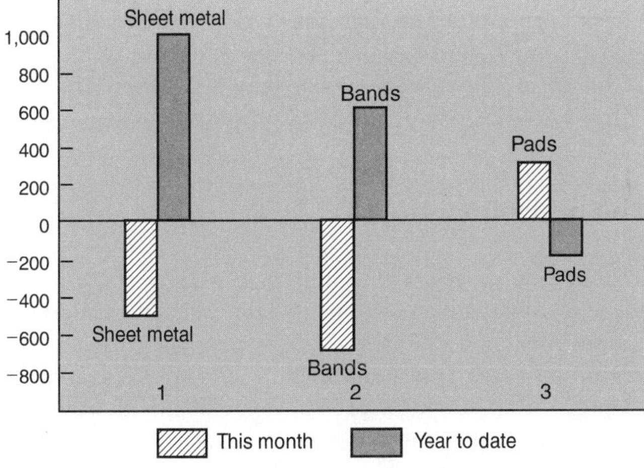

FIGURE 14.1 *Stamping department: variance analysis*

TABLE 14.3 *Some behavioural assumptions: why people work*

Traditional Assumptions

1. People work principally for money and do not derive any intrinsic satisfaction from work.
2. People are generally lazy, inefficient, and apt to avoid working unless closely supervised.
3. Two important jobs of the manager are to control workers through close supervision and to find more efficient ways for workers to accomplish their tasks (especially through making jobs simpler).
4. The role of the accounting and budgeting system is to provide information that helps managers to control their subordinates by highlighting inadequate performance.

Modern Assumptions

1. People work for many reasons, including satisfaction. They are motivated by many needs, which differ in relative importance over time.
2. Managers usually cannot be effective unless their subordinates accept their authority and believe that they will advance their own goals if they work towards their superiors' goals.
3. Accounting and budgeting systems should serve to communicate and to provide feedback that helps people to perform better. Accountants should recognise that the information they present, and the ways that they present it, can affect the behaviour of people receiving the reports.

Source: Hirsch and Louderback (1986: 535).

The traditional assumptions are now considered harsh by most people's standards, and if we accept these assumptions, we will be harsh in the expectations we have of ourselves and our subordinates. If we apply the traditional assumptions to reporting, we will have reports that are concerned solely with financial returns, detailed output information and so on. There will be strict criteria on which to base the results of subordinates, and deviations from those criteria could incur severe penalties. The modern assumptions are more realistic and give management accountants more of an insight into how people really want to carry out a reporting process. A more enlightened approach will lead to a more enlightened set of reporting requirements. Targets that are set by agreement between superior and subordinate, rather than imposed by the superior, would be one outcome of a more enlightened approach to be included in the reports prepared and published by the management accountant. We return to the behavioural aspects of budgeting later in this chapter.

The budgeting process

It would be easy to dismiss the budgeting process as beginning when the first budget is prepared, and as being complete when the master budget is finalised. In reality, the budgeting process begins for many organisations a long time before the budget period begins; and the process ends once the budget period has ended. This means the budgeting process is a very lengthy process – typically, for a large organisation, the pre-budgeting phase can begin up to a year before the budget period starts. For local government councils the budgeting process usually starts in June in the year preceding the budget period, with the draft budget manual being sent to finance officers, who will discuss this draft with their departmental staff (with a view to adoption or amendment). The budgetary planning phase is completed in March (ready for an April start) when the printed budget book is published and the approved estimates are put into the financial control system.

The budget period is the period for which a set of budgets is prepared: typically the budget period is of one year's duration, and will be designed to coincide with an organisation's financial, or fiscal, year. There is no reason why a budget period has to be one year, but typically it is. Most organisations have a budget period analysed between calendar months (or periods); others have thirteen period years (all periods of an equal four week period); and stockbrokers have their year divided into 'accounts' of two and three weeks' duration. These divisions of a budget period are control periods. The budget period is: 'The period for which a budget is prepared and used, which may then be subdivided into control periods' (CIMA 1991).

In a similar way to that in which the financial year is divided, the organisation will be divided up into budget centres. A budget centre is: 'A section of an entity for which control may be exercised and budgets prepared' (CIMA 1991). A budget centre, like a cost or profit centre, is a section of an organisation (division, department, building, individual) for which a separate budget is prepared. The overall budgeting process takes place within the planning cycle. The planning cycle incorporates corporate planning and budgetary control: CIMA defines corporate planning, under the heading of strategic planning, as: 'The formulation, evaluation and selection of strategies for the purpose of preparing a long term plan of action to attain objectives. Also known as corporate planning and long range planning' (ibid.).

Budgetary control

This present chapter is concerned with the evaluation stage in the long-term planning phase, and the short-term planning phase. We should stress that budgeting is **part of** corporate planning. If senior management did not develop any objectives for their organisation, and did not share those objectives with their subordinates, there would be no possibility of anyone preparing budgets, other than, perhaps, a rudimentary cash budget. The assessment stage in budgetary control concerns the organisation by looking at the economic environment external and internal to it. From the assessment of the organisation in its environment, the senior management will develop the objectives that it wishes its organisation to pursue. Having set its objectives, senior management will then set up a budget committee whose task is to find how the objectives may be met. It is usual for the budget committee to consider how to achieve the objectives in a variety of ways before one overall, acceptable, set of budgets is prepared. Once the evaluation stage is complete, the corporate plan can be completed. The corporate plan contains the following sections:

- introduction;
- forecast of relevant environmental factors;
- corporate objectives;
- strategies;
- divisional/departmental plans;
- personnel implications; and
- financial implications.

A budget committee is a crucial aspect of the budgeting process since it will contain in its membership senior, middle, and junior executives of the organisation. The work the budget committee carries out is central to the budgeting process since it is this committee that oversees the preparation of the functional, and other, budgets. The budget committee will base much of its work on the budget manual, which is a document that contains the organisation's budgeting procedures in detail, together with specimens of the forms to be used in the budgeting process. The work of the budget committee is outlined in the top half of Table 14.4.

TABLE 14.4 ***Budgetary planning and control***

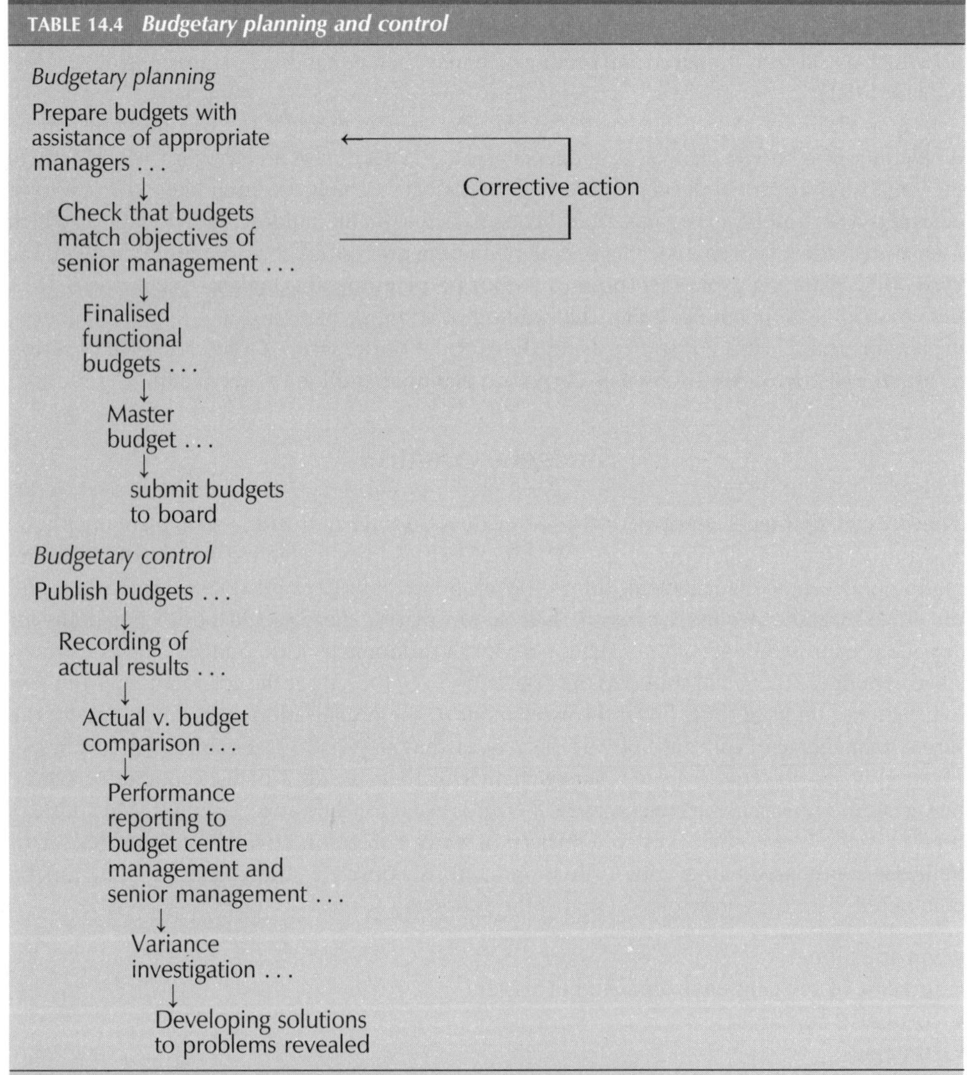

Note: This scheme ignores the capital budgeting aspects of the budgeting process: this is the subject of Chapter 17.

The rest of Table 14.4 concerns the implementation of budgetary control: that is, is the use of the budgets, the comparison of budgets with actuals, reporting back to management, taking corrective action, and drawing conclusions for future budget periods.

Interrelationship of budgets

One of the key reasons why management accountants and other planners are using spreadsheets more and more for budgeting purposes is because of the many interrelationships that exist in budgeting and budgetary-control. If we are preparing budgets for our organisation, we will quickly find that the sales budget has strong links with the stock budget, and it in turn has strong links with the cash budget. When, then, the sales budget is changed, the stock and cash budgets will also have to change. Similarly, if the stock levels are changed, say, as a result of a revision of managerial policy during the budgeting process, then that could impact on both the sales and cash budgets. This section uses an example to demonstrate the full impact of the interrelationships of budgets; it does so in a wholesaling environment. The kinds of changes we are discussing here are perfectly dealt with by using a spreadsheet, and we can carry out sensitivity analysis of our budgets relatively easily once we have properly programmed our spreadsheet.

WORKED EXAMPLE 14.1

Andy is a wholesaler of cricketing equipment and trades under the name of Andy's Bats. He trades in cricket bats, pads, gloves, sweaters and so on. Andy's territory covers much of the south and east of England and his business is sufficiently large that he needs to consider each product line as its own revenue centre. To this end, he prepares detailed budgets line by line. Consider the following details for his purchases and sales of cricket bats.

Andy's assessment of the coming season is that the weather will be hot and dry, and the demand for cricket bats will be high from June and for the rest of the season (until early September). After September, Andy will concentrate on his overseas business (selling to agents in India, Australia, New Zealand and South Africa).

Andy's Bats 19X4

	June	July	August	September	October	November	December
Sales (units)	950	950	750	600	600	500	600

Stock at the end of any month is to be set at the level of 100 bats plus 20% of the number of bats scheduled to be sold in the following month.

Required

For the seven-month period June to December 19X4, prepare the stock and purchases budget and the sales budget. The selling price per bat is £20 and the purchase price per bat is £15.

Solution to Worked example 14.1

The first part of the solution to this example is the purchases budget, expressed in terms of units. The format we are using is a familiar one, where we start the schedule with the opening stock, add purchases and subtract the closing stock to leave us with the sales amounts. We are using this format so that we are consistent with explanations in previous chapters.

If you prefer the purchases to be shown as the final item in the schedule, rework this schedule: you will arrive at the same solution, however.

Purchases budget (units): cricket bats

	19X4 June	July	August	September	October	November	December
Balance b/d	290	290	250	220	220	200	220
Purchases	950	910	720	600	580	520	640
	1,240	1,200	970	820	800	720	860
Balance c/d	290	250	220	220	200	220	260
Sales	950	950	750	600	600	500	600

Once we have the unit situation sorted out, it is a straight forward matter to multiply the relevant parts of the stock and purchases budget by the relevant cost and sales values, so that we obtain the stock, purchases and sales budgets expressed in terms of monetary amounts:

Stock Budget(£): Cricket bats

	June	July	August	September	October	November	December
Opening stock	4,350	4,350	3,750	3,300	3,300	3,000	3,300
Closing stock	4,350	3,750	3,300	3,300	3,000	3,300	3,900

Purchases budget(£): Cricket bats

	June	July	August	September	October	November	December
Purchases	14,250	13,650	10,800	9,000	8,700	7,800	9,600

Sales budget(£): Cricket bats

	June	July	August	September	October	November	December
Sales	19,000	19,000	15,000,	12,000	12,000	10,000	12,000

Interrelationship aspects

The interrelationship aspects of this example have probably not bothered us so far – the nature of interrelationships is that they often pass by unnoticed! In order to arrive at the purchases in units, we have had to determine the opening and closing stock amounts, and we were given the sales units. Thus, if we have calculated the stock budgets incorrectly, the purchase amounts will be wrong, and the purchases budget will be misleading. Similarly, an error in the sales budget guarantees an error in the purchase and stock budgets. We can assess the extent of the interrelationships between the various budgets we are preparing by, for example, changing one of the variables involved in this example. Assume the stock levels are to be set at 50 bats plus 20% of the sales units for the following month: What effect does that have on the purchases, opening and closing stock budgets? Expressing the results in units and values, the revised budgets are:

Stock and purchase ***revised*** *budget (units): cricket bats*

	19X4 June	July	August	September	October	November	December
Balance b/d	240	240	200	170	170	150	170
Purchases	950	910	720	600	580	520	640
	1,190	1,150	920	770	750	670	810
Balance c/d	240	200	170	170	150	170	210
Sales	950	950	750	600	600	500	600

Stock ***revised*** *budget (£): cricket bats*

	June	July	August	September	October	November	December
Opening stock	3,600	3,600	3,000	2,550	2,550	2,250	2,550
Closing stock	3,600	3,000	2,550	2,550	2,250	2,550	3,150

Purchases ***revised*** *budget (£): cricket bats*

	June	July	August	September	October	November	December
Purchases	14,250	13,650	10,800	9,000	8,700	7,800	9,600

The workings for these revised schedules are identical to the workings for the original budgets. The effects of what we have done are that the opening and closing stock units and values have changed, but the effect on purchases and sales has been nil. As far as sales are concerned, they are fixed anyway: everything else depends on them. Purchases can change with stock levels, but since the change to stock levels is constant between opening and closing stock, there is no overall change to purchases.

Limiting factors

We discussed limiting factors and limiting factor analysis when we considered costing for decision making. This chapter illustrates the point that limiting factor analysis is not a one topic subject. Limiting factors are all pervasive: that is, if an organisation has a limiting factor it affects many aspects of the work of that organisation. Hence, when we wish to consider a special decision, we might be faced with a limiting factor problem. Similarly, as we are about to see, limiting factors play a vital role in budgeting and budgetary control. In the discussion of the interrelationships of budgets, we said, for example, that as far as sales are concerned, they are fixed anyway: everything else depends on them. In the examples we were working through this was certainly true: everything the Andy's Bats organisation was doing centred around its sales levels: that is, both purchases and stock levels depended upon the level of sales for any given month. In this situation, sales is considered to be the limiting factor (which is also known as the principal budget factor, and the key factor).

CIMA (1991) define the limiting factor as:

> Anything which limits the activity of an entity. An entity seeks to optimise the benefit it obtains from the limiting factor. ... Examples are shortage of supply of a resource and a restriction on sales at a particular price.

The limiting factor is the one factor which dominates all other factors. As CIMA says, it is not necessarily sales that is the limiting factor – although very many examples found in textbooks, and examination questions say it is. The limiting factor can be '... shortage of supply of a resource' (ibid.): This means any factor that is important to the carrying out of the organisation's activities can be the limiting factor. Each of the following can be the limiting factor depending on the circumstances of the case; moreover, in some cases, a combination of these factors could become limiting, hence the need for linear programming:

1. cash;
2. raw materials;
3. skilled labour;
4. land;
5. equipment.

The overriding consideration that must be paid to the limiting factor is that since it is the dominating factor, this must be the budget that is prepared before all others. There is no point in preparing every budget except the raw materials budget, only to find that the assumptions built into all other budgets means that the amount of raw materials needed just cannot be acquired. Similarly, if cash is the limiting factor, preparing any budgets that take no account of the cash position will probably lead to a lot of unnecessary work having to be carried out.

Application of linear programming in a budgeting setting

We have used linear programming (LP) already: relevant costing. A second use shows how LP can help in the preparation of budgets. Since we are familiar with LP now, the example used to illustrate this point is given below as a cameo, in which we consider the case of a manufacturer who is attempting to schedule his output over a period of several months.

CAMEO

For the period May, June and July, Han Ltd is considering whether he can schedule the production of 6,000 units of output from one department of their factory. 1,000 units must be shipped in May, 3,000 units shipped in June and 2,000 units shipped in July. Han can make 1,500 units per month in normal working time and a further 750 units per month using overtime. The manufacturing cost per item made in normal time is £3 per unit; and £5 per unit if overtime is worked. The monthly storage cost is £1.

Required

Formulate and solve the LP model to help Han establish the budget for this production scheduling problem and at the same time minimise costs of production and storage.

Solution of Han's problem

The LP model is:

Minimise $c = 3a_{111} + 5a_{121} + 4a_{112} + 6a_{122} + 5a_{113} + 7a_{123} + 3a_{212} + 5a_{222} + 4a_{213} + 6a_{223} + 3a_{313} + 5a_{323}$

Subject to:

$$
\begin{aligned}
&a_{111} + a_{112} + a_{113} && \leqslant 1{,}500 \\
&a_{212} + a_{213} && \leqslant 1{,}500 \\
&a_{313} && \leqslant 1{,}500 \\[6pt]
&a_{121} + a_{122} + a_{123} && \leqslant 750 \\
&a_{222} + a_{223} && \leqslant 750 \\
&a_{323} + && \leqslant 750 \\[6pt]
&a_{111} + a_{121} && = 1{,}000 \\
&a_{112} + a_{122} + a_{212} + a_{222} && = 3{,}000 \\
&a_{113} + a_{123} + a_{213} + a_{313} + a_{323} && = 2{,}000 \\[6pt]
&a_{ijk} \geqslant 0
\end{aligned}
$$

This needs some explanation! The subscripts come in three parts i, j, k: i is the month in which to make the goods: May = 1, June = 2, July = 3; j is the shift used normal working = 1, overtime work = 2; and k represents the month in which the goods are shipped May = 1, June = 2 and July = 3. So, 111 means made in May, during normal working and shipped in May; 223 means Made in June during overtime working and shipped in July.

The model is in three parts: section one represents the restriction of output during normal working time; the second section represents the overtime working constraint; and the third section represents the shipping schedule. The cost schedule consists of units that cost £3 to make, £5 to make; £3 to make, store for one month then ship for a total of £4, £5 to make, store for one month then ship for a total of £6 . . . and so on.

The outcome of this model is:

Variable	Units to make
a111	750
a121	250
a112	750
a122	0
a113	0
a123	0
a212	1,500
a222	750
a213	0
a223	0
a313	1,500
a323	500
Total cost	£21,750

This is a complex problem to solve by hand and by using LP. Consider it carefully!

The preparation of functional budgets

Although we could prepare dozens of theoretical exercises concerning functional budget preparation, there is little point in doing so. We will limit our efforts to two exercises only:

1. to give us practice at working through situations that may initially be unfamiliar; and
2. to give us insight into the nature of a theoretical budgeting question.

The key to budget preparation questions is often in interpreting the situation itself. Many times, the person that constructs the question does so deliberately to be obscure on the one hand, or helpful on the other. Unfortunately, it is not always obvious which tack is being taken!

WORKED EXAMPLE 14.2

R Limited manufactures three products: A, B and C. You are required, using the information given below, to prepare budgets for the month of January for:

1. sales in quantity and value, including total value;
2. production quantities;

3. material usage in quantities; and
4. materials purchases in quantity and value, including total value;

(NB Particular attention should be paid to your layout of the budgets.)

Data for preparation of January budgets

Sales:

Product	Quantity	Price each (£)
A	1,000	100
B	2,000	120
C	1,500	140

Materials used in the company's products are:

Material	M1	M2	M3
Unit cost (£)	4	6	9

Quantities of material used:

	M1 (units)	M2 (units)	M3 (units)
Product A	4	2	–
B	3	3	2
C	2	1	1

Finished stocks:

	Product A	B	C
Quantities:			
1 January	1,000	1,500	500
31 January	1,100	1,650	550

Material stocks:

	M1 (units)	M2 (units)	M3 (units)
1 January	26,000	20,000	12,000
31 January	31,200	24,000	14,400

(CIMA Cost Accounting)

Solution to Worked example 14.2

Although budgeting questions can sometimes prove difficult to solve, they are basically an exercise in following through relationships and carrying out arithmetical calculations in a methodical way. The question specifically mentions paying particular attention to layout. This is a very valuable piece of advice to follow: the less clear and logical the layout, the less chance there is of completing a budgeting exercise successfully. The final layout of a schedule or budget is of equal importance whether we are dealing with a theoretical exercise or a real live situation. The budgets presented below should be found to be clearly and logically laid out. The need for an adequate layout is paramount since the recipient of a performance report will probably be a non-financial manager who will find the report less understandable *per se* than the management accountant who generates it.

1. *Sales budget*

	Product			
	A	B	C	Total
Sales units	1,000	2,000	1,500	
Sales values (£)	100,000	240,000	210,000	550,000

The workings here are very straightforward: the sales values are found by multiplying the number of units sold (given in the question) by the selling price per unit (also given in the question).

2. *Production budget*

	Product (units)		
	A	B	C
Opening stock	1,000	1,500	500
Production	1,100	2,150	1,550
	2,100	3,650	2,050
Closing stock	1,100	1,650	550
Sales	1,000	2,000	1,500

The production budget follows the layout that we have seen many times now, and have just discussed in connection with previous examples. Remember, in the case of a production budget, we are dealing with finished goods, not raw materials or work in progress. Hence, check where the opening and closing stock figures in this schedule have come from.

3. *Materials usage budget*

		Product			
		A	B	C	Total
Units produced		1,100	2,150	1,550	
Materials	M1	4,400	6,450	3,100	13,950
(units used):	M2	2,200	6,450	1,550	10,200
	M3	–	4,300	1,550	5,850

Here we see an example of the interrelationships between budgets that we discussed above. Having prepared the production budget, we use the outputs of that budget as the primary input of the materials usage budget: that is, the units produced. The material usages are found by multiplying together the number of units produced by the number of units of each raw material required for each product.

4. *Materials purchases budget*

	Material (units)			
	M1	M2	M3	Total (£)
Opening stock	26,000	20,000	12,000	
Purchases	19,150	14,200	8,250	
	45,150	34,200	20,250	
Closing stock	31,200	24,000	14,400	
Used in production	13,950	10,200	5,850	
Purchases (units)	19,150	14,200	8,250	
Cost per unit (£)	4	6	9	
Total cost of purhases (£)	76,600	85,200	74,250	236,050

Cash budgeting

Cash in an organisation is the equivalent of blood in a mammal! When we bleed sufficiently, we die: an organisation dies when it runs out of cash. When an organisation fails, it usually does so for a lack of cash: it has no notes and coins, lines of credit run dry, loans are called in, and so on. Because of this kind of chain of events, cash budgeting is of crucial importance since it can help organisations to anticipate its cash needs, and, in many cases, anticipation of such needs is the dividing line between the going concern and the liquidation. This section looks, via a short series of examples, at cash budgeting: what it is and how it works.

Vital elements of cash budgeting

There are three important points associated with cash budgeting:

1. the accuracy of forecasts;
2. include everything;
3. timing: the actual cash flow

A cash budget is of limited value (sometimes it will be of no value) if the forecasts on which it is based are inaccurate. Whilst it is not possible to attain decimal point accuracy with most forecasts, a large measure of accuracy is called for when dealing with a budget of such central importance as the cash budget. If significant items are left out of the cash budget, this will limit the impact of it. In the case of the organisation preparing a cash budget for the first time, covering all aspects of the cash budget may not be entirely possible. Very quickly, however, the organisation will have to ensure that all aspects are covered by the budget. Once we appreciate the elements of cash budgeting, cash budgeting is relatively straightforward. When using a spreadsheet, cash budgets can be, if properly programmed, updated instantly. Every change in a component cell of a spreadsheet leads to a change in every linked cell. Thus, for example, if sales changes, total revenue changes, net cash receipts changes, the cash balance carried down changes, and so on. When using a manual system, any changes to sales lead to the same changes as with the spreadsheet determined model, but the changes will take longer to work out.

Cash budget layout

Cash budget layout of any cash budget is:

Balance b/d
plus: Receipts/Revenue
= Total cash available

less: Expenditure
= Balance c/d

There are, or course, alternative layouts that we could use, but, again, this layout is consistent with the layout we have used in this book so far when we have discussed, for example, manufacturing accounts, trading accounts, and other budgets. The precise layout that we use is determined either by the requirements of an example or an exercise, or the situation we are in: for instance head office may send out pre-printed cash budget forms for us to fill in.

WORKED EXAMPLE 14.3

The information concerning an organisation is as follows:

19X4	Purchases (£)	Sales (£)	Administration overheads (£)
January	84,000	144,000	26,000
February	192,000	132,000	27,500
March	72,000	120,000	29,000
April	108,000	156,000	28,000
May	120,000	132,000	29,000

The balance brought down on the debtors' account from December was made up as as follows:

- from sales made in November, 19X3, and due to be paid in January, £13,050;
- from sales made in December, 19X3, and due to be paid in January, £30,000; and
- from sales made in December, 19X3, and due to be paid in February, £13,500.

70% of debtors pay, on average, their full account in the month of sale (sales are billed as and when the sale is completed), 20% of debtors pay in full in the month following sale and 9% pay in the month following that.

This organisation is offered, and takes full advantage of, a 2% discount on its purchases: to earn this discount creditors must be paid within 14 days of being invoiced (assume creditors invoice on the final day of the month in which goods and services are supplied). The purchases made in December, 19X3 were worth £105,000. Administration overheads are planned to be paid for as they arise; and the balance brought down on the cash account at the start of January 19X4 is estimated to be £18,475.

Required

From the above information:

1. prepare a cash budget;
2. derive the sales values for both November and December, 19X3 and
3. calculate the balance carried down on debtors as at the end of May

Solution to Worked example 14.3

This is not a difficult situation to deal with, but since it contains ideas that are new to us, the workings are presented in full. The debtors' budget is often, as in this case, the most complex part of the solution to a situation such as this. The schedule below shows the values needed for the cash budget; the schedule is followed by the relevant explanations:

Debtors' budget

	January	February	March	April	May
	£	£	£	£	£
sales	144,000	132,000	120,000	156,000	132,000
Debtors (1)	100,800	92,400	84,000	109,200	92,400
(2)	30,000	28,800	26,400	24,000	31,200
(3)	13,050	13,500	12,960	11,880	10.800
	143,850	134,700	123,360	145,080	134,400

The sales information is included in this budget to allow managers to assess the debtors' turnover ratio, for example, and to make any other comparisons they might choose. In budgets carefully drawn up, with the full needs of the user in mind, the management accountant will include as much non-financial information as is felt necessary, in addition to the financial information. Debtors (1) . . . (2) . . . (3) are classifications given to distinguish those debtors who pay very quickly (1), those who pay after one month (2), and those who pay after two months (3). Debtor (1) is 70% of the current month's sales value: this clearly reflects the information given: '70% of debtors pay, on average, their full account in the month of sale'. For January, this is 70% × £144,000 = £100,800. Debtors (2) and (3) for January relate entirely to the sales made in November and December, 19X3, respectively. We are not given the sales values for either of November or December: part (ii) of the question, which follows now, asks us to calculate what these values are.

Value of sales

The value of sales for November is derived from the receipts from debtors given in the information supplied: receipts in February that relate to November's sales amount to £13,050; since receipts in February relating to November's sales represent 9% of November's sales, the value of sales we are looking for must be:

$$\frac{£13,050}{0.09}$$

$$= £145,000$$

Similarly, the receipt in January relating to December's sales amounts to 20% of December's sales. The calculation is:

$$\frac{£30,000}{0.20}$$

$$= £150,000$$

We can confirm that December's sales value is £150,000 by working through debtors (3) for January: this gives the same sales value for December as we have just derived (check it for yourself). Confirming the other calculations for receipts for January and February, we have:

Received in the month of sale:

70% × £144,000 = £100,800

Sales made in January, 20% of which are paid for with a delay of one month:

20% × £144,000 = £28,800, received in February

Sales made in January, 9% of which are paid for with a delay of two months:

9% × £144,000 = £12,960

All other calculations for this schedule follow along these lines. Check the workings to your own satisfaction.

Creditors' budget

	January £	February £	March £	April £	May £
Purchases	84,000	192,000	72,000	108,000	120,000
Paid to creditors	102,900	82,320	188,160	70,560	105,840

The values for purchases are given in this schedule for the same reason that sales were given in the debtors' budget; they do not **need** to be there. Creditors are budgeted for by allowing for the full amount of cash discounts being offered to the organisation. The discount to be earned is 2% of the purchase price, and we are told that the organisation takes full advantage of the 2% discount. Consequently, the calculation for each month, for the amount payable to creditors, is 100% − 2% = 98% of that month's purchases. The creditors are paid 14 days after the purchase invoice is received; and we are told to assume that invoices are made out on the final day of the month in which the goods and services are supplied. For January's purchases, therefore, the calculation is:

98% × £84,000 = £82,320

and this is the amount to be paid to creditors in February. Check all subsequent creditors' payments to your own satisfaction.

Administration overheads

The amounts for administration overheads are paid as they arise: it is just a matter of writing the relevant amounts in the cash budget, therefore. No further workings are needed for this part of the solution.

Balance on debtors' account

The balance on debtors' account is relatively straightforward to calculate. As the schedule below demonstrates, we need to know the opening balance on the account (this is given in the information), the total sales for the period (this is also given), and the amounts that debtors have paid during the period (we have already determined this amount in the previous schedule). Thus the balance carried down on the debtors' account is given below:

	£
Balance b/d	56,550
Sales	684,000
	740,550
Received from debtors	681,390
Balance c/d	59,160

Notice that, given the way the question is designed, bad debts amount to 1% of sales. The value of bad debts is included in the final balance carried down of £59,160. Having carried out all of these calculations, we can now put together the cash budget. The cash budget is shown in full below.

Cash budget

	January	February	March	April	May
	£	£	£	£	£
Balance b/d	18,475	33,425	58,305	(35,495)	11,025
Receipts					
Debtors	143,850	134,700	123,360	145,080	134,400
Cash available	162,325	168,125	181,665	109,585	145,425
Payments					
Creditors	102,900	82,320	188,160	70,560	105,840
Administration overheads	26,000	27,500	29,000	28,000	29,000
Total payments	128,900	109,820	217,160	98,560	134,840
Balance c/d	£33,425	58,305	(35,495)	11,025	10,585

As with many of the exercises and examples shown in this book, although there are often lengthy explanations to read through, the technical and arithmetical content of what we have done is not too great. The cash budget is a case along these lines. We have spent a long time working through a reasonably simple example.

The master budget

A master budget is, essentially, an overall budget for an entire organisation. For some organisations, the master budget is taken to be only the balance sheet; in other organisations the master budget consists of the income statement and the balance sheet; in yet other organisations, the master budget includes the income statement, the balance sheet, and a cash budget. We could define the master budget as circumstances determine. However for the purposes of this book, we will define it as the income statement, balance sheet, and cash budget. The example that follows is aimed at preparing these statements when we are asked to construct the master budget. There is little need to spend too much time on the preparation of the master budget since consideration of such budgets can be very time consuming; there are books which takes several hundred pages to do just that! Working through the following example will give us further practice at the construction of functional budgets, as well as the master budget.

WORKED EXAMPLE 14.4

Dooley Ltd started business on 1 July 19X3. The proposals and estimates for the next three months to 30 September 19X3 are as follows:

1. The company will issue 15,000 £1 shares on 1 July 19X3, on which date all amounts are due to be paid in full.
2. Fixtures and fittings costing £4,000 will be bought and paid for on 1 July 19X3.
3. Five delivery vans costing £3,000 each are to be bought on 1st July, 19X3. A deposit of £400 cash on each van is required. The balance is to be paid in eight equal instalments starting on 31 July 19X3. Ignore interest payments.
4. An initial stock of goods is to be bought on 1 July 19X3 at a cost of £22,500 (£3 per unit), and subsequent purchases at £3 per unit are to be made so that this stock level is maintained at the end of each month. Suppliers are paid during the month following purchase.
5. All sales are on credit at £5 per unit, and the estimated sales are:

July	6,000 units
August	7,000 units
September	8,000 units

   Debtors will pay in the second month after the month of sale.
6. Administration expenses are expected to be 20% of sales and are paid during the month in which they are incurred.
7. Ignore depreciation throughout this exercise.

Required

1. A cash budget for the three months ended 30 September 19X3.
2. A budgeted income statement for the three months ended 30 September 19X3.
3. A budgeted balance sheet as at 30 September 19X3.

Solution to Worked example 14.4

The purpose of this question is really to allow us to put together the master budget; the aspects concerning the functional budgets and so on are of secondary importance to us now. The solution that follows, therefore, concentrates only on the new point. Thus there are not always explanations to accompany the schedules presented below.

Cash Budget

	July	August	September
	£	£	£
Balance b/d	—	1,375	(47,750)

Receipts			
Share issue	15,000	–	–
Receipts from debtors	–	–	30,000
Cash available	15,000	1,375	(17,750)
Payments			
Fixtures and fittings	4,000	–	–
Delivery vans	3,625	1,625	1,625
Payments to creditors	–	40,500	21,000
Administration expenses	6,000	7,000	8,000
Total Payments	13,625	49,125	30,625
Balance c/d	1,375	(47,750)	(48,375)

The workings for this cash budget are presented in full, without further explanation.

	July	August	September
	£	£	£
Debtors budget			
Balance b/d	0	30,000	65,000
Sales	30,000	35,000	40,000
	30,000	65,000	105,000
Receipts from debtors	0	0	30,000
Balance c/d	30,000	65,000	75,000
Delivery vans budget			
Total value of vans bought	15,000	–	–
Deposit	2,000	–	–
Balance to pay	13,000	11,375	9,750
Instalments	1,625	1,625	1,625
balance c/d	11,375	9,750	8,125
Stock and purchases budget (units)			
Opening stock	0	7,500	7,500
Purchases	13,500	7,000	8,000
	13,500	14,500	15,500
Closing stock	7,500	7,500	7,500
Sales	6,000	7,000	8,000

Stock and purchases budget (£)

Opening stock	0	22,500	22,500
Purchases	40,500	21,000	24,000
	40,500	43,500	46,500
Closing stock	22,500	22,500	22,500
Sales	18,000	21,000	24,000

Creditors budget

Balance b/d	0	40,500	21,000
Purchases	40,500	21,000	24,000
Payments	0	40,500	21,000
Balance c/d	40,500	21,000	24,000

Note that there are no budgets presented for the share issue and the purchases of the fixtures because of the simplicity of the schedules that would be presented.

Income statement for the three months ended 30 September 19X3

	£	£
Sales		105,000
less: Cost of sales:		
Opening stock	0	
purchases	85,500	
closing stock	(22,500)	63,000
Gross profit		42,000
Administration expenses		21,000
Net profit		21,000

Balance sheet as at 30 September 19X3

	£	£	£
Fixed assets			
Fixtures			4,000
Delivery vans			15,000
			19,000
Current assets:			
stocks	22,500		
debtors	75,000	97,500	
less: Current liabilities:			
creditors	24,000		
bank	48,375	72,375	25,125
Net assets			44,125

Represented by:	
Issued share capital fully paid	15,000
Profit and loss account	21,000
Loan (for delivery vans)	8,125
	44,125

Budgetary control: an introduction to variance analysis

There is little point in an organisation committing large amounts of resources to the budgeting exercise only to ignore the fruits of that labour. The key to the success of the budgetary control exercise lies in using the budgets, and taking any necessary action as a result of having used them. The CIMA (1991) definition of budgetary control helps us to see what is involved in it:

> the establishment of budgets relating the responsibilities of executives to the requirements of a policy, and the continuous comparison of actual with budgeted results, whether to secure by individual action the objectives of that policy or to provide a basis for its revision.

The essence of this definition is that, having prepared and circulated the budgets, the organisation **must** continuously compare what has happened with what it felt should have happened (the budget): that is, variance analysis. Once the difference between the actual and the budget has been determined (the variance), investigations are carried out to determine why there is a difference and what, if anything, should be done about that difference. The principle of *management by exception* will be applied by any organisation using a system of budgetary control.

The performance report is the perfect vehicle for the management accountant to let his or her management team know how near or far they are to having achieved their targets: such performance reports may be prepared daily, weekly, monthly . . . or however frequently they are needed. The performance report that follows is indicative of the kind of report that a management accountant might issue:

Department A **John Smith, Manager**

February, 19X4

	Current month			Year to date		
	Actual	Budget	Variance	Actual	Budget	Variance
	£	£	£	£	£	£
Direct materials	10,554	10,000	(554)	21,367	20,000	(1,367)
Direct labour	27,923	28,000	77	55,494	57,000	1,506
Prime cost	38,477	38,000	(477)	76,861	77,000	139

Overheads	35,987	33,500	(2,487)	70,286	71,000	714
Total costs	74,464	71,500	(2,964)	147,147	148,000	853

This performance report for department A is a simplified version of what John Smith, the manager, would probably receive. However, for our purposes it will suffice. The first point to notice is that all items of expenditure have a variance: some have brackets round them and others do not. The bracket around a variance means that the *variance is adverse* or unfavourable. An adverse expenditure variance arises when the actual expenditure exceeds the budgeted expenditure. A *favourable variance* has no bracket round it and represents the situation where actual expenditure is less than the expected, budgeted, expenditure. The second point we should look at is the significance of the variance, so that we can determine whether, applying management by exception, we ought to bother ourselves with investigating the variance. The level of significance, we have discussed several times already, is set by the organisation either intuitively or as a result of statistical analysis. We can assume the significance level for this department is 6% of budget. In this case, then, the only significant variance is the overheads variance: the variance is 7.42% of the budget of £33,500. John Smith will now have to look into the reason, or reasons, why this variance has arisen. Once the reasons are known, action may have to be taken to ensure that the variance does not arise again; or, if it does, that it is not as serious as this time.

Note that the direct materials variance for the year to date is not significant (although it is greater than 6% of the budget amount) since it has already been investigated in both January and/or February, as necessary.

The control aspects of budgetary control

By control we mean being able to direct something or someone to behave in the way we want. In terms of budgetary control, we aim to control the outcomes of our planning and target-setting exercise that led to the development and use of our budgets. Control, however, exists on many different levels, especially in a business setting. Drury (1988) and others start to discuss control by speaking in terms of a thermostat: an electromechanical device that is used, *inter alia*, for controlling central heating mechanisms, or the water temperature in a car engine. In the case of the thermostat, we have inputs, energy; we have a process, the boiler or engine; and we have an output, heat. The element of this procedure that Drury and others leave out is the aim or objective of the desired temperature: if there is no upper or lower limit to the temperature we are aiming to control, there is no need for a thermostat! One further aspect of the thermostat that we need to consider is the feedback loop. Again, there is no possibility of controlling the water temperature if no attempt is made to regulate some or all of the inputs, process and outputs. Hence, a thermostat has a feedback loop that works this way:

1. Switch on the central heating system.
2. The boiler operates (inputs and process) until the outputs have achieved the desired level (objectives).

3. Once the objective is achieved, close down the boiler but keep monitoring the desired temperature levels (feedback).
4. If the temperature falls below the desired level (feedback), switch back on the boiler until the desired temperature is reached again

See the example of a thermostat used in this context in Chapter 1 of this book. Note the interplay of all aspects of this system. Budgets can be viewed in the same way that the thermostat system operates insofar as we have objectives that have been translated into targets: value of sales, labour hours, kilogrammes of raw material. We have the inputs and processes that our organisation is set up to operate around: manufacturing, banking, word processing bureau. We have our outputs: goods, services. Once we have completed a budget period, we report on our findings to management: this is the beginning of the feedback loop. Having reported back to management, comparisons take place to evaluate how near to or how far away from the objectives and targets they were: we are monitoring just like the thermostat. Once we have agreed which variances away from budget need corrective action to be taken, we take it. Hence the feedback loop feeds back into the input cycle as relevant.

When we discussed the significance of variances above, we discussed them in terms of being adverse and favourable. We should emphasise the point that the level of significance applies to both positive and negative feedback scenarios. Many management accountants, textbooks and journal articles give the impression that favourable variances are good, whilst adverse variances are bad. This is too simplistic. When we talk in terms of management by exception, we say that we might set a level of significance of, say, 10% away from budget. We mean ±10%: emphasising the fact that both adverse and favourable variances that are found to be significant must be investigated and acted upon as necessary. There are many scenarios we could develop to prove the point we have just made, but it is not really necessary. Simply consider any situation you like and look at a favourable variance that is found to be significant: carry out a brainstorming exercise on this variance and before long you will arrive at a whole list of reasons why even favourable variances can have a negative impact on our organisation's wellbeing.

We can discuss now a feedforward control system. A feedforward system seeks to anticipate any deviations between the desired outcome and the actual outcome: thus avoiding any deviations. The main difference between the two systems, feedback and feedforward, is that the feedback system reacts to a situation: that is, it merely monitors the outputs of the process under review and reports back on it. The feedforward system monitors both the process and its outputs and the environment in which the process is operating. If we have an 'intelligent' thermostat, it may be programmed to operate under feedforward conditions. In this case its feedback will work its way into the input phase, the process phase, as well as back into the objective-setting phase. Any variable that is part of the process is subject to review and revision as necessary: not just the input phase. After all, we may be putting poor raw materials into process, the processing machinery might be faulty, or the manager who set the production targets may have programmed his or her spreadsheet wrongly.

Budgeting is a feedforward system, whilst budgetary control is a feedback system.

The amount and quality of corrective action that is and can be taken will vary according to circumstance, of course, but there is often a need for corrective action to be taken if our inputs and processes are considered to be out of control, or going out of control. If our budgetary controls have been badly estalished, we could be attempting to achieve our budget targets oblivious to the fact that our inventories are getting more and more out of control. If this is the case, and we agree that something is wrong, we need to correct for it. Obvious? Not always. Look at the Maxwell Communications Corporation (MCC): using the benefit of hindsight at least, it was obvious that something was clearly wrong with the accounting and other controls within that organisation long before it finally collapsed. However, nothing was done to correct the problems at MCC and so it went further and further out of control, to the great chagrin of a large number of people.

The way that organisations tend to use budgetary control systems is to establish a system of variance analysis, along the lines that we have already discussed. As we will see in Chapter 15, management accountants have a large array of variances at their disposal that allow them to break down the operations and processes of their organisation. Having broken down their organisation, the management accountant can then set about helping his or her management colleagues to control their operations. We have variances that help us control materials, in terms of prices and usage; variances that help us control people costs; and variances that help us control overheads, sales, and anything else for which we can establish standards. Such variances are known as operational variances and we will be working our way through them in Chapter 15.

Finally, we need to make ourselves fully aware that a budgeting and budgetary control system will achieve nothing unless it is properly used. Furthermore, unless the control aspects of budgetary control are fully appreciated and acted upon, little can change for the benefit of our organisation.

Budgeting can be implemented and/or improved at any time

CAMEO

The story which follows relates to a small 'high-tech' business in the United States. The article from which this story is taken is written by the company's accountant, Mr C. L. Grant.

The company was in "survival mode" when Grant joined the company: 'It was in desperate need of a management accounting budget.' Once the budget had been devised, the company developed three 'what if?' scenarios:

1. *Best case*: everything goes according to plan.
2. *Worst case*: nothing goes right.
3. *Most likely case*: a realistic mixture of 1 and 2.

Unlike large corporations, when we go through the options of how to spend money, we are still concerned about meeting payroll and cash flow . . . we need a quicker reaction time to turn projects on and off.

Consider, further, the case of the company which is expanding: it may be acquiring or developing a subsidiary, or its mainstream operations may be growing. If this company does not change its budgetary requirements, then the budgets it prepares will be severely flawed.

Reference: Grant (1991: 30–1).

The section that follows takes us away from the quantitative aspect of budgeting and budgetary control and into the area of the organisational and behavioural aspects of the subject: the qualitative aspects of budgeting and budgetary control. Whilst much has been written on the subject of the quantitative aspects of budgeting, budgetary control, corporate planning, the setting of objectives and so on, the qualitative aspects are, it seems, clear, less well known and understood by management accountants. There are still stories of budgets having been set that are considered foolish, a joke, unattainable . . . when the person or people who set those budgets were far from jocular types! Having said that, it is Hofstede who recommended that managers should treat budgetary control as less than serious . . . as a game!

Organisational goals

Ackoff defined objectives as desired outcomes of behaviour which may be unattainable but must be approachable within a planning period. Alternatively, he defined goals as objectives which must be attainable within the planning period but need not necessarily be attained. For example, my objective may be to be wealthy but my goal could be to earn a given sum in a given year. Furthermore an organisation is a social unit deliberately constructed to seek specific goals. In a sense, organisational goals may become self-perpetuating through a process of internalisation. That is, they may acquire an existence independent of the personal motives of the participants. Goals have been classified into two separate categories:

1. Goals **for** the organisation: products offered, range of customers served.
2. Goals **of the** organisation: future domains intended for the organisation by the dominant coalition.

Thus, goals, in these senses, reflect authority and power.

Organisational goals are established by individuals – but interdependent individuals who collectively have sufficient control of organisational resources to commit them in certain directions and to withhold them from others. This does not mean that all goals are set by top management only. For example, goals for the organisation can be set at a variety of levels, whereas goals of the organisation are the domain of senior management. We have spoken above of goals as if all goals are similar. However, goals do cover a very wide variety of aspects of a business. Hence, the classification shown in Table 14.5.

TABLE 14.5 *Organisational goals*

Societal goals	How to respond to society's needs and demands: pollution, recreation, safety.
Output goals	Kinds of products, business to be in, how many businesses to be in.
Systems goals	Operating characteristics: for example, productivity, stability.
Product characteristics	Safety characteristics and product goals quality (part of systems goals).
Derived goals	Support for political parties, provision of staff facilities

When setting objectives and preparing corporate plans and budgets, the management of an organisation quite commonly allow for these differences. We can see this more and more as organisations try to convince us of the environmental friendliness, for example, of their products and services. An organisation can be viewed as the centre of a complex process in which the conflicting aims of participants are managed on the basis of contractual relations. Goal congruence exists when the goals of the manager or worker are in accord with those of the organisation. For example, earning a satisfactory profit is a common goal for a business, but it is not possible to evaluate all units based on profitability. Therefore sub-goals have to be set, but ensuring these sub-goals match the primary goals can be difficult. Do goals evolve or are they static? If they evolve, how do they do so? A variety of models have been developed to try to answer these sorts of questions. With the entrepreneurial model, goals are set by entrepreneurs although a principal–agent relationship exists. Therefore, organisational participants agree with such goals in return for esteem, security, prestige, transfer of money. The entrepreneur is the principal and the employee is the agent in this relationship. This model implies the pre-eminence of the interests of one group (entrepreneurship) all the time.

The bargaining model shows organisations are more evenly balanced coalitions of participants, who can be both internal and external to the organisation. These participants may be further sub-divided into sub-coalitions: bargaining may take place between internal and/or external sub-coalitions. For example:

- *External* Quality considerations determined by customers.
- *Internal* Efficiency of employees determined by employees.

As environmental forces change, the dominant group or individual changes. In the case of a new business, the dominant force will be the owner of the business. As the product develops, engineers may gain dominance; and as long-term market share is enhanced, professional managers will become the dominant force. Quasi-resolution of conflict may be attained through a bargaining process involving the dominant coalition and other interest groups. For many years, economic theory stated that all firms have a prime objective: to maximise profits. More enlightened thought has shown a variety of such models exist, including:

1. *Profit maximisation models* Surveys have shown that profitability is the primary goal of 77% of large companies. (Although this does not necessarily relate to profit maximisation.)
2. *Managerial models* These models are concerned with the behaviour of the management of large firms where the management has a degree of latitude in directing the affairs of the corporation. Examples of such managerial models include sales revenue maximisation models and sales revenue growth models.
3. *Satisfying models* Such models attempt to explain goals setting behaviour in terms of levels of satisfaction achieved by organisations.

Dent found that in the United States 96% of companies have more than one goal and 80% of companies have more than four goals. For the purposes of a recent study, a UK based researcher (Belkaoui) tested 43 undergraduates on their reactions to tests in which there were varying degrees of certainty about the outcomes and in which there were varying levels of difficulty in achieving goals. Research shows that setting difficult goals leads to an improved level of performance over setting moderate or easy goals. However, the certainty of a task may be a moderating variable. Belkaoui (1990: 43) found, furthermore, that the more certain the task, the higher the performance *and* effort put into a job: However, 'To motivate task interest, some degree of task uncertainty seems to be beneficial.'

In contrast to Belkaoui's findings, several researchers have shown that uncertainty relating to the task to be performed leads to insecurity, loss of self-confidence, tension and reduced job satisfaction.

Stedry's analysis showed those with high budget targets where aspiration levels were set after receiving their budget, performed best of all, with the poorest performance coming from those who had set high budget targets with aspiration levels set before the budget was received. Hofstede, writing in 1968, also found that budgets only motivate significantly if they represent challenging targets which carry a risk that they will not be met. Indeed, it was Hofstede who first concluded, in terms of Europe at least that:

- Budgets have no motivational effect unless they are accepted by the managers involved as their own personal target.
- Up to the point where the budget target is no longer accepted, the more demanding the budget target, then the better are the results achieved; providing the targets are not too difficult to achieve.
- Managers' personalities play a role in the acceptance of budgets: some managers simply do not like budgets, others thrive on them.

It has long been argued that one of the primary goals, if not the primary goal, of a limited company is the maximisation of shareholder wealth. A great deal of material has been generated on the idea of shareholder wealth maximisation, and we should appreciate that it may be important to a consideration of organisational goals and budgetary control. However, there is now increasing evidence that the goal of shareholder wealth maximisation is either a myth or has been modified. Nevertheless, when dealing with an organisation, and in particular dealing with the establishment of objectives, plans and targets for that organisation, we need to make ourselves aware that shareholders are a vital group of people and institutions and that they need to be considered carefully when budgets are being prepared.

Budgets as pressure devices

Since Argyris's work in the early 1950s, budgets have been recognised as capable of being seen or used as pressure devices by superiors and subordinates alike. Argyris reported that employees seek ways to overcome the pressure by, for example, forming groups which often stay together when the pressure is removed. The reason postulated for the groups remaining together is that they may be anticipating future pressure. Argyris also reported that supervisors under pressure adopted one of three broad strategies:

1. blame other supervisors
2. blame budgeting staff, production staff, and sales staff;
3. internalise the pressure.

Becker and Green observed in the United States that 'imposed' budgets were used as an instrument of control over employees and that this resulted in some dissatisfaction. Emphasising budget attainment resulted in many employees being task centred and supervisors being department centred, overemphasising individual departments even to the detriment of the business as a whole. Hughes described budgetary control as an endless cycle characterised by continuous unresolved conflict between top management and lower management.

Participation in the budgeting process

McGregor, Coch and French, and many others have found that those who are able to participate in the budget-setting process had higher levels of productivity than those who were not so allowed. Similarly, those who did not participate were more likely to be dissatisfied with the organisation and to quit to seek alternative employment. According to Hirsch and Louderback (1986: 543), the benefits attributed to employee participation in the budgeting process are:

1. Employees who participate will be more likely to internalise the goals in the budget, to accept them because they had a hand in developing them. Participation should increase the commitment of employees to the budget.
2. Employees who participate in developing budgets are experiencing job enlargement. Their responsibilities are greater than those of employees who do not participate. Enlarging an employee's job should bring greater satisfaction and self-esteem.
3. Employees who participate are likely to have more positive attitudes toward the firm, which should lead to higher levels of performance and morale.

Whether participation is allowed for or not, there is always the danger of budgetary slack.

Budgetary slack

Budgetary slack is the building into budgetary estimates of an allowance over and above that necessary to achieve a given objective: such allowances include underoptimistic sales targets, overestimated expense levels, and so on. Cooper (1981: 187) states:

> Galbraith argues that organisations will inevitably but unconsciously increase slack resources or reduce performance standards if there is no conscious design strategy in the face of increasing complexity and environmental uncertainty.

CAMEO

A study of a retail store revealed the following:

1. When the reward system was based on performance, targets were set so that they were easy to achieve.
2. Company history shows sales growth as an important factor, therefore targets were submitted which showed further sales growth (even if this is unrealistic in the circumstances).
3. A manager's performance had been poor so he submitted targets which showed that his future performance would be good.

It has been found that if slack can be detected by superiors, greater emphasis is attached to meeting targets and greater participation in setting targets being allowed led to less slack being created.

Slack may be created deliberately or unintentionally. Estimates show that budgetary slack may account for as much as 20–25% of budgeted operating expenses. One report suggested that 80% of managers created slack in their budgets.

Alternative budgeting systems

In order for there to be an alternative budgeting system, there has to be an orthodox or accepted one. In this discussion, this orthodox system is known as incremental budgeting, and everything designated as an alternative will be seen to be different to that system. We will be discussing only two major alternative systems, zero base budgeting (ZBB) and programming, planning, budgeting, system (PPBS) although there are several alternatives which could be discussed. Having briefly described incremental budgeting, and the first two 'alternative' systems, we will discuss ZBB and PPBS in more detail.

Incremental budgeting is the type of budgeting system with which most people are familiar; and it is the system implied by CIMA's definition of a budget 'drawn up showing incremental effects on former budgeted or actual figures'. By the term 'incremental', we mean that something is increased by a factor over and above something else. In the context of budgeting, we usually mean that this period's budget allowance is x% greater (or less) than the previous period's. Thus, if my budget for last year for travel had been, say, £350, then, allowing for inflation of 10%, this year's allowance for travel will be £350 + (£350 × 10%) = £350 + 35 = £385. Within the guidelines of common sense and obvious and necessary changes, this is how the entire incremental budget is generated.

Rolling or continuous budgets are a variation on incremental budgets and are defined by CIMA (1991) as follows: 'A budget continuously updated by adding a further period, say a month or quarter and deducting the earliest period. Beneficial where future costs and/or activities cannot be forecast reliably.' With a rolling budget, there is always a year's budget available: we start with a year's budget covering the period January to December, for example and proceed as follows. At the end of January, we cross off January's budget and add on the budget for January for the following year. Thus we still have a year's budget available.

Sunset budgets are very common in governmental and international organisations. The term derives, very simply, from the idea that a project is set into motion on which the 'sun will set' after a predetermined time. That is, it will be a six-month, or 2-year, or 15-year project, and after this time, no further funding will take place, or the project will naturally be wound down. There are, however, many examples whereby, although the sun was intended to have set, circumstances had changed so much that further funding, or allowing the project to continue, was a good and viable proposition. Foreign aid and Third World development projects are examples of where sunset projects are easy to find.

The following two sections contain discussions of zero base budgeting (ZBB) and programming, planning, budgeting, system (PPBS) respectively. Whilst it is true that the implementation of both systems has not been too widespread throughout industry and commerce, they have both been successfully used in many organisations in their respective settings (profit-making organisations and non-profit-making organisations, respectively, in general).

The inclusion of these two systems here is justified on the grounds that both systems have a lot to offer as planning and controlling devices. The advantage of both systems is that they provide management with significant insights into their operations – insights that incremental budgeting simply cannot give. Both systems have significant disadvantages, otherwise they would probably have been implemented across a much broader spectrum of organisations than they have. The biggest disadvantage of both systems is the amount of resources that have to be applied to them. A more detailed review of ZBB than is being given here clearly reveals the amount of effort that is required in setting up the ZBB process each time it is used.

Zero base budgeting (ZBB)

The first point to note is that we are dealing with zero base budgeting, not zero-based budgeting. Many articles and books wrongly use the variant zero-based: this shows a lack of understanding. There is no such thing as 'zero-based budgeting'.

Zero base budgeting (ZBB) is defined by CIMA (1991) as: 'A method of budgeting whereby all activities are reevaluated each time a budget is set. Discrete levels of each activity are valued and a combination chosen to match funds available.'

The best known exponent of ZBB was President Jimmy Carter of the United States of America. Figure 14.2 shows a memorandum that was issued by the President shortly after he took office.

Attachment

Bulletin

No. 77–9
THE WHITE HOUSE
WASHINGTON

February 14, 1977

MEMORANDUM FOR THE HEADS OF EXECUTIVE DEPARTMENTS AND AGENCIES

During the campaign, I pledged that immediately after the inauguration I would issue an order establishing zero base budgeting throughout the Federal Government. This pledge was made because of the success of the zero base budget system adopted by the State of Georgia under my direction as Governor.

A zero base budgeting system permits a detailed analysis and justification of budget requests by an evaluation of the importance of each operation performed.

An effective zero base budgeting system will benefit the Federal Government in several ways. It will

- Focus the budget process on a comprehensive analysis of objectives and needs.
- Combine planning and budgeting into a single process.
- Cause managers to evaluate in detail the cost effectiveness of their operations.
- Expand management participation in planning and budgeting at all levels of the Federal Government.

The director of the Office of Management and Budget will review the Federal budget process for the preparation, analysis, and justification of budget estimates and will revise those procedures to incorporate the appropriate techniques of the zero base budgeting system. He will develop a plan for applying the zero base budgeting concept to preparation, analysis, and justification of the budget estimates of each department and agency of the Executive Branch.

I ask each of you to develop a zero base system within your agency in accordance with instructions to be issued by the Office of Management and Budget. The Fiscal Year 1979 budget will be prepared using this system.

By working together under a zero base budgeting system, we can reduce costs and make the Federal Government more efficient and effective.

Jimmy Carter

FIGURE 14.2 *White House memorandum*

The basic mechanics of zero base budgeting

The details of ZBB are beyond the scope of this book. The basis of the system, however, is that every time the budgeting process is carried out, every budget centre starts with a zero budget allocation – literally. If the system is being applied literally and fairly across the organisation, even the managing director's pet project starts with nothing. Once this has been established, the budget centre then builds up a budget – at a variety of levels such as minimum requirement to keep the centre operating at the lowest level of performance. The influence of flexible budgeting (see Chapter 15) is felt very strongly within this system. At the end of the budget preparation process, each proposal is voted on. So we would submit our proposals to our immediate superior and he or she would select the level of our operation he or she is prepared to support: nothing, minimum, minimum plus 10%, and so on. At the end of this stage, the next higher level of management will vote on the portfolios for which it is responsible. At the end of the line, the board of directors has before it a refined package of budgets that they wish to support.

Criticisms of zero base budgeting

Whilst ZBB has many stated advantages, there are several journal papers and books around which categorically deny that ZBB is in any way effective. The following is an extract from a chapter in a book aimed almost solely at destroying ZBB as a useful alternative budgeting system:

> there has been a substantial reallocation of financial resources within state government during Governor Carter's administration – especially during his first year of office.
>
> All the evidence suggests that ZBB played a negligible role ... there had been no apparent shifting of financial resources as a result of employing the ZBB system. This story is repeated across Texas, New Jersey and Delaware. (Hammond and Knott 1980: 61)

The rest of the chapter concentrates, negatively, on quotations and evidence (much of it anecdotal) which 'proves' that ZBB never works. It should be pointed out, however, that the book was written after only one year of ZBB being in operation in the Federal Government.

Florida Power and Light and ZBB

On a more optimistic note, comes a report from a US electricity utility where ZBB is reported as being a success. Early benefits of having installed the system are reported to be:

1. It can be used to control indirect labour and expenses.
2. It can be used effectively to require supervisors to set priorities on proposed new work.
3. It can be used as an effective communications tool to identify what was being done now that would not be done in the future and gain concurrence up the line that it was all right to stop it.
4. By applying resource constraints in forcing setting of priorities, we could squeeze out the low payoff work rather than keep it forever, and thereby protect our ability to limit growth in staff areas. (Dady 1979: 3)

Dady also gives guidance to those who feel they would like to install a system of ZBB.

(a) an orthodox sophisticated budgeting system must already be in place;
(b) MBO must run alongside ZBB;
(c) top management must be prepared to say 'No' to pet projects, even of other senior managers, which do not measure up.

Programming, Planning, Budgeting, System (PPBS)

PPBS involves the preparation of a long-term corporate plan which clearly establishes the objectives that the organisation aims to achieve. These objectives do not necessarily follow the existing organisational structure. For example, a local authority provides many different services. The provision of these activities may be undertaken by separate departments, such as housing, parks and gardens, recreation. A programme budget cuts across departmental barriers by providing estimates of a programme rather than these estimates being included within the two ... three ... four ... or more budgets for each of the departments which have an input into the service being provided. It takes a matrix view of organisations. The aim of PPBS is to enable the management of non-profit-making organisations to take more informed decisions about the allocation of resources to meet the overall objectives of the organisation. The first stage in the process is to review the organisational objectives for the activities which it performs. Stage two involves identifying programmes which can be undertaken to achieve the organisation's objectives. The third stage involves identifying and evaluating alternative methods of achieving the objectives for each specific programme. The final stage is to select the appropriate programmes on the basis of cost/benefit principles.

> PPBS forces management to identify the activities, functions or programmes to be provided, thereby establishing a basis for evaluating the worthiness of the programme. In addition, PPBS provides information which will enable management to assess the effectiveness of its plans. The programme structure should correspond to the principal objectives of the organisation and enable management to focus on the organisation's output (the objectives to be achieved) rather than just on the inputs (resources available to be used). (Drury 1988:) 468–9

Activity-based budgeting

As we saw in Chapters 6 and 7, activity-based costing and activity-based costing management (ABC and ABCM) have much to offer modern management and modern management accountants. Not the least of the areas in which the management accountant can apply his or her ABC and ABCM skills is in the area of budgeting: activity-based budgeting (ABB). Again, as with ABC itself, there is nothing in ABB that we do not already know. As we should expect, ABB is the application of ABC and ABCM principles in a budgetary control setting. Consequently, any exercise, whether in a textbook or in reality, concerning the application of ABB simply follows ABC principles and guidelines. Any of the exercises we worked through in Chapters 6 and 7 that applied to ABC could be reworked in this chapter as if they were budgeting exercises. The benefits of ABB, of course, are that by applying all of the principles of ABC and ABCM to budgeting and budgetary control, we gain greater insight into our organisation than we otherwise would. ABB allows us to establish budgeted values for activities and for cost drivers. Having established all of the values for activities and drivers, we then have the basis for ABB and ABCM.

Contingency budgeting

By contingency budgeting, we mean that each organisation or group of organisations has features and factors unique to it which mean, in the current context, that its budgetary control systems are contingent upon them. A manufacturer of wallpaper has systems and procedures that are different to the systems and procedures of a manufacturer of gloss and emulsion house paint. Hence, given the differences between organisations, we expect systems and procedures to be different. This is the contingency effect. A reading of management accounting texts, journal articles and case studies will reveal that there are many budgeting systems in use throughout the world. The few that we have considered above are the ones that are most commonly used and discussed. Many budgeting systems are idiosyncratic in that they are based on principles and guidelines drafted by the management of an organisation for its own use and understanding. Idiosyncratic budgeting systems include back-of-an-envelope type budgeting systems that we might easily come across in very small organisations!

Large organisations in particular have budgeting systems that have been designed with their own organisation in mind and which might not be found elsewhere. This will be especially true of organisations that work in unique environments: banks and building societies come to mind here. With banks and buildings societies, we are dealing with relatively few organisations nationwide, and yet they have budgeting systems that are designed to fit each of their own requirements. The specific application of budgeting in a bank will be radically different to that of a manufacturer of ceramic tableware, for example – except for cash budgeting, perhaps. Cash budgeting is one aspect of budgeting that is common to all budgeting systems, whether they be a profit-making organisation or not, a manufacturer or not. Not only do banks have their own budgeting requirements, but the forms and procedures they use are also unique to them. As we would expect, working through the requirements of the budgeting procedures and budgetary control system itself, almost every organisation we would care to look at will have its own inputs and outputs in terms of raw data and actual data.

The exceptions to the uniqueness of budgeting requirements might come when organisations are using the same computer software as each other. In the case of two organisations using the same bookkeeping, accounting and finance software package, the forms they generate and use will be similar if not the same. Of course, there are exceptions to this generalisation: for example, when the two organisations are using the same package, but organisation A has had its version adapted for its own contingency factors, its forms and procedures could easily be different to those of organisation B.

Flexible budgeting and standard costing

We have spoken in this chapter about budgeting and budgetary control in terms that allow us to accept all outputs from such systems. The reality is that, as presented here, budgeting and budgetary control have their limitations. One of the most serious limitations that budgeting and budgetary control have relates to the volume of output. If we take an elementary example, we can see the problems that budgeting systems have with levels of volume.

WORKED EXAMPLE 14.5

Bass Ltd is a pencil manufacturer and one extract from their cost accounting records show that their budget for manufacturing overheads is £120,000 for the year: this amount accrues evenly over the year. Bass's performance report for May shows:

	Actual	Budget	Variance
Sales	xxx	xxx	xxx
Direct materials	xxx	xxx	xxx
Direct labour	xxx	xxx	xxx
Direct expenses	xxx	xxx	xxx
Manufacturing overheads (£)	13,500	10,000	3,500 adv
Units made in the month	50,000	45,000	5,000 fav

where:

adv means adverse or unfavourable;
fav means favourable

Required

Comment on Bass Ltd's performance report for May.

Solution to Worked example 14.5

In terms of variance analysis, from the reporting to and from management of the deviations from budget for a period, we see that manufacturing overheads are overspent by £3,500 for the period. However, we also notice that we made 5,000 units more in the period than the budget had anticipated. What should we make of this situation? Flexible budgeting, the subject of the next chapter, helps us with the solution to this problem. In anticipation of Chapter 15, we can solve Bass's problem here quite simply.

Flexible budgeting: elementary example

We are told that the fixed cost element of manufacturing overheads is £3,000 for the month. The revised performance report for Basss Ltd is as follows:

	Actual	Budget	Variance
Manufacturing overheads	12,500	11,000	(1,500)
Units made in the month	50,000	40,000	(10,000)
Fixed costs	3,000	3,000	
Variable costs as per performance report	9,500	8,000	(1,500)
Flexible budget variable costs (based on manufacture of 50,000 units)	9,500	10,000	500

When we rework the variable cost element of the performance report, we base the calculation on the actual volume of production that was achieved, not the amount that was budgeting during the budgeting process. This gives us the flexible budget amount. The calculation is:

$$\frac{\text{variable budgeted overhead}}{\text{budgeted output}} \times \text{actual output}$$

$$= \frac{£11{,}000 - 3{,}000}{40{,}000 \text{ units}} \times 50{,}000 \text{ units}$$

$$= £10{,}000$$

We can now conclude that, taking a more realistic view, the true variances our management colleagues need to consider show that there are no variances on fixed manufacturing costs; but the variable costs are now found to be £500 favourable, not £1,500 adverse. For the full implications of this, turn to the next chapter.

CAMEO

The Barings débâcle, management control and the wine chemist

Controls failed, audits were ineffective and the Bank of England erred in judgement

That was the subheading of an article that appeared in *The Times* on 19 July 1995. The article was discussing the official report into the Barings Bank collapse that was caused by one of its traders, Nick Leeson, based in Singapore, who was allowed to trade without let or hindrance. By the time Barings Bank had collapsed, Mr Leeson had overstretched Barings by an amount in excess of £825 million. Whilst there are many facets to the Barings collapse, we are concerned here with the aspects of management control that come through this case.

> Mr Leeson had no authority to maintain open positions overnight. He was given certain specific limits on intraday trading. He had no authority to trade in options (save as execution broker on behalf of clients). (The Times, 19 July 1995, p. 9)

However, all reports indicate that senior managers within Barings had some idea of what was going on, yet they did nothing to prevent Mr Leeson working outside the bounds of his terms of reference. In August 1994, six months or so before Barings finally collapsed, Barings' internal auditors warned its senior executives of 'significant risk' that Leeson was putting Barings under.

If we were privy to all the facts of the Barings/Leeson case, we would determine the extent of the controls imposed on traders like Leeson. As it is, we can only speak in general terms. In terms of budegary control and management control, there is a very simple message to be learned here: namely, that it is simply not enough merely to install a system of controls – those controls also have to be made to work. So, it is clear that all of the work we have done so far would come to naught if we did not operate budgetary control, with the emphasis on the control aspects.

On a much less grand scale, there is the story of the wine chemist who was overseeing the introduction of a new wine into the range being offered by a UK-based wines and spirits bottler. This wine chemist's boss was an overbearing, powerful man who wanted the new wine introduced under almost any circumstances. Hence, the chemist did one thing and told his boss and his cost accountant another. The chemist began to operate like Leeson, without any regard for the controls under which he should have been operating. However, since the accountant had all of the control data – wine recipe, throughput times and so on – he knew by the end of the first two accounting periods that the new wine was a financial problem. A meeting between cost accountant, overbearing boss and wine chemist resolved the issues. From the cost accountant's point view the issue centred around the use of budgetary and standard costing controls. From the boss's point of view, he was more interested in the control of his wine chemist . . . !

Putting the two stories together we see the benefits and deficiencies of management, budgetary and standard costing controls. Without anyone monitoring and reporting on performance, with reference to the contol limits imposed, managers, traders and wine chemists are likely to exceed their authority, limits of operating, and so on. Merely setting limits is not sufficient: they have to be policed.

SUMMARY

This concludes our introduction to budgeting and budgetary control. In this chapter we have discussed a very wide range of issues, including the behavioural and technical aspects of budgeting.

As far as the behavioural aspects of budgeting are concerned, we have reviewed much of current theory and practice to discover that it is not merely sufficient to prepare a budget, or series of budgets, and hope that this will solve many of an organisation's problems. We know that people react to budgets in differing ways, and the structure of organisations vary, and such variations are important in assessing the budgeting procedures that should be adopted. When we discussed the technical aspects of budgeting we started by seeing the need for budgeting. Although medium- and large-sized organisations have relatively very complex budgeting procedures, manuals and reports, the essence of the work we did in this chapter covers the principles that such organisations should follow.

In this chapter we have appreciated that it is not only industrial concerns which can benefit from budgeting: commercial organisations and non-profit-making organisation, as well as individuals, of course, all benefit from having prepared budgets and operating a system of budgetary control. There are, however, organisations known to each of us that have never considered, and may never even in the future consider, implementing a budgetary control system. If the organisation is relatively small, and the management is sufficiently close to the operation of daily events, there is a good chance that the organisation will survive. Nevertheless, there are organisations that do not use a system of budgetary control, where the management is aware of what happens on a day-to-day basis, but the orginsation is run more by instinct than by proper planning and procedures. In the latter situation, management is known to sign cheques even when it is aware that there may or may not be any money to cover that cheque today, tomorrow, the day after tomorrow . . . who can tell?

We also had a look at some of the organisational and behavioural theory surrounding budgetary control. We know that some managers react badly to the sight of a budget; others welcome a budget as a comforter. Some managers take a pride in beating the budget: Scrooge is a role model for them! Hofstede's work on budget complexity, Argyris's work on participation, and so on, all demonstrate the human side of budgetary control. Even though much of this chapter dwells on the quantitative side of budgeting and budgetary control, anyone who has ever used them knows this is only one aspect. The human side of the contents of this chapter are important.

Finally, we had a very brief look at flexible budgeting, partly by way of an introduction to the work of the next chapter, but primarily as a statement which says that although budgeting and budgeting control has a great deal to offer all organisations, we need to be wary of how we interpret the outputs from our budgeting systems.

KEY TERMS

You should satisfy yourself that you have noted all of these terms and can define and/or describe their meaning and use, as appropriate.

Budget (p. 452)	Interrelationships of budgets (p. 459)
Budgetary control (p. 452)	Functional budgets (p. 464)
Limiting factor (p. 453)	Variance analysis (p. 476)
Behavioural aspects of budgeting (p. 456)	Participation (p. 483)
Master budget (p. 456)	Incremental budgeting (p. 484)
Planning cycle (p. 457)	Zero base budgeting (p. 484)
Corporate planning (p. 457)	Programming, planning, budgeting, system (p. 484)
Short-term planning (p. 457)	Activity-based budgeting (p. 488)
Cash budget (p. 457)	Contingency budgeting (p. 488)

RECOMMENDED READING

For an update on much classical work on the behavioural side of budgeting read Belkaoui (1990). Colville (1989) is not well written, but gives a realistic insight. Jones and Pendlebury (1984) is much better written than Colville, but may be a little advanced for the general reader. DuPree (1987) is essential reading, while Pyhhr (1970) is the classic in this area.

QUESTIONS

Review questions

1. What is the link between responsibility accounting and budgetary control?

2. What is a budget?
3. Discuss the common pitfalls of the way in which the management accountant has historically communicated with his fellow managers.
4. Define each of the following:

   (a) planning cycle;
   (b) budget period;
   (c) budget committee;
   (d) budget manual; and
   (e) budget centre.

5. In what ways can budgets be interrelated? Give examples.
6. What is a master budget?
7. What are the behavioural aspects of budgeting concerned with?
8. Are the 'alternative budgeting systems' really alternative?

Answers to review questions 2, 3, 5 and 8 can be found in the Student Workbook.

Graded practice questions

Level I

1. Umapathy (1987) discusses the findings to a research project based on the following two questions:

   (a) Are the budgetary practices in successful firms different from those in unsuccessful firms?
   (b) Is there a systematic approach to improving budgetary effectiveness?

   What are his findings?

2. To what extent is the budgetary control system employed by organisations part of the planning aspect of a manager's work?
3. At the beginning of August the Carpet 'n' Rug Company had 100,000 square metres of rugs and 400,000 kg of raw materials on hand. Budgeted sales for the next three months are as follows:

August	200,000 sq. m.
September	180,000 sq. m.
October	150,000 sq. m.

The company wants to have sufficient raw material on hand at the end of each month to meet 50% of the following month's production requirement and sufficient square metres of finished products on hand at the end of each month to meet 40% of the following month's sales. Five kg of raw materials are required to produce each square metre of carpeting. The standard cost per kg of raw materials is £1.5.

   (a) Prepare a production budget for August and September.
   (b) Prepare a purchases budget in units and £s for August.

4. Draw up a cash budget for Dan E. Ell from the following information for the six months ended 30 June 1994:

   (a) Opening cash (including the bank account) balance is £800.
   (b) Production in units:

1993			1994						
Oct.	Nov.	Dec.	Jan.	Feb.	Mar.	Apr.	May	June	July
300	400	460	540	700	640	560	500	420	380

(c) Raw materials used in production cost £3 per unit. Of this, one-third is paid one month before production and two-thirds in the same month as production.
(d) Direct labour costs of £5 per unit of production are payable in the same month as production.
(e) Variable expenses are £4 per unit of production, payable three-quarters in the same month as production and one-quarter in the month following production.
(f) Sales at £15 per unit; sales in units:

1993			1994					
Oct.	Nov.	Dec.	Jan.	Feb.	Mar.	Apr.	May	June
240	360	480	580	620	720	680	520	360

Debtors pay their accounts: one-fifth as a deposit in the month of the sale and the remainder two months later.

(g) Fixed expenses are £300 per month payable each month.
(h) Extensions to the premises costing £6,000 are to be paid for in February 1994.

Level II

5. From the detail presented below, you are required to prepare:

(a) a cash budget for the three months ended 31 March;
(b) a budgeted income statement for the period ended 31 March; and
(c) a budgeted balance sheet as at 31 March

(i) ABC plc issued 100,000 £1 shares on 1 January.
(ii) Fixtures were purchased and paid for on 1 January for £20,000.
(iii) 10 machines costing £2,000 each were purchased on 1 January: a deposit of £500 each is paid. The balance is paid off at £1,000 per month, commencing January.
(iv) An initial stock of goods is bought on 1 January at a cost of £40,000 (£2 per unit). This purchase price is static throughout and the level of stock maintained (suppliers are paid during the month following purchase).
(v) All sales are on credit at £4 per unit.
(vi) Estimated sales are:

January	8,000 units
February	9,000 units
March	10,000 units

Debtors will pay during the second month after sales.
(vii) Administration expenses are expected to be 20% of sales.

6. The Victoria Hospital is located in a holiday resort which attracts visitors to such an extent that the population of the area is trebled for the summer months of June, July, and August. From past experience this influx of visitors doubles the activity of the hospital during these months. The annual budget for the hospital's laundry department is broken down into four quarters, that is, April–June, July–September, October–December and January–March by dividing the annual budgeted figures by four. This budgeting work has been done for the current year by

the secretary of the hospital using the previous year's figures and adding 16%. It is realised by the hospital authority that management information for control purposes needs to be improved and you have been recruited to help introduce a system of responsibility accounting.

Required

From the information given:

(a) Comment on the way in which the quarterly budgets have been prepared and suggest improvements which could be introduced when preparing budgets for 1979/80.
(b) State what information you would like to flow from the actual against budget comparison (NB: calculated figures are *not* required).
(c) State the amendments that would be needed to the current practice of budgeting and reporting to enable the report below to be used as a measure of the efficiency of the laundry manager.

Report

Victoria Hospital – Laundry Department

Report for quarter ended 30 September 1978

	Budget	Actual
Patient days	9,000	12,000
Weight processed, (lbs)	180,000	240,000
Costs:	£	£
Wages	8,800	12,320
Overtime premium	1,400	2,100
Detergents and other supplies	1,800	2,700
Water, water softening and heating	2,000	2,500
Maintenance	1,000	1,500
Depreciation of plant	2,000	2,000
Manager's salary	1,250	1,500
Overhead apportioned:		
for occupancy	4,000	4,250
for administration	5,000	5,750

(CIMA Cost Accounting 1)

7. Tomm Ltd has three manufacturing departments. One of these is regarded, for responsibility accounting purposes, as a cost centre, whereas the other two are classified as profit centres. Cost centre I (CCI) produces two joint products, P12 and P13. P12 is processed further in profit centre 2 (PC2) to yield P2. P13 is processed further in profit centre 3 (PC3) to yield P3.

The draft budgets for the three departments are as follows:

	Departments CC1	PC2	PC3
Budgeted output	20,000 kg of P12 40,000 kg of P13	40,000 units of P2	20,000 units of P3
	£'000	£'000	£'000
Budgeted sales revenue	0	1600	800
Cost of goods sold:			
Bought in raw material	100	20	30
Internal transfers	−600	200	400
Direct labour	120	150	110
Processing cost	150	115	145
Administrative salaries	55	135	150
General overhead allocation	175	30	15
		650	850
Budgeted profit (loss)	0	950	(50)

The processing costs can by analysed as follows:

	Departments CCI	PC2	PC3
	£'000	£'000	£'000
Variable			
Identifiable with individual departments and varying with output	120	20	5
Fixed			
Identifiable with individual departments and controllable by departmental management	25	90	130
Central computer services not controllable by departmental management, but allocated on basis of floor area	5	5	10

If the centrally provided computer facilities were obtained from outside the organisation on an individual basis by the individual departments, it is estimated that this would cost:

CCI	PC2	PC3
£'000	£'000	£'000
25	20	5

The costs of CCI have been allocated to PC2 and PC3 on the basis of the weight of material transferred during the period. This basis has been used in the past, but it is now being questioned as it seems to bias the figures in favour of PC2. An investigation of this, and other aspects of the budgeting system, has been undertaken and the following recommendations have been made:

(a) Fixed and variable costs should be separated in the budgets.
(b) Controllable and uncontrollable costs should be clearly distinguished.
(c) Joint costs (both fixed and variable) should be allocated so that both profit centres show the same profit rate (as a percentage of sales value).
(d) Central computer costs should be allocated in a manner which recognises the cost savings achieved by using a central facility.

Required

You are required to redraft the budget in a way that conforms to these recommendations. Make (and state) any assumptions that you consider necessary or appropriate.

ACCA 2.4 Management Accounting
December 1986

Solutions to practice questions 2, 4 and 7 can be found in the Student Workbook. Solutions to practice question numbers in red can be found at the end of this book.

Projects

1. Jain (1989) discusses the approach being taken to budgeting for the operations of a sugar cane farm in Jamaica. Apply what Jain says to your own organisation, or to any organisation that you choose to study.
   Look at the budgetary control system you are studying under the headings suggested by Jain's article:

- Objectives
- Available resources
- Limiting factor
- Sensitivity analysis
- Variety of budgets prepared
- Checking validity

2. Conduct a survey of two or three organisations in each of industry, commerce, and the non-profit-making sectors, and determine the extent to which the management of these organisations is using a system of budgetary control.

Also attempt to assess how effective the managers of the organisations you have chosen to study consider the system of budgetary control they are using.

REFERENCES

Ashford, J. K. (1989), 'Management accounting process in non profit making organisations', *Management Accounting* (CIMA) (December), 36–7.

Belkaoui, A. (1990) 'The effects of goal setting and task uncertainty on task outcomes', *Management Accounting Research* vol. 1, pp. 91–100.

CIMA (1991), *Management Accounting Official Terminology* (Chartered Institute of Management Accountants).

Colville, I. (1989), 'Scenes from a budget or: helping the police with their accounting enquiries', *Financial Accountability and Management*, 5 (2)(Summer), 89–106.

Cooper, D. (1981), 'A sociological and managerial view of management accounting' in Bromwich and Hopwood (eds), *Essays in British Accounting Research* (Pitman).

Dady, B. L. (1979), 'How Florida power and light installed ZBB', *Management Accounting* (NAA) (March), 31–4.

Drury, J. C. (1988), *Management and Cost Accounting*, 2nd edn (Van Nostrand Reinhold).

DuPree, J. M. (1987), 'How management accountants can communicate better', *Management Accounting* (US) (February), 40–3.

Grant, C. L. (1991), 'High tech budgeting', *Management Accounting* (NAA) (May), 30–1.

Hammond, T. H. and Knott, J. E. (1980), *A Zero Based Look at Zero Base Budgeting* (Transaction Books).

Hirsch, M. L. and Louderback, J. G. (1986), *Cost Accounting: Accumulation, analysis and use* (Kent Publishing Company).

Jain, S. K. (1989), 'Budgeting for a sugar cane farm', *Management Accounting* (CIMA) (September), 40–2.

Jones, R. and Pendlebury, M. (1984), *Public Sector Accounting* (Pitman).

Morse, W. J. and Roth, H. P. *Cost Accounting: processing, evaluating, and using cost data*, 3rd edn (Addison-Wesley).

Pyhrr, P. A. (1970), 'Zero-base budgeting', *Harvard Business Review* (Nov–Dec.) 99–109.

Straat, E. B. Information needs in an era of change. From The control function outside the business organisation . . . 329–39.

Umapathy, S. (1987), 'How successful firms budget', *Management Accounting* (NAA) (February), 25, 27.

CHAPTER FIFTEEN

Flexible budgeting and standard costing

CHAPTER OBJECTIVES

After reading this chapter you should be able to:

- discuss the link between flexible budgeting and marginal costing
- appreciate the relationship between flexible budgeting and standards
- appreciate the reasons for variances
- analyse the fixed overhead variances
- discuss the standard setting process
- appreciate the role of normal activity in the setting of fixed overhead rates
- calculate the total standard cost of a product
- prepare a standard manufacturing cost summary

Introduction

As we saw at the end of the previous chapter, unless we take changes in volume into account we could be convinced that budgeting and budgetary control are the panacea for all managerial ills. We could easily be fooled into thinking that by identifying variances and acting on the significant ones, we are likely to solve all of our organisation's problems quickly and effectively. Because we appreciate this problem, however, in this chapter we cover both flexible budgeting and standard costing, and not just standard costing by itself. A lot of standard costing variances stem directly from the nature and behaviour of flexible budgeting. Once we have appreciated the underlying nature of flexible budgeting, we will then be in an excellent position to move on to a full discussion of standard costing and variance analysis.

We will also discuss, in this chapter, the relationship between flexible budgeting and variable costing. Whilst we will not dwell on this link, we ought to be aware of it since in reality the two aspects of management accounting are likely to be found together.

Flexible budgeting defined

Taking allowance of volume differences is known as flexible budgeting, which is defined as: 'A budget which, by recognising different cost behaviour patterns, is designed to change as volume of output changes' (CIMA 1991). A flexible budget is defined as: 'The budgeted cost ascribed to the level of activity achieved in a budget centre in a control period.

It comprises variable costs in direct proportion to volume achieved and fixed costs as a proportion of the annual budget' (ibid.). CIMA gives the alternative title of budget cost allowance to the flexed budget.

Example of flexible budgeting

When we prepared the budget for a business before the budget period actually got under way, we set the hours and costs of the maintenance of plant and machinery for a period as we see in Table 15.1. Based on the work of the previous chapter, we would prepare a performance report for this situation as shown in Table 15.2.

TABLE 15.1 ***Budget and actual figures for maintenance of plant and machinery***

40,000 hours production time

	£
Fixed costs	800
Variable costs	1,200
Total costs	2,000

Now that we have arrived at, and concluded, the period to which the budget relates, we find the actual figures to be as follows:

48,000 hours production time

	£
Fixed costs	800
Variable costs	1,400
Total costs	2,200

TABLE 15.2 ***Fixed budget performance report (£)***

	Actual	Budget	Variance
Maintenance	2,200	2,000	(200)

This budget may be known as the fixed budget. The adverse variance of £200 is 10% of the budgeted amount and, assuming a significance level of, say, 6%, we would need to investigate why that difference has arisen. One of the factors that the investigators will discover when they look into the reasons for the variance is that the budget allowed for 40,000 hours' production time to be worked, whereas 48,000 production hours were actually worked (that is, actual output is 20% higher than the budgeted output). This is important because of its influence on the variable costs of the department. By definition, variable costs vary with output; and since the actual output is 20% higher than the budgeted output, the variable costs can be expected to be radically different to the budgeted variable costs prepared during the budgeting process. In the case of the maintenance costs, the flexible budget performance report is found in Table 15.3.

TABLE 15.3 ***Flexible budget performance report (£)***

	Actual	Flexible	Variance
Maintenance	2,200	2,240	40

Note: The flexible budget amount is made up as follows:

	£
Fixed costs	800
Variable costs $\frac{48{,}000 \times £1{,}200}{40{,}000}$	= 1,440
Total costs	2,240

Only the variable costs are flexed to allow for the differences arising because of volume differences: fixed costs remain fixed!

A flexible budget can only be constructed *after* the period to which it relates has finished, and the actual output levels are known. So now, having fully allowed for the influence of the differing levels of output between budget and actual, we can see that the variance has changed from being 10% of the total budgeted cost to less than 2% – much less significant. The flexible budget gives a fairer representation of the period's results because the variable costs are made to relate directly to the level of output which was actually attained. The flexible budget report gives us a much more realistic insight into the performance of a department or an organisation than does the fixed budget report. By allowing for actual levels of output rather than possibly unrealistic levels of output, we are comparing like with like: that is, we are looking at two sets of information that are closely related, rather than two sets of data that may be grossly unrelated. The flexing of a budget for differences in levels of output gets rid of the influence of volume, but it does not get rid of any other influences. The other influences that will remain in the results of a department's performance include: materials, labour costs per unit or per hour, labour efficiency, power consumption, costs associated with buying and running fixed assets, and so on.

Flexible budgeting and variable costing

Since flexible budgeting concerns itself with the effects of changes of volume of activity on both fixed and variable costs, we can usefully consider linking flexible budgeting with variable costing. We should be careful to note that we do not need to employ variable costing in order to use flexible budgeting, but we should be aware of the possible links.

WORKED EXAMPLE 15.1

From the following information prepare fixed and flexible budgetary control statements using the variable costing approach:

	Per unit based on a budget of 1,000 units	Actual for the period 1,100 units
	£	£
Sales	25	28,600
Direct materials	9	10,450
Direct labour	10	10,920
Variable overheads	1	1,300
Contribution	5	5,930
Fixed overhead	2	2,500
Profit	3	3,430

Solution to Worked example 15.1

There are two aspects to this solution. First, the fixed budget has been prepared to allow us to see clearly the differences that can arise when the flexible budgeting system is *not* in place; and secondly, the statements are presented in the variable costing format.

Fixed budget statement

	Per unit based on a budget of	Fixed budget	Actual for the period	Variance
Units	1,000	1,000	1,000	
		£	£	£
Sales	25	25,000	28,600	3,600

Direct materials	9	9,000	10,450	(1,450)
Direct labour	10	10,000	10,920	(920)
Variable overheads	1	1,000	1,300	(300)
Contribution	5	5,000	5,930	930
Fixed overhead	2	2,000	2,500	(500)
Profit	3	3,000	3,430	430

Workings

To get from the per unit budget data to the fixed budget column, all that needs to happen is for us to multiply the per unit costs by the number of units that the fixed budget has been based on: 1,000 units in this case. For example:

The fixed budget sales are:

1,000 units × £25 per unit = £25,000

similarly, the total fixed budget direct materials cost is:

1,000 units × £9 per unit = £9,000

The variance column is included since we are being required to prepare a budgetary control statement, and a variance column must be part of such a statement. Table 15.4 shows the variances as a percentage of the fixed budget. Assuming for the sake of argument, a 20% exception level, all variances except the direct labour variance are exceptional and would need to be investigated. We can use Table 15.4 to help us with our analysis of these variances.

TABLE 15.4 ***Variances as a percentage of the fixed budget***

	Variance percentages
Sales	−14.40
Direct materials	−16.11
Direct labour	−9.20
Variable overheads	−30.00
Contribution	18.60
Fixed overhead	−25,00
Profit	14.33

The flexible budget, based on the number of units actually produced during the period, is shown in Table 15.5.

TABLE 15.5 ***Flexible budget statement***

	Per unit (based on a budget of 1,000) £	Flexible budget (1,100 units) £	Actual for the period (1,100 units) £	Variance £
Sales	25	27,500	28,600	1,100
Direct materials	9	9,900	10,450	(550)
Direct labour	10	11,000	10,920	80
Variable Overheads	1	1,100	1,300	(200)
Contribution	5	5,500	5,930	430
Fixed overhead	2	2,000	2,500	(500)
Profit	3	3,500	3,430	(70)

In terms of the workings, Table 15.5 is different in only one respect to the fixed budget statement, and that is that **the number of flexible budget units is the same as the actual number of units**: Remember, this is one of the key foundations of flexible budgeting. The other key foundation is that the fixed costs remain the same as they were in the fixed budget – fixed costs do not vary in relation to changes in output. So, for example, the flexible budgeted sales amount is:

1,100 actual units sold × £25 per unit = £27,500

and the flexible budgeted direct materials amount is:

1,100 actual units made × £9 per unit = £9,900

The flexible budget variances are radically different to the fixed budget statement variances; and this is confirmed by the percentage variation from budget that we see below in Table 15.6. From this table we can see that instead of all but one variance being significant, with a significant level of 20%, only one variance is significant: the fixed overhead. All other variances have changed dramatically from the values given by the fixed budget statement.

TABLE 15.6 ***Variances as a percentage of the flexible budget***

	Variance percentages
Sales	4.00
Direct materials	−5.56
Direct labour	0.73
Variable overheads	−18.18
Contribution	7.82
Fixed overhead	−25.00
Profit	−2.00

Flexible budgeting only explains volume effects

We have flexed a budget in terms of its volume, as we should. This only takes care of the variations between the fixed and flexible budget for reasons of volume effect. Whilst adjusting for changes in volume is a valid thing to do, there are usually many more variables at work in an organisation than just volume of output and sales. The rest of this discussion on flexible budgeting will highlight some of the other reasons for variations between budgeting and the actual outturn. This will lead us into standard costing.

Standards and standard costing

In the examples we have dealt with in this chapter we have used such items as unit selling prices, unit costs and other unit-based information. These unit-based pieces of information are standards, and a standard is: 'A predetermined measurable quantity set in defined conditions' (CIMA 1991).

By a predetermined measurable quantity, we mean precisely what we have been seeing: by means of detailed analyses of all of our operations, we have a very good idea what our selling price per unit will be, the standard selling price; we know what our material cost per unit should be, the standard material cost; and so on. Since we are generating these standards as part of the budgeting process, they are, by definition, predetermined: that is, set in advance. The term 'standard' is a general term; it can cover any eventuality. A standard cost is:

> A standard expressed in money. It is built up from an assessment of the value of cost elements. Its main uses are providing bases for performance measurement, control by exception reporting, valuing stock and establishing selling prices. (ibid.)

As far as this definition is concerned, we have already seen some of its aspects: performance measurement, and exception reporting. We have not yet seen how we can build up a standard cost 'from an assessment of the value of cost elements'. In terms of valuing stock, once we know all other aspects of this definition, together with what we have learned in several previous chapters of this book, this will become apparent.

In assessing standards, we also need one further definition before we progress. A standard hour is: 'The quantity of work achievable at standard performance in an hour or minute' (ibid.). A standard hour is *not* 60 minutes: it is 1,000 units, or 200 square metres, or 5 cars made. For example, if, working at standard performance (working at an average rate of output for the relevant grade of labour) I can mix 100 kilogrammes of cement in 15 minutes, and, in one working day I actually mix, say, 350 kilogrammes of cement, then I have achieved:

$$\frac{350 \text{ kg}}{100 \text{ kg}}$$

$$= 3.5 \text{ standard hours}$$

We might have attended work for eight hours to mix that amount of cement, but at a standard rate of performance, we have achieved 3.5 standard hours. Precisely how we arrive at the standard rate of performance is a matter for work measurement and work study. We will be assuming that these departments have done their work and have established standards for us. For production standards, such as rates of output from the factory, we would rely on the production departments.

Standards and flexible budgeting

This discussion now takes us back to budgeting. In the examples we have already seen, we have concerned ourselves only with total sales, total material costs, total labour costs, and so on. Whilst we are interested in these total costs, a consideration of standard costs and hours means that we can take a two-level view of an organisation. The two-level view means we look at both the unit-based information and the total information concerning our organisation. Consider the following example.

WORKED EXAMPLE 15.2

Analyse the variance in the following statement:

Flexible budget statement

	Fixed budget	Flexible budget	Actual for the period	Variance
Units	160,000	200,000	200,000	
	£	£	£	£
Sales	160,000	200,000	184,800	(15,200)
less: Factory variable cost of sales:				
Material	80,000	100,000	85,350	14,650
Labour	30,000	37,500	35,450	2,050
Variable overheads	20,000	25,000	21,000	4,000
Contribution	30,000	37,500	43,000	5,500
Admin and marketing costs	10,000	10,000	9,000	1,000
Profit	20,000	27,500	34,000	6,500

In addition to the information in the table, you are told that the standard selling prices and costs of all units are to be found by dividing the total sales or individual items of cost by the number of units sold. This keeps this example as simple as possible by assuming that the number of units made equals the number of units sold, which in turn equals the number of hours worked.

Solution to Worked example 15.2

The solution to this worked example starts to highlight the power of standard costing variance analysis. Derivation of standards and actual revenues/costs per unit is as follows:

	Standard	Actual per unit
Selling price	1.00	0.924
Material	0.50	0.42675
Labour	0.1875	0.17725
Variable overheads	0.125	0.105

These standards are derived by applying the additional information given in the example: divide the relevant revenue of cost item by the budgeted number of units (for the standards); divide by the actual number of units for the actual unit items. We can now analyse the variances in detail and provide management with a lot of guidance as a result.

Sales price variance

The sales price variance indicates the impact on revenues of a change in selling price, given the actual sales volume. In algebraic terms this is

(actual selling price − budgeted selling price) × actual sales

= (AP − BP) AS

= £(1.00 − 0.924) × 200,000 units

= £0.076 × 200,000 units

= £15,200 favourable

Satisfy yourself why this variance is favourable.

Look at the table for the flexible budget statement above. The variance of £15,200 favourable is there. What this variance is telling us is that we have actually been able to sell our goods at a price higher than the standard selling price: set during the budgeting process. Therefore, since by flexing the budget we have got rid of the effects of volume on profit, the reason for the variance of 15,200 is due to this difference in selling price.

Materials price variance

At this stage, we are going to consider two aspects of the purchase and usage of materials: the price of those materials, and the usage of the same materials. As we might expect from our discussion, and given what we have just discovered about the sales price variance, there may be a materials price variance, and it has the following formula:

standard cost of the actual material − actual cost of material

= SC − AC

The standard cost of the material is the actual quantity of the material used multiplied by the standard cost per unit:

= £(0.5 × 200,000) – (0.42675 × 200,000)

= £100,000 – 85,350

= £14,650 favourable

Again, satisfy yourself why this variance is favourable. Note how this variance works: the standard cost of the actual materials used is the flexible budget cost; and the actual cost is just the actual cost, as per the statement given in the example.

Labour rate variance

There may be a labour price variance, but its usual name is the labour rate variance. It is called the rate variance because labour usually receives a rate of pay rather than a price. Again, the guidance we have received under the headings of the sales and material price variances is helpful here. And again, all we need to do is to compare the flexible budget costs with the actual costs to give us this variance. In algebraic terms, however, it is:

standard cost of labour – actual cost of labour

= SC – AC

The standard cost of labour is the actual hours worked multiplied by the standard rate of pay per hour:

= £(0.1875 × 200,000) – (0.17725 × 200,000)

= £37,500 – 35,450

= £2,050 favourable

Again, satisfy yourself why this variance is favourable.

Variable overheads spending variance

Another change of name of variance, but the meaning is exactly the same as in the previous three examples. The formula for this variance is

standard cost of variable overheads – actual cost of variable overheads

= SC – AC

The standard cost of the variable overheads is the variable overhead absorption rate per unit multiplied by the number of units actually made:

= £(0.125 × 200,000) – (0.105 × 200,000)

= £25,000 – 21,000

= £4,000 favourable

Again, satisfy yourself why this variance is favourable.

A more advanced view of the variances

Whilst the variances we have just isolated are genuine variances, the information they were based on was rather simplistic. The information only allowed us to isolate and calculate price variances. However, in this section we will see that there are usage variances to consider in addition to price variances.

Let us first define the new materials, labour and overhead variances.

Material usage variance

standard cost – standard cost of actual usage

Labour efficiency variance

standard cost – standard cost of actual hours worked

Variable overhead efficiency variance

standard cost – standard cost of actual hours worked

Consider now the following worked example.

WORKED EXAMPLE 15.3

The flexible budgeting manufacturing cost statement for a company shows for February:

	Standards	Flexible budget	Actual costs	Total variances
Units		10,000	10,000	
	£	£	£	£
Manufacturing costs				
Direct materials	20	200,000	208,250	(8,250)
Direct labour	15	150,000	164,800	(14,800)
Variable overheads	12	120,000	112,000	8,000

The additional information in support of this statement, derived from the cost accounting records is:

1. The standard costs per unit are based on the following relationships:
   (a) Direct materials are used at the rate of 4 kg at £5 per kg; direct labour takes 1.5 hours at £10 per hour
   (b) Variable overheads are absorbed on the basis of direct labour hours at £8 per direct labour hour.
2. For February, the actual materials and labour data was:

Actual usage of materials	42,500 kg
Actual labour hours	16,000 hours

Required

Calculate the materials and labour variances.

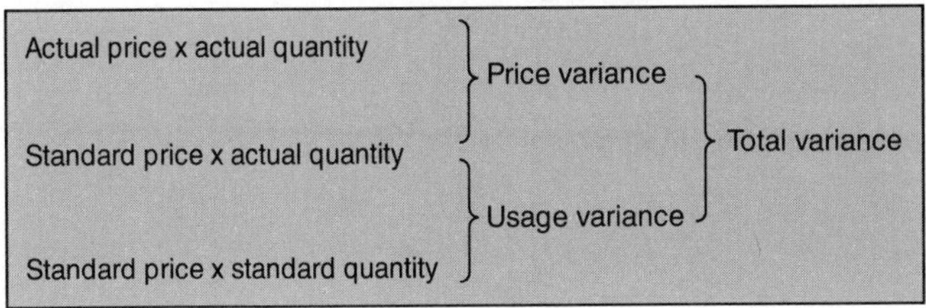

FIGURE 15.1 *Layout for materials*

Solution to Worked example 15.3

There are many ways to set out the solution to questions such as this one. The method I derived can be seen demonstrated in Williamson (1990), and it is this method that will be followed throughout this chapter. Many American textbooks follow a similar, but usually more complex, version of this layout. The layout we will follow is, for example, for materials as shown in Figure 15.1.

Using the layout in Figure 15.1 saves effort over other methods and is also very easy to learn since there is a pattern to the layout. Using symbols instead of words gives us the revised version found in Figure 15.2.

For this example, then, the solution is as follows:

Materials variances

	Actual or flexible costs £	Price or usage variances £		Direct materials variance £
AP × AQ	208,250			
	Price variance	4,250		
SP × AQ	212,500		Direct materials	(8,250)
	Usage variance	(12,500)		
SP × SQ	200,000			

The workings here are:

- the actual materials cost is given and is £208,250;
- SP × AQ = £5 per kg × 42,500 kg used = £212,500;
- SP × SQ = £5 per kg × (4 kg × 10,000 units) = £200,000.

This represents the kilogrammes of materials that should have been used at standard efficiencies, given the actual output of 10,000 units of the finished product.

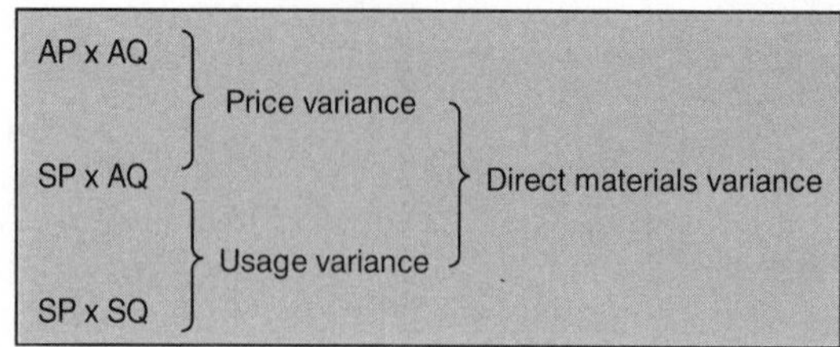

FIGURE 15.2 *Revised layout for materials*

Labour variances

	Actual or flexible costs £	Price or usage variances £	Direct labour variance £
AR × AH	164,800		
	Rate variance	(4,800)	
SR × AH	160,000	Direct labour	(14,800)
	Efficiency variance	(10,000)	
SR × SH	150,000		

The workings here are:

- the actual labour cost is given and is £164,800;
- SR × AH = £10 per kg × 16,000 hours worked = £160,000;
- SR × SH = £10 per kg × (1.5 hours per unit made × 10,000 units actually made) = £150,000.

This represents the direct labour hours that should have been used at standard efficiencies, given the actual output of 10,000 units of the finished product.

The joint variance: a case of the emperor's new clothes

Someone somewhere had a brilliant idea and probably had a paper published on the strength of it. The brilliant idea was that if we draw graphs of a price and a usage variance, there is often an area of overlap. When they looked into the gap, they revised their view of standard costing variances and invented the notion of the joint variance. Given that this seemed such a brilliant idea, many textbook writers have adopted it. When we look at that area of overlap in detail, we can start to analyse it and see a cornucopia of ideas to discuss. Figure 15.3 shows the kind of diagram referred to.

The joint variance now unfolds along the lines of the example that follows:

- 100 kg of material are needed at a standard cost of 5 per kg;
- 110 kg of this material are used, at a cost of £5.2 per kg.

The buyer is now said to be unhappy because of the price variance on the extra 10 kg that were used in manufacture: it was not his fault they used more material than

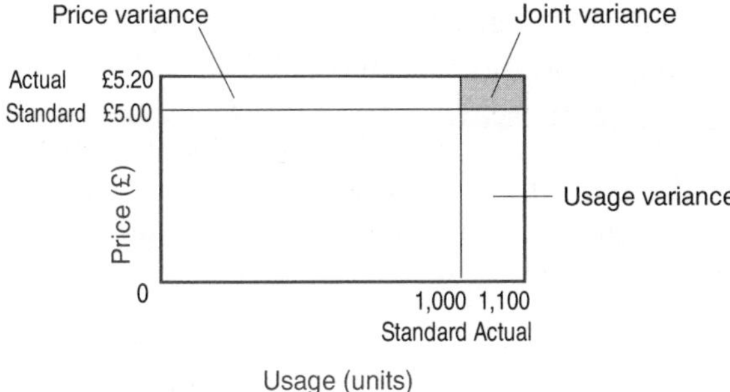

FIGURE 15.3 *The joint variance*

standard; he cannot control that. Similarly, the factory manager will not accept the price variance of £0.2 (£5.2 − £5) per kg: he cannot control that, although he is happy to take the blame for the additional 10 kg he used. A mathematical foundation can now be given to this problem, to 'prove' it exists . . . a case of the emperor's new clothes, unfortunately! There is absolutely no problem here at all. Like Santa Claus, the joint variance does not exist; and there is no overlap on any graph either. When we work through an example carefully, we will see the joint variance idea evaporate.

Price variance

We buy 100 kg of material at £5.2 per kg when the standard cost is £5 per kg: the price variance is

$$(SP - AP) \times AQ = (£5 - £5.20) \times 100\text{kg} = £20 \text{ adv}$$

All of this is the responsibility of the buyer: no one is asking the production manager to be accountable for any of this variance *at all*. In fact, of course, at this stage the production manager may not even have seen the material yet.

Usage variance

The standard rate of material usage is 0.1 kg per unit of output and in a period, we make 900 units. We actually used all of the 110 kg of material we bought, as discussed under the price variance. The usage variance is:

$$(SQ - AQ) \times SP = (90 \text{ kg} - 110 \text{ kg}) \times £5 = £100 \text{ adv}$$

The production manager is responsible for *all* of this variance. The buyer has nothing to do with the usage of material in the ordinary course of events.

Where is the joint variance? There is no joint variance. Draw a graph if you like and plot the above data on it: draw it properly and there will be no two sections of it overlapping. Consider it carefully and you will see that the so-called overlap is not an overlap at all. The shaded area that is often claimed to be a joint variance actually belongs to the price variance: that is, it is all due to the effects of price. Take the idea a stage or two further and draw a graph where the price variance is adverse but the usage variance is favourable. Where is the joint variance now? We can find the joint variance mathematically, but the emperor still has no clothes on! See Dopuch, Birnberg and Demski (1982: 248–9) for the wrong and then the corrected diagram!

Drury (1992) makes this mistake. Dopuch *et al.* made this mistake too, but then, almost by default, give the correct answer. Wright (1994) also makes this mistake. There are some very elaborate explanations and justifications on this topic too!

Variable overheads variances

	Actual or Flexible costs £	Price or Usage variances £	Direct overheads variance £
AR x AH	112,000		
	Spending variance	16,000	
SR × AH	128,000		Variable overheads variance 8,000
	Efficiency variance	(8,000)	
SR × SH	120,000		

The workings for the variable overheads variances are:

- the actual overhead cost is given and is £112,000;
- SR × AH = £8 per kg × 16,000 hours worked = £128,000;
- SP × SQ = £8 per kg × (1.5 hours per unit made x 10,000 units actually made) = £120,000.

This represents the direct labour hours that should have been used at standard efficiencies, given the actual output of 10,000 units of the finished product.

Reasons for variances

The precise questions that arise from variance analysis are bound to vary from case to case, but we can generalise to give ourselves some insights into such questions. We can do this by taking examples from each of the variance sets. As we consider such reasons we should constantly bear in mind that when we are seeking to question the variance we do so with the expectation that there may be scope for corrective action. When considering corrective action that might be taken, we need to establish precisely what scope there is for it. In some cases there may be little scope, whilst in others there will be a lot. Remember, 90% of all manufacturing is carried out away from the shop floor; thus our scope for corrective action might well be limited.

Direct materials variances

Price variance

The questions that arise here would be directed at the person who can control, or have some influence on, the prices that are paid for the materials that are bought and used:

Assuming an adverse variance, the questions are:

- Is the price different because discounts were lost (assuming that discounts were built into the standard cost)?
- Is the price different because quantity discounts were not secured?
- Is the price different because a new supplier was used, and he or she charged a higher price?

Assuming a favourable variance, the questions are:

- Were previously unaccounted for discounts taken?
- Has there been a period of deflation in the supplier's sector of the economy?

Usage variance

The questions arising here will be directed at the person best able to control the usage of materials, which will normally be the production director and his or her staff.

Assuming an adverse variance, the questions are:

- Has there simply been inefficient usage of materials?
- Was a machine faulty, causing unexpected losses?
- Were the materials substandard, causing more to be used?

Assuming a favourable variance, the questions are:

- Has a higher, more skilled, grade of labour been used?
- Were higher quality than normal grade materials used?

Note that in the favourable section of the materials usage variance, there is an example of a materials variance that interrelates with a labour variance. A higher grade of labour has been used on a job or task, leading to a saving in materials used. The saving comes because the labour is more skilled and more efficient, so they are less likely to waste materials. On the other hand, if a higher than normal grade labour has been used, the labour rate variance, for example, will probably be adverse for that person or group of people.

Fixed overhead variances

By definition, fixed costs are not expected to change despite even wide fluctuations in output or production. For this reason, a standard fixed cost per unit of output is not a useful concept for managerial planning and control purposes. However, we know from earlier discussions that standard fixed costs are useful for product costing purposes: in absorption costing we derived fixed overhead absorption rates for product costing purposes, for example. The idea behind using a standard fixed overhead absorption rate is for it to be used to calculate job and product costs as soon as they are complete, rather than waiting until after an (artificial) accounting period end. Similarly, it assists the bookkeeping function if the accountant can debit job and product accounts as jobs and products are completed, rather than wait until the period end, when, possibly, thousands of entries will have to be caught up with. Finally, using predetermined fixed overhead absorption rates allows for constant fixed cost allocation throughout the period: thus product prices will not fluctuate wildly from period to period as they might otherwise do.

When we use a standard fixed overhead absorption rate, the total fixed production overheads absorbed behave like a variable cost: that is, as production increases, the total fixed overhead absorbed by production increases. However, since the total budgeted fixed overhead does not vary, differences arise between budgeted and absorbed fixed overhead. We will be discussing three fixed production overhead variances in this section. They are defined as follows.

Fixed production overhead total variance

'(Standard absorbed cost) – (Actual fixed overhead production overhead)' (CIMA 1991). Algebraically, we can represent this variance as:

SC – AC

Fixed production overhead expenditure variance

'(Budgeted fixed production overhead) – (Actual fixed production overhead)' (ibid.). Algebraically, we can represent this variance as:

BFO – AFO

Fixed production overhead volume variance

'(Standard absorbed cost) – (Budgeted fixed production overhead). May be subdivided according to the needs of management' (ibid.). Algebraically, we can represent this variance as:

SC – BFO

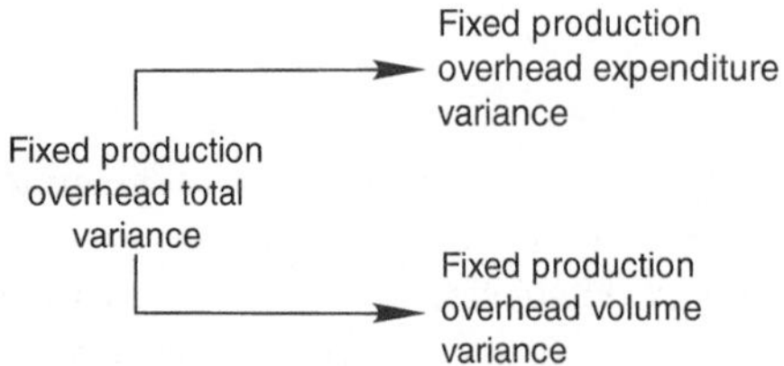

FIGURE 15.4 *Interrelationship of fixed production overhead variances*

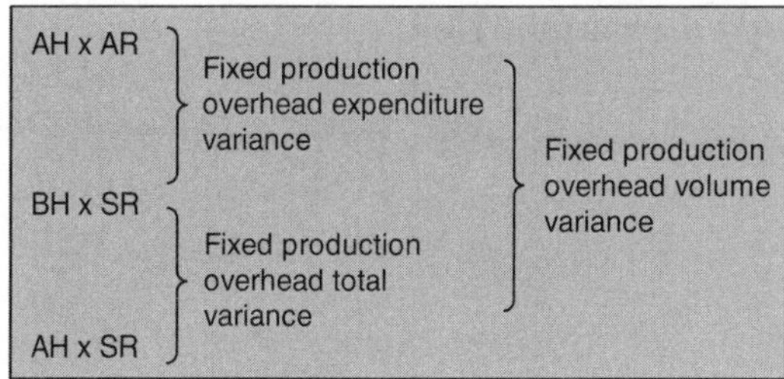

FIGURE 15.5 *Calculation of fixed production overhead variances*

These variances can be shown as being interrelated in Figure 15.4, and because of the way they interrelate, we can deal with them in a similar way to the way in which we dealt with the direct materials, direct labour, and the variable overheads variances. First, we should define the terms we are using:

1. The **actual fixed production cost** is either the total fixed production overhead cost as given in the ledgers, or it is the actual hours worked multiplied by the actual fixed overhead cost per hour:

   AH × AR

2. The **budgeted fixed overhead cost** is the budgeted hours multiplied by the standard fixed overhead absorption rate per hour:

   BH × SR

3. The **standard fixed overhead cost** is the standard hours allowed multiplied by the standard fixed overhead absorption rate per hour:

   SH × SR

The layout for calculating the variances is shown in Figure 15.5, and an example will clearly illustrate this calculation.

WORKED EXAMPLE 15.4

A. Wagner plc manufactures ladies' lingerie and, at the end of an accounting period, has taken the following data from its records:

	£
Actual fixed production overheads	400,000
Budgeted fixed production overheads	396,000

The actual activity level for the period was 40,000 units, representing 40,000 standard hours of output. The budgeted and standard information on which the budgeted fixed production overhead was based is as follows: budgeted activity level 44,000 units, representing 44,000 hours.

Solution to Worked example 15.4

Based on this information, the standard fixed overhead absorption rate is:

$$\frac{£396{,}000}{44{,}000 \text{ hours}} = £9 \text{ per hour}$$

	Actual or flexible costs £	Price or usage variances £	Direct overheads variances £
AH × AR			
	400,000		
BH × SR		4,000 adverse	
	396,000		10,000 adverse
AH × SR		6,000 adverse	

40,000 hours × £9 = £390,000

Note that the standard hours used in the calculation of the standard fixed overhead production cost is the standard hours derived from the actual production: that is, it is the number of standard hours that should have been produced, given the actual units made in the period.

Meaning of the variances

The fixed production overhead expenditure variance represents the difference between the actual fixed overheads and the budgeted fixed overhead. The variance is caused by a combination of price and volume factors related to the use of fixed overhead inputs: for example, indirect materials, indirect labour and other indirect expenditures. As Drury(1988) says, however:

> The total of the fixed overhead expenditure variance on its own is not particularly informative. Any meaningful analysis of this variance requires a comparison of the actual expenditure for each individual item of fixed overhead expenditure against the budget.

The fixed production overhead volume variance does not indicate whether production performance has been either good or bad. It merely tells us the difference between the activity used in the absorption of fixed costs and the activity level used in calculating the standard fixed overhead absorption rate. Hence, if there is a volume variance, it indicates that production facilities are over- or underused relative to management's expectations at budget preparation time.

Reconciliation of budgeted and actual profit

It is possible to reconcile the differences between the budgeted and the actual net profit for an organisation. This is done by generating a report that starts with the budgeted net profit and then adding or subtracting variances, as relevant, to that profit and arriving at the actual net profit. The reason for carrying out such a reconciliation is partly to prove that the workings have been correctly carried out: if they had not been correctly carried out, then the actual profit on the reconciliation statement would not agree with the actual profit on the profit and loss account! Additionally, the reconciliation statement is prepared to illustrate to management the relationship between the budgeted and actual profits. The statement, shown in Table 15.7, illustrates how such a report works: to reconcile the budgeted with the actual profit, add to the budgeted profit the favourable variances, and subtract the adverse variances.

Setting standards

Standard costing is most effective where products or services and their processes are standardised. For example, when there is only one product; and where processes are continuous. Examples of where standard costing can be used include:

1. Oil refining.
2. Pharmaceuticals.
3. Process industries where the same products are being made continuously: such as cars, canned fruit and vegetables.
4. Engineering products where the same product is made continuously.
5. A standardised service, such as word processing.

TABLE 15.7 ***Reconciliation statement for Mozart plc: budget versus actual net profit***

	£	£	£
Budgeted net profit			175,000
		22,000 fav.	
Direct materials variances			
Price variance	7,500 fav.		
Usage variance	2,500 adv.	5,000 fav.	
Direct labour variances			
Rate variance	3,750 adv.		
Efficiency variance	2,250 adv.	6,000 adv.	
Production overhead variances			
Fixed expenditure	7,000 adv.		
Fixed volume	3,500 fav.	3,500 fav.	
Variable expenditure	750 fav.		
Variable efficiency	250 adv.	500 fav.	25,000 fav.
Actual profit			200,000

Standards have to be set for every aspect of a business's activities which are to be controlled by the standard costing reporting routine. Thus, we need to set standards for: direct materials; direct labour; and overheads.

Setting standards for direct materials

There are several basic principles which ought to be appreciated in setting standards for direct materials. Cost depends on both quantity and price, therefore it will be necessary to forecast standard quantities and prices for all direct materials used in the manufacture of each product or the provision of each service. The buyer, the production manager and the accountant should work together on setting such standards since the actual amount of material used in the past may not be that laid down in the current material specifications for each product. The reasons for this situation include changing specifications: changes due, for example, to design changes, or cost efficiencies, or changes in technology. The standard quantity of each material issued to production should include an allowance for normal production losses. Even with the best and most efficient machinery and technology, losses are almost certain to occur in the production of a product or the provision of a service.

In setting standard prices, we should consider historic prices, but make ourselves aware that past prices are not relevant unless they remain unchanged. If prices are expected to remain relatively stable, an average of the expected prices could be used. Rapid inflation and/or exchange rate fluctuations can soon render standard prices out of date. If this is the case, they may have to be reviewed at shorter intervals than one year to ensure that reports on variances and stock valuations are realistic. Standard prices are the responsibility of the purchasing department. The cheapest prices might not always be the best: delivery, quality and continuity of supply should also be considered.

WORKED EXAMPLE 15.5

Last year the cost of 2,500 metres of material was £27,500. Next year the price of material is expected to rise by 10% and discounts of 12% of the new purchase price are being offered. Assuming all discounts are to be expected to be earned, what will the standard cost per unit and in total of material be next year?

Solution to Worked example 15.5

The solution to this example consists of two calculations: first, calculating the new purchase prices; and secondly, calculating the purchase price net of the discounts:

New purchase price per unit:

$$\frac{£27{,}500}{2{,}500 \text{ units}} \times 110\%$$

$$= £12.1$$

New purchase price net of discounts:

$$£12.1 \times (100\% - 12\%)$$

$$= £10.648$$

In total, the calculation is:

$$£27{,}500 \times 110\% \times (100\% - 12\%)$$

$$= £26{,}620$$

Setting standards for direct labour

The procedures for setting standard costs for direct labour follows the same approach as for direct materials. The basic approach is to determine the quantity of labour required and the price that will have to paid for it. The most important aspect here is that of standard hours. A standard hour is defined as being: 'The quantity of work achievable at standard performance in an hour or minute' (CIMA 1991).

For example, at standard performance it takes 10 minutes to repair a leaky value. Therefore, if 30 leaky values are repaired, 5 standard hours are recorded. That is, each valve is repaired in ten sixtieths (one-sixth) of an hour; this is one-sixth of a standard hour. Therefore, when 30 leaky valves are repaired, the number of standard hours achieved is:

$$\frac{1}{6} \times 30 \text{ leaky valves repaired}$$

$$= 5 \text{ standard hours}$$

Calculate the standard labour cost for manufacturing metal shapes

Dept	Operation	Standard hours for this batch	Standard rate of pay/hour (£)	Standard labour cost (£)
Cutting	Cut and shape	40	1.50	60
Drilling	Drill metal	50	1.60	80
Fitting	Fit rod	20	1.70	34
Packing	Pack	20	1.40	28
		130	-	202

Notes:

1. The standard hours per batch will be determined by, for example, a detailed analysis of previous batches of the same product or estimates of what should happen when making this product. Such an analysis will include work study, method study and so on.

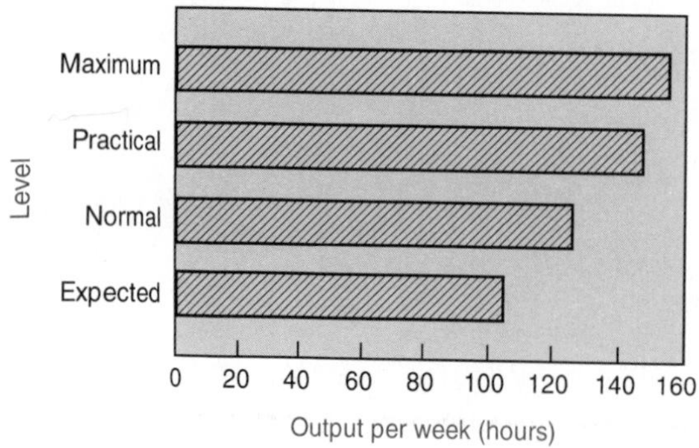

FIGURE 15.6 *The various levels of overheads to be consulted*

2. Therefore, the standard cost of labour for a product or service includes: standard hours to be worked; *and* the standard rates of pay for each hour.

Setting standards for overheads

Overheads are always a problem. Even with standard costing, we cannot eliminate all of the problems which arise. One of the critical problems with setting standards for overheads is the one of output or activity levels. Look at Figure 15.6, which illustrates the various levels of overhead that might be considered when evaluating standard costs and overheads. The 100% ideal level of output is the absolute physically possible maximum number of hours that can be worked or operated. The practical level of output represents the ideal less some allowance for the absolute minimum of interruptions: such interruptions might be due to planned maintenance and so on. The normal level of output allows, over and above the practical level of output, for breaks in activity for reasons such as meal breaks, potential stoppages due to breakdowns, stockouts and so on. The expected attainable level of output adds further allowances onto the normal stoppages and results in an activity level that management can **really** expect to be achieved.

Activity levels and fixed overhead rates

As we have seen several times in this book, when fixed costs and activity levels are put together, interesting results can emerge. The relationship between levels of activity and fixed costs is that the more units are produced, assuming a constant fixed cost, the lower the average fixed cost per unit becomes.

WORKED EXAMPLE 15.6

If the fixed overhead cost for an organisation is £10,000, calculate the fixed overhead absorption rate if the expected attainable levels of output are established at any of 10,000, 8,000, 6,000, 4,000, 2,000, and 1,000 standard hours.

Solution to Worked example 15.6

Simply dividing the total fixed costs by the number of units given, gives the results, which are presented in the form of a table:

Activity (units)	Total fixed costs (£)	Fixed cost per unit (£)
10,000	10,000	1.00
8,000	10,000	1.25
6,000	10,000	1.67
4,000	10,000	2.50
2,000	10,000	5.00
1,000	10,000	10.00

Moving ahead a little, we can extend the examples to include consideration of a slightly more realistic example. The following worked example gives us all the details we need.

WORKED EXAMPLE 15.7

The fixed costs for next year in the canning department of Katisha Beans Ltd are estimated to be £150,000. Variable costs are estimated at £120 for each hour that the production line operates, and beans are canned at the rate of 20 cans a minute. The company works an eight-hour day, five days a week for 50 weeks a year, but normal production interruptions amount to 10% of the ideal capacity.

Required

Prepare a cost schedule to show what the standard overhead costs rate per 1,000 cans would be at practical level and at 75% , 50% and 25% of ideal capacity.

Solution to Worked example 15.7

Before constructing the table, there are two calculations to carry out: establishing the ideal capacity; and the number of cans that can be filled during the ideal capacity.

Ideal capacity:

= 8 hours per day × 5 days per week × 50 weeks per year

= 2,000 hours

Number of cans:

= 2,000 hours × 60 minutes per hour × 20 cans per minute

= 2,400,000 cans

The variable costs are calculated, as should be expected, by multiplying the number of hours to be worked by the costs per hour. The schedule shows the results. Note that the question asks us to calculate the cost per 1,000 cans, rather than per can. This is perfectly normal in that since the volume of cans is so large, and the costs relatively small, it makes more sense to talk in terms of a cost per 1,000 cans rather than any other smaller denomination.

Cost schedule: costs per 1,000 cans filled

	Level of output as a percentage of ideal capacity			
	100%	90%	75%	50%
Hours	2,000	1,800	1,500	1,000
Cans	2,400,000	2,160,000	1,800,000	1,200,000
	£	£	£	£
Fixed costs	150,000	150,000	150,000	150,000
Variable costs	240,000	216,000	180,000	120,000
	£	£	£	£
Fixed costs per 1,000 cans	62.50	69.44	83.33	125.00
Variable costs per 1,000 cans	100.00	100.00	100.00	100.00
Total costs per 1,000 cans	162.50	169.44	183.33	225.00

Again, such a schedule shows the influence of volume of output on the fixed costs per unit (or 1,000 units in this case).

Total standard cost of a product

We can conclude this section by looking in detail at one product and putting together a complete standard cost schedule.

WORKED EXAMPLE 15.8

Mikado Ltd are planning to introduce standard costing into their accounting system, and the management accountant has been given the responsibility of co-ordinating the compilation of cost standards for all their products. One of the company's recently introduced but very popular products is a machinery component. Last year, the direct material and labour cost of producing 2,500 of these components was as follows:

		£
Materials		
2,550 basic frames		38,250
300 sq metres sheet steel		2,700
250 litres of paint		1,000
Labour		
Cutting sheet steel (230 hours)		460
Assembling and finishing (5,400 hours)		13,500
Overheads		
Cutting sheet steel:	total overhead	18,700
Assembling and finishing:	total overhead	24,000
Direct labour hours available		
Cutting sheet steel		500
Assembling and finishing		7,500

Further investigation showed that:

- The same number of products will be made this year as last.
- The wastage rate on basic frames should be 4% of finished units.
- Because of a drop in the value of the pound, the expected imported cost for each basic frame will be £1 more next year than last.
- Assembling and finishing time should be extended by 20 hours in total; this would reduce last year's usage of sheet steel by 25 sq metres.
- The price of sheet steel will not change next year, nor will that of paint.
- Labour hourly rates of pay are expected to increase by 10% next year.
- Assembling and finishing time should be 2 hours for each finished unit produced.
- Variable overhead is based on practical capacity hours and is expected to increase by 20% in value next year.
- Practical capacity for each department achieved last year, and expected to be repeated this year was as follows: cutting sheet steel = 90% of direct labour hours available; assembling and finishing = 85% of direct labour hours available.

→

- Fixed overhead is estimated as follows:

	Last year £	Next year £
Cutting sheet steel	11,950	2,600
Assembling and finishing	9,125	9,520

Required

Compile a detailed standard manufacturing cost summary for one component for next year.

Solution to Worked example 15.8

For once, there is no explanation at all for the solution that follows. Ensure all details are fully understood, however.

Standard manufacturing cost summary

Units	2,500	
Materials	£	£
Basic frames	2,600	41,600
Sheet steel	275	2,475
Paint	250	1,000
Labour		
Cutting sheet steel	230	506
Assembling and finishing	5,000	13,750
Variable overheads		
Cutting sheet steel	500	22,440
Assembling and finishing	7,500	28,800
Fixed overheads		
Cutting sheet steel		12,600
Assembling and finishing		9,520
		132,691

Limitations of standard costing

Standards and standard costing have been used successfully for a long time; but there are aspects of standard costing that call the subject into question. Many of the problems revolve around three central themes:

1. Standards remaining up to date.
2. The introduction of different technology.
3. The standard setting process.

CAMEO

Standards are predetermined, hence they are set in advance of something happening! An extreme consequence of how standards can cause problems came with the oil price crisis of 1973/1974. Anyone setting standards around the time of the oil price crisis of the mid-1970s and whose organisation was affected by the price of oil, will recall the problems ensuing. The effect of the significant oil price rises that took place was that standards already established became out of date before they had even been used. The scenario was that many management accountants and their staffs had spent many man months establishing standards and budgets for the coming year, only to find that a lot of the work needed to be repeated after OPEC had dealt everyone a cutting oil price blow. Of course, this is an extreme event that is not repeated very often, but it does illustrate what happens at the extreme.

The introduction of different technologies into our organisation will affect the standard setting process. If we introduce new computer-controlled machinery, for example, we might find that either labour has been replaced, or a different grade of labour is now employed. Whatever the final outcome of the introduction of new technology, the standards that need to be set will be different now: fewer labour hours and more machine hours; no grade A labour hours but 100 grade B labour hours per unit and more machine hours, and so on. (See Drury (1992) for a detailed discussion of standard costing and the introduction of advanced manufacturing technology into an organisation.)

There is also the problem of setting some of the standards in the first place. There is the delightful story from Emmanuel *et al.* (1990: 167) of the dustmen and the way a poor unfortunate work study officer was trying to establish standards:

> The authors well recollect a slow motion ballet that was performed by local dustmen outside their office windows. The strange performance only became explicable when a young man with a clip-board and stop-watch was observed in one corner. The following week he was absent and the dustbins were once more emptied at their usual speed!

This kind of story is repeated daily all over the world, no doubt. It leads to a serious outcome, of course, in that the young man with the clip-board and stop-watch may be necessary but he will often need to do his work in secret or in such a way that he has to be able to eliminate the time effects of the ballet from his results! This therefore calls the results of his efforts into question: secrecy breeds discontent and eliminating the ballet by means of guesstimates will almost inevitably lead to errors of estimation.

SUMMARY

This chapter has shown the links between the outputs of the budgeting process (the budgets) and the data resulting from organisations when the actual outputs are achieved. We have seen that a budget prepared in advance is known as a fixed budget; and that it is limited in its value for managerial planning and control purposes. The limitations are caused by the actual output varying, sometimes significantly, from the expected, or budgeted output. To solve the mismatch of levels of output, the management accountant uses the concept of flexible budgeting. This chapter has shown that flexible budgeting changes the variable aspects of a budget to allow for variations in volumes of output, thus making a budget a better control tool from a managerial point of view.

Having seen that flexible budgeting gives a manager a more realistic view of his or her performance, we then demonstrated that standard costing can be a direct development out of flexible budgeting. We saw that when we flex a budget, we do so by taking allowance of standards, predetermined costs and revenues per unit, and applying them to the actual outputs achieved. The ideas underlying standard costing were then developed and we considered the variances in performance that may be found by comparing standard performance with actual performance. Variances can be derived for direct costs, variable overheads and fixed overheads. Furthermore the budgeted profit and the actual profit can be reconciled by means of a relatively simple statement. Finally, we discussed the limitations of standard costing. Many management accountants and their management colleagues have been distrustful of standard costing for a long time now, standards having been seen as artificial in every sense. With the advent of global marketing and advanced technology, the setting of standards is an even more critical subject than perhaps it used to be. Using standard costing systems, then, requires that we use flexible budgeting carefully and that we fully understand both the implications of standard setting and our own technological environment.

KEY TERMS

You should satisfy yourself that you have noted all of these terms and can define and/or describe their meaning and use, as appropriate.

Flexible budgeting (p. 500)
Standard costing (p. 500)
Volume effects (p. 506)
Standard hour (p. 506)
Labour rate variance (p. 509)
Variable overheads (p. 509)
Fixed production overhead (p. 516)
Setting standards (p. 520)

RECOMMENDED READING

Blowing one's own trumpet! Williamson (1990) is an abridged version of part of this chapter.

QUESTIONS

Review questions

1. Define a fixed budget and contrast it with a flexible budget.
2. What relationship, if any, is there between flexible budgeting and variable costing?
3. Define the terms 'standard hour' and 'standard cost'.
4. (a) How can the total materials cost variance be subdivided?
   (b) How can the total labour cost variance be subdivided?
   (c) How can the total variable overheads cost variance be subdivided?
   (d) How can the total fixed overheads cost variance be subdivided?
5. Give possible reasons why a materials, or a labour, or an overheads variance might arise.

Answers to review questions 1, 2, 4(b) and 5 can be found in the Student Workbook.

Graded practice questions

Level I

1. Construct a table giving general examples of the reasons for:
   (a) the variable overheads spending variance; and
   (b) the variable overheads efficiency variance.
   Give examples of possible interrelationships between a labour variance, a materials variance and a variable overheads variance.

2. By means of examples of your own devising demonstrate your understanding of the terms
   (a) price/rate/spending variance; and
   (b) usage/efficiency variance.

3. Prepare a statement reconciling the budgeted and actual profits of Normansco from the information that follows. Normansco manufactures jars of preserves from fruits and nuts gathered from the hedgerows around the area in which the business is based. For one full financial year, the variances were as follows.

   Direct materials: price variance £35,000 adv; usage variance £13,000 fav. The direct labour variances were: rate £1,200 fav and efficiency £27,500 fav. The variable overhead variances amounted to expenditure £350 fav, and efficiency £1,000 adv. The fixed production variances were overhead expenditure £3,000 adv and overhead volume £12,000 fav. The budgeted production profit for the period was £125,000.

4. A flexible budget is often prepared to show the effects on revenues and costs of a variety of levels of output. The following data relate to one accounting period for Hale and Harty Ltd:

	Fixed budget	Production levels (as percentages of maximum output) 80%	100%	110%
Sales units	10,000			

	Per unit
	£
Sales	42.50
Direct materials	3.00
Direct labour	2.50
Variable overheads:	
Indirect materials	2.50
Indirect labour	1.25
Electricity	0.35
Water	0.36
Contribution	32.54
Fixed overheads annually:	
Depreciation	100,000
Supervision	75,000
Insurance	12,500
Maintenance	23,500
Rent	50,000

Required

Prepare the flexible budgeting statement at the three levels of output indicated on the pro forma statement.

Level II

5. McCarty makes one product, the direct materials for which have a standard cost of £1.50 per unit. During January, 11,000 units of materials were bought at £1.55 per unit. Of the 11,000 units that were bought in the period (and opening stocks were nil) only 10,000 units were actually used.

Required

(a) Calculate the materials price variance assuming that materials costs are the responsibility of the buyer.
(b) Calculate the materials price variance assuming that materials costs are the responsibility of the production manager.

6. The standard materials costs for a product are £20: based on a usage of 4 units of that material at £5 per unit. Two hours of direct labour, at standard, are used in the manufacture of the product at an hourly rate of £12. Variable overheads are recovered on the basis of standard direct labour hours at the rate of £2.50 per standard direct labour hour. Fixed costs are budgeted at £10,000 per month. This product is being made by a new business, the first month's financial results for which are:

Materials bought at £4.90/unit	9,000 units
Materials used in production	7,000 units
Direct labour used at £12.50/hour	3,600 hours
Variable overhead costs incurred	£8,900
Fixed overhead costs incurred	£13,000

A total of 1,700 units of finished goods were produced in the period.

Required

(a) Calculate all relevant standard costing variances.
(b) Calculate the standard variable cost of the 1,700 units produced. Show all the main elements of cost separately.

7. A business manufactures a single product which has the following specifications:

Component No.	Standard quantity	Standard price each (£)
345	5	20
789	6	25

Number of standard direct labour hours	20
Standard wage rate per hour	£3.50
Budgeted production overhead (all fixed) per month	£14,000
Budgeted production per month, in units	200

A summary profit statement for the month of October is stated below:

	£	£
Sales		90,000
Materials used	47,480	
Direct wages	12,480	
Production overhead	14,200	
		74,160
Gross profit		15,840
Administration costs	3,000	
Selling and distribution costs	5,500	
		8,500
Net profit		7,340

Additional information:

180 units were produced and sold during October, at the standard selling price. It should be assumed that work-in-progress stocks at the end of the month were the same as at the beginning of October.

Component	Stock at		Purchases during October	
				Price
No.	1 Oct.	31 Oct.	Quantity	each (£)
345	200	250	1,000	19
789	240	150	1,000	27

Direct labour: actual hours worked during the month were 3,900.

Required

(a) Calculate the following variances for the month of October:
- (i) direct materials price for each component and in total, based on usage;
- (ii) direct materials usage for each component and in total;
- (iii) direct wages rate;
- (iv) direct labour efficiency;
- (v) fixed production overhead expenditure;
- (vi) fixed production overhead volume.

(b) Utilising the variances you have calculated, present a statement for management reconciling the standard gross profit with the actual profit.

(c) Explain the meaning of the term 'fixed production overhead volume variance' and its significance to management.

CIMA Cost Accounting 1
November 1981

Solutions to practice questions 1, 3 and 7 can be found in the Student Workbook. Solutions to practice question numbers in red can be found at the end of this book.

Project

1. Consider any organisation and determine the main characteristics of its processes. By analysing those processes say whether standard costing is appropriate for that organisation.

   To help with this project you should first analyse an organisation for which standard costing *is* appropriate: an organisation such as those discussed in Chapter 15. Once this has been done, select an organisation that may not so obviously apply standard costing and analyse it fully.

REFERENCES

CIMA (1991), *Management Accounting Official Terminology* (Chartered Institute of Management Accounting.)

Dopuch, N., Birnberg, J. G. and Demski, J. S. (1982), *Cost accounting: accounting data for management decisions*, 3rd edn (Harcourt Brace Jovanovich).

Drury, C. (1988), *Management and cost accounting*, 2nd edn (Van Nostrand Reinhold).

Drury, C. (1992), *Standard costing* (Academic Press).

Emmanuel, C., Otley, D. and Merchant, K. (1990), *Accounting for management control*, 2nd edn (Chapman & Hall).

Williamson, D. (1990), 'Standard costing made simple', *ACCA Students' Newsletter* (January).

Wright, D. (1994), *A Practical Foundation in Costing* (Routledge).

CHAPTER SIXTEEN

Risk and uncertainty

CHAPTER OBJECTIVES

After reading this chapter you should be able to:

- define risk, uncertainty and certainty
- appreciate the expected value criterion
- apply decision tree analysis to risk and uncertainty
- apply Monte Carlo simulation methods to risk and uncertainty
- discuss and apply risk-adjusted discount rate methods to risk and uncertainty
- define and discuss the capital asset pricing model
- critically analyse the assumptions of the capital asset pricing model
- appreciate the real-world uses of the capital asset pricing model

Introduction

As Benjamin Franklin rightly said, in this world only two things are certain: death and taxes. Given that the previous statement is true, we must cast some doubt over some aspects of the work of this book. As examples, we can cite the chapters on relevant costing and budgeting and budgetary control as being subject to further consideration since we were dealing with aspects of the future in each of them. Even though we know that when we toss a fair coin, it has a 50% chance of landing with the head side uppermost, we also know that there is a 50% chance that the same coin will land with the tail side uppermost. What we cannot know with certainty is what will happen on the next toss of the coin. Business decisions have the same characteristics as coin tossing but with one significant difference. The difference between tossing a fair coin and a business decision is that a business decision may have many uncertain elements or aspects to it and many possible outcomes, whilst the tossing of a fair coin really only has one element to it, with two possible outcomes.

In this chapter we will look at business decisions in order to understand their elements and the nature of their outcomes. There are three aspects to the work we are going to do: risk, certainty, uncertainty. Definitions of these terms are as follows:

1. Risk can be defined as: 'being a situation where there are several different outcomes and there is material statistical evidence relating to them' (Arnold and Hope 1983: 60).
2. Certainty is defined as: 'the situation where one knows in advance the exact future values of all relevant parameters' (Clark, Hindeland & Pritchard 1989: 197).
3. Uncertainty exists where there are: 'several possible outcomes but where there is little previous statistical evidence to guide the decision maker in predicting them' (Arnold and Hope 1983: 60).

Risk

First we will deal with the several different aspects of risk since risk comes in many forms:

- business risk
- investment risk
- portfolio risk
- systematic risk
- cataclysmic risk
- financial risk
- political risk
- environmental risk

Each of these forms of risk can be defined in fairly simple terms before we expand on them.

Business risk

Business risk concerns the way that earnings vary due to the interaction of an organisation's normal activities and management's decision with respect to the level of capital investment in their organisation: for example, more capital equipment means higher fixed costs. A greater investment in capital equipment leads to variability of profit with output. Business risk is independent of financial risk, as discussed below. We saw the way that business risk affects organisations in Chapter 11 when we looked at cost volume profit analysis (see Figures 11.3 and 11.4 to see the effect on profit of varying levels of capital investment). Management takes a risk when it decides to invest in capital assets: the risk is that as capital investment increases, the incidence of fixed costs will tend to increase and thus there will be a once and for all decrease in profits. One of the outcomes of capital investment, therefore, is that the amount of profit available for distribution to shareholders may suffer, at least in the short term.

Investment risk

Following directly on from business risk is the risk that an investment project will return variable profits: the investment risk. Investment risk stems from the possibility that incorrect

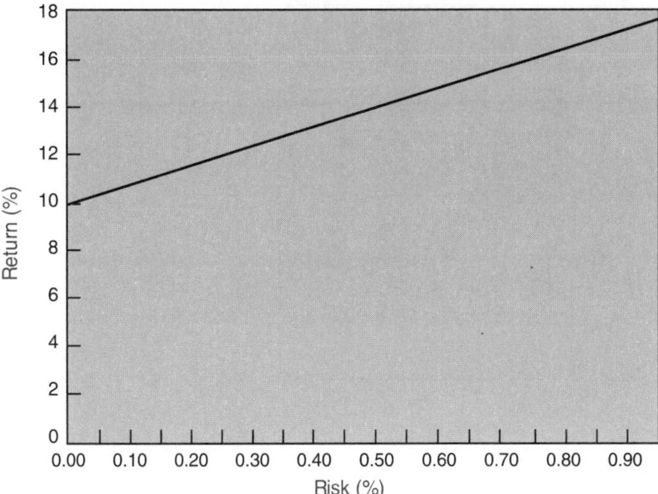

FIGURE 16.1 *Risk versus return*

forecasts will cause profits to fluctuate; similarly with, unforeseen changes in technology, changes in cash flows and changes in costs and the cost structure. The level of investment risk can be associated with the expected rate of return, which is well described in Figure 16.1. This figure clearly illustrates the relationship between an investment, the risk associated with it and the likely returns from it. It almost goes without saying that the greater the risk associated with an investment, the greater return an investor will require. Taking an extreme example, we should ask ourselves under what conditions we would invest in a project in an area of the world currently involved in military unrest: Bosnia during 1994, Chechniya in 1994, and so on. Very few investors would suggest opening a new facility if there is a possibility that it will be destroyed in the foreseeable future. The investors who are prepared to invest in such areas of conflict will demand a significant chance of earning a large return, perhaps of the order of hundreds, if not thousands, of percent return on investment. Note also that the curve begins at a return of 10% even when risk is nil. 10% is known as the risk free rate, and is the lowest rate of return that anyone who is likely to invest in this kind of project will demand. The risk-free rate is usually taken to be the return that it is possible to earn on government bonds or securities. Government bonds are classed as risk free in that there is an excellent chance that the government will not default on its own securities. (This is not true of every government, of course!).

Portfolio risk

A portfolio is a group or bundle of investments or projects which have been bought or acquired with a view to spreading risk. Risk is spread within a portfolio by buying or acquiring a spread of types of investment, from relatively riskless to relatively risky. Portfolio

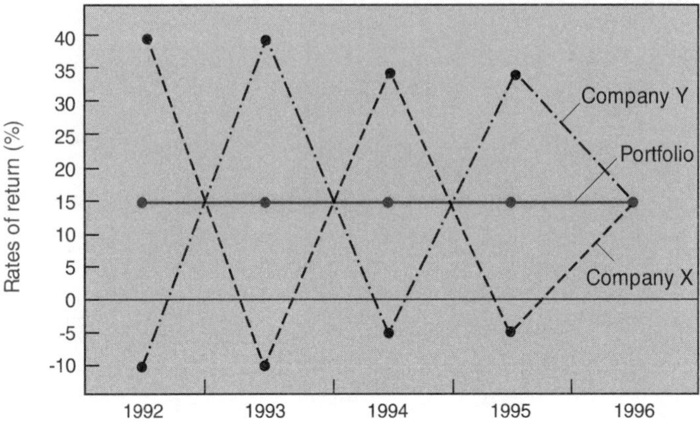

FIGURE 16.2 *The portfolio effect*

analysis is based on the idea that, given a choice, most of us would spread our risks in such a way that if one decision proved to be a loser then others would turn out to be winners. In a portfolio, we diversify our investments. Arnold and Hope (1983) give an example of a diversified business as being one that would sell both umbrellas and ice cream. At any one time in the summer, an umbrella and ice cream salesman might constantly be able to sell something, whatever the weather! Table 16.1 and Figure 16.2 illustrate the way that portfolios are meant to behave. At any time, if company X is doing badly, we hope that company Y is doing well. Overall, our portfolio investment in both X and Y provides us with an average acceptable project.

Because management has the discretion to invest in a portfolio, portfolio risk is otherwise known as diversifiable or specific risk. The reason for the name 'diversifiable risk' is that a portfolio diversifies the chances of substantial problems or variations in earnings. The name 'company specific risk' suggests that the problem which an organisation faces is unique to it and is essentially random. A portfolio that covers many aspects of potential risk is known as a well-diversified portfolio.

TABLE 16.1 ***The portfolio effect***

	X	Y	Average
1992	40	−10	15
1993	−10	40	15
1994	35	−5	15
1995	−5	35	15
1996	15	15	15
Average returns	15	15	15
Standard deviations	20.25	20.25	0.00

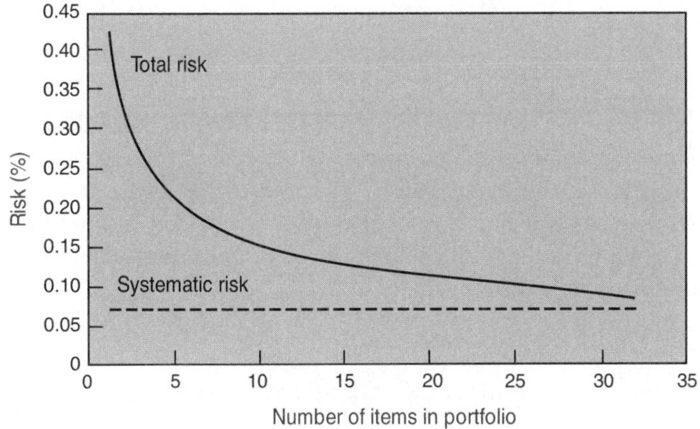

The difference between total risk and systematic risk is unsystematic risk.

FIGURE 16.3 *Systematic risk: diversification*

Systematic risk

Systematic risk, or market risk, stems from external events such as war, economic depression, falling exchange rates and so on that impact on all organisations. Since all organisations are affected at the same time by such external events, diversification cannot eliminate the risk involved. Figure 16.3 illustrates how some of the total risk associated with individual securities can be avoided by diversification.

Cataclysmic risk

Cataclysmic risk arises when the variability of earnings is a function of events beyond managerial control and anticipation. Examples of cataclysmic situations include:

- *Changes in laws*: significant increases in level of taxation on consumer goods or imports, for example.
- *Severe energy shortages*: for instance, coal miners' strikes can lead to such situations.
- *Earthquakes*: Japan had a serious earthquake early in 1995 that affected many business and commercial organisations cataclysmically.

Cataclysmic risks have an influence on the earnings of an organisation by, for example, taking away the possibility of earning some or all of their revenues. In the case of a chemical plant that relies on its supply of coal to manufacture its products, it will not be able to make anything if coal is suddenly not available. Similarly, Toyota Motors fell foul of cataclysmic risk early in 1995 when they were most unfortunately affected by the terrific earthquake that hit Japan at that time. Notice, in this case, Toyota were sited away from the epicentre of the earthquake zone, but were still affected by it.

Financial risk

Financial risk is the variability in earnings resulting from the firm's financial structure and the necessity of meeting obligations on fixed income securities. The use of more debt or preference shares results in greater compulsory payments, which thereby increases the variability of earnings after taxes and earnings per share. That gives us the long-term view of financial risk. There is also short-term financial risk, of course, that relates to liquidity, solvency and interest cover. Taking both long- and short-term views tells us that financial risk is inherent in the way a business finances its activities.

Example of variability in earnings arising from differing financial structure

Table 16.2 illustrates the variability of earnings arising from differing financial structures of different organisations. The implications of financial risk are plain to see from Table 16.2. When company A decides to structure its £1 million capital employed in such a way that its debt amounts to £100,000, rather than company B structuring whereby its debt amounts to £900,000, it has an advantage. Interest cost obligations are radically different between the organisations. Hence the flexibility in the income statement of company A is clearly revealed.

TABLE 16.2 ***Variability of earnings from differing financial structures***

	Company A Low gearing	Company B High gearing
	£	£
Balance sheets (part of)		
Share capital	900,000	100,000
10% Debentures (Loans)	100,000	900,000
Capital employed	1,000,000	1,000,000
Therefore, annual interest payments	10,000	90,000
Income statements		
Sales	1,000,000	1,000,000
Total costs	800,000	800,000
Net profit before interest	200,000	200,000
Interest costs	10,000	90,000
Net profit before tax	190,000	110,000
Net profit before tax (%)	19	11

Political risk

If there is political instability in a country or region, there is a good chance that earnings from that country or region may be subject to variability. Such variability stems from political strife leading to strikes, riots, sequestration of assets and so on. This takes us back to the discussion on investment risk where we discussed the risk-versus-return idea. In an area that is known, or felt, to be politically unstable, the short-term return from that area will need to be higher than from a more stable environment: the higher the risk involved in undertaking an investment, the greater the return that will be required.

Environmental risk

Earnings may vary when an organisation falls foul of environmental issues. Consider the case where power stations in the United States have to ensure that emissions from the coal they burn to generate electricity are cleaner than before. In this case, power stations suffer a penalty if they do not or cannot match the new emission requirements. For this reason we can talk about variability of earnings due to environmental issues. As the world becomes greener and greener – that is, individuals, organisations and governments are more and more concerned to protect our environment – organisations need to pay greater attention to their environmental policies. There are now 'Green portfolios' in which investors only invest in those organisations that are seen to behave responsibly with respect to their environment. Hence, organisations acting in a non-acceptable way with respect to their environment may suffer reductions in sales and hence reductions in profit as a result of consumer or investor actions.

Internal versus external aspects of the various forms of risk

We should consider that the various types of risk arise from different sources. Thus we can see that financial risk, for example, arises from internally driven decisions: management decides their own levels of gearing. On the other hand, the amount of cataclysmic risk arises from outside the organisation and is thus not controllable by the management of that organisation. The source of the risk will determine management's attitude to it. If a risk emerges from inside the organisation, that risk can be controlled to a lesser or greater degree. If a risk emanates from outside an organisation, management can merely anticipate it and offset its effects as efficiently as possible as time goes by.

What is the usefulness of a knowledge of risk?

Having examined several of the various forms that risk can take, but before moving on to the way that management can quantify and deal with risk, we should consider whether a knowledge of the existence of risk and its forms is of any use to us as managers. Ho and Pike (1992) provide us with a most useful insight into the way that managers perceive a knowledge of risk when concerned with capital investment decisions. Based on 146 responses

TABLE 16.3 ***Formal risk analysis***

Incentive effect
■ Provides a useful insight into the project.
■ Improves quality of investment decisions.
■ Increases confidence in investment decisions.
■ Improves efficiency of investment decisions.
■ Enhances communications among managers.
■ Improves ultimate project performance.
Disincentive effect
■ Makes it more difficult to accept proposals.
■ Reduces managers' enthusiasm to generate/accept projects.
■ Leads to lower capital investment.

Source: Ho and Pike (1992: 40).

to a survey of 350 firms in *The Times* 1000, 1987, Ho and Pike's findings are shown in Table 16.3. They say:

> an examination of the means revealed a general agreement that . . . risk analysis provides useful insights into the project, improves decision quality and increases decision confidence. There was general disagreement that it reduces enthusiasm for project generation or leads to lower capital expenditure. (Ho and Pike 1992: 400)

As Table 16.3 shows, they found that the incentive effects of knowing more about the risk involved in capital investment projects were reasonably strong: that is, it is better to know about the risk of what one is doing than not to know. Furthermore the same survey reveals that 54% of respondents felt that risk analysis will become more important over the next five years. Management accountants and their clients, their management colleagues, are better off knowing about risk. But risk is something of an abstract concept since we cannot usually feel and see it. We do not tangibly know that risk is present or absent from a proposal or situation. Nevertheless, as accountants, we need to be able to attempt to quantify the effects of risk on our decisions before they are taken, in an attempt to minimise our potential losses.

What of management's attitude to risk?

Having discussed many aspects of risk, we need to ask the questions: What are managers' attitudes to risk? Is risk a problem? Do all managers suffer from risk nightmares? The answer is no, they do not. There are other managers, however, who are inherently afraid of risk: they not only do not like it, they are opposed to it and will avoid it at all costs. There are other managers, however, who thrive on risk; they love it. Managers who like risk will happily enter into a deal on the basis that there is a risk element attached to it. Any deal that does not have a risky edge to it is simply not exciting enough for them. Finally, there are those managers who are neither risk averse nor risk lovers (or seekers): they are said to be indifferent to risk. Someone who is indifferent to risk is not afraid of it – but neither

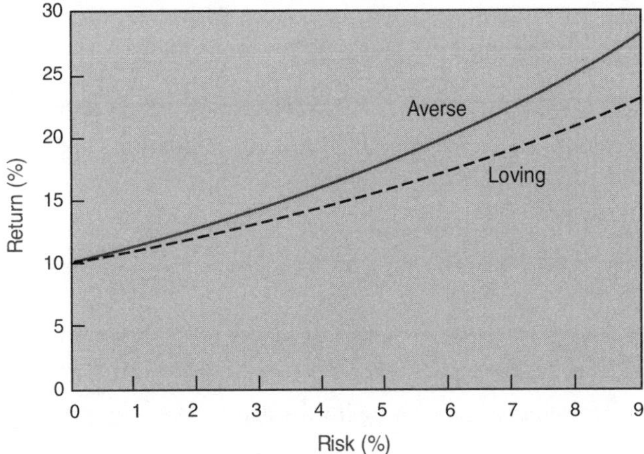

FIGURE 16.4 *Risk versus return: attitudes to risk*

does he or she go looking for it. Figure 16.4 illustrates a risk versus return graph for two of the three types of managers we have just discussed: risk averse, and risk loving. The figure shows that the risk-averse manager needs a higher rate of return at almost all levels of risk than his or her risk-loving colleague.

Dealing with risk

In the simplest of all worlds, management simply adds a risk premium to the profit it requires from a project before deciding to undertake it. That is, before investing large amounts of money in a capital project, management may determine that a project will return, say, £10 million over a life of seven years. Having found such a return, management will then, to cover the possibility of greater or lesser variability in it, add a premium of, say, £4 million. Hence the required return is now £14 million, not £10 million for the project. Hertz (1964) reports a number of ways by which businessmen have attempted to cope with risk:

1. More accurate forecasts.
2. Empirical adjustments: for example, a comparison of actual results and budgeted data reveal that costs are 90% accurately forecast; hence forecasts are adjusted in the light of this experience.
3. Revising cut off rates: selecting higher rates of return to protect against uncertainty, inflation and so on.
4. Three-level estimates: management prepare high, middle and low values of estimated factors; although these are not necessarily empirically based.
5. Selected probabilities: these may be objective (based on historic data) or subjective (I feel 10% of the time . . .); or on the basis of statistical or computer simulations.

These are not, on the whole, very scientific approaches, of course. However, they have existed in this or similar forms both before and after Hertz wrote about them in 1964.

Here we are concerned to make our estimates more scientifically based than merely making the kind of adjustments that may or may not be realistic. To try to overcome the problems facing us, we will consider three methods: expected value criteria; simulation; and risk adjusted rates.

CAMEO

Examples of how organisations cope with their own risk factors

Even organisations that enjoy monopoly privileges operate under one or more forms of risk. In the case of a true monopoly, the largest risk could be managerial competence, or incompetence. However, most organisations do not operate under the benefits of monopoly power, hence they have risk to be coped with or diversified. Shapiro (1992) gives several examples of the ways in which risk can be managed, and he does so under a variety of headings. Under the heading of the marketing management of exchange risk, Shapiro discusses the way that American textile mills have competitive advantages in terms of the success with which they can manufacture certain fabrics, and also in their inventory management systems and procedures. Shapiro then goes on to report that because it is clear that America is the place to be to reap the rewards of such expertise, Japanese and Korean organisations are setting up their textile operations there rather than in their home countries.

Under the heading of production management of exchange risk, Shapiro gives the example of Japanese car manufacturers who are outsourcing their components. Outsourcing means having the component parts, in this example, made by independent third parties. In the case of Japan, the benefits of outsourcing in third-party countries – not only in third-party organisations – is that they are protecting themselves from the effects of the rising value of the yen on the world currency markets.

Shapiro gives several more examples along the lines of the two given here. The most important point that should be borne in mind when reading what he has to say is that the changes which Japanese organisations have gone through have happened against a background of: 'The 100% appreciation of the Japanese yen against the dollar from 1985 to 1988' (Shapiro (1992: 262).

Taking Shapiro's examples, including one final one reported below, the Japanese have clearly been operating on a 'needs must when the devil drives' philosophy. Toshiba, according to Shapiro were faced, in 1988, with the situation where the effects of a rising yen value were eating away at any cost advantage they had. Overall, Toshiba is estimated to have saved ¥115 billion by restructuring its organisation to cope with the effects of the exchange rate fluctuations.

Source: Shapiro (1992).

The expected value criterion

The expected value criterion of a project is the projected or budgeted result multiplied by the probability that this result will occur.Thus to apply the expected value technique, we need both budgetary information and estimates of the likelihood of each outcome. We can illustrate the expected value technique by using a coin tossing example. Assume that we are gambling on the outcome of tossing a coin – you and I are betting against each other. Toss by toss, one of us will win something from the other. However, overall, we can anticipate the final outcome by matching the sum waged with the likely outcomes; and this will give us the expected value or payoff. We know that when we toss a fair coin, we expect it to land heads up 50% of the time: the probability of obtaining a head is 50% or 0.5. Similarly, the probability of obtaining a tail is 50% or 0.5. Hence, we can calculate our expected payoffs now, by assuming we are gambling to win £25 and that we are gambling on heads being uppermost on every occasion. The expected payoff is shown in Table 16.4.

Hence, when a head appears, we win, when a tail appears, we lose. Consequently, we expect to win 50% of the time, therefore our expected payoff is 50% of the possible winnings of £25 which is £12.50.

Interpreting the expected value

On a toss-by-toss basis we may win or lose: all or nothing. In the long run, however, we would win 50% of the time. The expected value or payoff, then, is the weighted average outcome of a large number of trials. However the expected value criterion is presented, it is never any more than the weighted average of the various outcomes.

Dealing with uncertainty

We know from the definitions at the beginning of this chapter that a risky situation is one in which there are several different outcomes, but there is sufficient knowledge on which to base a decision. In reality, there are often several outcomes but there is not sufficient evidence on which to base a decision: in other words, outcomes are uncertain. For the rest of this chapter we will be dealing with an uncertain situation, not a risky one. That is, there will be several outcomes, and the statistical evidence on which our calculations are based is relatively scarce.

TABLE 16.4 *Expected payoff from gambling on heads only*

Possible winnings (£)	Outcome	Probability of outcome	Expected value of outcome (£)	Total expected payoff (£)
25	Heads	0.5	12.5	12.5
0	Tails	0.5	0.0	

Decision tree analysis

As we saw in Chapter 11, one most useful application of expected value criterion is decision tree analysis in which we can model a whole series of events and possible outcomes and from there calculate an expected value or payoff. Decision tree analysis follows the logic of the coin tossing example we have just seen in the previous section. However, Worked example 16.1 takes us through the components of decision tree analysis and uncertainty.

WORKED EXAMPLE 16.1

An investment opportunity has arisen for OurCo Ltd that has the following characteristics. The initial investment is to be £1 million, and there are three possible outcomes to this investment. The outcomes and the financial results associated with them are given below:

Outcome classification	Probability of occurrence	Contribution (£)	Probability of achieving contribution
Excellent	0.1	500,000	0.3
		600,000	0.5
		400,000	0.2
Moderate	0.6	500,000	0.4
		400,000	0.4
		300,000	0.2
Poor	0.3	300,000	0.3
		150,000	0.6
		50,000	0.1

The fixed costs associated with all of these outcomes amount to £275,000.

Required

1. What is the expected value of this opportunity?;
2. Interpret the result.

Solution to Worked example 16.1

Expected value of opportunity

Here we have one opportunity, each with three possible outcomes; and each outcome has three possible sub-outcomes: a total of nine possible results. To calculate the total expected value for this opportunity, we need to construct a decision tree that will evaluate each element of the decision. The table that follows gives us the result we are looking for:

Invest	Prob (outcome)	Contribution (contrib)	Pr	FC	Profit	EV
		800	0.3	275	525	15.750
	0.1	600	0.5	275	325	16.250
		400	0.2	275	125	2.500
		500	0.4	275	225	54.000
1,000	0.6	400	0.4	275	125	30.000
		300	0.2	275	25	3.000
		300	0.3	275	25	2.250
	0.3	150	0.6	275	(125)	−2.500
		50	0.1	275	(225)	−0.750
Total expected value						94.500

Notes: Pr = probability.
All monetary values are given in £'000.
Here we are dealing with conditional probabilities: conditional in the sense that the probability of any outcome is dependent upon which event it is. That is, the [excellent, excellent] outcome has a joint probability of 3% conditional upon the excellent outcome having a probability of 10% and the excellent contribution outcome being 30% (10% × 30% = 3%).

This decision tree works this way:

1. The decision point is whether to invest £1 million.
2. If we invest, there are three possible outcomes (often referred to as states of nature):

   (a) excellent results;
   (b) moderate results; and
   (c) poor results.

3. For each outcome we have a further classifcation of their worth:

   (a) excellent results;
   (b) moderate results; and
   (c) poor results.

4. Each row of the tree contains a combination of the probabilities and the financial values. For example, excellent, excellent results:

   (a) there is a 10% chance (0.1 probability) of excellent results overall; and given this excellent result, there is 30% chance (0.3 probability) that the contribution derived from this project will be £800,000.
   (b) Hence, the total probability of this outcome is:

   $$0.1 \times 0.3 = 0.03$$

   and the financial outcome is:

£800,000 − £275,000 = £525,000

(c) Consequently, the expected value of this row is

0.03 × £525,000 = £15,750

From our knowledge of probability analysis, we know that the sum of all probabilities for a given set of outcomes must be 1.0, or 100%. We should check that this is the case. For the initial outcomes, the probabilities are:

Excellent results	0.1
Moderate results	0.6
Poor results	0.3
Total probabilities	1.0

For the sub-outcomes, for excellent, excellent results, the probabilities are:

Excellent results	0.3
Moderate results	0.5
Poor results	0.2
Total probabilities	1.0

Finally, for the whole decision tree, the overall total probabilities must sum to 1, and they do:

Outcome	Sub-outcome	Probabilities (sum)
Excellent	Excellent	0.03
Excellent	Moderate	0.05
Excellent	Poor	0.02
Moderate	Excellent	0.24
Moderate	Moderate	0.24
Moderate	Poor	0.12
Poor	Excellent	0.09
Poor	Moderate	0.18
Poor	Poor	0.03
Total probability		1.00

Interpreting the decision tree

What does the final result of an expected value of £94,500 mean? The final overall expected value is interpreted as meaning that if this investment opportunity were carried out a large number of times, we would expect, on average, the final profit figure to be £94,500. That is, 3% of the time the profit would be £15,750 (excellent, excellent); 5% of the time the profit would be £16,250 (excellent, moderate); 24% of the time the expected profit would be £54,000 (moderate, excellent); and 3% of the time the expected profit would be £(6,750) (poor, poor). The benefit of the decision tree analysis approach is that we do not need to have carried out this investment opportunity a large number of times: in fact, this is usually impossible. By carrying out normal project analysis and assigning realistic probabilities to them, we are effectively taking a short cut and simulating a large number of trials.

Probabilities

Where do the probabilities come from?

When we looked at the way Hertz (1964) reported a number of ways by which businessmen have attempted to cope with uncertainty, we mentioned subjective and objective probabilities. These are the two types of probability assignment that may be used in decision tree analysis.

Subjective probabilities

Subjective probabilities are those probabilities that arise from intuition. That is, we assign probabilities on the basis of how we feel a situation will arise. For example, we might say we believe there is a 10% chance that this project will give us excellent results (excellent, excellent), and so on. If we accept subjective probabilities, we are accepting our subjective assessment and understanding of the situation: that is, we trust our intuition. The problem with being subjective is that it is subject to significant amounts of bias. There is no way of measuring how realistic the manager's assessment is. We do not know whether a 10% probability rating for an excellent, excellent result is realistic or far from it. Hence, we would prefer objective probabilities where possible.

Objective probabilities

Objective probabilities, on the other hand, are more scientifically based. By objective probabilities, we mean that we take historical data or statistically analysed data as the basis of our probability analysis. This means that we are no longer using our intuition in order to arrive at expected values. Using objective probabilities has no effect other than that they provide a more scientific base for our work. The methods and procedures we have already gone through in worked example 16.1 remain unchanged whether we are using either subjective or objective probabilities.

Cumulative probability distributions

One further useful aspect of our work with probabilities arises from our ability, having prepared our decision tree, to derive a cumulative probability distribution (CPD). A CPD allows us to answer such questions as, what is the probability of, say, breaking even; or making a profit of at least £55,000. Worked example 16.2 illustrates a CPD.

WORKED EXAMPLE 16.2

Required

1. Prepare a CPD from the decision tree derived in the solution to Worked example 16.1.
2. Calculate the probability of making:

   (a) a profit of at least £2,500; and
   (b) a loss of £6,750 (that is, a loss of £6,750 or better)

Solution to Worked example 16.2

1. Note that CPDs follow on naturally from decision tree analysis.

   All we need to do to be able to prepare a cumulative distribution is to sort our final profitability data in ascending order and then calculate cumulative probabilities. First, in order to derive this distribution, we have to rank the expected values, EV, ranging from the smallest outcome to the largest. Secondly, we list the total probabilities associated with each of the nine outcomes (Pr(sum)). Thirdly, we derive the cumulative probabilities (Cum Pr(sum)) by adding together the successive probabilities from outcome one to outcome two to outcome three, and so on:

EV	Pr(sum)	Cum Pr(sum)
(22,500)	0.18	
(6,750)	0.03	0.18
2,250	0.09	0.21
2,500	0.02	0.30
3,000	0.12	0.32
15,750	0.03	0.44
16,250	0.05	0.47
30,000	0.24	0.52
54,000	0.24	0.76
		1.00
94,500	1.00	

2. We can now answer questions such as: what is the probability of making a profit of at least £2,500? And a loss of £6,750 (that is, a loss of £6,750 or better)?

   (a) The probability of making a profit of at least £2,500 is 32%.
   (b) The probability of making a loss of at most £6,750 is 21%.

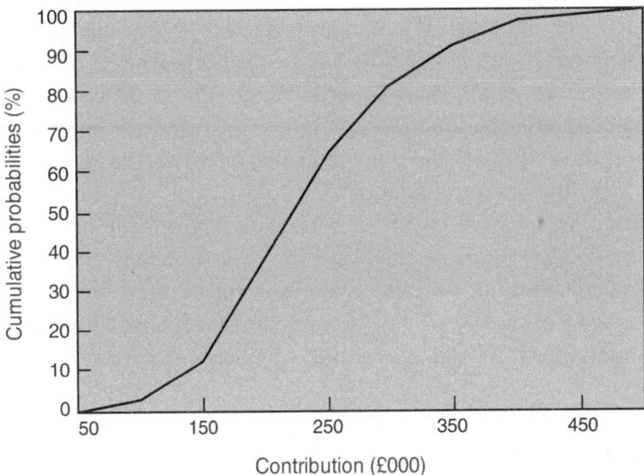

FIGURE 16.5 *Cumulative probability distribution*

Limitations of the cumulative probability distribution

Whilst the CPD gives us a lot of useful information, it does have its limitations. For example, from the solution to Worked example 16.2, what is the probability of making a profit of at least £20,000? The answer is that we cannot say, because of a lack of information. Such a CPD does not give us complete information. The solution to this general problem has two possible solutions: graphical; and mathematical.

Again based on the solution to Worked example 16.2, Figure 16.5 presents us with the graph of the CPD. From this graph we can estimate the value we are looking for: that is, the cumulative probability of earning a profit of at least £20,000. By inspection, the solution appears to be a probability of approximately 47% that profits will be at least £20,000. We can repeat this exercise for any level of expected profit and we will obtain a useful answer. However, as we know from the previous work we have done on scattergraph analysis, we are certain to face problems using graphical analysis, problems which stem from the inaccuracy of our graph and so on. Additionally, looking at Figure 16.5 closely, we see that between the profit/loss regions of − £6,750 to + £10,000, we have a curiously shaped curve. How do we interpret this section? Given the curiosity of the shape, do we believe it without question or do we attempt to model it more carefully?

The nature of the data and curve contained in Figure 16.5 could cause us problems as we have just admitted. How can we overcome these problems? When we deal with data that tends to behave in a linear way, we can approximate the data and curve reasonably easily: we use the high–low method, the scattergraph method or ordinary least squares. With the example we have now, we are dealing with curvilinear data. Mathematically, we could be dealing with a complex situation that is not easy to model. Transforming these data by logarithms does not help our analysis. When regressing the profits against the cumulative probabilities, the *r* squared value is 0.9547; yet when both sets of data are transformed by logarithms and regressed again, the *r* squared value falls to 0.9094. With CPDs we might be dealing with an exponential function to the power of three or even four. Deriving such functions is beyond the scope of this book; but the interested reader could refer to Kaplan and Atkinson (1989) for further guidance.

One way to improve on the situation we have just described is to carry out the proposed investment a large number of times. By working in this way, we have sufficient data to be sure not only that our results are meaningful, but also that they can be used with more confidence than is otherwise perhaps the case. One way to carry out investment projects a large number of times is by simulation, so we are now going to discuss the Monte Carlo simulations technique.

Monte Carlo simulations

Although there is a wealth of statistical theory underlying Monte Carlo simulations (MCs), including advanced integral calculus, the aspects of it we will be dealing with here will be much more user friendly:

> The [Monte Carlo] method itself does not directly improve a model but it can assist in highlighting where improvement is needed. In particular, it can provide valuable insights into the dynamic behaviour of a model in response to risk. (Rouse 1993: 113–14)

MCs are eminently suitable for spreadsheet analysis since almost any spreadsheet contains a sufficient number of functions and commands to enable us to generate random numbers and carry out statistical analysis. Rouse's paper is written specifically for use with Lotus 1-2-3, but it can be readily modified by users of, for example, Excel, SuperCalc, Joe Spreadsheet and so on. The essence of MCs is that they are based on the generation and use of random numbers drawn from a normally distributed set of random numbers. Whilst most, if not all spreadsheets have problems with the integrity of their random number generators, they tend to work within acceptable tolerances. By assigning the random numbers we generate carefully, we can build in a simulation of risk. For example, if we have two possible outcomes 'A' and 'B', with probabilities of occurrence of 40% and 60% respectively, we could assign random numbers 0 to 39 for outcome 'A' and random numbers 40 to 99 to outcome 'B'. On average, therefore, if the numbers are truly randomly generated, we twould draw out a number for outcome 'A' 40% of the time and a number for 'B' 60% of the time. So far this is simple! The power of MCs is that we can combine many different possible outcomes in any one simulation and, rather than becoming bogged down in a hideously complex spreadsheet or decision tree, we would have a simulation that was relatively easy both to construct and to use. Worked example 16.3 takes us through a small MC.

WORKED EXAMPLE 16.3

MyCo Ltd has carried out extensive marketing research on a product it is wishing to launch nationwide. Once the product had been launched, Joseph Psmith would be assigned profit centre responsibilities for the product. Hence, Psmith classes this launch in terms of an investment project. The summary data, including the objective probabilities derived for them, are given below:

Selling price per unit	Prob.	Volume	Prob.	VC per unit	Prob.
100	0.15	10,000	0.05	75	0.20
95	0.15	9,000	0.20	70	0.20
90	0.30	8,000	0.25	65	0.25
85	0.30	7,000	0.30	60	0.20
80	0.10	6,000	0.20	55	0.15

where:
Prob. = probability
VC = variable cost

Required

Carry out a Monte Carlo simulation analysis of the above data and report your findings to your management colleagues. Use the non-dependent format for your solution. (There is a table of 400 randomly generated numbers at the end of the practice questions for this chapter that you might find useful in answering this question.)

Solution to Worked example 16.3

Most of the work for this solution was carried out in a spreadsheet. You are encouraged to do the same. Such analysis takes a significant amount of time to carry out, but the results are interesting, complex and a lot of spreadsheet programming learning can take place! The first section of the spreadsheet developed to deal with this problem is shown below. The first point to note is that we are dealing here with a **non-dependent model**. To keep the model simple at this stage, we can assume that selling prices, sales volumes and variable costs are all independent of each other. In other words, the selling price does not depend upon the number of units sold, or vice versa. Similarly with the variable costs per unit.

Partial outputs: non-dependent model

Trial number	Volume (Random number)	Total sales volume	Sales (Random number)	Selling price (£)	Total sales (£)
1	58	7,000	53	90	630,000
2	62	7,000	16	95	665,000
3	40	8,000	37	90	720,000
4	91	6,000	14	100	600,000

Note: the random numbers in this schedule are not taken from the table of random numbers found at the end of this chapter.

Each trial in the above table simulates one investment in the project under review. That is, the row containing trial one shows us the volume achieved, at the relevant selling price, together with the variable cost per unit (not shown in the table). From these data we can simply derive the total sales revenues and variable costs and hence derive the total contribution. For the first trial, we generate a random number. In the case of volume, the first number generated was 58. We use the number 58 to identify how many units this simulates having been sold. In this case, this is 7,000 units. Similarly, for the selling price, we generate another random number, 53, and this tells us that the selling price per unit is £90 per unit. Hence, total sales value is £630,000. To handle the random numbers generated and the volumes and values determined by them, we use a LOOKUP table in the spreadsheet. Rouse demonstrates a full LOOKUP table in his article. However, the LOOKUP table that is required in this case is given below: we need only tabulate a LOOKUP table that contains the relevant class intervals (different for each variable in this example). Rouse admits that his full version is not required, but he does not demonstrate it.

LOOKUP Tables

Random number	Volume	Random number	Sales	Random number	VC per unit
0	10,000	0	100	0	75
5	9,000	15	95	19	70
24	8,000	29	90	39	65
49	7,000	59	85	64	60
79	6,000	89	80	84	55

The question now arises: How many trials do we carry out? How many investments do we simulate? In this exercise, two series of trials were carried out: 40 trials per simulation run; and 130 trials per simulation run. At the end of 10 simulations runs, each of 40 trials, then of 130 trials, the overall average results were:

Trials	40
Mean	187,950
Standard deviation	70,475
Maximum	358,000
Minimum	52,500

Trials	130
Mean	180,835
Standard deviation	73,589
Maximum	345,100
Minimum	38,500

These results are our expected values or payoffs. Thus, if we simulate our investment opportunity 40 × 10 times, we average a contribution of £187,950, with a standard deviation of £70,475. If we simulate our investment 130 × 10 times, we average a contribution level of £180,835 which has a standard deviation of £73,589. In general, the more complex the simulation, the more trials we ought to have. There is a danger that with only a total of 40 trials, we have not provided enough of a spread of possible outcomes to give us a proper idea of the likely outcomes we will face. In Worked example 16.3, 400 trials gave an average contribution of £187,950 whereas 1,300 trials gave an average contribution of less than that, at £180,835. Since we are dealing with random numbers, there is no guarantee that we can replicate these results, of course. If we carry out a further simulation of 400 or 1,300 trials, we could easily obtain significantly different results. The table below shows two separate continuous sets of simulations of 400 then 1,300 trials. In each case, the 400 trial simulation is part of the 1,300 trial simulation: it is a subset of it.

Contributions

Trials	400	1,300	400	1,300
Mean	183,625	185,096	177,463	182,462
Standard deviation	72,496	71,830	71,766	73,799
Maximum	405,000	405,000	405,000	450,000
Minimum	30,000	30,000	30,000	30,000

Note that despite the large number of trials simulated in every case, no two sets of results are the same.

Recommendations to Psmith

Finally, we have to report our findings to Psmith. Should he undertake the launch of the product and become the manager of the profit centre that would go with the launch? To help Psmith with his problem, we should now prepare a cumulative probability distribution (see Table 16.5). The data in Table 16.5 are shown in Figure 16.6.

We now know that the average contribution is around £180,000. Provided total fixed costs for this profit centre and product are significantly less than this, Psmith's department will be profitable. Similarly, from the CPD, we know that there is a 62.7% chance of achieving a contribution of greater than £200,000. All Psmith needs to know now are his fixed costs and he can make his final decision.

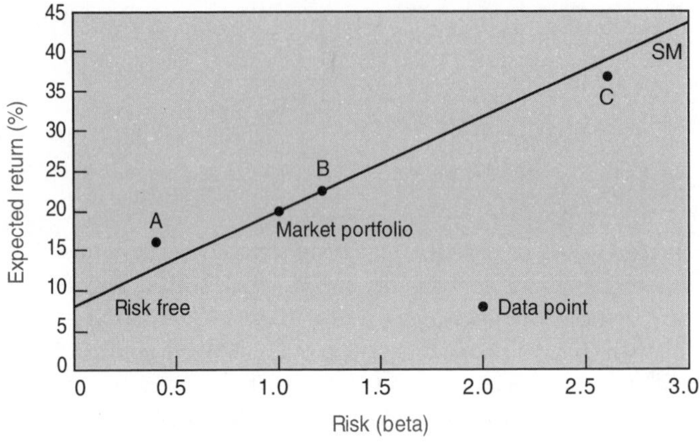

FIGURE 16.6 *Risk, return, beta, and SML*

TABLE 16.5 *Cumulative probability function*

Contribution (£)	Cumulative frequency (%)	Frequency (%)
less than:		
50,000	2.5	–
100,000	10.0	2.5
150,000	24.7	12.5
200,000	26.2	37.2
250,000	17.5	63.4
300,000	10.5	80.9
350,000	6.0	91.4
400,000	1.8	97.4
450,000	0.8	99.2
	–	100.0

Note: n = 400.

Benefits of the Monte Carlo method

Worked example 16.3 should have helped to demonstrate the flexibility of the MC method, providing we have all worked through a spreadsheet of that example (Rouse's (1993) paper is also helpful here). We have worked through simulations of 40 trials, 130 trials, 400 trials and 1,300 trials – all with relative ease once the spreadsheet is established. Depending on the memory available on our computer, we can simulate thousands of outcomes with the MC method. Furthermore we could have set up an example involving a lot more than the three variables shown in Worked example 16.3. For instance, Hertz (1964) simulated an investment planning exercise and used nine different variables in arriving at his overall rate-of-return distribution. Setting up an MC model on a computer is much easier than trying to draft the equivalent decision tree. Although it has not been demonstrated here, the interested reader can attempt to set up the decision tree to answer Worked example 16.3 – not overly horrific, but it will not fit easily on to one piece of paper. Finally, the MC can easily incorporate even complex interdependencies. Worked example 16.3 has excluded such dependencies, but check the practice questions at the end of this chapter for an example of a model calling for the setting up of an MC model with dependencies. Additionally, see Rouse (1993) for a fully worked example containing dependencies.

Useful though the Monte Carlo method is, another way of discounting the risk element of a decision is to calculate what is called the certainty equivalent adjustment.

Certainty equivalent method for risk adjustment

The certainty equivalent coefficient (CEC) allows adjustment for risk by incorporating the manager's utility preference for risk versus return directly into the capital investment process. The CEC reflects management's perceptions of the degree of risk associated with the established cash flow distribution as well as management's degree of aversion to perceived risk. A value of 1 for a CEC indicates that management does not associate any risk with established cash flows. Therefore, it accepts it as certain. Because the certainty equivalents method compensates for risk in its entirety, the correct discount rate to use in all calculations is the risk-free rate of return. For the application of the certainty equivalent method we need to devise or calculate a series of risk factors.

The certainty equivalent formula is:

$$\bar{CE} = \sum_{t=0}^{n} \frac{\Sigma_t \bar{R}_t}{(1+\mathrm{i})^t}$$

where:

$\bar{CE}$ = the expected certainty equivalent value over the life of the project
$\bar{R}_t$ = the expected cash flow in period t
Σ_t = the certainty equivalent factor that converts the expected risky cash flow into its perceived certainty equivalent factor
i = the risk-free rate that is assumed to remain constant over the life of the project
n = the life of the project in years

Worked example 16.4 takes us through a relatively simple example of the application of the certainty equivalent method.

WORKED EXAMPLE 16.4

The Hermanns project has an initial cost of £13,000 and the firm's risk-free interest rate is 10%. The certainty equivalents and net cash flows for the project are as below.

Year	Certainty equivalents	Net cash flows (£)
1	0.90	8,000
2	0.85	7,000
3	0.80	7,000
4	0.75	5,000
5	0.70	5,000
6	0.65	5,000
7	0.60	5,000

Required

Should this project be accepted for further review by management?

Solution to Worked example 16.4

To solve all problems such as this one, we need to set out the kind of table we see below. All of the relevant workings are shown in that table. Read the appendix to Chapter 17 if you do not know discounted cash flow theory.

Year	ENCF £	CEC_t	ENCF × CEC_t £	DF(10%)	Present value £
0	−13,000	1.00	−13,000	1.0000	−13,000
1	8,000	0.90	7,200	0.9091	6,546
2	7,000	0.85	5,950	0.8264	4,917
3	7,000	0.80	5,600	0.7513	4,207
4	5,000	0.75	3,750	0.6830	2,561
5	5,000	0.70	3,500	0.6209	2,173
6	5,000	0.65	3,250	0.5645	1,835
7	5,000	0.60	3,000	0.5132	1,540
Certainty equivalent					10,779

(ENCF = expected net cash flow; DF = discount factor.)

The value of £10,779 tells us that, discounting all elements of risk, the net present value of this project is £10,779. Since this is a positive result, this project is acceptable and worthy of further consideration. It is rarely the case that rates of interest are fixed even in the short and medium term. The following worked example illustrates the effect of changing interest rates on the certainty equivalent method of project evaluation. In fact, the worked example provides us with a general solution to the problem of fluctuating interest rates.

WORKED EXAMPLE 16.5

Assume the estimated cash flows for a project, the risk-free rate of return, and the certainty equivalent coefficients are as follows:

Year	Σ_t	R_t	Risk free return
0	1.00	−£3,000	0
1	0.95	1,000	0.05
2	0.92	1,500	0.06
3	0.89	1,700	0.07

Required

Determine the certainty equivalent value.

Solution to Worked example 16.5

Year	ENCF £	CEC_t	ENCF × CEC_t £	DF*	Present value £
0	−3,000	1.00	−3,000	1.0000	−3,000
1	1,000	0.95	950	0.9524	905
2	1,500	0.92	1,380	0.8985	1,240
3	1,700	0.89	1,513	0.8397	1,270
Certainty equivalent					£ 415

Note: *the discount factor calculations are as follows:

$DF_1 = 1/(1.05) = 0.9524$

$DF_2 = 1/((1.05)(1.06)) = 0.8985$

$DF_3 = 1/((1.05)(1.06)(1.07)) = 0.8397$

The questions may have arisen in your minds: Where does Σ_t come from? How can I calculate it? It can be found from the following transposed formula:

$$\Sigma_t = \frac{PV_t(1+i)^t}{\overline{X}_t} = \frac{\dfrac{\overline{X}_t}{(1+r)^t} \times (1+i)^t}{\overline{X}_t} = \frac{(1+i)^t}{(1+r)^t}$$

The following worked example is added simply to provide those of us who need practice at using formulæ such as the one above.

WORKED EXAMPLE 16.6

1. Calculate Σ_t from the following:

t	r	i
0	15%	8%
1	15%	8%
2	15%	8%
3	15%	8%
4	15%	8%

2. In this case, find r when:

$\bar{X}_1 = 1{,}000$ $\quad i = 6\%$ $\quad \Sigma_1 = 0.86$

Solution to Worked example 16.6

1. Without further comment, the results of this exercise are given in the following table.

t	r	i	Σ_t
0	15%	8%	1.0000
1	15%	8%	0.9391
2	15%	8%	0.8820
3	15%	8%	0.8283
4	15%	8%	0.7779

2. Similarly, without comment, $r = 18.87\%$

Risk-adjusted discount rates

A discount rate, or the cost of capital or the required rate of return, is the rate of return that we require to be earned by a project or investment. The discount rate is the rate of return that we will be applying to the discussion of capital budgeting projects in subsequent chapters. A discount rate is the equivalent of the rate of interest that we might have to pay to generate financing for our projects or assets. In general terms, the discount rate, or the required rate of return, is:

risk free rate + average past risk premium

where the average past risk premium is defined by Drury (1992: 399) as: 'the difference between the average past return on long term gilts and the average past return on ordinary shares over the long term'.

Thus, if the average past return on long-term gilts is 6% and the average past return on ordinary shares over the long term is 14%, then the average past risk premium is

14% – 6% = 8%. Consequently, if the current risk-free rate of return is 7%, then the discount rate, or required rate of return is 7% + 8% = 15%. When we worked through the meaning of Figure 16.1, above, we noted that there is a relationship between the amount of risk associated with an investment and the return we are likely to achieve. The higher the risk, the higher return we are likely to need to be persuaded to invest in that project. Ziobrowski and Ziobrowski (1995), in discussing exchange rate risk and its diversification in internationally diversified portfolios, give data on historical rates of return. Table 16.6 shows extracts of mean and standard deviations of returns taken from Ziobrowski and Ziobrowski's paper.

TABLE 16.6 *Mean and standard deviations of risk*

Asset	Mean annual return	Standard deviation (%)	Return/risk ratio (%)
US stocks	13.00	17.94	0.72
US Gov LT bonds	9.81	12.56	0.78
UK stocks	19.22	37.17	0.52
UK Gov LT bonds	12.65	22.42	0.56
Japanese stocks	17.98	29.08	0.62
Jap. Gov LT bonds	14.59	19.85	0.74

Note: Gov LT bonds = government long-term bonds
Source: Ziobrowski and Ziobrowski (1995: 69), table 1.

The kind of data shown in Table 16.6 is the kind of data that we need to use help us assess the required rate of return as defined at the beginning of this section.

The risk-adjusted discount rate method of risk adjustment

Quite simply, the risk-adjusted discount rate (RADR) is found by:

$$r' = \mathrm{i} + u + a$$

where:

r' = the RADR
i = the risk-free rate
u = adjustment for the firm's normal risk
a = adjustment for risk is greater or less than the firm's normal risk level.

In a similar manner to the certainty equivalent method, the RADR method requires a table to be drafted of the required rates of return for each class of investment. For example, if an investment is of the kind that has historically proven to be slightly risky, we might determine that the RADR for that project should be the risk free rate plus, say, 3%. Worked example 16.7 introduces and develops the RADR method.

WORKED EXAMPLE 16.7

Helen Ltd builds ships and is about to launch a new design of container carrier. This will entail a large investment in new plant, equipment and machinery. The management of Helen Ltd is not entirely risk averse, but it wants to take a rational investment decision with as little risk left undiscounted as possible. Historically, Helen's management has set the following required rates of return, or hurdle rates, for the three kinds of projects that it has previously invested in:

Project type	Hurdle rate
Replacement investment	Risk-free rate + 3%
New investment	Risk-free rate + 6%
Widening investment	Risk-free rate + 9%

Helen Ltd believes that since this is a new investment opportunity, it should use the RADR of risk-free plus 6%, where the risk-free rate is the equivalent of government bond rates of 7% per annum. The cash flows have been estimated for this project as follows:

	£m.
Initial cost	−51
Year 1	−3
Year 2	−1
Year 3	9
Year 4	10
Year 5–15	12

Required

Advise the management of Helen Ltd as to the acceptability of this new investment opportunity.

Solution to Worked example 16.7

The formula for determining the expected present value of an investment opportunity such as this one, using the RADR is:

$$RAR = \sum_{t=0}^{n} \frac{R_t}{(1+r)^t}$$

The following table shows, in full, the workings and application of the risk-adjusted discount rate formula:

Year	Cash flow	Discount rate	Present value £
0	−51	1.0000	−51.00
1	−3	0.8850	−2.65

2	−1	0.7831	−0.78
3	9	0.6931	6.24
4	10	0.6133	6.13
5	12	0.5428	6.51
6	12	0.4803	5.76
7	12	0.4251	5.10
8	12	0.3762	4.51
9	12	0.3329	3.99
10	12	0.2946	3.54
11	12	0.2607	3.13
12	12	0.2307	2.77
13	12	0.2042	2.45
14	12	0.1807	2.17
15	12	0.1599	1.92
Net present value			−0.21

The interpretation of this solution is that at an initial capital cost of £51 million, and a cash flow profile as given in the example, this opportunity is not worth while undertaking since the net present value (NPV) is negative. That is, it will return a negative change to the wealth of Helen Ltd over the entire life of the project.

Notes

1. The concept of present values is developed in detail in the appendix to Chapter 17. Some readers will find it profitable to read this appendix before going any further.
2. Kennedy's (1983) article on this topic is fairly comprehensive and well worth a read through since it is written in an easy-to-understand style.

We can extend our discussion now to encompass a much more scientifically based method involving the use of betas and the capital asset pricing model.

Betas

A beta is a measure of the level of risk inherent in a project, investment or security. The higher the beta value, the higher the risk involved in owning and operating that asset and the higher the return that will be required to persuade the investor to invest in that asset. It is accepted that a beta value of 1.0 represents the average market portfolio, where the market portfolio is a security, investment or project with a beta of 1.0. The market portfolio may also be defined as being the average stock, that is, a stock which is defined as one which tends to move up and down in line with the general market as measured by an index such as the *Financial Times* Ordinary Share Index. Thus, if the market moves up by 10%, the stock will also move upwards by 10%. A beta is defined as being the

$$\frac{\text{covariance of return on the security with return on market portfolio}}{\text{variance of return on market portfolio}}$$

A portfolio of low beta securities will itself have a low beta, since the beta of any set of securities is the weighted average of the individual securities' betas. Because a project's beta measures its contribution to the riskiness of a portfolio, beta is the appropriate measure of the stock's riskiness. The beta values for all quoted companies are calculated by a variety of organisations. In the United Kingdom, for example, the London Business School and Datastream do our work for us; in the United States, it is Merrill Lynch. Beta values are useful of themselves, and beta values are the basis of a lot of analysis that investors may wish to carry out. In this chapter, however, we will be using betas in connection with the capital asset pricing model

Capital asset pricing model (CAPM)

The CAPM relates the return of a project to a broad-based economic indicator of returns on risky assets, as signified by stock market indices. The model asserts a linear relationship existing between the returns on a risky asset and the relevant index. We use the outputs of the CAPM in the same way that we use the outputs of the RADR.

> A capital asset is an asset with a life of greater than one year, expected to earn an income sufficient to cover the amortization of its acquisition cost and operation expenses plus a net yield commensurate with the time value of money and risk. The term includes long-lived physical assets (plant and equipment) plus claims on such assets (common stocks, bonds, and other securities). (Clark, Hindelang and Pritchard 1989: 269 n.)

Using market data, the CAPM determines the required rate of return that we mentioned above; it provides us with an estimate of the cost of capital of a project, investment or asset; and it can be used to value a firm and a firm's incremental debt capacity if the project is accepted. The capital asset pricing model allows us to calculate both the capital market line (CML) and the security market line (SML).

Capital market line

The CML represents the aggregate view of the various individual portfolio preferences of the market: it is the line representing the whole market for securities. The average portfolio on the CML – the equilibrium portfolio – must contain every risky asset in the exact proportion to that asset's fraction of the total market value of all risky assets.

Security market line

Of more interest to us in this chapter is the SML, the line that describes the view of individual securities or investments or projects.

SML formula:

$$\text{expected return on a security} = \text{risk-free rate} + \left(\text{expected return on market portfolio} - \text{risk-free rate}\right) \times \text{Beta}$$

Hence, for a security where the risk-free rate is 8%, the expected return on the market portfolio is 20% and the security's beta is 1, the expected return on this security is

$$8\% + (20 - 8\%) \times 1$$

$$= 20\%$$

We need a return of 20% on this security given the level of risk built into this situation. Figure 16.6 shows the effect of the above on Figure 16.1. We now have a Figure where we have defined risk in terms of betas. From Figure 16.6 we can estimate the expected return on a security for any known level of risk. Conversely, we could estimate the riskiness of a security, given the rate of return experienced. Also shown on Figure 16.6 are three securities that do not lie along the SML; we can interpret the meaning of these results now. We need to ask a structured question to analyse what is going on in this figure: Would we invest in any of securities A, B, or C? We would invest in security A, we should invest in security B, but we would not invest in security C. The reasoning here is that A and B lie above or on the SML, and therefore offer at least the market rate of return, whereas C lies below the SML and the return on that security is therefore less than the market is offering for that level of risk.

Because the CAPM is a model, it is based on a series of assumptions. Because it is based on a series of assumptions, it is open to criticism. We will look at the assumptions first, then the criticisms of those assumptions.

Assumptions of the CAPM

The assumptions of the CAPM are widely reported but Clark *et al.* (1989) present them under two subheadings: assumptions about investor behaviour and assumptions about the market.

Investor behaviour

- All investors are single-period expected utility of terminal wealth maximisers who choose among alternative portfolios on the basis of each portfolio's expected return and standard deviation.
- Investors have homogeneous expectations.
- Investors choose only efficient portfolios.
- Investors are risk averse.

Market behaviour

- All investors can borrow or lend at the risk-free rate of interest and in unlimited quantities.
- All assets are perfectly divisible and perfectly liquid and there are no transactions costs.
- There are no taxes.
- The cost of insolvency or bankruptcy is zero.
- Information is freely available to all investors.

Question marks over the CAPM

If all of the above assumptions were perfectly valid, the CAPM would be true. However, since the assumptions do tend to oversimplify reality, the CAPM is not entirely accurate. Question marks hang over full diversifiability and borrowing at rates other than the risk-free rate, and taxes and transactions costs do exist. (See Brigham and Gapenski (1987: 61 ff.) and Clark *et al.* (1989: 310–25) for a full discussion of these points and other operational problems with the CAPM model.)

Empirical work and the CAPM

The CAPM has been the subject of a very large amount of analysis worldwide over the last four decades or so. We will discuss in this section a few of the findings of some of the investigations into the validity of the CAPM model and its component parts.

Logue and Merville (1972) have shown that the value assigned or calculated for betas of organisations is significantly correlated to that organisation's financial policy: expressed in terms of its liquidity ratios, its gearing ratios, dividend payout and profitability. This may not be a surprise, given that analysts look at an organisation's results with a view to its liquidity, profitability and dividend policy. However, Clark *et al.* (1989) report that Levy's work does not necessarily follow on from that of Logue *et al.* Levy found that average betas can be predicted for large portfolios but not necessarily for smaller portfolios; forecasts are better over longer periods than over shorter periods; and for portfolios of 25 stocks or more over forecasts intervals of 26 weeks and longer, historical betas seem to be fairly good and stable indicators of future risk. Finally, Clark *et al.* also report Levitz's findings that betas for individual securities are not reliable indicators of risk whereas portfolios of as few as 10 securities have reliable betas.

Finally, Gregory (1985a: 56), quoting Rutterford, says: 'that by holding ten randomly selected shares in equal amounts, an investor may, on average, diversify away 80% of the shares' non-market [unsystematic] risk'. (1985a and b) Both of Gregory's two articles (1985a and b) are well worth reading as excellent introductions to this topic.

Empirical use of CAPM type models

Whilst this book is not directly concerned with international financial management, one recent paper from a journal in this area that is of interest should be noted. Ziobrowski and Ziobrowski (1995) work through their research on exchange rate risk and diversification.

In their paper they make use of a model that is similar to the CAPM. Fortunately, the paper is relatively easy to read and it does contain actual data that is also of relevance to our discussion on the CAPM.

SUMMARY

In this chapter we have taken an introductory view of risk, uncertainty and certainty. We started our discussion by looking at the various forms that risk can take in the business environment. We also emphasised the important influence that a knowledge of risk has on the manager's daily life.

A variety of methods were applied to the solution of the problems of risk and uncertainty, including decision tree analysis, Monte Carlo simulations, the certainty equivalent method, and the risk-adjusted discount rate method of adjusting for risk. We concluded our overview of risk and uncertainty by looking at the offerings of the capital asset pricing model. Whilst we found that this model has much to offer, it suffers from being based on a series of assumptions that are not always helpfully drafted. However, we concluded that the capital asset pricing model is used in reality.

KEY TERMS

You should satisfy yourself that you have noted all of these terms and can define and/or describe their meaning and use, as appropriate.

Risk (p. 534)	Probabilities (p. 547)
Certainty (p. 534)	Cumulative probability distribution (p. 547)
Uncertainty (p. 534)	Monte Carlo simulation (p. 550)
Attitudes to risk (p. 540)	Certainty equivalents method (p. 555)
Expected value criterion (p. 543)	Risk-adjusted discount rate (p. 559)
Decision tree analysis (p. 544)	Capital asset pricing model (p. 562)

RECOMMENDED READING

Brigham and Gapenski (1987) is a good starting point. Clark *et al.* (1989) is an excellent book that covers everything in this chapter and the next in a very readable way. Already lauded are Gregory (1985a) and (1985b). Hertz (1964) and (1968) are the classics to start us off on Monte Carlo simulations. Kennedy (1983) is an easy read, while Rouse (1993) is good to work through for those who like MC simulations.

QUESTIONS

Review questions

1. Define the following different forms of risk:
   (a) business;
   (b) investment;
   (c) portfolio;
   (d) cataclysmic; and
   (e) financial.
2. What are:
   (a) certainty; and
   (b) uncertainty?
3. How can decision trees help with our understanding of risk and uncertainty?
4. What is meant by the term 'cumulative probability distribution'?
5. Develop your own example of a Monte Carlo simulation by:
   (a) not building in dependencies between the variables; and
   (b) building in dependencies between the variables.
6. What is meant by the risk adjusted discount rate and how might one be used?
7. What is the capital asset pricing model?
8. What are the limitations of the capital asset pricing model and how is the model used in practice?

Answers to review questions 2, 3, 6 and 7 can be found in the Student Workbook.

Graded practice questions

Level I

1. The NPV probability distributions for projects X and Y are given below:

Probability	Project X	Project Y
	£	£
0.2	2,000	0
0.6	3,000	3,000
0.2	4,000	6,000

   Calculate the expected NPV, the standard deviation, the semi-variance, and coefficient of variation for each project. Which of these mutually exclusive projects would you accept?

2. (a) EZ Enterprises Ltd has a proposal costing £800. Using a 10% cost of capital, compute the expected NPV, standard deviation and coefficient of variation, assuming independent interperiod cash flows.

	Year 1	Year 2
Probability	NCF	NCF
0.2	400	300
0.3	500	400
0.3	600	500
0.2	700	600

(b) Recalculate the above, assuming perfectly dependent cash flows.

3. A Chemical Company Ltd has two investment proposals under the following states of the economy: normal, deep recession, mild recession, minor boom and major boom. The probabilities of the various states of the economy are as follows:

State	Proposal A Probability	Cash flow	Proposal B Probability	Cash flow
Deep recession	0.1	3,000	0.1	2,000
Mild recession	0.2	3,500	0.2	3,000
Normal	0.4	4,000	0.4	4,000
Minor boom	0.2	4,500	0.2	5,000
Major boom	0.1	5,000	0.1	6,000

Determine and interpret the following measures:

(a) expected return;
(b) mean absolute deviation;
(c) variance;
(d) standard deviation;
(e) semivariance; and
(f) coefficient of variation.

Level II

4. A machine with a 4-year life is being replaced with a modern, more efficient piece of equipment with a longer expected life. The equipment will require a payment of £55,000 for the first 30 days of its operation. The expected return and standard deviation are as follows:

Year	Expected return	Standard deviation
1	14,000	1,200
2	16,000	1,800
3	18,000	2,000
4	20,000	1,950
5	22,000	3,000

The risk-free rate of return is 5%. The CEC values and the coefficient of variation are as follows for the 5-year period:

	Certainty equivalent coefficient				
Coefficient of variation	Year 1	2	3	4	5
$v \leqslant 0.10$	0.92	0.88	0.85	0.80	0.74
$0.10 \leqslant v \leqslant 0.25$	0.86	0.82	0.78	0.73	0.69

(a) Determine the certainty equivalent value.

(b) Calculate the value of *r* for each of *t* from years 1 to 5.

5. A boiler manufacturing company uses a certainty equivalent approach in its evaluation of risky investments. Currently, the company is faced with two alternative projects. Project A's projected cash flow distribution is as follows:

Year	A £	CEC_A	B £	CEC_B	Risk-free return
0	−40,000	1.00	−50,000	1.00	–
1	20,000	0.90	20,000	0.86	0.05
2	20,000	0.86	25,000	0.82	0.06
3	20,000	0.82	30,000	0.78	0.07

Which alternative should be selected and why?

6. A business is considering two projects and will choose one or the other based upon their RAR. The business's cost of capital is 14%; the firm estimates the risk-free rate will be 10%; and project A represents the kind of investment that calls for a risk premium loading of 2% over risk-free rates, whereas project B calls for a risk premium of 8% over risk-free rates.

	Certainty equivalent coefficient				
Project	year 1	2	3	4	5 & 6
Project A	0.90	0.86	0.82	0.77	0.74
Project B	0.86	0.82	0.78	0.73	0.69

Projects A's projected cash flow distribution is as follows:

Original cost		Cash flows for years 1–6	
Probability	Amount (£)	Probability	Amount(£)
0.3	100,000	0.15	20,000
0.3	110,000	0.25	25,000
0.4	120,000	0.25	30,000
		0.15	35,000
		0.10	45,000
		0.10	45,000

Projects B's projected cash flow distribution is as follows:

Original cost		Cash flows for years 1–6	
Probability	Amount (£)	Probability	Amount(£)
0.5	225,000	0.25	50,000
0.2	210,000	0.25	50,000
0.3	200,000	0.15	70,000
		0.15	75,000
		0.10	80,000
		0.10	85,000

(a) Determine the RAR for each project using each of the certainty equivalent method and the risk-adjusted discount rate method.
(b) Discuss which of the two projects should be chosen for further investigation and possible adoption.

7. This question is the same as Worked example 16.3 from the chapter with the exception that for this question, we are required to build dependencies into our model.

MyCo Ltd has carried out extensive marketing research on a product it is wishing to launch nationwide. Once the product had been launched, Joseph Psmith would be assigned profit centre responsibilities for the product. Hence, Psmith classes this launch in terms of an investment project. The summary data, including the objective probabilities derived for them, are given below:

Selling price	Probability	Volume	Variable costs	Probability
100	0.15	10,000	83	0.05
		9,000	83	0.20
		8,000	84	0.25
		7,000	84	0.30
		6,000	85	0.20
99	0.15	11,000	82	0.10
		10,000	83	0.15
		9,000	83	0.30
		8,000	84	0.30
		7,000	84	0.15
98	0.30	13,000	81	0.05
		12,000	82	0.25
		11,000	82	0.20
		10,000	83	0.25
		9,000	83	0.25
97	0.30	15,000	80	0.05
		14,000	81	0.25
		13,000	81	0.25
		12,000	82	0.25
		11,000	82	0.20
96	0.10	18,000	79	0.05
		17,000	70	0.30
		16,000	80	0.30
		15,000	80	0.20
		14,000	81	0.15

Note: This table reads from left to right in order that the full interdependencies can be appreciated. For example, if the random number that is generated means that a selling price of £98 per unit is to be selected, then the volume range that is then selected must fall in the range 13,000 to 9,000 units, with the relevant probabilities assigned as per the extreme right-hand column.

Similarly, the variable costs per unit are directly related to the output volumes – variable costs depend to an extent on the volume of output.

Required

Carry out a Monte Carlo simulation of the above data and report your findings to your management colleagues.

Table of 400 random numbers

The following table of random numbers may be helpful with the Monte Carlo simulation questions in this chapter:

14	74	65	30	22	2	2	97	25	61
29	33	32	2	49	85	99	31	39	66
72	57	79	46	25	57	40	1	66	70
86	59	82	14	5	38	13	72	76	70
74	99	55	50	68	11	12	29	57	98
77	50	2	30	61	34	56	59	30	38
15	91	95	55	66	94	60	13	13	94
72	85	11	48	85	78	18	50	57	75
93	80	86	16	40	24	74	88	83	62
84	19	79	43	86	88	35	93	77	80
80	60	50	29	99	99	82	18	30	47
33	17	25	10	29	90	33	92	35	57
10	65	75	6	8	33	10	17	65	21
5	42	8	82	88	39	80	90	12	74
67	18	94	80	30	72	84	15	4	85
33	82	8	46	68	93	42	11	74	69
5	86	6	45	25	28	35	6	89	44
31	21	98	41	47	84	38	51	8	83
3	66	62	55	15	16	36	52	91	34
60	77	23	83	65	40	91	99	95	37
48	17	46	23	92	43	45	62	36	30
81	33	10	27	69	46	76	30	1	16
91	77	9	77	67	49	2	74	16	88
98	35	31	7	24	28	97	34	47	63
4	64	78	24	73	52	58	95	90	29
33	58	37	93	93	48	60	76	72	60
56	6	92	38	20	33	39	37	67	29
97	19	88	56	16	71	77	25	77	81
68	21	86	12	5	42	99	40	23	8
93	76	58	38	33	83	48	8	89	99
96	27	12	90	10	82	7	98	85	52
61	64	98	66	10	0	3	46	3	89
56	93	73	77	13	70	32	13	13	94

63	82	71	46	59	73	22	10	83	21
11	69	57	78	90	65	31	42	54	83
22	88	78	25	8	35	18	9	17	48
6	67	0	75	60	65	57	70	2	95
66	91	60	62	79	36	58	97	2	77
70	85	95	8	91	90	29	20	32	30
65	18	92	96	40	56	94	68	60	76

Source: Random numbers generated using Microsoft Works version 3 software.

Solutions to practice questions 2(a), 2(b) and 7 can be found in the Student Workbook. Solutions to practice question numbers in red can be found at the end of this book.

REFERENCES

Arnold, J. and Hope, A. (1983), *Accounting for Management Decisions* (Prentice Hall).

Brigham, E. F. and Gapenski, L. C. (1987), *Intermediate Financial Management*, 2nd edn (Dryden).

CIMA (1991), *Management Accounting Official Terminology* (Chartered Institute of Management Accounting).

Clark, J. J., Hindeland, T. J. and Pritchard, R. E. (1989), *Capital Budgeting: Planning and control of capital expenditures*, 3rd edn (Prentice Hall).

Drury, C. (1992), *Management and Cost Accounting* (Chapman & Hall).

Gregory, A. (1985a), 'Handling risk: implications of project risk financing and project risk – part 1' *Management Accounting* (October), 56–8.

Gregory, A. (1985b), 'Handling risk: implications of project risk financing and project risk – part 2', *Management Accounting* (November), 40–3.

Hertz, D. B. (1964), 'Risk analysis in capital investment', *Harvard Business Review* (Jan.–Feb.),

Hertz, D. B. (1968), 'Investment policies that pay off', *Harvard Business Review* (Jan.–Feb.),

Ho, S. S. and Pike, R. H. (1992), 'Adoption of probabilistic risk analysis in capital budgeting and corporate investment', *Journal of Business Finance and Accounting*, **19** (3), 387–405.

Kaplan, R. S. and Atkinson, A. (1989), *Advanced Management Accounting* (Prentice Hall).

Kennedy, A. (1983), 'The risk adjusted discount rate in investment appraisal', *Management Accounting* (July/August) (CIMA) 28–31.

Logue, D. E. and Merville, L. J. (1972), 'Financial policy and market expectations', *Financial Management* (Summer), 44.

Rouse, P. (1993), 'Construcing Monte Carlo simulations in Lotus 1–2–3', *Journal of Accounting Education*, **11** pp. 113–32.

Shapiro, A. C. (1992), *Multinational Financial Management*, 4th edn (Allyn & Bacon).

Ziobrowski, B. J. and Ziobrowski, A. J. (1995), 'Exchange rate risk and internationally diversified portfolios', *Journal of International Money and Finance*, **14** (1) (February), 65–81.

CHAPTER SEVENTEEN

Capital budgeting

CHAPTER OBJECTIVES

After reading this chapter you should be able to:

- define capital budgeting
- define and describe capital investments
- appreciate the different kinds of investment
- appreciate the nature of investments and the nature of assets
- describe the capital budgeting process
- define capital investment appraisal
- evaluate capital budgeting projects using five main methods of analysis
- appreciate the real-world uses of the five capital investment appraisal methods discussed in this chapter

Introduction

Capital budgeting is a very broad area. It covers the investment in large assets by organisations and, because the investments are large, they need to be controlled carefully. This chapter looks at capital budgeting decisions from their beginning to their end. Unlike many texts and journal articles, this chapter looks at the entire capital budgeting process. Some texts merely leap into the middle of the process and look at capital investment appraisal. Capital investment appraisal is the mathematical approach to deciding which asset, if any, to invest in. Dealing only with capital investment appraisal is, however, a very limiting thing to do as there is so much that happens before the decision stage and so much that should happen after the decision stage.

Definition of capital budgeting

By capital budgeting, we mean the acquisition and/or disposal of capital assets such as land, buildings, plant, equipment, and vehicles. The capital budgeting decision is one that involves the entire process of whether to make a capital investment decision. The process should start with an organisation looking for investment opportunities that are consistent with its objectives and strategies. The process finishes with a proper evaluation of whether the decision finally taken and implemented went according to plan. The types of projects investigated include, for example, whether to set up and operate a new factory, warehouse or shop; or whether a process should be mechanised or left as a manual one. Capital budgeting also includes consideration of the optimal time to make such investments: thus, although a project may not be worthwhile now, it might be viable if delayed for, say, twelve months.

Bierman and Smidt (1980: 4) capture much of the nature and content of capital budgeting activities with their definition:

> Capital budgeting is a many sided activity that includes searching for new and more profitable investment proposals, investigating engineering and marketing considerations to predict the consequences of accepting the investment, and making economic analyses to determine the profit potential of each investment proposal.

However, they do not talk about implementing a project, or about post-auditing. Post-auditing (or post-completion auditing) is the review of a project once it is underway. The purpose of it is to see whether the project has proven worthwhile. Depending on a variety of factors, post-auditing will be comprehensively or sketchily carried out.

Importance of capital budgeting

We can see the importance of capital budgeting when we consider that in the United Kingdom in 1990, total investment in capital assets in the economy amounted to £92 billion. This figure represents £1,618 for every man, woman and child in the country; or approximately £2,466 for every man and woman of working age. The amounts actually invested by organisations will vary widely across the economy, of course. For example, in the financial year ended 31 December 1988, Unilever invested £832 million by way of capital expenditure (this represents 4.86% of Unilever's total turnover for the year). On the other hand, Radio Mercury plc, with a total turnover for the year ended 30 September 1989 of £2.2 million, invested a total of £63,798 in studios, equipment, vehicles and sundry equipment (this represents 2.87% of total turnover). A further aspect is the consideration of capital budgeting from the point of view of the shareholder. Financial management and economic theory often contend that the primary objective of a business is to maximise shareholder wealth. Whether we agree with this assertion is not really appropriate to a discussion of management accounting issues. However, the organisations we are concerned with will be seeking to increase the value of that organisation by enhancing their earning capacity; or at least by minimising its cost outflows. Whether they maximise shareholder wealth is not of direct consequence to our deliberations here.

Capital investments

When we speak of investment we need to be clear about precisely what sort of investments we are talking about. The three principal features of a capital investment are:

1. The amounts of money spent on them are relatively large.
2. The time horizon of the investment is relatively long.
3. The money spent on them will be expected to be recovered.

The key word in the first two of these features of a capital investment is **relatively**. The amounts spent being relatively large means that the organisation undertaking the investment considers it a large investment: my organisation, with a sales turnover of £1 million, might consider a capital investment of £50,000 to be large, whereas your organisation, with a sales turnover of £750 million, might consider expenditure of £50,000 still comes under the heading of revenue expenditure in certain circumstances.

The word 'relative', when discussing the time horizon, needs clarification too. As in many examples concerned with management accounting, the example of the relative lengths of time horizons must be qualified with reference to the nature of the business. For example, designing, building and commissioning an electricity generating station will take a very long time (upwards, possibly, of ten years); whereas designing and installing a computerised stock control system in an organisation will take a much shorter time. In terms of the profit and loss account and balance sheet, the accountant's short term is anything occurring (or to be settled) within one year; and the long term relates to anything occurring or to be settled after more than one year has elapsed. Since we are studying aspects of accountancy, we can accept this as our benchmark for the relevant time horizon.

Recovery of money invested

Carsberg's (1979: 28) definition of an investment is: 'An investment normally involves setting aside some cash at one time in return for the expectation for the receipt of a larger amount of cash at a later time.' Merging this definition with what we have just said about the time horizon of capital investments, we can see that we invest in capital assets knowing that our investment will take a relatively long time to be recovered. For example, we must expect that if we buy or set up a furniture manufacturing unit costing, say, £15 million, that it may take four, five, or ten years for that investment to pay for itself.

Conventional and non-conventional investments

Speaking of the recovery of a project's investment outlay, we can classify a project as being conventional or non-conventional in nature. By a conventional investment, we mean an investment for which we pay out a sum immediately and from then onwards we reap positive rewards. By a non-conventional investment, we mean an investment for which benefits flow in an irregular fashion. For a conventional investment, we will spend a capital sum today and receive cash inflows in all future years. For a non-conventional investment, cash outflows will occur in more than one period and may alternate with cash inflows. Table 17.1 illustrates these points.

TABLE 17.1 ***Fund flows for conventional and non-conventional investments***

	Conventional investment	Non-conventional investments		
		1	2	3
Year 0	−	−	−	−
Year 1	+	−	+	−
Year 2	+	+	−	−
Year 3	+	−	+	+
Year 4	+	+	+	+

Note: '−' means an outflow of funds occurs; '+' means an inflow of funds occurs; and year 0 means the start of the very first day of the first year of the project. Year 0 is taken to be the start of the project. Year 1 is, literally, one calendar year after year 0; year 2 is one calendar year after year 1, and so on. We will assume that all flows of funds, except that which takes place at year 0, take place at the end of the relevant years. This means that any income and expenditure for year 1 takes place on the very last day of year 1. The same applies to all other years during the life of a project.

Summary definition of capital investments

We can agree a summary definition of a capital investment now:

> A capital investment is large relative to the total resources of the business as a whole, and the time frame over which a capital investment extends is greater than one year. A typical capital investment involves spending money now in return for its recovery later.

Kinds of investment

Having described capital investments in general terms, we should now refine our definition and consider capital investments in more detail. We can consider capital investments under five different headings: generative investments; sustaining investments; replacement investments; expanding investments; and safety and environmental investments.

Generative investments

Generative investments are investments undertaken with the promise of economic improvement for the organisation undertaking the investment. Examples of such investments include:

- a new materials handling system (to save labour costs);
- a refrigerator (to minimise or eliminate losses of perishable items);
- a lorry (to reduce distribution costs).

Sustaining investments

Sustaining investments are necessary investments that the organisation cannot, on average, fail to undertake. Such investments include:

- new computer network (old one is slow and cannot be upgraded to cope with present work flows);
- new inspection equipment (needed by the quality control department as part of a drive for zero defects).

Replacement investments

1. *Replacement: maintenance of business* concerns such matters as whether to continue to produce the products and services that are currently being provided; and whether to use the existing plant and equipment.
2. *Replacement: cost reduction* concerns capital investments that will result in the lowering of materials and/or labour and/or overhead costs.

Expanding investments

1. *Expansion of existing products and markets* relates to capital investment decisions that seek out new opportunities within the framework of the products and markets within which the organisation already operates.
2. *Expansion into new products and markets* concerns the development of capital investment projects that enhance the products and markets currently served. By expanding into new products and markets, we mean developing products that we have not considered up to now; or selling in areas of the country we never sold in before. It could all mean, of course, expanding internationally rather than operating purely from within the home country.

Safety and environmental investments

Safety and environmental projects are, finally, those capital investments that are needed to comply with government directives, with labour agreements, or with insurance policy terms. This means they are mandatory investments: that is, the organisation has no choice but to undertake them. These investments are often called non-revenue-producing projects. In other words, they will probably not enhance an organisation's revenue earning capacity, and may, in fact, reduce it.

Nature of investments

Under each of the headings we have just seen, generative investments, sustaining investments, and so on, we can further classify each kind of investment as:

- purely complementary;
- independent; or
- mutually exclusive.

Figure 17.1 helps to summarise the meaning of each of these terms.

Referring to Figure 17.1, by a complementary investment we mean that if project 'a' is to be invested in, then project 'b' must be invested in as well. For example, if we are to

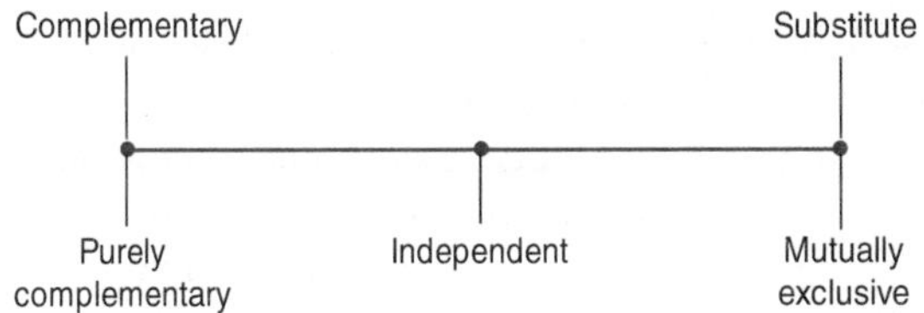

FIGURE 17.1 *Investment classification continuum (Source: Archer et. al. (1983: 164))*

consider the setting up of a biscuit-making factory, we need equipment for mixing and baking as complementary to a storage area. That is, there is little point in setting up a biscuit-making factory if we do not have the buildings in which to store the finished products. On the other hand, substitute investments are those whereby if one investment is undertaken, the other(s) are not. A good example here would be the consideration of different machines for carrying out the same or similar tasks; or situations where, because of lack of funds, the organisation can afford to undertake only one project from the two, three, or four alternatives available. Complements and substitutes are at extreme ends of the spectrum. In the middle we have independent investments which do not depend upon another aspect of the project to be in place simultaneously; neither are they substitutes for other projects.

Real and financial assets

Pike and Dobbins (1986: 1) add an extra dimension to capital investment classification with their discussion of real and financial assets:

> Most of these assets will be real assets employed within the business to produce goods or services to satisfy consumer demand. Real assets may be tangible, such as land and buildings, plant and equipment, and stocks, or intangible, such as patents, trademarks and 'know-how'. Sometimes a firm may choose to invest in financial assets outside the business in the form of short term securities and deposits.

This definition concludes our overview of capital investments. We now know precisely what a capital investment is. We know that they are relatively expensive investments, and that once invested in, they may be retained for many years (if not indefinitely). We also know that assets may be real or financial; and that the recovery of the initial outlay could take several years. Now, however, we must turn our attention to the way that capital investments are identified by organisations, how such investments come to be accepted (or rejected) by the management of the organisation, and how, if at all, such investments are monitored once the project has been implemented. This is the capital budgeting process.

The capital budgeting process

Many practitioners and academics have researched the capital budgeting process. Referring to two or three of the references found at the end of this chapter will give some idea of just how extensively the process has been researched. We will, however, only have time to summarise some of the work carried out in this area. One of the most interesting pieces of work on the capital budgeting process was carried out by McIntyre and Coulthurst (1985). Their diagram (reproduced as Figure 17.2 below) is excellent because it covers virtually all aspects of the capital budgeting process. The only aspect of the capital budgeting process not covered by this diagram is that of setting objectives and implementing the strategy of the organisation. They do, however, refer to 'management by plan' when discussing their diagram: and they have 'top management' involved at the outset by having them: 'Develop systematic means of searching for investment projects both to identify opportunities and to anticipate problems' (McIntyre and Coulthurst 1985: 29).

In summary, we should agree that capital budgeting is part of corporate planning and as such, the objectives for the capital budgeting process are set by senior management as part of their normal corporate planning review procedures. Thus, in terms of McIntyre and Coulthurst's diagram, the setting of objectives and strategy predates the creation phase. To cover this aspect of the capital budgeting process we can amend their diagram so that the setting of objectives and the implementation of strategies are clearly seen. The amended diagram is displayed as Figure 17.2. This figure ensures that we appreciate that all aspects of the capital budgeting process are governed by the objectives and strategy of the organisation. Let us take each of the eight processes from the figure and discuss them in turn.

Creation phase

Stage 1 Search for ideas

Large organisations may have entire departments or divisions devoted to the creative search for ideas for capital investment. These organisations will tend to undertake capital investments by design. Many other organisations will undertake this search when it fits in with its objectives and strategies, and they will also undertake capital investment by design. Yet other organisations, however, will carry out the search on an *ad hoc* basis: that is, when an opportunity presents itself or when the need arises. Such organisations will often undertake capital investment by accident (because they suddenly find they have to, in order to compete, for example), or never invest at all. By searching for ideas, we mean, for example, looking for a new business to buy, which could result in either vertical or horizontal integration. A business integrating vertically will be looking to buy forwards or backwards along the value chain: a cigarette manufacturer, for example, will integrate vertically backwards by buying a tobacco farm: that is, buying an organisation that produces the raw materials, or produces at a stage nearer to its raw materials. That same cigarette manufacturer will integrate horizontally by buying another cigarette manufacturer: namely, a related business. By looking to improve a manufacturing process the organisation could be undertaking a generative investment or a sustaining investment. By looking to expand the range of services offered to customers the organisation will be undertaking an expansion of its activities, which could be an expansion of existing products and services or an expansion into new products and services.

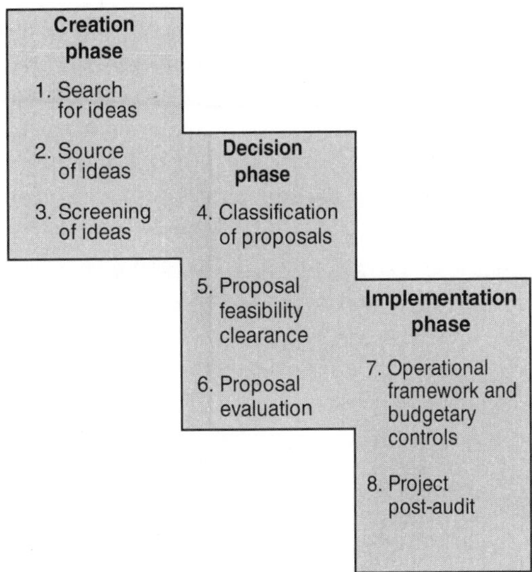

FIGURE 17.2 *Organisational objectives set and strategies implemented (Source: McIntyre and Coulthurst (1985: 28))*

Stage 2 Source of ideas

No one has the monopoly on good ideas. Ideas can be generated from anywhere. If the organisation has a department dedicated to the creative search process, it is this department that will be expected to be the main source of ideas. Additionally, other departments in the organisation should be able to contribute to the process. For example, the marketing department 'must have' a lot to offer by way of detailed intelligence gained by sales representatives as they meet their customers, and travel around as part of their daily activities. The research department will also have a lot to contribute since part of its function will be the generation of new ideas for both existing and new products and services. One of the simplest ways of collecting ideas is the suggestion box: that is, boxes placed around the organisation in which employees (and others) can make suggestions for improving service, efficiency and so on around the organisation. Quite often, cash prizes are given as a reward for useful and usable ideas. Regular employee/employer open meetings are a further source of excellent idea generation. At these sessions, management sit around a table with the junior employees and discuss possible improvements. There are benefits other than the organisational benefits that accrue from such meetings, such as the fostering of positive employee/employer relationships.

Stage 3 Screening of ideas

The screening of ideas will be simplified when the organisation has specific objectives. For example, if we are concerned to produce and distribute high-quality products, we would not consider a product or project that meant producing and distributing low-quality products.

On the other hand, if a project is, at the moment, not acceptable, it is possible that it may fit in with the natural development of the organisation's product portfolio for, say, two years' time; therefore it may be put on hold until then. There are many different levels at which the screening process will operate. If we take the example of a change to a part of the production process, that change may be initiated at shop floor level. If this is the case, then screening could take place at the following levels up the organisation (moving from lower to senior levels):

- shop floor/department management;
- factory management;
- division management; and
- organisation management (board of directors).

A proposal could be rejected at any stage, of course: it is not guaranteed to be discussed at every level up to, and including, the board.

Decision phase

Stage 4 Classification of proposals

Having reached the end of stage 3 in the creation phase, a proposal enters the decision phase: projects are now considered as being suitable for consideration on their own merits. The fourth stage, the classification of proposals stage, seeks to categorise projects so that they can be ranked according, for example, to whether they are 'must have' projects, or are desirable but not 'must have' projects, and so on.

The classification system used could be the one we have already discussed: generative investments; sustaining investments; replacement investments; expanding investments; and safety and environmental investments. We can now see the usefulness of this categorisation. For example, if a project is classified under safety and environmental investments, there is no choice but to invest in it. If the law says that project X is needed, then project X must be invested in. Similarly, if a project is classified as generative, it may receive more support from management than, say, a project proposing an expansion into new products or services. McIntyre and Coulthurst (1985) quote Piper and add a further classification, that of the risk inherent in the proposal. As we saw in Chapter 17, risk aversion is a common human trait, and it can be applied to capital budgeting. If a project is considered risky, then a risk averse management will either not be interested in the project, or they will require a larger than normal return on that project. Knowledge of the riskiness of the project is useful at the decision stage.

Stage 5 Proposal feasibility clearance

The single most important question arising here is: 'Is this project viable?' Factors important and applicable at the time the project was initially researched may no longer apply. If these factors do not apply, can the project still be considered viable? Moreover a full evaluation of the viability of a project may be expensive. Arriving at the final stage of accept or reject could involve the organisation in a large amount of expense: for instance, market research may have to be carried out, preliminary design work may be necessary. We should aim, therefore, to be in the position of assessing the feasibility of projects for which there is a good chance of acceptance. Otherwise large amounts of money may be wasted in pre-evaluation expenditure.

Stage 6 Proposal evaluation

We will be discussing this section of the capital budgeting process in much more detail later in this chapter under the heading of the quantitative aspects of capital budgeting. Nevertheless, at this stage we can say that, having reached stage 6 of the process, a proposal will be subject to a detailed analysis. We will see that there are several methods available for the purposes of proposal evaluation. At the moment, though, we should be content to know that these methods exist. In addition to the quantitative aspects of capital investment appraisal, there are also the qualitative aspects. Lumijärvi (1991) has demonstrated that, despite the findings of many other researchers, the quantitative aspects of project appraisal may not be as important as it has seemed up to now. He was investigating, within one large company (Scandinavia Corp), how subordinates attempt to influence decision makers so that they achieve the desired capital investment funds, and he classified the arguments that subordinates used as follows:

1. Economic arguments, e.g., profitability of an investment
2. Strategic arguments, e.g., an investment's strategic applicability
3. Non-economic arguments, e.g., social factors pertaining to an investment
4. Production technology arguments, e.g., new manufacturing system. (Lumijärvi 1991: 178)

He continued:

> It was observed ... that economic arguments were emphasized extremely frequently although they did not seem to have much influence on the decision-makers. Strategic arguments were employed very often and they had more effect on the superiors than economic arguments. Non-economic arguments were applied rarely, but when employed they were effective. Finally, proposers emphasized production technology arguments frequently and the decision-makers seemed to value them very high. (ibid. 179–80)

Finally, he concluded:

> Observations gave evidence that in general proposers use economic arguments when their units' profitability is poor, an investment is small, or the project represents standard technology in the company. Strategic arguments are prevalent in situations characterized by a unit's good profitability, a large investment project, or an investment in standard technology. On the other hand, non-economic arguments are used when the project is not based on economic factors. Finally, production technology arguments are dominant when a unit's profitability is good and a project represents new technology in the company. (ibid. 185)

Whilst Lumijärvi is not presenting a case that might be universally applicable, since he has surveyed just one organisation, he is providing very useful insights into the need for greater consideration of techniques other than quantitative techniques in capital investment appraisal.

Implementation Phase

Stage 7 Operational framework and budgetary controls

At this stage of the proceedings, we must be assuming that the proposal has been accepted and is being or has been implemented. Therefore, there will be a manager in charge of the project, and he will be subject to the rigours of responsibility accounting. He will be held responsible for the operation of the project on a day-to-day basis. He will also be held accountable for his management of the project by means of his monthly performance reports, and at the end of the year, he may receive a bonus as a result of his handling of the project. In order to be held responsible for his project management, he will be set targets for sales, costs, output rates, after-sales service productivity, and whatever else is relevant to his project. Thus he will have a budget for his activities and the project will be monitored under normal budgetary control procedures, as detailed in Chapters 15 and 16.

Stage 8 Project post-audit

Post-auditing has been the subject of much research over recent years, and the general conclusion is that not everyone who could carry it out does so. From a management accounting point of view, this must be classed as a serious problem for the management of an organisation. It is serious because by not carrying out post-auditing, managers are denying themselves vital information relating to the reasons for the success or failure of a project.

Neale and Holmes (1988: 27) define post-auditing as:

> An objective and independent appraisal of the measure of success of a capital expenditure project in progressing the business as planned. The appraisal should cover the implementation of the project from the authorisation to commissioning and its technical and commercial performance after commissioning.

The reason why vital information is lost becomes clear from this definition. A post-audit of a project is objective and independent; and it covers the project from authorisation to commissioning – and performance after commissioning. If something is done well during the commissioning and running of the project, the valuable lessons that could be learned by others may be lost. Similarly, if a project goes badly, the lessons to be learned could also be lost if no one is monitoring what is happening. Merrett and Sykes (1969: 388) give a clue to why some organisations do not carry out post-auditing procedures: 'They are sometimes held to discourage initiative and to produce a policy of over caution . . . and to give executives the sense of being hounded.'

Another reason that will often not be admitted is that the organisation will consider a post-audit an expensive luxury. As with all audits, the true benefits are commonly not fully quantifiable. The post-audit is no exception. Thus unless the accounting function (since it must take a lead here) can convince the management of the organisation (and it must be the senior management) that a post-audit is a valuable management tool, many projects will be unmonitored, and the lessons we discussed above will be lost forever. This concludes our overview of the theory of capital budgeting. We have seen that capital budgeting is part of the overall budgeting process of an organisation, and deals with the acquisition and/or disposal of capital assets. The theory of capital budgeting tells us that the process begins with the identification of objectives, followed by the implementation of strategies designed to achieve those objectives. McIntyre and Coulthurst (1985) provided us with a flowchart which we were able to modify and which described in detail the process of capital budgeting. The modification we carried out was to encompass their process in the objectives and strategies with which, any capital budgeting process must start.

Capital investment appraisal

We turn our attention now to the quantitative aspects of capital budgeting: namely, capital investment appraisal. In this part of the chapter we will be discussing how we can sort out, in financial and mathematical terms, which project, of several alternatives possible, we should choose. If alternatives are mutually exclusive – that is, we can only choose one out of, say, four or five possible projects – then we need to decide which one it should be. If a project is mandatory, we still need to assess it financially: that is, we need to know the impact it will have on the costs of the organisation.

Accounting profit and cash flow

Of the five methods of capital investment appraisal that we will be looking at, all except one method uses cash flow as their basic input data. The one exception uses accounting profit data. The significance of this is that cash flow concerns itself only with the relevant aspects of a project that involve the movement of cash. Accounting profit, on the other hand, concerns itself with items such as provisions for depreciation and bad debts that do not involve the movement of cash. If we base our decisions on accounting profit, we must be including sunk costs in our analysis: we would be charging to projects, for example, depreciation of machinery and equipment from investments made, perhaps, several years ago. Sunk costs are not relevant to the choices being made among alternative projects. What we are looking for, therefore, are costs and charges that are relevant to the project under review. Table 17.2 illustrates the differences between accounting profit and cash flow.

Table 17.2 also helps us to define recurring or periodic cash flow: that is, cash flow that will be generated period after period. Cash flow literally measures the cash implications only of the outcomes of a project. Anything which does not affect the cash position of the project is ignored. Note also that the additional interest on debt is not taken into account in determining the cash flow figure. This means that we treat the financing aspects of a project as being a part of the financing of the business as a whole: in other words, we do not separate one part of the organisation from any others. In addition to the periodic cash flow there is the initial capital cost itself, and we need to assess the cash flow implications of this. As well as the cost of the building, machine, and equipment, there are other aspects that we should take into account:

TABLE 17.2 *Difference between accounting profit and cash flow*

	Accounting Profit	Cash Flow
	£	£
Additional sales receipts	50,000	50,000
Savings in labour and materials	12,000	12,000
Cash benefits	62,000	62,000
less:		
Depreciation on new equipment	9,000	
less:		
Depreciation on old equipment	4,000	
Additional depreciation expense	5,000	
Additional administration expense	7,000	7,000
Additional sellingt expenses	6,000	6,000
Additional interest on debt	3,000	–
Additional taxes	5,000	5,000
Net accounting profit	36,000	
Periodic cash flow		44,000

- Investment in additional working capital required by the project.
- Residual or disposal value of old equipment.
- Tax gains or losses on disposal of old equipment.
- The liquidation value of stocks no longer required should be credited to the old project.

Table 17.3 shows the inclusion of these items in a capital investment:

TABLE 17.3 *Items included in a capital investment*

	£	£
Cost of new equipment		100,000
Additional working capital		25,000
Total		125,000
less:		
Salvage value of old equipment	15,000	
Liquidation value of spare parts no longer required	5,000	
Tax savings on disposal of old equipment	3,000	23,000
Investment cash flow		102,000

Anyone who has never studied compound interest and/or discounting should turn to the appendix to this chapter before proceeding any further. If you have studied compounding and discounting before, but that was some time ago, you should also revise your knowledge by turning to the appendix to this chapter now. Either way, make sure you understand the contents of the appendix before reading on.

The five main methods of capital investment appraisal

There are five main methods that we will discuss under the heading of capital investment appraisal: the payback period method; the accounting rate of return method; the net present value method; the profitability index method; and the internal rate of return method. We will discuss each of these five methods in turn, basing our discussions on the basic data found in Table 17.4: and using this data for demonstrations.

The payback period method

A definition of payback is:

'The period, usually expressed in years, which it takes the cash inflows from a capital investment project to equal the cash outflows' (CIMA 1991).

Of all of the methods that we could use to assess a capital investment project, the payback period is usually considered to be the simplest both to calculate and to understand. The arithmetic involved is certainly straightforward. We can see this by applying the method to project 1. The calculation centres around the cumulative cash flow: this will tell us when the cash inflows from the project exactly equal the initial capital cost. What we are looking

TABLE 17.4 ***Basic data for discussions of capital investment appraisal methods***

Project	Initial cost (£)	Cash flows (£)			
		Year 1	Year 2	Year 3	Year 4
1	10,000	6,000	6,000	6,000	6,000
2	14,000	6,000	6,500	8,500	9,000
3	15,000	9,000	7,000	6,000	4,500

Note: All transactions occur at the end of each year, except the initial investments in year 0.

The cost of capital is 12%, and it will remain at this level for the duration of all of the projects. The residual values of the projects are:

	£
Project 1	nil
2	4,000
3	5,300

For each of the five methods, determine which of the projects to undertake. The projects are mutually exclusive: only one of them can be chosen to be undertaken.

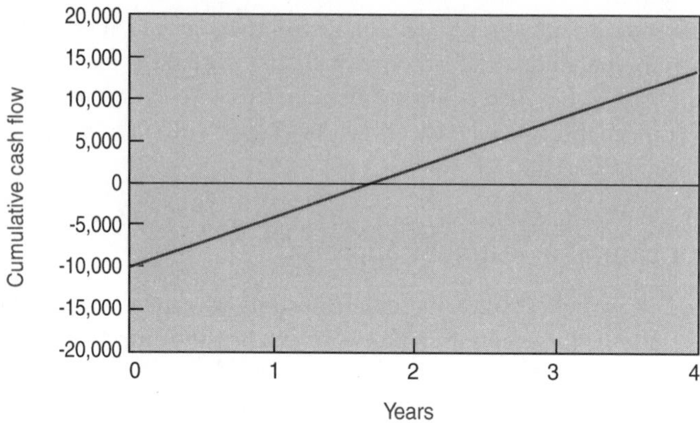

FIGURE 17.3 *Payback period for project 1*

for is the exact time at which the cumulative cash inflows pay back the initial capital cost. Figure 17.3 helps to illustrate this situation.

Figure 17.3 shows that, at the start of the project, the cumulative outflow of cash is £10,000: the initial capital cost. As the project gets under way, cash flows into the organisation and, bit by bit, will help to pay back (or pay off) the initial capital cost. In the case of Figure 17.3, we can estimate the payback period to be at the point where the cumulative cash flow line cuts the horizontal axis, which is at approximately 1.7 years. For some purposes, an estimate of the payback period might be sufficient, but we can calculate the exact payback period by considering Table 17.5 which is, in fact, the basis of Figure 17.3. The calculation that follows, however, tells us exactly what the payback period is:

The calculation works as follows. From the cumulative cash flow column, we see that the cumulative cash flow moves from negative to positive after the end of the first year, but before the end of the second year. Therefore the payback period occurs in less than two years. The fraction of 4,000/6,000 tells us how far into the second year it is before the payback finally occurs. To get from a £4,000 negative cumulative cash flow position to

$$\text{PB} = 1 \text{ year} + \frac{4{,}000}{6{,}000} \text{ years} = 1.67 \text{ years}$$

TABLE 17.5 *Payback period for project 1*

Year	Cash flow	Cumulative cash flow
0	−10,000	−10,000
1	6,000	−4,000
2	6,000	2,000
3	6,000	8,000
4	6,000	14,000

payback takes £4,000; and during that second year, a total of £6,000 cash flowed into the project. Hence, *assuming the cash flows accrue evenly throughout the year*, the payback period must have occurred at 1.67 years, as shown above.

Payback period decision rule

We were asked in Table 17.4 which project of the three we would choose, given that they are mutually exclusive projects. To make such a decision we need a decision rule. The decision rule for the payback period method is: the quicker a project pays back the better.

The accounting rate of return method (ARR)

The accounting rate of return method is the one exception, as stated above, that uses accounting profit data as the basis on which to differentiate between projects. The calculation for accounting profit is exactly as it is for any financial accounting problem. As we will see with the basic data, all we need to do to calculate accounting profit from cash flow information is to subtract depreciation. We find the net profit by subtracting depreciation from the cash flows for the whole project. The average annual net profit figure is then found by dividing the total project net profit by the number of years that the project is expected to be in existence. The average profit is then expressed as a percentage of the initial investment: this is the accounting rate of return (ARR). Table 17.6 gives us the result for project 1.

The version we have just worked through in Table 17.6 is based on the initial investment as at the start of the project. CIMA (1991), however, says that the accounting rate of return on investment can be defined as:

$$\frac{\text{Average annual profit from the investment} \times 100}{\text{Average investment}}$$

This is a common situation whereby there may be variations of methods that all have the same (or very similar) names. As far as the method in general is concerned, CIMA (1991) says ARR is 'not a recommended measure'.

Although CIMA does not recommend APR, it is worth remembering that businesses and industries are commonly assessed on their profitability rather than on their cash flows. The ARR decision rule, that helps us to sort out which project we should be investing in, says: if the ARR of Project 1 is greater than the ARR of Project 2, accept Project 1. There is often an addition to this rule which says that in order for a project to be acceptable in the first place, the ARR of that project must attain a predetermined level: namely, the hurdle rate

TABLE 17.6 *The accountancy rate of return for project 1*

Project	Initial cost (£)	Total cash flow (£)	Depreciation (£)	Net profit (£)	Life (yrs)	Average profit (£)	ARR (%)
1	10,000	24,000	10,000	14,000	4	3,500	35

(also known as the cut-off rate and the discount rate). This level will be determined by the management of the organisation in line with its corporate objectives.

ARR decision rule:

1. If the ARR of a project reaches a given level, that project is acceptable. and
2. If the ARR of Project 1 is greater than the ARR of Project 2, accept Project 1.

The net present value method

The academic literature presents the net present value as the best all-round method of capital investment appraisal. It takes into account all of the available data (the payback period method does not); it also takes into account the time value of money (the ARR method does not). It takes the time value of money into account by discounting the cash flows (neither the payback period method nor the ARR method does that). The net present value method takes the cash flow data of the whole project, from year 0 to the end of the project, and discounts those cash flows at the organisation's cost of capital. In Chapter 16, we discussed such ideas as the risk adjusted discount rates and the capital asset pricing model; these ideas included discussion of an organisation's cost of capital. Similarly, when discussing compounding and discounting in the appendix to this chapter, we assume that we are talking in terms of all investments being financed by or through a bank (or similar). However, many capital investment projects will be financed by the organisation itself. Therefore, the term 'interest rate' is not appropriate. We will, from now on, talk about an organisation's cost of capital.

We must now define the term cost of capital before we discuss the net present value method. An organisation's cost of capital is defined by CIMA (1991) as being: 'The cost of financing an investment, expressed as a percentage rate. The rate should be based on the overall pool of capital.' The rate has to be based on the overall pool of capital so that we are not tempted to try to identify individual projects with individual sources of capital. For example, any large organisation will usually have several different sources of financing – ordinary shares, preference shares, debentures and so on – and there may be different classes of finance within each of these categories. Consequently, we are viewing projects as being marginal. By being marginal we mean that the project can be implemented without the need to restructure the pool of capital of the organisation. CIMA (1991) defines the weighted average cost of capital as:

> A percentage discount rate used in capital investment appraisal to calculate the net present value of the costs and future revenues of the project.
>
> It is the average cost of the combined sources of finance (equity, debentures, bank loans) weighted according to the proportion each element bears to the total pool of capital available. Weighting is usually based on the current market valuations and current yields or costs.
>
> Example:

Capital	Market (£)		Rate (%)		Cost (£)
Equity	800,000	×	10	=	80,000
Debt	400,000	×	15	=	60,000

Total	1,200,000	140,000

Weighted average 11.67%

The weighted average given in the CIMA definition of the weighted average cost of capital (WACC), is found by expressing the total cost of the capital by the total market value of the capital. That is:

WACC = 11.67% = (£140,000 ÷ £1.2 million) × 100

The 'rates' given in the CIMA example refers to the rates obtained based on market value and on being net of tax. For example, by being based on market values, we mean an 11% debenture currently being traded at £97.5% has a market yield of:

$$\frac{11}{97.5} \times 100 = 11.282\%$$

That is, the interest actually receivable is based on how much we bought the debenture for, not its nominal value (which, in fact, no one may ever have actually paid). If tax is payable on this amount at the rate of, say, 30%, the relevant tax-adjusted rate is:

$$\frac{11\% \times 0.70}{97.5} = 7.90\%$$

We can include our discussion of discount rates and the capital asset pricing model here.

Illustration of the net present value method

We can use the basic data now, to work through the net present value method. Following on from what we say about the similarity between the net present value method and the discounting of a stream of earnings (see chapter appendix, p. 602), we will see that we need to revise the discounting of the stream of earnings method only slightly (See Table 17.7).

TABLE 17.7 *Calculation of net present value for project 1*

Project 1	Discount factors	Cash flows (12%)	Present values
		£	£
Year 0	1.0000	−10,000	−10,000.00
1	0.8929	6,000	5,357.14
2	0.7972	6,000	4,783.16
3	0.7118	6,000	4,270.68
4	0.6355	6,000	3,813.11
Net present value			8,224.10

The revision we have made to the discounting of a stream of earnings method in arriving at the net present value method in Table 17.7, is that we have taken into account the initial (capital) cost. When we take the capital cost into account, we have to include it in the final calculation in order to arrive at the net present value. We can see that the net present value of a capital budgeting project is the present value of the stream of earnings of the project less the initial capital cost of the project. For project one, we can see that the total present value of the stream of earnings is £18,224.10; and the capital cost of the project is £10,000. Therefore, the net present value is £8,224.10: as given in the table above. The interpretation of the net present value of Project 1 is that the organisation is being asked to pay £10,000 in exchange for an asset that will generate cash flows which have a net present value of £8,224.10. This means the organisation will be getting a 'bargain': that is, it is being asked to pay £10,000 for an asset that generates a stream of earnings with a total present value of £18,224.10.

Net present value decision rule

1. If the net present value of a project is positive, that project is acceptable for investment purposes.
2. If the net present value of Project 1 is greater than the net present value for Project 2, Project 1 should be accepted in preference to Project 2.

Part (1) of this rule tells us that, generally, projects with a negative net present value do not increase the wealth of the organisation considering the investment, and should therefore not be considered. Part (2) confirms that, in the case of two or more alternative projects, the project providing the largest net present value is the preferred project.

The profitability index method

The profitability index method is otherwise known as the benefit/cost ratio; and it is an extension of the net present value. The index is derived by dividing the net present value of a project by the present value of the cash outflows of the project. The index thus overcomes one of the serious limitations of the net present value rules which is that the net present value rule considers the net present values only in terms of their absolute value. The profitability index rule considers the net present values of a project relative to the capital cost. We can consider an extreme example of the need to consider the relative values of projects rather than the absolute values. Assume we have to choose between two different projects (they are mutually exclusive). Project A has a net present value of £50,000; and Project B has a net present value of £150,000. Applying the NPV rule tells us to choose Project B. However, if we are now told that Project A requires £55,000 as its initial outlay, but Project B needs £3 million, we immediately see that the return on Project A is far superior to Project B.

For Project A the profitability index:

$$= \frac{\text{net present value of Project A}}{\text{net present value of cash outflows of Project A}}$$

$$= \frac{£50{,}000}{£55{,}000}$$

$$= 0.90900$$

For every £1 invested in Project A, we obtain a net present value of £0.90909. For Project B, the profitability index is 0.05: for every £1 invested in this project, the present value is only £0.05.

Profitability index rule

If the profitability index for Project A is greater than the profitability index for Project B, choose Project A.

The internal rate of return method

The internal rate of return (IRR) (otherwise known as the yield or the DCF yield, among other names) has a very simple definition. It is that cost of capital at which the NPV of a project is exactly £0. It gives us a breakeven view of a project: that is it tells us the maximum cost of capital we should be prepared to suffer before a project becomes unacceptable. Unfortunately, the IRR is much easier to define than it is to calculate. Apart from using financial calculators and computers, there is no quick way of calculating the IRR for a project (unless we are dealing with an annuity). There are two basic approaches for calculating the IRR of a project: graphically, and by trial and error. We will look at each in turn.

Graphical method

To derive the IRR for a project graphically, we draw the net present value profile of that project. The NPV profile is the graphical representation of the NPVs derived for a project at a number of different levels of cost of capital. That is, for any project, we calculate the NPVs at 5, 10, or more different costs of capital and plot the resulting NPVs on a graph. Let's work through Project 1 from our basic data. Table 17.8 shows, in summary, the NPVs for that project at a variety of costs of capital. We then plot these values along the '*y*' (vertical) axis, with the costs of capital on the '*x*' (horizontal) axis.

Table 17.8 shows us that the IRR lies somewhere between a cost of capital of 40% and one of 50%: that is where the NPV turns to zero (it goes from £1,095 to £−370). It does not, however, tell us precisely what the value of the IRR of Project 1 is. The NPV profile does a better job for us here. Look at Figure 17.4.

TABLE 17.8 *Net present values at various costs of capital*

Cost of capital (%)	NPV (£)
0	14,000
10	9,019
20	5,532
30	2,997
40	1,095
50	(370)
60	(1,526)
70	(2,455)
80	(3,214)
90	(3,845)
100	(4,375)

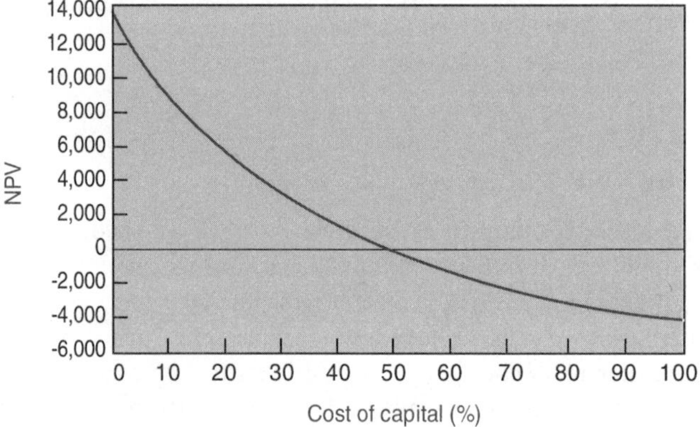

FIGURE 17.4 *NPV profile for project 1*

An accurately drawn graph, such as the one in Figure 17.4, allows us to estimate the value of the IRR for Project 1. A reasonable estimate of the IRR taken from this graph is 47.5%. This is taken from the graph by following the NPV profile down to the point at which it cuts the horizontal axis. The horizontal axis represents a NPV of £0. Thus, when NPV = £0, '*r*' = IRR. In fact, the actual IRR for Project 1 is 47.23%. There are several reasons why the graph did not give us the precise answer of 47.5%. The first is that it is actually drawn in a piecewise manner: that is, we have taken the cost of capital in steps of 10%. Had we taken the cost of capital in steps of 1% (or even less) we would have been able to refine our estimate. The second reason is that it has been drawn to fit into a very confined space; a larger version of the graph would have been more helpful. Finally, the thickness of the lines coupled with a small graph, help to mislead us. Nevertheless, the graphical method, taking the above three limitations into account, gives a good estimate of the IRR of a project. It is worthwhile noting that at any cost of capital below the IRR, the NPV of a conventional project is positive, and at any cost of capital above the IRR of a conventional project, the NPV must be negative.

Trial and error

The trial and error method is based on the same principles as the graphical method: two or more costs of capital need to be used to derive the NPVs at those costs of capital in order to establish the IRR. The reason for this method being known as the trial and error method is that, even though there is a mathematical representation of what we must do, found in Table 17.9, it is not possible to solve for '*r*' without going through the trial and error method, as we are about to do.

TABLE 17.9 ***Mathematical representations of internal rate of return method***

Any project's IRR is the discount rate at which:

PV (Investment costs) = PV (Inflows).

Rearranging this, we get:

PV (Investment costs) − PV (Inflows) = 0

which translates to:

$$\frac{CF_0}{(1+r)0} + \frac{CF_1}{(1+r)1} + \ldots + \frac{CF_n}{(1+r)1} = 0$$

and which gives:

$$\sum_{t=0}^{n} \frac{CF_t}{(1+r)t} = 0.$$

The starting point for the method outlined in Table 17.9 is to take any value for '*r*' (the cost of capital of 12% given in the basic data for the three problems we are discussing will do), and use this to evaluate the first trial NPV value. We have already done this under the NPV method and found the NPV, at a 12% cost of capital, to be £8,224.10. This is good enough to provide us with a starting point. We now know that 12% is not the IRR! However, from what we know from the NPV profile, since the NPV at '*r*' = 12% is positive, the IRR must be greater than 12%. We know this because the NPV profile tells us that when the NPV is positive, the internal rate of return is greater than the cost of capital. All we can do now is to guess at what cost of capital we should use in our search for the IRR of Project 1. At '*r*' = 12%, the NPV is £8,224.10 with a capital cost of £10,000. Thus the NPV is still large relative to the capital cost. This should tell us that 12% is a long way away from the true IRR. Let us try '*r*' = 30% as our next estimate of Project 1's IRR. At '*r*' = 30%, the NPV of Project 1 is £2,997.44 – a lot nearer to the IRR than 12%, but still quite a way away. Our next guess might be that the IRR is 50%. This gives a NPV of £−370.37. Not bad, but now we have an estimate of the IRR that is greater than the IRR – we know this because the NPV of the project at '*r*' = 50% is negative, and if the NPV is negative, the internal rate of return is less than the cost of capital. We can guess at 'r' being equal to 45%. This gives a value for NPV of £317.08. Again, we are below the value of the IRR now, but at both 'r' = 45% and 'r' = 50% we are very close to our objective. Once we have estimates of the IRR reasonably close to the true IRR, the final stage in our search for the IRR of Project 1 is to carry out linear interpolation. With linear interpolation, we take our final two close estimates of the IRR and assume that between these two points the NPV profile is a perfectly straight line. Taking 'r' being equal to 45% as our starting point, our estimate of the IRR becomes:

$$= 45\% + \frac{317.08}{(317.08 + 370.37)} \times (50\% - 45\%)$$

$$= 45\% + (0.46124 \times 5\%)$$

$$= 45\% + 2.31\%$$

$$= 47.31\%$$

Our estimate of the IRR of Project 1 is that it is 47.31%. This compares very favourably with the computer generated estimate of the IRR of Project 1 of 47.23%. The basis of this calculation is that we are estimating the IRR of the project by taking the £317.08 that it takes for 'r' to move along the NPV profile from 45% to the IRR as a proportion of the whole distance between the 45% and 50% estimates of 'r'. We should check our result by making 'r' equal to 47.31%. If this gives us a NPV of £0, we should be happy that we have found the IRR. If we do this, we obtain a NPV of £−10.90; not zero, but not a very significant distance from it. As a proportion of the capital cost of the project of £10,000, this is a very small error. There is a way to overcome this problem and that is to fine tune the answer we obtained by finding estimates of the IRR nearer than we did, before interpolating. For example, if we had estimated 'r' at 47% (when the NPV is £32.05) and £47.5% (when the NPV is £−37.06) and then interpolated, our estimate of the IRR would have been:

$$47\% + \frac{32.05}{(32.05 + 37.06)} \times (47.5\% - 47\%)$$

$$= 47\% + (0.46357 \times 0.5\%)$$

$$= 47\% + 0.2319$$

$$= 47.2319\%$$

This is clearly very close to the true value of 47.23%. The accuracy required for the estimate of IRR depends largely on the situation we are in and the resources available to us. In an examination where we are required to calculate the IRR as we have just seen, pinpoint accuracy cannot be expected. In reality, however, where we have access to computers, sophisticated calculators, and time, accuracy to several places of decimals could be required. As with the other four methods, we now need a decision rule to help us decide which of the projects we should recommend for adoption.

IRR decision rule

1. If the IRR of a project is greater than the hurdle rate, consider the project further; and
2. If the IRR of Project 1 is greater than the IRR of Project 2, accept Project 1.

The reason for the second part of this rule behaving in this way is because the higher the IRR, the greater the leeway a project has. For example, an IRR of 100% when general interest rates are, say, 15%, indicates a project has a very large margin of safety built into it; the project would have to suffer a very serious setback in order to fail. On the other hand, if general interest rates are 15% and a project has an IRR of 15.5%, our estimates of cash flow and so on need only be slightly optimistic and the whole project could crash.

The annuity factor method

If we are dealing with an annuity, the situation where the cash inflows of a project are the same year after year, the calculation of the IRR is greatly simplified. Consider the following example.

Capital cost of the project is £25,730, the cost of capital is 11% per year, and annual inflows for the life of the project are all the same at £6,000 per year for seven years. The annuity factor of the IRR for this project is found by applying the following formula:

$$\frac{\text{capital cost of the project}}{\text{annual cash flows}}$$

In this example, this gives:

$$\frac{£25,730}{£6,000}$$

$$= 4.2883$$

Applying the annuity factor table at the back of the book, we can determine the IRR by looking along the year 7 row until we come to the value of 4.2883. When we do this we find that the IRR for this project is 14%. If, however, the capital cost of the project had been £16,500 for the same stream of earnings, the annuity factor for the IRR would have been 2.7500. When we look at the annuity factor table now, we find the 2.7500 lies between 28% and 32%. To solve this problem, we can use the linear interpolation approach we used under the trial and error method above. If we do, we obtain:

$$28\% + \frac{2.9370 - 2.7500}{2.9370 - 2.6775} \times (32\% - 28\%)$$

$$= 28\% + (0.72062 \times 4\%)$$

$$= 30.8825\%$$

Check the annuity factor table very carefully to ensure you know where all of these figures come from.

The computer generated value for the IRR for this revised project is that it is 30.81721%. As with the trial and error method, the linear interpolation method can give rise to errors in estimation.

Real world use of capital investment appraisal techniques

> It is now well established that investment appraisal practices do not correspond to theoretical prescriptions. (Collier and Gregory 1995: 33)

There has been a long-running debate over the gap between management accounting theory and practice. One area where a lot of useful work has been done is attempting to find out which capital investment appraisal methods managers really use. Additionally, a lot of useful work has been done in attempting to discover why techniques that are theoretically superior are not as widely used as they ought to be. In this section of this chapter, we will look at two studies that will help us to discover how widely the methods we have reviewed are used, if at all, in British organisations.

CAMEO

Study 1

Collier and Gregory undertook a study of six hotel groups from the United Kingdom. They were interested in learning about how the groups appraised capital budgeting problems.

This study is interesting for at least two reasons. First, they found a wide disparity in the methods used, which is interesting insofar as they were surveying apparently homogenous organisations. Secondly, they found that the leadership style of the chief executive might influence the methods of investment appraisal in use.

Collier and Gregory suggest that since all the organisations surveyed were from the same industry and sector, some conformity in the investment appraisal methods might be expected to be used. They did not find this at all. Four of the hotel groups in the survey used formal investment appraisal methods, whereas the other two used more informal methods. It is Collier and Gregorys' view that the informal techniques are used in organisations where the chief executive is essentially the decision maker. Of course, this does not suggest that all chief executives take decisions on the fly! Collier & Gregory do say that the chief executive might use numeric techniques, but this is not known.

Overall, however, the six hotel groups did use the payback method, the ARR method, the NPV method and the IRR method. Furthermore the survey suggests that one of the hotel groups may have been using the capital asset pricing model to assess its cost of capital.

Study 2

Sangster carried out two surveys in Scotland: one of large companies and one of small companies. The survey sought to answer:

- What is the current usage of payback, IRR, NPV and ARR?
- What changes have occurred in usage?
- Are larger companies more sophisticated in investment appraisal than smaller companies?
- Is ARR still popular despite its theoretical deficiencies?

Table 17.10 gives the rates of usage found in Sangster's study and the rates of usage found by some previous studies. Generally, Sangster has confirmed what just about every other researcher in this area has found: that the payback method is the single most important method in use in industry, with 78% of all companies using that technique, compared with a usage rate of only 73% for all other DCF techniques combined.

TABLE 17.10 ***Use of quantitative evaluation methods***

	Current study	McIntyre and Coulthurst (1985)	Mills and Herbert .	Pike 1980	Pike 1975
IRR	58	28	68	54	42
NPV	48	36	51	38	32
PB	78	82	78	79	71
ARR	31	33	44	51	51
DCF	73	45		69	60
Other	2	4		7	5
None	8	0		0	4

Source: Sangster (1993: 315), table 4.

When comparing the investment appraisal methods in use, where multiple methods are in use and where single methods are in use, Sangster's findings reflected those of McIntyre and Coulthurst and of Pike: the payback method is the most widely used, whether used singly or alongside other methods. The IRR method is the second 'most popular' method in both Sangster's and Pike's studies. (See Sangster's paper, table 11 for full details of these findings.) Overall, Sangster summarises his findings as follows:

- ARR is being used less than before.
- DCF techniques are gaining in popularity.
- NPV use is increasing at a greater rate than IRR.
- Individual companies are using more of the methods than before.

References: Collier and Gregory (1995); Sangster (1993).

There is evidence of change, therefore. Sangster's study shows that both large and small companies are becoming increasingly more sophisticated in their use of capital investment appraisal techniques. However, old habits die hard: the payback technique, the simplest technique of all, is still the front runner by far.

SUMMARY

This chapter has given us a detailed look at capital budgeting. Starting with the nature of capital budgeting and the procedures surrounding it, we saw how organisations should be operating their capital budgeting procedures.

We have also seen much of the basic theory surrounding capital investment appraisal. We looked at the five basic methods that are used in practice to assess which projects are acceptable and which are not. The chapter concluded with a brief review, through the use of two recent studies, of the real-world use of the numerical techniques discussed in this chapter. By way of the appendix to this chapter, we also saw how to use compounding and discounting formulæ and tables, and how to assess the present value of annuities.

KEY TERMS

You should satisfy yourself that you have noted all of these terms and can define and/or describe their meaning and use, as appropriate.

Capital assets (p. 572)
Capital budgeting (p. 573)
Post-auditing (p. 573)
Non-conventional investment (p. 574)
Search for ideas (p. 578)
Source of ideas (p. 579)
Screening of ideas (p. 579)
Classification of proposals (p. 580)
Cash flow (p. 583)
Payback period (p. 585)
Accounting rate of return (p. 587)
Net present value (p. 588)
Cost of capital (p. 588)
Weighted average cost of capital (p. 588)
Profitability index (p. 590)
Internal rate of return (p. 591)
DCF (p. 591)
NPV profile (p. 591)

RECOMMENDED READING

Bierman and Smidt (1980) is one from the 'they don't write like that any more' category, but heavy going except for the specialist. Similarly, Merrett and Sykes (1969). Another scholarly although dated work is Carsberg (1979). Service sector knowledge is always worth gleaning, so read Collier and Gregory (1995). Fairly recent knowledge on what's happening in reality is found in Sangster (1993).

QUESTIONS

Review questions

1. Define capital budgeting.
2. Outline the five kinds of investment discussed in this chapter.
3. What are complementary investments?
4. Outline McIntyre and Coulthurst's (1985) view of the capital budgeting process.

5. Define capital investment appraisal.
6. What are the five major quantitative methods of capital investment appraisal?
7. Define the weighted average cost of capital.
8. What is a net present value profile?

Answers to review questions 1, 3, 5 and 7 can be found in the Student Workbook.

Practice questions

Level I

1. Calculate the present value of the cash flows in the table below:

Years	Cash flow (£)
1–5	10,000
6–10	12,000
11–20	9,000

The cost of capital for discounting purposes is 10%.

2. My Company is undergoing an expansion programme that will increase its sales. The expansion will be completed and fully operational by the beginning of January. A full schedule of all relevant costs and revenues is shown below. Calculate the periodic cash flows for the first two years of the project.

Sales will be £3,600,000 per year and, on average, debtors' collection schedule shows 20% of gross sales are received from debtors within one month of being invoiced, 70% received within two months and 10% received within 3 months. Sales are invoiced at the end of the month of sale.

Raw material 1 will cost £900,000 per year and 2 months' stock will be carried which needs to be bought immediately. Raw material 2 will cost £300,000 per year and 1 month's stock is carried which needs to be bought immediately. Payment for raw materials attracts a discount of 2.5% providing payment is made within 30 days of being invoiced. Purchases are invoiced on the last day of the month of purchase.

Sundry materials will cost £480,000 per year, and one month's stocks will be carried, which needs to be bought immediately. A discount of 1.5% is usually earned for payment within 25 days. Purchases of sundry raw materials are usually invoiced at the same time as raw materials 1 and 2. All discounts are always earned.

Electricity will cost £18,000 per year; fuel oil will cost £25,000; water will cost £13,000; hourly labour will earn £301,600 gross, payable weekly with one week payable in arrears. Packaging and containers will cost £450,000; and they will carry 2 months' stocks which has to be bought immediately. Except for hourly labour, all payments are made on the final day of the month.

3. Your company is looking into replacing an old lorry with a newer model, which will reduce costs (excluding depreciation) from £40,000 to £24,000 per year. Sales are £65,000 per year. The old lorry cost £45,000 when bought nearly 5 years ago, had an estimated useful life of 15 years, nil residual value, and is being depreciated on the straight-line basis. At present, its resale value is estimated to be £15,000 if sold outright. The new lorry costs £75,000 and would be depreciated on the straight-line basis to a nil residual value over a 10-year life. Your Company

has a relevant tax rate of 40%, and for tax purposes you are to assume the straight-line method is employed with the useful lives given above being used.

Required

(a) Calculate the outflow required to acquire the new lorry assuming the old one is sold now.
(b) Calculate the yearly post taxation profits from operations resulting from the old lorry and the new lorry.
(c) Summarise the cash flows and calculate the differential cash flows of the new lorry over the 10-year period. (Ignore any tax adjustments arising from the sale of the old lorry.)

4. Lewis Boxer Ltd is evaluating two mutually exclusive capital investment projects. The post-tax cash flows for the proposals are as below:

Year	Project A (£)	Project B (£)
0	–20,000	–28,000
1	5,000	8,000
2	5,000	8,000
3	6,000	8,000
4	6,000	8,000
5	6,000	8,000

Project A will have a residual value of £5,000 and project B one of £4,000.

Required

(a) Assuming a cost of capital for this business of 10%, evaluate these projects in terms of the five methods discussed in the chapter.
(b) Using costs of capital of 0%, 5%, 10%, 15%, 20%, and 25%, prepare an estimated net present profile of projects A and B. Plot both profiles on the same graph, and discuss the use of such a profile in helping management to choose between alternative investment proposals.

Level II

5. Gray City General Hospital comprises many old buildings, and these buildings are thought to be the source of a serious drain on the financial resources of the hospital. A study by the hospital's Administration team has recommended that the present buildings can be updated for £5,000,000. Having carried out these renovations, the hospital's annual budget would be £3,000,000. They also say that they can build an entirely new building for £7,500,000. The new building would have an annual operating budget of £2,500,000. An Area Health Authority planning officer has been asked to decide which project would be the least costly alternative. This planning officer has determined:

(a) Both projects would have a useful life of 25 years with a salvage value of 30% of the initial capital costs.
(b) Expenses are expected to increase equally over the years for both projects due to inflation.
(c) An 11% cost of capital is felt to be appropriate for this kind of decision.

Required

Prepare an analysis that would indicate the least costly alternative, using whichever method(s) you prefer. Comment on the decision to be made in the light of the net present value rule.

6. Your Company is seeking investment projects and has identified three alternative proposals for its capital expenditure budget for next year.

   Although the projects are similar, their profiles are radically different to each other. An inflation rate of 10% per year has been estimated as being appropriate.

   (a) *Project 1* Requires an immediate outlay of £200,000 and is expected to give rise to an annual cash flow of £50,000 for each of the next 10 years. At the end of year 10, the residual value of the project is expected to be £30,000.
   (b) *Project 2* has no capital outlay and has an expected useful life of 12 years. During this time, annual cash flows are anticipated to arise at the level of £50,000. However, in years 2, 5 and 9 repair and maintenance payments will arise amounting to £225,000 in year 2, £250,000 in year 5 and £100,000 in year 9.
   (c) *Project 3* requires an immediate capital outlay of £525,000. Cash flows arising over the 13-year life of the project will be £79,000 for years 1–5 (inclusive) and £110,000 for years 6–13 (inclusive). This project has a residual value of £140,000.

   Your Company's permanent capital comprises: 200,000 Ordinary shares whose market value is currently £1.35 per share; £1.5 million 11% Debentures, currently trading at £97.5%. Ordinary dividends are currently being paid at the rate of 15 pence per share.

Required

Use the NPV method to assess which, if any, of the three alternatives you would advise the management of Your Company to invest in.

7. Florence Ltd is considering the selection of one of a pair of mutually exclusive investment projects. Both would involve purchase of machinery with a life of 5 years.

- *Project 1* would generate annual cash flows of £200,000; the machinery would cost £556,000 and have a scrap value of £56,000.
- *Project 2* would generate annual cash flows of £500,000; the machinery would cost £1,616,000 and have a scrap value of £301,000.

Florence uses the straight-line method for providing for depreciation. Its cost of capital is 15% per year. Assume that annual cash flows arise on the anniversaries of the initial outlay, and that inflation will be insignificant over the project lives.

Required

(a) Calculate for each project:
   (i) the ARR to the nearest;
   (ii) the NPV;
   (iii) the profitability index;
   (iv) the IRR to the nearest;
   (v) the payback period.

(b) State which, if any, project you would select for acceptance. Give your reasons.

Solutions to practice questions 2, 5 and 7 can be found in the Student Workbook. Solutions to practice question numbers in red can be found at the end of this book.

Projects

1. Find a variety of sets of published accounts for small, and medium, and large profit-making organisations and investigate the importance of capital budgeting for those organisations:

   (a) Look for the absolute levels of capital investment in the organisations.
   (b) Look for the relative levels of capital investment in the organisations.

   Try to assess, from the accounting evidence as well as any evidence contained elsewhere in the report, the nature of the capital investments undertaken. Can you see evidence of investments under the headings discussed in the chapter:

   (a) generative;
   (b) sustaining;
   (c) replacement;
   (d) expanding; and
   (e) safety and environmental?

2. As you walk around the town or city that you live in, look for capital investment projects undertaken by non profit-making organisations. Assess the basis on which these investments are, or have been, made.

   Examples to look out for would include: Why has the Local Authority built a new link road? Why has the hospital added a new ward? Why has your church built a new hall?

   If possible, get copies of the report and accounts of these organisations and carry out the analysis from project (1) above. Additionally, try to contact these organisations and find out the reasoning behind these developments.

3. Assuming you have carried out both of projects (1) and (2), are there significant differences in the way the different types of organisation undertake capital investment projects?

   If there are differences, how do you think these differences arise?

   (a) Is it because of the differences in objectives (for example, profit-making or non-profit-making objectives)?
   (b) Is it because of the nature of the financing of the organisations?
   (c) Is it for some other reason?

Appendix: Introduction to compounding and discounting

Introduction

Compounding and discounting are the keys to understanding much of the theory and practice of capital investment appraisal. Of all the techniques we will be looking at under this heading the most important aspects of them involve the use of the concepts underlying compound interest and discounting.

Compound interest

The term 'compounding' refers to the situation which usually exists when we invest money (known as the principal) at the bank or building society. That is, we not only earn interest on our original investment but, if we leave an investment untouched and not only do not withdraw the principal but also do not withdraw the interest either, the interest itself earns interest.

Assume we invest £100 today; the interest rate payable is 10% per year, compounded annually; and we intend to leave our investment untouched for four whole years. We want to know, first, how much our investment will be worth at the end of the four-year period, and second, how much interest will be earned over the four years.

We calculate the balance carried down (c/d) at the end of a year by taking the balance at the start of the year and inflating it by the interest rate. The calculation we need to perform here is, for year 1:

principal × compound interest factor = balance c/d

£100 × (1 + 0.10) = £110.00

Therefore, the balance carried down at the end of year 1 is £110.00.

Notice that we always add one to the rate of interest (which we use in the form of a decimal, not a percentage) to give us the compound interest factor: this is, the number we multiply the principal by.

Starting with the balance brought down from year 1, the calculation of the balance for the end of year 2, and any subsequent year, becomes:

Balance b/d × compound interest factor = balance c/d

£110.00 × (1 + 0.10) = £121.00

For years 3 and 4 respectively we have.

£121.00 × (1 + 0.10) = £133.10

£133.10x (1 + 0.10) = £146.41

WORKED EXAMPLE 17.A1

Calculate the final balance c/d at the end of each year on the following investment: £250 invested for five years at 12% per year, compounded annually.

Solution to Worked example 17.A1:

Year 1	£250.00 × (1 + 0.12) = £280.00
Year 2	£280.00 × (1 + 0.12) = £313.60
Year 3	£313.60 × (1 + 0.12) = £351.23

Year 4	£351.23 × (1 + 0.12) = £393.38
Year 5	£393.38 × (1 + 0.12) = £440.59

The balance on our account at the end of year 5 is £440.59 (worked to the nearest penny).

Although there is nothing wrong with the way we are preparing this account, it is not *generally* useful. If we wish to work through a 20- or 30-year investment problem, we would find the effort involved was tedious and time consuming. We are looking for a method that will simplify our work as much as possible. We are, after all, looking to solve capital investment appraisal problems, and such problems can easily involve investments covering decades rather than just a few years.

If we look at the logic of what we have just done, we will see the way compound interest works. We can generalise our workings by assigning letters to the numbers:

let P be the principal
let r be the rate of interest

Our workings become:

	Balance at the end of the year
Year 1	$P \times (1 + r)$
Year 2	$P \times (1 + r) \times (1 + r)$
Year 3	$P \times (1 + r) \times (1 + r) \times (1 + r)$
Year 4	$P \times (1 + r) \times (1 + r) \times (1 + r) \times (1 + r)$

Notice how we have incorporated the way that the interest earns interest by multiplying $(1 + r)$ by $(1 + r)$ for each successive year.

When we get rid of the unnecessary multiplication signs, and simplify what we have done, we get:

	Balance at the end of the year
Year 1	$P(1 + r)^1$
Year 2	$P(1 + r)^2$
Year 3	$P(1 + r)^3$
Year 4	$P(1 + r)^4$

There is a definite pattern to the calculation: for year 1, we find the balance carried down by multiplying the principal by $(1 + r)$ raised to the power of 1; we raise $(1 + r)$ for year 2 to the power 2; for year 3 the power is 3, and so on. For any year, which we can designate as 'n', we can specify a general formula for compound interest factors:

The balance on deposit at the end of a period of investment, which is usually called S_n, is given by:

$$S_n = P(1 + r)^n$$

This is the general formula we have been looking for. We can see its usefulness immediately by reworking the two examples above by substituting for P, r and n as appropriate and evaluating S_n.

Example 1

$$S_4 = £100(1.10)^4 = £100(1.46410) = £146.41$$

Example 2

$$S_5 = £250(1.12)^5 = £250(1.76234) = £440.59$$

Notice how S_n becomes S_4 when we are dealing with a four-year problem, and it becomes S_5 when we are dealing with a five-year problem.

WORKED EXAMPLE 17.A2

Evaluate S_n in each of the following cases:

	Interest rate (%)	Principal (£)	Term (years)
1.	15.50	15,000	10
2.	12.00	30,000	12
3.	108.75	1,000	5
4.	25.00	125,000	11

Keep your compound interest factors to five decimal places for now; and think carefully about how to deal with 108.75% for part (3).

Solution to Worked example 17.A2

1. £15,000 $(1.155)^{10}$ = £15,000 (4.22493) = £63,373.95
2. £30,000$(1.120)^{12}$ = £30,000 (3.89598) = £116,879.40
3. £1,000 $(2.0875)^5$ = £1,000 (39.63989) = £39,639.89
4. £125,000$(1.250)^{11}$ = £125,000(11.64153) = £1,455,191.25

For part (3), the solution to dealing with 108.75% is to make 108.75% into a decimal, giving 1.0875; one is then added to that number (as we agreed it should be, above) to give 2.0875. This is a general rule: convert the interest rate into a decimal number and add one to it. Therefore:

198.12% becomes 1.9812 + 1.0000 = 2.9812
312.00% becomes 3.1200 + 1.0000 = 4.1200
684.63% becomes 6.8463 + 1.0000 = 7.8463

Calculation of interest earned

At any time the interest earned to date, I, can be calculated by subtracting the principal, P, from the final balance carried down:

final
balance c/d − principal = interest earned
$P(1 + r)^n - P = I$

We can apply this new formula to the data from Worked example 17.A2, and calculate the interest earned on each of the investments:

	Final balance c/d (£)	−	Principal (£)	=	Interest earned (£)
1.	63,373.95	−	15,000	=	48,373.95
2.	116,879.40	−	30,000	=	86,879.40
3.	39,639.89	−	1,000	=	38,639.89
4.	1,455,191.25	−	125,000	=	1,330,191.25

Compound interest factors

As with many things mathematical, the good news about compound interest calculations is that the compound interest factors we have already met – and the ones we haven't – are all constants. This means that the compound interest factor for 10% for 10 years is *always* 2.59374; and the factor for 6% for 25 years is *always* 4.29187.

The significance of compound interest factors being constant is that we can use compound interest factor tables, such as the one found in Table A.1 in the Appendix at the back of this book, an extract of which is found below.

TABLE A17.1 ***Compound interest factors***

	Interest rate (%)						
Year	1	5	10	15	20	25	30
1	1.0100	1.0500	1.1000	1.1500	1.2000	1.2500	1.3000
2	1.0201	1.1025	1.2100	1.3225	1.4400	1.5625	1.6900
3	1.0303	1.1576	1.3310	1.5209	1.7280	1.9531	2.1970
4	1.0406	1.2155	**1.4641**	1.7490	2.0736	2.4414	2.8561
5	1.0510	1.2763	1.6105	2.0114	2.4883	3.0518	3.7129
6	1.0615	1.3401	1.7716	2.3131	2.9860	3.8147	4.8268
7	1.0721	1.4071	1.9487	2.6600	3.5832	4.7684	6.2749
8	1.0829	1.4775	2.1436	3.0590	4.2998	5.9605	8.1573
9	1.0937	1.5513	2.3579	**3.5179**	5.1598	7.4506	10.6045
10	1.1046	1.6289	2.5937	4.0456	6.1917	9.3132	13.7858

Note, Table A17.1, and Table A.1, at the end of the book, is based on interest being compounded annually, although we could just as readily calculate discount factors based on interest being compounded daily, weekly, monthly, or on any other basis.

For Worked example 17.A1, we could have used Table A17.1 to find the compound factor for 10% for four years. From the Table A17.1 above it is 1.4641, which we find at the intersection of the 10% column and the year 4 row (it is highlighted in Table A17.1). Similarly, when the interest rate is 15% and we are considering a 9-year investment, the relevant compound factor is 3.5179 (again, this factor is highlighted in Table A17.1).

WORKED EXAMPLE 17.A3

Using the compound interest factors from Table A17.1 only, calculate S_n for each of the following cases:

	Interest rate (%)	Principal (£)	Term (years)
1.	5	10,000	8
2.	20	10,000	8
3.	15	10,000	8
4.	1	10,000	8

Solution to Worked example 17.A3

1. £10,000 × 1.4775 = £14,775
2. £10,000 × 4.2998 = £42,998
3. £10,000 × 3.0590 = £30,590
4. £10,000 × 1.0829 = £10,829

Problems with compound interest factor tables

There is one significant problem to overcome with compound interest factor tables. The problem is that they usually do not cater for fractional interest rates. For example, in Table A17.1, the interest rates are shown as whole numbers only. Suppose we needed to evaluate an investment based on an interest rate of, say, 11.125% per year, compounded annually? We could not do that from Table A17.1, nor Table A.1 at the end of the book.

Unless we can find a table containing fractional interest rates, we have to use the compound interest factor formula. Whatever the rate of interest, the compound interest formula will cope with it. Worked example 17.A4 contains some fractional interest rates for us to use.

WORKED EXAMPLE 17.A4

Calculate S_n from the following:

1. £5,000 is invested for eight years at 9.75125% p.a., compounded annually.
2. £12,345 is invested for eleven years at 12.003733% p.a., compounded annually.
3. £2,464 is invested for 18 years at 8.0101% p.a., compounded annually.
4. £45,543 is invested for four years at 11.11111% p.a., compounded annually.

Solution to Worked example 17.A4

Applying the formula $S_n = P(1 + r)^n$ (and working with five places of decimals for the compound interest factor) gives:

1. £5,000 × $(1.0975125)^8$
   = £5,000 × 2.10511 = 10,525.55
2. £12,345 × $(1.12003733)^{11}$
   = £12,345 – 3.47983 = £42,958.50
3. £2,464 × $(1.080101)^{18}$
   = £2,464 × 4.00275 = £9,862.78
4. £45,543 × $(1.111111)^4$
   = £45,543 × 1.52416 = £69,414.82

Whatever the compound interest problem is, whether it be for 10% or 3.333857% interest, whether it be for three or 83 years, and whether it be for £1 or £1 billion, the formula we have will always provide us with the interest earned and the balance carried down.

Compounding on a basis other than annual

Throughout this appendix, we have compounded interest calculations on an annual basis. Although we have not said why, it is vital that we know what the compounding basis is, but it need not be done on an annual basis.

In reality (and we can check with our banks that this is true), interest is compounded on a daily basis rather than on an annual basis. Whilst the concepts involved in such a change of compounding base remain as they have been so far, the formula we need to use for daily compounding is different to the one we have been using. The formula for calculating interest earned (or paid) on a daily basis on a one year investment is:

$$S_n = \left(1 + \frac{r}{365}\right)^{365}$$

Therefore, to calculate the interest earned on an investment when the interest is compounded on a daily basis, we divide the rate of interest by 365 (days in a year) and raise the resulting compound factor to the power of 365 multiplied by the number of years of the investment. When we compare the two compounding bases, we can see whether we are better off being paid interest earned when it is compounded yearly or daily. Calculate the interest earned on an investment of £1,000 for one year at 15%, using (i) annual and (ii) daily compounding:

Compounded annually

£1,000 × 1.15 = £1,150

Compound daily

$$£1{,}000 \times \left(1 + \frac{0.15}{365}\right)^{365}$$

$$= £1{,}000 \times 1.161799 = £1.161.80$$

From this example, we can see that a difference arises of £11.80 between compounding daily and compounding annually on our investment of £1,000 for year at 15% per year.

The general rule is that the more frequently the compounding is carried out, the more interest will be earned.

Making this formula more general now, we can vary the number of times we compound our interest payments and modify the new formula. For any investment, with any rate of interest, and compounding any number of times per year, the formula is:

$$S_n = \left(1 + \frac{r}{m}\right)^{nm}$$

Where:

S_n, r, and n are all as we defined earlier. m is the number of times compounding takes place in the period.

Consequently, m can be any number: 365 for daily compounding, 2 for compounding every half year, 12 for compounding every month, and so on. We can use these variations to the basic formula in Worked example 17.A5.

WORKED EXAMPLE 17.A5

Calculate the balances carried down for the following investments:

	Principal (£)	Times compounded per year	Years	Interest rate (%)
1.	3,500	365	10	11.00
2.	5,000	12	5	10.00
3.	2,750	2	8	10.75
4.	6,432	52	15	9.63

Solution to Worked example 17.A5

1. $£3,500(1 + (0.11 \div 365))^{10 \times 365} = £3,500(3.00367)$
   $= £10,523.45$
2. $£5,000£(1 + (0.10 \div 12))^{5 \times 12} = £5,000(1.64531)$
   $= £8,226.55$
3. $£2,750(1 + (0.1075 \div 2))^{8 \times 2} = £2,750(2.31101)$
   $= £6,355.28$
4. $£6,432(1 + (0.0963 \div 52))^{15 \times 52} = £6,432(4.23407)$
   $= £27,233.54$

Continuous compounding

In the case we have just been examining, with compounding on a daily basis, we can make our work a little simpler by knowing that as m tends to infinity, all we need to do to calculate the compounding factor is to solve the following expression:

$$e^r$$

where:

e is the base of natural logarithms (and is equal to approximately 2.718282).
r is the rate of interest or cost of capital.

Taking a value of m of 365 compounding periods per year to represent a large value (tending to infinity), we can compare the compound factors using daily and continuous compounding based on an investment of £10,000 at 10% per annum:

daily compounding result = £11,051.56
continuous compounding result = £11,051.71

The daily compounding calculation is familiar now; but the continuous calculation is:

$$£10,000 \times e^{0.1}$$

$$= £10,000 \times 2.718282^{0.1}$$

$$= £11,051.71$$

Discounting

The reason for discussing compound interest in such detail will now become apparent.

With compounding we look *forward* from today in order to predict what the future will bring. That is, we assume an investment takes place now and, given a particular rate of interest, calculate what that will increase to over a given period.

In capital budgeting, however, we usually arrive at this part of the answer first! That is, by preparing detailed analyses, we will have estimates of likely cash flows. Thus we will have the outcomes of our investments before we know the value, at today's values, of that investment. We are looking, therefore, to reverse the compounding process in order to find out how much we should invest today to receive the benefits we have estimated for tomorrow.

We can apply the principles of discounting to the first example we looked at under compounding. When we invested £100 for four years at 10% per year compounded annually, the final balance carried down was £146.41. By discounting, we want to work from the final balance to find out how much we should invest at the very beginning of year 1 in order to have £146.41 at the end of the four-year period. All we need do to discover the initial investment required is to reverse the compounding process and divide £146.41 by the compound interest factor:

$$\frac{£146.41}{1.4641} = £100.00$$

Simple! This is always the way it works. In Worked example 17.A2 (2), we had a final balance of £116,879.40 on our investment which had been earning interest at the rate of 12% per year, compounded annually, for 12 years. How much would we need to invest now to have this sum left after those 12 years?

$$\frac{£116,879.40}{3.89598} = £30,000$$

WORKED EXAMPLE 17.A6

Calculate the sum needed to be invested now in each of the following cases:

1. £10,000 receivable in five years' time when interest rates are 10% per year, compounded annually.
2. £15,750 receivable in nine years' time when interest rates are 8% per year, compounded annually.
3. £1,000 receivable in 15 years' time when interest rates are 12.3% per year, compounded annually.
4. £25,000 receivable in 13 years' time when interest rates are 10.09% per year, compounded annually.

Solution to Worked example 17.A6

1. £10,000 ÷ 1.61051 = £6,209.21
2. £15,750 ÷ 1.99900 = £7,878.92
3. £ 1,000 ÷ 5.69766 = £ 175.11
4. £25,000 ÷ 3.48917 = £7,165.02

Look at part (1) of Worked example 17.A6. The full interpretation of this result is that if we invest £6,209.21 today, when the interest rate is (and remains at) 10% per year compounded annually, we will have £10,000 in our account at the end of five years. Another way of saying this is that £10,000 receivable in exactly five years' time, when interest rates are 10% per year compounded annually, has a present value of £6,209.21. For part (2) of Worked example 17.A6, £7,878.92 is the present value of £15,750 receivable in nine years' time when the rate of interest is to be 8% per year, compounded annually.

Discount factors

We saw under the heading of compound interest that tables of compound interest factors can be prepared for general use since any rate of interest for a given period gives rise to a constant compound interest factor. The same applies to discounting, but not in the format we have been discussing.

When we calculate compound interest, we multiply by the compound interest factor. When we have discounted, we have divided by the compound interest factor. The difficulty with this method of discounting is that it is difficult to represent dividing by a compound interest factor in a table in the way we have described so far. However, if we check the logic of what we are doing, we will see how we can derive discount factors.

The present value of £146.41 receivable in four years' time when the rate of interest is 10% per year, compounded annually, is £100.00. We derived this as we saw above. If we generalise this, we get:

$$\text{present value} = \frac{\text{final balance carried down}}{\text{compound interest factor}}$$

We should refer to the final balance carried down as the future value, from now on:

$$\text{present value} = \frac{\text{future value}}{\text{compound interest factor}}$$

If we assume that our future value will be £1, the formula for calculating the present value is the discount factor formula, which is:

$$P = \frac{1}{(1 + r)^n}$$

where P is the principal, as it was for calculations for compound interest. If r is 10% per year, compounded annually and n is 1 year, the present value is:

$$P = \frac{1}{(1 + 0.1)^1}$$

$$= 0.909091$$

Taking this generalisation, we can now derive a table of discount factors for any rate of interest and for any number of years; and rather than dividing by a compound interest factor, we now multiply by the discount factor. Thus instead of:

$$\frac{£146.41}{1.4641} = £100.00$$

We have:

$$£146.41 \times 0.68301 = £100$$

The discount factor of 0.68301 is calculated as follows:

$$\frac{1}{(1 + 0.1)^4} = 0.68301$$

WORKED EXAMPLE 17.A7

1. Calculate the discount factors for the following:

   (a) 15% for 6 years;
   (b) 7% for 18 years;
   (c) 12.5% for 10 years; and
   (d) 13.125% for 11 years.

2. Now apply those discount factors by using them to find the present values in the following situations:

   (a) Apply the discount factor found in part (1)(a) of this exercise to find the present value of £2,000 receivable in six years' time.
   (b) Apply the discount factor found in part (1) (b) of this exercise to find the present value of £9,000 receivable in 18 years' time.
   (c) Apply the discount factor found in part (1) (c) of this exercise to find the present value of £8,600 receivable in 10 years' time.
   (d) Apply the discount factor found in part (1) (d) of this exercise to find the present value of £14,800 receivable in 11 years' time.

Solution to Worked example 17.A7

1. (a) $1 \div 2.31031 = 0.43284$
   (b) $1 \div 3.37993 = 0.29586$
   (c) $1 \div 3.24732 = 0.30795$
   (d) $1 \div 3.88280 = 0.25755$

2. (a) $0.43284 \times £2,000 = £856.68$
   (b) $0.29586 \times £9,000 = £2,573.64$
   (c) $0.30795 \times £8,600 = £2,648.37$
   (d) $0.25755 \times £14,800 = £3,811.74$

Discount factor tables

We can now look at a discount factor table (Table A17.2). The discount factors are calculated as we have been discussing, and the table works in the same way that Table A17.1 worked for compound interest factors. Therefore, the discount factor for 20% for 9 years is 0.1938 (it is highlighted in Table A17.2); and the discount factor for 5% for 3 years (also highlighted) is 0.8638.

TABLE A17.2 *Discount factors*

	Interest rate (%)						
Year	1	5	10	15	20	25	30
1	0.9901	0.9524	0.9091	0.8696	0.8333	0.8000	0.7692
2	0.9803	0.9070	0.8264	0.7561	0.6944	0.6400	0.5917
3	0.9706	**0.8638**	0.7513	0.6575	0.5787	0.5120	0.4552
4	0.9610	0.8227	0.6830	0.5718	0.4823	0.4096	0.3501
5	0.9515	0.7835	0.6209	0.4972	0.4019	0.3277	0.2693
6	0.9420	0.7462	0.5645	0.4323	0.3349	0.2621	0.2072
7	0.9327	0.7107	0.5132	0.3759	0.2791	0.2097	0.1594
8	0.9235	0.6768	0.4665	0.3269	0.2326	0.1678	0.1226
9	0.9143	0.6446	0.4241	0.2843	**0.1938**	0.1342	0.0943
10	0.9053	0.6139	0.3855	0.2472	0.1615	0.1074	0.0725

Note that the extract of a discount factor table, Table A17.2, and Table A.2 in the Appendix at the end of the book is based on interest being compounded annually, although we could just as readily calculate discount factors based on interest being compounded daily, weekly, monthly, or on any other basis.

WORKED EXAMPLE 17.A8

Using the discount factors to be found in Table A17.2, calculate the present values in each of the following situations:

	Interest rate (%)	Future value (£)	Term (years)
1.	10	75,000	5
2.	15	53,500	10
3.	25	100,000	2
4.	5	1,250	9

Solution to Worked example 17.A8

1. £75,000 × 0.6209 = £46,567.50
2. £53,500 × 0.2472 = £13,225.20
3. £100,000 × 0.6400 = £64,000.00
4. £1,250 × 0.6446 = £805.75

The present value of a stream of earnings

Given that a capital investment project is one that will carry on for a relatively long time, it should be clear that such a project will pay out and earn money over several different years. Consequently, we need to consider the present value of an asset when cash does flow over several years.

Imagine we are offered a deal whereby we invest a sum today in return for:

1. £1,000 payable in exactly one year's time;
2. £2,000 payable in exactly two years' time; and
3. £6,000 payable in exactly three years' time.

The rate of interest is to be 10% for the whole period.

We want to know how much we should pay for this stream of earnings. In other words, what is the present value of that stream of earnings?

The solution to this problem is to find the present value of each of the sums of money receivable, and then add those results together to provide us with the overall present value of the stream:

Year	Discount factor (10%)	Cash flow (£)	Present value (£)
1	0.9091	1,000	909.10
2	0.8264	2,000	1,652.80
3	0.7513	6,000	4,507.80
Present value			7,069.70

The present value of this stream of earnings is £7,069.70. This means that the amount we should invest now in order to receive the stream of earnings indicated is £7,069.70. If the project were negotiable, securing the stream of earnings for, say, £7,000 or £6,500 would be even better because we would be financially better off as a result. However, if we were to pay, say, £7,500 or £8,000 for the stream of earnings, we would be losers on the deal. Therefore, £7,069.70 is the *maximum* we should pay for that stream of earnings.

We can prove that this method works by considering the behaviour of the investment account that this stream is coming from. We can consider the opening balance at the start of each year, add on the interest earned for the year by that investment, and then determine the balance carried down by subtracting the withdrawal at the end of each year. Finally, we will arrive at a nil balance carried down at the end of the project period.

Year	Balance (£)	Interest earned (£)	Withdrawal (£)	Balance (£)
1	7,069.70	706.97	−1,000	6,776.67
2	6,776.67	677.67	−2,000	5,454.34
3	5,454.34	545.43	−6,000	−0.23

To be consistent with the problem, the final balance carried down should be exactly £0.00. However, because of the rounding errors that arise by working with only four places of decimals, a small discrepancy has arisen of £0.23: not a significant error. With full decimal accuracy, this problem disappears.

WORKED EXAMPLE 17.A9

Consider the following stream of earnings and say how much should be paid to secure the asset giving rise to that stream.

1. £3,000 payable in exactly one year's time;
2. £3,000 payable in exactly two years' time; and
3. £2,500 payable in exactly three years' time.

The rate of interest is to be 14% for the whole period.

Solution to Worked example 17.A9

Year	Discount factor (14%)	Cash flow (£)	Present value (£)
1	0.8772	3,000	2,631.60
2	0.7695	3,000	2,308.50
3	0.6750	2,500	1,687.50
Present value			£6,627.60

So, we would pay no more than £6,627.60 to ensure that we would receive the stream of earnings promised by the problem.

The present value of an annuity

An annuity is an asset that gives rise to a stream of earnings that is constant over the life of the asset. For example, if we invest £10,000 now, and that investment gives a return of, say, £2,000 each year for the life of that investment of eight years, we have an annuity. Assuming the rate of interest applicable to this investment is 12% per year, compounded annually, we can calculate the present value of that stream of earnings by using the annuity factor formula, which is:

$$\frac{1 - \dfrac{1}{(1+r)^n}}{r}$$

For this example, the annuity factor is:

$$\frac{1 - \dfrac{1}{(1+0.12)^8}}{0.12}$$

$= 4.96764$

We apply this to our problem by multiplying the annuity factor by the annual cash inflow. The result of this calculation is the present value of the annuity of £2,000 per year for eight years:

£2,000 × 4.96764

= £9,935.28

Since we are being asked to pay £10,000 for this investment, we should refuse it since its present value is only £9,935.28.

Although we do not need to know the derivation of the annuity factor formula, we should be aware of the logic behind it. For example, consider an annuity of £1,000 each year for three years at 10% each year. The present value calculation of this annuity can be shown in the familiar layout:

Year	Discount factor (10%)	Cash flow (£)	Present value (£)
1	0.9091	1,000	909.10
2	0.8264	1,000	826.40
3	0.7513	1,000	751.30
Present value			2,486.80

We can derive the annuity factor from this example by adding together the discount factors for the three years:

$0.9091 + 0.8264 + 0.7513 = 2.4868$

Multiplying this factor by the constant annual stream of 1,000 gives us the present value of that stream:

2.4868 × £1,000 = £2,486.80

We can confirm this result by applying the annuity factor to this example. The annuity factor is:

$$\frac{1 - \dfrac{1}{(1 + 0.1)^3}}{0.1}$$

= 2.486851991.

And multiplying this factor by the constant annual stream of £1,000 for each of three years gives:

2.48685 × £1,000

= £2,486.85

That is, to within a few pence of agreeing with our initial result.

As with compounding and discounting factors, annuity factors are also constant. Table A17.3, an extract from the annuity factor table (Table A.3 to be found at the end of the book) can be used for Worked example 17.A10.

TABLE A17.3 ***Extract from the annuity factor table***

	Interest rates (%)					
Year	10	11	12	13	14	15
1	0.90909	0.900901	0.892857	0.884956	0.87719	0.869565
2	1.73553	1.712523	1.690051	1.668102	1.64666	1.625709
3	2.48685	2.443715	2.401831	2.361153	2.32163	2.283225
4	3.16986	3.102446	3.037349	2.974471	2.91371	2.854978
5	3.79078	3.695897	3.604776	3.517231	3.43308	3.352155
6	4.35526	4.230538	4.111407	3.997550	3.88866	3.784483
7	4.86841	4.712196	4.563757	4.422610	4.28830	4.160420
8	5.33492	5.146123	4.967640	4.798770	4.63886	4.487322
9	5.75902	5.537048	5.328250	5.131655	4.94637	4.771584
10	6.14456	5.889232	5.650223	5.426243	5.21611	5.018769
11	6.49506	6.206515	5.937699	5.686941	5.45273	5.233712
12	6.81369	6.492356	6.194374	5.917647	5.66029	5.420619
13	7.10335	6.749870	6.423548	6.121812	5.84236	5.583147
14	7.36668	6.981865	6.628168	6.302488	6.00207	5.724476
15	7.60608	7.190870	6.810864	6.462379	6.14216	5.847370

WORKED EXAMPLE 17.A10

1. Use the annuity factor formula to calculate the present value of an annuity that costs £100,000 to buy today and that gives a rise in earnings of £15,000 each year for twelve years when the rate of interest is 14% per year compounded annually. Would you buy this annuity?
2. Use the annuity factor tables at the end of the book to determine the present value of the annuity in part (1) of this exercise.

Solution to Worked example 17.A10

1. Using the annuity factor formula gives:

$$\frac{1 - \dfrac{1}{(1 + 0.14)^{12}}}{0.14}$$

$$= 5.660292125$$

Therefore, the present value of the stream of earnings generated by the annuity is:

$$£15,000 \times 5.660292125$$

$$= £84,904.38188$$

Given that the annuity costs £100,000 to buy, this appears not to be a worthwhile investment since it costs £15,095.61812 more to buy than it is worth. It is worth only £84,904.38188.

2. Using the tables at the end of the book gives a very similar solution:

$$£15,000 \times 5.6602$$

$$= £84,904.38$$

Again, a deficit arises by buying this annuity of the difference between the purchase price and the present value of the stream of earnings produced by that annuity.

Modified annuities

We can consider assets that give rise to streams of earnings which are not annuities but which can be analysed by what we can call the modified annuity method. For example, use the annuity factor tables at the end of the book to determine whether the following is a good investment.

An asset costs £30,000 if bought today. It will give rise to £3,000 cash flow per year for the first six years and £1,000 per year for each of years 7 to 11. Assume the interest rate will be 15% throughout the period. Would you invest in this asset?

The calculations require that the problem be split into two parts:

1. Treat the earnings from years 1 to 6 as an ordinary annuity.
2. Treat the earnings from years 7 to 11 as an incremental annuity.

Years	Annuity factor	Cash flow (£)	Present value (£)
1 to 6	3.7844	3,000	11,353.44
7 to 11	1.4492	1,000	1,449.22
Present value			12,802.66

The question might arise of where does the annuity factor of 1.4492 come from for years 7 to 11? This comes from what we called the incremental annuity. The derivation of this factor is as follows. Take the annuity factor for year 11 and subtract from it the annuity factor for year 6. This gives us the difference between the annuity factor for years 1 to 11 and the annuity factor for years 1 to 6, the difference being the annuity factor for years 7 to 11:

Factor for years 1 to 11	5.2337
Factor for years 1 to 6	3.7844
Factor for years 7 to 11	1.4493

Perpetual annuity

It can happen that an annuity is received in perpetuity: for ever! In this case, as was the case with continuous compounding, the mathematics are greatly simplified. The formula for finding the present value of an annuity is

$$\frac{c}{r}$$

That is, the capital cost divided by the rate of interest or cost of capital.

If I receive £1,000 per year by way of a perpetual annuity and the rate of interest is 10% per annum, the present value of the stream of earnings generated by that annuity is:

$$\frac{£1,000}{10\%}$$

$$= £10,000$$

This can be demonstrated quite simply to be true by setting up a situation such as £1,000 for ever and finding the annuity factor for, say, thirty years or fifty years at 10% per annum, and then comparing the result of that calculation with the one we have just seen, which has a present value of an annuity factor of 10.

That concludes this appendix. You should now return to the main part of the chapter. However, if you have any further difficulties you can either rework this appendix, or consult any one or more of the many excellent business mathematics texts that are available.

REFERENCES

Archer, S. H., Choate, G. M. and Racette, G. (1983) *Financial Management*, 2nd edn (Wiley).

Bierman, H. Jr. and Smidt, S. (1980), *The Capital Budgeting Decision: Economic analysis of investment projects*, 5th edn (Macmillan).

Carsberg, B. V. (1979), *Economics of Business Decisions* (Pitman).

CIMA (1991), *Management Accounting Official Terminology* (Chartered Institute of Management Accountants).

Collier, P. and Gregory, A. (1995), 'Investment appraisal in service industries: a field study analysis of the UK hotels sector', *Management Accounting Research* vol. **6** (March), 33–57.

Lumijärvi, O.P. (1991), 'Selling of capital investment to top management', *Management Accounting*, research vol. **3** (2)(September), 161–225.

McIntyre, A. D. and Coulthurst, N. J. (1985), 'Theory and practice in capital budgeting: with particular reference to medium-sized UK companies', *British Accounting Review* vol. 17(2) (Autumn), 24–70.

Merrett, A. J. and Sykes, A. (1969), *Capital budgeting and company finance*, 2nd edn (Longmans).

Neale, B. and Holmes, D. (1988), 'Post completion audits: the costs and benefits', *Management Accounting* (CIMA) (March), 27–30.

Pike, R. H. and Dobbins, R. (1986), *Investment decisions and financial strategy* (Philip Allan).

Sangster, A. (1993), 'Capital investment appraisal techniques: a survey of current usage', *Journal of Business Finance and Accounting* **20** (3) (April), 307–32.

PART FOUR

Evaluation of divisional performance

Both chapters in Part IV are concerned with the evaluation of divisional performance. First, in Chapter 18 we look at the issues surrounding divisionalisation (or segmentation), and take both a financial and a management accounting view of the issues involved. After a discussion of the benefits of segmentation, the conclusion reached is that many organisations can benefit from segmenting their operations.

The content of Chapter 19 follows the same line directly. Transfer pricing only concerns organisations that are segmented in some way, and transfer prices are the prices set by one segment of an organisation when selling, or transferring goods to another segment of the same organisation. Many issues are involved in transfer pricing, and consequently many problems too, to which there are a complex variety of solutions.

CHAPTER EIGHTEEN

Divisional performance: segmental analysis

CHAPTER OBJECTIVES

After reading this chapter you should be able to:

- define, describe and discuss segmentation of organisations
- define and apply what is meant by performance assessment: weighted factor analysis; the strategic funds approach; the combined approach; return on investment; residual income; cash indicators; non-financial indicators
- apply the principles of segment reporting

Introduction

Divisional performance is concerned with monitoring and assessing managerial performance in organisations that are divided into two or more responsibility centres. Whether the responsibility centres are investment centres, profit centres or cost centres does not matter. What we are concerned about is that a divisional manager has targets set for or by him or her and that he or she is responsible for achieving those targets. This chapter reviews some of the work found under the heading of divisional performance and segmental analysis. The chapter looks at both the technical accounting and legal requirements surrounding divisional performance and some of the behavioural or qualitative aspects of divisional performance.

The extent of segmentation and the setting of performance targets

Emmanuel, Otley and Merchant (1990) report on four studies that sought to answer the question of to what extent organisations are segmented, or divisionalised. The general result is that the vast majority of organisations surveyed have profit or investment centres, and can thus be considered to be segmented. Segmentation is an important issue, therefore. We will be discussing later in this chapter several methods by which we can assess whether a segment manager is achieving his or her targets. Emmanuel *et al.* again provide the information we need to start our discussion of what methods are used to assess managers. They show that the return on investment method (ROI) is the single most important method of performance assessment in use. A significant number of organisations use a combination of both ROI and the residual income method (RI). We should say, however, that of the three studies cited, one shows that the combination of ROI and RI is by far the most important variant in use (Tomkins 1973). Whatever the precise rates of usage are, there is evidence that the two methods of performance assessment mentioned so far are widely used.

Segmentation

A segment is a part of an organisation. In the case of a profit-making organisation it is an investment centre, a profit centre or a cost centre. In the case of a non-profit-making organisation it is an area of responsibility such as a functional department. Normally, we would expect only medium-sized or large organisations to be segmented, but that is by no means always bound to be the case. Similarly, there is no rule or code that prescribes how large a segment has to be, either in relative or in absolute terms. Finally, organisations do not have to divisionalise if they do not wish to; but see the proposals of Exposure Draft 45 (ED 45) below. An exposure draft is a draft of an SSAP issued by the Accounting Standards Board and is equivalent to a Government White Paper in that it is a discussion document. ED45 was intended to add to the segmental disclosure requirements of the Companies Act 1985 (CA85). If the management of an organisation can operate successfully without divisionalisation, why divisionalise? There are several ways in which an organisation can segment itself. Overall, the following general classification is useful:

- geographical;
- product line;
- classes of business;
- demographic; and
- psychographic.

We are free to segment our organisation under any of these kinds of headings, although it is common for profit-making organisations to use geographical and product line classifications. A geographical segment can be further segmented into

- continent;
- country;
- region;
- city.

The accounting profession in the UK uses SSAP 25 (Segmental Reporting) to regulate the reports that emanate from a segmented or divisionalised organisation. International Accounting Standard 14 (IAS 14) (IASC) also deals with segmental reporting and provides us with definitions of geographical segments, segment revenue and segment expense. IAS 14 says industry segments are the distinguishable components of an enterprise each engaged in providing a different product or service, or a different group of related products or services, primarily to customers outside the enterprise.

> **Geographical segments** are the distinguishable components of an enterprise engaged in operations in individual countries or groups of countries within particular geographical areas as may be determined to be appropriate in an enterprise's circumstances.
>
> **Segment revenue** is revenue that is directly attributable to a segment, or the relevant portion of revenue that can be allocated on a reasonable basis to a segment, and that is derived from transactions with parties outside the enterprise and from other segments of the same enterprise.
>
> **Segment expense** is expense that is directly attributable to a segment or the relevant portion of an expense that can be allocated on a reasonable basis to the segments. (IASC: para. 4)

Looking at the way organisations can be segmented geographically gives an insight into the kind of control issues that segmentation can give rise to. If one geographical segment of an organisation is situated in, say, the Middle East, it is important that this is recognised so that the manager of that segment can be carefully and properly assessed for his or her performance since such a location has characteristics peculiar to it.

CAMEO

The General Accident Company, a British insurance company, is segmented on two levels:

Geographical segments

- United Kingdom
- United States
- Canada
- Pacific
- Europe
- Other overseas

Examples of sub-segmentation for three of these segments:

United Kingdom

- Profit for the year.
- Claim frequency.
- Number of fraudulent claims.
- Personal motor business.
- Home insurance.
- Property insurance.
- Commercial motor insurance.
- Commercial liability.
- Reorganisation.

United States

- Property and casualty insurance.
- Personal motor insurance.
- Personal property.
- Commercial casualty.
- Commercial property.

Canada

- Motor insurance.
- Involuntary market.

The overall purposes of presenting segmental information where a company carries on operations in different classes of business or in a different geographical area include that a segment:

(a) earns a return on investment that is out of line with the remainder of the business; or
(b) is subject to different degrees of risk; or
(c) has experienced different rates of growth; or
(d) has different potentials for future development (Stein 1989: 6)

Financial accounting has recognised the need for segmentation of organisations for quite a while now. From IAS 14, we learn the following information for each reported segment is generally considered necessary:

(a) a depreciation of the activities of each reported industry segment and an indication of the composition of each reported geographical area,
(b) sales or other operating revenues, distinguishing between revenue derived from customers outside the enterprise and revenue derived from other segments,
(c) segment result, and
(d) segment assets employed, expressed either in money amounts or as percentages of the consolidated totals. (IASC: para. 19)

These are specific accounting rules that are to be applied by segmented organisations. We might consider them useful ideas in helping us to decide on the performance indicators to use when assessing managerial performance.

ED45, for example, proposed (Stein 1989: 6):

> When deciding whether a company operates in different classes of business, the directors should take into account the following factors:
>
> (a) the nature of the products or services
> (b) the nature of the production processes
> (c) the markets in which the products or services are sold
> (d) the distribution channels for the products
> (e) any separate legislative framework relating to part of the business, for example, a bank or insurance company.

In financial accounting terms, therefore, managers are being told they must segment their business (if the rules of CA85 apply in the first place) if they believe that two or more areas of its business display the characteristics shown in ED 45. ED 45 went on to discuss the information that must be disclosed by the segments of the organisation. ED 45 says that turnover is an important indicator of an organisation's performance and is therefore essential in assessing the performance of a segment. Additionally, it says, turnover should be disclosed segmentally both by source and destination in order to give the user of the financial statements a fuller understanding of the company's exposure to those factors.

Problems with segmentation

Lev (1974: 45) has identified one of the main problems with segmentation. This problem is one that we came across in Chapters 6 and 7: the assignment of common costs:

> The main problem involved in the segmentation of financial statements of diversified companies concerns the allocation of common costs (eg interest, administration expenses etc) to the various segments . . . such allocations are . . . arbitrary . . .

Of course, as management accountants, we have a solution to this problem in that we are not reliant on financial accounting constraints as far as having to follow prescribed accounting practices. To this end, Lev continues:

> It would . . . seem preferable for the analyst to base the profitability analysis on the contribution margin of each segment (ie revenues less traceable costs) rather than on net income figures which involve common cost allocations. (ibid.)

Perhaps the classic case of problems arising from a kind of divisionalisation of an organisation comes with the case study known as Joe's Peanuts. This case study has been around for a long time now, but it is still an excellent example of what goes wrong when someone who does not really understand what he or she is doing sets upon solving a problem. This case is a tongue in cheek dig at management accountants and 'efficiency experts' and should be read with the thought firmly in our minds that this is the extreme of what happens when common costs are badly assigned. Joe's Peanuts case study is given at the end of the chapter. (A follow up to Joe's Peanuts appeared in CIMA's *Management Accounting* journal; and although it does not read as well as the original case, it is a brave attempt at providing a solution for us. For copyright reasons that case cannot be reproduced here; but see the list of references at the end of this chapter. Both cases can also usefully be read in conjunction with the material found in Chapters 6, 7 and 12.)

Performance assessment

As we agreed in the very first sentence of this chapter, divisional performance is concerned with monitoring and assessing managerial performance in organisations that are divided into two or more responsibility centres.

We have also agreed that divisionalisation is a good idea in that it can give excellent insights into the idiosyncratic performance of segments. What we must now do, having considered the background to segments, is to consider how to assess managerial performance and help management control the idiosyncrasies of their segment or division. The performance assessment methods we will be looking at in this chapter are:

1. Performance rating.
2. Return on investment.
3. Residual income.
4. Cash measures of performance.
5. Non-financial measures of performance.

We will complete our review of segment performance assessment by considering segment reports.

Performance rating

CAMEO

Performance rating at USI

This cameo is specific to one organisation: US Industries Inc (USI). USI had a turnover of $81 million in 1972. USI's performance-rating system evaluates the performance of segment managers by setting actual performance against agreed-upon standards. At the time that USI's segment assessment system was being reported on, it had already been used successfully for more than ten years. USI's assessment system looks at three areas

1. Profits are compared to prior years.
2. Profits are compared to budget.
3. Managing cash and capital.

In general, USI takes an assessment criterion and assigns a number of points to it. As the extract below shows, the common points value for each criterion is one (see Table 18.1). So, if our current pre-tax dollar profit exceeds our pre-tax dollar profit for the same period last year, we earn one point. There are 12 criteria in total, with the potential to earn a maximum of a total of 13 points.

For copyright reasons it is not possible to show the whole of USI's points allocation, but examples of the headings against which managers are assessed are clearly shown. The essence of the system is that on the one hand we can see what are essentially textbook-type criteria being used to assess performance. On the other hand, we can also see that USI uses criteria that are specific to itself. The three areas we identified above that USI use are better translated in Table 18.1 as

1. Doing better than last year.
2. Planning realistically.
3. Managing cash and capital.

Reference: Tanzola, in Thomas (1983: 456).

TABLE 18.1 *USI assessment criteria*

Criteria	Value
1. Doing better than last year	1 point
2. Pre-tax dollar profit exceeds same period in previous year	1 point
3. Pre-tax dollar profit exceeds same period in previous year by 15% or more	1 point
4. Pre-tax profit percentage on sales	1 point
5. Return on average investment	1 point
6. Planning realistically	1 point
7. Pre-tax dollar profit for the period: not less than 90% nor more than 125% of budget	1 point
8. Pre-tax percentage profit on sales for the period	1 point
9. Return on average capital employed	1 point
10. Managing cash and capital	1 point
11. Investment criteria	1 point
12. Cash transfers to headquarters: more than or equal to year-to-date budgeted transfers	2 points
Maximum points per period	13 points

Note: 12 points achieves standard of excellence
Source: Tanzola, in Thomas (1983: 457).

The USI system essentially takes a broad view of a manager's performance. Within the broad view, it weights each criterion almost equally, with only the final criterion being given a double weighting. Hence cash transfers to headquarters that are more than or equal to year-to-date budgeted transfers must clearly be twice as important to USI than each of the other criteria taken individually. All assessments are sent to corporate headquarters where they are reviewed and the divisions ranked according to points earned. One vital issue here that USI allows for is that the results of the assessment process must be seen to be absolutely transparent: the assessment system is fully and fairly applied. To achieve the objective of transparency, each segment's results are widely publicised. The system also has the interest and support of top management. The perceived benefits of USI's system are threefold:

1. Management can see at a glance the performance standing of divisions
2. Lost points act as red flags
3. Discussions of lost points leads to in depth discussions of problems (ibid 461)

Further evidence of USI's desire to ensure transparency is the fact that the reasons for lost points are verified by internal audit. Such a check ensures that when someone has a poor performance reported, they really are returning a poor performance. The key point, in concluding this section is that **the system works for USI**. Furthermore, the system that USI operates fulfils the requirement spelled out by Stonich (in Thomas 1983: 474): 'It is important to tailor the details of the measurement and reward process to the company's specific strategy and situation.'

The weighted factor approach (wfa)

The weighted factor approach is, perhaps, a step beyond USI's approach in that it takes a variety of factors, assigns weights to those factors, and assesses performance on the basis of the actual outcome compared with the standard. Table 18.2 illustrates how one large manufacturer used the wfa method. This organisation recognised that different segments do, indeed, have different characteristics, as we agreed above. Hence, they changed the relative importance of four key results according to whether the segment was a high-, medium- or low-growth business. What happens now, of course, is that once the results of the segments are published, the relative weights are applied to them and the overall performance of the management of each segment can be assessed. It would be interesting to learn why, for example, cash flow is not considered important to high-growth segments (it has a zero weighting here), yet for a low-growth segment it has a 50% weighting. High-growth segments were measured in terms of market share, sales growth, cash flow potential, and progress of several future-oriented strategic projects. Low-growth strategic business units (SBUs) were measured in terms of their cash-generating ability. The wfa can be fine-tuned to reflect each individual strategy by using such additional points as target market share, productivity levels, product quality measures, product development measures, and personnel development measures.

One of the problems that has been facing British industry for a long time now is short-termism. It is often reported that the average British manager takes only a short-term view of his or her organisation and its prospects. Short-termism leads to sub-optimal

TABLE 18.2 ***A weighted factor approach to rewarding achievement of strategic goals***

SBU category	Factor	Weight (%)
High growth	ROA	10
	Cash flow	0
	Strategic funds programmes	45
	Market share increase	45
		100
Medium growth	ROA	25
	Cash flow	25
	Strategic funds programmes	25
	Market share increase	25
		100
Low growth	ROA	50
	Cash flow	50
	Strategic funds programmes	0
	Market share increase	0
		100

Source: Stonich (1984), in Thomas (1988: 475).

behaviour in that short-term returns are generally considered to be inferior to long-term returns. Stonich develops the weighted factor approach to help the manager take a longer-term view of his or her operations. A long-term view has been found to be particularly important where a manager's bonus is linked to his or her performance.

> This method explicitly motivates managers toward a future orientation by compensating managers for achieving set goals over a multiyear period. Long-term evaluation usually involves deferred income or incentive compensation, typically deferred stock awarded on the basis of attaining an earnings growth target over an extended period. (Stonich, in Thomas 1983: 476)

The long-term evaluation approach should tie the interest of the firm's managers to the long-term interest of the firm's shareholders. The approach does, however, pose two problems:

1. One manager can have little impact on the whole organisation, unless he or she is a senior manager.
2. Unless everyone is working to optimise the same targets, sub-optimal behaviour can still be found since each manager may be trying to optimise a different ratio, for example.

A method that takes a strategic view of the deployment of funds is called the strategic funds approach. With the strategic funds approach, we take the view that the aspects of the organisation's financial commitments that relate to future, strategic, oriented investments in fixed assets are highlighted in financial reports.

The strategic funds approach

The strategic funds approach encourages executives to consider certain developmental expenses apart from current operations. Table 18.3 shows a profit and loss statement that is based on the strategic funds approach and that is therefore different to the type that accountants require for external reporting purposes.

TABLE 18.3 ***Strategic business unit profit and loss account, illustrating segregation of strategic funds ($)***

	$
Sales	12,300,000
Cost of sales	6,900,000
Gross margin	5,400,000
Operating expense (general and administrative)	3,700,000
Operating profit (return on sales)	1,700,000
Strategic funds	1,000,000
Pre tax profit	700,000

Source: Stonich (1984) in Thomas (1988: 477).

Note, from Table 18.3, that the manager is measured on two bases. The top part of the income statement is familiar in that it shows sales, cost of sales, gross margin, operating expenses, and operating profit. The bottom part of the statement shows what are termed strategic funds. Strategic funds are conventionally included in the operating administrative account, but here they are separated out below operating return on sales. Strategic funds are identified during the programming process, and are the resources devoted to future-oriented activities. The strategic funds approach gives managers a practical way to combine short- and long-term views of their organisation.

The combined approach

In keeping with the general theme that each segment is unique, an organisation might take the view that some aspects of the approaches discussed so far are appealing. Consequently, the best way to assess segment performance may be through a combined approach: that is, to combine the three approaches in some way:

> First, segregate future oriented strategic funds from short term funds, list them, and report them as in the strategic funds approach. Second, develop a weighted factor chart for each strategic business unit, including return on assets, cash flow, strategic funds programs, market share increase, and others. (Specific factors taken into account depend on the strategy of the particular business unit.) Third, measure performance on three bases: the bottom line in the strategic funds approach, the weighted factors, and long term evaluation of the corporation's and SBU's performances. The relative weights that can be assigned to each of these in a combined approach will vary from SBU to SBU and from company to company depending on its business environment and the organisation's culture. (Stonich, in Thomas 1983: 478)

The previous two assessment methods are either specific to one organisation or have been developed in response to a particular piece of research. Traditionally, however, the assessment of segment managers has been discussed in terms of two principal measures:

1. return on investment; and
2. residual income.

The next two sections look at each of these in turn.

Return on investment (ROI)

Return on investment is calculated as a ratio of net divisional profits (before tax) to the net assets (at book values) employed in the division; the normal divisional objective is to maximise that return. Table 18.4 can be used to illustrate the return on investment of two divisions, A and B. The return for division A is

$$\frac{\text{net divisional profit before tax}}{\text{divisional capital employed}} \times 100$$

$$= \frac{£286{,}000}{£725{,}000} \times 100$$

$$= 39.4\%$$

For division B the ROI is 50.2%.

TABLE 18.4 *Income statements and balance sheets for divisions A and B*

	Division A	Division B
	£	£
Sales revenue	858,000	236,050
less: Cost of goods sold	405,000	101,500
Gross profit	453,000	134,550
less: Operating expenses (including allocated overheads)	167,000	53,820
Net profit before tax	286,000	80,730
Net fixed assets	630,000	139,550
Net current assets	95,000	21,250
Net capital employed	725,000	160,800

Source: Fanning (Cowe, 1988: 222).

If we allow for taxation now, by making a notional charge against each division for corporation tax (say, at a rate of 40%), would reduce each division's profits to £171,600 and £48,438 respectively. On that basis, the return on investment from division A would be calculated at 23.7% and for division B it would be 30.1%.

Depending on the precise nature of what we are trying to achieve, the next possible step might be to relate these calculated returns to the company's cost of capital. This then gives us a relative measure of the efficiency of our capital. A refinement to that approach is to use sensitivity analysis that compares the rate of return after tax for each division with the excess of those earnings over different costs of capital. Table 18.5 illustrates this procedure.

TABLE 18.5 *Earnings for divisions A and B*

	Division A	Division B
Net capital employed (£)	725,000	160,800
Net profit after tax (£)	137,280	38,750
Rate of return on capital invested (%)	18.9	24.1
Excess of net profit after tax over cost of capital:	£	£
at 12%	50,280	19,454
at 16%	21,280	13,022
at 20%	(7,720)	6,590

Source: Fanning (Cowe, 1988: 223).

The table shows that, on the face of it, division B has a superior return on investment. However, this analysis highlights one of the main drawbacks to the development of the return on investment criterion. The manager of division B will want to act to maintain his or her superior position over division A. Furthermore he or she may be rewarded on the basis of this return. If, though, the organisation's actual cost of capital is less than 18%, the manager of division A is performing better in the interests of the firm as a whole. Table 18.5 shows examples of the organisation's cost of capital being set at 12%, 16% and 20% respectively. The excess of net profit after tax over cost of capital figures confirms this viewpoint. Additionally, the inclusion of depreciation charges in an organisation's profit and loss account means that a manager's return on investment will increase over time, even if his or her actual profitability remains static or declines slightly. For example, if the manager of division B depreciated the fixed assets shown in Table 18.4 by 15% per annum on a straight-line basis, and if the average life of those assets is six years, the depreciation charge for the next period will be around £38,000. If depreciation charge changes mean that the division's profits decline to £32,000, the calculated rate of return on investment will be 26.1% (£32,000/£122,800), suggesting an increase in divisional profitability. The reality, of course, is that there has been no real improvement. As we know from financial accounting, the book values of the assets may bear little or no relation to real underlying values. Depreciation charges may be calculated in any one of several different ways, none of which might reflect the true levels of depreciation of the assets under review.

For the group as a whole, the rate of return on investment criterion lends itself to short-term judgements and may act as a dysfunctional influence on divisional managers. Fanning (Cowe, 1988: 224) gives the example of the investment opportunity that provides a return of 22.2% on investment over its lifetime. However, in years one, two and three of the project, the returns are 15%, 16.5% and 18% respectively. On this basis, the manager will reject this proposal if his or her hurdle rate, or minimum required rate of return, is 20% since he or she cannot, then, apparently, meet his or her target. In years four, five and six, however, the returns on this opportunity are 55%, 60.5% and 66.66% respectively.

Advantages of ROI

The return on investment criterion has two significant advantages:

1. It provides a direct comparison of the financial performance of dissimilar businesses or types of investment.
2. It is a measure so comprehensive that it is affected by changes in any item on either the balance sheet or the income statement. (Dearden 1988: 485)

These advantages clearly spell out that the ROI criterion has a great deal to offer any organisation. It is generally applicable where a return can be calculated and where capital employed can be evaluated. However, as with everything that has an advantage, there are disadvantages to the ROI criterion.

Disadvantages of ROI

The most serious problem with using ROI is that it can discourage managers of divisions with high rates of return from making new investments. If an organisation's hurdle rate is

15%, for example, and the current divisional ROI objective is 30%, investments above the hurdle rate but below 30% would reduce the divisional ROI. Hence, the manager of the division has no incentive to invest in the new project. For the same reason, the lack of goal congruency, divisions with low rates of return can improve their ROI by investing in projects that return ROIs that are less than the organisation's hurdle rate. We looked at the example above from Fanning, where a new investment opportunity that will eventually yield a satisfactory ROI earns a low rate of return at the outset. We saw this as a reason for discouraging investment. The end result to all of this is that maximising divisional ROI will not necessarily ensure maximisation of the organisation's financial performance. The organisation's financial performance

> is maximised when divisional managers maximise the long run cash flow from the resources at their disposal and invest in new resources when, and only when, the additional investment will earn a true financial rate of return higher than the organisation's cost of capital. (Dearden 1988: 486)

There may be problems with intercompany comparisons and with intra-company comparisons if the basis on which segmental income is assessed varies from segment to segment. We have taken the view that profit is profit before taxation. We could take an alternative view that profit for segmentation analysis purposes should be profit after taxation. The problem that might arise here, however, is that the profit basis we use might be different to the profit basis that another segment or organisation uses. For example, yet another profit basis is profit before taxation but after head office cost allocations. We must be consistent with the bases on which we assess our segments. If a segment manager is suffering from a relatively high level of committed costs, he or she will not be in a position fully to control his or her ROI. This takes us back to Chapter 1 and controllability issues, of course, the problem being that if a manager cannot directly control all of his or her costs and revenues, it is difficult to distinguish between the manager's performance and that of the division.

That concludes our overview of return on investment. We turn, now, to an alternative criterion, residual income. The significant feature of the residual income criterion is the notion of controllability.

Residual income (RI)

This criterion is really relevant when managers of divisions are accountable for their performance and make their own decisions on capital investment. In such a situation, ROI has been shown to be ineffective, so a residual income (RI) approach may be utilised. RI is the profit remaining after deduction of the cost of capital in investments or the excess of net earnings over the cost of capital. The RI technique deducts a charge for the use of assets from divisional profits, and bases this charge on the organisation's cost of capital. The emphasis of the RI approach is to determine an absolute value for divisional income, as adjusted, rather than a percentage value. If a division is to be charged for the use of capital and the RI derived, it is reasonable to expect that the profit figure adjusted for that capital charge should be one that reflects all items subject to any substantial degree of control or influence by the divisional manager. Following on from our work on controllability in

Chapter 1, we know that items over which the divisional manager has little control should not be included. According to Mauriel and Anthony (1966), about one-third of the companies they surveyed for their research used the RI approach either on its own or in combination with the return on investment yardstick, to measure divisional performance. Such an approach can be applied to the income statement for division A given in Table 18.4. Adjusted to distinguish between controllable and non controllable items of expenditure, the income statement would then appear as in Table 18.6.

From Table 18.6, we see that such a statement reveals three possible measurements of divisional profit: net profit before tax; contribution margin; and controllable profit. Which should be used? Divisional income statements should clearly reveal a figure of controllable operating profit against which to set the charge for use of capital in the division during the period. The charge for the cost of capital is based on the corporate cost of capital. Such a statement, described as a divisional RI statement, is shown in Table 18.7 where the corporate cost of capital has been estimated at 18%, and the division applied capital employed of £725,000 during the period (from Table 18.4), leading to a charge on controllable investment of £76,500.

As shown in Table 18.7, controllable RI for division A is calculated at £286,500, representing a rate of return of 67.4% on controllable capital invested in the division. Net RI before tax was calculated at £155,500, representing a rate of return of 21.4% on capital invested in the division.

TABLE 18.6 *Income statements for division A, adjusted to distinguish between controllable and non-controllable items*

	£	£
Sales revenue		858,000
less:		
Variable cost of goods sold	405,000	
Variable divisional selling and administration expenses	27,300	432,300
Variable profit		425,700
less: Controllable divisional overhead		62,700
Controllable profit		363,000
less: Fixed non-controllable divisional overhead		41,700
Contribution margin		321,300
less: Allocated extradivisional fixed non-controllable expenses		35,300
Net profit before tax		286,000

Source: Fanning (Cowe, 1988: 226).

TABLE 18.7 *Residual income statement for division A*

	£	£
Sales revenue		858,000
less: Variable cost		432,300
Variable profit		425,700
less: Controllable division overhead		62,700
Controllable profit		363,000
less: Interest on controllable investment		76,500
Controllable RI		286,500
less:		
Interest on non-controllable divisional investment	54,000	
Fixed non-controllable divisional overhead	41,700	
Allocated extradivisional fixed non-controllable expenses	35,300	131,000
Net profit before tax		155,500

Source: Fanning (Cowe, 1988: 226).

For division B, the controllable RI is calculated at £92,300 (after a charge of £29,700 on controllable investment), which represents a rate of return of 55.9% on controllable capital invested in the division. Net RI before tax was calculated at £31,230, representing a rate of return of 13.6% on capital invested in the division.

The most obvious outcome of the revision of divisional earning measurements – that is, RI instead of ROI – is that the relative positions of divisions A and B are reversed.

Advantages of the RI method

A beneficial effect of the use of the RI approach is that it encourages divisional managers to take more notice of, and even to become aware of, the real costs of using capital. The argument is that if managers have to pay for the use of the capital they employ, that capital will be used more effectively and efficiently. A manager found guilty of underusing his or her resources may prompt a rationalisation of capital requirements. RI corrects the most serious problems of ROI because the RI charge can be made equal to the organisation's hurdle rate. In such a case, divisional investment objectives can be made consistent with the organisation's cost of capital. No matter how high the rate of return a division is currently earning, the RI can be improved by investing in any project that earns more than the organisation's cost of capital. All managers, therefore, are motivated to take advantage of any investment that exceeds this rate.

Disadvantages of the RI method

From Dearden (1988: 487):

> The problem of new investment in fixed assets still exists. Although the return on an investment may exceed the hurdle rate over its life, it may not do so in the first few years. Thus a desirable investment may reduce RI initially. Also, the RI will increase over time as the fixed assets are simply allowed to get older. The basic problem is, there is no satisfactory way to include fixed assets in the investment base.
>
> The RI calculation requires a profit investment calculation. There is an almost universal tendency also to calculate ROI. All that is required is a transposition of the figures Since ROI appears to be a much easier concept to understand, managers then tend to make judgements based on the ROI and more or less ignore the RI.

In the next section, we discuss two further systems for measuring performance in a segmented organisation: cash indicators, and non-financial indicators.

Cash indicators

Cash and cash flow is the basis on which a great many investment decisions are made by management teams around the world. Since a great deal of evidence supports the view given in the previous sentence, it makes sense to attempt to measure a manager's performance in terms of his or her cash flow performance. A cash flow view of performance is in contradistinction to the previous two methods: ROI and RI. There are two important advantages to cash flow performance assessment

1. It relates directly to the method of assessment used to establish the project (centre, department or organisation).
2. It eliminates subjective criteria such as accounting adjustments – for example, depreciation, accruals and the arbitrary assignment of common costs – which we have berated many times now.

Non-financial indicators

In the first and final chapters of this book we discuss some of the ways the management accountant has suffered from severe problems relating his or her work to that of management colleagues. One way we carried out our discussion was in terms of non-financial indicators. Non-financial indicators (NFIs) are exactly what they sound like: they are ratios, values and expressions that give, in non-financial terms, the results of an accounting period or operation or process. That is, rather than saying that sales amounted to £100,000, we say that we sold 2,000 units; or instead of spending £50,000 on repairs and maintenance in the previous period, repairs and maintenance spent 450 man hours in fulfilling their duties. There is potentially an infinite number and variety of NFIs. There are as many NFIs as the whole of humanity can think of! With NFIs, we are not tied down to any particular scheme, unlike financial indicators that have now become very firmly established and prescribed, over the last two decades in particular. So much so that many financial accounting textbooks that discuss financial indicators do so by using the same, or almost the same, ratios as any other financial accounting book. It is not our aim in this section to give out a list of NFIs which everyone can commit to memory and apply every time an examination question comes along that asks us to recite such indicators. What we will do here is to give a few examples of what an NFI might be. We should then attempt to define an NFI on every occasion they seem applicable – remembering of course that the NFIs we use today may not be appropriate for the situation we come across tomorrow.

The benefits of NFIs include the fact that they are not tied to an imaginary reference point. Conversely, money and monetary values are tied to an entirely imaginary reference point. Moreover money and monetary values are tied to moving targets if anything is. Imagine the situation where we are importing goods from Denmark into the United Kingdom. At the beginning of January 1995 the rate of exchange was approximately £1 = DKr 10 (DKr = Danish kroner). Hence, when we received an invoice in January 1995 for goods from Denmark asking us to pay DKr 100,000, we paid £10,000 (ignoring transactions costs for the sake of simplicity). In June 1995, we received another invoice for another DKr 100,000 but this time paid £11,364: the exchange rate in June 1995 was £1 = DKr 8.8. When someone is analysing our organisation's accounting records, they will see that our imports into the United Kingdom from Denmark have increased by 13.64% from January to June 1995 ... but they haven't. In financial terms they have increased by 13.64% without a doubt – the monetary values have changed. However, in this example we find that the NFIs associated with these two deals have not changed at all: for example, the number of units for each transaction was 2,000. Whilst not all NFI problems are related to the importation of goods from Denmark, this does help to illustrate the point that monetary values are unrealistic bases for true and fair comparisons. Smith (1990: 24–5) provides an extensive list of examples – 65 in all – of NFIs, including the following:

Factor to be measured	Non-financial indicator
Quality of purchased components	Zero defects
Overtime	Overtime hours/total hours
Reliability	Warranty claims/costs
Market share	% local/domestic/worldwide volume
Growth	% increase in market share

Taking any situation we care to name, there will be a series of NFIs that we can devise which may be more useful to us than any number of financial indicators. Therefore, why do financial indicators seem to persist at the expense of what appear to be more reliable indicators of performance? One answer to this apparent conundrum is that financial reports are relatively easy to produce now. There are many software packages the job of which is to simplify the generation of financial reports; the basic versions of such packages doing nothing but generate financial information. More important than software packages that generate financial data is the veritable wealth of legislation that prescribes the work of the accountant: he or she must account for every penny raised or used in his or her organisation. The annual financial audit has as one of its primary purposes the reconciliation of cash with accounting documents – to attempt to account for stewardship and so on. The last ten years has seen the emergence of books, journal articles and so on that all extol the virtue of the NFI. These books will readily be found in any university library and many libraries of colleges of further education: books by Kaplan, Kaplan and Johnson, and so on, are all in this league and are well worth reading.

Inflation: non-stable prices

One of the very good reasons for using NFIs rather than financial indicators is that they can help us to overcome the influence of inflation. As is usually clear, inflation is an insidious problem that simply refuses to go away! For the majority of economies, inflation is an ever-present problem. When we suffer hyperinflation, our problems multiply. There has been extensive debate on this topic over the last three decades or so, but only rarely has this debate ever sought refuge in NFIs! If we look at the example of importing from Denmark, we can see that the effects of exchange rate fluctuations are real and can be explained away by using NFIs rather than financial results. By being explained away, we mean that we can monitor our performance with reference to units rather than total costs. Thus in this example we have a constant frame of reference, which is units and not costs. With inflation we are facing similar issues. If we deflate actual prices by the inflation rate, we obtain constant prices. This is not a bad idea, but even so, it is not a perfect solution because prices and costs change for reasons other than external factors led by inflationary pressures. We can change our own costs by changing suppliers, we can increase our selling prices, and so on. To return again to NFIs, if we deal in units not related to prices or anything with a monetary orientation, we are able to monitor our activity constantly over time: a unit is a unit is a unit! Once we are happy with our indicators of performance, we have to report it to our management colleagues. The next section looks at some of the issues that are important to the adequate reporting of segmental information.

CAMEO

Non-financial indicators in the real world

We already know about non-financial indicators (NFIs); and we have discussed some real-world uses of them. This cameo adds to the list of the kind of NFIs in use in reality. We will look at two organisations and their NFIs in this cameo. The first organisation is the international hotel chain we first came across in the cameos in Chapters 3 and 9; secondly, we will look at the NFIs used by The General Electric Co.

Hotel chain

In their annual report and accounts, this organisation used the following NFIs,among others, when discussing its annual results with shareholders:

- average room occupancy for the year: percentage of maximum number of hotels
- square feet of casino space
- number of table games
- number of slot machines
- number of restaurants

From these data, we could calculate, given the necessary segmental, non-financial, information, for example:

- average sales per hotel
- average income per gaming table
- average profit per restaurant

The General Electric Co. (GE)

GE has evolved eight key result areas for the measurement of departments (but not managers):

1. Profitability.
2. Market position, measured in terms of market share.
3. Productivity.
4. Product leadership, in terms of leadership re innovation and development.
5. Personnel development.
6. Employee attitudes.
7. Social responsibilities.
8. Balance between long-term and short-term goals

This list was devised by GE in 1952 and has obviously served them well for a long time now. Measuring some of these NFIs might cause problems, of course, and GE's definition of productivity might not fit in with the definitions we have used in this book. However, once a measure has been determined and agreed on within an organisation, and provided that measure is used in a consistent manner, its use will prove beneficial. There are, of course, behavioural implications in the use of NFIs – the kind of issues we discussed in Chapter 14 when we discussed budgeting and budgetary control.

Reference: Coates, Rickwood and Stacey (1989), for source of GE indicators.

Performance indicators in context

The role of performance indicators

Despite the debate that we have just had over performance indicators, Bowerman (1995: 174) raises the problem that there is no consensus as to what performance indicators are intended to do. Whilst Bowerman is talking about performance indicators in terms of government reporting, it may still be a valid question for other forms of organisation. He goes on to point out that performance can vary due to factors other than efficiency, such as different objectives, needs, modes of service delivery or accounting methods. As a word of warning for those who see performance indicators as less than helpful, we should heed the findings of Bowerman in relation to government use of such things: 'apathy of the public towards local government affairs ... gives rise to the possibility that the performance indicators will make little impact' (ibid. 175). Furthermore: 'The majority of indicators deal with activity or cost. Others require details of procedures only and few require performance to be compared to a predetermined target' (ibid. 176).

If we take a simplistic view and simply translate public into management colleagues and government into management accountant, we might be in the position of being able to point fingers! Performance indicators have the aim of helping managers to manage. If the performance indicators we use can be, and are, ignored, or do not help us to manage our resources better, why bother with them? Bowerman seems to be suggesting the latter train of thought is prevalent in local and central government circles.

The use of performance indicators

We have spoken a great deal about the technicalities of a variety of assessment methods but we have not really said how we might use them. We could discuss the use of such measures under a variety of headings: for example, productivity; efficiency; bonus calculation; fitness for appointment held; eligibility for promotion; and eligibility for further investment.

As we said when we discussed NFIs, the precise assessment measures we use may be determined by the individual circumstances of each case – in spite of the surveys Emmanuel *et al.* (1990) reported concerning the uses of the ROI and other methods. Even if we set our basic assessment of a segment manager on the basis of the ROI, we will, for productivity assessment purposes, need to enhance our analysis by devising and using more specific indicators. The same comments apply to efficiency. Hence, we would need to work our way down, or along, a pyramid of ratios such as is found in a DuPont analysis. Emmanuel *et al.* provide a useful introductory discussion to many of the issues on this point in chapter 10 of their book.

Segment reports

The purposes for which divisional reports will be drawn up can be given under three main headings:

1. the guidance of the divisional management in making decisions;
2. the guidance of corporate management in making decisions;
3. the appraisal of divisional management by corporate management. (Fanning in Cowe, 1988: 230)

Morse, Davis and Hartgraves (1991: 434) say there are four most common types of segment reports:

1. income statements for each plant or division
2. income statements for each product line
3. income statements for each sales territory
4. cost reports for cost centres (segments without sales or revenues)

Segment reporting requires careful control over data collection and storage because of the different reporting formats. To properly compute the income for each segment or product, all costs (fixed and variable) must be considered. To effectively report the activities of a business segment, management should use the contribution approach. Each reporting objective must be identified and described as precisely as possible to ensure that only relevant revenues and costs are assigned to each reporting segment. Segment reporting is an excellent example of how the contribution margin approach can be used for evaluation purposes. This approach can be used for determining the effect on profit of certain types of short-run changes when other variables are held constant. Examples include changes in sales volume, product mix, temporary changes in capacity, special orders and product promotions (see Morse *et al.* for a full debate in this area). Morse *et al.* demonstrate an organisation reporting by means of several different segment reports for an oil drilling and refining organisation:

Report 1: segments are geographical territories
TOTAL ORGANISATION
Report 2: segments are divisions
TOTAL ORGANISATION
Report 3: segments are products
EACH DIVISION HAS A REPORT
Report 4: segments are geographical territories
EACH PRODUCT HAS A REPORT

We have seen management accounting uses of segment reporting when we discussed closure decisions under the heading of costing for decision making: relevant costing. Morse *et al.* (1991: 444) give an example of the use of segment reporting when discussing the decision of whether to close the yogurt department of a dairy products organisation. They also also have a very useful case – 'Music Teachers Inc.' (ibid. 464–6) – for helping us to appreciate some of the issues involved with the preparation of segment reports.

SUMMARY

In this chapter we have undertaken a comprehensive review of divisional or segmental reporting, looking in detail at both financial and management accounting aspects of such reporting requirements. The financial accountant is interested in segmental reporting because, when dealing with the segmented organisation, he or she has issues to deal with that cut across the ordinary work that he or she usually does. Segmented organisations often have to assign costs and revenues. Such organisations work in diverse areas simply because the nature of the work of their segments is diverse. The management accountant is interested in segmental reporting and analysis because his or her management colleagues need sufficiently detailed information to allow them to review not only their own operations, but also those of their management colleagues in other segments of their organisation. The management accountant takes his or her own information and systems and those of the financial accountant, and provides management colleagues with the information they require.

As we saw in this chapter, there is no single way that segment performance can be analysed and reviewed. We have discussed a variety of methods here. Each method has its uses, and its advantages and disadvantages. We have discussed methods that are unique to the organisation reporting it and we have discussed methods that are generally applicable. The outcome of our discussion is that each method has its merits and can be applied providing it is found to be suitable for the organisation seeking to use it. Perhaps the best solution is to measure performance with a range of measures that take into account both financial and non-financial factors as well as the short term and long term.

KEY TERMS

You should satisfy yourself that you have noted all of these terms and can define and/or describe their meaning and use, as appropriate.

Segmentation (p. 625)	Weighted factor approach (p. 632)
Return on investment (p. 626)	Strategic funds approach (p. 633)
Residual income (p. 626)	Combined approach (p. 634)
Divisionalisation (p. 626)	Non-financial indicators (p. 640)
Performance assessment (p. 630)	Segment reporting (p. 644)

RECOMMENDED READING

There is a veritable wealth of information relating to divisional performance and segmental analysis. The selection you are advised to consult is literally just the tip of the iceberg! A good, up-to-date start is Bowerman (1995). Emmanuel and Otley (1985) and Emmanuel *et al.* (1990) provide well considered views and reviews of the topic. A book with a viewpoint other than the management accounting one but that should prove interesting is Leontiades (1985). I find Porter (1986) unreadable, but the book sells well and many people swear by it, so consider trying it. Smith, M. (1990) is a good paper for this level of work, while Smith, T. (1992) provides a cynical view from someone who was inside, put himself on the outside, and was then castigated by those on the inside! Woodward (1992) and Woodward and Spink (1992) give another run through of an excellent case study and a good attempt at a follow up.

QUESTIONS

Review questions

1. What is meant by the segmentation of organisations?
2. Define and describe each of the following

   (a) weighted factor analysis;
   (b) the strategic funds approach;
   (c) the combined approach;
   (d) return on investment;
   (e) residual income;
   (f) cash indicators; and
   (g) non-financial indicators.

3. Define and describe each of the following

   (a) performance rating at USI;
   (b) return on investment;
   (c) residual income;
   (d) cash measures of performance;
   (b) non-financial measures of performance.

4. Compare and contrast ROI and RI
5. What role do non-financial indicators play in the assessment of divisional performance?
6. What are the general guidelines that can be drawn up for segment reporting?

Answers to review questions 1, 5 and 6 can be found in the Student Workbook.

Graded practice questions

Level I

1. Cobbold Ltd, a long-established, highly centralised, company, has grown to the extent that its chief executive, despite having a good supporting team, is finding difficulty in keeping up with the many decisions of importance.

   Consideration is therefore being given to reorganising the company into profit centres. These would be product divisions, headed by a divisional managing director, who would be responsible for all the division's activities relating to its products.

   Required

   Explain in outline:

   (a) The types of decision area that should be transferred to the new divisional managing directors if such a reorganisation is to achieve its objectives.
   (b) The types of decision area that might reasonably be retained at company head office.
   (c) The management accounting problems that might be expected to arise in introducing effective profit centres.

2. At a recent meeting of the board of the Alpha Omega Group, the group finance director proposed that all properties owned by operating companies should be transferred to a newly formed group property company and that the properties should be leased back to the operating companies at a rental of 10% of their value as assessed by professional valuers.

   AB Ltd, one of the operating companies, currently owns a factory that was valued at £150,000 ten years ago when the company was acquired by the Alpha Omega Group. The company expects the factory to be valued at £300,000 now.

   In calculating its profits hitherto, it has been charging depreciation on a straight-line basis of 1.5% per annum on the value ten years ago of this factory.

   In the year just ended, AB Ltd's sales were £1,100,000, its profits were £91,000 and its return on capital employed (ROI) was 26%.

   Required

   (a) Calculate the change in AB Ltd's ROI that would result from acceptance of the group's proposal if all other relevant factors did not change.
   (b) Discuss briefly the extent to which the results of the above proposed transaction cast doubt on the validity of the use of ROI as a means of measuring company performance within the group.

3. As management accountant for a group of four similar companies you have recently introduced an interfirm comparison scheme. A summary of basic information received from each company for the period under review is as follows:

Operating profit	A	B	C	D
	£	£	£	£
Net current assets	221	209	315	162
Fixed assets	520	385	525	315
Sales	930	715	975	585
Production cost	2,470	1,980	2,925	1,665
Selling cost	1,605	1,228	1,784	1,016
Administration cost	370	317	497	187
Companies	74	226	329	187

Required

(a) Present the information to management in such a way as to compare clearly the results achieved by each company with those of the rest of the group.
(b) Write a short constructive report to the directors of company A, setting out the possible reasons for the differences in their results as compared with the rest of the group.

Level II

4. A group of companies is divided into ten operating divisions, each of which is autonomous. The cost of capital for the group is 12% per annum and it is currently earning 15% on its capital employed.

In the ROI calculation, return is equated with net profit and capital employed is the figure at the beginning of the financial year. All fixed assets are depreciated on a straight-line basis. Investments in new projects include incremental working capital. Projects sold or withdrawn from operation are treated as consisting of fixed assets only.

If no new capital expenditure transactions take place the position of four of the divisions would be:

Division	Capital employed as at 1 January 19X0 (£000)	Budgeted for 19X0 Net profit (£000)	Sales (£000)
P	320	80	800
Q	450	150	1,400
R	280	84	700
S	200	26	200

The following transactions are proposed:

Division P: Investment of £100,000 to yield sales of £150,000 per annum and net profit of £20,000 per annum.

Division Q: Sales for £75,000 of a project that is budgeted to yield a net profit of £15,000 in 19X0. The original equipment cost £600,000 seven years ago with an expected life of eight years.

Division R: (i) Sale of product line at book value. The original equipment cost £60,000 two years ago with an expected life of three years. This line is budgeted to yield a net profit of £20,000 in 19X0, combined with

(ii) replacement of (i) above by investing £100,000 in a new product to yield £30,000 per annum.

Division S: Investment of £80,000 in a project to yield sales of £36,000 per annum and a net profit of £11,200 per annum.

Note: In connection with each of the above transactions, you are to assume that the sale and/or investment would be completed by 1 January 19X0 so as to be included in the relevant ROI calculations for the year 19X0. Ignore taxation and inflation and assume that actual results are as budgeted.

Required

(a) On the assumption that each transaction goes ahead:

(i) Calculate the new ROI for each division for the year ending 31 December 19X0.
(ii) Identify those divisional managers whose bonuses will be higher if they receive annual bonuses related to the level of their respective ROI.
(iii) State in respect of each division whether the group's interests will be favourably or adversely affected by the proposed transactions. Explain briefly why in each case.

(b) Identify, with brief reasons, which proposals the group would approve if its new capital expenditure were limited to 200,000 for the four divisions.

(c) (i) Compare the old results of division P and division S, both of which are in the same type of business, and briefly advise the divisional manager of division S how he might improve his performance based on the data concerning division P.
(ii) Comment briefly on how the new project for division S fits in with the advice given in (c) (i) above.

(d) Calculate the lowest price at which the equipment should be sold by division Q if the transaction proposed is to break even financially for the group.

(e) (i) Explain briefly the concept of 'residual income' in the context of performance evaluation.
(ii) Calculate the residual income for each division for 19X0 on the assumption that each transaction goes ahead.

Solutions to practice questions 1 and 3 can be found in the Student Workbook. Solutions to practice question numbers in red can be found at the end of this book.

Appendix: Joe's Peanuts

Cost allocation and contribution margin

This case concerns the restaurateur who has the good idea of putting a rack of peanuts at one end of his counter. The idea being that customers would make impulse purchases of these peanuts when they are standing at the counter paying their bill, ordering a drink ... at least, he thought it was a good idea!

In discussing the costs incident to various types of operations the analogy was drawn of the restaurant that adds a rack of peanuts to the counter, intending to pick up a little additional profit in the usual course of business. This analogy was attacked as an oversimplification. However, the accuracy of the analogy is evident when one considers the actual problem faced by the restaurateur (Joe) as revealed by this accountant-efficiency expert.

Scenario

EFF EX: Joe, you said you put in these peanuts because some people ask for them, but do you realise what this rack of peanuts is costing you?

JOE: It ain't gonna cost. 'sgonna be a profit. Sure, I paid £25 for a fancy rack to hold the bags, but the peanuts cost 6p a bag and I sell 'em for 10p. Figger I sell 50 bags a week to start. It'll take weeks to cover the cost of the rack. After that I gotta clear profit of 4p a bag. The more I sell, the more I make.

EFF EX: That is an antiquated and completely unrealistic approach, Joe. Fortunately, modern accounting procedures permit a more accurate picture which reveals the complexities involved.

JOE: Huh?

EFF EX: To be precise, those peanuts must be integrated into your entire operation and be allocated their appropriate share of business overhead. They must share a proportionate part of your expenditure for rent, heat, light, equipment depreciation, decorating, salaries for your waitresses, cook . . .

JOE: The cook? What's he gotta do wit'a peanuts? He don't even know I got 'em.

EFF EX: Look, Joe, the cook is in the kitchen, the kitchen prepares the food, the food is what brings people in here, and the people ask to buy peanuts. That's why you must charge a portion of the cook's wages, as well as part of your own salary to peanut sales. This sheet contains a carefully calculated cost analysis which indicates the peanut operation should pay exactly £1,278 per year toward these general overhead costs.

JOE: The peanuts? £1,278 a year for overhead? The nuts?

EFF EX: It's really a little more than that. You also spend money each week to have the windows washed, to have the place swept out in the mornings, keep soap in the washroom, and provide free Cokes to the police. That raises the total to £1,313 per year.

JOE: [*thoughtfully*] But the peanut salesman said I'd make money . . . put 'em on the end of the counter, he said . . . and get 4p a bag profit.

EFF EX: [*with a sniff*] He's not an accountant. Do you actually know what the portion of the counter occupied by the peanut rack is worth to you?

JOE: Ain't worth nothing – no stool there . . . Just a dead spot at the end.

EFF EX: The modern cost picture permits no dead spots. Your counter contains 60 square feet and your counter business grosses £15,000 a year. Consequently, the square foot of space occupied by the peanut rack is £250 per year. Since you have taken that area away from general counter use, you must charge the value of the space to the occupant.

JOE: You mean I gotta add £250 a year more to the peanuts?

EFF EX: Right. That raises their share of the general operating costs to a grand total of £1,563 per year. Now then, if you sell 50 bags of peanuts per week, these allocated costs will amount to 60p per bag.

JOE: What?

EFF EX: Obviously, to that must be added your purchase price of 6p per bag, which brings the total to 66p. So you see by selling peanuts at 10p per bag, you are losing 56p on every sale.

JOE: Somethin's crazy!

EFF EX: Not at all! Here are the figures. They prove your peanuts operation cannot stand on its own feet.

JOE: [*brightening*] Suppose I sell lotsa peanuts ... thousands bags a week 'stead of fifty?

EFF EX: [*tolerantly*] Joe, you don't understand the problem. If the volume of peanuts sales increases, our operating costs will go up ... you'll have to handle more bags with more time, more depreciation, more everything. The basic principal of accounting is firm on that subject: 'The bigger the operation, the more general overhead costs that must be allocated.' No, increasing the volume of sales won't help.

JOE: Okay, you so smart, you tell me what I gotta do.

EFF EX: [*condescendingly*] Well ... you could first reduce operating expenses.

JOE: How?

EFF EX: Move to a building with cheaper rent. Cut salaries. Wash the windows bi-weekly. Have the floor swept only on Thursday. Remove the soap from the washrooms. Decrease the square-foot value of your counter. For example, if you can cut your expenses 50%, that will reduce the amount allocated to peanuts from £1,563 to £781.50 per year, reducing the cost to 36p per bag.

JOE: [*slowly*] That's better?

EFF EX: Much, much better. However, even then you would lose 26p per bag if you only charge 10p. Therefore, you must raise your selling price. If you want a net profit of 4p per bag you would have a charge 40p.

JOE: [*flabbergasted*] You mean even after I cut operating costs 50% I still gotta charge 40p for a 10p bag of peanuts? Nobody's that nuts about nuts! Who'd buy 'em?

EFF EX: That's a secondary consideration. The point is, at 40p you'd be selling at a price based upon a true and fair evaluation of your then reduced costs.

JOE: [*eagerly*] Look! I gotta better idea. Why don't I just throw the nuts out ... put 'em in the dustbin.

EFF EX: Can you afford it?

JOE: Sure. All I got is about 50 bags of peanuts ... cost about three bucks... so I lose £25 on the rack, but I get outta this nutty business and so no more grief.

EFF EX: [*shaking head*] Joe it isn't that simple. You are in the peanut business! The minute you throw those peanuts out you are adding £1,563 of annual overhead to the rest of your operation. Joe ... be realistic ... can you afford to do that?

JOE: [*completely crushed*] It's unbelievable! Last week I was making money. Now I'm in trouble ... just because I believe 50 bags of peanuts a week is easy.

EFF EX: [*with raised eyebrow*] that is the object of modern cost studies, Joe ... to dispel those false illusions.

Required

1. Is Joe losing 26p on every sale of peanuts? Explain.

2. Do you agree that if the volume of peanut sales is increased, operating losses will increase? Explain.
3. Do you agree with the 'efficiency expert' that, in order to make the peanut operation profitable, the operating costs in the restaurant should be decreased and the selling price of the peanuts should be increased? Give reasons.
4. Do you think that Joe can afford to get out of the peanut business? Give reasons.
5. Do you think that Joe should eliminate his peanut operations? Why or why not?

Acknowledgement

This case has appeared in many books and journals over the years. Unfortunately the identity of the author seems to have been lost. I am indebted to the author for writing such a fine and interesting case study and I apologise if I have inadvertently infringed copyright on this case.

REFERENCES

Bowerman, M. (1995), 'Auditing performance indicators: the role of the Audit Commission in the Citizen's Charter Initiative', *Financial Accountability and Management* **11** (2), 171–83.

Coates, J., Rickwood, C. and Stacey, R. (1989), *Control and Audit in Management Accounting* (Heinemann).

Cowe, R. (ed.) (1988), *Handbook of Management Accounting*, 2nd edn (Gower).

Dearden, J. (1988), *Management Accounting* (Prentice Hall).

Emmanuel, C. and Otley, D. (1985), *Accounting for Management Control* (Van Nostrand Reinhold).

Emmanuel, C., Otley, D. and Merchant, K. (1990), *Accounting for Management Control* 2nd edn (Chapman & Hall).

IASC, International Accounting Standard 14 (International Accounting Standards Committee).

Leontiades, J. C. (1985), *Multinational Corporate Strategy: Planning for world markets* (Lexington Books).

Lev, B. (1974), *Financial Statement Analysis: A new approach,* Foundations of Finance Series (Prentice Hall).

Mauriel, J. J. and Anthony, R. N. (1966), 'Misevaluation of investment centre performance', *Harvard Business Review*, March/April, 98–105.

Morse, W. J., Davis, J. R. and Hartgraves, A. L. (1991), *Management Accounting*, 3rd edn (Addison-Wesley).

Porter, M. (ed.) (1986), *Competition in Global Industries* (Harvard Business School Press).

Smith, M. (1990), 'The rise and rise the NFI', *Management Accounting* (CIMA) (May), 24–6.

Smith, T. (1992), *Accounting for Growth: Stripping the camouflage from company accounts* (Century Business).

Stein, N. D. (1989), 'ED45 segmental reporting', *ACCA Students' Newsletter* (June), 6–7.

Stonich, P. J. (1984), 'The performance measurement and reward system: critical to strategic management' *Organisational Dynamics* (Winter), republished in Thomas (1988), op. cit.

Thomas, W. E. (ed.) (1983), *Readings in Cost Accounting, Budgeting and Control*, 6th edn (South-Western).

Tomkins, G. (1973) *Financial Planning in Divisional Companies* (Haymarket).

Woodward, D. S. (1992), 'Joe's Bistro and the peanut problem', *Management Accounting* (CIMA), **70** (4) (April), 40.

Woodward, D. S. and Spink, B. (1992), 'Joe's Bistro and the peanut solution', *Management Accounting* (CIMA), **70**(5) (May), 56–7.

CHAPTER NINETEEN

Transfer pricing

CHAPTER OBJECTIVES

After reading this chapter you should be able to:

- describe how to set a transfer price using: cost-based prices; cost-plus prices; market prices; linear programming prices; negotiated prices; and profit-sharing-based prices
- appreciate the use of transfer pricing methods in reality
- discuss the external monitoring and control of transfer pricing

Introduction

To illustrate the potential minefield that this chapter is about to step into, the following quotation is apt:

> Many PhD dissertations in accounting explore the theoretical never-never land of transfer pricing, thereby assuring the writer of almost complete obscurity. We have read a number of these dissertations and suggest that you wait for the movie. (Keegan and Howard (1986), quoted in Hirsch 1988: 557)

Meer-Kooistra (1994: 123) opens with a discussion that says there are many studies on transfer pricing but very few of them integrate the whole transfer pricing picture, and:

> there had been relatively few empirical studies ... there is only a small amount of research dealing with the behavioural aspects of transfer pricing. The vast majority of studies are analytical in nature and mostly *ad hoc* approaches.

Tomkins' (1990) paper is an example of the type of study that is analytical and *ad hoc* in nature. Whilst Tomkins' article appears mathematically and qualitatively sound, there is little in it to recommend it to the average management accountant in industry.

Based on the above sentiments, the material that follows provides an overview of the material relating to transfer pricing. A scrutiny of the references given at the end of this chapter will give a more detailed insight into most of the aspects of this topic.

Definition of a transfer price

A transfer price is: 'an administered (or notional) intra company charge at which goods or services are "sold" by one division to another in the same organisation or by central management to a division' (Mepham 1980: 240).

The role of transfer prices frequently extends beyond that of being a passive bookkeeping device. In particular, the system may be intended to:

1. Help central management judge divisional performance.
2. Provide a surrogate selling price for internal work, enabling a division to earn a 'profit' on such work when divisions are given a profit earning objective.
3. Encourage divisional managers to adopt policies which lead to achieving both divisional and organisational goals (goal congruency).

The first point we should make in this discussion of transfer pricing is that we have already met transfer pricing before in this book. In Chapter 8 on job, batch and process costing, we worked through transfer pricing calculations for process costing situations. In the examples of process costing, we were taking an absorption costing view. In this chapter, we will be taking a much broader view, and we will, in fact, be rather critical of the absorption costing approach to transfer pricing in the process costing situation. Many observers of the transfer pricing situation see transfer pricing as something of a battleground, with winners and losers amongst the many players: 'Transfer pricing systems function in decentralized firms and influence the balance between, on the one hand, the profit centre managers' room for manoeuvre and, on the other hand, the need for integration between the profit centre activities' (Meer-Kooistra 1980:129).

One of the reasons why we might talk in terms of winners and losers is that the level at which transfer prices are set often impinge upon a manager's annual remuneration package. If a manager is paid at least partly by results, he or she will be keen to ensure that his or her results are as good as possible. Hence a manager with profit centre responsibilities might be most keen to see the highest possible transfer price in order to ensure the highest possible divisional profit.

How to set a transfer price

Many (perhaps thousands) of articles, books, monographs, working papers and so on have been written and presented on the subject of transfer prices and how they might be set. However, there seems to be no single answer on how to set a transfer price. Every new paper and book discusses similar approaches and no one ever gets nearer to solving this problem. Sizer (1989: 482–3) quotes Anthony and Dearden who have developed a set of guidelines for establishing transfer prices:

1. Use standard cost-plus-profit transfer prices for goods transferred between divisions that are likely never to be made outside the company.
2. Use estimated long-run competitive prices for goods that management might be willing to buy from outside but only on a relatively long-term basis because their manufacture requires a significant investment in facilities and skills.
3. Use market-based prices for goods that can be made outside the company without any significant disruption to present operations. Use actual competitive prices for those products that are:
   (a) sold to both the company and outside sources; or
   (b) produced from outside and within the company.

The reality of the setting of transfer prices is, of course, that there are many agendas for it. Setting transfer prices in my organisation may be based on the internal politics of my organisation; setting transfer prices for Lever Brothers (Malawi) Ltd may be done by head office in the United Kingdom in an attempt to minimise foreign exchange losses; setting transfer prices elsewhere may be done deliberately to result in maximising cash flow into head office; and so on. However, we have many options to consider in setting our transfer prices, including:

1. *Cost-based prices*
   (a) actual absorption cost;
   (b) standard absorption cost;
   (c) actual marginal cost;
   (d) standard marginal cost.
2. *Cost-plus prices*
   (a) actual absorption cost plus profit;
   (b) standard absorption cost plus profit;
   (c) actual marginal cost plus profit;
   (d) standard marginal cost plus profit.
3. *Market prices*
   (a) actual market price;
   (b) modified market price.
4. *Linear programming prices*
5. *Negotiated prices*
6. *Profit sharing-based prices*

Cost-based prices

Standard cost-based prices may be preferred so that the inefficiencies of the transferring segment are not passed on to the receiving segment. This may be so because the selling division would have no incentive to control production costs, since any cost increases can be passed on to the buying division. Transfers at standard cost impose cost discipline on selling divisions and enable buying divisions to plan with the security of certain prices for transferred inputs.

Problems with cost-based prices

What is a cost-based price? We know from the work of several earlier chapters, that cost behaviour analysis, overhead apportionment, the non-use of activity-based costing, and so on, may distort product costs. Hence, if a cost basis has been used that is inaccurate, how can a fair transfer price be established. We know from the work on activity-based costing that the production manager often has a keener eye for his or her costs than the management accountant! Consequently, if the production manager is aware of his or her true costs and the management accountant is setting transfer prices based on his or her own notion of costs, there is bound to be conflict and a lack of motivation somewhere along the line. There is also the possibility that the divisional manager will be playing games with the cost schedules. In such a case, the costs that are being presented as being actual costs will be nothing of the sort. If the buying division has no choice but to pay the price demanded by the selling division, where is the incentive for the selling division to be efficient? The selling division has no incentive to keep costs under control and improve efficiency if it can merely pass on all cost increases to the next division in the chain. One way round the problem of inefficient supplying divisions is to treat them as real profit centres along the lines of the Weyehaeuser organisation we looked at in a previous chapter. If a selling division genuinely has to compete with external organisations who are keen to compete with it at every level, and if the buying division genuinely has the right to buy goods and/or services from outside its own organisation, there will be an incentive for the selling division to perform well. As an end result, we must ensure that all managers are working together for the greater benefit of the entire organisation: in other words, that they are working goal congruent. One manager trying to optimise his or her own performance may do so at the expense of all other divisions in the organisation. In a situation where the goals of the manager of division A are self-set and are in conflict with the goals of all other divisions, goal congruence is lacking.

Cost plus prices

By cost-plus prices, we mean exactly the same under the heading of transfer pricing as we did under the heading of pricing. The same problem faces the divisional manager as faced the marketing manager: What should be the profit margin?

Market prices

One surrogate for a transfer price is to look outside the organisation and find the price at which the goods or services can be obtained on the open market. For example, if the goods coming out of my division can be bought in the same state on the open market, my transfer price is the price at which the goods can be bought outside the organisation: 'when the selling division is operating at capacity it should transfer goods at the external market price because this represents the opportunity cost of selling the goods' (Wilson and Chua 1993: 304).

The principal benefit of a market-based selling price is, of course, its inherent fairness. A market-based transfer price is an unbiased estimate of the worth of the goods. Secondly, if a market price exists for a good or service, there is no requirement for a sophisticated cost accounting system to calculate the transfer price: it is a ready-made estimate. In some cases – monopolies, for example – no ready market exists for a product since no one else is making and selling it. Alternatively, there is no open market for the goods or services because they are always intermediate goods and services. That is, they are always and only transferred between processes and are never brought to the open market. Thirdly, as Cats-Baril *et al.* (1988) point out, in the introduction phase in the product life cycle, the firm frequently has a near monopoly on its product, hence no market price will exist. If it is not possible to obtain quotations from outside suppliers, it may be possible to:

1. Adjust for differences in design the price of a similar product or service, for which a market price does exist.
2. Adjust a past market price for changes in product group market levels since that price became effective.

Linear programming prices

Refer back to the appendix to Chapter 12 if necessary to remind yourself of the solving of linear programming (LP) problems.

Linear programming is used in establishing transfer prices. However, there are problems with it! The problems largely stem from reconciling who sets the organisation's objectives and who sets the transfer prices. If divisional managers set both objectives and prices, there will probably be few problems. Wilson and Chua (1993) provide a very simple example of the application of linear programming to the transfer pricing problem. With linear programming prices we examine all of the relevant variables of a situation, and set up a linear programming model, which we then solve. The outputs of the linear programming model are the number of units to be made. Worked example 19.1 is an exercise similar to that found in Wilson and Chua (1993: 305–6).

WORKED EXAMPLE 19.1

An organisation has two divisions, A and B. Division A's products can be sold on the open market for £10 per unit, with variable costs of £7 per unit. Division B can take the output of division A and process it further at an additional £1.5 per unit. Division B sells its product at an enhanced selling price of £13 per unit.

Both divisions operate under a capacity constraint: A's capacity is 1,000 units and B's capacity is 600 units. Note: stocks of these products are not kept.

Required

How many units should division A produce and sell; and how many units should division B produce and sell?

Solution to Worked example 19.1

The first step here is to set up the linear programming (LP) model, as follows:

Let:
a be the output from division A to the external market;
b be the output from division B to the external market.

The optimal solution is found by solving the following model:

$$\begin{aligned} \text{Maximise} \quad & p = 3a + 4.5b \\ \text{Subject to:} \quad & a + b \leq 1{,}000 \\ & b \leq 600 \\ & a, b \geqslant 0 \end{aligned}$$

The objective function says, maximise the contributions for a and b where the contribution per unit for a is £3 per unit and for b it is £4.50 per unit. The constraints say that the total output of a and b cannot exceed 1,000 units; and total output of b cannot exceed 600 units. Finally, neither a nor b can have negative values: this is known as the non-negativity constraint. Compared to the examples we have used so far, this example is so simple that all we need to do is to transform the model into simultaneous equations and solve them:

$$a + b = 1{,}000 \tag{19.1}$$
$$b = 600 \tag{19.2}$$

All we need to do in this very simple example is to substitute equation 2 into equation 1:

$$a = 1{,}000 - 600 = 400$$
$$b = 600$$

The solution is to produce 400 units from division A and 600 units from division B. This is the optimum solution and returns a total contribution of

400 units × £3	= £1,200
600 units × £4.50	= £2,700
Total	£3,900

The above example is a very simplified one, as we have already mentioned. Goal congruence problems are, however, well illustrated when objective setting is divorced from pricing setting. Emmanuel *et al.* (1990) discuss examples to deal with these problems. Essentially, the issues surrounding the latter case, where objective and price setting are divorced are grouped under the heading of decomposition methodology The essence of the situation is:

1. divisions solve divisional LPs
2. solutions sent to HQ
3. HQ sends out new transfer prices
4. when optimum is reached, divisions informed of quantities to produce. (Emmanuel *et al.* 1990: 147)

The arguments should be clear. In the divisional situation, management at headquarters are the ones with the final say in the setting of transfer prices and so on. Hence, whilst divisional managers can solve their problems using LP, they do so only as an interim measure; and their results are subject to revision. Otherwise, the problems of goal congruence may impact upon the rest of the organisation. As Emmanuel *et al.* say: 'Note that step 4 is necessary because knowledge of the transfer prices alone does not give divisions enough information to calculate optimum production quantities' (ibid. 146).

As Emmanuel *et al.* also demonstrate, the solution to the LP solution of transfer pricing problems is to build an LP model with linking constraints. That is, we develop an LP for division A, a model for division B, a model for division C . . . then build in the constraints that link the requirements of the whole organisation as they impact upon division A . . . B . . . C . . . Such a model appears as follows:

$$\begin{array}{llrrrrl}
\text{Maximise} & p = 10a + 12b + 9c + 11d & & & & & \\
\text{Subject to:} & & 2a + & b + & & & \leqslant 1{,}200 \text{ machine A} \\
& & 4a + & 7b & & & \leqslant 5{,}000 \text{ machine B} \\
& & & & 3c + & 4d & \leqslant 890 \text{ machine C} \\
& & & & 23c + & 15d & \leqslant 2{,}750 \text{ machine D} \\
& & -a & & +\,2c + & 4d & \leqslant 0 \text{ link 1} \\
& & & -b & + & 9d & \leqslant 0 \text{ link 2}
\end{array}$$

This model is built around two divisions, each with two machines: division A has machines A and B; and so on. The linking constraints are necessary to ensure that enough of the products from division A are produced to allow the products of division B to be made. We can solve this problem in three parts to view the overall effects of what should happen:

1. variables *a* and *b* belong to division A;
2. variables *c* and *d* belong to division B;
3. the link constraints belong to the whole organisation.

The solutions are:

Division A only (units)	Division B only (units)	Organisation (units)
a 340		*a* 340
b 520		*b* 520
	c 156.667	*c* 95.161
	d 183.333	*d* 37.419
Profit (£):		
9,640	2,016.66	10,908.07

Rework these problems and discover the shadow prices and so on. The message is clear from this example. Working as independent divisions, A and B produce the levels of output as given in their respective columns. When the linking constraints are included to give the overall model, B has to reduce its output significantly. Hence, as independent divisions, A and B would ostensibly earn a total profit of £11,656.66; whereas, when working as an entire organisation, total profit becomes £10,908.07. (See Emmanuel *et al.* for a full discussion of this kind of problem.)

Although the development of LP models in the context of transfer pricing has helped considerably, there are still limitations associated with them. First, the models assume goal consensus: that is, managers from different divisions are working towards achieving the same goals. They also assume, of course, that everyone is trading openly and honestly in terms of the information they submit to head office! Secondly, uncertainty is usually left out – of textbook models, at least; yet each manager will probably be faced with a probability distribution of transfer prices in many situations. Thirdly, there are organisational and behavioural issues to be faced in transfer pricing situations: for instance, when corporate and divisional optimality come into conflict, who makes the final sacrifice? As Ezzamel *et al.* say these arguments do not invalidate LP theory and practice. In cases of doubt or non-applicability of an LP model, remodelling may be all that is needed.

Negotiated prices

If divisions are free to negotiate prices with each other, the agreement may not be in the group's interests even though the prices satisfy the two divisions concerned. The prices may be different from the linear programming price and from the market price. Negotiated prices depend upon the divisions involved being able to reach agreement, a process which can, of course, waste large amounts of time. Disagreements are likely if changes in market prices are expected soon or one of the parties has a stronger bargaining position.

Additionally, of course, there may be disagreements that the respective managers of the two divisions involved in the negotiations cannot resolve. What then? Meer-Kooistra (1994) reports that in the situation where divisions cannot agree, the organisations researched in his survey go to arbitration with central management.

CAMEO

Transfer pricing around the world

This chapter is looking at many of the issues facing managements of organisations that have two or more divisions or segments. One particular aspect of transfer pricing that is the subject of an OECD report concerns organisations with divisions in more than one country.

Writing in *The Times*, the head of international tax at accountants KPMG, Jim Marshall (1995), spells out some of the issues arising out of transfer pricing for multinational corporations. Marshall spells out that for multinationals, transfer pricing reviews are expensive: travel, salary and associated costs of consultants/accountants, documentation costs, training costs, communication costs – all add to the transfer pricing bill. Furthermore Marshall points out that we are not only dealing with physical goods when we discuss transfer pricing. Transfer pricing may also be relevant to the provision of services between segments, such as royalty payments, or research and devlopment.

Since Marshall is a tax expert, it is not surprisng that much of his article is aimed at the taxation aspects of transfer pricing. However, Marshall does point out that the United States and Australia have highly regulated transfer pricing environments, whereas the United Kingdom has a much looser regime. Nevertheless, every organisation where transfer pricing is an issue needs to be aware that whatever the legal and regulatory background to the setting of transfer prices, it is unlikely that organisations will merely be allowed to set a policy one day and revise it the next. From the management accountant's point of view, therefore, transfer pricing takes on an important sheen, in that we have one aspect of our work that is subject to external monitoring and review.

Marshall gives us a four-point checklist of how we can establish a defensible transfer pricing position that the Inland Revenue, in the United Kingdom, will almost certainly wish to review from time to time.

1. Background documention must be maintained.
2. Agreements between segments must be formalised.
3. Formal documentation of real transfers must be issued and kept.
4. Details of competitor information, market price information, and forecasts of sales, etc., that are used in arriving at transfer prices, must be maintained.

Marshall's final piece of advice to anyone involved in the transfer price setting business is: 'Looking forward and anticipating transfer pricing reviews is really the key to avoiding the tax penalties and costs of transfer pricing investigations in future years.'

Reference: Marshall (1995).

Profit sharing-based prices

We may need to develop such ideas as profit-sharing models in the situation where three departments or divisions exist within an organisation, but only one of them sells the final product, with the other two divisions processing the ingredients to make it. The question is: How, if at all, can divisions 1 and 2 share in the profit that division 3 has apparently earned by selling the product? The Massachusetts formula is one model that allows us to apportion the profit earned by the group over the separate divisions of that group. Worked example 19.2 explains how the formula works. Although this example is only one of many such models, it does beg the question of how appropriate it is. Two possible issues might arise:

1. Need we bother with assigning profit anyway?
2. Is such a method the best one, given that profit must be assigned?

Whether the profit needs to be assigned will be a question that the management accountant and his or her management colleagues will have to resolve. We cannot really anticipate all of the arguments in general here for what will be a specific question on an organisation-by-organisation basis. If we feel we do have to assign profit across departments or divisions, we can possibly improve on the situation here by considering the use of non-financial indicators in helping us to sort out such assignments. If we take throughput times, productivity rates and so on, instead of trying to use what are essentially artificial methods of profit assignment, we would be better able both to assess management and to assign profits.

WORKED EXAMPLE 19.2

A product generates £100,000 profit and is made by three divisions in the group: 1, 2 and 3. The profit is apportioned to each division in proportion to its:

- net tangible assets
- labour costs; and
- responsibility for sales.

The relevant data for this organisation are:

	Divisions		
	1	2	3
	£	£	£
Net tangible assets	1m.	2m.	0.5m.
Labour costs	200,000	500,000	300,000
Sales	nil	nil	3m.

Required

Calculate the transfer prices and the final selling price of the product made by this organisation

Solution to Worked example 19.2

The Massachusetts formula is:

$$MF_{profit} = \left(\frac{\text{division assets}}{\text{total assets}} + \frac{\text{division labour}}{\text{total labour}} + \frac{\text{division sales}}{\text{total sales}}\right) \times \text{total profit}$$

This gives:

$$1_{profit} = \left(\frac{£1m.}{£3.5m.} + \frac{£200,000}{£1m.} + \frac{£0m.}{£3m.}\right) \times £100,000$$

$$= £16,190$$

$$2_{profit} = 1/3\left(\frac{£2m.}{£3.5m.} + \frac{£500,000}{£1m.} + \frac{£0m.}{£3m.}\right) \times £100,000$$

$$= £35,714$$

$$3_{profit} = 1/3\left(\frac{£0.5m.}{£3.5m.} + \frac{£300,000}{£1m.} + \frac{£3m.}{£3m.}\right) \times £100,000$$

$$= £48,096$$

Division 3 sells 8,095 units to the final consumer and unit costs are £4 for each division except division 1 which has a conversion cost of £2 and materials cost of £2. Hence:

Profit apportioned per unit

	1	2	3
	£	£	£
	16,190	35,714	48,096
	8,095	8,095	8,095
	= 2.00	4.41	5.94

Costs per unit

	1	2	3
	£	£	£
Costs from previous process	nil	6.00	14.41
Materials and conversion costs	4.00	4.00	4.00
Profit allocation	2.00	4.41	5.94
Transfer/selling price	6.00	14.41	24.35

The Massachusetts formula is an idiosyncratic method of profit apportionment and has both merits and demerits. However, the application of the method does at least give us one view of how the problem of assigning profits can be achieved. Its most serious problem comes with the assessment of departmental or divisional costs, assets and sales. As with any apportionment exercise, some or all of these three variables may be estimates rather than actual amounts.

Transfer prices and the product life cycle

We discussed some of the work of Cats-Baril, Gatti and Grinnell (1988) when we looked at product life cycle pricing under the main heading of pricing. Cats-Baril *et al.* (1988: 32) also give an example of the product life cycle and transfer pricing, illustrating the product life cycle and the respective pricing mechanisms. They also discuss the development of the microprocessor in terms of product life-cycle transfer pricing. Table 19.1 contains an extract from their article that is relevant here. Cats-Baril *et al.* say:

TABLE 19.1 ***Life-cycle stages and their respective pricing mechanisms***

Life cycle stages	Introduction	Growth	Maturity/decline
Pricing mechanism	Cost plus fixed fee, or cost plus profit share	Price associated with closest substitute, or bids solicited, or prices charged by second sources	Price of identical products

Source: Cats-Baril *et al.* (1988: 32).

> As each internally transferred product moves through the life cycle from unique to homogeneous, the available benchmark changes, requiring a timely change in the transfer price. If that adjustment does not occur, and the transfer price remains at a level that corresponds to a different stage of the life cycle, suboptimal decision making will occur. . . . Given the different rates at which products move from unique to homogeneous, it is impossible to establish any general rule concerning the length of each pricing phase of the product life cycle. Therefore it is also impossible to generalize about how frequently transfer prices must be adjusted. . . . The risk of suboptimal decision making is greatest during the early stages of the plc. This is due to the lack of clarity of a market reference price early in the life cycle when the product is unique. (ibid. 32–3)

The use of transfer pricing methods in reality

A number of surveys have been undertaken and reported over the last twenty years or so. Table 19.2 shows the average of the five surveys found in Emmanuel *et al.* (1990: 293); the columns 'maximum' and 'minimum' mean the largest and the smallest return respectively for each of the categories from the five surveys reported. Additionally, Emmanuel *et al.* report on the setting of transfer prices and product design characteristics. The research on which this aspect is based differentiated between standardised products, customised products and specialised products. Table 19.3 shows the hypothesised schema that transfer pricing setting should follow. The hypothesis on which this table is based is developed from research reported in 1988. Emmanuel *et al.* report that over 50 empirical studies have been undertaken world wide into transfer pricing since 1960, yet evidence to substantiate Spicer's hypothesised table is limited. Nevertheless, the table is presented here as a useful starting point for consideration of whether design characteristics are important in the setting of transfer prices. Note that Emmanuel *et al.* were writing in 1990; since then even more research papers on transfer pricing have been written.

External monitoring and control of transfer pricing

Economists often get hot under the collar about transfer prices when the transfer price set by, for example, a multinational organisation relates to business taking place between two countries. The problem here is that the organisation may set an artificial transfer price such that the tax exposure in one country is minimised. Alternatively, the transfer price may be

TABLE 19.2 *Average of five surveys of transfer pricing methods*

	Average	Maximum	Minimum
Variable costs	4.5	5.8	2.9
Full cost	28.0	44.5	13.4
Cost plus	14.3	16.7	12.0
Market price	39.4	46.2	31.0
Negotiated	21.3	23.0	19.1
Other	2.9	2.9	2.9

TABLE 19.3 ***Transfer prices and product design characteristics***

	Standardized	Customized	Specialized
Recommended transfer price	Market price	Negotiated on manufacturing cost	Manufacturing cost
Divisional autonomy over make or buy decision	Total	Required to negotiate initially	
	Low	Transactions costs	High

Source: Emmanuel *et al.* (1990: 296), reporting Spicer.

set with the intention of repatriating as much profit as possible from the country containing the subsidiary organisation. Many of the arguments under this heading tend to revolve around organisations with investments in developing countries. Thus a multinational that has investments in Africa might take as much profit as possible by means of its manipulation of transfer prices of the products developed in the African subsidiary. The purpose of our discussion here is to reassure anyone who believes that multinationals have it all their own way. Whilst it is probably still true that large organisations have experts working on this kind of problem all of the time, the tax authorities in many countries have for several years attempted to control the situation through external monitoring

If necessary, tax authorities are often prepared to dictate to an organisation what they feel is the correct transfer price for a subsidiary's outputs if they believe that tax evasion is taking place. Nevertheless, transfer pricing is a sufficiently serious issue for the tax authorities to devote such a relatively large amount of their energies towards regulating it.

SUMMARY

In this chapter we have had a comprehensive overview of both transfer pricing theory and practice. We have seen that there has been much discussion on transfer pricing over the years in management accounting, and other, literature, and it has to be said that the debate will continue since there are so many aspects to transfer pricing. Given the conclusion to the linear programming discussion in this chapter, we know that there are issues entwined in the transfer pricing debate that extend beyond management accounting issues. Organisational and behavioural issues are important; manager reward systems often impact on transfer pricing systems; and at the end of it all, the bullying of one manager by another might be the way that transfer prices are actually set in an organisation.

We also reviewed a large body of knowledge containing a number of mathematical and quasi-mathematical techniques that are designed to smooth the ruffled feathers of any organisation's transfer pricing problems!

KEY TERMS

You should satisfy yourself that you have noted all of these terms and can define and/or describe their meaning and use, as appropriate.

Goal congruency (p. 654)
Cost-based prices (p. 655)
Cost-plus prices (p. 656)
Market price (p. 657)
Linear-programming prices (p. 657)
Decomposition methodology (p. 658)
Negotiated prices (p. 660)
Massachusetts formula (p. 661)
Product life cycle (p. 663)
External monitoring (p. 665)

RECOMMENDED READING

Although they both relate to pricing, Corey (1980) and (1982) are still a good, general starting point here. Emmanuel *et al.* give a good, considered, overview of many of the issues. Meer-Kooistra (1994) is worth a read as it is an up-to-date view and extensive. For those who need mathematical detail, Mepham (1980) is recommended, while Tomkins (1990) works through a mathematical nicety!

QUESTIONS

Review questions

1. Define the term 'transfer price'.
2. Why might an organisation divisionalise?
3. In the context of transfer pricing describe how the following methods work:

   (a) cost-based prices;
   (b) cost-plus prices;
   (c) market prices;
   (d) linear programming prices;
   (e) negotiated prices; and
   (f) profit-sharing based prices.

4. Which transfer pricing methods are used in reality?
5. (a) What role can linear programming play in the setting of transfer prices?
   (b) What are the limitations of the linear programming approach to the setting of transfer prices?
6. How can transfer pricing and the product life cycle work together?

Answers to review questions 1, 3 and 5 can be found in the Student Workbook.

Graded practice questions

Level I

1. A company operates four factories. Each makes components which are incorporated into the products sold by one or more of the other factories. To encourage a competitive environment the directors have decided that each factory should become a separate profit centre. This will necessitate the use of transfer prices for the interfactory components.

Required

(a) Describe three different methods of establishing the transfer prices.
(b) State which method you would recommend for the company described, giving reasons for your choice.
(c) Prepare a policy statement for the one method chosen, outlining how the pricing system would be operated among the different factories.

2. (a) Quoin Ltd, an abrasives manufacturer, has two divisions. Division M manufactures abrasive grain, an intermediate product, which it can sell either to division D (where it is incorporated into coated grain final products) or on the open market (where there is perfect competition). In order to maintain a sufficient element of divisional autonomy division D is allowed to buy abrasive grain in the open market if it so wishes. There are no extra costs of buying or selling in the open market as compared with buying and selling between the divisions.

   State and explain the optimal transfer pricing policy which will maximise the profits of Quoin Ltd as a whole, showing how this profit would accrue to the two divisions.

   (b) Son of Quion Ltd has three divisions. Division S supplies a special grain to divisions X and Y (in lots of 100 tonnes), which each utilises in the preparation of its own final products. There is no other market for the special grain.

   Division S has the following cost structure:

Tonnage produced	400	500	600	700	800	900	1,000
Total cost (£'000)	400	420	450	485	525	585	665

Divisions X and Y can generate total net revenues (after meeting their own respective independent processing costs) as follows, in relation to the tonnage of special grain processed:

Division X

Tonnage processed	100	200	300	400
Total net revenues (£'000)	120	180	220	240

Division Y

Tonnage processed	100	200	300	400	500	600
Total net revenues (£0'00)	120	240	360	420	460	480

Show the price at which the special grain should be transferred from division S to divisions X and Y, stating your reasons.

3. The Philadelphia Company has two divisions, A and B. For one of the company's products division A produces a major sub-assembly and division B incorporates this sub-assembly into the final product. There is a market for both the sub-assembly and the final product, and the divisions have been delegated profit responsibility. The transfer price for the sub-assembly has been set at long-run average market price.

The following data are available to each division:

	£
Estimated selling price for final product	300
Long-run average selling price for intermediate product	200
Outlay cost for completion in division B	150
Outlay cost in division A	120

The manager of division B has made the following calculation:

	£	£
Selling price: final product		300
Transferred in cost (market)	200	
Outlay cost for completion	150	350
Contribution (loss) on product		(50)

Required

(a) Should transfers be made to division B if there is no excess capacity in division A? Is the market price the correct transfer price?

(b) Assume that division A's maximum capacity for this product is 1,000 units per month and sales to the intermediate market are presently 800 units. Should 200 units be transferred to division B? At what relevant transfer price? Assume for a variety of reasons that A will maintain the £200 selling price indefinitely; that is, A is not considering cutting the price to outsiders regardless of the presence of idle capacity.

(c) Suppose A quoted a transfer price of £150. What would be the contribution to the firm as a whole if the transfer were made? As manager of B, would you be inclined to buy at £150?

(d) The manager of division A has the option of:

(i) cutting the external price to £195 with the certainty that external sales will rise to 1,000 units; or

(ii) maintaining the outside price of £200 for the 800 units, and transferring the 200 units to B at a price that would produce the same total contribution for A

State the minimum transfer price that should be used, and demonstrate whether it leads to the most desirable decision for the company as a whole.

4. (a) CB Division of the Meldon Group manufactures a single component which it sells externally and can also transfer to other divisions within the group. CB Division has been set the performance target of a budgeted residual income of £300,000 for the coming financial year.

The following additional budgeted information relating to CB Division has been prepared for the coming financial year:

(i) maximum production/sales capacity: 120,000 components;

(ii) sales to external customers: 80,000 components at £20 each;

(iii) variable cost per component: £14;

(iv) fixed costs directly attributable to the division: £16,000;

(v) capital employed: £1,600,000 with a cost of capital of 15%.

The XY Division of the Meldon Group has asked CB Division to quote a transfer price for 40,000 components.

Calculate the transfer price per component which CB Division should quote to XY Division in order that its budgeted residual income target will be achieved.

(b) Explain why the transfer price calculated in (a) may lead to sub-optimal decision making from a group viewpoint.

(c) XY Division now establishes that it requires 50,000 components. External Company L is willing to supply 50,000 components at £15.50 each but is not willing to quote for only part of the requirement of XY Division. External Company M is willing to supply any number of components at £18 each.

For each of the cases below (taken separately), state the source or sources from which XY Division should purchase the components in order to maximise its own net profit and explain why the particular source or sources have been chosen, assuming that CB Division is willing to supply the components to XY Division:

(i) at an average price per component for the quantity required, such that the budget residual income of CB Division will still be achieved;

(ii) at an average price per component which reflects the opportunity cost of components transferred;

(iii) at prices per component which reflect the opportunity cost of each component.

(d) State which of the bases for transfer prices in (c) should lead to group profit maximisation and calculate the reduction in group profit which should arise from the operation of each of the other transfer price bases in comparison.

ACCA 2.4 Management Accounting
December 1987

5. This question could equally well appear in this chapter's practice questions and the practice questions for Chapter 12 since it covers material from both chapters.

Two of the divisions of Sanco Limited are the Intermediate division and the Final division. The Intermediate division produces three products A, B, and C. The products are sold to overseas specialist producers as well as to the Final division at the same prices. The Final division uses products A, B and C in the manufacture of products X, Y and Z respectively. Recently the Final division has been forced to work below capacity because of difficulties in obtaining sufficient supplies of products A, B and C. Consequently the Intermediate division has been instructed by the board of directors to sell all its products to the Final division.

The price and cost data is as follows:

Intermediate division

	Product A	B	C
	£	£	£
Transfer price	20	20	30
Variable manufacturing cost per unit	7	12	10
Fixed costs	50,000	100,000	75,000

The Intermediate division has a maximum monthly capacity of 50,000 units. The processing constraints are such that capacity production can only be maintained by producing at least 10,000 units of each product. The remaining capacity can be used to produce 20,000 units of any combination of the three products.

Final division

	Product X	Y	Z
	£	£	£
Final selling price	56	60	60
Variable costs per unit:			
Internal purchase	20	20	30
Processing in Final division	10	10	16
Fixed costs	100,000	100,000	200,000

The Final division has sufficient capacity to produce up to 20,000 units more than it is now producing, but, because of the lack of products A, B and C, is limiting production. Further the Final division is able to sell all the products that it can produce at the final selling prices.

Required

(a) From the viewpoint of the Intermediate division, compute the products and quantities which would maximise its divisional profits and calculate the total company profit, given that all Intermediate production is transferred internally.

(b) From the viewpoint of the Final division, compute the products and quantities purchased from the Intermediate division which would maximise its divisional profits, and indicate the effect on the total company profits.

(c) Compute the product mix which would maximise the total company profits assuming all transfers were internal.

(d) If there were no transactions costs involved for either division in buying or selling A, B or C outside the company, what, if anything, is lost by the policy of internal transfers only?

(e) Discuss the effectiveness or otherwise of the transfer pricing system currently used at Sanco Limited.

ACCA 2.4 Management Accounting
June 1987

Solutions to practice questions 2, 3 and 5 can be found in the Student Workbook. Solutions to practice question numbers in red can be found at the end of this book.

REFERENCES

Cats-Baril, W., Gatti, J. F. and Grinnell, D. J. (1988), 'Transfer pricing in a dynamic market', *Management Accounting* (NAA) (February), 30–3.

Corey, E. R. (1980), 'Note on pricing', Note 580–091 (Harvard Business School).

Corey, E. R. (1982), 'Note on pricing strategies for industrial products', Note 9–582–124 (Harvard Business School) 124.

Emmanuel, C., Otley, D. and Merchant, K. (1990), *Accounting for Management Control*, 2nd edn (Chapman & Hall).

Keegan, D. P. and Howard, P. D. (1986), 'Transfer pricing for fun and profit,' *Review*, no. 3. (Price Waterhouse) 38, quoted in Hirsch (1988), op. cit.

Marshall, J. (1995), 'Pricing a reality for business life', *The Times*, Accountancy section (3 August 1995), 28.

Meer-Kooistra, J. (1994), 'The coordination of internal transactions: the functioning of transfer pricing systems in the organizational context', *Management Accounting Research* vol. 5, pp. 123–52.

Mepham, M. (1980), *Accounting models* (Polytech Publishers).

Hirsch, M. L. (1988), *Advanced Management Accounting* (PWS-Kent Publishing).

Sizer, J. (1989), *An Insight into Management Accounting* (Penguin Books)

Tomkins, C. (1990), 'Making sense of cost-plus transfer prices where there are imperfect intermediate good markets by a "pragmatic-analytic" perspective', *Management Accounting Research* vol. 1 (3), pp. 199–217.

Wilson, R. M. S. and Chua, W. F. (1993), *Managerial Accounting: Method and meaning* 2nd edn (Chapman & Hall).

PART FIVE

Management accounting: developments, dynamics and dichotomy

Part V comprises a personal view of the development of management accounting. Taking a number of sources, observations and viewpoints, we conclude that the management accounting profession, having solved many problems since the turn of the twentieth century, still faces many other problems that have yet to be resolved.

One particular hypothesis of this chapter is that management accountants may be guilty of being accountants first, last and foremost. Yet any rational view of the work of management accountants will conclude that they need to understand not only the environment in which they work, but also scientific principles, engineering principles, sociological principles, and a whole host of other knowledge and skills. Perhaps their greatest asset will be their ability to relate to their management colleagues, from whatever background they come.

A main conclusion, therefore, is that in order to acquire the necessary depth and variety of learning to ensure success in the profession, the management accountant's education needs to continue well past the final examination at university or accounting institution, and must be diversified beyond the subject boundaries of accountancy.

CHAPTER TWENTY

Management accounting: past, present and future

CHAPTER OBJECTIVES

After reading this chapter you should be able to:

- accept why management accounting is undergoing a revolution
- define the need for, and application of, non-financial indicators
- assess the potential future of management accounting and the part it will play in the management information system of the future

A revolution is taking place

Is management accounting the toppled ruler?

The principal objective of this book is to provide its reader with a comprehensive guide to cost and management accounting techniques. This final chapter looks at several aspects of the techniques we have studied and either raises questions for which there is yet no definitive answer, or raises questions and provides us with viewpoints other than the management accountant's own. In this chapter we will take a broad view of the relevance of the work of the management accountant. This will provide us with insights into the way that the work of management accountants is both perceived and received by his or her management colleagues. We will see reasons why there seems to be a revolution taking place in the manufacturing and service sector environments – revolution that can be interpreted as being aimed at overthrowing the place of the management accountant in the management information system of organisations.

Why the revolution is happening

Drury (1992) takes us through many of the issues concerning two major problem areas for the management accountant: the gap between theory and practice; and the relevance of management accounting. We are concerned here with the second of these issues: the relevance of management accounting.

Although there are many critics of management accounting techniques and practice, there is little evidence to suggest that all management accounting should be abandoned. Nevertheless, there is one particular area of criticism, namely, that the management accountant is using systems and techniques that his or her father used, and his father before him. Johnson (1990) reminds us of this when he describes some of the work that Kaplan undertook in 1982–3. Kaplan carried out research in a variety of organisations and concluded that the management accounting system was lagging behind the technological system by about seventy-five years. As a result of the way that management accountants seem reluctant to change, managers in organisations are turning away from the output of the management accountant in their desire to find performance indicators that tell them something useful about the way their business is operating. One of the most serious criticisms levelled at the management accountant is that he or she is more concerned with providing information based on financial accounting bases than information that is decision useful. Having addressed their questionnaire for their survey to the chief executive of 300 large organisations, one of Armitage and Atkinson's (1990: 92) conclusions was that: 'Most of the productivity measures that we observed were based on nonfinancial data, such as production rates, yield rates, and defect rates rather than on financial measures such as profits or costs.'

They also learned that managers were reluctant to rely on financial information because a financial number might obscure performance (ibid. 104), and that:

> the outputs from these cost accounting practices are not considered useful in measuring or directing productivity improvement efforts. Rather, their principal value appears to be in providing periodic, aggregate comparisons of the organization's performance with that of its competitors. (ibid. 108–9)

Johnson, Kaplan, and Armitage and Atkinson are not alone in their concern over the way management accountants are perceived as being monolithic in their approach to their place in the greater management information system. However, Johnson (1990: 84) provides a key thought that may be the reason why management accountants are behaving as they are: 'When one asks managers why they spend time managing accounting numbers, they usually answer, "Capital markets (or investors) ultimately judge us by the bottom line".' Thus the charge is that the management accountant is not working for his or her management colleagues at all, but for the shareholders or the industry analyst who works for an influential City stockbroker.

Management's reaction to the management accounting problem

We have seen the problem of the management accountant identified quite clearly, but what are the management accountant's colleagues doing about such inadequacies? Newspapers, magazines and journal articles have, from time to time, given accounts of organisations that have found a way to skirt round the work of their management accountant. Managers the world over have concluded that they need useful and realistic information to help them to manage their situation – but some of them have found that they have had to provide this information by and for themselves. Managers no longer want to work their way through a mountain of period-end printouts and reports provided by the accounting department in order to try to discover their key result factors. In one case, fifteen charts are printed on one side of a piece of A4-size paper, acting as a monthly condensed summary for the management team. When a manager wants to look at the detail behind a chart, he or she of course has access to the relevant data, but if that manager does not need to see the supporting data, he or she does not get it!

Developing further the idea of reporting in a style that is comfortable for non-financial managers, the non-financial manager also feels the need to concentrate on the positive aspects of his or her performance rather than be scolded for having got something wrong. Armitage and Atkinson (1990: 95) report an executive in one of the firms they visited as saying: 'that the key to achieving success is to focus on, and control, the factors that create success rather than focus on profit or cost – the often imperfect and clumsy artefacts of success or failure'. The manager does not find it useful to be told that his or her materials usage variance is adverse or favourable, or that flexible budget profit is £15,500 for the period. He or she does, however, find it useful to know that productivity ratios are improving, or that throughput time is lower this period than it was last period.

People problems

That we are still discussing such matters is disappointing since a lot of research work has been confirming such findings since at least 1953 when Argyris published his important work 'Human problems with budgets'. Argyris found, as have many others since, that workers and managers need to be able to participate in the setting of their own targets and performance indicators. Furthermore, any indicators of performance used to measure a manager's effectiveness must be both understandable by him or her as well as offering little scope for the manager to be able to manipulate his or her results. Finally, any indicator that is used as part of a reward system, must be compatible with that reward system.

Specific examples: non-financial indicators

There are many examples now of how a management accountant can help management colleagues to assess their operations without overwhelming them with data they neither understand nor need. Smith (1990) lists 65 separate non financial indicators (NFIs) in his discussion of the monitoring and control aspects of manufacturing industry. Smith's discussion covers ratios for: inputs; work performance; product; market; employees; and customers.

Each of these areas of a manufacturing business covers several focuses of measurement. For example, in the inputs analysis, Smith suggests an NFI for the quality of purchased components, namely zero defects; and he offers serious industrial injury rate as the appropriate NFI for safety when discussing product analysis. Similarly, for the market section, he proposes the NFI '% new product innovation' when measuring market leadership.

Do financial and non-financial performance measures have to agree?

McNair, Lynch and Cross (1990) take the kind of discussion offered by Smith a stage further and ask: 'Do financial and non-financial performance measures have to agree?' Such an article is obviously aimed at the management accountant who may feel that non-financial indicators are useful, but who also feels that they do not reconcile with the financial aspects of his or her work:

> An operating manager in a computer company implements a just-in-time work cell and witnesses a dramatic improvement in quality, cycle time, and work in process inventory – but gets whacked over the head with a stack of financial reports telling him that he has large volume variances, under absorbed costs, and poor productivity. (ibid. 28)

A symptom of tension, according to McNair *et al.*; and the message is that the accountant relies on accounting results. The accountant concludes that he or she must follow what the accounting figures are saying, rather than the non-financial indicators. McNair *et al.* go on to discuss what may be a particular problem for organisations that have significantly changed the way they manufacture or provide services. An organisation implemented JIT and reported striking successes: work in process down by 85%, throughput time went down from 20 days to under three. However, the management accountant recorded the new system of manufacturing as a failure. How can one view report success and the other failure? Simply, say McNair *et al.*, because the management accountant did not change when manufacturing changed: that is, the old accounting systems were not designed to deal with JIT and they could not. The output from the management accountant's office was, therefore, little short of useless, thus echoing Kaplan's findings of the early 1980s. McNair *et al.* (1990) have four key suggestions to offer all management accountants:

1. Provide the right information at the right time.
2. Switch from scorekeeper to coach.
3. Focus on what counts the most.
4. Know when to play second fiddle.

A reading of McNair's article will be illuminating for both the management accountant and his or her management colleagues.

Selim and Woodward (1992: 155) also provide examples of performance measures: they discuss non-financial measures in use in Thames Water and British Coal. For example, for Thames Water:

> *Water supply*
> Percentage of supplies which are:
> metered potable
> metered non-potable
> unmetered
> percentage of normal population on supply

For British Coal:

> Productivity (tonnes)
> coalface output per manshift
> overall output per manshift
> output per man year

Willcocks and Harrow also say the accounting figures used in computing some of these ratios are all dependent on the accounting concepts used in the preparation of these statements, with their associated limitations (ibid. 158). Thus, even when non-financial measures are used, they may depend upon the accounting system to provide the basic data on which they are based; and this is not always a certain way of providing good information!

The management accountant's education to blame?

Jones, Currie and Dugdale (1994) give us a comprehensive summary of the many thoughts that have been expressed on the differences between accounting and manufacturing performances in Britain and Japan. Among the more relevant aspects of their article are the following observations:

> there is evidence that industrial accountants in Britain have less technological awareness than their counterparts elsewhere . . .
>
> Accountants are either remote from production, or are restricted in their participation in planning teams by their narrowly specialized knowledge and skills. (ibid. 125)

To an engineer or other technical manager trying to justify an investment, or his or her periodic performance, there must be nothing more frustrating than to be faced with a management accountant who really does not appreciate what is happening in the warehouse, on the shop floor, or in the laboratory. Are we dealing with the truth, however, when we point the finger at undereducated management accountants? Is it really the case that management accountants do not know one end of a circlip from another? Only management accountants and their colleagues will really be aware of this.

However, if we look at some of the ways that British manufacturing industry is responding to the challenge of the global market, it might give management accountants food for thought. Farish (1994) reports on developments within the Rover Group and managerial education. Farish tells us about Rover's Continuing Professional Development (CPD) programme. In this comprehensive programme aimed at improving the quality of Rover's people, engineers are learning about such areas as corporate management, finance, quality, statistics, and information technology. Rover believes improving the quality of its people is crucial to its overall business success. All of this, says Farish, costs Rover around £35 million per year in direct charges and time lost from immediate productive work, but Rover feels it is worth the expense.

Baxter (1994) discusses concurrent engineering in the context of a specialist engineering group. Concurrent engineering means using teamwork to get new and better products to the market more rapidly. Thus a full-time manager will use colleagues from different disciplines to ensure that the objectives of the organisation are met, and that the right product is developed at the right time. Continuing professional development and concurrent engineering are solutions developed by engineering organisations to their problems. Such organisations are aware that they cannot succeed without working on aspects of business life other than their own. The engineer is aware that he or she needs financial and legal knowledge, that information technology experts have a lot to offer, and that only by co-operating with colleagues will he or she fulfil his or her own ambitions.

What is the management accountant doing in similar circumstances? What does the management accountant do when faced with a new situation or a problem? Picking at random a copy of CIMA's monthly *Management Accounting* journal and looking at the Mastercourses it runs regularly, the list of courses for October 1993 includes the following topics:

- Financial awareness for personal assistants.
- Treasury management.
- Business process management.
- Activity-based budgeting.
- The influential accountant.
- Management accounting in Germany.
- Financial reporting in France.
- Project management.
- Improving overhead cost effectiveness.

Without having attended any of these courses, we might be forgiven if we misrepresent some aspect of the contents of them. However, it does not appear from this list that engineering, technology, or scientific fundamentals are considered important in the continuing education of the management accountant.

Furthermore, looking through the job vacancies in the same issue of *Management Accounting* reveals the kind of environments that management accountants work in: for example, software house; engineering company; oil and gas; manufacturer and distributor; head office; retail; management consultancy; and business analysis. By the nature of the work the management accountant is undertaking he or she needs skills outside finance and accounting. The syllabuses of the major, and minor, accounting institutes do include cost accounting and management accounting, financial accounting, information technology, operations research and so on, but is this enough? By coincidence, the letters page of the October 1993 edition of *Management Accounting* contains three letters arguing about the content and style of the journal. The three correspondents were all critical of the content and appeal of the magazine and all called for additional material to be included in it. Not one of them called for more articles concerning engineering, technology . . .

CIMA, it is clear, also insist that all its members complete a comprehensive training programme before they are admitted to associate membership. Is that enough? Jones *et al.* tell us that the accountant does not feature too largely in the work of Japanese factory management – the engineer rules the roost. And we all know of the success of Japanese industry and commerce in recent years!

A solution to this debate

Is there a solution to this debate? Is it possible that the next essay written on this subject will be able to report a significant improvement in this situation? It is difficult to assess what the answer to such a question will be, of course, but the starting point must be to begin with another question: Why is there a gap between what is provided and what is needed? This should not take us into an infinite loop of questioning and soul searching, but into an area where a possible answer might lie. Imagine that one day I decide to invest £50,000 in a business: I decide that I want to make my fortune in order to be able to retire early, and then spend the remainder of my days lazing in a tax haven! On the evidence we have seen and discussed, the management accountant would buy something, anything, set up shop and *hope* to make some money out of it. The astute business person would research his or her market. He or she would take great care in finding out what the market is interested in – new products that are ready for exploitation, a gap in a market – and what customers' needs are, and he or she would then work towards satisfying those needs. The management accountant seems to be guilty of saying, 'I have these tools at my disposal; and with these tools I can make this product. This is the product I will supply you with, take it or leave it'. In response, more and more non-financial managers are deciding to take the latter option and leave it. The simple remedy is for the management accountant to talk to colleagues and find out what they need from him or her. Once he or she knows what they need, the management accountant either uses his or her skills to provide the information needed, or sets about learning those skills in order to satisfy his colleagues. If he or she cannot enhance those personal skills, he or she could hire a consultant with the relevant skills to set up the necessary systems.

The future of management accounting

Whilst several aspects of this chapter have been critical of management accounting and management accountants, we will finish on a hopeful and optimistic note. The developments that have taken place in industry and commerce in terms of both technological and systems developments over the last twenty years have often had far-reaching consequences for everyone concerned with them. We have discussed the findings of some researchers who have concluded that the management accountant is sometimes slow to update his or her systems and methods of reporting. We have also discussed some of the ways in which the management accountant's colleagues would like to be monitored: that is, in non-financial rather than financial terms. Alongside the changes in engineering technology, there have been changes in accounting systems technology. We now talk quite freely about life-cycle costing, activity-based costing, backflush costing and so forth. We have computer-based management accounting software; the financial accountant is directly concerned with JIT, MRPI and MRPII by way of EDI. The management accountant and the financial accountant can share computer-based information systems so that, by using integrated accounting systems, they can both can extract data and information for their own purposes.

The cost of computerised accounting and allied systems, and their power, is such that even small and medium-sized businesses can often afford to own and operate a computer-based accounting system. On the other hand, even though they are affordable, computer-based systems can still be relatively difficult to learn. Hence some organisations will rely on buying in computer-based expertise. The opportunities for sophistication in the application of accounting knowledge and expertise have never been as great as they are today, and such opportunities are increasing almost daily. Furthermore the research base on which modern management accounting is based is also being expanded rapidly. In addition to the work that is carried on in universities and other seats of further and higher learning, areas of the world are being opened up to the extent that we can all share in each other's experiences.

Moreover there are thousands of articles published each year on myriad management accounting and related topics; and there are hundreds of conferences held worldwide each year that discuss those same topics. The work contained in such articles and conferences has but two destinations: management accounting practice, and the bookshelf. If we were to take a look at the journals and textbooks written over the last eighty or ninety years, we would see the evidence on which this final assertion has been made. Some research never really sees the light of day, while other research has immediate practical appeal and is implemented quickly.

The clear message for management accounting is that it offers a great deal. The true management accountant knows his or her way around the shop floor. He or she needs to know and understand the processes taking place in factory, office or shop. Unless the management accountant can appreciate what the production manager, the purchaser, the chemist, and others are doing and trying to achieve, he or she will not succeed in his or her mission, which is, remember:

> The provision of information required by management for such purposes as:
>
> 1 formulation of policies,
> 2 planning and controlling the activities of the enterprise,
> 3 decision taking on alternative courses of action,
> 4 disclosure to those external to the entity (shareholders and others),
> 5 disclosure to employees,
> 6 safeguarding assets (CIMA 1991)

Thus the management accountant's proactive stance is, according to CIMA's definition, the provision of information. In other words, the definition tells the management accountant that he or she has to go and do something useful and positive. The management accountant's task is to *provide information*, not simply just to help or work with management.

The management accountant who has been tied to his or her desk, and who genuinely does not know one end of a circlip from another, needs serious attention. Imagine going to a doctor suspecting that you have high blood pressure, and he says to you: 'I don't know a great deal about blood pressure problems, but I know a fair amount about stomach disorder, so I'll treat you for that.' What would *you* do?

As a starting point, perhaps, and to help this debate on its way, the following short introduction to world-class manufacturing illustrates some of the issues that the modern management accountant must absorb.

World-class manufacturing

By world-class manufacturing organisations, we mean organisations which have appreciated that in order to compete both at home and overseas, they it must pay attention to four specific aspects listed by Turney (1992: 25). Customers:

1. are interested in quality;
2. desire good service;
3. want flexibility; and
4. covet value.

Following on from Turney's list, world-class manufacturers build in quality, rather than detect it and try to correct for poor quality once it has occurred. In a world-class manufacturing organisation, the quality controllers are now stationed with suppliers, in most senses, rather than at the end of the production line. The world-class manufacturer carries out benchmarking for some if not all of its operations to ensure that it is at least as good as the other world-class manufacturers in its industry. Benchmarking is the process whereby an organisation looks for the best organisation in the field in which it is operating. Once the best has been found, a detailed analysis is carried out of how it does what it does. The analysis undertaken then provides the data on which the world-class manufacturer bases his or her operating standards. The world-class manufacturer uses JIT techniques, and involves its employees in decision making at all levels of operation. As Turney says, because of the involvement of employees within world-class manufacturing organisations, management structures tend to be flat, eliminating much bureaucracy – it doesn't seem to eliminate huge salary disparities, however! Quite simply, the world-class manufacturer seeks to work alongside the best and aims to be the best in its chosen field. With the globalisation of the market place that we discussed earlier, the larger organisations throughout the world are all now working within the world-class manufacturer framework.

The concept of the world-class manufacturer has had a significant impact on the way that industries throughout the world are operating. The management accountant has his or her part to play in the development of the world-class manufacturer since management colleagues are relying on him or her more than ever to provide them with the information they need to implement what is essentially a fundamental new way of arranging and operating their organisation.

SUMMARY

Every day it seems, a new book comes off the presses that is relevant to the continuing debate on today's management accountant and his or her management colleagues. Once a chapter such as this has been written it very quickly needs updating. However, the debate presented above has attempted to summarise and address several issues that have proven resistant to treatment over an extended period. There will be management accountants for whom this chapter highlights a series of problems from which they suffer. There are management accountants who have met these problems, considered them and then overcome them. Academic accountants often go to conferences that practising accountants and consultants also attend and learn that they are not the only ones who have read all the books and journal articles. The academic is not necessarily the know-all that practitioners may sometimes think he or she would like to be. However, academics do tend to make their livelihood from doing a fair amount of reading and thinking. The debate in this chapter, therefore, is aimed at the management accounting profession in general, and even if it is felt to be missing the point in some organisation, it is right on target in others. Furthermore accountants ostensibly working as management accountants in countries that are classed as developing are often guilty of heinous management accounting practices – either by default or by design. A reading of this book is essential for people such as them.

If nothing else, this chapter aims to send out the message that management accounting best practice does not just leap into an organisation, but has to be brought in, carefully and in a considered way. Similarly, this entire book is a plea not only for aspiring and practising management accountants to buy it, but also for them to consider carefully at least some of what it has to say.

RECOMMENDED READING

In terms of modern management accounting, Berliner and Brimson (1988) is already old, but one of the first of its kind. Also not new, but insightful, is Johnson (1990). Smith (1990) is recommended for the second time. Finally, Yoshikawa *et al.* (1993) is not lengthy, easy to read, and definitely worth the effort.

REFERENCES

Addonzio, M. L. (1991), 'Chrysler Corporation: JIT and EDI (A)', Case No. 9–191–146 (Harvard Business School).

Armitage, H. M. and Atkinson, A. A. (1990), 'The choice of productivity measures in organizations', in Kaplan (1990), op. cit.

Baxter, A. (1994), 'Teamwork discovers fresh territory', *Financial Times Engineering Review* (25 March), 14.

Berliner, C. and Brimson, J. A. (1988), *Cost Management for Today's Advanced Manufacturing: The CAM-I conceptual design* (Harvard Business School Press).

CIMA (1991), *Management Accounting Official Terminology* (Chartered Institute of Management Accounting).

Cushing, B. E. and Romney, M. B. (1990), *Accounting Information Systems*, 5th edn, World Student Series (Addison-Wesley).

Drury, J. C. (1992), *Management and Cost Accounting*, 3rd edn (Chapman & Hall).

Farish, M. (1994) 'Back to the school desk with Rover', *Financial Times Engineering Review* (25 March), 7.

Johnson, H. T. (1990), 'Performance measurement for competitive excellence' in Kaplan (1990), op. cit.

Jones, T. C., Currie, W. L. and Dugdale, D. (1994), 'Accounting and technology in Britain and Japan: learning from field research', *Management Accounting Research* vol. 4 (2), pp. 109–37.

Kaplan, R. S. (ed.) (1990), *Measures for Manufacturing Excellence* (Harvard Business School Press).

Karmarkar, U.S., Lederer, P. J. and Zimmerman, J. L., 'Choosing manufacturing production control and cost accounting systems', in Kaplan (1990) op. cit.

McNair, C. J., Lyne, R. L. and Cross, K. F. (1990), 'Do financial and nonfinancial performance measures have to agree?', *Management Accounting* (NAA) (November), 28–31, 34–6.

Selim, G. M. and Woodward, S. A. (1992), 'The manager monitored', in L. Willcocks and J. Harrow (eds), *Rediscovering Public Services Management* (McGraw-Hill), 141–69.

Smith, M. (1989), 'Towards decision useful management accounting', *Management Accounting* (CIMA) (September), 70–1, 73.

Smith, M. (1990), 'The rise and rise of the NFI', *Management Accounting* (CIMA) (May), 24–6.

Turney, P. B. B. (1992), *Common Cents: The ABC performance breakthrough* (Cost Technology).

Yoshikawa, T., Innes, J., Mitchell, F. and Tanaka, M. (1993), *Contemporary Cost Management* (Chapman & Hall).

Solutions to selected practice questions

Chapter 1

1. Mr and Mrs Smith probably typify many business organisations across the world. Many entrepreneurs start their life in business in a small way and then, as they grow, they run out of expertise to run their business effectively. Fortunately, the Smiths have realised that they need a management accountant to help them develop further and properly. The type of help the management accountant can give is summarised by the CIMA definition of management accounting that we discussed in the body of the chapter. The rest of the answer to this question is taking that definition as its reference point, although not in too literal a way.

Management accounting helps organisations with policy formulation by focusing on a whole variety of costs and indicators. When an accounting report is produced, a lot of useful information is generated that helps managers and owners appreciate the direction that the organisation might be going in. Policy formulation is a precursor to planning in organisations. Management accounting helps here by preparing forecasts and budgets for all main areas of the organisation, including a cash budget.

Once plans are laid the Smiths would have a basis for control. The management accountant has helped them to appreciate their aims and objectives, as set out in their policy and planning schedules. Now the Smiths know whether they have matched those aims and objectives. If the aims and objectives are not matched, the Smiths can take appropriate action.

Textbooks usually present the control period as if it were always a month; and for many items such as some sales and cost items, a monthly reporting routine will probably still be appropriate. However, in most cases we should say that the mechanism for control is the control period. In reality the control period varies with the production or output cycle. In the case of an engineering organisation like the Smiths', the output cycle could be one day for a small job, and six months for a large job. Therefore, for some aspects of the business, a monthly reporting procedure will not be relevant. The control cycle will reflect the variability of the nature of the business. The management accountant can also provide special reports as seems necessary as a result of any special situations that arise. In order to provide the routine aspects of his or her services, the management accountant will formalise his recording and reporting systems for the Smiths. The outputs of the management accounting function will include:

(a) Detailed production/departmental statements: revenues, costs, and profit. These statements would include variances from budget, financial and non-financial indicators, and product costs per unit.
(b) Stock valuation statements/schedules.

(c) Budgets, especially the cash budget.

(d) Special, *ad hoc*, exercises including costs analysed by product, over time, and so on.

7.

(a) (i) The schedules given in the question have to be redrafted as per the requirements of the question. The schedule should also be redrafted to help with its readability; at the moment it is far too long to be easily readable. and several of the costs are out of place, because we have materials costs mixed up with transport costs and rates costs.

Three new schedules have been prepared, in an attempt to overcome the problems just identified:

(1) Summary profit statement: this statement is a summary of the net effects of schedules 1 and 2.

(2) Sales schedule: showing sales data.

(3) Expenses data: showing expenses data classified by major item of expense.

The first schedule, the **profit summary**, is relatively straightforward. This schedule should be the first to be presented because it is the executive summary schedule. It does not contain the percentages found in the other schedules. If the percentages were left in this schedule it would be too cluttered: even though it is only a small schedule.

The schedule does include the variances called for by the question, however.

Austins Bakery Ltd: Profit summary
for the month of October

	Actual	Budget	Variances
	£	£	£
Total sales	26,551	30,760	(4,209)
Less: Total costs			
Total ingredients	13,073	14,920	1,847
Total wages	5,600	7,000	1,400
Total expenses	4,518	5,160	642
Net Profit	3,360	3,680	(£320)

The **sales schedule** includes two additional features, over and above the original schedule given in the question:

(1) the variance column has been added as required; and

(2) a column showing each item of sales as a percentage of total sales has also been added, for further enlightenment.

Otherwise, these data are exactly as they were in the question.

Austins Bakery Ltd: Sales report
for the month of October

	Actual		Budget		Variances	
	£	%	£	%	£	%
Bread	9,500	35.78	11,875	38.61	−2,375	−56.43
Cakes	11,475	43.22	14,000	45.51	−2,525	−59.99
Pies:						
meat	3,500	13.18	3,375	10.97	125	2.97
fruit	1,950	7.34	1,450	4.71	500	11.88
Sweets	126	0.47	60	0.20	66	1.57
Total sales	26,551	100.00	30,760	100.00	−4,209	100.00

The following version of the cost schedule is only one of many possible variations. What this schedule does is to take the costs and show them under the headings of the three elements of costs: materials, wages and expenses.

Three separate schedules have been prepared: one for ingredients, one for wages, and one for expenses.

The important point to bear in mind here is how much more pleasing the finished result is to the reader. If the reader of these schedules feels comfortable with the presentation, then the redesigned schedule will have served its purpose. If not, then modify the layout even further.

As with the sales schedule, the cost schedule includes the variance and percentage columns. The percentages this time represent each cost as a percentage of total costs.

One of the reasons why the initial schedule is difficult to read and understand in the first instance is that it is far too long. We have used the device of breaking up the schedule further by inserting lines every five items or so. Generally speaking, this device should be used when the number of items in a table or schedule exceeds, say, eight or nine. We have chosen to split the schedule up every five lines or so, but we could have done so every four lines, or every six lines: there is no magic formula here, except that its effect must be easy on the eye.

Notice, also, just to demonstrate the differences in presentation that are possible, this schedule has negative values with a ' – ' sign in front of it: in the sales schedule, a negative value had '()' round it. For consistency, we should choose one of these conventions to work with, and use it permanently.

As far as the cost items themselves are concerned, they are presented in order of magnitude of cost: the largest cost item at the top of the list, the lowest cost item at the bottom of the list. The disadvantage here is that similar cost items (for example, margarine/butter and other shortening) are split apart from each other. Splitting similar cost items may mean that comparisons become difficult. An alternative presentation to overcome this problem might be considered worthwhile. The alternative presentations include:

- arranging the cost items alphabetically; and
- arranging the cost items in order of their account number in the relevant ledger (these account numbers are not given here).

Note, however, that whatever alternative form of layout we finally choose, we need to maintain that layout since these reports are presented month by month. Changes cannot just be made for the sake of it, otherwise everyone will end up confused.

Austins Bakery Ltd: Ingredients cost report
for the month of October

	Actual		Budget		Variances	
	£	%	£	%	£	%
Ingredients						
plain white flour	2,675	7.5	3,300	8.0	625	11.2
wholemeal flour	1,900	5.3	2,200	5.3	300	5.4
self-raising flour	1,350	3.8	1,700	4.1	350	6.3
caster sugar	3,500	9.8	3,500	8.5	0	0.0
icing sugar	950	2.7	950	2.3	0	0.0
margarine/ butter	865	2.4	1,080	2.6	215	3.9

eggs	500	1.4	625	1.5	125	2.2
meat	400	1.1	500	1.2	100	1.8
dried fruit	365	1.0	465	1.1	100	1.8
other shortening	293	0.8	265	0.6	−28	−0.5
jams	100	0.3	125	0.3	25	0.4
yeast	75	0.2	95	0.2	20	0.4
baking cases	70	0.2	80	0.2	10	0.2
spices	25	0.1	30	0.1	5	0.1
salt	5	0.0	5	0.0	0	0.0
Total ingredients	13,073	36.8	14,920	36.3	1,847	33.2

Even though the wages data are given in total only, a separate statement is prepared.

Austins Bakery Ltd: Wages cost report
for the month of October

	Actual		Budget		Variances	
	£	%	£	%	£	%
Total wages	5,600	15.7	7,000	17.0	1,400	25.2

Austins Bakery Ltd: Expenses cost report
for the month of October

	Actual		Budget		Variances	
	£	%	£	%	£	%
electricity	850	2.4	1,060	2.6	210	3.8
telephone	600	1.7	550	1.3	−50	−0.9
repairs and maintenance	512	1.4	640	1.6	128	2.3
rates	481	1.4	600	1.5	119	2.1
water	300	0.8	375	0.9	75	1.3
plant depreciation	300	0.8	300	0.7	0	0.0
cleaning materials	255	0.7	320	0.8	65	1.2
plastic bags	150	0.4	90	0.2	−60	−1.1
vehicle depreciation	150	0.4	150	0.4	0	0.0
overalls cleaning	125	0.4	100	0.2	−25	−0.4
paper bags	95	0.3	100	0.2	5	0.1
overalls replacement	50	0.1	60	0.1	10	0.2
transport	650	1.8	815	2.0	165	3.0
Total expenses	4,518	12.7	5,160	12.5	642	11.5
Total costs	£35,564		£41,125		£5,561	

(a) (ii) There is a lot of data generated by this question as far as variances are concerned. It would be wise to start at the top of the organisation, with the summary profit statement, and work our way down. For reasons of brevity, we will look at a selection of variances only.

The first thing we should do is to eliminate those variances that are causing no problems at all; we are going to use management by exception (MBE). Management by exception says, if something is not exceptional, leave it alone. If it ain't broke, don't fix it, as the Americans say. We have, first of all, to decide on what is exceptional, therefore. By exceptional, we mean that a variance is greater than a predetermined margin more or less than our target. For example, if we find (by statistical analysis, or some other scientific means) that our margin is ±10%, we say that if a variance is in the region +10% to −10%, it is not exceptional, and that variance does not need investigation, or action. So, we will only look at variances outside that acceptable region.

All variances except the net profit variance are significant: they are outside the range ±10%. The net profit variance is −8.70% (the variance of −£320 as a percentage of the budgeted net profit of £3,680, that is.)

The sales variance is, overall, −13.68%. This means that the actual sales were 13.68% less than the budgeted sales. Since this is a significant variance, we need to investigate it. How do we do this? The answer is, we now go to the sales schedule and look at each item of sales, determine whether the individual sales variances are significant, and investigate the ones that are:

Sales item	Variance as % of budget
Bread	−20.00
Cakes	−18.04
Pies	
meat	3.70
fruit	34.48
Sweets	110.00

All variances are significant except meat pies: meat pies, at a variance that is only 3.70% away from budgeted sales, falls within the acceptable range of variation, and we need not look into their performance further.

So, we need to investigate all other sales items: adverse as well as favourable. We have a problem of lack of data now. However, the management of Austins Bakery Ltd would have the knowledge and expertise to look into the sales that are causing the problems. They would be looking at such items as sales prices; quality of ingredients; quality of output; and presentation in the shop. No stone should be left unturned in their attempt to discover why the relatively large variance occurred. It could be that the budget was wrong, of course!

Sweets has a variation of 110%, but should not be bothered with. After all, sales of sweets, with only £126 out of £26,551 total sales, is not that important. In fact, as we say in part 'b' of the answer to this question, the sweets sales counter should be closed. Similarly, the variance on spices is 16.67% away from budget, yet the total spices budget is only £30. With a total expenses budget of £27,080, £30 is not that important. In summary, every variance is looked into provided it is worthwhile. Use MBE, and discretion, to make sure we don't waste management's time (and our own) on trivial items.

You should find it useful to carry out some of the variance analysis for yourselves before moving on to the next chapter.

(b) The accountant would look at this business and contemplate setting up separate profit centres, if that is feasible. If the duties of bread making can be successfully separated from cake and pie making, then all sales and costs can be successfully properly identified in this way and separate profit statements prepared. Thus the bread department manager can be assessed on his performance, as can the cake department manager and the pie department manager. A thorough investigation would confirm whether this is a good idea.

Why bother with sweets? It is a tiny addition to the organisation, and unless there are very good reasons for continuing with it, get rid of it.

It would be useful to everyone if the wages information could be split between the different baking functions, the administration, and the sales assistants. This would provide much more useful managerial information.

Other data must be able to be identified and added on to these statements. For example, data relating to units of output and sales; man hours to make the bread, cakes, and pies; and machine hours – all would be useful indicators of efficiency.

Chapter 2

4. The Craft Shop Statement of cost of goods manufactured and income for the period ended . . .

	£	£	£	£
Direct materials:				
Opening stock of timber		1,200		
plus: Purchases		24,500		
		25,700		
less: Closing stock of timber		800		24,900
Direct labour			9,000	9,000
Prime cost				33,900
Indirect costs:				
Indirect materials				
opening stock of glue	250			
plus: purchases	700	950		
less: closing stock				
of glue	300	650		
Rent (60% × £12,000)		7,200		
Fringe benefits of				
Production workers		4,000		
Electricity and water				
(60% × £4,600)		2,760	14,610	14,610
Conversion costs			23,610	
Cost of goods manufactured				£48,510
Sales				175,000
Cost of goods sold:				
Opening stock of finished goods				12,000
plus: Cost of goods manufactured				48,510
				60,510
less: Closing stock of finished goods				8,000

Cost of goods sold				52,510
Gross profit				122,490
Selling and administration costs:				
Office supplies				
opening stocks	75			
plus: purchases	210	285		
	90	195		
less: closing		4,800		
rent (40% × £12,000)				
electricity and water				
(40% × £4,600)		1,840		
advertising expenses		3,350		
selling and distribution wages		12,000	22,185	
Net profit				£100,305

Note that the title 'Indirect costs' means exactly the same as factory overheads, but since it is the one given by the question we should stick with it.

5. Ray Charles Production Company Statement of cost of goods manufactured and income for the period ended . . .

Direct materials:	£	£	£	£
Opening stock of materials			17,000	
plus: Purchases			70,000	
			87,000	
less: Closing stock			15,000	72,000
Direct labour			104,000	104,000
Prime cost				176,000
Indirect costs:				
Manufacturing supplies:				
Opening stock	1,500			
plus: Purchases	3,500	5,000		
less: closing stock	3,000	2,000		
Production expenses:				
Fringe benefits		4,000		
Production supervisor's salaries		7,200		
Depreciation on plant		14,000		
Plant maintenance		10,000		
Plant water and electricity		35,000		
Production equipment rent		6,000		
			78,200	78,200
Conversion costs			182,200	

Total manufacturing cost				254,200
Work in progress adjustment:				
Opening stock			51,000	
less: Closing stock			40,000	11,000
Cost of goods manufactured				265,200
Sales				425,700
Cost of goods sold:				
Opening stock of finished goods				35,000
Plus: Cost of goods manufactured				265,200
				300,200
less: Closing stock of finished goods				27,100
Cost of goods sold				273,100
Gross profit				152,600
Administration expenses:				
Office supplies:				
Opening stocks	600			
plus: Purchases	1,200	1,800		
less: Closing		1,000	800	
Administration salaries			12,000	
Depreciation of office equipment			20,000	
Office water and electricity			8,000	
Office maintenance			2,000	
Office equipment and rent			1,300	
			44,100	
Selling expenses:				
Sales commissions		50,000		
Advertising costs		11,000		
Depreciation on salespeople's cars		7,000		
Sales office equipment rent and maintenance		2,600	70,600	
Finance expenses:				
Interest on overdraft		2,000		
Interest on mortgage		6,000	8,000	122,700
Net profit				£29,900

Chapter 3

2. The graph showing variable costs per unit should look like Figure Q3.1, which represents a perfectly variable cost. Irrespective of how many units are produced, the variable cost per unit remains constant.

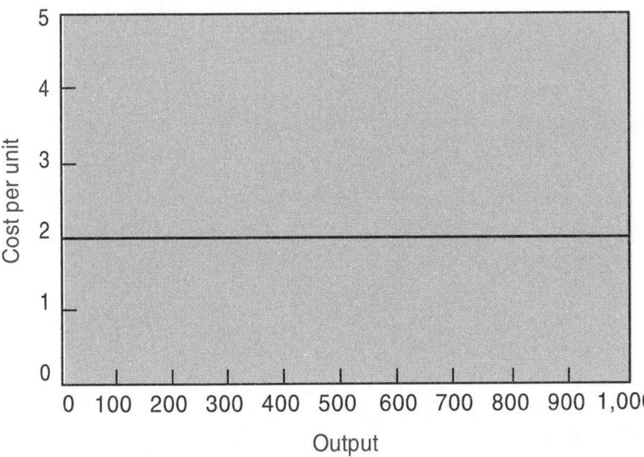

FIGURE Q3.1 *Variable costs per unit*

The graph showing the fixed costs per unit should look like Figure Q3.2.

In Figure Q3.2 we have a perfectly fixed cost. In total, fixed costs remain unchanged no matter how many units are made. On a unit basis, however, the more units made, the lower the fixed cost per unit becomes. It is this behaviour that gives rise to the assertion that the more we make, the cheaper our products become.

Organisations that have relatively high fixed costs should be very careful about their output levels, compared with organisations that have relatively low fixed costs. The reason for the need for such care is that fixed costs tend to be strategic in nature, as we have seen. Strategic costs are therefore likely to be committed and hence cannot be reduced in the short term. An organisation with high total fixed costs therefore needs large output levels to reduce fixed costs per unit to as low a level as possible.

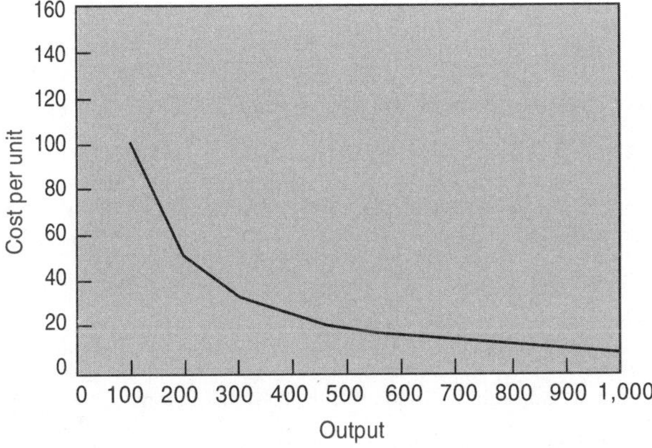

FIGURE Q3.2 *Fixed costs per unit*

6. Business Assistance Bureau income statement for the word processing pool for the period ended . . .

	£	£	£
Income			50,000
Variable costs:			
Paper		1,000	
Printer ribbons		100	
Floppy discs		25	
Binders/covers (250 × £4)		1,000	
Wages (£1 × 2,500 pages)		2,500	
Photocopying (22,500 × £0.05)		1,125	
Electricity (500 × £0.50)		250	
		6,000	
Fixed costs:			
Electricity	100		
Photocopying	400		
Supervision	1,000		
Depreciation:			
Computer hardware	1,500		
Software	500		
Furniture and fittings	2,000	5,500	11,500
Word processing profit			£38,500

Workings to accompany the statement

The total number of jobs completed is 250. This is derived from the information that a total of 25,000 sheets of paper were used and that every job needs 100 pieces of paper. The 100 pieces of paper per job figure is derived from each job needing 90 pieces for photocopying and 10 pieces for word processing. Therefore, total number of jobs:

$$= \frac{25{,}000 \text{ pieces of paper used altogether}}{100 \text{ pieces of paper per job}}$$

= 250 jobs

The variable costs of photocopying must be £1,125, based on the workings we have just done:

£0.05 × (25,000 ÷ (100 × 90)) = £1,125

Similarly, if 22,500 pieces of paper were used for photocopying, then 25,000 − 22,500 = 2,500 pieces must have been used for the word processing part of the job.

Variable costs

Paper: the total cost of paper is £1,000, made up of 500 reams of paper used at a cost of £2 per ream.

Printer ribbons: 20 printer ribbons are used at a cost of £5 per ribbon: thus, the total ribbons cost is £100.

Floppy discs: since 100 floppy discs are used at a cost of £0.25 per disc, the total cost for floppy discs must be £25.

Cost of binders/covers: this amounts to £1,000, made up of 250 covers at a cost of £4 each.

Wages: wages amount to a total of £2,500: this is 2,500 pages processed at a cost of £1 per page.

Photocopying expenses: these amount to £1,125, being the cost of 22,500 copies at a cost of £0.05 per copy.

Electricity costs: a total cost of £250 since the costs are based on the usage of 500 reams of paper: the cost per ream, we are told in the question is £0.50.

Fixed costs

These are as stated in the income statement.

Chapter 4

2. This question is split into cases: one and two, so that is how we should present our solutions. However, if we wanted to present our solutions in a tabular format, there is no reason why we should not do that. That is not the format that will be followed here, since we need to see some of the workings in detail.

The formulæ that we will be using to answer this question are:

Reorder level

maximum consumption × maximum reorder period

Minimum stock level

reorder level - (normal consumption × normal reorder period)

Maximum stock level

reorder level - (minimum consumption × minimum reorder period) + reorder quantity

Average stock

$$\frac{\text{minimum stock level} + \text{maximum stock level}}{2}$$

or

$$\text{minimum stock level} + \frac{\text{reorder quantity}}{2}$$

Case 1

(a) Reorder level:

= 4,200 units × 14 weeks = 58,800 units

(b) Minimum stock level:

= 58,800 units – (3,200 units × 12 weeks) = 20,400 units

(c) Maximum stock level:

= 58,800 units – (2,200 units × 10 weeks) + 35,000 units

= 71,800 units

(d) Average stock level:

$$\frac{20{,}400 + 71{,}800}{2}$$

$= 46{,}100$ units

or

$$20{,}400 + \frac{35{,}000}{2}$$

$= 37{,}900$ units

Case 2

(a) i) Reorder level:

$= 1{,}500 \text{ units} \times 4 \text{ weeks} = 6{,}000$ units

(b) ii) Minimum stock level:

$= 6{,}000 \text{ units} - (1{,}200 \text{ units} \times 3 \text{ weeks}) = 2{,}400$ units

(c) iii) Maximum stock level:

$= 6{,}000 \text{ units} - (800 \text{ units} \times 2 \text{ weeks}) + 6{,}000$ units

$= 10{,}400$ units

(d) iv) Average stock level:

$$\frac{2{,}400 + 10{,}400}{2} = 6{,}400 \text{ units}$$

or

$$2{,}400 + \frac{6{,}000}{2}$$

$= 5{,}400$ units

6.

(a) It is the FIFO method of stock valuation that corresponds to the physical movement of stocks. We discussed in the chapter the example of the boxes of biscuits found in a supermarket: the oldest biscuits must be sold first, before any new boxes are opened. This is the way that any reasonable store keeper would operate, and physically, he would be operating the FIFO method of stock movement, irrespective of the stores valuation method in use.

(b) The best way to answer a question such as this one, especially if the answers don't immediately suggest themselves, is to construct a small simple example and work from there. The following example should help with the understanding of the answers to the seven parts of the question.

The following stores ledger cards are based on the FIFO and LIFO methods of stock valuation, the details on which they are based can be deduced from the cards themselves. The example also simulates a period of inflation since the cost prices of the material being received is increasing with each receipt. We can assume that the events shown in the stores ledger card takes place over a two-week period.

FIFO

Receipts Quantity	Each	Amount	Quantity	Issues Each	Amount	Quantity	Balance Each	Amount
						100	1.0	100
100	1.1	110				100	1.0	100
						100	1.1	110
			100	1.0	100	100	1.1	110
100	1.2	120				100	1.1	110
						100	1.2	120
			100	1.1	110	100	1.2	120
		230			210			

LIFO

Receipts Quantity	Each	Amount	Issues Quantity	Each	Amount	Quantity	Balance Each	Amount
						100	1.0	100
100	1.1	110				100	1.1	110
						100	1.0	100
			100	1.1	110	100	1.0	100
100	1.2	120				100	1.2	120
						100	1.0	100
			100	1.2	120	100	1.0	100
		230			230			

The formula for calculating the stock turnover ratio is:

$$\frac{\text{average stock}}{\text{average weekly cost of sales}}$$

where the average stock can be taken in this example to be the average of the opening and the closing stock balances.

We can now determine whether it is the FIFO or the LIFO method that overstates stock turnover in a period of inflation:

FIFO

$$\frac{0.5(100 + 120)}{210 \div 2}$$

$$= \frac{110}{105}$$

= 1.048 weeks

LIFO

$$\frac{0.5(100 + 100)}{230 \div 2}$$

$= \frac{100}{115}$

= 0.870 weeks

Since these methods behave consistently, we can safely conclude that it is the FIFO method that overstates stock turnover in a period of inflation.

(c) It is the LIFO method that matches current costs with current revenues. It does this by charging into the costs the latest prices that the organisation has paid.

(d) We can use the example we generated in answering part (b) of this question to help us sort out the question of which of the methods depresses profits in a period of inflation.

Assume that the sales revenues are a total of £400, the trading account will be:

	FIFO	LIFO
Sales	400	400
Cost of sales	210	230
Gross profit	190	170

Check where all of these figures are coming from.

Again, we can safely conclude that it is the LIFO method that generally depresses profits in periods of inflation, since the methods behave consistently over time.

(e) It is the FIFO method that values stocks approximately at replacement cost. It does this because all issues from stock are made at the oldest possible price. Therefore, any stock remaining in the business is valued at a later price. This will be nearer the replacement value than would be the case with LIFO, since LIFO issues out at the latest price, and keeps stocks valued at the oldest possible price.

(f) As we have just agreed with the solution to part (e), since LIFO is issuing materials at the latest available cost, it must be the LIFO method that matches old costs with new prices.

(g) We can construct an example similar to the one we constructed for part (b) of this question to check on the behaviour of the two methods of stock valuation under deflationary influences.

FIFO

Receipts Quantity	Each	Amount	Issues Quantity	Each	Amount	Balance Quantity	Each	Amount
						100	1.2	120
100	1.1	110				100	1.2	120
						100	1.1	110
			100	1.2	120	100	1.1	110
100	1.0	100				100	1.1	110
						100	1.0	100
			100	1.1	110	100	1.0	100
		210			230			

LIFO

Receipts Quantity	Each	Amount	Issues Quantity	Each	Amount	Balance Quantity	Each	Amount
						100	1.2	120
100	1.1	110				100	1.1	110
						100	1.2	120
			100	1.1	110	100	1.2	120
100	1.0	100				100	1.0	100
						100	1.0	120
			100	1.0	100	100	1.2	120
		210			210			

To finish the example, we can assume the same level of sales as we did in part (b) of this question (£400 for the period) and then determine the levels of profit thrown up by the situation we have here.

Trading Account . . .

	FIFO	LIFO
Sales	400	400
Cost of sales	230	210
Gross profit	170	190

Thus we can see that the FIFO method gives us lower profits in a period of deflation.

Chapter 5

3. The analysis of the Square Table window cleaning team revolves around the performance per hour and per team cleaner. Table Q5.1 and Figure Q5.1 show the raw averages (per hour and per cleaner) as well as

TABLE Q5.1 ***Window cleaning performance***

Week	Windows per hour	Index	Windows per cleaner	Index
1	19.70	100.00	162.50	100.00
2	21.72	110.26	173.75	106.92
3	20.39	103.50	126.40	77.78
4	18.00	91.38	162.00	99.69
5	21.90	111.17	211.67	130.26
6	18.75	95.19	135.00	83.08
7	17.97	91.25	133.00	81.85
8	19.35	98.26	150.00	92.31
9	18.12	92.00	119.60	73.60
10	18.11	91.96	126.80	78.03
Average	19.40	98.50	150.07	92.35
Standard Deviation	143	7.25	26.83	16.51
Range	3.92	19.92	92.07	56.66

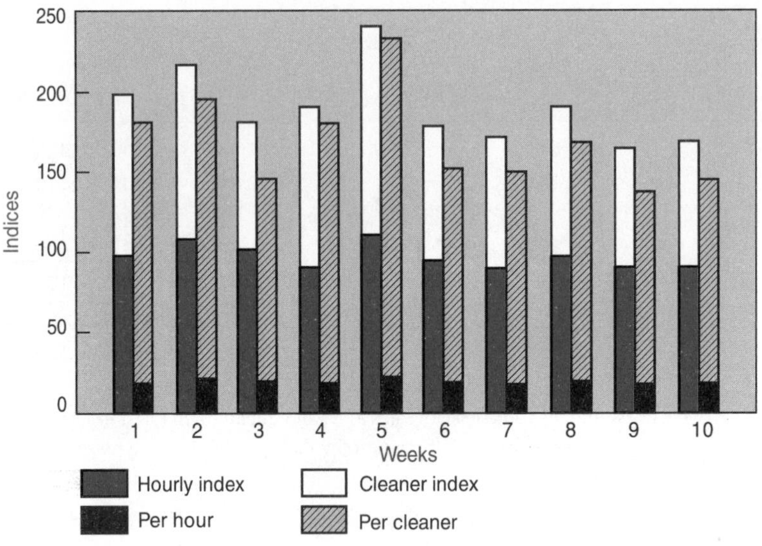

FIGURE Q5.1 *Window cleaning analysis: Square Table*

the performance indices derived from them. There is nothing complicated about any of the sets of information derived from the question. It should not be necessary, therefore, to illustrate any of the workings for this question!

The reason for the compilation of an index for each set of statistics (per hour and per cleaner) allows us to contrast the two on a comparable basis. Without an index of the kind presented in the table and on the graph, there would be little possibility of comparing the rate per hour with the rate per cleaner. With the indices, however, we can start both sets of information at 100.0 at the beginning of week one and monitor their progress over the ten-week period.

The standard deviations contained in the table show that, on a per cleaner basis, performance is very volatile, with a standard deviation of 26.83 windows per cleaner, as opposed to the standard deviation of 1.43 windows per hour. The conclusion here is that it does not matter how many cleaners there are, the number of windows cleaned is reasonably constant; the fifth cleaner may not be necessary!

6. A tabular and graphical approach is the best way of presenting our answer to this question. To see the data most clearly, the table we were given needs to be turned around so that the efficiencies are on the left-hand side of the table rather than across the top. Otherwise, there is no significant change to the presentation of the data.

Efficiency %	$y = 0.85x^2$	Earnings £
80	0.54	190.40
90	0.69	240.98
100	0.85	297.50
110	1.03	359.98
120	1.22	428.40
130	1.44	502.78
140	1.67	583.10
150	1.91	669.38
160	2.18	761.60

The calculations that are needed are relatively simple, and they are therefore not shown here. Do check them for you own satisfaction, however.

As the table shows, at any rate of efficiency below the 'breakeven point' of 108.465% (where George's basic and bonus-related pay are exactly the same), George will be earning less than his basic rate of pay of £350 per week. There is no suggestion in the question that the £350 is a fall-back (or guaranteed) rate: George's department may need to operate at greater than 108.465% in order for George to achieve his basic level of earnings.

However, once the breakeven barrier has been achieved and surpassed, the accelerating premium bonus scheme operates along the lines suggested by its name: the earnings quickly accelerate away from the basic £350. At the 110% efficiency level, George would earn £359.98; add only 10% more efficiency onto the 110% efficiency rate and a further £68.42 is earned, over and above the £359.98; add a further 10% on to that and £74.38 extra is earned over and above the 120% level of efficiency. And so it goes on: earnings increase at an ever increasing pace.

From what we have just been saying, we can now conclude that the accelerating premium bonus scheme is a progressive payments scheme. At greater levels of efficiency, earnings increase disproportionately.

Given the information in the question, it seems that there are no limits to the earnings that George could enjoy. This is not to say that management would not impose an upper limit on George's earnings; they might. Similarly, there must be limits to George's department's efficiency potential. His department could not operate at infinite levels or efficiency, for example. To that extent, therefore, the realistic limit to George's earnings; is the physical limit imposed by his department's maximum achievable efficiency level. At 1,000% efficiency, for example, George would be paid £29,750 for a week! If it were possible for George's department to operate at this level, however, we should conclude that the bonus scheme has been based on bogus efficiency assessments!

Chapter 6

5. Midland Ltd

Workings

Before we calculate a job cost for job 1-2-3, we should work out the respective OARs:

	A	B	C
(a) *Direct wages cost rate*			
	$\frac{£24,000}{£16,000}$	$\frac{£20,000}{£15,000}$	$\frac{£12,600}{£\ 8,400}$
	150%	$33.\dot{3}\dot{3}$%	150%
(b) *Direct labour hour rate*			
	$\frac{£24,000}{16,000 \text{ dlh}}$	$\frac{£20,000}{10,000 \text{ dlh}}$	$\frac{£12,600}{7,000 \text{ dlh}}$
	£1.50	£2.00	£1.80

We can then calculate the overheads to be absorbed:

(a) Using the direct wages cost rate:

Dept A £13.00 × 1.50 = £19.50

B 13.50 × 1.3̇3̇ = 18.00
C 12.50 × 1.50 = 18.75

(b) Using the direct labour hour rate:

Dept A	11 dlh × £1.50	= £16.50
B	9 dlh × 2.00	= 18.00
C	10 dlh × 1.80	= 18.00

Cost cards: Job 1-2-3

	Using direct wages cost rate		Using direct labour hour rate	
	£	£	£	£
Materials:				
Dept A	12.00			
B	14.00			
C	12.00	38.00		38.00
Labour:				
Dept A	13.00			
B	13.50			
C	12.50	39.00		39.00
Prime cost		77.00		77.00
Overheads:				
Dept A	19.50		16.50	
B	18.00		18.00	
C	18.75	56.25	18.00	52.50
Total cost		133.25		129.50

In summary, if the direct wages cost rate is used for product cost evaluation, the total cost of Job 1-2-3 is £133.25. If the direct labour hour overheads absorption rate is used, the cost of Job 1-2-3 becomes £129.50.

Remember the crucial point here. We do not accept the lower cost as the basis for our pricing or other decisions just because it gives us the better, more competitive price, or higher profit; we use the absorption basis that makes most sense. We need to determine the most effective way of absorbing costs and using that method: not just choosing the basis that *looks* the best!

7. Flowers Ltd

(a) (i) **Repeated distribution method**

The reapportionment of overheads is a familiar task now, but the whole of the **repeated distribution**-based overhead distribution summary is shown below anyway:

Overhead distribution summary

	Production			Service	
	M	T	F	A	B
	£	£	£	£	£
Total	25,000	20,000	30,000	10,000	20,000

Reapportionments

A	4,000	5,000	6,000	5,000	(20,000)
B	4,500	3,000	3,750	(15,000)	3,750
A	750	937	1,125	937	(3,750)
B	281.25	187.50	234.38	(937.5)	234.38
A	46.88	58.59	70.31	58.59	(234.38)
B	17.58	11.72	14.65	(58.59)	14.65
A	2.93	3.66	4.39	3.66	−14.65
B	1.10	0.73	0.92	(3.66)	0.92
A	0.18	0.23	0.27	0.23	−0.92
B	0.07	0.05	0.06	(0.23)	0.06
A	0.01	0.01	0.02	0.02	−0.06
B	0.00	0.01	0.00	(0.01)	0.00
	34,600	29,200	41,200	–	–

Note that there are more than the four to six iterations we mentioned would be necessary when we first discussed the repeated distribution method. This is to ensure as far as possible that all three methods we will be using give as near as possible the same solution, for the purposes of demonstration.

(ii) **Simultaneous equations method**

We will consider all five simultaneous equations for the solution to this problem initially, but then, as before, we will be solving for A and B using only the first two equations: we will eventually consider the final three equations, to solve for M, T, and F.

The equations are:

$$A = 10{,}000 + \qquad 0.25B \qquad (8.1)$$
$$B = 20{,}000 + 0.25A \qquad (8.2)$$
$$M = 25{,}000 + 0.30A + 0.20B \qquad (8.3)$$
$$T = 20{,}000 + 0.20A + 0.25B \qquad (8.4)$$
$$F = 30{,}000 + 0.25A + 0.30B \qquad (8.5)$$

where:

A = the overheads of department A after all reapportionments;
B = the overheads of department B after all reapportionments;
M = the overheads of department M after all reapportionments;
T = the overheads of department T after all reapportionments;
F = the overheads of department F after all reapportionments;

Solving for A and B in equations (8.1) and (8.2), by the elimination method gives:

Rearrange the equations first:

$$A - 0.25B = 10{,}000 \qquad (8.1)$$

$$-0.25A + \qquad B = 20{,}000 \qquad (8.2)$$

Divide equation (8.2) by 0.25:

$$-A + \qquad 4B = 80{,}000 \qquad (8.6)$$

Add equation (8.6) to equation (8.1):

$3.75B = 90{,}000$

Therefore:

$B = 24{,}000$

Substitute for B in equation (8.1):

$A - 0.25 \times 24{,}000 = 10{,}000$

$A = 10{,}000 + 6{,}000$

$A = 16{,}000$

Applying the results of A = £16,000 and B = £24,000 in equations (8.3) to (8.5) gives:

$M = 25{,}000 + (0.30 \times 16{,}000) + (0.20 \times 24{,}000) = £34{,}600$

$T = 20{,}000 + (0.20 \times 16{,}000) + (0.25 \times 24{,}000) = 29{,}200$

$F = 30{,}000 + (0.25 \times 16{,}000) + (0.30 \times 24{,}000) = 41{,}200$

These results agree exactly with the results of the repeated distribution method. We can see this if we translate the results we have just got into the form of an overhead distribution summary.

Overhead distribution summary

Production			Service	
M	T	F	A	B
£	£	£	£	£
34,600	29,200	41,200	–	–

(iii) **Matrix algebra method**

As before, since the simultaneous equations and matrix algebra methods are so closely linked, we will just work through the matrix that contains the first two simultaneous equations, solving for A and B only. We can then call upon the results for M, T, and F from the simultaneous equations part of the solution, as necessary.

initial matrix:

$$\left[\begin{array}{rr|r} 1 & -0.25 & 10{,}000 \\ -0.25 & 1 & 20{,}000 \end{array}\right]$$

Remember, this initial partitioned matrix derives its left-hand side from simultaneous equations one and two, above.

Add 0.25 of row one to row two:

$$\left[\begin{array}{rr|r} 1 & -0.25 & 10{,}000 \\ 0 & 0.9375 & 22{,}500 \end{array}\right]$$

Divide row two by 0.9375:

$$\left[\begin{array}{cc|c} 1 & -0.25 & 10{,}000 \\ 0 & 1 & 24{,}000 \end{array}\right]$$

Add 0.25 times row two to row one:

$$\left[\begin{array}{cc|c} 1 & 0 & 16{,}000 \\ 0 & 1 & 24{,}000 \end{array}\right]$$

We now have a unit matrix on the left-hand side of this partitioned matrix. We therefore have the solutions we are looking for:

A = £16,000
B = £24,000

Again, this agrees with the repeated distribution method, and the simultaneous equations method, and the values of M, T, and F can be derived from here.

Now that we have all of the information we need, we can calculate the OARs as per part (b) of the question.

(b) Based on our solutions to part (a) of this question, the OARs are:

	M	T	F
	£	£	£
Total overheads	34,600	29,200	41,200
(i) Direct labour hour rate	£34,600 / 17,300 dlh	£29,200 / 7,300 dlh	£41,200 / 41,200 dlh
	= £2/dlh	£4/dlh	£1/dlh
(ii) Tonne mile rate	£34,600 / 346,000 tm	£29,200 / 29,200tm	£41,200 / 4,120tm
	= £0.1/tm	£1/tm	£10/tm

where:

dlh = direct labour hours
tm = tonne miles

Chapter 7

1. In view of the type of calculations that we need to carry out to answer this question, it makes sense to combine the calculations for parts (a) and (c), and to combine the workings for parts (b) and (c)

(a + c) Overheads absorbed on a machine hour basis

The workings for this part of the question are very straightforward. All we have to do is to add together the overhead costs and then divide them by the total number of machine hours to be used:

Total overheads:

	£
Machine department costs (rent, business rates, depreciation and supervision)	10,430
Set-up costs	5,250
Stores receiving	3,600
Inspection/quality control	2,100
Materials handling and dispatch	4,620
Total overheads	26,000

The total machine hours are found by multiplying the number of machine hours per unit of a product by the total number of units of that product that are being made. In the case of product A, for example, the calculation is 4 machine hours per unit multiplied by 120 units of output: 480 machine hours. Adding together the results for all four products gives us total machine hours of 1,300:

	Product A	B	C	D	Total
Total machine hours	480	300	160	360	1,300

The machine hour rate is, therefore:

$$\frac{\text{total overheads}}{\text{total machine hours}}$$

$$= \frac{£26{,}000}{1{,}300\ \text{MHR}}$$

$$= £20 \text{ per MHR}$$

To find the costs per unit per product, we multiply this absorption rate by the number of machine hours per unit. For product A, for example, this is £20 per MHR multiplied by 4 MHR per unit: £80 per unit.

Unit costs per product:

	Product A	B	C	D	Total
	£	£	£	£	£
Direct material	40	50	30	60	180
Direct labour	28	21	14	21	84
Overheads absorbed	80	60	40	60	240
Cost per unit	148	131	84	141	504

Finally, to arrive at the total costs applied to each product, all we have to do is to multiply the costs per unit by the number of units of each product made. Using product A as the example again,this gives £148 per unit multiplied by 120 units of output: £17,760.

	Product A	B	C	D	Total
	£	£	£	£	£
Total costs per product	17,760	13,100	6,720	16,920	54,500

(b + c) Overheads assigned on an ABC basis

Before we can determine the costs per unit and in total for any of the four products under review, we need to determine the different OARs required by the ABC approach. In this case, we are given specific advice on four of the OARs we need to use. There is a fourth OAR, of course, and that is the one needed to assign the machine department costs. There is no guidance in the question on which basis the machine department's overheads are to be absorbed. In the absence of any information to the contrary, there is no reason why we should not use the machine hour basis – it is, after all, a machine department!

The other OAR's are calculated as we should expect, using the information supplied in the question. For example the set-up rate is derived by dividing the total set up costs of £5,250 by the total number of production runs of 21 : this gives £250 per production run, or set up. All the relevant data are given in Table Q7.1 following the rates to be used. Check the calculations in case of doubt.

TABLE Q7.1 ***Comparison of methods used***

Machine department (MHR)	8.0231 per MHR
Set up costs	250 per production run
Stores receiving	45 per requisition
Inspection/QC	100 per production run
Materials handling and dispatch	110 orders executed

Product	A	B	C	D	Total
Number of production runs	6	5	4	6	21
Number of stores requisitions	20	20	20	20	80
Sales orders (deduced from information)	12	10	8	12	42

Applying the data and information we now have allows us to calculate the costs per unit and the total costs of each product.

Product	A	B	C	D
Direct material	£40.00	£50.00	£30.00	£60.00
Direct labour	28.00	21.00	14.00	21.00
Machine department (MHR)	32.09	24.07	16.05	24.07
Set up costs	12.50	12.50	12.50	12.50
Stores receiving	7.50	9.00	11.25	7.50
Inspection/QC	5.00	5.00	5.00	5.00
Materials handling and dispatch	11.00	11.00	11.00	11.00
Cost per unit	£136.09	132.57	99.80	141.07
Total costs per product	£16,331.08	13,256.92	7,983.69	16,928.31

→

Table Q7.1 cont.

Finally, in direct response to part (c) of the question in which we are asked to comment on differences between the results of the two methods, the tables that follow provide a summary of the differences between the Machine hour method and the ABC method of overhead assignment.

Summary: comparison of the two methods

Unit costs: MHR		148.00	131.00	84.00	141.00
ABC		136.09	132.57	99.80	141.07
Differences		£11.91	(1.57)	(15.80)	(0.07)
Total costs:					Total
MHR	17,760.00	13,100.00	6,720.00	16,920.00	54,500
ABC	16,331.08	13,256.92	7,983.69	16,928.31	54,500
Differences	£1,428.92	(156.92)	(1,263.69)	(8.31)	
Overheads per unit					
MHR	£80.00	60.00	40.00	60.00	
ABC	£68.09	61.57	55.80	60.07	
Overheads as a percentage of total costs					
MHR	54.05	45.80	47.62	42.55	
ABC	50.03	46.44	55.91	42.58	

The conclusions to be drawn from this analysis is that in terms of units and in total, there are significant differences between the costs assigned by the two methods we have used. In general terms, products A and C give rise to the largest differences in costs, whereas products B and D are not significantly different. Depending Cupon the market that this organisation is operating in, the cost differences might have serious consequences for pricing and profit. In a highly competitive market, this organisation could now adjust its prices and be more competitive, in terms of product A particularly. Product C represents a problem in that if prices are based on product cost, the selling price of this product would now have to be increased. The evidence to date suggests that even though ABC has revealed cost differences, the marketing department often feels it difficult to translate such changes into price changes.

Furthermore there is the possibility, assuming this organisation is already profitable, that it may notice little difference to its profitability in the short to medium term providing the product mix remains as it is at the moment. Any big change in the product mix could have serious implications for organisational profitability. Substantial changes to the product mix involving products A and C would have the greatest impact, of course.

Chapter 8

1. The economic batch quantity (EBQ) is the optimal number of units to be made in any one batch of products or services, given cost and other resource input constraints. To a large extent the EBQ is equivalent to the EOQ that we saw in Chapter 4. There is a significant difference, however, between EOQ and EBQ: in an EBQ

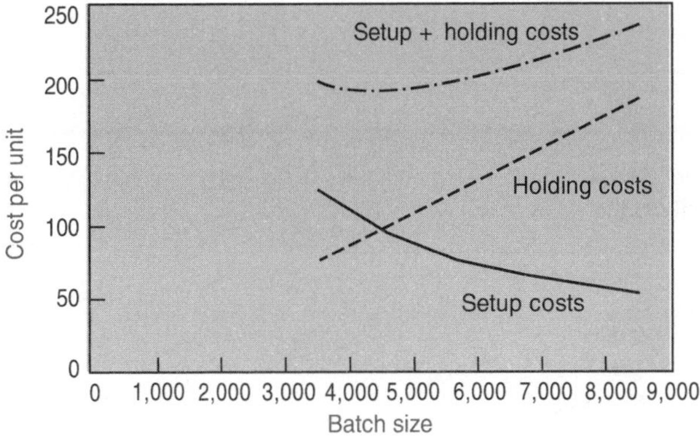

FIGURE Q8.1 *Economic batch size*

situation, the stocks are being produced gradually over time. That is, when we are making our own products we are assuming we are producing at a constant rate and consuming at a (different) constant rate. This means that there are probably no sudden intakes of stocks as is the case when we are buying goods. The goods are gradually being added to stocks and gradually taken away.

The economic batch size graph does look just like the economic order quantity graphs we saw in Chapter 4. An example of an economic batch size graph is contained in Figure Q8.1.

This figure relates to the data given in the question and shows an economic batch quantity of 4,500 units per batch. That is, to optimise the levels of cost, we should produce 4,500 units then cease production, until we need to produce again.

In the EOQ formula, holding costs are taken as annual storage and interest charges. In the EBQ formula, the holding costs are taken as the annual storage and interest charges weighted as between production and demand.

The interpretation of this result is that in order to optimise resource allocation and usage, this organisation should produce this product, or provide this service, in batches of 4,500 units. Table Q8.1 shows that producing greater than or less than 4,500 units per batch is not the optimal thing to do.

TABLE Q8.1

Units per batch	3,500	4,500	5,500	6,500	7,500	8,500
	£	£	£	£	£	£
Variable costs	32,400	32,400	32,400	32,400	32,400	32,400
Setup costs	125	97	80	67	58	51
Holding costs	75.60	97.20	118.80	140.40	162.00	183.60

7. Cleansing agent

(a) We are using the FIFO method throughout.

We are told quite specifically that there are no losses in process. Hence, there is no need to concern ourselves with either normal or abnormal losses. We need to consider the possibilities of abnormal gains, however. The question implies that there is no abnormal loss when it talks of the remaining items in work in progress. The following statement reflects the assumptions we have just made.

Inputs into process:

ingredient A		2,000 kg
ingredient B		3,000 kg
ingredient C		6,000 kg

Outputs from the process:

to finished goods	8,600	
work in progress c/d	2,400	11,000 kg

Equivalent units: the only equivalent units calculations, therefore, are:

work in progress c/d:		
ingredient A	100% × 2,400 kg	= 2,400 eu
ingredient B	100% × 2,400 kg	= 2,400 eu
ingredient C	100% × 2,400 kg	= 2,400 eu
labour	25% × 2,400 kg × 60%	= 360 eu
labour	75% × 2,400 kg × 25%	= 450 eu
other direct costs	25% × 2,400 kg × 60%	= 360 eu
other direct costs	75% × 2,400 kg × 25%	= 450 eu

Units started and completed in the period: since there is no work in progress b/d in the period, the units that were both started and completed during the period is the same as the units sent to finished goods as fully completed.

Evaluation statement

The evaluation statement contains all of the rest of the workings that we need in order to complete the process account, and the other ledger accounts as per the question.

	Costs (£)			Costs (£)		
	Ingredient			Labour	other	total
	A	B	C		direct costs	
For the period	1,600	1,500	2,400	3,764	1,882	11,146

Equivalent units

Since the information is available to us, we should use it to keep the two sets of work in progress c/d separate. Table Q8.4 reflects this.

TABLE Q8.4

Started and completed	8,600	8,600	8,600	8,600	8,600	8,600
work in progress c/d 1	600	600	600	360	360	600
2	1,800	1,800	1,800	450	450	1,800
cost per eu	£$0.1\dot{4}\dot{5}$	$0.1\dot{3}\dot{6}$	$0.2\dot{1}\dot{8}$	0.400	0.200	$1.0\dot{9}\dot{9}$
evaluation:						
process A	1,251	1,173	1,876	3,440	1,720	9,460
work in progress c/d 1	87	82	131	144	72	516
2	262	245	393	180	90	1,170
	1,600	1,500	2,400	3,764	1,882	11,146

We have rounded off all of the values in the evaluation part of the evaluation statement, for simplicity.

Process B account	Dr Kg	£	Cr Kg	£
Ingredients A	2,000	1,600		
Ingredients B	3,000	1,500		
Ingredients C	6,000	2,400		
Labour		3,764		
Overheads		1,882		
Finished goods			8,600	9,460
Work in progress c/d			2,400	1,686
	11,000	11,146	11,000	11,146

Since there are no losses or gains, there are no other accounts to present for this solution.

(b) (i) A by-product is a product that is an incidental output of a process. Generally speaking, the management accountant means that the output is incidental if it is relatively insignificant in cost or sales value to the rest of the output. In the chapter, we talked of oddments as being products that are incidental to the main output of the cardboard factory.

(ii) An abnormal gain arises when the loss that was expected in a process (the normal loss) is not as high as it should have been. If a process normally gives rise to 100 kg loss per 1,000 kg of input, and the actual loss was only 80 kg for an input of 1,000 kg, then there is an abnormal gain of 100 kg – 80 kg = 20 kg.

(iii) Equivalent units is a concept whereby we can compare unlike items of output. We cannot ordinarily add together 100 units that are half-finished and 50 units that are completely finished. However, if we say that 100 half-finished units is equal to 50 equivalently complete units, then we can add together the two sets of output, and arrive at a solution that there are 100 equivalent units of output.

Chapter 9

2.

(a) As we saw in the chapter, to answer this part of the question, to estimate the regression equation, we need to prepare a table, such as table Q9.2, in order to solve the 'normal equations'.

TABLE Q9.2

Cars and bikes made ('000)	Total costs (£m)		
X	Y	X^2	XY
385	9,400	148,225	3,619,000
410	11,420	168,100	4,682,364
450	13,738	202,500	6,181,965
465	16,155	216,225	7,511,843
482	17,778	232,324	8,568,948
480	17,177	230,400	8,245.104
490	19,085	240,100	9,351,503
510	24,092	260,100	12,287,022
540	26,129	291,600	14,109,876
550	26,780	302,500	14,728,890
4,762	181,754	2,292,074	89,286,514

In summary:

$\Sigma X = 4{,}762$
$\Sigma Y = 181{,}754$
$\Sigma X^2 = 2{,}292{,}074$
$\Sigma XY = 89{,}286{,}514$

We can now substitute the relevant values in the normal equations, including the value 'n', which is 10.

$$\Sigma y = na + b\tilde{o}x \qquad (9.1)$$

$$\Sigma x = a\tilde{o}x + b\tilde{o}x \qquad (9.2)$$

$$181{,}754 = 10a + 4{,}762b \qquad (9.1)$$

$$89{,}286{,}514 = 4{,}762a + 2{,}292{,}074b \qquad (9.2)$$

We can solve for 'b' in this case by multiplying equation (9.1) by 476.2 to give equation (9.3)

$$86{,}551{,}254.8 = 4{,}762a + 2{,}267{,}664.4b \qquad (9.3)$$

Subtract equation (9.3) from equation (9.2), to give:

$$2{,}735{,}259.2 = 0a + 24{,}409.6b \qquad (9.4)$$

Therefore:

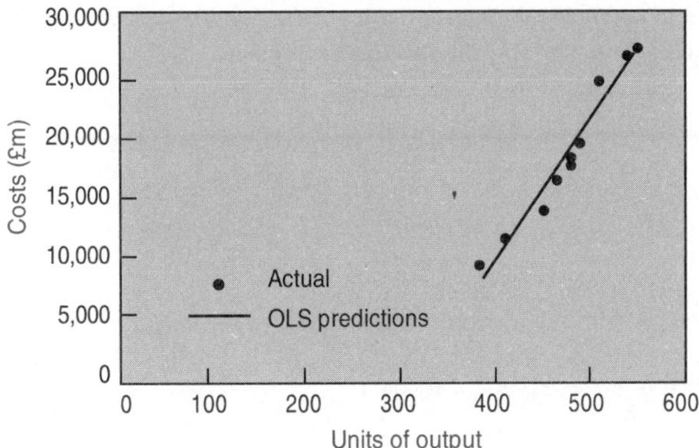

FIGURE Q9.2 *Car manufacturer's costs*

$$b = \frac{2,735,259.2}{24,409.6}$$

$$= 112.056699$$

Substitute for '*b*' now in equation (9.2):

$$89,286,514 = 4,762a + 2,292,074 \times 112.056699 \quad (9.2)$$

$$89,286,514 = 4,762a + 256,842,246.3 \quad (9.2)$$

$$89,286,514 \times 256,842,246.3 = 4,762a \quad (9.2)$$

$$-167,555,732.3 = 4,762a \quad (9.2)$$

Therefore:

$$a = \frac{-£167,555,732.3}{4,762}$$

$$= -35,186$$

Rounding off to two decimal places:

$$Y' = a + bX$$

$$= -35,186 + 112.06X$$

(b) Plotting the actual data and the regression line derived from the normal equations on a graph gives Figure Q9.2.

Although a comment is not called for by this question, it is worth noting the nature of the analysis that has been carried out. If we slavishly use the regression equation, we will find that at approximately 310,000 units of output, total production costs are £nil. Since zero production costs are clearly unrealistic, this observation confirms more than anything else the need to use the relevant range idea very carefully indeed.

(c) To prepare confidence bands, we need to determine the standard error of the estimate and the standard error of the coefficient. The fully worked solution to this part of the question follows:

The calculation of the standard error of the estimate is found by solving the following formula:

$$S_e = \frac{\sqrt{\Sigma(Y - Y')^2}}{n - 2}$$

Where:

S_e is the standard error of the estimate;
Y is the total cost;
Y' is the estimate of total cost derived from the regression equation;
$n - 2$ are the degrees of freedom.

Cars and bikes made ('000)	Total costs (£m.)				
X	Y	X^2	XY	Y'	$(Y - Y')^2$
385	9,400	148,225	3,619,000	7,957.1	2,081,960.4
410	11,420	168,100	4,682,364	10,758.6	437,979.2
450	13,738	202,500	6,181,965	15,241.0	2,259,910.9
465	16,155	216,225	7,511,843	16,921.9	588,902.8
482	17,778	232,324	8,568,948	18,826.9	1,100,443.0
480	17,177	230,400	8,245,104	18,602.8	2,032,050.3
490	19,085	240,100	9,351,503	19,723.4	407,937.7
510	24,092	260,100	12,287,022	21,964.6	4,526,681.8
540	26,129	291,600	14,109,876	25,326.4	644,809.0
550	26,780	302,500	14,728,890	26,447.0	110,755.8
4,762	181,754	2,292,074	89,286,514	181,769.7	14,191,430.8

Applying the formula to the relevant data in the table above gives us the *standard error* of the estimate:

$$S_e = \frac{\sqrt{\Sigma(Y - Y')^2}}{n - 2}$$

gives:

$$S_e = \frac{\sqrt{1\ 114{,}191{,}430.8}}{10 - 2}$$

$$= 1{,}331.89$$

We use the standard error of the estimate to give us an idea of how close we can expect our predicted costs to come to the actual costs. To do this, we calculate *confidence intervals*: that is, intervals within which population parameters should lie. From the confidence interval we will prepare a confidence band, which is a band of values lying above and below an estimated regression line and indicating the limits of the prediction interval for each value of X and Y.

We know that when we are dealing with a sample size of less than 30 observations, we should use the Student t tables for evaluating our confidence intervals; otherwise, we use the normal distribution tables. In

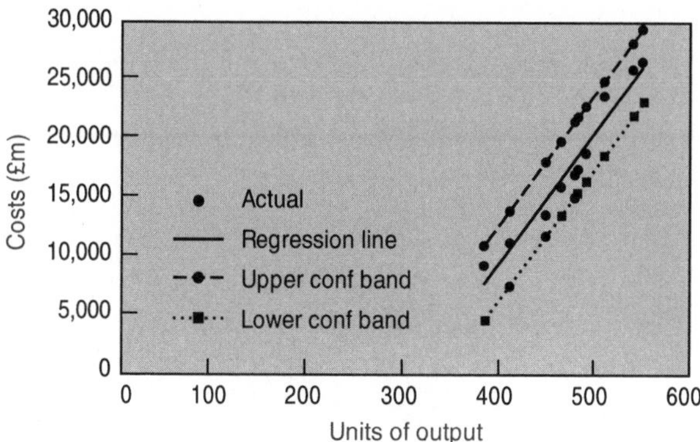

FIGURE Q9.3 *Confidence intervals added*

the example we are currently working through, the number of observations we are dealing with is only 10, therefore we must use the Student *t* tables. In this case, a 95% confidence interval is based on:

$$Y' \pm (t_{0.025})(S_e)$$

at 10 − 2 (10 − 2 = 8) degrees of freedom.

This confidence interval allows us to say, with 95% confidence, that the true production cost at 385 units of output is:

£9,400 ± (2.306)(£1,331.89)

that is:

£9,400 − (2.306)(£1,331.89) to

£9,400 + (2.306)(£1,331.89)

£9,400 − 3,071.34 to £9,400 + 3,071.34

£12,471.34 to £6,328.66

For 95% of all observations taken at 385 units of output, we would expect total production cost to lie within this confidence band.

Figure Q9.3 above shows the confidence band for all of the data from 385 units of output to 550 units of output, in addition to the regression line and the actual data.

The standard error of the '*b*' coefficient is calculated by:

$$S_b = \frac{S_e}{\sqrt{\Sigma x^2 - nx^2}}$$

and the confidence interval is calculated by:

$$B = b \pm t\alpha \frac{S_e}{\sqrt{\Sigma x^2 - nx^2}}$$

where α is half of the level of confidence. We have used a 95% confidence interval so far in this chapter, so α is half of 0.05 (5%).]

The standard error of the coefficient is:

$$\frac{1{,}331.89}{\sqrt{2{,}292{,}074 - (10)(476.2)^2}}$$

$= 8.5248751$

The 95% confidence interval is:

$$B = 112.06 \pm (2.306)\frac{1{,}331.89}{2{,}292{,}074 - (10)(476.2)^2}$$

$= 112.06 \pm (2.306)(8.5248751)$

$= 112.06 \pm 19.65836198$

$= 92.40163802$ to 131.718362

The meaning of this result is that we are 95% confident that B is greater than zero (and it is between 92.401 and 131.718): this is significant because if the observations on which all of these calculations were based were randomly distributed, the value of '*b*' would be close to zero. A value of '*b*' = zero indicates that changes in volume are not accompanied by changes in costs (that is total costs will be zero, or consist almost entirely of fixed costs). Alternatively, we could assess whether *B* were greater than zero by calculating the *t* statistic actually obtained from the data by dividing the value of 'b' by the standard error of the coefficient and setting the result against the theoretical value of t from a table of t statistics, given the relevant number of degrees of freedom for the exercise under review.

In this case, we have:

$$t = \frac{112.06}{8.5248751}$$

$= 13.1451$

Since $t_{(0.025)}$ with 8 degrees of freedom equals 2.306, which is considerably less than 13.1451, we are 95% confident that *B* is not equal to zero.

7. This question, on A Company Ltd, demonstrates the use of learning curve theory in production planning, and budgeting. The situation is that a new prospect has opened up for the company, and we are asked to assess whether the company can fulfil the order without disrupting the existing affairs of the company. We are therefore concerned to find out whether there are enough hours left in the current accounting period to enable the company to take on the new order.

(a) The time the company has available for this new job, of supplying 35 newly designed machines, is 3,500 hours: that is 11,000 hours available to the company less the 7,500 hours that are already committed to existing orders. To assess whether the new order will take more or less than the 3,500 hours available, we will use the following formula:

$$\ln XY = \ln a + (b + 1)\ln X$$

The learning rate is 75%, hence the value of '*b*' is −0.415037499, the estimated time to make the first machine ('*a*') is 450 hours and 35 machines are to be made. Therefore:

$\ln XY = \ln 450 + (-0.415037499 + 1)\ln 35$

$= 6.10925 + (0.58496 \times 3.55535)$

$= 8.18899$

$XY = 3{,}601.07$ hours

So, the total time needed to fulfil the order for 35 machines is 3,601.07 hours. Since the total time available for the job is only 3,500 hours, the job cannot be undertaken. However, if the job is sufficiently rewarding in terms of profitability and so on, efforts should be made to find ways of carrying out the job. Ideas that should be suggested would include further training (although with a reported learning rate of 75% this would seem unlikely to provide any benefits), subcontracting parts of the work, working overtime (if this is not already included in the 3,500 hours available), and redesigning the product, if possible.

(b) This part of the question is reasonably straightforward: finding the learning rate that will allow for the company to undertake the job of providing the 35 machines. Again we use the formula we have just used in the previous part of the solution to this question to enable us to find the relevant learning rate, and solve for 'b':

$$\ln XY = \ln a + (b + 1)\ln X$$

The total time available is 3,500 hours, the estimated time to make the first machine ('a') is 450 hours, and 35 machines are to be made. Therefore,

$$\ln 3500 = \ln 450 + (b + 1)\ln 35$$

$$8.16052 = 6.10925 + (b + 1) \times 3.55535$$

$$8.16052 - 6.10925 = (b + 1) \times 3.55535$$

$$2.05127 = (b + 1) \times 3.55535$$

$$\frac{2.05127}{3.55535} = (b + 1)$$

$$(b + 1) = 0.57695$$

$$b = 0.57695 - 1$$

$$b = -0.42305$$

$$b = \ln \text{learning rate}/\ln 2 = -0.42305$$

$$\ln \text{learning rate} = -0.42305 \times 0.69315$$

$$= -0.29323$$

$$\text{learning rate} = 0.7458 = 74.58\%$$

Assuming that the learning rate of 75% given in the question is a fair and accurate representation of the true rate of learning for this order, a rate of 74.58% seems within the grasp of the workers. Perhaps a small amount of rescheduling, training, or overtime working will help the company to achieve the target of 3,500 hours.

Chapter 10

2.

(a) Absorption costing profit = £250,000

The stock 'adjustment' is 2,000 units × £25 per unit = £50,000: this represents the difference in valuation as per the absorption costing method and the variable costing method. From this, we can readily determine the variable costing profit:

Variable costing profit = £250,000 − £50,000 = £200,000.

Note closing stock units are greater than opening stock units, therefore, the variable costing profit should be lower than the absorption costing profits, and it is!

(b) Variable costing profit = £250,000
Absorption costing profit = £200,000
The fixed overhead absorption rate is £12.50

We already know that the difference between the absorption and variable costing profits is due to the differences in stock levels as at the beginning and end of a period; and this equates to the difference between sales and output. Therefore, the number of units different between the sales and output is:

$$\frac{\text{variable costing profit} - \text{absorption costing profit}}{\text{fixed overhead absorption rate}}$$

$$= \frac{£250{,}000 - 200{,}000}{£12{,}50 \text{ per unit}}$$

$$= 4{,}000 \text{ units}$$

Since variable costing profit is greater than absorption costing profit, we can conclude that sales are 4,000 units greater than output.

(c) Variable costing profit = £150,000
Absorption costing profit = £250,000
Fixed overhead absorption rate = £5 per unit

The difference between the opening and closing stock is:

$$\frac{£250{,}000 - 150{,}000}{£5 \text{ per unit}}$$

$$= 20{,}000 \text{ units}$$

Since absorption costing profit is greater than variable costing profit, closing stocks are greater than opening stocks by 20,000 units.

4. The following quotation from Hirsch and Louderback (1986: 459) will help us to explore the avenues opened up by this question:

> It should not be difficult to see why the Internal Revenue Service would not allow variable costing. In most years, inventories will rise because most firms grow. Even if physical inventories do not rise, the dollar value of inventories is likely to rise because prices rise. In such periods, tax payments would be lower if firms used variable costing than if they used absorption costing.

Note that for UK purposes, for Internal Revenue Service you should read Inland Revenue, and for dollars read pounds.

From our discussion, we know that when closing stocks are larger than opening stocks, variable costing profit is lower than absorption costing profit. In general, this is always true. We also know, that over any period of time when, for example, production equals sales, the two costing methods give the same overall profit result, albeit with period-by-period variations. Although we could set up a series of examples to demonstrate the points being made by Hirsch and Louderback given the generalisations we have been making, we can continue to talk in general terms.

In any situation, when physical stocks rise (and costs and revenues per unit remain static), absorption costing will always give rise to higher profit levels, in every period. In any situation, when physical stocks remain static and costs rise period by period (but revenues remain unchanged), there will be no difference whatsoever between the profits reported by the marginal and the absorption costing methods. In any situations where physical stocks rise and costs rise (but revenues remain unchanged), the absorption costing profit will always be higher than the variable costing profit. Finally, in a situation where physical stocks fall and costs rise, the variable costing profit will exceed the absorption costing profit.

Depending on the circumstances of the case under review, then, it is not always the case that the assertion that Hirsch and Louderback made about the likely effects on taxable profits will prove true. In a scenario where physical stocks are rising and costs are increasing, absorption costing will be the favoured costing method. Nevertheless, there are real examples of situations where physical stocks can fall, and, at the same time, costs can also decline. A good illustration of this latter point comes with an interesting discussion of throughput accounting in Darlington *et al*. (1992) where, as a result of the implementation of throughput accounting in its factory, a business was able to reduce its stock level *and* reduce unit costs. Any organisation that has implemented just-in-time materials management systems will have experienced similar results.

We should consider situations such as the latter two if only to challenge Hirsch and Lauderback's provocative assertion that: 'In most years, inventories will rise because most firms grow.' The inference of this statement is that if a firm is to grow, its stocks must increase. Throughput accounting and just-in-time materials control systems, at least, help to show that this is not necessarily the case.

Chapter 11

3.

(a) A straightforward first part to the question. A reasonably straightforward p/v chart is all that is required (see Figure Q11.1).

The breakeven point, derived by inspecting the chart, is £240,000; and the margin of safety can be seen to be £60,000.

To prove the accuracy of our graph in Figure Q11.1, we should check our estimation of the breakeven point and margin of safety, by carrying out the necessary arithmetical calculations.

Breakeven point calculation

The breakeven point = total fixed costs ÷ C/S ratio.

The C/S ratio is contribution ÷ sales:

= (£300,000 - (£60,000 + 40,000 + 50,000)) ÷ £300,000

= 0.5

Therefore, the breakeven point.

= £120,000 ÷ 0.5

= £240,000

Margin of safety

The margin of safety is the difference between the maximum sales and the sales at the breakeven point

= £300,000 − 240,000 = £60,000

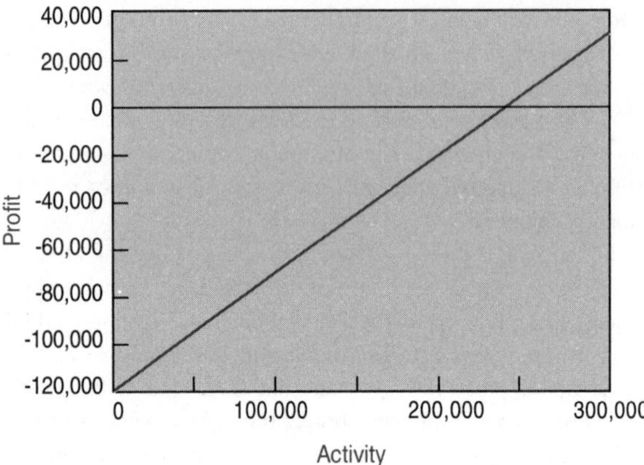

FIGURE Q11.1 *Profit/volume chart*

(b) We are required to discuss, in general terms, the effects that each of the four different scenarios have on B. Day Ltd's costs and profits. To answer this kind of question most effectively, a simple example should be devised for each part of the question; this example should, of course, relate to the data given in part (a) for maximum impact.

(i) An increase in fixed costs. If we assume that B Day Ltd has a fixed cost increase of £20,000, over the £120,000 it already incurs, the effects are that the breakeven point will become, all other factors remaining unchanged:

$= £140{,}000 \div 0.5$

$= £280{,}000;$

Similarly, the margin of safety becomes:

$= £300{,}000 - 280{,}000$

$= £20{,}000$

Generally speaking, any increase in fixed costs will cause the breakeven point to increase (that is, to worsen), and the margin of safety to shrink (that is, also to worsen).

(ii) If we assume that variable costs decrease by 10% overall, the effect on the breakeven point and the margin of safety is:

the C/S ratio is contribution ÷ sales

$= (£300{,}000 - (£150{,}000 \times 0.9)) \div £300{,}000$

$= (£300{,}000 - 135{,}000) \div £300{,}000$

$= 0.55$

Therefore the breakeven point:

$= £120{,}000 \div 0.55$

$= £218{,}181.82$

Note that the fixed costs have been returned to the level they were at in the original question.

The margin of safety now becomes:

= £300,000 − 218,181.82

= £81,818.18

Generally speaking, any decrease in variable costs will cause the breakeven point to fall (an improvement), and the margin of safety will increase (also an improvement).

(iii) We will see that an increase in selling price will have exactly the same kind of effect on the breakeven point and the margin of safety as does a decrease in variable costs. Let us assume a 10% increase in the sales revenues to demonstrate that this assertion is true:

The C/S ratio is contribution ÷ sales:

= ((£300,000 − 1.1) − £150,000) ÷ (£300,000 × 1.1)

= (£330,000 − 150,000) ÷ £330,000

= 0.5455

Therefore the breakeven point:

= £120,000 ÷ 0.5455

= £219,981.67

Note that the fixed and variable costs have been returned to the level they were at in the original question.

The margin of safety is now:

= £300,000 − £219,981.67

= £80,018.33

As we expected, the breakeven point does fall from its original position of £240,000 to £219,981.67 and the margin of safety increases from £60,000 to £80,018.33.

(iv) An increase solely in sales volume will have no effect on the breakeven point, providing discounts are neither given nor earned because of such an increase. If selling prices, variable costs and fixed costs all remain at their prior levels, then the breakeven point cannot change.

However, if we assume an increase in sales volume of 10%, taking total sales to £330,000, the margin of safety will become:

= £330,000 − 240,000

= £90,000

Note, yet again, all other costs and relationships remain as they were in the original question.

6. Our company

(a) There is an element of the brain teaser in this question. It appears, at first reading, that there is not enough information to calculate sufficient data to prepare a p/v chart, let alone prepare further p/v charts.

The key to starting off the workings for this solution is to assume, for example, that sales are 1,000 units (or 2,000 units or any other number of units), and then apply the information supplied.

When we make and sell 1,000 units, we sell 500 units of product 1 (the question says 'half of the total sales volume was made up of sales of product 1'); the question then goes on to say that four times as many units of product 2 were sold as product 3. This means that of the 500 units to be shared between products 2 and 3, four parts go to product 2 and one part to product 3, five parts altogether. Therefore, product 2 sells 400 units and product 3 sells 100 units.

Applying this logic to the requirements of the question, we should prepare a table, *part of which* is as follows:

Sales

		Units			
		1,000	1,000	2,000	4,000
Units	1	500	500	1,000	2,000
	2	400	400	800	1,600
	3	100	100	200	400
		1,000	1,000	2,000	4,000
		£	£	£	£
Values	1	175,000	175,000	350,000	700,000
	2	120,000	120,000	240,000	480,000
	3	25,000	25,000	50,000	100,000
Total		320,000	320,000	640,000	1,280,000
Contribution					
		£	£	£	£
	1	17,500	17,500	35,000	70,000
	2	24,000	24,000	48,000	96,000
	3	10,000	10,000	20,000	40,000
Total		51,500	51,500	103,000	206,000
Fixed costs		280,000	280,000	280,000	280,000
Profit		−228,500	−228,500	−177,000	−74,000

Although we don't see all of the workings for this table, it does contain all the information that could be of interest to us in answering this question.

The p/v chart we are looking for is as Figure Q11.2.

(b) This part of the question asks us to add a new profit line to the graph we have just found for part (a). To do this we had to rework the table given in part (a) in order to asses the effects on profit of the new product mix being suggested by the chief marketing executive.

Although the whole table is not reproduced here, the profit figures, at 0, 1,000, 2,000, and 8,000 units of total output are:

	Units			
	0	1,000	2,000	8,000
	£	£	£	£
Profit	−280,000	−219,500	−159,000	204,000

The revised p/v chart, is shown in Figure Q11.3.

(c) Our conclusions are, very briefly, that the marketing executive's proposals lead to a significant increase in profits – providing, of course, actual sales achieved exceed the break even point. At 8,000 units, for example, the total profit, based on historical data is £132,000; but following the marketing executive's advice would return a profit of £204,000 at that sales level.

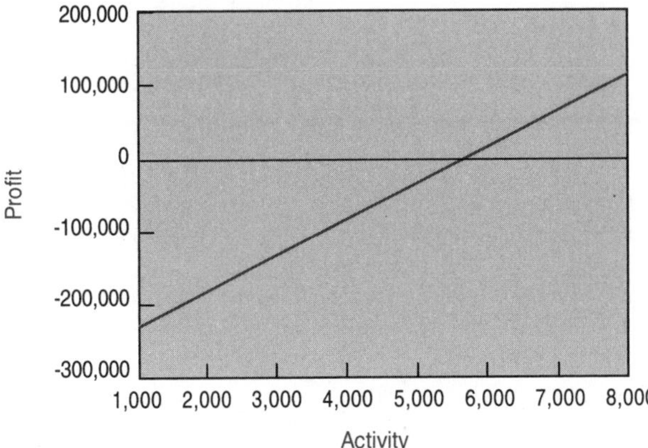

FIGURE Q11.2 *Profit/volume chart*

Given that this is a multiproduct company, we might be interested in trying to asses the breakeven points under the scenarios presented to us. Under the first (original) scenario, we have overall breakeven points of

5,437 units; and
£1,739,840

These results are based on total fixed costs of £280,000, the overall contribution per unit of £51.50, and an overall C/S ratio of 16.094%. (Check these calculations, to make sure you agree with them.)

For the second scenario, the equivalent results are overall breakeven points of

4,628 units; and
£1,411,570

In this case the overall contribution per unit is £60.5; and the overall C/S ratio is 19.836%.

The marketing executive's suggestions improve the prospects for the company, providing they are sustainable.

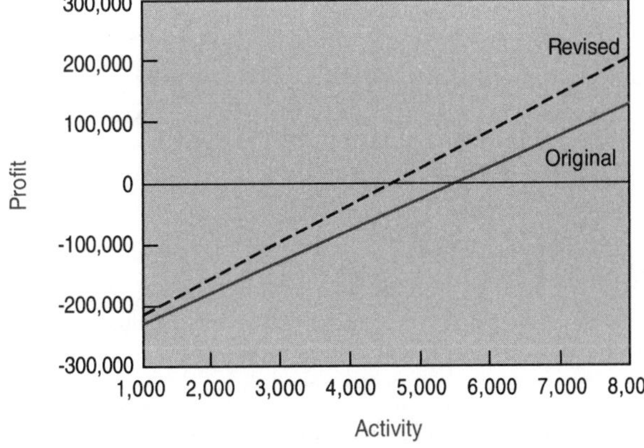

FIGURE Q11.3 *Revised profit/volume chart*

Chapter 12

1.

(a) On the evidence supplied by the question, Strouzer should accept the deal being offered. The analysis is as follows.

The capacity of the organisation is 4,000 units per year, and at the moment only 3,000 units are being produced, therefore the organisation has the capacity to cope with the order for an additional 500 units. The incremental profit, therefore, is:

	£
Sales income from the offer	50
less: Variable costs	45
Contribution	5

Every unit to be bought by the potential customer contributes £5 to fixed costs and profits. **Accept the offer**.

(b) A production problem causing the organisation's capacity to fall to 3,000 units per year puts an entirely different complexion on this problem. In order to fill the proposed order, existing business would have to be displaced. The differential analysis is as follows:

Workings

- The revenues from the new contract amount to 500 units × £50 per unit = £25,000.
- The revenues from the existing business that would be displaced by the new contract would be 500 units × £80 per unit = £40,000.
- Since the relevant costs for the existing and the new business are the same, the net effect on costs of the decision is nil.

Differential statement

	£
Revenues:	
New contract	25,000
Existing business displaced	40,000
Net change in profits	(15,000)
Costs:	
Additional costs	22,500
Savings in costs	22,500
Net addition to costs	0

The overall position, therefore, is:

Net change in profits	(15,000)
Net addition to costs	0
Overall impact on profits	(15,000)

In this situation, the contribution per unit of the new contract is significantly below the contribution being earned by the existing business, therefore, the proposal for the 500 units to be supplied at a price of £50 must be rejected.

5. The solution to this question, as with many relevant costing questions, revolves around the preparation of a schedule. To this end, the schedule that follows gives us all of the information we need on which to base our advice to the management of WP Ltd.

There are no really complicated calculations to do with this question. Consequently, we should go straight to the schedule and if there are any points of difficulty we can clear them up afterwards.

WP Ltd: analysis of proposed entry into new markets

Prices/costs per job

	Basic products	Premium products
	£	£
Revenues	50.00	142.50
Variable costs:		
Paper: basic	4.00	6.00
vellum		11.25
Covers: basic	0.50	0.50
premium		1.20
Salaries: basic	22.50	33.75
premium		30.00
Consumables	0.50	0.75
Contribution	22.50	59.05
Fixed costs:		
Depreciation	1.00	1.30
Profit per job	21.50	57.75
Total annual profit	57,749.00	57,750.00

A very finely balanced situation! The outcome of both alternatives is that the premium product returns an annual profit of £1 per annum more than the basic product. On the face of it, then, we would recommend that the premium product be the choice of marketing strategies to follow. However, a number of points should be made before this decision is taken:

(a) The difference between the two profits is only £1: this is a very small margin, and the question has to be asked about how confident WP Ltd can be about the accuracy of its forecasts. It would only take a very small error of forecasting to turn the situation round from the premium product being favoured to the basic product being the favoured one. The c/s ratio of 45% for the basic products, compared with 41% for the premium products, suggests selecting the former product.

(b) Moving from the basic product to the premium product means reducing the volume of activity from 2,686 jobs per year to 1,000 per year. The implications for this are that either some staff will have to be made redundant (and we have already discussed elsewhere the effects that this might have on morale), or staff costs will, in fact, behave like a fixed cost and any hoped for savings may not materialise. Further analysis should be carried out here.

(c) Given the reduction in volume, it might be worthwhile for WP Ltd to consider phasing in the premium product, rather than changing over entirely, as seems to be the suggestion implicit in the question. A mixture of products would, initially at least, cushion the business from any of the errors of forecasting that we discussed in point (a) above.

Chapter 13

4.

(a) The following is the logical way to work through this excercise, which is ostensibly a pricing exercise, but containing a large element of CVP analysis. Take each line step by step and follow the logic through to the final line of the solution, which gives the additional volumes that need to be sold to maintain profits at their present level, in value terms.

	Per unit			
Selling price (£)	9.00	8.55	8.10	7.65
Variable costs (£)	5.00	5.00	5.00	5.00
Contribution (£)	4.00	3.55	3.10	2.65
C/S ratio	0.44	0.42	0.38	0.35
Total fixed costs plus profit	800,000	800,000	800,000	800,000

	Selling price			
	Present	Less 5%	Less 10%	Less 15%
Sales	1,800,000	1,926,761	2,090,323	2,309,434
Variable costs	1,000,000	1,126,761	1,290,323	1,509,434
Fixed costs	500,000	500,000	500,000	500,000
Total costs	1,500,000	1,626,761	1,790,323	2,009,434
Profit	300,000	300,000	300,000	300,000
Units	200,000	225,352	258,065	301,887
Additional Units		25,352	32,712	43,822

(b) The progressively larger increases in volume are needed because of the compound effect of the changes.

(c) There is a whole host of factors that should be taken into account here before a reduction in selling prices is carried out. The first point relates to the data on which our calculations are based: are they reliable? What is the impact of accounting conventions? To what extent has creative accounting been used in arriving at the results we are given?

Secondly, we have taken no account of demand analysis so far. That is, we have calculated the new levels of sales, but have made no attempt to say whether it is possible to sell the additional units required. It is all very well assuming that since the price falls, the volume will increase; but that ignores the elasticity of demand for the product under review.

Thirdly, we have concentrated on selling prices, but what about investigating savings that could be made in terms of cost reduction exercises? Could we install activity-based costing and reap rewards from that?

6.

(a) The calculation of the absorption rates per hour are as follows:

Product	Labour hours (000s)	Machine hours (000s)
A	40	160
B	80	20
	120	180
Absorption rate per hour (£)	6	4

(i) *Cost per unit*

	Labour hours absorption method A (£000)	B (£000)	Machine hours absorption method A (£000)	B (£000)
Direct labour	200	280	200	280
Direct materials	240	160	240	160
Directly attributable overhead	120	280	120	280
General factory overhead	240	480	640	80
Total cost	680	1,200	1,200	800
Units produced (000s)	40	10	40	10
Cost per unit (£)	20	120	30	80
Price at cost + 20% (£)	24	144	36	96

(ii) and (iii) *Closing stock values and disclosed profit*

	Labour hour absorption method A	B	Total	Machine hour absorption method A	B	Total
Cost per unit (£)	20	120	30	80		
Price per unit (£)	24	144	36	96		
Sales quantity (000)	36	7	18	10		
	(£'000)					
Sales revenues	864	1,008	1,872	648	960	1,608
Opening stock						
Manufacturing costs	800	1,200	2,000	1,200	800	2,000
	800	1,200	2,000	1,200	800	2,000
Less: Closing stocks	80	360	440	660	0	660
Cost of goods sold	720	840	1,560	540	800	1,340
Disclosed profit	144	168	312	108	160	268

Note that sales have been limited to the maximum possible production level.

(b) The word price is mentioned several times in this question. Price is important to Wagner, therefore! Following on from this, we see in the above calculations that the cost figures derived above are heavily dependent on the accounting convention used. There is no guarantee that this procedure will give rise to an optimal selling price result. In Wagner's circumstance, it would be better if prices were derived after considering cost structures and demand analysis to price levels, and not merely as a consequence of accounting costs, remembering that apportionments of fixed costs are not normally useful for pricing decisions.

(c) In order to provide information useful for this pricing decision, the correct value per unit of closing stocks must be derived. This value of closing stock is the opportunity value of closing stock and can be derived as follows:

(i) In year 2 demand is lower than productive capacity. Here the only benefit that stock in hand at the end of year 1 actually bestows on Wagner is that such stocks save them from having to produce them in the following year. Therefore, their variable costs of £11 and £44 are relevant as they are the per unit costs saved in year 2.

(ii) In year 2, the demand is substantially in excess of productive capacity.

As demand exceeds productive capacity, any units of stock in hand at the end of year 1 will assist extra sales in year 2. These sales would be lost if the stock in hand were not available. Hence the relevant opportunity values are the sales prices of £30 and £130 per unit for X and Y respectively. Wagner should now seek to maximise the following:

sales revenue for year 1; *plus*

opportunity value of closing stock
(based on revenues or cost savings
to be realised in year 2); *less*

total costs incurred.

However, as total costs incurred in year 1 are constant at £2,000,000 they may be ignored for the purposes of this decision. Hence the management of Wagner should seek to maximise the other two items.

Calculation of optimum prices for year 1 (£'000)

Product A

Price per unit	Sales quantity	Revenue	Closing stock quantity	Case 1 Worth of closing stock	Total worth	Case 2 Worth of closing stock	Total worth
24	36	864	4	44	908	120	984
30	32	960	8	88	1,048	240	1,200
36	18	648	22	242	890	660	1,308
42	8	336	32	352	688	960	1,296

Product B

Price per unit	Sales quantity	Revenue	Closing stock quantity	Case 1 Worth of closing stock	Total worth	Case 2 Worth of closing stock	Total worth
96	10	960	0	0	960	0	960
108	10	1,080	0	0	1,080	0	1,080
120	9	1,080	1	44	1,124	130	1,210
132	8	1,056	2	88	1,144	260	1,316
144	7	1,008	3	132	1,140	390	1,398
156	5	780	5	220	1,000	650	1,430

For Case 1:

Wagner should adopt the following prices:

A £ 30 per unit
B £132 per unit

These will give the highest overall benefit to Wagner.

For Case 2:
Wagner should adopt the following prices:

A £ 36 per unit
B £156 per unit

These prices will give lower sales quantities and sales revenues in year 1 than will result from the case 1 prices. However, this will help give greater sales in year 2 which will outweigh the benefits previously foregone.

Chapter 14

3. Carpet 'n' Rug Company

Given the nature of the question, the most efficient way of presenting the solution to the question is to present the budget schedules first and then present any workings that need to be explained.

(a) **Production budget: August and September**

	August (sq.m.)	September (sq.m.)	October (sq.m.)
Opening stocks	100,000	72,000	60,000
Production	172,000	168,000	n/a
	272,000	240,000	
Closing stocks	72,000	60,000	n/a
Sales	200,000	180,000	150,000

Workings
The only workings here, apart from the arithmetic that is always involved in such schedules, relate to the closing stock. The information in the question says that: 'The company wants to have ... sufficient sq. m. of finished products on hand at the end of each month to meet 40% of the following month's sales.' This requirement explains why the schedule above includes the October column. It is for memorandum purposes only, but is useful!

For August, the closing stock calculation is that 40% of September's projected sales of rugs must be in stock:

40% × 180,000 sq. m. = 72,000 sq. m.

For September, the calculation is:

40% × 150,000 sq. m. = 60,000 sq. m.

Otherwise, the only point to appreciate is that the production amount for each of August and September is the balancing figure in each month.

(b) **Purchases budget: August**

	August		September
	£	kg.	kg.
Opening stock	600,000	400,000	420,000
Purchases	1,320,000	880,000	n/a
	1,920,000	1,280,000	n/a
Closing stock	630,000	420,000	n/a
Production	1,290,000	860,000	840,000

Workings

(i) We are confronted by an issue concerning the interrelationship of two budgets. That is, the purchases budget depends upon the production budget having been done, and on it being correct. This is so because in order to calculate the value and quantity of purchases, the production volume for the relevant month must be available. Furthermore we need to know that for every square metre of carpeting produced, five kilogrammes of raw materials are required.

(ii) Following on from what we have just said in point (i) above, we can now confirm that the production requirements of raw material for August and September are:

output of carpets × five kg. per sq. m.

August = 5 kg. × 172,000 sq. m. = 860,000 kg.
September = 5 kg. × 168,000 sq. m. = 840,000 kg.

(iii) As with part (a) of this question, we need to know of any stock holding requirements that relate to the raw materials. The information we are supplied with says: 'The company wants to have sufficient raw material on hand at the end of each month to meet 50% of the following month's production requirement'. For August, therefore, we need to know the weight of materials required for September's production, which we then multiply by 50% to satisfy the requirements we are given:

50% × 840,000 kg. = 420,000 kg.

The value column is simply the weight column multiplied by the standard cost per kilogramme. For the opening stock, for example, this is 400,000 kg. £1.50 per kg. = £600,000.

Finally, appreciate that the purchase amount for September is the balancing figure in both the value and the weight columns.

6. The question, concerning the Victoria Hospital, is a chance to apply the principles of budgetary control in a non-profit making or service-type organisation. Much of the theory concerning the functional budgets, the behavioural aspects of budgeting, and so on, are universally applicable, but this is the first example we have used specifically aimed at the service sector.

(a) This question is written in such a way that it should scream at us, 'Who on earth could be so dim as to prepare budgets this way?' Knowing that the hospital is located in a tourist resort, with a large influx of visitors in one quarter of the year, yet dividing the total budget amounts by four to derive the quarterly totals is clearly nonsensical.

The information in the question relating to patient days and the weight of articles processed in the laundry indicate that the budget is not in line with reality. However, the information given that the activity of the hospital doubles during the months of June, July and August, may not be borne out by the information supplied. In the information supplied, the budgeted patient days are 9,000, whereas the actual patient days for the quarter July/September are 12,000 (not doubled).

Following on directly from the previous point is the fact that the key tourist season revolves around June, July and August, whereas the question asks us to deal with the period July, August and September. If nothing else, the financial year, or its quarterly allocations and apportionments, should help to reflect the important parts of the year. A report for the quarter June–August would be most helpful to the management of the hospital. We could construct a budget for the quarter June–August based on the information supplied, but we do not have any actual information relating to June.

To improve the situation, we would recommend, as a minimum, that rather than the total annual budget being divided by four to obtain the quarterly amounts, we weight the year to reflect the increase in the activity of the hospital. The ways this works is best shown by way of an example.

Consider the budget for the wages. We are told that for the quarter for which we have information, the budgeted wage bill is £8,800. Thus, the annual budgeted wage bill is:

4 × £8,800 = £35,200

To weight the quarterly budgets as we are suggesting, we allow for the activity of the hospital to double in the July–September quarter and give that a weighting of two, rather than one. Thus the total annual wage bill is £35,200, and the quarterly wages budgets become:

	£
April–June	7,040
July–September	14,080
October–December	7,040
January–March	7,040
	35,200

These calculations are carried out by dividing the total annual budget by *five* now, and multiplying every budget by its weighting of one except the quarter July–September, which has the weighting of two. The weighting of the quarters would apply to all of the budgeted amounts, as relevant, not just the wages budget. Even more realistically, the hospital management would be best served by being presented with a set of budgets that are based on likely outcomes. Merely dividing by four will very rarely be of use to any business or anyone at any time. Only in exceptional circumstances will any organisation be providing the same level of service at a constant level of costs, all of the time. To allow for fluctuations in output and activity, the budget should be prepared along the lines that a fair analysis of actual activity levels month by month determine. The likely outcome of this analysis is that each quarter's budget will be different to each other quarter's budget; but, for the quarter July–September, the hospital management will have a realistic performance report on which to assess the quarterly performance of the departmental managers.

The final way in which the reports can be improved, would be to present reports monthly, or even more frequently if necessary. Since the control period for a laundry, or any other department, is likely to be a lot less than a quarter of a year, performance reports should reflect that and be prepared and distributed for the control period.

(b) As a general point, it is worth noting what Ashford (1989) had to say concerning budgeting in non-profit-making organisations: (see Chapter 14 for reference details). The following extract from Ashford's article is given to enhance our discussion on the justification for non-profit-making organisations preparing budgets. In a survey of 316 non-profit-making organisations (NPOs), Ashford found that 92% of them had budgets of one form or another; and that budgets were an important part of the reporting framework. Ashford also found that in the absence of a pricing mechanism based on profitability, the budget was likely to assist NPOs in the decisions relating to resource allocation. The respondents to Ashford's survey ranked the purposes for budgets in the following order:

Rank order	Purpose
1	Control spending
2	Planning
3	Control income
4	Co-ordination
5	Pricing
6	Setting standards
7	Performance evaluation
8	Motivation
9	Donors

These rankings are consistent with NPOs being involved almost entirely in achieving non-monetary results by spending allocated funds rather than earning money – and many have limited income which needs to be used wisely.

Finally, Ashford reported that although accountants are often involved in the budgeting process, this is by no means always and entirely the case; and in a majority of organisations, the board of finance is involved in the final decision on the level of expenditure.

In the simplest of all cases, the information that should flow from a comparison of the actual against the budgeted figures given in the performance report in the question, would be the variances. By presenting the variances in such a report, the managers of the relevant department can see at a glance the extent of their department's deviations from the expectations stemming from the budgeting exercise.

We can also see scope, based on the information supplied, to enhance the information the management accountant could provide. He or she could be providing actual versus budgeted costs per patient day, and actual versus budgeted costs per weights processed (in lbs): both patient days and weights processed are given in the performance report in the question.

There is often value in providing cumulative actual and budgetary data. Along the lines of some of the reports we have seen in this book so far, year-to-date columns of actual and budgeted information can be given, and can be analysed in the same way that we have been suggesting for the period figures.

Finally, there is always scope for the introduction of percentage (relative) comparisons and common size statements. In the case of the hospital laundry department, we could, for example, set total costs at 100%, and express the individual costs as a percentage of that (common sizing).

(c) We mentioned in part (b) of this solution that we could consider providing costs per patient day or costs per lb processed. Such an amendment to the performance report would help us to give the manager of the laundry an idea of his efficiency.

Secondly, using flexible budgeting would help the laundry manager to assess the level of his or her efficiency by comparing his or her actual performance with the performance he or she would have achieved had he or she been working at standard, or expected, rates of output.

Thirdly, preparing a common size statement would indicate the way the costs are incurred relative to each other, and that would be of great use to the laundry manager in that it would indicate the ways, if any, in which the incidence of costs are changing.

The following three statements are examples of the three ways in which the level of the laundry manager's efficiency might be assessed. Each statement should speak for itself! In the first report, the variance column has been omitted for reasons of space.

Victoria hospital – Laundry department

Report for the quarter ended 30 September 1978

	Patient days		Lbs processed	
	9,000	12,000	180,000	240,000
	Per patient days		Per lb processed	
	Budget	Actual	Budget	Actual
	£	£	£	£
Costs:				
Wages	0.9778	1.0267	0.0489	0.0513
Overtime premium	0.1556	0.1750	0.0078	0.0088
Detergents and other supplies	0.2000	0.2250	0.0100	0.0113
Water, water softening, and heating	0.2222	0.2083	0.0111	0.0104
Maintenance	0.1111	0.1250	0.0056	0.0063
Depreciation of plant	0.2222	0.1667	0.0111	0.0083
Manager's salary	0.1389	0.1250	0.0069	0.0063
Overhead apportioned:				
For occupancy	0.4444	0.3542	0.0222	0.0177
For administration	0.5556	0.4792	0.0278	0.0240

Victoria hospital – Laundry department

Flexible budget report for the quarter ended 30 September 1978

	Fixed budget	Flexible budget	Actual	
	£	£	£	£
Variance:				
Quarterly weighting	1	2		
Variable costs:				
Wages	8,800	14,080	12,320	1,760
Overtime premium	1,400	2,240	2,100	140
Detergents and other supplies	1,800	2,880	2,700	180
Water, water softening and heating	2,000	3,200	2,500	700
Maintenance	1,000	1,600	1,500	100
Overhead apportioned:				
For occupancy	4,000	6,400	4,250	2,150
For administration	5,000	8,000	5,750	2,250
Fixed costs:				
Depreciation of plant	2,000	2,000	2,000	0
Manager's salary	1,250	1,250	1,500	(250)
	27,250	41,650	34,620	7,030

Victoria hospital – Laundry department

Common size report for the quarter ended 30 September 1978

	Budget		Actual	
	£	%	£	%
Costs:				
Wages	8,800	32.29	12,320	35.59
Overtime premium	1,400	5.14	2,100	6.07
Detergents and other supplies	1,800	6.61	2,700	7.80
Water, water softening, and heating	2,000	7.34	2,500	7.22
Maintenance	1,000	3.67	1,500	4.33
Depreciation of plant	2,000	7.34	2,000	5.78
Manager's salary	1,250	4.59	1,500	4.33
Overhead apportioned:				
For occupancy	4,000	14.68	4,250	12.28
For administration	5,000	18.35	5,750	16.61
	27,250	100.00	34,620	100.00

Chapter 15

4. The calculations on which the flexible budget-type statement that follows is based should be very familiar now. We have been given the fixed budget, consisting of standard costs and total annual budgets, as appropriate. All that is necessary is to determine the number of units to be sold and produced at the relevant levels of activity (80% of maximum output, 100% and 110%), and then multiply that number of units by each of the standard costs for materials, labour and variable overheads. In the case of fixed costs, they remain fixed, of course.

Although the solution could have provided subtotals for each of the prime costs and the total variable costs, they have been omitted.

	Production levels (as percentages of maximum output)			
		80%	100%	110%
Sales units	10,000	8,000	10,000	11,000

		Production levels		
	Per unit	80%	100%	110%
	£	£	£	£
Sales	42.50	340,000	425,000	467,500
Direct materials	3.00	24,000	30,000	33,000
Direct labour	2.50	20,000	25,000	27,500
Variable overheads:				
Indirect materials	2.50	20,000	25,000	27,500
Indirect labour	1.25	10,000	12,500	13,750
Electricity	0.35	2,800	3,500	3,850

Water	0.36	2,880	3,600	3,960
Contribution	33.00	260,320	325,400	357,940
Fixed overheads (annually):				
Depreciation		100,000	100,000	100,000
Supervision		75,000	75,000	75,000
Insurance		12,500	12,500	12,500
Maintenance		23,500	23,500	23,500
Rent		50,000	50,000	50,000
Net profit		−680	64,400	96,940

6.

(a) The calculations for this situation are set out in full below in the style adopted in Chapter 15.

Materials

AP × AQ £4.90 × 7,000 units = £34,300

Price variance = £700 fav

SP × AQ £5 × 7,000 units = £35,000

Materials variance = £600 fav

Usage variance = £100 adv

SP × SQ £5 × 6,800 units = £34,000

Note: that the 7,000 units represent the actual usage of raw materials. The standard quantity is the flexible budget amount of 1,700 actual units of goods made multiplied by the standard usage of material per unitL that is, four units of raw material per unit of finished goods.

Labour

AR × AH £12.50 × 3,600 hours = £45,000

Rate variance = £1,800 adv

SR × AH £12.00 × 3,600 hours = £43,200

Labour variance = £4,200 adv

Efficiency variance = £2,400 adv

SR × SH £12.00 × 3,400 hours = £40,800

Note that actual hours worked are 3,600. The standard hours required for the process are 3,400. This represents the multiplication of the 1,700 units made and the standard hours per unit required to make those goods, at two hours per unit.

Variable overheads

AR × AH	= £8,900
Expenditure variance	= £100fav
SR × AH £2.50 × 3,600 hours = £9,000	
Variable overheads	= £400 adv
Efficiency variance	= £500 adv
SR × SH £2.50 × 3,400 hours = £8,500	

Note that the hours here are the same as they were for the labour variance calculations. This is because the absorption rates for the variable overheads are based on direct labour hours.

The actual variable overheads cost is given in total and there is no real need to split it into the actual rate per hour and the actual number of hours: expressing it as £8,900 only is fine.

(b) The statement we are required to prepare here consists only of the standard costs per unit or per hour as relevant, multiplied by the standard inputs per hour or per unit. All of the workings are shown in the table:

Standard variable costs of 1,700 units made

	£
Materials £5.00 per unit × 6,800 units	34,000
Labour £12.00 per hour × 3,400 hours	40,800
Variable overheads £2.50 per hour × 3,400 hours	8,500
Total standard variable costs	83,300

Chapter 16

1. Although we did not discuss the relevance of standard deviations, semi-variances and so on as required by this question, we have discussed many of the technical aspects of them in our chapters on the behaviour of costs. The solution that follows discusses these points, anyway.

Project X

Pr	Outcome	EV	Deviation	(Deviation)^2	Variance
0.2	2,000	400	−1,000	1,000,000	200,000
0.6	3,000	1,800	0	0	0
0.2	4,000	800	1,000	1,000,000	200,000
		3,000		2,000,000	400,000

Note: Pr = probability
EV = expected net present value (NPV)

Standard deviation = 632.46

Semi-variance = 0.2(2,000 − 3,000)2 = 0.2 × 1,000,000 = 200,000
Coefficient of variation = 632.46/3,000 = 0.21082

Project Y

Pr	Outcome	EV	Deviation	(Deviation)^2	Variance
0.2	0	0	−3,000	9,000,000	1,800,000
0.6	3,000	1,800	0	0	0
0.2	6,000	1,200	3,000	9,000,000	1,800,000
		3,000		18,000,000	3,600,000

Standard deviation = 1,897.37

Semi-variance = $0.2(0 - 3{,}000)^2 = 1{,}800{,}000$

Coefficient of variation = 1,897.37/3,000 = 0.21082

Interpretation of the above results:

(a) The standard deviation of project Y is greater than that of project X, therefore prefer project X.
(b) The semi-variance of project Y is greater than that of project X, therefore prefer project X – the semi-variance quantifies the downside risk of a project. The semi-variance only considers the deviations below the mean, since these are the unfavourable, downside, deviations.
(c) The coefficient of variation of project Y is greater than that of project X, therefore prefer project X.

On all three counts, project X is preferred.

6. The initial workings for this question involve calculating the expected values for both the original cost of each project and the cash flows for each of the six years of the lives of the projects. The solution is as follows:

Project A

EV original cost		EV cash flows	
30,000		3,000	
33,000		6,250	
48,000	111,000	7,500	
		5,250	
		4,500	
		4,500	31,000

The EVs are simple to calculate by multiplying the probability for each element by its associated monetary value. For example, for project A, the EV of £30,000 for the original cost is:

Pr(0.3) × £100,000 = £30,000

All other calculations in this table and the equivalent table for project B are done in this way.

Project B

EV original cost		EV cash flows	
112,500		12,500	
42,000		12,500	
60,000	214,500	10,500	
		11,250	
		8,000	
		8,500	63,250

We can now carry out the relevant present value calculations using both of the methods prescribed by the question.

Certainty equivalent method

Project A

Year	EV	CEC		DF (risk free) (10%)	PV £
0	(111,000)	1.00	(111,000)	1.0000	(111,000)
1	31,000	0.90	27,900	0.9091	25,364
2	31,000	0.86	26,660	0.8264	22,033
3	31,000	0.82	25,420	0.7513	19,098
4	31,000	0.77	23,870	0.6830	16,304
5	31,000	0.74	22,940	0.6209	14,244
6	31,000	0.74	22,940	0.5645	12,949
Net present value					(1,008)

Project B

Year	EV	CEC		DF (risk-free) (10%)	PV £
0	(214,500)	1.00	(214,500)	1.0000	(214,500)
1	63,250	0.86	54,395	0.9091	49,450
2	63,250	0.82	51,865	0.8264	42,864
3	13,250	0.78	49,335	0.7513	37,066
4	63,250	0.73	46,173	0.6830	31,536
5	63,250	0.69	43,643	0.6209	27,099
6	63,250	0.69	43,643	0.5645	24,635
Net present value					(1,850)

Our conclusion here is that neither project is acceptable since the NPV for both projects is negative; reject them both.

Risk adjusted discount rate method

Project A

Year	EV	DF (risk-adj,) (12%)	PV £
0	(111,000)	1.0000	(111,000)
1	31,000	0.8929	27,679
2	31,000	0.7972	24,713
3	31,000	0.7118	22,065
4	31,000	0.6355	19,701
5	31,000	0.5674	17,590
6	31,000	0.5066	15,706
Net present value			16,454

Project B

Year	EV	DF (risk-adj.) (18%)	PV £
0	(214,500)	1.0000	(214,500)
1	63,250	0.8475	53,602
2	63,250	0.7182	45,425
3	63,250	0.6086	38,496
4	63,250	0.5158	32,624
5	63,250	0.4371	27,647
6	63,250	0.3704	23,430
Net present value			6,723

Note here that project A has a risk adjusted rate of 10% + 2% = 12%, consistent with the requirements of the question; and project B has a risk adjusted rate of 10% + 8% = 18%.

We can conclude now that both projects are acceptable since they both return a positive net present value. Project A has the more favourable of the two NPVs and should be considered further.

Before we leave this question, by way of comparison we should carry out one further set of calculations and prepare the ordinary NPV calculations using the firm's cost of capital: by way of comparison.

Project A

Year	EV	DF (cost of capital) (14%)	PV £
0	(111,000)	1.0000	(111,000)
1	31,000	0.8772	27,193
2	31,000	0.7695	23,853
3	31,000	0.6750	20,924
4	31,000	0.5921	18,354
5	31,000	0.5194	16,100
6	31,000	0.4556	14,123
Net present value			9,549

Project B

Year	EV	DF (cost of capital) (14%)	PV £
0	(214,500)	1.0000	(214,500)
1	63,250	0.8772	55,482
2	63,250	0.7695	48,669
3	63,250	0.6750	42,692
4	63,250	0.5921	37,449
5	63,250	0.5194	32,850
6	63,250	0.4556	28,816
Net present value			31,458

Here we have a third set of results and a third set of recommendations to make. In this case, we recommend that both projects are suitable for further consideration, but we prefer project B since it is returning the highest NPV of the two projects under consideration.

The question now is, of course, since there are three sets of results and three sets of recommendations, which should we accept?

Essentially, the answer as to which result we accept stems from our own personal attitudes to risk. In this example, it would seem that the certainty equivalent method has taken the position of an extremely risk-averse investor whereas the NPV method has taken us to the other extreme.

As between the methods, however, only the certainty equivalent method is consistent in returning results that are reasonably close to each other.

In a case such as this, we ought, perhaps, to call for further investigation and carry out more tests. We could, for example, calculate profitability indices, the IRR and so on for each project. Alternatively, we simply present our findings to management and ask them to make their own final decision.

Chapter 17

3.

(a) The outflow needed to acquire the new lorry is made up of two parts: the cash price of the vehicle, and the residual value of the old lorry. The calculation is:

	£
Purchase price of new lorry	75,000
less: Resale price of old lorry	15,000
Cash needed to buy new lorry	60,000

(b) The calculation of the post-tax profits accruing to both the old and the new lorries should be straightforward. The schedule below should confirm that:

Profit statement: old and new lorries

	Old lorry £	New lorry £
Sales	65,000	65,000
Costs (excluding depreciation)	40,000	24,000
Depreciation	3,000	7,500
Profit before taxation	22,000	33,500
Taxation (40%)	8,800	13,400
Profit after taxation	13,200	20,100
plus: Depreciation	3,000	7,500
Annual cash flow	16,200	27,600

(c) *Incremental cash flows per year*:

Incremental profit after taxation:

= £11,400

Summary of the cash flows for years 1 to 10:

Year(s)	Cash flow
0	−60,000
1–10	11,400

The differential cash flows for years 1 to 10 can also be derived as follows:

	£
Savings in cash costs	16,000
Increase in tax payable	4,600
Differential cash flows	11,400

6. The solution to this question is relatively difficult to present, so we should consider each project on its own. Notice the cost of capital calculation that follows the three project NPV calculations.

Project 1

Year(s)	Discount or annuity factors	Cash flows £	Present values £
0	1.00000	(200,000)	(200,000.00)
1–10	5.82669	50,000	291,334.39
10	0.34418	30,000	10,325.47
Net present value			101,659.86

With this project, we have two possible ways of determining the NPV (assuming we have realised we can save a lot of effort by recognising the annuity aspects of the project). The first way is to carry out the calculations as we have here. The alternative is to treat years 1 to 9 as the annuity and calculate the whole of the cash flows for year 10 as one figure. Whichever way we do the calculations is largely irrelevant: the solution should be the same; and these comments relating to project 1 also relate to projects 2 and 3.

Project 2

Year(s)	Discount or annuity factors	Cash flows £	Present values £
1–12	6.41412	50,000	320,705.75
2	0.80790	(225,000)	(181,777.54)
5	0.58667	(250,000)	(146,667.64)
9	0.38292	(100,000)	(38,292.15)
Net present value			(46,032.00)

Project 3

Year(s)	Discount or annuity factors	Cash flows £	Present values £
0	1.00000	(525,000)	(525,000.00)
1–5	3.67227	79,000	290,109.59
6–13	2.99178	110,000	329,095.33
13	0.24993	140,000	34,990.74
Net present value			129,195.66

At a weighted average cost of capital of 11.26%, the rank order of the projects is:

(a) project 3 with an NPV of £129,195.66;
(b) project 1 with an NPV of £101,659.86.

The NPV for project 2 is negative at this discount rate and should not be considered further.

Cost of capital calculation

Permanent capital	Market price	Market value	Rate	Cost
Ordinary shares	1.35	270,000	11.1111%	30,000
Debentures	97.50	1,462,500	11.2821%	165,000
Total		1,732,500		195,000

Note that the rates given in the question are the rates based on the nominal values of the capitals. We need to calculate their market rate equivalents, as follows:

$$\text{Ordinary dividend} = \frac{£0.15}{1.35} \times 100$$

$$= 11.1111\%$$

$$\text{Debentures} = \frac{0.11}{0.975} \times 100$$

$$= 11.2821\%$$

$$\text{WACC} = \frac{£195{,}000}{£1{,}732{,}500} \times 100$$

$$= 11.26\%$$

Chapter 18

2.

(a) The present book value of the factory would be:

£150,000 − (10 × 1.5% × £150,000) = £127,500

As we are told that profits of £91,000 represent a rate of return of 26% on capital employed, the total book value of the capital employed by AB Ltd must be:

£91,000/0.26 = £350,000

The value of net assets other than the factory would therefore be: £222,500.

As a result of the group's proposal, the declared profit of AB Ltd would be:

	£
Existing profits	91,000
Add depreciation charge, no longer made ($1\frac{1}{2}$% × £150,000)	2,250
Deduct rent (10% × £300,000)	(30,000)
Adjusted profit	63,250

The new rate of return on capital employed would therefore be £63,250/£222,500 = 28.43%, that is, 2.43% higher than the rate of return currently calculated.

(b) In assessing the performance of an individual company, the only requirement relating to the valuation of assets and the calculation of profit is that both target (or budget) and actual figures shall be calculated on the same basis. If the performance of a company is to be compared with that of other companies, either within or outside the group, it is essential that the 'actual' figures of all of them shall be on a common basis. In particular:

(i) It is not valid to compare rates of return on capital employed when similar assets in different companies were acquired at different prices (and thus give rise to different depreciation charges) for reasons not connected with operating requirements. A common solution to this difficulty is to revalue the assets of all companies at a common – normally, a current – price level.

(ii) It is not valid to compare rates of return on capital employed when some companies occupy purchased premises and others are renting the premises they use. A common solution is to delete the value of premises from the figure of capital employed, and to charge the profit and loss account with an economic rental for the premises occupied. The group in this question therefore has proposed a correct solution to one of the problems of intercompany comparison, and at the same time has created a property-holding company from the results of which the benefit of property investment can be judged.

4. (a) (i)

	Division P (£'000)	Q (£'000)	R (£'000)	S (£'000)
Profit original I9X0 budget	80	150	84	26
Proposals:				
Additions to profit	20		30	11.2
Reductions of profit		15	20	
Revised profit	100	135	94	37.2
Capital employed:				
Original 1980 budget	320	450	280	200
Proposals:				
Additions to C/E	100		100	80

Reductions of C/E		75	20	
Revised capital employed	420	375	360	280
ROI (%)	23.8	36	26.1	13.3

(ii) ROI on original budget

	Division			
	P	Q	R	S
Percentage	25	33	30	13

Therefore the divisional managers of Q and S will benefit from increased bonus payments in 19X0.

(iii) The group's cost of capital is stated to be 12% and this is therefore the hurdle rate for investment and divestment decisions in the divisions. The 12% rate would preferably be used as a discount rate to be applied to the incremental cash flows. This is not possible in this question since the inclusion of working capital in the investments makes it impossible to establish depreciation figures and therefore cash flows. As a result the ROI approach to this part of the question will have to be taken using l9X0 figures, even though we know that ROI will tend to increase year by year since depreciation reduces the investment base.

	Division			
	P	Q	R	S
	(£'000)	(£'000)	(£'000)	(£'000)
Incremental or (lost) profit	20	(15)	10	11.2
Incremental or (lost) C/E	100	(75)	80	80
	%	%	%	%
	20	(20)	12.5	14
ROI for proposal	20	(20)	12.5	14
ROI for original budget	25	33	30	13
Group cost of capital	12	12	12	12

Thus in almost every case the ROI for the proposal exceeds the group cost of capital. This means that the proposals for divisions P, R and S are favourable to the group interest, despite the fact that it has already been shown in part (a)(i) that divisional ROI for P and R will deteriorate. The proposal for division Q should not be undertaken since it deprives the group of a return in excess of the group cost of capital. However, there is the unanswered question of what return may be earned on the reinvestment of the sales proceeds of £75,000.

(b) As suggested under (a)(iii), the 12% cost of capital should be used as a discount rate, and the proposal for division Q eliminated from the range of possibilities. Available new investment funds are £200,000.

Competing projects:

	Finance required (£)	ROI (%)	Residual income (£)
Division P	100,000	20.0	8,000
Division R	80,000 (net)	12.5%	400
Division S	80,000	14.0	1,600

The board would therefore choose the projects in divisions P and S, as having the highest ROI figures and the highest aggregate residual income.

(c) (i) The term 'old results' is taken to mean the I9X0 budget on the assumption that none of the proposals is to be implemented.

	Division P	S
ROI (%)	25	13
Profit/sales (%)	10	13
Capital turnover rate	2.5	1

Hence:

Division P 2.5 × 10% = 25%

Division S 1 × 13% = 13%

The profit/sales % in division S compares favourably with that of division P. This suggests that division S's problems may not be cost inefficiency, low product volume, etc. The real problem seems to be the turnover of capital employed. If this figure could be raised to 2, for example, ROI would become 26%. Whilst additional volume would tend to increase both the profit/sales % and the capital turnover rate (and therefore ROI), it may pay the divisional manager in S to question asset utilisation, stock levels credit control, etc., to see if the same level and profitability of sales is possible on a lower level of net asset investment.

(ii) The proposal in division S was:

ROI	£11,200/£80,000 = 14%
Profit/sales %	£11,200/£36,000 = 31%
Capital turnover, etc.	£36,000/£80,000 = 0.45 times

It is evident, therefore, that whilst the proposal offers an ROI marginally in excess of the 12% cost of capital, it does so by margin profitability, since the capital turnover rate is less than half the existing one. In this sense, then, it is not consistent with the advice given in (c)(i).

(d) In part (a)(iii) it was suggested that the divestment decision should be made incrementally. Because of this view the proposal for division Q was rejected, since by depriving the division of £75,000 income from the sale of a project the division was also deprived of £15,000 profits: that is, a return of 20%, considerably in excess of the 12% cost of capital. The decision changes, therefore, when the rising disposal value makes the potential profit equal to 12% of that disposal value: that is, £15,000 is to equal 12%, and breakeven disposal value is £125,000

(e) (i) The concept of residual income attempts to give recognition to the investment base. In this way comparisons of residual income are valid, in that a financing cost has already been taken out of profits made.

(ii)

	Division P (£'000)	Q (£'000)	R (£'000)	S (£'000)
Profit forecast	100.0	135.0	94.0	37.2
Cost of capital	50.4	45.0	43.2	33.6
Residual income	49.6	90.0	50.8	3.6

Note that the above calculations could have been made using the return on capital employed figure of 15%.

Chapter 19

1.

(a) **Alternative methods of transfer pricing**

(i) *At market prices*. The price would be that at which an outside competitor would be prepared to supply. Provided the supplier factory is able to produce the components at a variable *cost* which is lower than the competitive price, it is in the company's interest that it should be given the order. There may be instances where none of the company's factories is technically equipped to compete economically, in which case the work should be ordered outside.

(ii) *At cost plus*. The price would include not only full cost, but also an added profit margin. This is a fair basis for the supplying factory but, unless exceptions are made, it could result in the buying factory paying more than a fair market price. Where cost is an element in arriving at a price, such cost may be actual or standard. Standards are preferable as unpredictable month by month fluctuations are avoided and there is also a fairer sharing of the inefficiency factor. No factory operates to perfection and the buyer should be prepared to pay a reasonable amount towards the difficulties and lapses from perfection inherent in manufacture, but he or she should not be charged with additional cost arising from exceptional carelessness or lack of control. Standard costs provide an excellent basis, as they are usually based on good attainable performance and include only reasonable allowances for lapses from perfection. A modification of full cost often encountered in practice is to exclude from the cost figure those selling and administration costs which are specific to external sales but are not necessary to the achievement of internal sales. At the extreme, this may be equivalent to transferring at manufacturing cost. It is sometimes listed as a separate method.

(iii) *At negotiated price*. Where competitive prices are not available, prices could be negotiated between the factories concerned. These would be regarded as commercially based and would be in lieu of market prices. Not being linked with some firm base they could be unrealistic.

(b) **Preferred method**

When it can be used, the preferred method is the open market price, which gives the following advantages:

(i) It offers a fair reward to the supplying factory as well as an incentive to produce efficiently.
(ii) It leaves the buying factory in the same position as it would have been if the associated factory had not existed.
(iii) It cannot lead to controversy as to the efficiency or inefficiency of the manufacturing unit.
(iv) Executive time is not devoted to the bargaining process.

If, however, the components transferred are destined purely for incorporation into the company's end product and no outside market for them exists, there will be no market price. Under such circumstances, goal congruence is best achieved by making the transfers at variable cost. This however, provides no incentive to the transferor division, and two main alternative solutions to the problem are suggested:

(i) to transfer at full cost (plus profit if desired) but to declare to the buying division the variable cost content of that price; or
(ii) to transfer at variable cost, but to allow the selling division to make periodic lump-sum charges to cover its fixed costs and profit mark-up: that is, to have a two-part tariff.

(c) **Policy statement for transfers at market price**

(i) Interfactory sales will be effected at market price.
(ii) No factory will be obliged to accept an order from an associated factory at market price if the former is not equipped to manufacture at a cost which at least allows a reasonable contribution towards its fixed costs, or if the acceptance of such an order would result in more profitable work being displaced.

(iii) Where a factory is prepared to supply components at market price, the buying factory will be obliged to buy therefrom, unless it can be established that there are reasons to doubt that quality or delivery will be satisfactory.

(iv) Where it is not reasonably possible to obtain an outside quotation for a component the transfer price will be full standard cost plus 10% profit.

(v) Difficulties arising concerning interfactory pricing will be referred to the chief accountant who will give a ruling based on the overriding company interest.

4. (a)

	£
Variable cost 120,000 × £14	1,680,000
Fixed cost	60,000
Imputed interest £1,600,000 × 15%	240,000
Residual income	300,000
	2,280,000
External sales revenue 80,000 × £20	1,600,000
Revenue required from transfers	680,000
Units transferred	40,000
Hence transfer price per unit	£17

(b) XY division may be able to purchase the component from an external source at a price less than £17 per unit. In this case it will choose the external source of supply unless there is a group diktat that it must purchase from CB division. The cost to the group in cash flow terms of the 40,000 units available for transfer from CB division is the variable cost of £14 per unit. Assuming there is no other opportunity available:

Transfer price

= Variable cost + opportunity cost to the group

= £14 + £0

= £14

Hence if XY division purchases externally at, say, £16.50 per unit, the group will spend an extra £2.50 per unit, that is, £100,000 in total.

(c) (i) To achieve target residual income:

	£
40,000 units at £17	680,000
10,000 units at £20	200,000
50,000 units	880,000

The average price per component is £17.60. If XY Division is quoted a price of £17.60 per component it will choose external Company L as the cheapest source at £15.50 per component. Total cost to the group is:

50,000 × £15.50 = £775,000.

(ii) To reflect the opportunity cost of components transferred:

	£
40,000 × £14	560,000
10,000 × £20	200,000
50,000	760,000

The average price per component is £15.20. XY Division will now choose to purchase from CB Division at £15.20 which is a lower unit price than that quoted by external companies L and M. The total cost to the group is £760,000. This is the variable cost for 50,000 units plus the contribution forgone on the 10,000 units of external sales given up.

(iii) CB Division will quote for 40,000 units at £14 per unit and 10,000 units at £20 per unit. This gives additional information to XY Division who will now choose 40,000 units from CB Division at £14 per unit and 10,000 units from Company M at £18 per unit. Note that Company L is not willing to supply 10,000 units at £15 50 per unit and this is not, therefore, a possible source. Total cost to the group is:

	£
40,000 × £14	560,000
10,000 × £18	180,000
	740,000

(d) Group profit is maximised where method (iii) is implemented, since costs are minimised at £740,000. If method (ii) is implemented group profits are reduced by £760,000 – £740,000 = £20,000. If method (i) is implemented group profits are reduced by £775,000 – £740,000 = £35,000. Methods (i) and (ii) have led to sub optimal group decisions because of incomplete information flow between (FR Division and XY Division).

Appendix

TABLE A.1 ***Compound interest factors: Based on annual compounding periods***

Year	Cost of capital 1%	2%	3%	4%	5%	6%	7%	8%	9%	10%
1	1.010	1.020	1.030	1.040	1.050	1.060	1.070	1.080	1.090	1.100
2	1.020	1.040	1.061	1.082	1.103	1.124	1.145	1.166	1.188	1.210
3	1.030	1.061	1.093	1.125	1.158	1.191	1.225	1.260	1.295	1.331
4	1.041	1.082	1.126	1.170	1.216	1.262	1.311	1.360	1.412	1.464
5	1.051	1.104	1.159	1.217	1.276	1.338	1.403	1.469	1.539	1.611
6	1.062	1.126	1.194	1.265	1.340	1.419	1.501	1.587	1.677	1.772
7	1.072	1.149	1.230	1.316	1.407	1.504	1.606	1.714	1.828	1.949
8	1.083	1.172	1.267	1.369	1.477	1.594	1.718	1.851	1.993	2.144
9	1.094	1.195	1.305	1.423	1.551	1.689	1.838	1.999	2.172	2.358
10	1.105	1.219	1.344	1.480	1.629	1.791	1.967	2.159	2.367	2.594
11	1.116	1.243	1.384	1.539	1.710	1.898	2.105	2.332	2.580	2.853
12	1.127	1.268	1.426	1.601	1.796	2.012	2.252	2.518	2.813	3.138
13	1.138	1.294	1.469	1.665	1.886	2.133	2.410	2.720	3.066	3.452
14	1.149	1.319	1.513	1.732	1.980	2.261	2.579	2.937	3.342	3.797
15	1.161	1.346	1.558	1.801	2.079	2.397	2.759	3.172	3.642	4.177
16	1.173	1.373	1.605	1.873	2.183	2.540	2.952	3.426	3.970	4.595
17	1.184	1.400	1.653	1.948	2.292	2.693	3.159	3.700	4.328	5.054
18	1.196	1.428	1.702	2.026	2.407	2.854	3.380	3.996	4.717	5.560
19	1.208	1.457	1.754	2.107	2.527	3.026	3.617	4.316	5.142	6.116
20	1.220	1.486	1.806	2.191	2.653	3.207	3.870	4.661	5.604	6.727
21	1.232	1.516	1.860	2.279	2.786	3.400	4.141	5.034	6.109	7.400
22	1.245	1.546	1.916	2.370	2.925	3.604	4.430	5.437	6.659	8.140
23	1.257	1.577	1.974	2.465	3.072	3.820	4.741	5.871	7.258	8.954
24	1.270	1.608	2.033	2.563	3.225	4.049	5.072	6.341	7.911	9.850
25	1.282	1.641	2.094	2.666	3.386	4.292	5.427	6.848	8.623	10.835
26	1.295	1.673	2.157	2.772	3.556	4.549	5.807	7.396	9.399	11.918
27	1.308	1.707	2.221	2.883	3.733	4.822	6.214	7.988	10.245	13.110
28	1.321	1.741	2.288	2.999	3.920	5.112	6.649	8.627	11.167	14.421
29	1.335	1.776	2.357	3.119	4.116	5.418	7.114	9.317	12.172	15.863
30	1.348	1.811	2.427	3.243	4.322	5.743	7.612	10.063	13.268	17.449
31	1.361	1.848	2.500	3.373	4.538	6.088	8.145	10.868	14.462	19.194
32	1.375	1.885	2.575	3.508	4.765	6.453	8.715	11.737	15.763	21.114
33	1.389	1.922	2.652	3.648	5.003	6.841	9.325	12.676	17.182	23.225
34	1.403	1.961	2.732	3.794	5.253	7.251	9.978	13.690	18.728	25.548
35	1.417	2.000	2.814	3.946	5.516	7.686	10.677	14.785	20.414	28.102

TABLE A.1 ***Continued***

Year	Cost of capital 11%	12%	13%	14%	15%	16%	17%	18%	19%	20%
1	1.110	1.120	1.130	1.140	1.150	1.160	1.170	1.180	1.190	1.200
2	1.232	1.254	1.277	1.300	1.323	1.346	1.369	1.392	1.416	1.440
3	1.368	1.405	1.443	1.482	1.521	1.561	1.602	1.643	1.685	1.728
4	1.518	1.574	1.630	1.689	1.749	1.811	1.874	1.939	2.005	2.074
5	1.685	1.762	1.842	1.925	2.011	2.100	2.192	2.288	2.386	2.488
6	1.870	1.974	2.082	2.195	2.313	2.436	2.565	2.700	2.840	2.986
7	2.076	2.211	2.353	2.502	2.660	2.826	3.001	3.185	3.379	3.583
8	2.305	2.476	2.658	2.853	3.059	3.278	3.511	3.759	4.021	4.300
9	2.558	2.773	3.004	3.252	3.518	3.803	4.108	4.435	4.785	5.160
10	2.839	3.106	3.395	3.707	4.046	4.411	4.807	5.234	5.695	6.192
11	3.152	3.479	3.836	4.226	4.652	5.117	5.624	6.176	6.777	7.430
12	3.498	3.896	4.335	4.818	5.350	5.936	6.580	7.288	8.064	8.916
13	3.883	4.363	4.898	5.492	6.153	6.886	7.699	8.599	9.596	10.699
14	4.310	4.887	5.535	6.261	7.076	7.988	9.007	10.147	11.420	12.839
15	4.785	5.474	6.254	7.138	8.137	9.266	10.539	11.974	13.590	15.407
16	5.311	6.130	7.067	8.137	9.358	10.748	12.330	14.129	16.172	18.488
17	5.895	6.866	7.986	9.276	10.761	12.468	14.426	16.672	19.244	22.186
18	6.544	7.690	9.024	10.575	12.375	14.463	16.879	19.673	22.901	26.623
19	7.263	8.613	10.197	12.056	14.232	16.777	19.748	23.214	27.252	31.948
20	8.062	9.646	11.523	13.743	16.367	19.461	23.106	27.393	32.429	38.338
21	8.949	10.804	13.021	15.668	18.822	22.574	27.034	32.324	38.591	46.005
22	9.934	12.100	14.714	17.861	21.645	26.186	31.629	38.142	45.923	55.206
23	11.026	13.552	16.627	20.362	24.891	30.376	37.006	45.008	54.649	66.247
24	12.239	15.179	18.788	23.212	28.625	35.236	43.297	53.109	65.032	79.497
25	13.585	17.000	21.231	26.462	32.919	40.874	50.658	62.669	77.388	95.396
26	15.080	19.040	23.991	30.167	37.857	47.414	59.270	73.949	92.092	114.475
27	16.739	21.325	27.109	34.390	43.535	55.000	69.345	87.260	109.589	137.371
28	18.580	23.884	30.633	39.204	50.066	63.800	81.134	102.967	130.411	164.845
29	20.624	26.750	34.616	44.693	57.575	74.009	94.927	121.501	155.189	197.814
30	22.892	29.960	39.116	50.950	66.212	85.850	111.065	143.371	184.675	237.376
31	25.410	33.555	44.201	58.083	76.144	99.586	129.946	169.177	219.764	284.852
32	28.206	37.582	49.947	66.215	87.565	115.520	152.036	199.629	261.519	341.822
33	31.308	42.092	56.440	75.485	100.700	134.003	177.883	235.563	311.207	410.186
34	34.752	47.143	63.777	86.053	115.805	155.443	208.123	277.964	370.337	492.244
35	38.575	52.800	72.069	98.100	133.176	180.314	243.503	327.997	440.701	590.668

TABLE A.1 ***Continued***

Year	Cost of capital 21%	22%	23%	24%	25%	26%	27%	28%	29%	30%
1	1.210	1.220	1.230	1.240	1.250	1.260	1.270	1.280	1.290	1.300
2	1.464	1.488	1.513	1.538	1.563	1.588	1.613	1.638	1.664	1.690
3	1.772	1.816	1.861	1.907	1.953	2.000	2.048	2.097	2.147	2.197
4	2.144	2.215	2.289	2.364	2.441	2.520	2.601	2.684	2.769	2.856
5	2.594	2.703	2.815	2.932	3.052	3.176	3.304	3.436	3.572	3.713
6	3.138	3.297	3.463	3.635	3.815	4.002	4.196	4.398	4.608	4.827
7	3.797	4.023	4.259	4.508	4.768	5.042	5.329	5.629	5.945	6.275
8	4.595	4.908	5.239	5.590	5.960	6.353	6.768	7.206	7.669	8.157
9	5.560	5.987	6.444	6.931	7.451	8.005	8.595	9.223	9.893	10.604
10	6.727	7.305	7.926	8.594	9.313	10.086	10.915	11.806	12.761	13.786
11	8.140	8.912	9.749	10.657	11.642	12.708	13.862	15.112	16.462	17.922
12	9.850	10.872	11.991	13.215	14.552	16.012	17.605	19.343	21.236	23.298
13	11.918	13.264	14.749	16.386	18.190	20.175	22.359	24.759	27.395	30.288
14	14.421	16.182	18.141	20.319	22.737	25.421	28.396	31.691	35.339	39.374
15	17.449	19.742	22.314	25.196	28.422	32.030	36.062	40.565	45.587	51.186
16	21.114	24.086	27.446	31.243	35.527	40.358	45.799	51.923	58.808	66.542
17	25.548	29.384	33.759	38.741	44.409	50.851	58.165	66.461	75.862	86.504
18	30.913	35.849	41.523	48.039	55.511	64.072	73.870	85.071	97.862	112.455
19	37.404	43.736	51.074	59.568	69.389	80.731	93.815	108.890	126.242	146.192
20	45.259	53.358	62.821	73.864	86.736	101.721	119.145	139.380	162.852	190.050
21	54.764	65.096	77.269	91.592	108.420	128.169	151.314	178.406	210.080	247.065
22	66.264	79.418	95.041	113.574	135.525	161.492	192.168	228.360	271.003	321.184
23	80.180	96.889	116.901	140.831	169.407	203.480	244.054	292.300	349.593	417.539
24	97.017	118.205	143.788	174.631	211.758	256.385	309.948	374.144	450.976	542.801
25	117.391	144.210	176.859	216.542	264.698	323.045	393.634	478.905	581.759	705.641
26	142.043	175.936	217.537	268.512	330.872	407.037	499.916	612.998	750.468	917.333
27	171.872	214.642	267.570	332.955	413.590	512.867	634.893	784.638	968.104	1192.533
28	207.965	261.864	329.112	412.864	516.988	646.212	806.314	1004.336	1248.855	1550.293
29	251.638	319.474	404.807	511.952	646.235	814.228	1024.019	1285.550	1611.022	2015.381
30	304.482	389.758	497.913	634.820	807.794	1025.927	1300.504	1645.505	2078.219	2619.996
31	368.423	475.505	612.433	787.177	1009.742	1292.668	1651.640	2106.246	2680.902	3405.994
32	445.792	580.116	753.292	976.099	1262.177	1628.761	2097.583	2695.995	3458.364	4427.793
33	539.408	707.741	926.550	1210.363	1577.722	2052.239	2663.930	3450.873	4461.290	5756.130
34	652.683	863.444	1139.656	1500.850	1972.152	2585.821	3383.191	4417.118	5755.064	7482.970
35	789.747	1053.402	1401.777	1861.054	2465.190	3258.135	4296.653	5653.911	7424.032	9727.860

TABLE A.2 ***Present value factors: Based on annual compounding periods***

Year	Cost of capital 1%	2%	3%	4%	5%	6%	7%	8%	9%	10%
1	0.9901	0.9804	0.9709	0.9615	0.9524	0.9434	0.9346	0.9259	0.9174	0.9091
2	0.9803	0.9612	0.9426	0.9246	0.9070	0.8900	0.8734	0.8573	0.8417	0.8264
3	0.9706	0.9423	0.9151	0.8890	0.8638	0.8396	0.8163	0.7938	0.7722	0.7513
4	0.9610	0.9238	0.8885	0.8548	0.8227	0.7921	0.7629	0.7350	0.7084	0.6830
5	0.9515	0.9057	0.8626	0.8219	0.7835	0.7473	0.7130	0.6806	0.6499	0.6209
6	0.9420	0.8880	0.8375	0.7903	0.7462	0.7050	0.6663	0.6302	0.5963	0.5645
7	0.9327	0.8706	0.8131	0.7599	0.7107	0.6651	0.6227	0.5835	0.5470	0.5132
8	0.9235	0.8535	0.7894	0.7307	0.6768	0.6274	0.5820	0.5403	0.5019	0.4665
9	0.9143	0.8368	0.7664	0.7026	0.6446	0.5919	0.5439	0.5002	0.4604	0.4241
10	0.9053	0.8203	0.7441	0.6756	0.6139	0.5584	0.5083	0.4632	0.4224	0.3855
11	0.8963	0.8043	0.7224	0.6496	0.5847	0.5268	0.4751	0.4289	0.3875	0.3505
12	0.8874	0.7885	0.7014	0.6246	0.5568	0.4970	0.4440	0.3971	0.3555	0.3186
13	0.8787	0.7730	0.6810	0.6006	0.5303	0.4688	0.4150	0.3677	0.3262	0.2897
14	0.8700	0.7579	0.6611	0.5775	0.5051	0.4423	0.3878	0.3405	0.2992	0.2633
15	0.8613	0.7430	0.6419	0.5553	0.4810	0.4173	0.3624	0.3152	0.2745	0.2394
16	0.8528	0.7284	0.6232	0.5339	0.4581	0.3936	0.3387	0.2919	0.2519	0.2176
17	0.8444	0.7142	0.6050	0.5134	0.4363	0.3714	0.3166	0.2703	0.2311	0.1978
18	0.8360	0.7002	0.5874	0.4936	0.4155	0.3503	0.2959	0.2502	0.2120	0.1799
19	0.8277	0.6864	0.5703	0.4746	0.3957	0.3305	0.2765	0.2317	0.1945	0.1635
20	0.8195	0.6730	0.5537	0.4564	0.3769	0.3118	0.2584	0.2145	0.1784	0.1486
21	0.8114	0.6598	0.5375	0.4388	0.3589	0.2942	0.2415	0.1987	0.1637	0.1351
22	0.8034	0.6468	0.5219	0.4220	0.3418	0.2775	0.2257	0.1839	0.1502	0.1228
23	0.7954	0.6342	0.5067	0.4057	0.3256	0.2618	0.2109	0.1703	0.1378	0.1117
24	0.7876	0.6217	0.4919	0.3901	0.3101	0.2470	0.1971	0.1577	0.1264	0.1015
25	0.7798	0.6095	0.4776	0.3751	0.2953	0.2330	0.1842	0.1460	0.1160	0.0923
26	0.7720	0.5976	0.4637	0.3607	0.2812	0.2198	0.1722	0.1352	0.1064	0.0839
27	0.7644	0.5859	0.4502	0.3468	0.2678	0.2074	0.1609	0.1252	0.0976	0.0763
28	0.7568	0.5744	0.4371	0.3335	0.2551	0.1956	0.1504	0.1159	0.0895	0.0693
29	0.7493	0.5631	0.4243	0.3207	0.2429	0.1846	0.1406	0.1073	0.0822	0.0630
30	0.7419	0.5521	0.4120	0.3083	0.2314	0.1741	0.1314	0.0994	0.0754	0.0573
31	0.7346	0.5412	0.4000	0.2965	0.2204	0.1643	0.1228	0.0920	0.0691	0.0521
32	0.7273	0.5306	0.3883	0.2851	0.2099	0.1550	0.1147	0.0852	0.0634	0.0474
33	0.7201	0.5202	0.3770	0.2741	0.1999	0.1462	0.1072	0.0789	0.0582	0.0431
34	0.7130	0.5100	0.3660	0.2636	0.1904	0.1379	0.1002	0.0730	0.0534	0.0391
35	0.7059	0.5000	0.3554	0.2534	0.1813	0.1301	0.0937	0.0676	0.0490	0.0356

TABLE A.2 ***Continued***

Year	Cost of capital 11%	12%	13%	14%	15%	16%	17%	18%	19%	20%
1	0.9009	0.8929	0.8850	0.8772	0.8696	0.8621	0.8547	0.8475	0.8403	0.8333
2	0.8116	0.7972	0.7831	0.7695	0.7561	0.7432	0.7305	0.7182	0.7062	0.6944
3	0.7312	0.7118	0.6931	0.6750	0.6575	0.6407	0.6244	0.6086	0.5934	0.5787
4	0.6587	0.6355	0.6133	0.5921	0.5718	0.5523	0.5337	0.5158	0.4987	0.4823
5	0.5935	0.5674	0.5428	0.5194	0.4972	0.4761	0.4561	0.4371	0.4190	0.4019
6	0.5346	0.5066	0.4803	0.4556	0.4323	0.4104	0.3898	0.3704	0.3521	0.3349
7	0.4817	0.4523	0.4251	0.3996	0.3759	0.3538	0.3332	0.3139	0.2959	0.2791
8	0.4339	0.4039	0.3762	0.3506	0.3269	0.3050	0.2848	0.2660	0.2487	0.2326
9	0.3909	0.3606	0.3329	0.3075	0.2843	0.2630	0.2434	0.2255	0.2090	0.1938
10	0.3522	0.3220	0.2946	0.2697	0.2472	0.2267	0.2080	0.1911	0.1756	0.1615
11	0.3173	0.2875	0.2607	0.2366	0.2146	0.1954	0.1778	0.1619	0.1476	0.1346
12	0.2858	0.2567	0.2307	0.2076	0.1869	0.1685	0.1520	0.1372	0.1240	0.1122
13	0.2575	0.2292	0.2042	0.1821	0.1625	0.1452	0.1299	0.1163	0.1042	0.0935
14	0.2320	0.2046	0.1807	0.1597	0.1413	0.1252	0.1110	0.0985	0.0876	0.0779
15	0.2090	0.1827	0.1599	0.1401	0.1229	0.1079	0.0949	0.0835	0.0736	0.0649
16	0.1883	0.1631	0.1415	0.1229	0.1069	0.0930	0.0811	0.0708	0.0618	0.0541
17	0.1696	0.1456	0.1252	0.1078	0.0929	0.0802	0.0693	0.0600	0.0520	0.0451
18	0.1528	0.1300	0.1108	0.0946	0.0808	0.0691	0.0592	0.0508	0.0437	0.0376
19	0.1377	0.1161	0.0981	0.0829	0.0703	0.0596	0.0506	0.0431	0.0367	0.0313
20	0.1240	0.1037	0.0868	0.0728	0.0611	0.0514	0.0433	0.0365	0.0308	0.0261
21	0.1117	0.0926	0.0768	0.0638	0.0531	0.0443	0.0370	0.0309	0.0259	0.0217
22	0.1007	0.0826	0.0680	0.0560	0.0462	0.0382	0.0316	0.0262	0.0218	0.0181
23	0.0907	0.0738	0.0601	0.0491	0.0402	0.0329	0.0270	0.0222	0.0183	0.0151
24	0.0817	0.0659	0.0532	0.0431	0.0349	0.0284	0.0231	0.0188	0.0154	0.0126
25	0.0736	0.0588	0.0471	0.0378	0.0304	0.0245	0.0197	0.0160	0.0129	0.0105
26	0.0663	0.0525	0.0417	0.0331	0.0264	0.0211	0.0169	0.0135	0.0109	0.0087
27	0.0597	0.0469	0.0369	0.0291	0.0230	0.0182	0.0144	0.0115	0.0091	0.0073
28	0.0538	0.0419	0.0326	0.0255	0.0200	0.0157	0.0123	0.0097	0.0077	0.0061
29	0.0485	0.0374	0.0289	0.0224	0.0174	0.0135	0.0105	0.0082	0.0064	0.0051
30	0.0437	0.0334	0.0256	0.0196	0.0151	0.0116	0.0090	0.0070	0.0054	0.0042
31	0.0394	0.0298	0.0226	0.0172	0.0131	0.0100	0.0077	0.0059	0.0046	0.0035
32	0.0355	0.0266	0.0200	0.0151	0.0114	0.0087	0.0066	0.0050	0.0058	0.0029
33	0.0319	0.0238	0.0177	0.0132	0.0099	0.0075	0.0056	0.0042	0.0032	0.0024
34	0.0288	0.0212	0.0157	0.0116	0.0086	0.0064	0.0048	0.0036	0.0027	0.0020
35	0.0259	0.0189	0.0139	0.0102	0.0075	0.0055	0.0041	0.0030	0.0023	0.0017

TABLE A.2 ***Continued***

Year	Cost of capital 21%	22%	23%	24%	25%	26%	27%	28%	29%	30%
1	0.8264	0.8197	0.8130	0.8065	0.8000	0.7937	0.7874	0.7813	0.7752	0.7692
2	0.6830	0.6719	0.6610	0.6504	0.6400	0.6299	0.6200	0.6104	0.6009	0.5917
3	0.5645	0.5507	0.5374	0.5245	0.5120	0.4999	0.4882	0.4768	0.4658	0.4552
4	0.4665	0.4514	0.4369	0.4230	0.4094	0.3968	0.3844	0.3725	0.3611	0.3501
5	0.3855	0.3700	0.3552	0.3411	0.3277	0.3149	0.3027	0.2910	0.2799	0.2693
6	0.3186	0.3033	0.2888	0.2751	0.2621	0.2499	0.2383	0.2274	0.2170	0.2072
7	0.2633	0.2486	0.2348	0.2218	0.2097	0.1983	0.1877	0.1776	0.1682	0.1594
8	0.2176	0.2038	0.1909	0.1789	0.1678	0.1574	0.1478	0.1388	0.1304	0.1226
9	0.1799	0.1670	0.1552	0.1443	0.1342	0.1249	0.1164	0.1084	0.1011	0.0943
10	0.1486	0.1369	0.1262	0.1164	0.1074	0.0992	0.0916	0.0847	0.0784	0.0725
11	0.1228	0.1122	0.1026	0.0938	0.0859	0.0787	0.0721	0.0662	0.0607	0.0558
12	0.1015	0.0920	0.0834	0.0757	0.0687	0.0625	0.0568	0.0517	0.0471	0.0429
13	0.0839	0.0754	0.0678	0.0610	0.0550	0.0496	0.0447	0.0404	0.0365	0.0330
14	0.0693	0.0618	0.0551	0.0492	0.0440	0.0393	0.0352	0.0316	0.0283	0.0254
15	0.0573	0.0507	0.0448	0.0397	0.0352	0.0312	0.0277	0.0247	0.0219	0.0195
16	0.0474	0.0415	0.0364	0.0320	0.0281	0.0248	0.0218	0.0193	0.0170	0.0150
17	0.0391	0.0340	0.0296	0.0258	0.0225	0.0197	0.0172	0.0150	0.0132	0.0116
18	0.0323	0.0279	0.0241	0.0208	0.0180	0.0156	0.0135	0.0118	0.0102	0.0089
19	0.0267	0.0229	0.0196	0.0168	0.0144	0.0124	0.0107	0.0092	0.0079	0.0068
20	0.0221	0.0187	0.0159	0.0135	0.0115	0.0098	0.0084	0.0072	0.0061	0.0053
21	0.0183	0.0154	0.0129	0.0109	0.0092	0.0078	0.0066	0.0056	0.0048	0.0040
22	0.0151	0.0126	0.0105	0.0088	0.0074	0.0062	0.0052	0.0044	0.0037	0.0031
23	0.0125	0.0103	0.0086	0.0071	0.0059	0.0049	0.0041	0.0034	0.0029	0.0024
24	0.0103	0.0085	0.0070	0.0057	0.0047	0.0039	0.0032	0.0027	0.0022	0.0018
25	0.0085	0.0069	0.0057	0.0046	0.0038	0.0031	0.0025	0.0021	0.0017	0.0014
26	0.0070	0.0057	0.0046	0.0037	0.0030	0.0025	0.0020	0.0016	0.0013	0.0011
27	0.0058	0.0047	0.0037	0.0030	0.0024	0.0019	0.0016	0.0013	0.0010	0.0008
28	0.0048	0.0038	0.0030	0.0024	0.0019	0.0015	0.0012	0.0010	0.0008	0.0006
29	0.0040	0.0031	0.0025	0.0020	0.0015	0.0012	0.0010	0.0008	0.0006	0.0005
30	0.0033	0.0026	0.0020	0.0016	0.0012	0.0010	0.0008	0.0006	0.0005	0.0004
31	0.0027	0.0021	0.0016	0.0013	0.0010	0.0008	0.0006	0.0005	0.0004	0.0003
32	0.0022	0.0017	0.0013	0.0010	0.0008	0.0006	0.0005	0.0004	0.0003	0.0002
33	0.0019	0.0014	0.0011	0.0008	0.0006	0.0005	0.0004	0.0003	0.0002	0.0002
34	0.0015	0.0012	0.0009	0.0007	0.0005	0.0004	0.0003	0.0002	0.0002	0.0001
35	0.0013	0.0009	0.0007	0.0005	0.0004	0.0003	0.0002	0.0002	0.0001	0.0001

TABLE A.3 ***Annuity factors: Based on annual compounding periods***

Year	Cost of capital 1%	2%	3%	4%	5%	6%	7%	8%	9%	10%
1	1.010	1.020	1.030	1.040	1.050	1.060	1.070	1.080	1.090	1.100
2	2.030	2.060	2.091	2.122	2.153	2.184	2.215	2.246	2.278	2.310
3	3.060	3.122	3.184	3.246	3.310	3.375	3.440	3.506	3.573	3.641
4	4.101	4.204	4.309	4.416	4.526	4.637	4.751	4.867	4.985	5.105
5	5.152	5.308	5.468	5.633	5.802	5.975	6.153	6.336	6.523	6.716
6	6.214	6.434	6.662	6.898	7.142	7.394	7.654	7.923	8.200	8.487
7	7.286	7.583	7.892	8.214	8.549	8.897	9.260	9.637	10.028	10.436
8	8.369	8.755	9.159	9.583	10.027	10.491	10.978	11.488	12.021	12.579
9	9.462	9.950	10.464	11.006	11.578	12.181	12.816	13.487	14.193	14.937
10	10.567	11.169	11.808	12.486	13.207	13.972	14.784	15.645	16.560	17.531
11	11.683	12.412	13.192	14.026	14.917	15.870	16.888	17.977	19.141	20.384
12	12.809	13.680	14.618	15.627	16.713	17.882	19.141	20.495	21.953	23.523
13	13.947	14.974	16.086	17.292	18.599	20.015	21.550	23.215	25.019	26.975
14	15.097	16.293	17.599	19.024	20.579	22.276	24.129	26.152	28.361	30.772
15	16.258	17.639	19.157	20.825	22.657	24.673	26.888	29.324	32.003	34.950
16	17.430	19.012	20.762	22.698	24.840	27.213	29.840	32.750	35.974	39.545
17	18.615	20.412	22.414	24.645	27.132	29.906	32.999	36.450	40.301	44.599
18	19.811	21.841	24.117	26.671	29.539	32.760	36.379	40.446	45.018	50.159
19	21.019	23.297	25.870	28.778	32.066	35.786	39.995	44.762	50.160	56.275
20	22.239	24.783	27.676	30.969	34.719	38.993	43.865	49.423	55.765	63.002
21	23.472	26.299	29.537	33.248	37.505	42.392	48.006	54.457	61.873	70.403
22	24.716	27.845	31.453	35.618	40.430	45.996	52.436	59.893	68.532	78.543
23	25.973	29.422	33.426	38.083	43.502	49.816	57.177	65.765	75.790	87.497
24	27.243	31.030	35.459	40.646	46.727	53.865	62.249	72.106	83.701	97.347
25	28.526	32.671	37.553	43.312	50.113	58.156	67.676	78.954	92.324	108.182
26	29.821	34.344	39.710	46.084	53.669	62.706	73.484	86.351	101.723	120.100
27	31.129	36.051	41.931	48.968	57.403	67.528	79.698	94.339	111.968	133.210
28	32.450	37.792	44.219	51.966	61.323	72.640	86.347	102.966	123.135	147.631
29	33.785	39.568	46.575	55.085	65.439	78.058	93.461	112.283	135.308	163.494
30	35.133	41.379	49.003	58.328	69.761	83.802	101.073	122.346	148.575	180.943
31	36.494	43.227	51.503	61.701	74.299	89.890	109.218	133.214	163.037	200.138
32	37.869	45.112	54.078	65.210	79.064	96.343	117.933	144.951	178.800	221.252
33	39.258	47.034	56.730	68.858	84.067	103.184	127.259	157.627	195.982	244.477
34	40.660	48.994	59.462	72.652	89.320	110.435	137.237	171.317	214.711	270.024
35	42.077	50.994	62.276	76.598	94.836	118.121	147.913	186.102	235.125	298.127

TABLE A.3 ***Continued***

Year	Cost of capital 11%	12%	13%	14%	15%	16%	17%	18%	19%	20%
1	1.110	1.120	1.130	1.140	1.150	1.160	1.170	1.180	1.190	1.200
2	2.342	2.374	2.407	2.440	2.473	2.506	2.539	2.572	2.606	2.640
3	3.710	3.779	3.850	3.921	3.993	4.066	4.141	4.215	4.291	4.368
4	5.228	5.353	5.480	5.610	5.742	5.877	6.014	6.154	6.297	6.442
5	6.913	7.115	7.323	7.536	7.754	7.977	8.207	8.442	8.683	8.930
6	8.783	9.089	9.405	9.730	10.067	10.414	10.772	11.142	11.523	11.916
7	10.859	11.300	11.757	12.233	12.727	13.240	13.773	14.327	14.902	15.499
8	13.164	13.776	14.416	15.085	15.786	16.519	17.285	18.086	18.923	19.799
9	15.722	16.549	17.420	18.337	19.304	20.321	21.393	22.521	23.709	24.959
10	18.561	19.655	20.814	22.045	23.349	24.733	26.200	27.755	29.404	31.150
11	21.713	23.133	24.650	26.271	28.002	29.850	31.824	33.931	36.180	38.581
12	25.212	27.029	28.985	31.089	33.352	35.786	38.404	41.219	44.244	47.497
13	29.095	31.393	33.383	36.581	39.505	42.672	46.103	49.818	53.841	58.196
14	33.405	36.280	39.417	42.842	46.580	50.660	55.110	59.965	65.261	71.035
15	38.190	41.753	45.672	49.980	54.717	59.925	65.649	71.939	78.850	86.442
16	43.501	47.884	52.739	58.118	64.075	70.673	77.979	86.068	95.022	104.931
17	49.396	54.750	60.725	67.394	74.836	83.141	92.406	102.740	114.266	127.117
18	55.939	62.440	69.749	77.969	87.212	97.603	109.285	122.414	137.166	153.740
19	63.203	71.052	79.947	90.025	101.444	114.380	129.033	145.628	164.418	185.688
20	71.265	80.699	91.470	103.768	117.810	133.841	152.139	173.021	196.847	224.026
21	80.214	91.503	104.491	119.436	136.632	156.415	179.172	205.345	235.438	270.031
22	90.148	103.603	119.205	137.297	158.276	182.601	210.801	243.487	281.362	325.237
23	101.174	117.155	135.831	157.659	183.168	212.978	247.808	288.494	336.010	391.484
24	113.413	132.334	154.620	180.871	211.793	248.214	291.105	341.603	401.042	470.981
25	126.999	149.334	175.850	207.333	244.712	289.088	341.763	404.272	478.431	566.377
26	142.079	168.374	199.841	237.499	282.569	336.502	401.032	478.221	570.522	680.853
27	158.817	189.699	226.950	271.889	326.104	391.503	470.378	565.481	680.112	818.223
28	177.397	213.583	257.583	311.094	376.170	455.303	551.512	668.447	810.523	983.068
29	198.021	240.333	292.199	355.787	433.745	529.312	646.439	789.948	965.712	1180.882
30	220.913	270.293	331.315	406.737	499.957	615.162	757.504	933.319	1150.387	1418.258
31	246.324	303.848	375.516	464.820	576.100	714.747	887.449	1102.496	1370.151	1703.109
32	274.529	341.429	425.463	531.035	663.666	830.267	1039.486	1302.125	1631.670	2044.931
33	305.837	383.521	481.903	606.520	764.365	964.270	1217.368	1537.688	1942.877	2455.118
34	340.590	430.663	545.681	692.573	880.170	1119.713	1425.491	1815.652	2313.214	2947.341
35	379.164	483.463	617.749	790.673	1013.346	1300.027	1668.994	2143.649	2753.914	3538.009

TABLE A.3 *Continued*

Year	Cost of capital 21%	22%	23%	24%	25%	26%	27%	28%	29%	30%
1	1.210	1.220	1.230	1.240	1.250	1.260	1.270	1.280	1.290	1.300
2	2.674	2.708	2.743	2.778	2.813	2.848	2.883	2.918	2.954	2.990
3	4.446	4.524	4.604	4.684	4.766	4.848	4.931	5.016	5.101	5.187
4	6.589	6.740	6.893	7.048	7.207	7.368	7.533	7.700	7.870	8.043
5	9.183	9.442	9.708	9.980	10.259	10.544	10.837	11.136	11.442	11.756
6	12.321	12.740	13.171	13.615	14.073	14.546	15.032	15.534	16.051	16.583
7	16.119	16.762	17.430	18.123	18.842	19.588	20.361	21.163	21.995	22.858
8	20.714	21.670	22.669	23.712	24.802	25.940	27.129	28.369	29.664	31.015
9	26.274	27.657	29.113	30.643	32.253	33.945	35.723	37.593	39.556	41.619
10	33.001	34.962	37.039	39.238	41.566	44.031	46.639	49.398	52.318	55.405
11	41.142	43.874	46.788	49.895	53.208	56.739	60.501	64.510	68.780	73.327
12	50.991	54.746	58.779	63.110	67.760	72.751	78.107	83.853	90.016	96.625
13	62.909	68.010	73.528	79.496	85.949	92.926	100.465	108.612	117.411	126.913
14	77.330	84.192	91.669	99.815	108.687	118.347	128.861	140.303	152.750	166.286
15	94.780	103.935	113.983	125.011	137.109	150.377	164.924	180.868	198.337	217.472
16	115.894	128.020	141.430	156.253	172.636	190.735	210.723	232.791	257.145	284.014
17	141.441	157.405	175.188	194.994	217.045	241.585	268.888	299.252	333.007	370.518
18	172.354	193.254	216.712	243.033	272.556	305.658	342.758	384.323	430.870	482.973
19	209.758	236.989	267.785	302.601	341.945	386.389	436.573	493.213	557.112	629.165
20	255.018	290.347	330.606	376.465	428.681	488.110	555.717	632.593	719.964	819.215
21	309.781	355.443	407.875	468.056	537.101	616.278	707.031	810.999	930.044	1066.280
22	376.045	434.861	502.917	581.630	672.626	777.771	899.199	1039.358	1201.047	1387.464
23	456.225	531.750	619.817	722.461	842.033	981.251	1143.253	1331.659	1550.640	1805.003
24	553.242	649.955	763.605	897.092	1053.791	1237.636	1453.201	1705.803	2001.616	2347.803
25	670.633	794.165	940.465	1113.634	1318.489	1560.682	1846.836	2184.708	2583.374	3053.444
26	812.676	970.102	1158.002	1382.146	1649.361	1967.719	2346.751	2797.706	3333.843	3970.778
27	984.548	1184.744	1425.572	1715.101	2062.952	2480.586	2981.644	3582.344	4301.947	5163.311
28	1192.513	1446.608	1754.683	2127.965	2579.939	3126.798	3787.958	4586.680	5550.802	6713.604
29	1444.151	1766.081	2159.491	2639.916	3226.174	3941.026	4811.977	5872.231	7161.824	8728.985
30	1748.632	2155.839	2657.404	3274.736	4033.968	4966.953	6112.481	7517.735	9240.043	11348.981
31	2117.055	2631.344	3269.836	4061.913	5043.710	6259.620	7764.121	9623.981	11920.946	14754.975
32	2562.847	3211.460	4023.129	5038.012	6305.887	7888.382	9861.703	12319.976	15379.310	19182.768
33	3102.254	3919.201	4949.678	6248.375	7883.609	9940.621	12525.633	15770.849	19840.600	24938.899
34	3754.938	4782.645	6089.334	7749.225	9855.761	12526.442	15908.824	20187.966	25595.664	32421.868
35	4544.685	5836.047	7491.111	9610.279	12320.952	15784.577	20205.477	25841.877	33019.696	42149.729

Index